California Code of Civil Procedure

2024 Edition

(Volume 3 of 3)

Aurum Codex Print™

Part 3 - OF SPECIAL PROCEEDINGS OF A CIVIL NATURE

Title 3 - OF SUMMARY PROCEEDINGS

Chapter 1 - CONFESSION OF JUDGMENT WITHOUT ACTION

Section 1132 - Judgment by confession unenforceable; applicability

(a) A judgment by confession is unenforceable and may not be entered in any superior court.

(b) This section does not apply to a judgment by confession obtained or entered before January 1, 2023.

Ca. Civ. Proc. Code § 1132

Amended by Stats 2022 ch 851 (SB 688),s 1, eff. 1/1/2023.

Amended by Stats 2002 ch 784 (SB 1316),s 77, eff. 1/1/2003.

Section 1133 - [Repealed]

Ca. Civ. Proc. Code § 1133

Repealed by Stats 2022 ch 851 (SB 688),s 2, eff. 1/1/2023.

Enacted 1872.

Section 1134 - [Repealed]

Ca. Civ. Proc. Code § 1134

Repealed by Stats 2022 ch 851 (SB 688),s 3, eff. 1/1/2023.

Amended by Stats 2005 ch 75 (AB 145),s 40, eff. 7/19/2005, op. 1/1/2006

Amended by Stats 2001 ch 812 (AB 223), s 9, eff. 1/1/2002.

Chapter 2 - SUBMITTING A CONTROVERSY WITHOUT ACTION

Section 1138 - Generally
Parties to a question in difference, which might be the subject of a civil action, may, without action, agree upon a case containing the facts upon which the controversy depends, and present a submission of the same to any Court which would have jurisdiction if an action had been brought; but it must appear, by affidavit, that the controversy is real and the proceedings in good faith, to determine the rights of the parties. The Court must thereupon hear and determine the case, and render judgment thereon, as if an action were depending.

Ca. Civ. Proc. Code § 1138
Enacted 1872.

Section 1139 - Judgment; judgment roll
Judgment must be entered as in other cases, but without costs for any proceeding prior to the trial. The case, the submission, and a copy of the judgment constitute the judgment roll.

Ca. Civ. Proc. Code § 1139
Amended by Stats. 1933, Ch. 745.

Section 1140 - Enforcement of judgment
The judgment may be enforced in the same manner as if it had been rendered in an action of the same jurisdictional classification in the same court, and is in the same manner subject to appeal.

Ca. Civ. Proc. Code § 1140
Amended by Stats. 1998, Ch. 931, Sec. 115. Effective September 28, 1998.

Chapter 2.5 - JUDICIAL ARBITRATION

Section 1141.10 - Legislative findings and declaration; legislative intent

(a) The Legislature finds and declares that litigation involving small civil cases can be so costly and complex that efficiently resolving these civil cases is difficult, and that the resulting delays and expenses may deny parties their right to a timely resolution of minor civil disputes. The Legislature further finds and declares that arbitration has proven to be an efficient and equitable method for resolving small civil cases, and that courts should encourage or require the use of arbitration for those actions whenever possible.

(b) It is the intent of the Legislature that:

(1) Arbitration hearings held pursuant to this chapter shall provide parties with a simplified and economical procedure for obtaining prompt and equitable resolution of their disputes.

(2) Arbitration hearings shall be as informal as possible and shall provide the parties themselves maximum opportunity to participate directly in the resolution of their disputes, and shall be held during nonjudicial hours whenever possible.

(3) Members of the State Bar selected to serve as arbitrators should have experience with cases of the type under dispute and are urged to volunteer their services without compensation whenever possible.

Ca. Civ. Proc. Code § 1141.10
Amended by Stats 2003 ch 449 (AB 1712),s 9, eff. 1/1/2004.

Section 1141.11 - Unlimited civil cases submitted to arbitration; limited civil cases; motor vehicle collisions

(a) In each superior court with 18 or more judges, all nonexempt unlimited civil cases shall be submitted to arbitration under this chapter if the amount in controversy, in the opinion of the court, will not exceed fifty thousand dollars ($50,000) for each plaintiff.

(b) In each superior court with fewer than 18 judges, the court may provide by local rule, when it determines that it is in the best interests of justice, that all nonexempt, unlimited civil cases shall be submitted to arbitration under this chapter if the amount in controversy, in the opinion of the court, will not exceed fifty thousand dollars ($50,000) for each plaintiff.

(c) Each superior court may provide by local rule, when it is determined to be in the best interests of justice, that all nonexempt, limited civil cases shall be submitted to arbitration under this chapter. This section does not apply to any action in small claims court, or to any action maintained pursuant to Section 1781 of the Civil Code or Section 1161.

(d)

(1) In each court that has adopted judicial arbitration pursuant to subdivision (c), all limited civil cases that involve a claim for money damages against a single defendant as a result of a motor vehicle collision, except those heard in the small claims division, shall be submitted to arbitration within 120 days of the filing of the defendant's answer to the complaint (except as may be extended by the court for good cause) before an arbitrator selected by the court.

(2) The court may provide by local rule for the voluntary or mandatory use of case questionnaires, established under Section 93, in any proceeding subject to these provisions. Where local rules provide for the use of case questionnaires, the questionnaires shall be exchanged by the parties upon the defendant's answer and completed and returned within 60 days.

(3) For the purposes of this subdivision, the term "single defendant" means any of the following:

(A) An individual defendant, whether a person or an entity.

(B) Two or more persons covered by the same insurance policy applicable to the motor vehicle collision.

(C) Two or more persons residing in the same household

when no insurance policy exists that is applicable to the motor vehicle collision.

(4) The naming of one or more cross-defendants, not a plaintiff, shall constitute a multiple-defendant case not subject to the provisions of this subdivision.

Ca. Civ. Proc. Code § 1141.11

Amended by Stats 2003 ch 449 (AB 1712),s 10, eff. 1/1/2004.

Amended by Stats 2002 ch 784 (SB 1316),s 78, eff. 1/1/2003.

Section 1141.12 - Uniform system provided by rule

In all superior courts, the Judicial Council shall provide by rule for a uniform system of arbitration of the following causes:

(a) Any cause, regardless of the amount in controversy, upon stipulation of the parties.

(b) Upon filing of an election by the plaintiff, any cause in which the plaintiff agrees that the arbitration award shall not exceed the amount in controversy as specified in Section 1141.11.

Ca. Civ. Proc. Code § 1141.12

Amended by Stats 2003 ch 449 (AB 1712),s 11, eff. 1/1/2004.

Amended by Stats 2002 ch 784 (SB 1316),s 79, eff. 1/1/2003.

Section 1141.13 - Prayer for equitable relief

This chapter shall not apply to any civil action which includes a prayer for equitable relief, except that if the prayer for equitable relief is frivolous or insubstantial, this chapter shall be applicable.

Ca. Civ. Proc. Code § 1141.13

Added by Stats. 1978, Ch. 743.

Section 1141.14 - Rules for practice and procedure

Notwithstanding any other provision of law except the provisions of this chapter, the Judicial Council shall provide by rule for practice and procedure for all actions submitted to arbitration under this chapter. The Judicial Council rules shall provide for and conform with the provisions of this chapter.

Ca. Civ. Proc. Code § 1141.14
Added by Stats. 1978, Ch. 743.

Section 1141.15 - Exception provided by rules
The Judicial Council rules shall provide exceptions for cause to
arbitration pursuant to subdivision (a), (b), or (c) of Section 1141.11.
In providing for such exceptions, the Judicial Council shall take into
consideration whether the civil action might not be amenable to
arbitration.

Ca. Civ. Proc. Code § 1141.15
Added by Stats. 1978, Ch. 743.

Section 1141.16 - Determination of amount in controversy
(a) The determination of the amount in controversy, under
subdivision (a) or (b) of Section 1141.11, shall be made by the court
and the case referred to arbitration after all named parties have
appeared or defaulted. The determination shall be made at a case
management conference or based upon review of the written
submissions of the parties, as provided in rules adopted by the
Judicial Council. The determination shall be based on the total
amount of damages, and the judge may not consider questions of
liability or comparative negligence or any other defense. At that
time the court shall also make a determination whether any prayer
for equitable relief is frivolous or insubstantial. The determination
of the amount in controversy and whether any prayer for equitable
relief is frivolous or insubstantial may not be appealable. No
determination pursuant to this section shall be made if all parties
stipulate in writing that the amount in controversy exceeds the
amount specified in Section 1141.11.
(b) The determination and any stipulation of the amount in
controversy shall be without prejudice to any finding on the value of
the case by an arbitrator or in a subsequent trial de novo.
(c) Except as provided in this section, the arbitration hearing may
not be held until 210 days after the filing of the complaint, or 240
days after the filing of a complaint if the parties have stipulated to a
continuance pursuant to subdivision (d) of Section 68616 of the

Government Code. A case shall be submitted to arbitration at an earlier time upon any of the following:

(1) The stipulation of the parties to an earlier arbitration hearing.

(2) The written request of all plaintiffs, subject to a motion by a defendant for good cause shown to delay the arbitration hearing.

(3) An order of the court if the parties have stipulated, or the court has ordered under Section 1141.24, that discovery other than that permitted under Chapter 18 (commencing with Section 2034.010) of Title 4 of Part 4 will be permitted after the arbitration award is rendered.

Ca. Civ. Proc. Code § 1141.16
Amended by Stats 2004 ch 182 (AB 3081),s 14, eff. 7/1/2005
Amended by Stats 2003 ch 449 (AB 1712),s 12, eff. 1/1/2004.

Section 1141.17 - Running of time periods not suspended

(a) Submission of an action to arbitration pursuant to this chapter shall not suspend the running of the time periods specified in Chapter 1.5 (commencing with Section 583.110) of Title 8 of Part 2, except as provided in this section.

(b) If an action is or remains submitted to arbitration pursuant to this chapter more than four years and six months after the plaintiff has filed the action, then the time beginning on the date four years and six months after the plaintiff has filed the action and ending on the date on which a request for a de novo trial is filed under Section 1141.20 shall not be included in computing the five-year period specified in Section 583.310.

Ca. Civ. Proc. Code § 1141.17
Amended by Stats. 1984, Ch. 1705, Sec. 6.

Section 1141.18 - Who may serve as arbitrators; compensation; assignment of arbitrator; disqualification

(a) Arbitrators shall be retired judges, retired court commissioners who were licensed to practice law prior to their appointment as a commissioner, or members of the State Bar, and shall sit individually. A judge may also serve as an arbitrator without compensation. People who are not attorneys may serve as arbitrators upon the stipulation of all parties.

(b) The Judicial Council rules shall provide for the compensation, if any, of arbitrators. Compensation for arbitrators may not be less than one hundred fifty dollars ($150) per case, or one hundred fifty dollars ($150) per day, whichever is greater. A superior court may set a higher level of compensation for that court. Arbitrators may waive compensation in whole or in part. No compensation shall be paid before the filing of the award by the arbitrator, or before the settlement of the case by the parties.

(c) In cases submitted to arbitration under Section 1141.11 or 1141.12, an arbitrator shall be assigned within 30 days from the time of submission to arbitration.

(d) Any party may request the disqualification of the arbitrator selected for his or her case on the grounds and by the procedures specified in Section 170.1 or 170.6. A request for disqualification of an arbitrator on grounds specified in Section 170.6 shall be made within five days of the naming of the arbitrator. An arbitrator shall disqualify himself or herself, upon demand of any party to the arbitration made before the conclusion of the arbitration proceedings on any of the grounds specified in Section 170.1.

Ca. Civ. Proc. Code § 1141.18

Amended by Stats 2003 ch 449 (AB 1712),s 13, eff. 1/1/2004.

Section 1141.19 - Arbitrator's powers

Arbitrators approved pursuant to this chapter shall have the powers necessary to perform duties pursuant to this chapter as prescribed by the Judicial Council.

Ca. Civ. Proc. Code § 1141.19

Added by Stats. 1978, Ch. 743.

Section 1141.19.5 - Pretrial discovery

In any arbitration proceeding under this chapter, no party may require the production of evidence specified in subdivision (a) of Section 3295 of the Civil Code at the arbitration, unless the court enters an order permitting pretrial discovery of that evidence pursuant to subdivision (c) of Section 3295 of the Civil Code.

Ca. Civ. Proc. Code § 1141.19.5

Amended by Stats. 1994, Ch. 327, Sec. 1. Effective January 1, 1995.

Section 1141.20 - Award final unless de novo trial or dismissal requested;; de novo trial

(a) An arbitration award shall be final unless a request for a de novo trial or a request for dismissal in the form required by the Judicial Council is filed within 60 days after the date the arbitrator files the award with the court.

(b) Any party may elect to have a de novo trial, by court or jury, both as to law and facts. Such trial shall be calendared, insofar as possible, so that the trial shall be given the same place on the active list as it had prior to arbitration, or shall receive civil priority on the next setting calendar.

Ca. Civ. Proc. Code § 1141.20

Amended by Stats 2011 ch 49 (SB 731),s 3, eff. 1/1/2012.

Section 1141.21 - Costs and fees if judgment upon trial de novo not more favorable than arbitration award

(a)

(1) If the judgment upon the trial de novo is not more favorable in either the amount of damages awarded or the type of relief granted for the party electing the trial de novo than the arbitration award, the court shall order that party to pay the following nonrefundable costs and fees, unless the court finds in writing and upon motion that the imposition of these costs and fees would create such a substantial economic hardship as not to be in the interest of justice:

(A) To the court, the compensation actually paid to the arbitrator, less any amount paid pursuant to subparagraph (D).

(B) To the other party or parties, all costs specified in Section 1033.5, and the party electing the trial de novo shall not recover his or her costs.

(C) To the other party or parties, the reasonable costs of the services of expert witnesses, who are not regular employees of any party, actually incurred or reasonably necessary in the preparation or trial of the case.

(D) To the other party or parties, the compensation paid by the other party or parties to the arbitrator, pursuant to subdivision (b) of Section 1141.28.

(2) Those costs and fees, other than the compensation of the arbitrator, shall include only those incurred from the time of election of the trial de novo.

(b) If the party electing the trial de novo has proceeded in the action in forma pauperis and has failed to obtain a more favorable judgment, the costs and fees under subparagraphs (B) and (C) of paragraph (1) of subdivision (a) shall be imposed only as an offset against any damages awarded in favor of that party.

(c) If the party electing the trial de novo has proceeded in the action in forma pauperis and has failed to obtain a more favorable judgment, the costs under subparagraph (A) of paragraph (1) of subdivision (a) shall be imposed only to the extent that there remains a sufficient amount in the judgment after the amount offset under subdivision (b) has been deducted from the judgment.

Ca. Civ. Proc. Code § 1141.21
Amended by Stats 2006 ch 538 (SB 1852),s 66, eff. 1/1/2007.
Amended by Stats 2005 ch 706 (AB 1742),s 14, eff. 1/1/2006

Section 1141.22 - Rules to specify grounds for correction, modification or vacation of award

The Judicial Council rules shall specify the grounds upon which the arbitrator or the court, or both, may correct, modify or vacate an award.

Ca. Civ. Proc. Code § 1141.22
Added by Stats. 1978, Ch. 743.

Section 1141.23 - Requirements of award; entry in judgment book; force and effect of award

The arbitration award shall be in writing, signed by the arbitrator and filed in the court in which the action is pending. If there is no request for a de novo trial or a request for dismissal in the form required by the Judicial Council and the award is not vacated, the award shall be entered in the judgment book in the amount of the award. Such award shall have the same force and effect as a judgment in any civil action or proceeding, except that it is not subject to appeal and it may not be attacked or set aside except as provided by Section 473, 1286.2, or Judicial Council rule.

Ca. Civ. Proc. Code § 1141.23
Amended by Stats 2011 ch 49 (SB 731),s 4, eff. 1/1/2012.

Section 1141.24 - Discovery after award

In cases ordered to arbitration pursuant to Section 1141.11, no discovery other than that permitted by Chapter 18 (commencing with Section 2034.010) of Title 4 of Part 4 is permissible after an arbitration award except by stipulation of the parties or by leave of court upon a showing of good cause.

Ca. Civ. Proc. Code § 1141.24
Amended by Stats 2004 ch 182 (AB 3081),s 15, eff. 7/1/2005
Amended by Stats 2003 ch 449 (AB 1712),s 14, eff. 1/1/2004.

Section 1141.25 - Reference to arbitration proceedings and award in subsequent trial constitutes irregularity

Any reference to the arbitration proceedings or arbitration award during any subsequent trial shall constitute an irregularity in the proceedings of the trial for the purposes of Section 657.

Ca. Civ. Proc. Code § 1141.25
Added by Stats. 1978, Ch. 743.

Section 1141.26 - Award or judgment in excess of amount in controversy

Nothing in this act shall prohibit an arbitration award in excess of the amount in controversy as specified in Section 1141.11. No party electing a trial de novo after such award shall be subject to the provisions of Section 1141.21 if the judgment upon the trial de novo is in excess of the amount in controversy as specified in Section 1141.11.

Ca. Civ. Proc. Code § 1141.26

Amended by Stats. 1981, Ch. 1110, Sec. 4.

Section 1141.27 - Applicability to public agency or public entity

This chapter shall apply to any civil action otherwise within the scope of this chapter in which a party to the action is a public agency or public entity.

Ca. Civ. Proc. Code § 1141.27

Added by Stats. 1978, Ch. 743.

Section 1141.28 - Administrative costs; actual costs of compensation of arbitrators

(a) All administrative costs of arbitration, including compensation of arbitrators, shall be paid for by the court in which the arbitration costs are incurred, except as otherwise provided in subdivision (b) and in Section 1141.21.

(b) The actual costs of compensation of arbitrators in any proceeding which would not otherwise be subject to the provisions of this chapter but in which arbitration is conducted pursuant to this chapter solely because of the stipulation of the parties, shall be paid for in equal shares by the parties. If the imposition of these costs would create such a substantial economic hardship for any party as not to be in the interest of justice, as determined by the arbitrator, that party's share of costs shall be paid for by the court in which the arbitration costs are incurred. The determination as to substantial economic hardship may be reviewed by the court.

Ca. Civ. Proc. Code § 1141.28
Amended by Stats 2000 ch 447 (SB 1533), s 3, eff. 1/1/2001.

Section 1141.29 - [Repealed]
Ca. Civ. Proc. Code § 1141.29
Repealed by Stats 2002 ch 784 (SB 1316),s 80, eff. 1/1/2003.

Section 1141.30 - Construction of chapter
This chapter shall not be construed in derogation of Title 9 (commencing with Section 1280) of Part 3, and, to that extent, this chapter and that title, other than Section 1280.1, are mutually exclusive and independent of each other.
Ca. Civ. Proc. Code § 1141.30
Amended (as added by Stats. 1978, Ch. 743) by Stats. 1990, Ch. 817, Sec. 1.

Section 1141.31 - Effective date
The provisions of this chapter shall become operative July 1, 1979, except that the Judicial Council shall adopt the arbitration rules for practice and procedures on or before March 31, 1979.
Ca. Civ. Proc. Code § 1141.31
Added by Stats. 1978, Ch. 743.

Chapter 4 - SUMMARY PROCEEDINGS FOR OBTAINING POSSESSION OF REAL PROPERTY IN CERTAIN CASES

Section 1159 - When person guilty of forcible entry
(a) Every person is guilty of a forcible entry who either:

(1) By breaking open doors, windows, or other parts of a house, or by any kind of violence or circumstance of terror enters upon or into any real property.

(2) Who, after entering peaceably upon real property, turns out

by force, threats, or menacing conduct, the party in possession.
(b) For purposes of this section, "party in possession" means any person who hires real property and includes a boarder or lodger, except those persons whose occupancy is described in subdivision (b) of Section 1940 of the Civil Code.

Ca. Civ. Proc. Code § 1159
Amended by Stats 2018 ch 92 (SB 1289),s 42, eff. 1/1/2019.

Section 1160 - When person guilty of forcible detainer

(a) Every person is guilty of a forcible detainer who either:

(1) By force, or by menaces and threats of violence, unlawfully holds and keeps the possession of any real property, whether the same was acquired peaceably or otherwise.

(2) Who, in the night-time, or during the absence of the occupant of any lands, unlawfully enters upon real property, and who, after demand made for the surrender thereof, for the period of five days, refuses to surrender the same to such former occupant.
(b) The occupant of real property, within the meaning of this section is one who, within five days preceding such unlawful entry, was in the peaceable and undisturbed possession of such lands.

Ca. Civ. Proc. Code § 1160
Amended by Stats 2018 ch 92 (SB 1289),s 43, eff. 1/1/2019.

Section 1161 - [Effective until 2/1/2025] When tenant for term less than life guilty of unlawful detainer

A tenant of real property, for a term less than life, or the executor or administrator of the tenant's estate heretofore qualified and now acting or hereafter to be qualified and act, is guilty of unlawful detainer:
1. When the tenant continues in possession, in person or by subtenant, of the property, or any part thereof, after the expiration of the term for which it is let to the tenant; provided the expiration is of a nondefault nature however brought about without the permission of the landlord, or the successor in estate of the

landlord, if applicable; including the case where the person to be removed became the occupant of the premises as a servant, employee, agent, or licensee and the relation of master and servant, or employer and employee, or principal and agent, or licensor and licensee, has been lawfully terminated or the time fixed for occupancy by the agreement between the parties has expired; but nothing in this subdivision shall be construed as preventing the removal of the occupant in any other lawful manner; but in case of a tenancy at will, it shall first be terminated by notice, as prescribed in the Civil Code.

2. When the tenant continues in possession, in person or by subtenant, without the permission of the landlord, or the successor in estate of the landlord, if applicable, after default in the payment of rent, pursuant to the lease or agreement under which the property is held, and three days' notice, excluding Saturdays and Sundays and other judicial holidays, in writing, requiring its payment, stating the amount that is due, the name, telephone number, and address of the person to whom the rent payment shall be made, and, if payment may be made personally, the usual days and hours that person will be available to receive the payment (provided that, if the address does not allow for personal delivery, then it shall be conclusively presumed that upon the mailing of any rent or notice to the owner by the tenant to the name and address provided, the notice or rent is deemed received by the owner on the date posted, if the tenant can show proof of mailing to the name and address provided by the owner), or the number of an account in a financial institution into which the rental payment may be made, and the name and street address of the institution (provided that the institution is located within five miles of the rental property), or if an electronic funds transfer procedure has been previously established, that payment may be made pursuant to that procedure, or possession of the property, shall have been served upon the tenant and if there is a subtenant in actual occupation of the premises, also upon the subtenant. The notice may be served at any time within one year after the rent becomes due. In all cases of tenancy upon agricultural lands, if the tenant has held over and retained possession for more than 60 days after the expiration of the term without any demand of possession or notice to quit by the landlord or the successor in estate of the landlord, if applicable, the tenant shall be deemed to be holding by permission of the landlord or successor in estate of the landlord, if applicable, and shall be entitled to hold under the terms of the lease for another full year, and shall not be guilty of an unlawful detainer during that year, and the holding over for that period shall be taken and construed as a consent on the part of a tenant to hold for another year.

An unlawful detainer action under this paragraph shall be subject to the COVID-19 Tenant Relief Act of 2020 (Chapter 5 (commencing with Section 1179.01)) if the default in the payment of rent is based upon the COVID-19 rental debt.

3. When the tenant continues in possession, in person or by subtenant, after a neglect or failure to perform other conditions or covenants of the lease or agreement under which the property is held, including any covenant not to assign or sublet, than the one for the payment of rent, and three days' notice, excluding Saturdays and Sundays and other judicial holidays, in writing, requiring the performance of those conditions or covenants, or the possession of the property, shall have been served upon the tenant, and if there is a subtenant in actual occupation of the premises, also, upon the subtenant. Within three days, excluding Saturdays and Sundays and other judicial holidays, after the service of the notice, the tenant, or any subtenant in actual occupation of the premises, or any mortgagee of the term, or other person interested in its continuance, may perform the conditions or covenants of the lease or pay the stipulated rent, as the case may be, and thereby save the lease from forfeiture; provided, if the conditions and covenants of the lease, violated by the lessee, cannot afterward be performed, then no notice, as last prescribed herein, need be given to the lessee or the subtenant, demanding the performance of the violated conditions or covenants of the lease. A tenant may take proceedings, similar to those prescribed in this chapter, to obtain possession of the premises let to a subtenant or held by a servant, employee, agent, or licensee, in case of that person's unlawful detention of the premises underlet to or held by that person.

An unlawful detainer action under this paragraph shall be subject to the COVID-19 Tenant Relief Act of 2020 (Chapter 5 (commencing with Section 1179.01)) if the neglect or failure to perform other conditions or covenants of the lease or agreement is based upon the COVID-19 rental debt.

4. Any tenant, subtenant, or executor or administrator of that person's estate heretofore qualified and now acting, or hereafter to be qualified and act, assigning or subletting or committing waste upon the demised premises, contrary to the conditions or covenants of the lease, or maintaining, committing, or permitting the maintenance or commission of a nuisance upon the demised premises or using the premises for an unlawful purpose, thereby terminates the lease, and the landlord, or the landlord's successor in estate, shall upon service of three days' notice to quit upon the person or persons in possession, be entitled to restitution of possession of the demised premises under this chapter. For purposes of this subdivision, a person who commits or maintains a public nuisance as described in Section 3482.8 of the Civil Code, or who commits an offense described in subdivision (c) of Section 3485 of the Civil Code, or subdivision (c) of Section 3486 of the Civil Code, or uses the premises to further the purpose of that offense shall be deemed to have committed a nuisance upon the premises.

5. When the tenant gives written notice as provided in Section 1946 of the Civil Code of the tenant's intention to terminate the hiring of the real property, or makes a written offer to surrender which is accepted in writing by the landlord, but fails to deliver possession at the time specified in that written notice, without the permission of the landlord, or the successor in estate of the landlord, if applicable.

6. As used in this section: "COVID-19 rental debt" has the same meaning as defined in Section 1179.02.

"Tenant" includes any person who hires real property except those persons whose occupancy is described in subdivision (b) of Section 1940 of the Civil Code.

7. This section shall remain in effect until February 1, 2025, and as of that date is repealed.

Ca. Civ. Proc. Code § 1161

Amended by Stats 2020 ch 37 (AB 3088),s 15, eff. 8/31/2020.

Amended by Stats 2018 ch 260 (AB 2343),s 1, eff. 1/1/2019.
Amended by Stats 2011 ch 128 (SB 426),s 2, eff. 1/1/2012.
Amended by Stats 2009 ch 244 (AB 530),s 5, eff. 1/1/2010.
Added by Stats 2008 ch 440 (AB 2052),s 3, eff. 9/27/2008.

Section 1161 - [Operative 2/1/2025] When tenant for term less than life guilty of unlawful detainer

A tenant of real property, for a term less than life, or the executor or administrator of the tenant's estate heretofore qualified and now acting or hereafter to be qualified and act, is guilty of unlawful detainer:

1. When the tenant continues in possession, in person or by subtenant, of the property, or any part thereof, after the expiration of the term for which it is let to the tenant; provided the expiration is of a nondefault nature however brought about without the permission of the landlord, or the successor in estate of the landlord, if applicable; including the case where the person to be removed became the occupant of the premises as a servant, employee, agent, or licensee and the relation of master and servant, or employer and employee, or principal and agent, or licensor and licensee, has been lawfully terminated or the time fixed for occupancy by the agreement between the parties has expired; but nothing in this subdivision shall be construed as preventing the removal of the occupant in any other lawful manner; but in case of a tenancy at will, it shall first be terminated by notice, as prescribed in the Civil Code.

2. When the tenant continues in possession, in person or by subtenant, without the permission of the landlord, or the successor in estate of the landlord, if applicable, after default in the payment of rent, pursuant to the lease or agreement under which the property is held, and three days' notice, excluding Saturdays and Sundays and other judicial holidays, in writing, requiring its payment, stating the amount that is due, the name, telephone number, and address of the person to whom the rent payment shall be made, and, if payment may be made personally, the usual days and hours that person will be available to receive the payment (provided that, if the address does not allow for personal delivery, then it shall be conclusively presumed that upon the mailing of any rent or notice to the owner by the tenant to the name and address provided, the notice or rent is deemed received by the owner on the date posted, if the tenant can show proof of mailing to the name and address provided by the owner), or the number of an account in a financial institution into which the rental payment may be made, and the name and street address of the institution (provided that the institution is located within five miles of the rental property), or if an electronic funds transfer procedure has been previously established, that payment may be made pursuant to that procedure, or possession of the property, shall have been served upon the tenant and if there is a subtenant in actual occupation of the premises, also upon the subtenant. The notice may be served at any time within one year after the rent becomes due. In all cases of tenancy upon agricultural lands, if the tenant has held over and retained possession for more than 60 days after the expiration of the term without any demand of possession or notice to quit by the landlord or the successor in estate of the landlord, if applicable, the tenant shall be deemed to be holding by permission of the landlord or successor in estate of the landlord, if applicable, and shall be entitled to hold under the terms of the lease for another full year, and shall not be guilty of an unlawful detainer during that year, and the holding over for that period shall be taken and construed as a consent on the part of a tenant to hold for another year.

3. When the tenant continues in possession, in person or by subtenant, after a neglect or failure to perform other conditions or covenants of the lease or agreement under which the property is held, including any covenant not to assign or sublet, than the one for the payment of rent, and three days' notice, excluding Saturdays and Sundays and other judicial holidays, in writing, requiring the performance of those conditions or covenants, or the possession of the property, shall have been served upon the tenant, and if there is a subtenant in actual occupation of the premises, also, upon the subtenant. Within three days, excluding Saturdays and Sundays and other judicial holidays, after the service of the notice, the tenant, or any subtenant in actual occupation of the premises, or any mortgagee of the term, or other person interested in its continuance, may perform the conditions or covenants of the lease or pay the stipulated rent, as the case may be, and thereby save the lease from forfeiture; provided, if the conditions and covenants of the lease, violated by the lessee, cannot afterward be performed, then no notice, as last prescribed herein, need be given to the lessee or the subtenant, demanding the performance of the violated conditions or covenants of the lease. A tenant may take proceedings, similar to those prescribed in this chapter, to obtain possession of the premises let to a subtenant or held by a servant, employee, agent, or licensee, in case of that person's unlawful detention of the premises underlet to or held by that person.

4. Any tenant, subtenant, or executor or administrator of that person's estate heretofore qualified and now acting, or hereafter to be qualified and act, assigning or subletting or committing waste upon the demised premises, contrary to the conditions or covenants of the lease, or maintaining, committing, or permitting the maintenance or commission of a nuisance upon the demised premises or using the premises for an unlawful purpose, thereby terminates the lease, and the landlord, or the landlord's successor in estate, shall upon service of three days' notice to quit upon the person or persons in possession, be entitled to restitution of possession of the demised premises under this chapter. For purposes of this subdivision, a person who commits or maintains a public nuisance as described in Section 3482.8 of the Civil Code, or who commits an offense described in subdivision (c) of Section 3485 of the Civil Code, or subdivision (c) of Section 3486 of the Civil Code, or uses the premises to further the purpose of that offense shall be deemed to have committed a nuisance upon the premises.

5. When the tenant gives written notice as provided in Section 1946 of the Civil Code of the tenant's intention to terminate the hiring of the real property, or makes a written offer to surrender which is accepted in writing by the landlord, but fails to deliver possession at the time specified in that written notice, without the permission of the landlord, or the successor in estate of the landlord, if applicable.

6. As used in this section, "tenant" includes any person who hires real property except those persons whose occupancy is described in subdivision (b) of Section 1940 of the Civil Code.

7. This section shall become operative on February 1, 2025.

Ca. Civ. Proc. Code § 1161

Added by Stats 2020 ch 37 (AB 3088),s 16, eff. 8/31/2020.

Section 1161.1 - Cases of possession of commercial property after default in payment of rent

With respect to application of Section 1161 in cases of possession of commercial real property after default in the payment of rent:

(a) If the amount stated in the notice provided to the tenant pursuant to subdivision (2) of Section 1161 is clearly identified by the notice as an estimate and the amount claimed is not in fact correct, but it is determined upon the trial or other judicial determination that rent was owing, and the amount claimed in the notice was reasonably estimated, the tenant shall be subject to judgment for possession and the actual amount of rent and other sums found to be due. However, if (1) upon receipt of such a notice claiming an amount identified by the notice as an estimate, the tenant tenders to the landlord within the time for payment required by the notice, the amount which the tenant has reasonably estimated to be due and (2) if at trial it is determined that the amount of rent then due was the amount tendered by the tenant or a lesser amount, the tenant shall be deemed the prevailing party for all purposes. If the court determines that the amount so tendered by the tenant was less than the amount due, but was reasonably estimated, the tenant shall retain the right to possession if the tenant pays to the landlord within five days of the effective date of the judgment (1) the amount previously tendered if it had not been previously accepted, (2) the difference between the amount tendered and the amount determined by the court to be due, and (3) any other sums as ordered by the court.

(b) If the landlord accepts a partial payment of rent, including any payment pursuant to subdivision (a), after serving notice pursuant to Section 1161, the landlord, without any further notice to the tenant, may commence and pursue an action under this chapter to recover the difference between the amount demanded in that notice and the payment actually received, and this shall be specified in the complaint.

(c) If the landlord accepts a partial payment of rent after filing the complaint pursuant to Section 1166, the landlord's acceptance of the partial payment is evidence only of that payment, without waiver of any rights or defenses of any of the parties. The landlord shall be entitled to amend the complaint to reflect the partial payment without creating a necessity for the filing of an additional answer or other responsive pleading by the tenant, and without prior leave of court, and such an amendment shall not delay the matter from proceeding. However, this subdivision shall apply only if the landlord provides actual notice to the tenant that acceptance of the partial rent payment does not constitute a waiver of any rights, including any right the landlord may have to recover possession of the property.

(d) "Commercial real property" as used in this section, means all real property in this state except dwelling units made subject to Chapter 2 (commencing with Section 1940) of Title 5 of Part 4 of Division 3 of the Civil Code, mobilehomes as defined in Section 798.3 of the Civil Code, or recreational vehicles as defined in Section 799.24 of the Civil Code.

(e) For the purposes of this section, there is a presumption affecting the burden of proof that the amount of rent claimed or tendered is reasonably estimated if, in relation to the amount determined to be due upon the trial or other judicial determination of that issue, the amount claimed or tendered was no more than 20 percent more or less than the amount determined to be due. However, if the rent due is contingent upon information primarily within the knowledge of the one party to the lease and that information has not been furnished to, or has not accurately been furnished to, the other party, the court shall consider that fact in determining the reasonableness of the amount of rent claimed or tendered pursuant to subdivision (a).

Ca. Civ. Proc. Code § 1161.1

Added by Stats. 1990, Ch. 890, Sec. 1.

Section 1161.2 - Access to limited civil case records filed under chapter
(a)

(1) The clerk shall allow access to limited civil case records filed under this chapter, including the court file, index, and register of actions, only as follows:

(A) To a party to the action, including a party's attorney.

(B) To a person who provides the clerk with the names of at least one plaintiff and one defendant and the address of the premises, including the apartment or unit number, if any.

(C) To a resident of the premises who provides the clerk with the name of one of the parties or the case number and shows proof of residency.

(D) To a person by order of the court, which may be granted ex parte, on a showing of good cause.

(E) Except as provided in subparagraph (G), to any person by order of the court if judgment is entered for the plaintiff after trial more than 60 days since the filing of the complaint. The court shall issue the order upon issuing judgment for the plaintiff.

(F) Except as provided in subparagraph (G), to any other person 60 days after the complaint has been filed if judgment against all defendants has been entered for the plaintiff within 60 days of the filing of the complaint, in which case the clerk shall allow access to any court records in the action. If a default or default judgment is set aside more than 60 days after the complaint has been filed, this section shall apply as if the complaint had been filed on the date the default or default judgment is set aside.

(G)

(i) In the case of a complaint involving residential

property based on Section 1161a as indicated in the caption of the complaint, as required in subdivision (c) of Section 1166, to any other person, if 60 days have elapsed since the complaint was filed with the court, and, as of that date, judgment against all defendants has been entered for the plaintiff, after a trial.

(ii) Subparagraphs (E) and (F) shall not apply if the plaintiff filed the action between March 4, 2020, and September 30, 2021, and the action is based on an alleged default in the payment of rent.

(2) This section shall not be construed to prohibit the court from issuing an order that bars access to the court record in an action filed under this chapter if the parties to the action so stipulate.

(b)

(1) For purposes of this section, "good cause" includes, but is not limited to, both of the following:

(A) The gathering of newsworthy facts by a person described in Section 1070 of the Evidence Code.

(B) The gathering of evidence by a party to an unlawful detainer action solely for the purpose of making a request for judicial notice pursuant to subdivision (d) of Section 452 of the Evidence Code.

(2) It is the intent of the Legislature that a simple procedure be established to request the ex parte order described in subparagraph (D) of paragraph (1) of subdivision (a).

(c) Upon the filing of a case so restricted, the court clerk shall mail notice to each defendant named in the action. The notice shall be mailed to the address provided in the complaint. The notice shall contain a statement that an unlawful detainer complaint (eviction action) has been filed naming that party as a defendant, and that access to the court file will be delayed for 60 days except to a party, an attorney for one of the parties, or any other person who (1) provides to the clerk the names of at least one plaintiff and one defendant in the action and provides to the clerk the address, including any applicable apartment, unit, or space number, of the subject premises, or (2) provides to the clerk the name of one of the parties in the action or the case number and can establish through proper identification that the person lives at the subject premises. The notice shall also contain a statement that access to the court index, register of actions, or other records is not permitted until 60 days after the complaint is filed, except pursuant to an order upon a showing of good cause for access. The notice shall contain on its face the following information:

(1) The name and telephone number of the county bar association.

(2) The name and telephone number of any entity that requests inclusion on the notice and demonstrates to the satisfaction of the court that it has been certified by the State Bar of California as a lawyer referral service and maintains a panel of attorneys qualified in the practice of landlord-tenant law pursuant to the minimum standards for a lawyer referral service established by the State Bar of California and Section 6155 of the Business and Professions Code.

(3) The following statement: "The State Bar of California certifies lawyer referral services in California and publishes a list of certified lawyer referral services organized by county. To locate a lawyer referral service in your county, go to the State Bar's internet website at www . calbar . ca . gov or call 1 – 866 – 442 - 2529."

(4) The name and telephone number of an office or offices funded by the federal Legal Services Corporation or qualified legal services projects that receive funds distributed pursuant to Section 6216 of the Business and Professions Code that provide legal services to low-income persons in the county in which the action is filed. The notice shall state that these telephone numbers may be called for legal advice regarding the case. The notice shall be issued

between 24 and 48 hours of the filing of the complaint, excluding weekends and holidays. One copy of the notice shall be addressed to "all occupants" and mailed separately to the subject premises. The notice shall not constitute service of the summons and complaint.

(5) The following statement, for a notice sent out pursuant to this section between October 1, 2021 and March 31, 2022: "IMPORTANT NOTICE FROM THE STATE OF CALIFORNIA - YOU MUST TAKE ACTION TO AVOID AN EVICTION: As part of the state's COVID-19 relief plan, money has been set aside to help renters who have fallen behind on rent or utility payments.
If you are behind on rent or utility payments, YOU SHOULD COMPLETE A RENTAL ASSISTANCE APPLICATION IMMEDIATELY! It is free and simple to apply. Citizenship or immigration status does not matter.
You can find out how to start your application by calling 1-833-430-2122 or visiting http://housingiskey.com right away."

(d) Notwithstanding any other law, the court shall charge an additional fee of fifteen dollars ($15) for filing a first appearance by the plaintiff. This fee shall be added to the uniform filing fee for actions filed under this chapter.
(e) This section does not apply to a case that seeks to terminate a mobilehome park tenancy if the statement of the character of the proceeding in the caption of the complaint clearly indicates that the complaint seeks termination of a mobilehome park tenancy.
(f) This section does not alter any provision of the Evidence Code.
Ca. Civ. Proc. Code § 1161.2
Amended by Stats 2021 ch 360 (AB 1584),s 7, eff. 1/1/2022.
Amended by Stats 2021 ch 27 (AB 832),s 11, eff. 6/28/2021.
Amended by Stats 2021 ch 2 (SB 91),s 11, eff. 1/29/2021.
Amended by Stats 2020 ch 37 (AB 3088),s 17, eff. 8/31/2020.
Amended by Stats 2020 ch 36 (AB 3364),s 25, eff. 1/1/2021.
Amended by Stats 2016 ch 336 (AB 2819),s 3, eff. 1/1/2017.
Amended by Stats 2012 ch 241 (AB 1865),s 1, eff. 1/1/2013.
Amended by Stats 2010 ch 641 (SB 1149),s 1, eff. 1/1/2011.
Amended by Stats 2005 ch 610 (AB 664),s 2, eff. 1/1/2006
Amended by Stats 2005 ch 75 (AB 145),s 41, eff. 7/19/2005, op.

1/1/2006
Amended by Stats 2004 ch 568 (SB 1145),s 6, eff. 1/1/2005
Amended by Stats 2003 ch 449 (AB 1712),s 15, eff. 1/1/2004.
Amended by Stats 2003 ch 787 (SB 345),s 2, eff. 1/1/2004.
Amended by Stats 2001 ch 824 (AB 1700), s 11, eff. 1/1/2002.

Section 1161.2.5 - Access to civil case records for actions seeking recovery of COVID-19 rental debt
(a)

(1) Except as provided in Section 1161.2, the clerk shall allow access to civil case records for actions seeking recovery of COVID-19 rental debt, as defined in Section 1179.02, including the court file, index, and register of actions, only as follows:

(A) To a party to the action, including a party's attorney.

(B) To a person who provides the clerk with the names of at least one plaintiff and one defendant.

(C) To a resident of the premises for which the COVID-19 rental debt is owed who provides the clerk with the name of one of the parties or the case number and shows proof of residency.

(D) To a person by order of the court, which may be granted ex parte, on a showing of good cause.

(2) To give the court notice that access to the records in an action is limited, any complaint or responsive pleading in a case subject to this section shall include on either the first page of the pleading or a cover page, the phrase "ACTION FOR RECOVERY OF COVID-19 RENTAL DEBT AS DEFINED UNDER SECTION 1179.02" in bold, capital letters, in 12 point or larger font.

(3) The Judicial Council shall develop forms for parties to utilize in actions brought pursuant to Section 116.223 and in civil actions for recovery of COVID-19 rental debt as defined in Section 1179.02.

The forms shall provide prominent notice on the first page that access to the records in the case is limited pursuant to this section.

(b)

(1) For purposes of this section, "good cause" includes, but is not limited to, both of the following:

(A) The gathering of newsworthy facts by a person described in Section 1070 of the Evidence Code.

(B) The gathering of evidence by a party to a civil action solely for the purpose of making a request for judicial notice pursuant to subdivision (d) of Section 452 of the Evidence Code.

(2) It is the intent of the Legislature that a simple procedure be established to request the ex parte order described in subparagraph (D) of paragraph (1) of subdivision (a).

(c) This section does not alter any provision of the Evidence Code.
Ca. Civ. Proc. Code § 1161.2.5
Amended by Stats 2021 ch 27 (AB 832),s 13, eff. 6/28/2021.
Amended by Stats 2021 ch 2 (SB 91),s 13, eff. 1/29/2021.
Added by Stats 2020 ch 37 (AB 3088),s 19, eff. 8/31/2020.

Section 1161.3 - Acts against tenant or tenant's household member constituting domestic violence

(a) For purposes of this section:

(1) "Abuse or violence" means domestic violence as defined in Section 6211 of the Family Code, sexual assault as defined in Section 1219, stalking as defined in Section 1708.7 of the Civil Code or Section 646.9 of the Penal Code, human trafficking as defined in Section 236.1 of the Penal Code, abuse of an elder or a dependent adult as defined in Section 15610.07 of the Welfare and Institutions Code, or any act described in paragraphs (6) to (8), inclusive, of subdivision (a) of Section 1946.7 of the Civil Code.

(2) "Documentation evidencing abuse or violence against the tenant, the tenant's immediate family member, or the tenant's household member" means any of the following:

(A) A temporary restraining order, emergency protective order, or protective order lawfully issued within the last 180 days pursuant to Section 527.6, Part 3 (commencing with Section 6240), Part 4 (commencing with Section 6300), or Part 5 (commencing with Section 6400) of Division 10 of the Family Code, Section 136.2 of the Penal Code, or Section 213.5 or 15657.03 of the Welfare and Institutions Code that protects the tenant, the tenant's immediate family member, or the tenant's household member from abuse or violence.

(B) A copy of a written report, written within the last 180 days, by a peace officer employed by a state or local law enforcement agency acting in the officer's official capacity, stating that the tenant, the tenant's immediate family member, or the tenant's household member has filed a report alleging that they are a victim of abuse or violence.

(C)

(i) Documentation from a qualified third party based on information received by that third party while acting in their professional capacity to indicate that the tenant, the tenant's immediate family member, or the tenant's household member is seeking assistance for physical or mental injuries or abuse resulting from an act of abuse or violence, which shall contain, in substantially the same form, the following:

Tenant Statement and Qualified Third Party Statement under Code of Civil Procedure Section 1161.3

Part I. Statement By Tenant

Title 3 - OF SUMMARY PROCEEDINGS

I, [insert name of tenant], state as follows:

I, my immediate family member, or a member of my household, have been a victim of:

[insert one or more of the following: domestic violence, sexual assault, stalking, human trafficking, elder abuse, dependent adult abuse, a crime that caused bodily injury or death, a crime that included the exhibition, drawing, brandishing, or use of a firearm or other deadly weapon or instrument, or a crime that included the use or threat of force against the victim.]

The most recent incident(s) happened on or about:

[insert date or dates.]

The incident(s) was/were committed by the following person(s), with these physical description(s), if known and safe to provide:

[if known and safe to provide, insert name(s) and physical description(s).]

(signature of tenant)(date)

Part II. Qualified Third Party Statement

I, [insert name of qualified third party], state as follows:

My business address and phone number are:

[insert business address and phone number.]

Check and complete one of the following:

_____I meet the requirements for a sexual assault counselor provided in Section 1035.2 of the Evidence Code and I am either engaged in an office, hospital, institution, or center commonly known as a rape crisis center described in that section or employed by an organization providing the programs specified in Section 13835.2 of the Penal Code.

_____I meet the requirements for a domestic violence counselor provided in Section 1037.1 of the Evidence Code and I am employed, whether financially compensated or not, by a domestic violence victim service organization, as defined in that section.

_____I meet the requirements for a human trafficking caseworker provided in Section 1038.2 of the Evidence Code and I am employed, whether financially compensated or not, by an organization that provides programs specified in Section 18294 of the Welfare and Institutions Code or in Section 13835.2 of the Penal Code.

_____I meet the definition of "victim of violent crime advocate" provided in Section 1946.7 of the Civil Code and I am employed, whether financially compensated or not, by an agency or organization that has a documented record of providing services to victims of violent crime or provides those services under the auspices or supervision of a court or a law enforcement or prosecution agency.

_____I am licensed by the State of California as a:

[insert one of the following: physician and surgeon, osteopathic physician and surgeon, registered nurse, psychiatrist, psychologist, licensed clinical social worker, licensed marriage and family therapist, or licensed professional clinical counselor.] and I am licensed by, and my license number is:

[insert name of state licensing entity and license number.]

The person who signed the Statement By Tenant above stated to me that they, a member of their immediate family, or a member of their household is a victim of:

[insert one or more of the following: domestic violence, sexual assault, stalking, human trafficking, elder abuse, dependent adult abuse, a crime that caused bodily injury or death, a crime that included the exhibition, drawing, brandishing, or use of a firearm or other deadly weapon or instrument, or a crime that included the use or threat of force against the victim.]

The person further stated to me the incident(s) occurred on or about the date(s) stated above.

(signature of qualified third party)(date)

(ii) The documentation may be signed by a person who meets the requirements for a sexual assault counselor, domestic violence counselor, a human trafficking caseworker, or a victim of violent crime advocate only if the documentation displays the letterhead of the office, hospital, institution, center, or organization, as appropriate, that engages or employs, whether financially compensated or not, this counselor, caseworker, or advocate.

(D) Any other form of documentation or evidence that reasonably verifies that the abuse or violence occurred.

(3) "Health practitioner" means a physician and surgeon, osteopathic physician and surgeon, psychiatrist, psychologist, registered nurse, licensed clinical social worker, licensed marriage and family therapist, or licensed professional clinical counselor.

(4) "Immediate family member" has the same meaning as defined in Section 1946.7 of the Civil Code.

(5) "Perpetrator of abuse or violence" means any of the following:

(A) The person against whom an order described in subparagraph (A) of paragraph (2) of subdivision (a) has been issued.

(B) The person who was named or referred to as causing the abuse or violence in the report described in subparagraph (B) of paragraph (2) of subdivision (a).

(C) The person who was named or referred to as causing the abuse or violence in the documentation described in subparagraph (C) of paragraph (2) of subdivision (a).

(D) The person who was named or referred to as causing the abuse or violence in the documentation described in subparagraph (D) of paragraph (2) of subdivision (a).

(6) "Qualified third party" means a health practitioner, domestic violence counselor, as defined in Section 1037.1 of the Evidence Code, a sexual assault counselor, as defined in Section 1035.2 of the Evidence Code, a human trafficking caseworker, as defined in Section 1038.2 of the Evidence Code, or a victim of violent crime advocate.

(7) "Tenant" means tenant, subtenant, lessee, or sublessee.

(8) "Tenant in residence" means a tenant who is currently residing in the unit and has full physical and legal access to the unit.

(9) "Victim of violent crime advocate" has the same meaning as defined in Section 1946.7 of the Civil Code.

(b)

(1) A landlord shall not terminate a tenancy or fail to renew a tenancy based on an act of abuse or violence against a tenant, a tenant's immediate family member, or a tenant's household member if the landlord has received documentation evidencing abuse or violence against the tenant, the tenant's immediate family member, or the tenant's household member.

(2) Notwithstanding paragraph (1), a landlord may terminate a tenancy or fail to renew a tenancy based on an act of abuse or violence against a tenant, a tenant's immediate family member, or a tenant's household member even after receiving documentation of abuse or violence against the tenant, the tenant's immediate family member, or the tenant's household member if either of the following apply:

(A) The perpetrator of abuse or violence is a tenant in residence of the same dwelling unit as the tenant, the tenant's immediate family member, or household member.

(B) Both of the following apply:

(i) The perpetrator of abuse or violence's words or actions have threatened the physical safety of other tenants, guests, invitees, or licensees.

(ii) After expiration of a three-day notice requiring the tenant not to voluntarily permit or consent to the presence of the perpetrator of abuse or violence on the premises, the tenant continues to do so.

(c) Notwithstanding any provision in a lease to the contrary, a landlord shall not be liable to any other tenants for any action that arises due to the landlord's compliance with this section.

(d) A defendant in an unlawful detainer action arising from a landlord's termination of a tenancy or failure to renew a tenancy that is based on an act of abuse or violence against a tenant, a tenant's immediate family member, or a tenant's household member may raise an affirmative defense as follows:

(1) If the perpetrator of the abuse or violence is not a tenant in residence of the same dwelling unit as the tenant, the tenant's immediate family member, or household member, then the defendant shall have a complete defense as to that cause of action, unless each clause of subparagraph (B) of paragraph (2) of subdivision (b) applies.

(2) If the perpetrator of the abuse or violence is a tenant in residence of the same dwelling unit as the tenant, the tenant's immediate family member, or household member, the court shall proceed in accordance with Section 1174.27.

(e)

(1) A landlord shall not disclose any information provided by a tenant under this section to a third party unless either of the following is true:

(A) The tenant has consented in writing to the disclosure.

(B) The disclosure is required by law or court order.

(2) A landlord's communication with the qualified third party

who provides documentation in order to verify the contents of that documentation is not a disclosure for purposes of this subdivision.
(f) The Judicial Council shall review its forms that may be used by a party to assert in the responsive pleading the grounds set forth in this section as an affirmative defense to an unlawful detainer action and, by January 1, 2025, make any changes to those forms that the Judicial Council deems necessary to conform them to this section.

Ca. Civ. Proc. Code § 1161.3
Amended by Stats 2023 ch 478 (AB 1756),s 16, eff. 1/1/2024.
Amended by Stats 2022 ch 558 (SB 1017),s 2, eff. 1/1/2023.
Amended by Stats 2018 ch 190 (AB 2413),s 2, eff. 1/1/2019.
Amended by Stats 2013 ch 130 (SB 612),s 3, eff. 1/1/2014.
Amended by Stats 2012 ch 516 (SB 1403),s 2, eff. 1/1/2013.
Added by Stats 2010 ch 626 (SB 782),s 4, eff. 1/1/2011.

Section 1161.4 - Causing tenant to quit involuntarily or bring action to recover possession because of immigration or citizenship status prohibited

(a) A landlord shall not cause a tenant or occupant to quit involuntarily or bring an action to recover possession because of the immigration or citizenship status of a tenant, occupant, or other person known to the landlord to be associated with a tenant or occupant, unless the landlord is complying with any legal obligation under any federal government program that provides for rent limitations or rental assistance to a qualified tenant.
(b) In an unlawful detainer action, a tenant or occupant may raise, as an affirmative defense, that the landlord violated subdivision (a).
(c) It is a rebuttable presumption that a tenant or occupant has established an affirmative defense under this section in an unlawful detainer action if the landlord did both of the following:

(1) Approved the tenant or occupant to take possession of the unit before filing the unlawful detainer action.

(2) Included in the unlawful detainer action a claim based on one of the following:

(A) The failure at any time of a previously approved tenant or occupant to provide a valid social security number.

(B) The failure at any time of a previously approved tenant or occupant to provide information required to obtain a consumer credit report under Section 1785.11 of the Civil Code.

(C) The failure at any time of a previously approved tenant or occupant to provide a form of identification deemed acceptable by the landlord.

(d) This section does not create a rebuttable presumption that a tenant or occupant has established an affirmative defense under this section if a landlord has requested the information described in paragraph (2) of subdivision (c) for the purpose of complying with any legal obligation under any federal government program that provides for rent limitations or rental assistance to a qualified tenant, or any other federal law, or a subpoena, warrant, or other order issued by a court.

(e) The rebuttable presumption in this section does not limit paragraph (2) of subdivision (c) of Section 1940.3 of the Civil Code.

(f) No affirmative defense is established under subdivision (b) if a landlord files an unlawful detainer action for the purpose of complying with any legal obligation under any federal government program that provides for rent limitations or rental assistance to a qualified tenant.

(g) For purposes of this section, "immigration or citizenship status" includes a perception that the person has a particular immigration status or citizenship status, or that the person is associated with a person who has, or is perceived to have, a particular immigration status or citizenship status.

Ca. Civ. Proc. Code § 1161.4
Added by Stats 2017 ch 489 (AB 291),s 8, eff. 1/1/2018.

Section 1161.5 - Declaration of forfeiture nullified upon timely performance after notice or waiver of breach

When the notice required by Section 1161 states that the lessor or the landlord may elect to declare the forfeiture of the lease or rental agreement, that declaration shall be nullified and the lease or rental agreement shall remain in effect if the lessee or tenant performs within three days after service of the notice or if the breach is waived by the lessor or the landlord after service of the notice.

Ca. Civ. Proc. Code § 1161.5
Added by Stats. 1984, Ch. 174, Sec. 1.

Section 1161a - Removal of persons holding over and continuing in possession of manufactured home, mobilehome, floating home or real property after three-day notice

(a) As used in this section:

(1) "Manufactured home" has the same meaning as provided in Section 18007 of the Health and Safety Code.

(2) "Mobilehome" has the same meaning as provided in Section 18008 of the Health and Safety Code.

(3) "Floating home" has the same meaning as provided in subdivision (d) of Section 18075.55 of the Health and Safety Code.
(b) In any of the following cases, a person who holds over and continues in possession of a manufactured home, mobilehome, floating home, or real property after a three-day written notice to quit the property has been served upon the person, or if there is a subtenant in actual occupation of the premises, also upon such subtenant, as prescribed in Section 1162, may be removed therefrom as prescribed in this chapter:

(1) Where the property has been sold pursuant to a writ of execution against such person, or a person under whom such person claims, and the title under the sale has been duly perfected.

(2) Where the property has been sold pursuant to a writ of sale, upon the foreclosure by proceedings taken as prescribed in this code of a mortgage, or under an express power of sale contained therein, executed by such person, or a person under whom such person claims, and the title under the foreclosure has been duly perfected.

(3) Where the property has been sold in accordance with Section 2924 of the Civil Code, under a power of sale contained in a deed of trust executed by such person, or a person under whom such person claims, and the title under the sale has been duly perfected.

(4) Where the property has been sold by such person, or a person under whom such person claims, and the title under the sale has been duly perfected.

(5) Where the property has been sold in accordance with Section 18037.5 of the Health and Safety Code under the default provisions of a conditional sale contract or security agreement executed by such person, or a person under whom such person claims, and the title under the sale has been duly perfected.

(c) Notwithstanding the provisions of subdivision (b), a tenant or subtenant in possession of a rental housing unit which has been sold by reason of any of the causes enumerated in subdivision (b), who rents or leases the rental housing unit either on a periodic basis from week to week, month to month, or other interval, or for a fixed period of time, shall be given written notice to quit pursuant to Section 1162, at least as long as the term of hiring itself but not exceeding 30 days, before the tenant or subtenant may be removed therefrom as prescribed in this chapter.

(d) For the purpose of subdivision (c), "rental housing unit" means any structure or any part thereof which is rented or offered for rent for residential occupancy in this state.

Ca. Civ. Proc. Code § 1161a
Amended by Stats. 1991, Ch. 942, Sec. 11.

Section 1161b - Tenant or subtenant in possession of rental housing unit at time property sold in foreclosure

(a) Notwithstanding Section 1161a, a tenant or subtenant in possession of a rental housing unit under a month-to-month lease or periodic tenancy at the time the property is sold in foreclosure shall be given 90 days' written notice to quit pursuant to Section 1162 before the tenant or subtenant may be removed from the property as prescribed in this chapter.

(b) In addition to the rights set forth in subdivision (a), tenants or subtenants holding possession of a rental housing unit under a fixed-term residential lease entered into before transfer of title at the foreclosure sale shall have the right to possession until the end of the lease term, and all rights and obligations under the lease shall survive foreclosure, except that the tenancy may be terminated upon 90 days' written notice to quit pursuant to subdivision (a) if any of the following conditions apply:

(1) The purchaser or successor in interest will occupy the housing unit as a primary residence.

(2) The lessee is the mortgagor or the child, spouse, or parent of the mortgagor.

(3) The lease was not the result of an arms' length transaction.

(4) The lease requires the receipt of rent that is substantially less than fair market rent for the property, except when rent is reduced or subsidized due to a federal, state, or local subsidy or law.

(c) The purchaser or successor in interest shall bear the burden of proof in establishing that a fixed-term residential lease is not entitled to protection under subdivision (b).

(d) This section shall not apply if any party to the note remains in the property as a tenant, subtenant, or occupant.

(e) Nothing in this section is intended to affect any local just cause eviction ordinance. This section does not, and shall not be construed to, affect the authority of a public entity that otherwise exists to regulate or monitor the basis for eviction.

Ca. Civ. Proc. Code § 1161b

Amended by Stats 2019 ch 134 (SB 18),s 3, eff. 1/1/2020.
Amended by Stats 2012 ch 562 (AB 2610),s 3, eff. 1/1/2013.
Added by Stats 2008 ch 69 (SB 1137),s 6, eff. 7/8/2008.

Section 1161c - [Repealed]
Ca. Civ. Proc. Code § 1161c
Amended by Stats 2012 ch 210 (SB 825),s 1, eff. 1/1/2013.
Added by Stats 2010 ch 641 (SB 1149),s 2, eff. 1/1/2011.

Section 1162 - Service of required notices
(a) Except as provided in subdivision (b), the notices required by Sections 1161 and 1161a may be served by any of the following methods:

(1) By delivering a copy to the tenant personally.

(2) If he or she is absent from his or her place of residence, and from his or her usual place of business, by leaving a copy with some person of suitable age and discretion at either place, and sending a copy through the mail addressed to the tenant at his or her place of residence.

(3) If such place of residence and business cannot be ascertained, or a person of suitable age or discretion there can not be found, then by affixing a copy in a conspicuous place on the property, and also delivering a copy to a person there residing, if such person can be found; and also sending a copy through the mail addressed to the tenant at the place where the property is situated. Service upon a subtenant may be made in the same manner.
(b) The notices required by Section 1161 may be served upon a commercial tenant by any of the following methods:

(1) By delivering a copy to the tenant personally.

(2) If he or she is absent from the commercial rental property, by leaving a copy with some person of suitable age and discretion at the property, and sending a copy through the mail addressed to the tenant at the address where the property is situated.

(3) If, at the time of attempted service, a person of suitable age or discretion is not found at the rental property through the exercise of reasonable diligence, then by affixing a copy in a conspicuous place on the property, and also sending a copy through the mail addressed to the tenant at the address where the property is situated. Service upon a subtenant may be made in the same manner.

(c) For purposes of subdivision (b), "commercial tenant" means a person or entity that hires any real property in this state that is not a dwelling unit, as defined in subdivision (c) of Section 1940 of the Civil Code, or a mobilehome, as defined in Section 798.3 of the Civil Code.

Ca. Civ. Proc. Code § 1162

Amended by Stats 2010 ch 144 (AB 1263),s 1, eff. 1/1/2011.

Amended by Stats 2002 ch 664 (AB 3034),s 49.5, eff. 1/1/2003.

Section 1162a - Service of copy of receiver's or levying officer's deed

In any case in which service or exhibition of a receiver's or levying officer's deed is required, in lieu thereof service of a copy or copies of the deed may be made as provided in Section 1162.

Ca. Civ. Proc. Code § 1162a

Amended by Stats. 1982, Ch. 497, Sec. 75. Operative July 1, 1983, by Sec. 185 of Ch. 497.

Section 1164 - Parties defendants

No person other than the tenant of the premises and subtenant, if there be one, in the actual occupation of the premises when the complaint is filed, need be made parties defendant in the proceeding, nor shall any proceeding abate, nor the plaintiff be nonsuited for the nonjoinder of any person who might have been made party defendant, but when it appears that any of the parties served with process, or appearing in the proceeding, are guilty of the offense charged, judgment must be rendered against him or her. In case a defendant has become a subtenant of the premises in controversy, after the service of the notice provided for by subdivision 2 of Section 1161 of this code, upon the tenant of the premises, the fact that such notice was not served on each subtenant shall constitute no defense to the action. All persons who enter the premises under the tenant, after the commencement of the suit, shall be bound by the judgment, the same as if he or they had been made party to the action.

Ca. Civ. Proc. Code § 1164
Amended by Stats. 1975, Ch. 1241.

Section 1165 - Applicability of procedures relating to civil actions

Except as provided in the preceding section, the provisions of Part II of this Code, relating to parties to civil actions, are applicable to this proceeding.

Ca. Civ. Proc. Code § 1165
Enacted 1872.

Section 1166 - Complaint requirements

(a) The complaint shall:

(1) Be verified and include the typed or printed name of the person verifying the complaint.

(2) Set forth the facts on which the plaintiff seeks to recover.

(3) Describe the premises with reasonable certainty.

(4) If the action is based on paragraph (2) of Section 1161, state the amount of rent in default.

(5) State specifically the method used to serve the defendant with the notice or notices of termination upon which the complaint is based. This requirement may be satisfied by using and completing all items relating to service of the notice or notices in an appropriate Judicial Council form complaint, or by attaching a proof of service of the notice or notices of termination served on the defendant.

(b) The complaint may set forth any circumstances of fraud, force, or violence that may have accompanied the alleged forcible entry or forcible or unlawful detainer, and claim damages therefor.

(c) In an action regarding residential real property based on Section 1161a, the plaintiff shall state in the caption of the complaint "Action based on Code of Civil Procedure Section 1161a."

(d)

(1) In an action regarding residential property, the plaintiff shall attach to the complaint the following:

(A) A copy of the notice or notices of termination served on the defendant upon which the complaint is based.

(B) A copy of any written lease or rental agreement regarding the premises. Any addenda or attachments to the lease or written agreement that form the basis of the complaint shall also be attached. The documents required by this subparagraph are not required to be attached if the complaint alleges any of the following:

(i) The lease or rental agreement is oral.

(ii) A written lease or rental agreement regarding the premises is not in the possession of the landlord or any agent or employee of the landlord.

(iii) An action based solely on subdivision (2) of Section 1161.

(2) If the plaintiff fails to attach the documents required by this subdivision, the court shall grant leave to amend the complaint for a five-day period in order to include the required attachments.

(e) Upon filing the complaint, a summons shall be issued thereon.

Ca. Civ. Proc. Code § 1166

Amended by Stats 2010 ch 641 (SB 1149),s 3, eff. 1/1/2011.

Added by Stats 2003 ch 787 (SB 345),s 4, eff. 1/1/2004 op. 1/1/2005.

Former §1166 repealed by Stats 2003 ch 787 (SB 345),s 3, eff. 1/1/2004

Section 1166a - Immediate possession upon motion by writ of possession

(a) Upon filing the complaint, the plaintiff may, upon motion, have immediate possession of the premises by a writ of possession of a manufactured home, mobilehome, or real property issued by the court and directed to the sheriff of the county or marshal, for execution, where it appears to the satisfaction of the court, after a hearing on the motion, from the verified complaint and from any affidavits filed or oral testimony given by or on behalf of the parties, that the defendant resides out of state, has departed from the state, cannot, after due diligence, be found within the state, or has concealed himself or herself to avoid the service of summons. The motion shall indicate that the writ applies to all tenants, subtenants, if any, named claimants, if any, and any other occupants of the premises.

(b) Written notice of the hearing on the motion shall be served on the defendant by the plaintiff in accordance with the provisions of Section 1011, and shall inform the defendant as follows: "You may file affidavits on your own behalf with the court and may appear and present testimony on your own behalf. However, if you fail to appear, the plaintiff will apply to the court for a writ of possession of a manufactured home, mobilehome, or real property."

(c) The plaintiff shall file an undertaking in a sum that shall be fixed and determined by the judge, to the effect that, if the plaintiff fails to recover judgment against the defendant for the possession of the premises or if the suit is dismissed, the plaintiff will pay to the defendant those damages, not to exceed the amount fixed in the undertaking, as may be sustained by the defendant by reason of that dispossession under the writ of possession of a manufactured home, mobilehome, or real property.

(d) If, at the hearing on the motion, the findings of the court are in favor of the plaintiff and against the defendant, an order shall be entered for the immediate possession of the premises.

(e) The order for the immediate possession of the premises may be enforced as provided in Division 3 (commencing with Section 712.010) of Title 9 of Part 2.

(f) For the purposes of this section, references in Division 3 (commencing with Section 712.010) of Title 9 of Part 2 and in subdivisions (e) to (m), inclusive, of Section 1174, to the "judgment debtor" shall be deemed references to the defendant, to the "judgment creditor" shall be deemed references to the plaintiff, and to the "judgment of possession or sale of property" shall be deemed references to an order for the immediate possession of the premises.

> *Ca. Civ. Proc. Code § 1166a*

Amended by Stats. 1996, Ch. 872, Sec. 20. Effective January 1, 1997.

Section 1167 - Summons; defendant's response

(a) The summons shall be in the form specified in Section 412.20 except that when the defendant is served, the defendant's response shall be filed within five days, excluding Saturdays and Sundays and other judicial holidays, after the complaint is served upon the defendant.

(b) If service is completed by mail or in person through the Secretary of State's address confidentiality program under Chapter 3.1 (commencing with Section 6205) of Division 7 of Title 1 of the Government Code, the defendant shall have an additional five court days to file a response.

(c) In all other respects the summons shall be issued and served and returned in the same manner as a summons in a civil action.

> *Ca. Civ. Proc. Code § 1167*

Amended by Stats 2022 ch 686 (AB 1726),s 3, eff. 1/1/2023.
Amended by Stats 2018 ch 260 (AB 2343),s 2, eff. 1/1/2019.

Section 1167.1 - Dismissal for failure to file proof of service

If proof of service of the summons has not been filed within 60 days of the complaint's filing, the court may dismiss the action without prejudice.

> *Ca. Civ. Proc. Code § 1167.1*

Added by Stats 2016 ch 336 (AB 2819),s 4, eff. 1/1/2017.

Section 1167.25 - [Repealed]

> *Ca. Civ. Proc. Code § 1167.25*

Repealed by Stats 2001 ch 115 (SB 153), s 4, eff. 1/1/2002.

Section 1167.3 - Time allowed defendant to answer

In any action under this chapter, unless otherwise ordered by the court for good cause shown, the time allowed the defendant to answer the complaint, answer the complaint, if amended, or amend the answer under paragraph (2), (3), (5), (6), or (7) of subdivision (a) of Section 586 shall not exceed five days.

Ca. Civ. Proc. Code § 1167.3
EFFECTIVE 1/1/2000. Amended September 7, 1999 (Bill Number: SB 210) (Chapter 344).
Amended July 12, 1999 (Bill Number: SB 966) (Chapter 83).

Section 1167.4 - Notice of motion as provided for in section 418.10(a) filed by defendant

Notwithstanding any other provision of law, in any action under this chapter:

(a) Where the defendant files a notice of motion as provided for in subdivision (a) of Section 418.10, the time for making the motion shall be not less than three days nor more than seven days after the filing of the notice.

(b) The service and filing of a notice of motion under subdivision (a) shall extend the defendant's time to plead until five days after service upon him of the written notice of entry of an order denying his motion, except that for good cause shown the court may extend the defendant's time to plead for an additional period not exceeding 15 days.

Ca. Civ. Proc. Code § 1167.4
Added by Stats. 1971, Ch. 1332.

Section 1167.5 - Number of days allowed in extension of time

Unless otherwise ordered by the court for good cause shown, no extension of time allowed in any action under this chapter for the causes specified in Section 1054 shall exceed 10 days without the consent of the adverse party.

Ca. Civ. Proc. Code § 1167.5
Added by Stats. 1971, Ch. 849.

Section 1169 - Default judgment

If, at the time appointed, any defendant served with a summons does not appear and defend, the clerk, upon written application of the plaintiff and proof of the service of summons and complaint, shall enter the default of any defendant so served, and, if requested by the plaintiff, immediately shall enter judgment for restitution of the premises and shall issue a writ of execution thereon. The application for default judgment and the default judgment shall include a place to indicate that the judgment includes tenants, subtenants, if any, named claimants, if any, and any other occupants of the premises. Thereafter, the plaintiff may apply to the court for any other relief demanded in the complaint, including the costs, against the defendant, or defendants, or against one or more of the defendants.

Ca. Civ. Proc. Code § 1169

Amended by Stats 2007 ch 263 (AB 310),s 13, eff. 1/1/2008.

Section 1170 - Appearance by defendant

On or before the day fixed for his appearance, the defendant may appear and answer or demur.

Ca. Civ. Proc. Code § 1170

Enacted 1872.

Section 1170.5 - Trial of proceeding

(a) If the defendant appears pursuant to Section 1170, trial of the proceeding shall be held not later than the 20th day following the date that the request to set the time of the trial is made. Judgment shall be entered thereon and, if the plaintiff prevails, a writ of execution shall be issued immediately by the court upon the request of the plaintiff.

(b) The court may extend the period for trial upon the agreement of all of the parties. No other extension of the time for trial of an action under this chapter may be granted unless the court, upon its own motion or on motion of any party, holds a hearing and renders a decision thereon as specified in subdivision (c).

(c) If trial is not held within the time specified in this section, the court, upon finding that there is a reasonable probability that the plaintiff will prevail in the action, shall determine the amount of damages, if any, to be suffered by the plaintiff by reason of the extension, and shall issue an order requiring the defendant to pay that amount into court as the rent would have otherwise become due and payable or into an escrow designated by the court for so long as the defendant remains in possession pending the termination of the action. The determination of the amount of the payment shall be based on the plaintiff's verified statement of the contract rent for rental payment, any verified objection thereto filed by the defendant, and the oral or demonstrative evidence presented at the hearing. The court's determination of the amount of damages shall include consideration of any evidence, presented by the parties, embracing the issue of diminution of value or any set off permitted by law.

(d) If the defendant fails to make a payment ordered by the court, trial of the action shall be held within 15 days of the date payment was due.

(e) Any cost for administration of an escrow account pursuant to this section shall be recoverable by the prevailing party as part of any recoverable cost in the action.

(f) After trial of the action, the court shall determine the distribution of the payment made into court or the escrow designated by the court.

(g) Where payments into court or the escrow designated by the court are made pursuant to this section, the court may order that the payments be invested in an insured interest-bearing account. Interest on the account shall be allocated to the parties in the same proportions as the original funds are allocated.

(h) If any provision of this section or the application thereof to any person or circumstances is held invalid, such invalidity shall not affect other provisions or applications of the section which can be given effect without the invalid provision or application, and to this end the provisions of this section are severable.

(i) Nothing in this section shall be construed to abrogate or interfere with the precedence given to the trial of criminal cases over the trial of civil matters by Section 1050 of the Penal Code.

Ca. Civ. Proc. Code § 1170.5
Added by Stats. 1982, Ch. 1620, Sec. 2.

Section 1170.7 - Motion for summary judgment

A motion for summary judgment may be made at any time after the answer is filed upon giving five days notice. Summary judgment shall be granted or denied on the same basis as a motion under Section 437c.

Ca. Civ. Proc. Code § 1170.7
Added by Stats. 1982, Ch. 1620, Sec. 3.

Section 1170.8 - Discovery motion

In any action under this chapter, a discovery motion may be made at any time upon giving five days' notice.

Ca. Civ. Proc. Code § 1170.8
Added by Stats 2007 ch 113 (AB 1126),s 1, eff. 1/1/2008.

Section 1170.9 - Rules prescribing time for filing and serving opposition and reply papers

The Judicial Council shall adopt rules, not inconsistent with statute, prescribing the time for filing and serving opposition and reply papers, if any, relating to a motion under Section 1167.4, 1170.7, or 1170.8.

Ca. Civ. Proc. Code § 1170.9
Added by Stats 2007 ch 113 (AB 1126),s 2, eff. 1/1/2008.

Section 1171 - Issue of fact tried by jury

Whenever an issue of fact is presented by the pleadings, it must be tried by a jury, unless such jury be waived as in other cases. The jury shall be formed in the same manner as other trial juries in an action of the same jurisdictional classification in the Court in which the action is pending.

Ca. Civ. Proc. Code § 1171
Amended by Stats. 1998, Ch. 931, Sec. 120. Effective September 28, 1998.

Section 1172 - Showing required by plaintiff in proceeding for forcible entry or forcible detainer; defendant's showing in defense

On the trial of any proceeding for any forcible entry or forcible detainer, the plaintiff shall only be required to show, in addition to the forcible entry or forcible detainer complained of, that he was peaceably in the actual possession at the time of the forcible entry, or was entitled to the possession at the time of the forcible detainer. The defendant may show in his defense that he or his ancestors, or those whose interest in such premises he claims, have been in the quiet possession thereof for the space of one whole year together next before the commencement of the proceedings, and that his interest therein is not then ended or determined; and such showing is a bar to the proceedings.

Ca. Civ. Proc. Code § 1172
Enacted 1872.

Section 1173 - Amendment of complaint when evidence shows defendant guilty of offense other than charged in complaint

When, upon the trial of any proceeding under this chapter, it appears from the evidence that the defendant has been guilty of either a forcible entry or a forcible or unlawful detainer, and other than the offense charged in the complaint, the Judge must order that such complaint be forthwith amended to conform to such proofs; such amendment must be made without any imposition of terms. No continuance shall be permitted upon account of such amendment unless the defendant, by affidavit filed, shows to the satisfaction of the Court good cause therefor.

Ca. Civ. Proc. Code § 1173
Amended by Stats. 1885, Ch. 121.

Section 1174 - Judgment if verdict or findings of court in favor of plaintiff; action brought by petroleum distributor against gasoline dealer

(a) If upon the trial, the verdict of the jury, or, if the case be tried without a jury, the findings of the court be in favor of the plaintiff and against the defendant, judgment shall be entered for the possession of the premises; and if the proceedings be for an unlawful detainer after neglect, or failure to perform the conditions or covenants of the lease or agreement under which the property is held, or after default in the payment of rent, the judgment shall also declare the forfeiture of that lease or agreement if the notice required by Section 1161 states the election of the landlord to declare the forfeiture thereof, but if that notice does not so state that election, the lease or agreement shall not be forfeited. Except as provided in Section 1166a, in any action for unlawful detainer brought by a petroleum distributor against a gasoline dealer, possession shall not be restored to the petroleum distributor unless the court in the unlawful detainer action determines that the petroleum distributor had good cause under Section 20999.1 of the Business and Professions Code to terminate, cancel, or refuse to renew the franchise of the gasoline dealer.

In any action for unlawful detainer brought by a petroleum distributor against the gasoline dealer, the court may, at the time of request of either party, require the tenant to make rental payments into the court, for the lessor, at the contract rate, pending the resolution of the action.

(b) The jury or the court, if the proceedings be tried without a jury, shall also assess the damages occasioned to the plaintiff by any forcible entry, or by any forcible or unlawful detainer, alleged in the complaint and proved on the trial, and find the amount of any rent due, if the alleged unlawful detainer be after default in the payment of rent. If the defendant is found guilty of forcible entry, or forcible or unlawful detainer, and malice is shown, the plaintiff may be awarded statutory damages of up to six hundred dollars ($600), in addition to actual damages, including rent found due. The trier of fact shall determine whether actual damages, statutory damages, or both, shall be awarded, and judgment shall be entered accordingly.

(c) When the proceeding is for an unlawful detainer after default in the payment of rent, and the lease or agreement under which the rent is payable has not by its terms expired, and the notice required by Section 1161 has not stated the election of the landlord to declare the forfeiture thereof, the court may, and, if the lease or agreement is in writing, is for a term of more than one year, and does not contain a forfeiture clause, shall order that a writ shall not be issued to enforce the judgment until the expiration of five days after the entry of the judgment, within which time the tenant, or any subtenant, or any mortgagee of the term, or any other party interested in its continuance, may pay into the court, for the landlord, the amount found due as rent, with interest thereon, and the amount of the damages found by the jury or the court for the unlawful detainer, and the costs of the proceedings, and thereupon the judgment shall be satisfied and the tenant be restored to the tenant's estate. If payment as provided in this subdivision is not made within five days, the judgment may be enforced for its full amount and for the possession of the premises. In all other cases the judgment may be enforced immediately.

(d) Subject to subdivision (c), the judgment for possession of the premises may be enforced as provided in Division 3 (commencing with Section 712.010) of Title 9 of Part 2.

(e) Personal property remaining on the premises which the landlord reasonably believes to have been lost shall be disposed of pursuant to Article 1 (commencing with Section 2080) of Chapter 4 of Title 6 of Part 4 of Division 3 of the Civil Code. The landlord is not liable to the owner of any property which is disposed of in this manner. If the appropriate police or sheriff's department refuses to accept that property, it shall be deemed not to have been lost for the purposes of this subdivision.

(f) The landlord shall give notice pursuant to Section 1983 of the Civil Code to any person (other than the tenant) reasonably believed by the landlord to be the owner of personal property remaining on the premises unless the procedure for surrender of property under Section 1965 of the Civil Code has been initiated or completed.

(g) The landlord shall store the personal property in a place of safekeeping until it is either released pursuant to subdivision (h) or disposed of pursuant to subdivision (i).

(h) The landlord shall release the personal property pursuant to Section 1965 of the Civil Code or shall release it to the tenant or, at the landlord's option, to a person reasonably believed by the landlord to be its owner if the tenant or other person pays the costs of storage as provided in Section 1990 of the Civil Code and claims the property not later than the date specified in the writ of possession before which the tenant must make his or her claim or the date specified in the notice before which a person other than the tenant must make his or her claim.

(i) Personal property not released pursuant to subdivision (h) shall be disposed of pursuant to Section 1988 of the Civil Code.

(j) Where the landlord releases personal property to the tenant pursuant to subdivision (h), the landlord is not liable with respect to that property to any person.

(k) Where the landlord releases personal property pursuant to subdivision (h) to a person (other than the tenant) reasonably believed by the landlord to be its owner, the landlord is not liable with respect to that property to:

(1) The tenant or to any person to whom notice was given pursuant to subdivision (f); or

(2) Any other person, unless that person proves that, prior to releasing the property, the landlord believed or reasonably should have believed that the person had an interest in the property and also that the landlord knew or should have known upon reasonable investigation the address of that person.

(l) Where personal property is disposed of pursuant to Section 1988 of the Civil Code, the landlord is not liable with respect to that property to:

(1) The tenant or to any person to whom notice was given pursuant to subdivision (f); or

(2) Any other person, unless that person proves that, prior to disposing of the property pursuant to Section 1988 of the Civil Code, the landlord believed or reasonably should have believed that the person had an interest in the property and also that the landlord knew or should have known upon reasonable investigation the address of that person.

(m) For the purposes of subdivisions (e), (f), (h), (k), and (l), the terms "owner," "premises," and "reasonable belief" have the same meaning as provided in Section 1980 of the Civil Code.

Ca. Civ. Proc. Code § 1174

Amended by Stats. 1993, Ch. 755, Sec. 2. Effective January 1, 1994.

Section 1174.2 - Affirmative defense of breach of landlord's obligations or warranty of habitability raised in unlawful detainer proceeding

(a) In an unlawful detainer proceeding involving residential premises after default in payment of rent and in which the tenant has raised as an affirmative defense a breach of the landlord's obligations under Section 1941 of the Civil Code or of any warranty of habitability, the court shall determine whether a substantial breach of these obligations has occurred. If the court finds that a substantial breach has occurred, the court (1) shall determine the reasonable rental value of the premises in its untenantable state to the date of trial, (2) shall deny possession to the landlord and adjudge the tenant to be the prevailing party, conditioned upon the payment by the tenant of the rent that has accrued to the date of the trial as adjusted pursuant to this subdivision within a reasonable period of time not exceeding five days, from the date of the court's judgment or, if service of the court's judgment is made by mail, the payment shall be made within the time set forth in Section 1013, (3) may order the landlord to make repairs and correct the conditions which constitute a breach of the landlord's obligations, (4) shall order that the monthly rent be limited to the reasonable rental value of the premises as determined pursuant to this subdivision until repairs are completed, and (5) except as otherwise provided in subdivision (b), shall award the tenant costs and attorneys' fees if provided by, and pursuant to, any statute or the contract of the parties. If the court orders repairs or corrections, or both, pursuant to paragraph (3), the court's jurisdiction continues over the matter for the purpose of ensuring compliance. The court shall, however, award possession of the premises to the landlord if the tenant fails to pay all rent accrued to the date of trial, as determined due in the judgment, within the period prescribed by the court pursuant to this subdivision. The tenant shall, however, retain any rights conferred by Section 1174.

(b) If the court determines that there has been no substantial breach of Section 1941 of the Civil Code or of any warranty of habitability by the landlord or if the tenant fails to pay all rent accrued to the date of trial, as required by the court pursuant to subdivision (a), then judgment shall be entered in favor of the landlord, and the landlord shall be the prevailing party for the purposes of awarding costs or attorneys' fees pursuant to any statute or the contract of the parties.

(c) As used in this section, "substantial breach" means the failure of the landlord to comply with applicable building and housing code standards which materially affect health and safety.

(d) Nothing in this section is intended to deny the tenant the right to a trial by jury. Nothing in this section shall limit or supersede any provision of Chapter 12.75 (commencing with Section 7060) of Division 7 of Title 1 of the Government Code.

Ca. Civ. Proc. Code § 1174.2

Amended by Stats. 1993, Ch. 589, Sec. 28. Effective January 1, 1994.

Section 1174.21 - Landlord's liability for attorney's fees and costs

A landlord who institutes an unlawful detainer proceeding based upon a tenant's nonpayment of rent, and who is liable for a violation of Section 1942.4 of the Civil Code, shall be liable to the tenant or lessee for reasonable attorneys' fees and costs of the suit, in an amount to be fixed by the court.

Ca. Civ. Proc. Code § 1174.21

Added by Stats 2003 ch 109 (AB 647),s 2, eff. 1/1/2004.

Section 1174.25 - Claim filed as prescribed by section 415.46 when occupant served with prejudgment claim of right of possession

(a)

(1) Except as provided in paragraph (2), an occupant who is served with a prejudgment claim of right to possession in accordance with Section 415.46 may file a claim as prescribed in Section 415.46, with the court within 10 days of the date of service of the prejudgment claim of right to possession as shown on the return of service, which period shall include Saturday and Sunday but exclude all other judicial holidays. If the last day for filing the claim falls on a Saturday or Sunday, the filing period shall be extended to and including the next court day. Filing the prejudgment claim of right to possession shall constitute a general appearance for which a fee shall be collected as provided in Section 70614 of the Government Code. Section 68511.3 of the Government Code applies to the prejudgment claim of right to possession.

(2) In an action as described in paragraph (2) of subdivision (e) of Section 415.46, an occupant may file a prejudgment claim of right to possession at any time before judgment is entered.
(b) At the time of filing, the claimant shall be added as a defendant in the action for unlawful detainer and the clerk shall notify the plaintiff that the claimant has been added as a defendant in the action by mailing a copy of the claim filed with the court to the plaintiff with a notation so indicating. The claimant shall answer or otherwise respond to the summons and complaint within five days, including Saturdays and Sundays, but excluding all other judicial holidays, after filing the prejudgment claim of possession. Thereafter, the name of the claimant shall be added to any pleading, filing or form filed in the action for unlawful detainer.
　　Ca. Civ. Proc. Code § 1174.25
Amended by Stats 2014 ch 913 (AB 2747),s 8, eff. 1/1/2015.
Amended by Stats 2005 ch 75 (AB 145),s 42, eff. 7/19/2005, op. 1/1/2006

Section 1174.27 - Unlawful detainer proceeding; documentation evidencing abuse or violence; affirmative defense

(a)This section shall apply to an unlawful detainer proceeding in which all of the following are true:

(1)The proceeding involves a residential premises.

(2) The complaint includes a cause of action based on an act of abuse or violence against a tenant, a tenant's immediate family member, or a tenant's household member.

(3)A defendant has invoked paragraph (2) of subdivision (d) of Section 1161.3 as an affirmative defense to the cause of action described in paragraph (2).

(b) For the purposes of this section, the definitions in subdivision (a) of Section 1161.3 apply.

(c) The court shall determine whether there is documentation evidencing abuse or violence against the tenant, the tenant's immediate family member, or the tenant's household member.

(d) If the court determines there is not documentation evidencing abuse or violence against the tenant, the court shall deny the affirmative defense.

(e) If the court determines that there is documentation evidencing abuse or violence against the tenant, the tenant's immediate family member, or the tenant's household member, and the court does not find the defendant raising the affirmative defense guilty of an unlawful detainer on any other grounds, then both of the following:

(1) The defendant raising the affirmative defense and any other occupant not found guilty of an unlawful detainer shall not be guilty of an unlawful detainer and shall not be named in any judgment in favor of the landlord.

(2) The defendant raising the affirmative defense and any other occupant not found guilty of an unlawful detainer shall not be held liable to the landlord for any amount related to the unlawful detainer, including, but not limited to, holdover damages, court costs, lease termination fees, or attorney's fees.

(f)

(1) If the court makes the determination described in subdivision (e), upon a showing that any other defendant was the perpetrator of the abuse or violence on which the affirmative defense was based and is guilty of an unlawful detainer, the court shall do both of the following:

(A) Issue a partial eviction ordering the removal of the perpetrator of abuse or violence and ordering that person be immediately removed and barred from the dwelling unit, but the court shall not order the tenancy terminated.

(B) Order the landlord to change the locks and to provide the remaining occupants with the new key.

(2) If a court issues a partial eviction order as described in subparagraph (A) of paragraph (1), then only a defendant found guilty of an unlawful detainer may be liable for holdover damages, court costs, lease termination fees, or attorney's fees, as applicable.

(3) If the court makes the determination described in subdivision (e), the court may, upon a showing that any other defendant was the perpetrator of the abuse or violence on which the affirmative defense was based and is guilty of an unlawful detainer, do any of the following:

(A) Permanently bar the perpetrator of abuse or violence from entering any portion of the residential premises.

(B) Order as an express condition of the tenancy that the remaining occupants shall not give permission to or invite the perpetrator of abuse or violence to live in the dwelling unit.

(4) In exercising its discretion under this subdivision, the court shall take into account custody or visitation orders or arrangements and any other factor that may necessitate the temporary reentry of the perpetrator of abuse or violence.
(g) The Judicial Council shall develop a judgment form for use in a ruling pursuant to subdivision (e) or (f).
(h) Notwithstanding any other law, a determination that a person is a perpetrator of abuse or violence under subdivision (e) or (f) shall not constitute a finding that the person is a perpetrator of abuse or violence for any other purposes and shall not be admissible as

evidence that the person committed a crime or is a perpetrator of abuse or violence in any other proceeding, including, but not limited to, a civil action or proceeding, a criminal action or proceeding, and a proceeding involving a juvenile for a criminal offense.

Ca. Civ. Proc. Code § 1174.27
Added by Stats 2022 ch 558 (SB 1017),s 3, eff. 1/1/2023.

Section 1174.3 - Claim of possession filed by occupant not named in judgment for possession

(a)

(1) Except as provided in paragraph (2), unless a prejudgment claim of right to possession has been served upon occupants in accordance with Section 415.46, any occupant not named in the judgment for possession who occupied the premises on the date of the filing of the action may object to enforcement of the judgment against that occupant by filing a claim of right to possession as prescribed in this section. A claim of right to possession may be filed at any time after service or posting of the writ of possession pursuant to subdivision (a) or (b) of Section 715.020, up to and including the time at which the levying officer returns to effect the eviction of those named in the judgment of possession. Filing the claim of right to possession shall constitute a general appearance for which a fee shall be collected as provided in Section 70614 of the Government Code. Section 68511.3 of the Government Code applies to the claim of right to possession. An occupant or tenant who is named in the action shall not be required to file a claim of right to possession to protect that occupant's right to possession of the premises.

(2) In an action as described in paragraph (2) of subdivision (e) of Section 415.46, an occupant may file a claim of right to possession at any time up to and including the time at which the levying officer returns to effect the eviction of those named in the judgment of possession, without regard to whether a prejudgment claim of right to possession has been served upon the occupant.

(b) The court issuing the writ of possession of real property shall set a date or dates when the court will hold a hearing to determine the validity of objections to enforcement of the judgment specified in subdivision (a). An occupant of the real property for which the writ is issued may make an objection to eviction to the levying officer at the office of the levying officer or at the premises at the time of the eviction. If a claim of right to possession is completed and presented to the sheriff, marshal, or other levying officer, the officer shall forthwith (1) stop the eviction of occupants at the premises, and (2) provide a receipt or copy of the completed claim of right of possession to the claimant indicating the date and time the completed form was received, and (3) deliver the original completed claim of right to possession to the court issuing the writ of possession of real property.

(c) A claim of right to possession is effected by any of the following:

(1) Presenting a completed claim form in person with identification to the sheriff, marshal, or other levying officer as prescribed in this section, and delivering to the court within two court days after its presentation, an amount equal to 15 days' rent together with the appropriate fee or form for proceeding in forma pauperis. Upon receipt of a claim of right to possession, the sheriff, marshal, or other levying officer shall indicate thereon the date and time of its receipt and forthwith deliver the original to the issuing court and a receipt or copy of the claim to the claimant and notify the plaintiff of that fact. Immediately upon receipt of an amount equal to 15 days' rent and the appropriate fee or form for proceeding in forma pauperis, the court shall file the claim of right to possession and serve an endorsed copy with the notice of the hearing date on the plaintiff and the claimant by first-class mail. The court issuing the writ of possession shall set and hold a hearing on the claim not less than five nor more than 15 days after the claim is filed with the court.

(2) Presenting a completed claim form in person with identification to the sheriff, marshal, or other levying officer as prescribed in this section, and delivering to the court within two court days after its presentation, the appropriate fee or form for proceeding in forma pauperis without delivering the amount equivalent to 15 days' rent. In this case, the court shall immediately set a hearing on the claim to be held on the fifth day after the filing is completed. The court shall notify the claimant of the hearing date at the time the claimant completes the filing by delivering to the court the appropriate fee or form for proceeding in forma pauperis, and shall notify the plaintiff of the hearing date by first-class mail. Upon receipt of a claim of right to possession, the sheriff, marshal, or other levying officer shall indicate thereon the date and time of its receipt and forthwith deliver the original to the issuing court and a receipt or copy of the claim to the claimant and notify the plaintiff of that fact.

(d) At the hearing, the court shall determine whether there is a valid claim of possession by the claimant who filed the claim, and the court shall consider all evidence produced at the hearing, including, but not limited to, the information set forth in the claim. The court may determine the claim to be valid or invalid based upon the evidence presented at the hearing. The court shall determine the claim to be invalid if the court determines that the claimant is an invitee, licensee, guest, or trespasser. If the court determines the claim is invalid, the court shall order the return to the claimant of the amount of the 15 days' rent paid by the claimant, if that amount was paid pursuant to paragraph (1) or (3) of subdivision (c), less a pro rata amount for each day that enforcement of the judgment was delayed by reason of making the claim of right to possession, which pro rata amount shall be paid to the landlord. If the court determines the claim is valid, the amount equal to 15 days' rent paid by the claimant shall be returned immediately to the claimant.

(e) If, upon hearing, the court determines that the claim is valid, then the court shall order further proceedings as follows:

(1) If the unlawful detainer is based upon a curable breach, and the claimant was not previously served with a proper notice, if any notice is required, then the required notice may at the plaintiff's discretion be served on the claimant at the hearing or thereafter. If the claimant does not cure the breach within the required time, then a supplemental complaint may be filed and served on the claimant as defendant if the plaintiff proceeds against the claimant in the same action. For the purposes of this section only, service of the required notice, if any notice is required, and of the supplemental complaint may be made by first-class mail addressed to the claimant at the subject premises or upon his or her attorney of record and, in either case, Section 1013 shall otherwise apply. Further proceedings on the merits of the claimant's continued right to possession after service of the Summons and Supplemental Complaint as prescribed by this subdivision shall be conducted pursuant to this chapter.

(2) In all other cases, the court shall deem the unlawful detainer Summons and Complaint to be amended on their faces to include the claimant as defendant, service of the Summons and Complaint, as thus amended, may at the plaintiff's discretion be made at the hearing or thereafter, and the claimant thus named and served as a defendant in the action shall answer or otherwise respond within five days thereafter.

(f) If a claim is made without delivery to the court of the appropriate filing fee or a form for proceeding in forma pauperis, as prescribed in this section, the claim shall be immediately deemed denied and the court shall so order. Upon the denial of the claim, the court shall immediately deliver an endorsed copy of the order to the levying officer and shall serve an endorsed copy of the order on the plaintiff and claimant by first-class mail.

(g) If the claim of right to possession is denied pursuant to subdivision (f), or if the claimant fails to appear at the hearing or, upon hearing, if the court determines that there are no valid claims, or if the claimant does not prevail at a trial on the merits of the unlawful detainer action, the court shall order the levying officer to proceed with enforcement of the original writ of possession of real property as deemed amended to include the claimant, which shall be effected within a reasonable time not to exceed five days. Upon receipt of the court's order, the levying officer shall enforce the writ of possession of real property against any occupant or occupants.

(h) The claim of right to possession shall be made on the following form: [SEE PRINTED VERSION OF THE BILL]

Ca. Civ. Proc. Code § 1174.3
Amended by Stats 2014 ch 913 (AB 2747),s 9, eff. 1/1/2015.
Amended by Stats 2005 ch 75 (AB 145),s 43, eff. 7/19/2005, op. 1/1/2006
Amended by Stats 2002 ch 664 (AB 3034),s 50, eff. 1/1/2003.
Amended by Stats 2001 ch 115 (SB 153), s 5, eff. 1/1/2002.

Section 1174.5 - Lessee not relieved from liability upon judgment declaring forfeiture of lease or agreement

A judgment in unlawful detainer declaring the forfeiture of the lease or agreement under which real property is held shall not relieve the lessee from liability pursuant to Section 1951.2 of the Civil Code.

Ca. Civ. Proc. Code § 1174.5
Added by Stats. 1982, Ch. 488, Sec. 1.

Section 1176 - Stay of judgment pending appeal

(a) An appeal taken by the defendant shall not automatically stay proceedings upon the judgment. Petition for stay of the judgment pending appeal shall first be directed to the judge before whom it was rendered. Stay of judgment shall be granted when the court finds that the moving party will suffer extreme hardship in the absence of a stay and that the nonmoving party will not be irreparably injured by its issuance. If the stay is denied by the trial court, the defendant may forthwith file a petition for an extraordinary writ with the appropriate appeals court. If the trial or appellate court stays enforcement of the judgment, the court may condition the stay on whatever conditions the court deems just, but in any case it shall order the payment of the reasonable monthly rental value to the court monthly in advance as rent would otherwise become due as a condition of issuing the stay of enforcement. As used in this subdivision, "reasonable rental value" means the contract rent unless the rental value has been modified by the trial court in which case that modified rental value shall be used.

(b) A new cause of action on the same agreement for the rental of real property shall not be barred because of an appeal by any party.

Ca. Civ. Proc. Code § 1176
Amended by Stats. 1985, Ch. 1279, Sec. 3.

Section 1177 - Applicability of Part II of Code
Except as otherwise provided in this Chapter the provisions of Part II of this Code are applicable to, and constitute the rules of practice in the proceedings mentioned in this Chapter.
Ca. Civ. Proc. Code § 1177
Enacted 1872.

Section 1178 - Applicability of Part 2 relative to new trials and appeals
The provisions of Part 2 of this code, relative to new trials and appeals, except insofar as they are inconsistent with the provisions of this chapter or with rules adopted by the Judicial Council, apply to the proceedings mentioned in this chapter.
Ca. Civ. Proc. Code § 1178
Amended by Stats. 1945, Ch. 40.

Section 1179 - Relief against forfeiture in case of hardship
The court may relieve a tenant against a forfeiture of a lease or rental agreement, whether written or oral, and whether or not the tenancy has terminated, and restore him or her to his or her former estate or tenancy, in case of hardship, as provided in Section 1174. The court has the discretion to relieve any person against forfeiture on its own motion.
An application for relief against forfeiture may be made at any time prior to restoration of the premises to the landlord. The application may be made by a tenant or subtenant, or a mortgagee of the term, or any person interested in the continuance of the term. It must be made upon petition, setting forth the facts upon which the relief is sought, and be verified by the applicant. Notice of the application, with a copy of the petition, must be served at least five days prior to the hearing on the plaintiff in the judgment, who may appear and contest the application. Alternatively, a person appearing without an attorney may make the application orally, if the plaintiff either is

present and has an opportunity to contest the application, or has been given ex parte notice of the hearing and the purpose of the oral application. In no case shall the application or motion be granted except on condition that full payment of rent due, or full performance of conditions or covenants stipulated, so far as the same is practicable, be made.

Ca. Civ. Proc. Code § 1179

Amended by Stats 2002 ch 301 (SB 1403),s 4, eff. 1/1/2003.

Section 1179a - Precedence of actions

In all proceedings brought to recover the possession of real property pursuant to the provisions of this chapter all courts, wherein such actions are or may hereafter be pending, shall give such actions precedence over all other civil actions therein, except actions to which special precedence is given by law, in the matter of the setting the same for hearing or trial, and in hearing the same, to the end that all such actions shall be quickly heard and determined.

Ca. Civ. Proc. Code § 1179a

Added by Stats. 1931, Ch. 885.

Chapter 5 - COVID-19 TENANT RELIEF ACT

Section 1179.01 - [Effective until 10/1/2025] Short title

This chapter is known, and may be cited, as the COVID-19 Tenant Relief Act.

Ca. Civ. Proc. Code § 1179.01

Amended by Stats 2021 ch 2 (SB 91),s 15, eff. 1/29/2021.

Chapter heading amended by Stats 2021 ch 2 (SB 91),s 14, eff. 1/29/2021.

Added by Stats 2020 ch 37 (AB 3088),s 20, eff. 8/31/2020.

Section 1179.01.5 - [Effective until 10/1/2025] Legislative intent; prohibited acts by court; unlawful detainer cover sheet

(a) It is the intent of the Legislature that the Judicial Council and the courts have adequate time to prepare to implement the new procedures resulting from this chapter, including educating and training judicial officers and staff.

(b) Notwithstanding any other law, before October 5, 2020, a court shall not do any of the following:

(1) Issue a summons on a complaint for unlawful detainer in any action that seeks possession of residential real property and that is based, in whole or in part, on nonpayment of rent or other charges.

(2) Enter a default or a default judgment for restitution in an unlawful detainer action that seeks possession of residential real property and that is based, in whole or in part, on nonpayment of rent or other charges.

(c)

(1) A plaintiff in an unlawful detainer action shall file a cover sheet in the form specified in paragraph (2) that indicates both of the following:

(A) Whether the action seeks possession of residential real property.

(B) If the action seeks possession of residential real property, whether the action is based, in whole or part, on an alleged default in payment of rent or other charges.

(2) The cover sheet specified in paragraph (1) shall be in the following form: "UNLAWFUL DETAINER SUPPLEMENTAL COVER SHEET

1. This action seeks possession of real property that is:

a. [] Residential

b. [] Commercial

2. (Complete only if paragraph 1(a) is checked) This action is based, in whole or in part, on an alleged default in payment of rent or other charges.

    a. [] Yes

    b. [] No Date:_____

_____

_____
Type Or Print Name Signature Of Party Or Attorney For Party"

    (3) The cover sheet required by this subdivision shall be in addition to any civil case cover sheet or other form required by law, the California Rules of Court, or a local court rule.

    (4) The Judicial Council may develop a form for mandatory use that includes the information in paragraph (2).
(d) This section does not prevent a court from issuing a summons or entering default in an unlawful detainer action that seeks possession of residential real property and that is not based, in whole or in part, on nonpayment of rent or other charges.
    Ca. Civ. Proc. Code § 1179.01.5
Added by Stats 2020 ch 37 (AB 3088),s 20, eff. 8/31/2020.

Section 1179.02 - [Effective until 10/1/2025] Definitions
For purposes of this chapter:
(a) "Covered time period" means the time period between March 1, 2020, and September 30, 2021.
(b) "COVID-19-related financial distress" means any of the following:

    (1) Loss of income caused by the COVID-19 pandemic.

    (2) Increased out-of-pocket expenses directly related to performing essential work during the COVID-19 pandemic.

    (3) Increased expenses directly related to the health impact of the COVID-19 pandemic.

(4) Childcare responsibilities or responsibilities to care for an elderly, disabled, or sick family member directly related to the COVID-19 pandemic that limit a tenant's ability to earn income.

(5) Increased costs for childcare or attending to an elderly, disabled, or sick family member directly related to the COVID-19 pandemic.

(6) Other circumstances related to the COVID-19 pandemic that have reduced a tenant's income or increased a tenant's expenses.
(c) "COVID-19 rental debt" means unpaid rent or any other unpaid financial obligation of a tenant under the tenancy that came due during the covered time period.
(d) "Declaration of COVID-19-related financial distress" means the following written statement: I am currently unable to pay my rent or other financial obligations under the lease in full because of one or more of the following:

1. Loss of income caused by the COVID-19 pandemic.

2. Increased out-of-pocket expenses directly related to performing essential work during the COVID-19 pandemic.

3. Increased expenses directly related to health impacts of the COVID-19 pandemic.

4. Childcare responsibilities or responsibilities to care for an elderly, disabled, or sick family member directly related to the COVID-19 pandemic that limit my ability to earn income.

5. Increased costs for childcare or attending to an elderly, disabled, or sick family member directly related to the COVID-19 pandemic.

6. Other circumstances related to the COVID-19 pandemic that have reduced my income or increased my expenses. Any public assistance, including unemployment insurance, pandemic unemployment assistance, state disability insurance (SDI), or paid family leave, that I have received since the start of the COVID-19 pandemic does not fully make up for my loss of income and/or increased expenses.

Signed under penalty of perjury:

Dated:

(e) "Landlord" includes all of the following or the agent of any of the following:

    (1) An owner of residential real property.

    (2) An owner of a residential rental unit.

    (3) An owner of a mobilehome park.

    (4) An owner of a mobilehome park space or lot.

(f) "Protected time period" means the time period between March 1, 2020, and August 31, 2020.

(g) "Rental payment" means rent or any other financial obligation of a tenant under the tenancy.

(h) "Tenant" means any natural person who hires real property except any of the following:

    (1) Tenants of commercial property, as defined in subdivision (c) of Section 1162 of the Civil Code.

    (2) Those persons whose occupancy is described in subdivision (b) of Section 1940 of the Civil Code.

(i) "Transition time period" means the time period between September 1, 2020, and September 30, 2021.

Ca. Civ. Proc. Code § 1179.02

Amended by Stats 2021 ch 27 (AB 832),s 14, eff. 6/28/2021.
Amended by Stats 2021 ch 2 (SB 91),s 16, eff. 1/29/2021.
Added by Stats 2020 ch 37 (AB 3088),s 20, eff. 8/31/2020.

Section 1179.02.5 - [Effective until 10/1/2025] Serving notice to high income tenant

(a) For purposes of this section:

(1)

(A) "High-income tenant" means a tenant with an annual household income of 130 percent of the median income, as published by the Department of Housing and Community Development in the Official State Income Limits for 2020, for the county in which the residential rental property is located.

(B) For purposes of this paragraph, all lawful occupants of the residential rental unit, including minor children, shall be considered in determining household size.

(C) "High-income tenant" shall not include a tenant with a household income of less than one hundred thousand dollars ($100,000).

(2) "Proof of income" means any of the following:

(A) A tax return.

(B) A W-2.

(C) A written statement from a tenant's employer that specifies the tenant's income.

(D) Pay stubs.

(E) Documentation showing regular distributions from a trust, annuity, 401k, pension, or other financial instrument.

(F) Documentation of court-ordered payments, including, but not limited to, spousal support or child support.

(G) Documentation from a government agency showing

receipt of public assistance benefits, including, but not limited to, social security, unemployment insurance, disability insurance, or paid family leave.

(H) A written statement signed by the tenant that states the tenant's income, including, but not limited to, a rental application.

(b)

(1) This section shall apply only if the landlord has proof of income in the landlord's possession before the service of the notice showing that the tenant is a high-income tenant.

(2) This section does not do any of the following:

(A) Authorize a landlord to demand proof of income from the tenant.

(B) Require the tenant to provide proof of income for the purposes of determining whether the tenant is a high-income tenant.

(C)

(i) Entitle a landlord to obtain, or authorize a landlord to attempt to obtain, confidential financial records from a tenant's employer, a government agency, financial institution, or any other source.

(ii) Confidential information described in clause (i) shall not constitute valid proof of income unless it was lawfully obtained by the landlord with the tenant's consent during the tenant screening process.

(3) Paragraph (2) does not alter a party's rights under Title 4 (commencing with Section 2016.010), Chapter 4 (commencing with Section 708.010) of Title 9, or any other law.

(c) A landlord may require a high-income tenant that is served a notice pursuant to subdivision (b) or (c) of Section 1179.03 to submit, in addition to and together with a declaration of COVID-19-related financial distress, documentation supporting the claim that the tenant has suffered COVID-19-related financial distress. Any form of objectively verifiable documentation that demonstrates the COVID-19-related financial distress the tenant has experienced is sufficient to satisfy the requirements of this subdivision, including the proof of income, as defined in subparagraphs (A) to (G), inclusive, of paragraph (2) of subdivision (a), a letter from an employer, or an unemployment insurance record.

(d) A high-income tenant is required to comply with the requirements of subdivision (c) only if the landlord has included the following language on the notice served pursuant to subdivision (b) or (c) of Section 1179.03 in at least 12-point font: "Proof of income on file with your landlord indicates that your household makes at least 130 percent of the median income for the county where the rental property is located, as published by the Department of Housing and Community Development in the Official State Income Limits for 2020. As a result, if you claim that you are unable to pay the amount demanded by this notice because you have suffered COVID-19-related financial distress, you are required to submit to your landlord documentation supporting your claim together with the completed declaration of COVID-19-related financial distress provided with this notice. If you fail to submit this documentation together with your declaration of COVID-19-related financial distress, and you do not either pay the amount demanded in this notice or deliver possession of the premises back to your landlord as required by this notice, you will not be covered by the eviction protections enacted by the California Legislature as a result of the COVID-19 pandemic, and your landlord can begin eviction proceedings against you as soon as this 15-day notice expires."

(e) A high-income tenant that fails to comply with subdivision (c) shall not be subject to the protections of subdivision (g) of Section 1179.03.

(f)

    (1) A landlord shall be required to plead compliance with this section in any unlawful detainer action based upon a notice that alleges that the tenant is a high-income tenant. If that allegation is contested, the landlord shall be required to submit to the court the proof of income upon which the landlord relied at the trial or other hearing, and the tenant shall be entitled to submit rebuttal evidence.

(2) If the court in an unlawful detainer action based upon a notice that alleges that the tenant is a high-income tenant determines that at the time the notice was served the landlord did not have proof of income establishing that the tenant is a high-income tenant, the court shall award attorney's fees to the prevailing tenant.

Ca. Civ. Proc. Code § 1179.02.5

Added by Stats 2020 ch 37 (AB 3088),s 20, eff. 8/31/2020.

Section 1179.03 - [Effective until 10/1/2025] Modification of notice demanding payment

(a)

(1) Any notice that demands payment of COVID-19 rental debt served pursuant to subdivision (e) of Section 798.56 of the Civil Code or paragraph (2) or (3) of Section 1161 shall be modified as required by this section. A notice which does not meet the requirements of this section, regardless of when the notice was issued, shall not be sufficient to establish a cause of action for unlawful detainer or a basis for default judgment.

(2) Any case based solely on a notice that demands payment of COVID-19 rental debt served pursuant to subdivision (e) of Section 798.56 of the Civil Code or paragraph (2) or (3) of Section 1161 may be dismissed if the notice does not meet the requirements of this section, regardless of when the notice was issued.

(3) Notwithstanding paragraphs (1) and (2), this section shall have no effect if the landlord lawfully regained possession of the property or obtained a judgment for possession of the property before the operative date of this section.

(b) If the notice demands payment of rent that came due during the protected time period, as defined in Section 1179.02, the notice shall comply with all of the following:

(1) The time period in which the tenant may pay the amount due or deliver possession of the property shall be no shorter than 15 days, excluding Saturdays, Sundays, and other judicial holidays.

(2) The notice shall set forth the amount of rent demanded and the date each amount became due.

(3) The notice shall advise the tenant that the tenant cannot be evicted for failure to comply with the notice if the tenant delivers a signed declaration of COVID-19-related financial distress to the landlord on or before the date that the notice to pay rent or quit or notice to perform covenants or quit expires, by any of the methods specified in subdivision (f).

(4) The notice shall include the following text in at least 12-point font: "NOTICE FROM THE STATE OF CALIFORNIA: If you are unable to pay the amount demanded in this notice, and have decreased income or increased expenses due to COVID-19, your landlord will not be able to evict you for this missed payment if you sign and deliver the declaration form included with your notice to your landlord within 15 days, excluding Saturdays, Sundays, and other judicial holidays, but you will still owe this money to your landlord. If you do not sign and deliver the declaration within this time period, you may lose the eviction protections available to you. You must return this form to be protected. You should keep a copy or picture of the signed form for your records.
You will still owe this money to your landlord and can be sued for the money, but you cannot be evicted from your home if you comply with these requirements. You should keep careful track of what you have paid and any amount you still owe to protect your rights and avoid future disputes. Failure to respond to this notice may result in an unlawful detainer action (eviction) being filed against you.
For information about legal resources that may be available to you,

visit lawhelpca . org."

(c) If the notice demands payment of rent that came due during the transition time period, as defined in Section 1179.02, the notice shall comply with all of the following:

(1) The time period in which the tenant may pay the amount due or deliver possession of the property shall be no shorter than 15 days, excluding Saturdays, Sundays, and other judicial holidays.

(2) The notice shall set forth the amount of rent demanded and the date each amount became due.

(3) The notice shall advise the tenant that the tenant will not be evicted for failure to comply with the notice, except as allowed by this chapter, if the tenant delivers a signed declaration of COVID-19-related financial distress to the landlord on or before the date the notice to pay rent or quit or notice to perform covenants or quit expires, by any of the methods specified in subdivision (f).

(4) For notices served before February 1, 2021, the notice shall include the following text in at least 12-point type: "NOTICE FROM THE STATE OF CALIFORNIA: If you are unable to pay the amount demanded in this notice, and have decreased income or increased expenses due to COVID-19, you may sign and deliver the declaration form included with your notice to your landlord within 15 days, excluding Saturdays, Sundays, and other judicial holidays, and your landlord will not be able to evict you for this missed payment so long as you make the minimum payment (see below). You will still owe this money to your landlord. You should keep a copy or picture of the signed form for your records.
If you provide the declaration form to your landlord as described above AND, on or before January 31, 2021, you pay an amount that equals at least 25 percent of each rental payment that came due or will come due during the period between September 1, 2020, and January 31, 2021, that you were unable to pay as a result of decreased income or increased expenses due to COVID-19, your landlord cannot evict you. Your landlord may require you to submit

a new declaration form for each rental payment that you do not pay that comes due between September 1, 2020, and January 31, 2021. For example, if you provided a declaration form to your landlord regarding your decreased income or increased expenses due to COVID-19 that prevented you from making your rental payment in September and October of 2020, your landlord could not evict you if, on or before January 31, 2021, you made a payment equal to 25 percent of September's and October's rental payment (i.e., half a month's rent). If you were unable to pay any of the rental payments that came due between September 1, 2020, and January 31, 2021, and you provided your landlord with the declarations in response to each 15-day notice your landlord sent to you during that time period, your landlord could not evict you if, on or before January 31, 2021, you paid your landlord an amount equal to 25 percent of all the rental payments due from September through January (i.e., one and a quarter month's rent).

You will still owe the full amount of the rent to your landlord, but you cannot be evicted from your home if you comply with these requirements. You should keep careful track of what you have paid and any amount you still owe to protect your rights and avoid future disputes. Failure to respond to this notice may result in an unlawful detainer action (eviction) being filed against you.

For information about legal resources that may be available to you, visit lawhelpca.org."

(5) For notices served on or after February 1, 2021, and before July 1, 2021, the notice shall include the following text in at least 12-point type: "NOTICE FROM THE STATE OF CALIFORNIA: If you are unable to pay the amount demanded in this notice, and have decreased income or increased expenses due to COVID-19, you may sign and deliver the declaration form included with your notice to your landlord within 15 days, excluding Saturdays, Sundays, and other judicial holidays, and your landlord will not be able to evict you for this missed payment so long as you make the minimum payment (see below). You will still owe this money to your landlord. You should keep a copy or picture of the signed form for your records.

If you provide the declaration form to your landlord as described above AND, on or before June 30, 2021, you pay an amount that equals at least 25 percent of each rental payment that came due or will come due during the period between September 1, 2020, and June 30, 2021, that you were unable to pay as a result of decreased income or increased expenses due to COVID-19, your landlord cannot evict you. Your landlord may require you to submit a new declaration form for each rental payment that you do not pay that comes due between September 1, 2020, and June 30, 2021.

If you were unable to pay any of the rental payments that came due between September 1, 2020, and June 30, 2021, and you provided your landlord with the declarations in response to each 15-day notice your landlord sent to you during that time period, your landlord could not evict you if, on or before June 30, 2021, you paid your landlord an amount equal to 25 percent of all the rental payments due from September 2020 through June 2021.

You will still owe the full amount of the rent to your landlord, but you cannot be evicted from your home if you comply with these requirements. You should keep careful track of what you have paid and any amount you still owe to protect your rights and avoid future disputes. Failure to respond to this notice may result in an unlawful detainer action (eviction) being filed against you.

YOU MAY QUALIFY FOR RENTAL ASSISTANCE. In addition to extending these eviction protections, the State of California, in partnership with federal and local governments, has created an emergency rental assistance program to assist renters who have been unable to pay their rent and utility bills as a result of the COVID-19 pandemic. This program may be able to help you get caught up with past-due rent. Additionally, depending on the availability of funds, the program may also be able to assist you with making future rental payments.

While not everyone will qualify for this assistance, you can apply for it regardless of your citizenship or immigration status. There is no charge to apply for or receive this assistance.

Additional information about the extension of the COVID-19 Tenant Relief Act and new state or local rental assistance programs, including more information about how to qualify for assistance, can be found by visiting http : // housingiskey . com or by calling 1 – 833 – 422 - 4255."

(6) For notices served on or after July 1, 2021, and before April 1, 2022, the notice shall include the following text in at least 12-point type: "NOTICE FROM THE STATE OF CALIFORNIA - YOU MUST TAKE ACTION TO AVOID EVICTION. If you are unable to pay the amount demanded in this notice because of the COVID-19 pandemic, you should take action right away.

IMMEDIATELY: Sign and return the declaration form included with your notice to your landlord within 15 days, excluding Saturdays, Sundays, and other judicial holidays. Sign and return the declaration even if you have done this before. You should keep a copy or a picture of the signed form for your records.

BEFORE SEPTEMBER 30, 2021: Pay your landlord at least 25 percent of any rent you missed between September 1, 2020, and September 30, 2021. If you need help paying that amount, apply for rental assistance. You will still owe the rest of the rent to your landlord, but as long as you pay 25 percent by September 30, 2021, your landlord will not be able to evict you for failing to pay the rest of the rent. You should keep careful track of what you have paid and any amount you still owe to protect your rights and avoid future disputes.

AS SOON AS POSSIBLE: Apply for rental assistance! As part of California's COVID-19 relief plan, money has been set aside to help renters who have fallen behind on rent or utility payments. If you are behind on rent or utility payments, YOU SHOULD COMPLETE A RENTAL ASSISTANCE APPLICATION IMMEDIATELY! It is free and simple to apply. Citizenship or immigration status does not matter. You can find out how to start your application by calling 1-833 – 430 - 2122 or visiting http : // housingiskey . com right away."

(7) For notices served on or after April 1, 2022, and before July 1, 2022, the notice shall include the following text in at least 12-point type: "NOTICE FROM THE STATE OF CALIFORNIA: If:

(1) Before October 1, 2021, you paid your landlord at least 25 percent of any rent you missed between September 1, 2020, and September 30, 2021, and you signed and returned on time any and all declarations of COVID-19 related financial distress that your landlord gave to you, or

(2) You completed an application for government rental assistance on or before March 31, 2022, You may have protections against eviction.
For information about legal resources that may be available to you, visit lawhelpca.org."

(d) An unsigned copy of a declaration of COVID-19-related financial distress shall accompany each notice delivered to a tenant to which subdivision (b) or (c) is applicable. If the landlord was required, pursuant to Section 1632 of the Civil Code, to provide a translation of the rental contract or agreement in the language in which the contract or agreement was negotiated, the landlord shall also provide the unsigned copy of a declaration of COVID-19-related financial distress to the tenant in the language in which the contract or agreement was negotiated. The Department of Housing and Community Development shall make available an official translation of the text required by paragraph (4) of subdivision (b) and paragraphs (4) to (6), inclusive, of subdivision (c) in the languages specified in Section 1632 of the Civil Code by no later than July 15, 2021.
(e) If a tenant owes a COVID-19 rental debt to which both subdivisions (b) and (c) apply, the landlord shall serve two separate notices that comply with subdivisions (b) and (c), respectively.
(f)A tenant may deliver the declaration of COVID-19-related financial distress to the landlord by any of the following methods:

(1) In person, if the landlord indicates in the notice an address at which the declaration may be delivered in person.

(2) By electronic transmission, if the landlord indicates an email address in the notice to which the declaration may be delivered.

(3) Through United States mail to the address indicated by the landlord in the notice. If the landlord does not provide an address pursuant to subparagraph (1), then it shall be conclusively presumed that upon the mailing of the declaration by the tenant to the address provided by the landlord, the declaration is deemed received by the landlord on the date posted, if the tenant can show proof of mailing to the address provided by the landlord.

(4) Through any of the same methods that the tenant can use to deliver the payment pursuant to the notice if delivery of the declaration by that method is possible.

(g) Except as provided in Section 1179.02.5, the following shall apply to a tenant who, within 15 days of service of the notice specified in subdivision (b) or (c), excluding Saturdays, Sundays, and other judicial holidays, demanding payment of COVID-19 rental debt delivers a declaration of COVID-19-related financial distress to the landlord by any of the methods provided in subdivision (f):

(1) With respect to a notice served pursuant to subdivision (b), the tenant shall not then or thereafter be deemed to be in default with regard to that COVID-19 rental debt for purposes of subdivision (e) of Section 798.56 of the Civil Code or paragraphs (2) and (3) of Section 1161.

(2) With respect to a notice served pursuant to subdivision (c), the following shall apply:

(A) Except as provided by subparagraph (B), the landlord may not initiate an unlawful detainer action before October 1, 2021.

(B)A tenant shall not be guilty of unlawful detainer, now or in the future, based upon nonpayment of COVID-19 rental debt that came due during the transition period if, on or before September 30, 2021, the tenant tenders one or more payments that, when taken together, are of an amount equal to or not less than 25 percent of each transition period rental payment demanded in one or more notices served pursuant to subdivision (c) and for which the tenant complied with this subdivision by timely delivering a declaration of COVID-19-related financial distress to the landlord.

(h)

(1)

(A) Within the time prescribed in Section 1167, a tenant shall be permitted to file a signed declaration of COVID-19-related financial distress with the court.

(B) If the tenant files a signed declaration of COVID-19-related financial distress with the court pursuant to this subdivision, the court shall dismiss the case, pursuant to paragraph (2), if the court finds, after a noticed hearing on the matter, that the tenant's failure to return a declaration of COVID-19-related financial distress within the time required by subdivision (g) was the result of mistake, inadvertence, surprise, or excusable neglect, as those terms have been interpreted under subdivision (b) of Section 473.

(C) The noticed hearing required by this paragraph shall be held with not less than five days' notice and not more than 10 days' notice, to be given by the court, and may be held separately or in conjunction with any regularly noticed hearing in the case, other than a trial.

(2) If the court dismisses the case pursuant to paragraph (1), that dismissal shall be without prejudice as follows:

(A) If the case was based in whole or in part upon a notice served pursuant to subdivision (b), the court shall dismiss any cause of action based on the notice served pursuant to subdivision (b).

(B) Before October 1, 2021, if the case is based in whole or in part on a notice served pursuant to subdivision (c), the court shall dismiss any cause of action based on the notice served pursuant to subdivision (c).

(C) On or after October 1, 2021, if the case is based in whole or in part on a notice served pursuant to subdivision (c), the court shall dismiss any cause of action based upon the notice served pursuant to subdivision (c) if the tenant, within five days of the court's order to do so, makes the payment required by subparagraph (B) of paragraph (2) of subdivision (g), provided that if the fifth day falls on a Saturday, Sunday, or judicial holiday the last day to pay shall be extended to the next court day.

(3) If the court dismisses the case pursuant to this subdivision, the tenant shall not be considered the prevailing party for purposes of Section 1032, any attorney's fee provision appearing in contract or statute, or any other law.

(i) Notwithstanding any other law, a notice which is served pursuant to subdivision (b) or (c) that complies with the requirements of this chapter and subdivision (e) of Section 798.56 of the Civil Code or paragraphs (2) and (3) of Section 1161, as applicable, need not include specific language required by any ordinance, resolution, regulation, or administrative action adopted by a city, county, or city and county.

Ca. Civ. Proc. Code § 1179.03

Amended by Stats 2022 ch 13 (AB 2179),s 1, eff. 3/31/2022.
Amended by Stats 2021 ch 27 (AB 832),s 15, eff. 6/28/2021.
Amended by Stats 2021 ch 5 (AB 81),s 8, eff. 2/23/2021.
Amended by Stats 2021 ch 2 (SB 91),s 17, eff. 1/29/2021.
Added by Stats 2020 ch 37 (AB 3088),s 20, eff. 8/31/2020.

Section 1179.03.5 - [Effective until 10/1/2025] Conditions for court to find tenant guilty of unlawful detainer

(a) Before October 1, 2021, a court may not find a tenant guilty of an unlawful detainer unless it finds that one of the following applies:

(1) The tenant was guilty of the unlawful detainer before March 1, 2020.

(2) In response to service of a notice demanding payment of

COVID-19 rental debt pursuant to subdivision (e) of Section 798.56 of the Civil Code or paragraph (2) or (3) of Section 1161, the tenant failed to comply with the requirements of Section 1179.03.

(3)

(A) The unlawful detainer arises because of a termination of tenancy for any of the following:

(i) An at-fault just cause, as defined in paragraph (1) of subdivision (b) of Section 1946.2 of the Civil Code.

(ii)

(I) A no-fault just cause, as defined in paragraph (2) of subdivision (b) of Section 1946.2 of the Civil Code, other than intent to demolish or to substantially remodel the residential real property, as defined in subparagraph (D) of paragraph (2) of subdivision (b) of Section 1946.2.

(II) Notwithstanding subclause (I), termination of a tenancy based on intent to demolish or to substantially remodel the residential real property shall be permitted if necessary to maintain compliance with the requirements of Section 1941.1 of the Civil Code, Section 17920.3 or 17920.10 of the Health and Safety Code, or any other applicable law governing the habitability of residential rental units.

(iii) The owner of the property has entered into a contract for the sale of that property with a buyer who intends to occupy the property, and all the requirements of paragraph (8) of subdivision (e) of Section 1946.2 of the Civil Code have been satisfied.

(B) In an action under this paragraph, other than an action to which paragraph (2) also applies, the landlord shall be precluded from recovering COVID-19 rental debt in connection with any award of damages.

(b)

(1) This section does not require a landlord to assist the tenant to relocate through the payment of relocation costs if the landlord would not otherwise be required to do so pursuant to Section 1946.2 of the Civil Code or any other law.

(2) A landlord who is required to assist the tenant to relocate pursuant to Section 1946.2 of the Civil Code or any other law, may offset the tenant's COVID-19 rental debt against their obligation to assist the tenant to relocate.

Ca. Civ. Proc. Code § 1179.03.5
Amended by Stats 2021 ch 27 (AB 832),s 16, eff. 6/28/2021.
Amended by Stats 2021 ch 2 (SB 91),s 18, eff. 1/29/2021.
Added by Stats 2020 ch 37 (AB 3088),s 20, eff. 8/31/2020.

Section 1179.04 - [Effective until 10/1/2025] Notice to tenants

(a) On or before September 30, 2020, a landlord shall provide, in at least 12-point type, the following notice to tenants who, as of September 1, 2020, have not paid one or more rental payments that came due during the protected time period: "NOTICE FROM THE STATE OF CALIFORNIA: The California Legislature has enacted the COVID-19 Tenant Relief Act of 2020 which protects renters who have experienced COVID-19-related financial distress from being evicted for failing to make rental payments due between March 1, 2020, and January 31, 2021.

"COVID-19-related financial distress" means any of the following:

1. Loss of income caused by the COVID-19 pandemic.

2. Increased out-of-pocket expenses directly related to performing essential work during the COVID-19 pandemic.

3. Increased expenses directly related to the health impact of the COVID-19 pandemic.

4. Childcare responsibilities or responsibilities to care for an elderly, disabled, or sick family member directly related to the COVID-19 pandemic that limit your ability to earn income.

5. Increased costs for childcare or attending to an elderly, disabled, or sick family member directly related to the COVID-19 pandemic.

6. Other circumstances related to the COVID-19 pandemic that have reduced your income or increased your expenses.This law gives you the following protections:

1. If you failed to make rental payments due between March 1, 2020, and August 31, 2020, because you had decreased income or increased expenses due to the COVID-19 pandemic, as described above, you cannot be evicted based on this nonpayment.

2. If you are unable to pay rental payments that come due between September 1, 2020, and January 31, 2021, because of decreased income or increased expenses due to the COVID-19 pandemic, as described above, you cannot be evicted if you pay 25 percent of the rental payments missed during that time period on or before January 31, 2021. You must provide, to your landlord, a declaration under penalty of perjury of your COVID-19-related financial distress attesting to the decreased income or increased expenses due to the COVID-19 pandemic to be protected by the eviction limitations described above. Before your landlord can seek to evict you for failing to make a payment that came due between March 1, 2020, and January 31, 2021, your landlord will be required to give you a 15-day notice that informs you of the amounts owed and includes a blank declaration form you can use to comply with this requirement.

If your landlord has proof of income on file which indicates that your household makes at least 130 percent of the median income for the county where the rental property is located, as published by the Department of Housing and Community Development in the Official State Income Limits for 2020, your landlord may also require you to provide documentation which shows that you have experienced a decrease in income or increase in expenses due to the COVID-19 pandemic. Your landlord must tell you in the 15-day notice whether your landlord is requiring that documentation. Any form of objectively verifiable documentation that demonstrates the financial impact you have experienced is sufficient, including a letter from your employer, an unemployment insurance record, or medical bills, and may be provided to satisfy the documentation requirement.

It is very important you do not ignore a 15-day notice to pay rent or quit or a notice to perform covenants or quit from your landlord. If you are served with a 15-day notice and do not provide the declaration form to your landlord before the 15-day notice expires, you could be evicted. You could also be evicted beginning February 1, 2021, if you owe rental payments due between September 1, 2020, and January 31, 2021, and you do not pay an amount equal to at least 25 percent of the payments missed for that time period.

For information about legal resources that may be available to you, visit lawhelpca.org."

(b) On or before February 28, 2021, a landlord shall provide, in at least 12-point type, the following notice to tenants who, as of February 1, 2021, have not paid one or more rental payments that came due during the covered time period: "NOTICE FROM THE STATE OF CALIFORNIA: The California Legislature has enacted the COVID-19 Tenant Relief Act which protects renters who have experienced COVID-19-related financial distress from being evicted for failing to make rental payments due between March 1, 2020, and June 30, 2021.

"COVID-19-related financial distress" means any of the following:

1. Loss of income caused by the COVID-19 pandemic.

2. Increased out-of-pocket expenses directly related to performing essential work during the COVID-19 pandemic.

3. Increased expenses directly related to the health impact of the COVID-19 pandemic.

4. Childcare responsibilities or responsibilities to care for an elderly, disabled, or sick family member directly related to the COVID-19 pandemic that limit your ability to earn income.

5. Increased costs for childcare or attending to an elderly, disabled, or sick family member directly related to the COVID-19 pandemic.

6. Other circumstances related to the COVID-19 pandemic that have reduced your income or increased your expenses.This law gives you the following protections:

1. If you failed to make rental payments due between March 1, 2020, and August 31, 2020, because you had decreased income or increased expenses due to the COVID-19 pandemic, as described above, you cannot be evicted based on this nonpayment.

2. If you are unable to pay rental payments that come due between September 1, 2020, and June 30, 2021, because of decreased income or increased expenses due to the COVID-19 pandemic, as described above, you cannot be evicted if you pay 25 percent of the rental payments missed during that time period on or before June 30, 2021. You must provide, to your landlord, a declaration under penalty of perjury of your COVID-19-related financial distress attesting to the decreased income or increased expenses due to the COVID-19 pandemic to be protected by the eviction limitations described above. Before your landlord can seek to evict you for failing to make a payment that came due between March 1, 2020, and June 30, 2021, your landlord will be required to give you a 15-day notice that informs you of the amounts owed and includes a blank declaration form you can use to comply with this requirement.
If your landlord has proof of income on file which indicates that your household makes at least 130 percent of the median income for the county where the rental property is located, as published by the Department of Housing and Community Development in the Official State Income Limits for 2020, your landlord may also

require you to provide documentation which shows that you have experienced a decrease in income or increase in expenses due to the COVID-19 pandemic. Your landlord must tell you in the 15-day notice whether your landlord is requiring that documentation. Any form of objectively verifiable documentation that demonstrates the financial impact you have experienced is sufficient, including a letter from your employer, an unemployment insurance record, or medical bills, and may be provided to satisfy the documentation requirement.

It is very important you do not ignore a 15-day notice to pay rent or quit or a notice to perform covenants or quit from your landlord. If you are served with a 15-day notice and do not provide the declaration form to your landlord before the 15-day notice expires, you could be evicted. You could also be evicted beginning July 1, 2021, if you owe rental payments due between September 1, 2020, and June 30, 2021, and you do not pay an amount equal to at least 25 percent of the payments missed for that time period.

YOU MAY QUALIFY FOR RENTAL ASSISTANCE. In addition to extending these eviction protections, the State of California, in partnership with federal and local governments, has created an emergency rental assistance program to assist renters who have been unable to pay their rent and utility bills as a result of the COVID-19 pandemic. This program may be able to help you get caught up with past-due rent. Additionally, depending on the availability of funds, the program may also be able to assist you with making future rental payments.

While not everyone will qualify for this assistance, you can apply for it regardless of your citizenship or immigration status. There is no charge to apply for or receive this assistance.

Additional information about the extension of the COVID-19 Tenant Relief Act and new state or local rental assistance programs, including more information about how to qualify for assistance, can be found by visiting http://housingiskey.com or by calling 1-833-422-4255."

(c)On or before July 31, 2021, a landlord shall provide, in at least 12-point type, the following notice to tenants who, as of July 1, 2021, have not paid one or more rental payments that came due

during the covered time period: "NOTICE FROM THE STATE OF CALIFORNIA: The California Legislature has extended the COVID-19 Tenant Relief Act. The law now protects renters who have experienced COVID-19-related financial distress from being evicted for failing to make rental payments due between March 1, 2020, and September 30, 2021.
"COVID-19-related financial distress" means any of the following:

1. Loss of income caused by the COVID-19 pandemic.

2. Increased out-of-pocket expenses directly related to performing essential work during the COVID-19 pandemic.

3. Increased expenses directly related to the health impact of the COVID-19 pandemic.

4. Childcare responsibilities or responsibilities to care for an elderly, disabled, or sick family member directly related to the COVID-19 pandemic that limit your ability to earn income.

5. Increased costs for childcare or attending to an elderly, disabled, or sick family member directly related to the COVID-19 pandemic.

6. Other circumstances related to the COVID-19 pandemic that have reduced your income or increased your expenses.This law gives you the following protections:

1. If you failed to make rental payments due between March 1, 2020, and August 31, 2020, because you had decreased income or increased expenses due to the COVID-19 pandemic, as described above, you cannot be evicted based on this nonpayment.

2. If you are unable to pay rental payments that come due between September 1, 2020, and September 30, 2021, because of decreased income or increased expenses due to the COVID-19

pandemic, as described above, you cannot be evicted if you pay 25 percent of the rental payments missed during that time period on or before September 30, 2021. You must provide, to your landlord, a declaration under penalty of perjury of your COVID-19-related financial distress attesting to the decreased income or increased expenses due to the COVID-19 pandemic to be protected by the eviction limitations described above. Before your landlord can seek to evict you for failing to make a payment that came due between March 1, 2020, and September 30, 2021, your landlord will be required to give you a 15-day notice that informs you of the amounts owed and includes a blank declaration form you can use to comply with this requirement.

If your landlord has proof of income on file that indicates that your household makes at least 130 percent of the median income for the county where the rental property is located, as published by the Department of Housing and Community Development in the Official State Income Limits for 2020, your landlord may also require you to provide documentation that shows that you have experienced a decrease in income or increase in expenses due to the COVID-19 pandemic. Your landlord must tell you in the 15-day notice whether your landlord is requiring that documentation. Any form of objectively verifiable documentation that demonstrates the financial impact you have experienced is sufficient, including a letter from your employer, an unemployment insurance record, or medical bills, and may be provided to satisfy the documentation requirement.

It is very important you do not ignore a 15-day notice to pay rent or quit or a notice to perform covenants or quit from your landlord. If you are served with a 15-day notice and do not provide the declaration form to your landlord before the 15-day notice expires, you could be evicted. You could also be evicted beginning October 1, 2021, if you owe rental payments due between September 1, 2020, and September 30, 2021, and you do not pay an amount equal to at least 25 percent of the payments missed for that time period.

YOU MAY QUALIFY FOR RENTAL ASSISTANCE. In addition to extending these eviction protections, the State of California, in partnership with federal and local governments, has created an emergency rental assistance program to assist renters who have been unable to pay their rent and utility bills as a result of the COVID-19 pandemic. This program may be able to help you get caught up with past-due rent. Additionally, depending on the availability of funds, the program may also be able to assist you with making future rental payments.

While not everyone will qualify for this assistance, you can apply for it regardless of your citizenship or immigration status. There is no charge to apply for or receive this assistance.

Additional information about the extension of the COVID-19 Tenant Relief Act and new state or local rental assistance programs, including more information about how to qualify for assistance, can be found by visiting http://housingiskey.com or by calling 1-833-430-2122."

(d) The landlord may provide the notice required by subdivisions (a) to (c), inclusive, as applicable, in the manner prescribed by Section 1162 or by mail.

(e)

   (1)A landlord may not serve a notice pursuant to subdivision (b) or (c) of Section 1179.03 before the landlord has provided the notice required by subdivisions (a) to (c), inclusive, as applicable.

   (2) The notice required by subdivision (a) may be provided to a tenant concurrently with a notice pursuant to subdivision (b) or (c) of Section 1179.03 that is served on or before September 30, 2020.

   (3) The notice required by subdivision (b) may be provided to a tenant concurrently with a notice pursuant to subdivision (b) or (c) of Section 1179.03 that is served on or before February 28, 2021.

   (4) The notice required by subdivision (c) may be provided to a tenant concurrently with a notice pursuant to subdivision (b) or (c) of Section 1179.03 that is served on or before September 30, 2021.

   Ca. Civ. Proc. Code § 1179.04

Amended by Stats 2022 ch 28 (SB 1380),s 27, eff. 1/1/2023.

Amended by Stats 2021 ch 27 (AB 832),s 17, eff. 6/28/2021.

Amended by Stats 2021 ch 2 (SB 91),s 19, eff. 1/29/2021.
Added by Stats 2020 ch 37 (AB 3088),s 20, eff. 8/31/2020.

Section 1179.04.5 - [Effective until 10/1/2025] Application of security deposit or rental payments to COVID-19 rental debt without tenant's consent prohibited

Notwithstanding Sections 1470, 1947, and 1950 of the Civil Code, or any other law, for the duration of any tenancy that existed during the covered time period, the landlord shall not do either of the following:

(a) Apply a security deposit to satisfy COVID-19 rental debt, unless the tenant has agreed, in writing, to allow the deposit to be so applied. Nothing in this subdivision shall prohibit a landlord from applying a security deposit to satisfy COVID-19 rental debt after the tenancy ends, in accordance with Section 1950.5 of the Civil Code.

(b) Apply a monthly rental payment to any COVID-19 rental debt other than the prospective month's rent, unless the tenant has agreed, in writing, to allow the payment to be so applied.

Ca. Civ. Proc. Code § 1179.04.5

Renumbered from Ca. Civ. Code §Civ. 1179.04.5 and amended by Stats 2021 ch 124 (AB 938),s 3, eff. 1/1/2022.
Renumbered from Ca. Civ. Code §Civ. 1179.04.5 and amended by Stats 2021 ch 5 (AB 81),s 2, eff. 2/23/2021.
Added by Stats 2021 ch 2 (SB 91),s 20, eff. 1/29/2021.

Section 1179.05 - [Effective until 10/1/2025] Laws or regulations adopted in response to pandemic to protect tenants

(a) Any ordinance, resolution, regulation, or administrative action adopted by a city, county, or city and county in response to the COVID-19 pandemic to protect tenants from eviction is subject to all of the following:

(1) Any extension, expansion, renewal, reenactment, or new adoption of a measure, however delineated, that occurs between August 19, 2020, and June 30, 2022, shall have no effect before

July 1, 2022.

(2) Any provision which allows a tenant a specified period of time in which to repay COVID-19 rental debt shall be subject to all of the following:

(A) If the provision in effect on August 19, 2020, required the repayment period to commence on a specific date on or before August 1, 2022, any extension of that date made after August 19, 2020, shall have no effect.

(B) If the provision in effect on August 19, 2020, required the repayment period to commence on a specific date after August 1, 2022, or conditioned commencement of the repayment period on the termination of a proclamation of state of emergency or local emergency, the repayment period is deemed to begin on August 1, 2022.

(C) The specified period of time during which a tenant is permitted to repay COVID-19 rental debt may not extend beyond the period that was in effect on August 19, 2020. In addition, a provision may not permit a tenant a period of time that extends beyond August 31, 2023, to repay COVID-19 rental debt.
(b) This section does not alter a city, county, or city and county's authority to extend, expand, renew, reenact, or newly adopt an ordinance that requires just cause for termination of a residential tenancy or amend existing ordinances that require just cause for termination of a residential tenancy, consistent with subdivision (g) of Section 1946.2, provided that a provision enacted or amended after August 19, 2020, shall not apply to rental payments that came due between March 1, 2020, and June 30, 2022.
(c) The one-year limitation provided in subdivision (2) of Section 1161 is tolled during any time period that a landlord is or was prohibited by any ordinance, resolution, regulation, or administrative action adopted by a city, county, or city and county in response to the COVID-19 pandemic to protect tenants from eviction based on nonpayment of rental payments from serving a notice that demands payment of COVID-19 rental debt pursuant to

subdivision (e) of Section 798.56 of the Civil Code or paragraph (2) of Section 1161.

(d) It is the intent of the Legislature that this section be applied retroactively to August 19, 2020.

(e) The Legislature finds and declares that this section addresses a matter of statewide concern rather than a municipal affair as that term is used in Section 5 of Article XI of the California Constitution. Therefore, this section applies to all cities, including charter cities.

(f) It is the intent of the Legislature that the purpose of this section is to protect individuals negatively impacted by the COVID-19 pandemic, and that this section does not provide the Legislature's understanding of the legal validity on any specific ordinance, resolution, regulation, or administrative action adopted by a city, county, or city and county in response to the COVID-19 pandemic to protect tenants from eviction.

Ca. Civ. Proc. Code § 1179.05
Amended by Stats 2022 ch 13 (AB 2179),s 2, eff. 3/31/2022.
Amended by Stats 2021 ch 27 (AB 832),s 18, eff. 6/28/2021.
Amended by Stats 2021 ch 5 (AB 81),s 9, eff. 2/23/2021.
Amended by Stats 2021 ch 2 (SB 91),s 21, eff. 1/29/2021.
Added by Stats 2020 ch 37 (AB 3088),s 20, eff. 8/31/2020.

Section 1179.06 - [Effective until 10/1/2025] Waiver void

Any provision of a stipulation, settlement agreement, or other agreement entered into on or after the effective date of this chapter, including a lease agreement, that purports to waive the provisions of this chapter is prohibited and is void as contrary to public policy.

Ca. Civ. Proc. Code § 1179.06
Added by Stats 2020 ch 37 (AB 3088),s 20, eff. 8/31/2020.

Section 1179.07 - [Effective until 10/1/2025] Repealer

This chapter shall remain in effect until October 1, 2025, and as of that date is repealed.

Ca. Civ. Proc. Code § 1179.07
Amended by Stats 2021 ch 27 (AB 832),s 19, eff. 6/28/2021.

Amended by Stats 2021 ch 2 (SB 91),s 22, eff. 1/29/2021.

Added by Stats 2020 ch 37 (AB 3088),s 20, eff. 8/31/2020.

Chapter 6 - COVID-19 RENTAL HOUSING RECOVERY ACT

Section 1179.08 - [Effective until 9/30/2024] Title

This chapter shall be known, and may be cited, as the COVID-19 Rental Housing Recovery Act.

Ca. Civ. Proc. Code § 1179.08

Added by Stats 2021 ch 27 (AB 832),s 20, eff. 6/28/2021.

Section 1179.09 - [Effective until 9/30/2024] Definitions

For purposes of this chapter:

(a) "Approved application" means an application for which a government rental assistance program has verified applicant eligibility, and the requested funds have been obligated to the applicant for payment.

(b) "COVID-19 recovery period rental debt" means a rental debt of a tenant under a tenancy that came due between October 1, 2021, and March 31, 2022.

(c) "COVID-19 rental debt" has the same meaning as defined in Section 1179.02.

(d)

(1) "Final decision" means either of the following determinations by a government rental assistance program regarding an application for rental assistance:

(A) The application is an approved application.

(B) The application is denied for any of the following reasons:

(i) The tenant is not eligible for government rental assistance.

(ii) The government rental assistance program no longer has sufficient rental assistance funds to approve the application.

(iii) The application for government rental assistance remains incomplete 15 days, excluding Saturdays, Sundays, and other judicial holidays, after the landlord properly completed the portion of the application that is the responsibility of the landlord because of failure on the part of the tenant to properly complete the portion of the application that is the responsibility of the tenant.

(2) "Final decision" does not include any of the following:

(A) The rejection of an application as incomplete or improperly completed by a landlord.

(B) Notification that an application is temporarily pending further action by the government rental assistance program or the applicant.

(C) Notification that the landlord or tenant applied to the wrong government rental assistance program for the property or rental debt at issue.

(e) "Government rental assistance program" means any rental assistance program authorized pursuant to Chapter 17 (commencing with Section 50897) of Part 2 of Division 31 of the Health and Safety Code.

(f) "Pertinent government rental assistance program" means a government rental assistance program for the city, county, or city and county in which the property at issue is located.

(g) "Rental debt" means an unpaid rent or other unpaid financial obligation of a tenant under the tenancy that has come due.

(h)

(1) "Rental debt that accumulated due to COVID-19 hardship" means COVID-19 rental debt, COVID-19 recovery period rental debt, or a combination of both, if it accumulated during a tenancy initially established before October 1, 2021.

(2)

(A) For purposes of this subdivision, a tenancy is initially established when the tenants first lawfully occupy the premises.

(B) Any of the following do not initially establish a tenancy:

(i) The renewal of a periodic tenancy.

(ii) The extension of an existing lease or rental agreement.

(iii) The execution of a new lease or rental agreement with one or more individuals who already lawfully occupy the premises.

Ca. Civ. Proc. Code § 1179.09
Added by Stats 2021 ch 27 (AB 832),s 20, eff. 6/28/2021.

Section 1179.10 - [Effective until 9/30/2024] Modification of notice demanding payment
(a) Before April 1, 2022, a notice for a residential rental property that demands payment of COVID-19 recovery period rental debt and that is served pursuant to subdivision (e) of Section 798.56 of the Civil Code or paragraph (2) or (3) of Section 1161 shall be modified as follows:

(1) The time period in which the tenant may pay the amount due or deliver possession of the property shall be no shorter than three days, excluding Saturdays, Sundays, and other judicial holidays.

(2) The notice shall include all of the following:

(A) The amount of rent demanded and the date each amount became due.

(B) The telephone number and internet website address of the pertinent government rental assistance program.

(C) The following bold text in at least 12-point font:
"IMPORTANT NOTICE FROM THE STATE OF CALIFORNIA -
YOU MUST TAKE ACTION TO AVOID AN EVICTION: As part of
the state's COVID-19 relief plan, money has been set aside to help
renters who have fallen behind on rent or utility payments.
If you cannot pay the amount demanded in this notice, YOU
SHOULD COMPLETE A RENTAL ASSISTANCE APPLICATION
IMMEDIATELY! It is free and simple to apply. Citizenship or
immigration status does not matter.
DO NOT DELAY! IF YOU DO NOT COMPLETE YOUR
APPLICATION FOR RENTAL ASSISTANCE WITHIN 15
BUSINESS DAYS, YOUR LANDLORD MAY BE ABLE TO SUE TO
OBTAIN A COURT ORDER FOR YOUR EVICTION.
You can start your application by calling 1-833-430-2122 or visiting
http://housingiskey.com."

(D) If the landlord was required, pursuant to Section 1632 of
the Civil Code, to provide a translation of the rental contract or
agreement in the language in which the contract or agreement was
negotiated, the landlord shall also provide the text of the notice in
subparagraph (C) to the tenant in the language in which the
contract or agreement was negotiated. The Business, Consumer
Services, and Housing Agency shall make available on the http : //
housingiskey . com internet website an official translation of the
text required by subparagraph (C) in the languages specified in
Section 1632 of the Civil Code by no later than September 15, 2021.
(b) On or after April 1, 2022, and before July 1, 2022, a notice for a
residential rental property that demands payment of COVID-19
recovery period rental debt and that is served pursuant to
subdivision (e) of Section 798.56 of the Civil Code or paragraph (2)
or (3) of Section 1161 shall be modified as follows: "NOTICE FROM
THE STATE OF CALIFORNIA:
If you completed an application for government rental assistance on
or before March 31, 2022, you may have protections against
eviction. For information about legal resources that may be
available to you, visit lawhelpca.org."

(c)

(1) A notice that demands payment of COVID-19 recovery period rental debt that does not meet the requirements of this section is not sufficient to establish a cause of action for unlawful detainer or a basis for default judgment.

(2) The court, upon its own motion or upon a motion by a defendant in the case, shall dismiss a cause of action for unlawful detainer that is based on a notice that demands payment of COVID-19 recovery period rental debt if the notice does not meet the requirements of this section.

(3) A defendant may raise the insufficiency of a notice pursuant to this section as a complete defense to an unlawful detainer.
Ca. Civ. Proc. Code § 1179.10
Amended by Stats 2022 ch 13 (AB 2179),s 3, eff. 3/31/2022.
Added by Stats 2021 ch 27 (AB 832),s 20, eff. 6/28/2021.

Section 1179.11 - [Effective until 9/30/2024] Procedures for unlawful detainer actions

On or after October 1, 2021, and before July 1, 2022, in an unlawful detainer action pertaining to residential real property and based, in whole or in part, on nonpayment of rental debt that accumulated due to COVID-19 hardship, all of the following shall apply:
(a) A court shall not issue a summons on a complaint for unlawful detainer that seeks possession of residential real property based on nonpayment of rental debt that accumulated due to COVID-19 hardship unless the plaintiff, in addition to any other requirements provided by law, also files any of the following:

(1) Both of the following:

(A) A statement verifying, under penalty of perjury, that before filing the complaint, the landlord completed an application for government rental assistance to cover the rental debt demanded from the defendants in the case, but the application was denied.

(B)A copy of a final decision from the pertinent government rental assistance program denying a rental assistance application for the property at issue in the case.

(2)A statement, under penalty of perjury, verifying that all of the following are true:

(A) Before filing the complaint, the landlord submitted a completed application, as defined in Section 50897 of the Health and Safety Code, for rental assistance to the pertinent government rental assistance program to cover the rental debt demanded from the defendants in the case.

(B) Twenty days have passed since the later of the following:

(i) The date that the landlord submitted the application as described in subparagraph (A).

(ii) The date that the landlord served the tenant with the three-day notice underlying the complaint.

(C) The landlord has not received notice or obtained verification from the pertinent government rental assistance program indicating that the tenant has submitted a completed application for rental assistance to cover the rental debt demanded from the defendants in the case.

(D) The landlord has received no communication from the tenant that the tenant has applied for government rental assistance to cover the unpaid rental debt demanded from the defendants in the case.

(3)A statement, under penalty of perjury, that the rental debt demanded from the defendant in the complaint accumulated under a tenancy that was initially established, as described in paragraph (2) of subdivision (h) of Section 1179.09, on or after October 1,

2021.

(4)A statement, under penalty of perjury, that a determination is not pending on an application, filed prior to April 1, 2022, for government rental assistance to cover any part of the rental debt demanded from the defendants in the case.

(b)A statement under penalty of perjury described in subdivision (a) shall be made on a form developed or revised by the Judicial Council for this purpose if the Judicial Council determines that this requirement is necessary to accomplish the purpose of the statement.

(c)

(1) In an action filed before April 1, 2022, judgment or default judgment shall not issue in favor of the plaintiff unless the court finds, upon review of the pleadings and any other evidence brought before it, that both of the following are true:

(A) Before filing the complaint, the plaintiff completed an application to the pertinent government rental assistance program for rental assistance to cover the rental debt demanded in the complaint.

(B) The plaintiff's application for rental assistance was denied because of lack of eligibility, lack of funding, or the application remained incomplete due to the tenant's failure to properly complete the portion of the application that is the responsibility of the tenant for 15 days, excluding Saturdays, Sundays, and other judicial holidays, after the landlord properly completed the portion of the application that is responsibility of the landlord.

(2) In an action filed on or after April 1, 2022, and before July 1, 2022, a judgment or default judgment shall not issue in favor of the plaintiff unless the court finds, upon review of the pleadings and any other evidence brought before it, that one of the following is true:

(A) Both of the following:

(i) Before April 1, 2022, the plaintiff completed an application to the pertinent government rental assistance program for rental assistance to cover that portion of the rental debt demanded in the complaint that constitutes rental debt that accumulated due to COVID-19 hardship.

(ii) The plaintiff's application for rental assistance was denied because lack of eligibility, lack of funding, or the application remained incomplete due to the tenant's failure to properly complete the portion of the application that is the responsibility of the tenant for 15 days, excluding Saturdays, Sundays, and other judicial holidays, after the landlord properly completed the portion of the application that is responsibility of the landlord.

(B)A determination is not pending on an application, filed prior to April 1, 2022, for government rental assistance to cover any part of the rental debt demanded from the defendants in the case.

(3) In making its findings pursuant to this paragraph, the court may take judicial notice of information available to the court pursuant to Section 1179.12.

(d) In addition to the summons, the complaint, and any other required document, the plaintiff shall serve the defendant with copies of the statement and final decision filed with the court pursuant to subdivision (a). The absence of these copies shall be sufficient grounds to grant a motion to quash service of the summons.

(e) If the defendant contests whether the plaintiff has met the requirements of subdivision (c), the plaintiff shall bear the burden of proving to the court that the plaintiff has met those requirements.

(f) The Legislature finds and declares all of the following:

(1) For rental debt that accumulated due to COVID-19 hardship that was incurred on or after October 1, 2021, and before April 1, 2022, a landlord must be compensated for all of the unpaid rent demanded in the notice that forms the basis of the complaint in order to prevent an unlawful detainer judgment based on that complaint.

(2) That for rental debt that accumulated due to COVID-19 hardship that was incurred on or after September 1, 2020, and before September 30, 2021, a landlord must be provided 25 percent of the unpaid rent demanded in the notice that forms the basis of the complaint before October 1, 2021, in order to prevent an unlawful detainer judgment based on that complaint.

(g)A summons on a complaint issued pursuant to paragraph (3) of subdivision (a) shall not be construed to subject the complaint to the requirements of this chapter.

Ca. Civ. Proc. Code § 1179.11

Amended by Stats 2022 ch 13 (AB 2179),s 4, eff. 3/31/2022.

Added by Stats 2021 ch 27 (AB 832),s 20, eff. 6/28/2021.

Section 1179.12 - [Effective until 9/30/2024] Requirements for government rental assistance program; noncompliance; privacy

(a) Each government rental assistance program shall, by no later than September 15, 2021, develop mechanisms, including, but not limited to, telephone or online access, through which landlords, tenants, and the court may do both of the following:

(1) Verify the status of an application for rental assistance based upon the property address and a unique application number.

(2) Obtain copies of any determination on an application for rental assistance. A determination shall indicate all of the following:

(A) The name of the tenant that is the subject of the application.

(B) The address of the property that is the subject of the application.

(C) Whether the application has been approved or denied.

(D) If the application has been approved, then the amount of the payment that has been approved and the period and type of rental debt to which the amount corresponds.

(E) If the application has been denied, the reason for the denial, which shall be any of the following:

(i) The tenant is ineligible for government rental assistance.

(ii) The government rental assistance program no longer has sufficient funds to approve the application.

(iii) The application remained incomplete 15 days, excluding Saturdays, Sundays, and other judicial holidays, after it was initially submitted because of failure on the part of the tenant to provide required information.

(b)A government rental assistance program that does not comply with this section shall be deemed ineligible to receive further block grant allocations pursuant to Section 50897.2 or 50897.2.1 of the Health and Safety Code.

(c) It shall be unlawful for a person to access or use any information available pursuant to subdivision (a) for any purpose other than to determine the status of an application for assistance.

Ca. Civ. Proc. Code § 1179.12
Amended by Stats 2022 ch 28 (SB 1380),s 28, eff. 1/1/2023.
Added by Stats 2021 ch 27 (AB 832),s 20, eff. 6/28/2021.

Section 1179.13 - [Effective until 9/30/2024] Application for relief due to COVID-10 financial hardship

(a) A court shall prevent the forfeiture of a lease or rental agreement, whether written or oral, and whether or not the tenancy has terminated, and restore the tenant to the former estate or tenancy, if necessary, if all of the following apply:

(1) The complaint for unlawful detainer is based on a demand for payment of rental debt that accumulated due to COVID-19 financial hardship.

(2)

(A) The tenant submits verification to the court that a government rental assistance program has approved an application for rental assistance corresponding to part or all of the rental debt demanded in the complaint.

(B) The verification described in this paragraph shall be in the form of either of the following:

(i) A copy of a final decision from the government rental assistance program showing the property address, the amount of payment approved, and the time period for which assistance was provided.

(ii) The property address and a unique application number to enable the court to obtain confirmation of the final decision, the corresponding property address, the amount of the payment approved, and the time period for which assistance was provided.

(3) The approved payment from the rental assistance program, together with any additional payments made by the tenant, constitute full payment of the rental debt demanded in the complaint.

(b) An application pursuant to this section may be made only at any time before restoration of the premises to the landlord.

(c)

(1) An application pursuant to this section shall consist of verification that a government rental assistance program has approved an application for rental assistance corresponding to the rental debt demanded in the complaint.

(2) The verification described in this subdivision shall consist of either of the following:

(A) A copy of the final decision from the government rental assistance program approving the application, showing the property address, and indicating the amount of payment approved.

(B) A property address and unique application number to enable the court to obtain confirmation of the final decision, the corresponding property address, and the amount of the payment approved.

(3)

(A) Except as provided in subparagraph (B), a tenant shall not be required to file any documentation not described in paragraph (1) or pleading with the court in order to apply for relief pursuant to this section.

(B) The verification required by this subdivision shall be provided on or accompanied by a form developed or revised by the Judicial Council for this purpose if the Judicial Council determines that this requirement is necessary to accomplish the purpose of the verification.

(d) Upon the filing of an application for relief pursuant to this section, the court shall do both of the following:

(1) Set a hearing on the matter on not less than 5 days' notice and not more than 10 days' notice to the parties, to be given by the court, and to be held separately or in conjunction with any regularly noticed hearing or trial in the case.

(2) Stay the action if no judgment has been entered in the case, immediately stay execution of any writ of possession issued in the case through the date of the hearing, and notify the sheriff accordingly.

(e)

(1) At the hearing set pursuant to paragraph (1) of subdivision (d), the court shall rule upon the application for relief pursuant to this section in one of the following ways:

(A) If the tenant does not qualify for relief pursuant to subdivision (a), the court shall deny the application. A denial pursuant to this subparagraph may be used as evidence in an unlawful detainer action between the parties.

(B) If the tenant qualifies for relief pursuant to subdivision (a), and the plaintiff has received all of the payments described in paragraph (3) of subdivision (a), then the court shall grant the application, set aside any judgment issued in the case, and dismiss the case.

(C) If the tenant qualifies for relief pursuant to subdivision (a), and the plaintiff has not received all of the payments described in paragraph (3) of subdivision (a), the court shall do all of the following:

(i) Set a followup hearing to be held within 15 days, excluding Saturdays, Sundays, and other judicial holidays.

(ii) Extend the stay of the action through the date of that followup hearing.

(iii) Extend the stay of execution of any writ of possession in the case through the date of that followup hearing.

(D) At any followup hearing pursuant to subparagraph (C), the court shall issue one of the following orders:

(i) If the government rental assistance program has withdrawn the approval of rental assistance, then the court shall deny the application.

(ii) If the plaintiff has received all of the payments described in paragraph (3) of subdivision (a), then the court shall grant the application, set aside any judgment issued in the case, and dismiss the case.

(iii) If the government rental assistance program has not withdrawn the approval of rental assistance, but the landlord has not received all of the payments described in paragraph (3) of subdivision (a) because the rental assistance program has not yet issued its part of the payment, then the court shall order another followup hearing in accordance with this subparagraph.

(iv) If the government rental assistance program has not withdrawn the approval of rental assistance, but the landlord has not received all of the payments described in paragraph (3) of subdivision (a) because the tenant has not yet paid the tenant's part of the payment, then the court shall deny the application with prejudice.

(2) If a court grants an application for relief pursuant to this section, the tenant shall not be considered the prevailing party for purposes of Section 1032, any attorney's fee provision appearing in contract or statute, or any other law.

Ca. Civ. Proc. Code § 1179.13

Added by Stats 2021 ch 27 (AB 832),s 20, eff. 6/28/2021.

Section 1179.14 - [Effective until 9/30/2024] 60 day time period

If the criteria for issuance of a summons pursuant to subdivision (a) of Section 1179.11 have not been satisfied within 60 days of the complaint's filing, the court shall dismiss the action without prejudice.

Ca. Civ. Proc. Code § 1179.14

Added by Stats 2021 ch 27 (AB 832),s 20, eff. 6/28/2021.

Section 1179.15 - [Effective until 9/30/2024] Repealer

This chapter shall remain in effect until September 30, 2024, and as of that date is repealed.

Ca. Civ. Proc. Code § 1179.15

Added by Stats 2021 ch 27 (AB 832),s 20, eff. 6/28/2021.

Title 4 - OF THE ENFORCEMENT OF LIENS

Chapter 1 - LIENS IN GENERAL

Section 1180 - Lien defined

A lien is a charge imposed upon specific property, by which it is made security for the performance of an act.

Ca. Civ. Proc. Code § 1180

Enacted 1872.

Chapter 2.5 - OIL AND GAS LIENS

Section 1203.50 - Title of act

This chapter shall be known and may be cited as the Oil and Gas Lien Act.

Ca. Civ. Proc. Code § 1203.50

Added by Stats. 1959, Ch. 2020.

Section 1203.51 - Definitions

Unless the context otherwise requires, the definitions set forth in this section shall govern the construction of this chapter.

(a) "Person" means an individual, corporation, firm, partnership, limited liability company, or association.

(b) "Owner" means a person holding any interest in the legal or equitable title or both to any leasehold for oil or gas purposes, or his or her agent and shall include purchasers under executory contract, receivers, and trustees.

(c) "Contract" means a contract, written or oral, express or implied, or partly express and partly implied, or executory or executed, or partly executory and partly executed.

(d) "Material" means any material, machinery, appliances, buildings, structures, casing, tanks, pipelines, tools, bits, or other equipment or supplies but does not include rigs or hoists or their integral component parts except wire lines.

(e) "Labor" means work performed in return for wages.

(f) "Services" means work performed exclusive of labor, including the hauling of material, whether or not involving the furnishing of material.

(g) "Furnish" means sell or rent.

(h) "Drilling" means drilling, digging, shooting, torpedoing, perforating, fracturing, testing, logging, acidizing, cementing, completing or repairing.

(i) "Operating" means all operations conducted on the lease in connection with or necessary to the production of oil or gas, either in the development thereof or in working thereon by the subtractive process.

(j) "Construction" means construction, maintenance, operation, or repair, either in the development thereof or in working thereon by the subtractive process.

(k) "Original contractor" means any person for whose benefit a lien is prescribed under Section 1203.52.

Ca. Civ. Proc. Code § 1203.51

Amended by Stats. 1994, Ch. 1010, Sec. 62. Effective January 1, 1995.

Section 1203.52 - Persons entitled to lien under chapter

Any person who shall, under contract with the owner of any leasehold for oil or gas purposes perform any labor or furnish any material or services used or employed, or furnished to be used or employed in the drilling or operating of any oil or gas well upon such leasehold, or in the constructing, putting together, or repairing of any material so used or employed, or furnished to be so used or employed, shall be entitled to a lien under this chapter, whether or not a producing well is obtained and whether or not such material is incorporated in or becomes a part of the completed oil or gas well, for the amount due him for any such labor performed, or materials or services furnished, within six months prior to the date of recording the statement of lien as provided in Section 1203.58, including, without limitation, shipping and mileage charges connected therewith, and interest from the date the same was due.

Ca. Civ. Proc. Code § 1203.52
Added by Stats. 1959, Ch. 2020.

Section 1203.53 - Lien extends to leasehold and appurtenances materials and fixtures and wells located on leasehold

Liens created under Section 1203.52 shall extend to:

(a) The leasehold for oil or gas purposes to which the materials or services were furnished, or for which the labor was performed, and the appurtenances thereunto belonging, exclusive of any and all royalty interest, overriding interests and production payments created by an instrument recorded prior to the date such materials or services were first furnished or such labor was first performed for which lien is claimed; and

(b) All materials and fixtures owned by the owner or owners of such leasehold and used or employed, or furnished to be used or employed in the drilling or operating of any oil or gas well located thereon; and

(c) All oil or gas wells located on such leasehold, and the oil or gas produced therefrom, and the proceeds thereof, except the interest therein owned by the owners of royalty interests, overriding royalty interests and production payments created by an instrument recorded prior to the date such materials or services were first furnished or such labor was first performed for which the lien is claimed.

Ca. Civ. Proc. Code § 1203.53
Added by Stats. 1959, Ch. 2020.

Section 1203.54 - Subcontractors entitled to lien

Any person who shall, under contract, perform any labor or furnish any material or services as a subcontractor under an original contractor or for or to an original contractor or a subcontractor under an original contractor, shall be entitled to a lien upon all the property upon which the lien of an original contactor may attach to the same extent as an original contractor, and the lien provided for in this section shall further extend and attach to all materials and fixtures owned by such original contractor or subcontractor to or for whom the labor is performed or material or services furnished and used or employed, or furnished to be used or employed in the drilling or operating of such oil or gas wells.

Ca. Civ. Proc. Code § 1203.54
Added by Stats. 1959, Ch. 2020.

Section 1203.55 - Forfeiture of estate; failure of equitable or contingent interest to ripen into legal interest

When a lien provided for in this chapter shall have attached to a leasehold estate, forfeiture of such estate shall not impair any lien as to material, appurtenances and fixtures located thereon and to which such lien has attached prior to forfeiture. If a lien provided for in this chapter attaches to an equitable interest or to a legal interest contingent upon the happening of a condition subsequent, failure of such interest to ripen into legal title or such condition subsequent to be fulfilled, shall not impair any such lien as to material, appurtenances and fixtures located thereon and to which said lien had attached prior to such failure.

Ca. Civ. Proc. Code § 1203.55
Added by Stats. 1959, Ch. 2020.

Section 1203.56 - Date lien arises; preference

The lien provided for in this chapter arises on the date of the furnishing of the first item of material or services or the date of performance of the first labor for which a lien is claimed under the provisions of this chapter. Upon compliance with the provisions of Section 1203.58, such lien shall be preferred to all other titles, charges, liens or encumbrances which may attach to or upon any of the property upon which a lien is given by this chapter subsequent to the date the lien herein provided for arises.

Ca. Civ. Proc. Code § 1203.56
Added by Stats. 1959, Ch. 2020.

Section 1203.57 - Liens arising upon same property

All liens arising by virtue of this chapter upon the same property shall be of equal standing except that liens of persons for the performance of labor shall be preferred to all other liens arising by virtue of this chapter.

Ca. Civ. Proc. Code § 1203.57
Added by Stats. 1959, Ch. 2020.

Section 1203.58 - Statement recorded by persons claiming liens

Every person claiming a lien under this chapter, shall record in the office of the county recorder for the county in which such leasehold, or some part thereof, is situated, a verified statement setting forth the amount claimed and the items thereof, the dates on which labor was performed or material or services furnished, the name of the owner of the leasehold, if known, the name of the claimant and his mailing address, a description of the leasehold, and if the claimant be a claimant under Section 1203.54, the name of the person for whom the labor was immediately performed or the material or services were immediately furnished. The statement of lien must be recorded within six months after the date on which the claimant's labor was performed or his materials or services were furnished to be effective as to such labor, materials, or services.

Ca. Civ. Proc. Code § 1203.58
Added by Stats. 1959, Ch. 2020.

Section 1203.59 - Notice of lien

Anything in this chapter to the contrary notwithstanding, any lien claimed by virtue of this chapter, insofar as it may extend to oil or gas or the proceeds of the sale of oil or gas, shall not be effective against any purchaser of such oil or gas until written notice of such claim has been delivered to such purchaser. Such notice shall state the name of the claimant, his address, the amount for which the lien is claimed, and a description of the leasehold upon which the lien is claimed. Such notice shall be delivered personally to the purchaser or by registered letter or certified mail. Upon receipt of such notice the purchaser shall withhold payments for such oil or gas runs to the extent of the lien amount claimed until delivery of notice in writing that the claim has been paid. The funds so withheld by the purchaser shall be used in payment of the lien judgment upon foreclosure. The lien claimant shall within 10 days give notice in writing that the claim has been paid.

Ca. Civ. Proc. Code § 1203.59
Added by Stats. 1959, Ch. 2020.

Section 1203.60 - Bond given by lessor or owner or contractor or subcontractor

(a) Whenever any lien or liens shall be claimed or recorded under the provisions of this chapter then the lessor or owner of the property on which the lien or liens are claimed or the contractor or subcontractor through whom such lien or liens are claimed, or either of them, may record a bond with the county recorder of the county in which the property is located as herein provided. Such bond shall describe the property on which lien or liens are claimed, shall refer to the lien or liens claimed in manner sufficient to identify them and shall be in an amount equal to 150 percent of the amount of the claimed lien or liens referred to and shall be payable to the party or parties claiming same. Such bond shall be executed by the party recording same as principal and by a corporate surety authorized to execute such bonds as surety and shall be conditioned substantially that the principal and surety will pay to the obligees named or their assigns the amounts of the liens so claimed by them with all costs in the event same shall be proven to be liens on such property.

(b) Such bond, when recorded, shall take the place of the property against which any claim for lien referred to in such bond is asserted. At any time within the period of time provided in Section 1203.61, any person claiming such lien may sue upon such bond but no action shall be brought upon such bond after the expiration of such period. One action upon such bond shall not exhaust the remedies thereon but each obligee or assignee of an obligee named therein may maintain a separate suit thereon in any court having jurisdiction.

Ca. Civ. Proc. Code § 1203.60
Added by Stats. 1959, Ch. 2020.

Section 1203.61 - Action to enforce lien

(a) Any lien provided for by this chapter shall be enforced in the same manner as provided in Chapter 4 (commencing with Section 8400) of Title 2 of Part 6 of Division 4 of the Civil Code. The action shall be filed within 180 days from the time of the recording of the lien. If a credit is given and notice of the fact and terms of the credit is filed in the office of the county recorder subsequent to the filing of the lien and prior to the expiration of the 180-day period, then the lien continues in force until 180 days after the expiration of the credit, but no lien continues in force by reason of any agreement to give credit for a longer time than one year from the time the work is completed. If the proceedings to enforce the lien are not prosecuted to trial within two years after commencement, the court may in its discretion dismiss the action for want of prosecution, and in all cases the dismissal of the action (unless it is expressly stated that it is without prejudice) or a judgment in the action that no lien exists is equivalent to the cancellation and removal from the record of the lien.

(b) As against any purchaser or encumbrancer for value and in good faith whose rights are acquired subsequent to the expiration of the 180-day period following the filing of the lien, no giving of credit or extension of the lien or time to enforce the lien shall be effective unless evidenced by a notice or agreement filed for record in the office of the county recorder prior to the acquisition of the rights of the purchaser or encumbrancer.

Ca. Civ. Proc. Code § 1203.61
Amended by Stats 2010 ch 697 (SB 189),s 24, eff. 1/1/2011, op. 7/1/2012.

Section 1203.62 - Personal action to whom debt due for work performed or materials and services furnished

Nothing in this chapter shall be construed to impair or affect the right of any person to whom any debt may be due for work performed or materials or services furnished to maintain a personal action against the person liable for such debt.

Ca. Civ. Proc. Code § 1203.62
Added by Stats. 1959, Ch. 2020.

Section 1203.63 - Waiver of lien

The taking of any note or any additional security by any person given a lien by this chapter shall not constitute a waiver of the lien given by this chapter unless made a waiver by express agreement of the parties in writing. The claiming of a lien under this chapter shall not constitute a waiver of any other right or security held by the claimant unless made a waiver by express agreement of the parties in writing.

Ca. Civ. Proc. Code § 1203.63
Added by Stats. 1959, Ch. 2020.

Section 1203.64 - Claims and actions assignable

All claims for liens and likewise all actions to recover therefor under this chapter shall be assignable upon compliance with the provisions of Section 1203.58 so as to vest in the assignee all rights and remedies herein given subject to all defenses thereto that might be raised if such assignments had not been made.

Ca. Civ. Proc. Code § 1203.64
Added by Stats. 1959, Ch. 2020.

Section 1203.65 - Subsequent perfection of unperfected lien arising prior to effective date of chapter

All liens granted by this chapter shall be perfected and enforced in accordance with the provisions hereof whether such liens arise before or after the effective date of this chapter; provided, however, that any unperfected lien granted under any statute in effect prior to the effective date of this chapter and which could be subsequently perfected in accordance with such prior statute were it not for the existence of this chapter may be perfected and enforced in accordance with the provisions of this chapter if the statement of lien required to be recorded under Section 1203.58 is recorded within the time therein required or within two months after the effective date of this chapter, whichever period is longer; and provided further, that the validity of any lien perfected prior to the effective date of this chapter in accordance with the requirements of any statute in effect prior to such effective date shall be determined on the basis of such prior statute but the enforcement thereof shall insofar as possible be governed by the provisions of this chapter.

Ca. Civ. Proc. Code § 1203.65
Added by Stats. 1959, Ch. 2020.

Section 1203.66 - Liberal construction

This chapter shall be given liberal construction in favor of all persons entitled to any lien under it.

Ca. Civ. Proc. Code § 1203.66
Added by Stats. 1959, Ch. 2020.

Chapter 3 - CERTAIN LIENS AND PRIORITIES FOR SALARIES, WAGES AND CONSUMER DEBTS

Section 1204 - Priority of claims when assignment made for benefit of creditors or assignor

When any assignment, whether voluntary or involuntary, and whether formal or informal, is made for the benefit of creditors of the assignor, or results from any proceeding in insolvency or receivership commenced against him or her, or when any property is turned over to the creditors of a person, firm, association or corporation, or to a receiver or trustee for the benefit of creditors, the following claims have priority in the following order:

(a) Allowed unsecured claims, but only to the extent of four thousand three hundred dollars ($4,300) for each individual or corporation, as the case may be, earned within 90 days before the date of the making of such assignment or the taking over of the property or the commencement of the court proceeding or the date of the cessation of the debtor's business, whichever occurs first, for either of the following:

Title 4 - OF THE ENFORCEMENT OF LIENS

(1) Wages, salaries, or commissions, including vacation, severance and sick leave pay earned by an individual.

(2) Sales commissions earned by an individual, or by a corporation with only one employee, acting as an independent contractor in the sale of goods or services of the debtor in the ordinary course of the debtor's business if, and only if, during the 12 months preceding the date of the making of the assignment or the taking over of the property or the commencement of the proceeding or the date of the cessation of the debtor's business, whichever occurs first, at least 75 percent of the amount that the individual or corporation earned by acting as an independent contractor in the sale of goods or services was earned from the debtor.

(b) Allowed unsecured claims for contributions to employee benefit plans arising from services rendered within 180 days before the date of the making of the assignment or the taking over of the property or the commencement of the court proceeding or the date of the cessation of the debtor's business, whichever occurs first; but only for each employee benefit plan, to the extent of the number of employees covered by the plan multiplied by four thousand three hundred dollars ($4,300), less the aggregate amount paid to the employees under subdivision (a), plus the aggregate amount paid by the estate on behalf of the employees to any other employee benefit plan.

(c) The above claims shall be paid by the trustee, assignee or receiver before the claim of any other creditor of the assignor, insolvent, or debtor whose property is so turned over, and shall be paid as soon as the money with which to pay same becomes available. If there is insufficient money to pay all the labor claims in full, the money available shall be distributed among the claimants in proportion to the amount of their respective claims. The trustee, receiver or assignee for the benefit of creditors shall have the right to require sworn claims to be presented and shall have the right to refuse to pay any such preferred claim, either in whole or in part, if he or she has reasonable cause to believe that a claim is not valid but shall pay any part thereof that is not disputed, without prejudice to the claimant's rights, as to the balance of his or her claim, and withhold sufficient money to cover the disputed portion until the claimant in question has a reasonable opportunity to establish the validity of his or her claim by court action, either in his or her own name or through an assignee.

(d) This section is binding upon all the courts of this state and in all receivership actions the court shall order the receiver to pay promptly out of the first receipts and earnings of the receivership, after paying the current operating expenses, such preferred labor claims.

Ca. Civ. Proc. Code § 1204

EFFECTIVE 1/1/2000. Amended July 28, 1999 (Bill Number: SB 219) (Chapter 202).

Section 1204.5 - Claims having priority but subordinate to priorities of labor claims

In any general assignment for the benefit of creditors, the following claims shall have priority, subordinate to the priorities for labor claims under Section 1204, but prior to all other unsecured claims: allowed unsecured claims of individuals, to the extent of nine hundred dollars ($900) for each such individual, arising from the deposit, before the commencement of the case, of money in connection with the purchase, lease, or rental of property, or the purchase of services, for the personal, family, or household use of such individuals, that were not delivered or provided. The priority granted by this section shall be subordinate to that granted by Sections 18933 and 26312 of the Revenue and Taxation Code.

Ca. Civ. Proc. Code § 1204.5

Amended by Stats. 1980, Ch. 135, Sec. 5.

Section 1205 - Unpaid wages preferred claims and liens upon sale or transfer of business not in ordinary and regular course of business

Upon the sale or transfer of any business or the stock in trade, in bulk, or a substantial part thereof, not in the ordinary and regular course of business or trade, unpaid wages of employees of the seller or transferor earned within ninety (90) days prior to the sale, transfer, or opening of an escrow for the sale thereof, shall constitute preferred claims and liens thereon as between creditors of the seller or transferor and must be paid first from the proceeds of the sale or transfer.

Ca. Civ. Proc. Code § 1205
Added by Stats. 1961, Ch. 1083.

Section 1206 - Statement of claim filed by persons performing work or rendering services upon levy under writ of attachment or execution

(a) Upon the levy under a writ of attachment or execution not founded upon a claim for labor, any miner, mechanic, salesman, servant, clerk, laborer or other person who has performed work or rendered personal services for the defendant within 90 days prior to the levy may file a verified statement of the claim with the officer executing the writ, file a copy with the court that issued the writ, and give copies, containing his or her address, to the plaintiff and the defendant, or any attorney, clerk or agent representing them, or mail copies to them by registered mail at their last known address, return of which by the post office undelivered shall be deemed a sufficient service if no better address is available, and that claim, not exceeding nine hundred dollars ($900), unless disputed, shall be paid by the officer, immediately upon the expiration of the time for dispute of the claim as prescribed in Section 1207, from the proceeds of the levy remaining in the officer's hands at the time of the filing of the statement or collectible by the officer on the basis of the writ.

(b) The court issuing the writ shall make a notation in the register of actions of every preferred labor claim of which it receives a copy and shall endorse on any writ of execution or abstract of judgment issued subsequently in the case that it is issued subject to the rights of a preferred labor claimant or claimants and giving the names and amounts of all preferred labor claims of which it has notice. In levying under any writ of execution the officer making the levy shall include in the amount due under the execution all preferred labor claims that have been filed in the action and of which the officer has notice, except any claims that may have been finally disallowed by the court under this procedure and of which disallowance the officer has actual notice. The amount due on preferred labor claims that have not been finally disallowed by the court shall be considered a part of the sum due under any writ of attachment or execution in augmentation of that amount and any person, firm, association, or corporation on whom a writ of attachment or execution is levied shall immediately pay to the levying officer the amount of the preferred labor claims, out of any money belonging to the defendant in the action, before paying the principal sum called for in the writ.

(c) If any claim is disputed within the time, and in the manner prescribed in Section 1207, and a copy of the dispute is mailed by registered mail to the claimant or the claimant's attorney at the address given in the statement of claim and the registry receipt is attached to the original of the dispute when it is filed with the levying officer, or is handed to the claimant or the claimant's attorney, the claimant, or the claimant's assignee, must within 10 days after the copy is deposited in the mail or is handed to the claimant or the claimant's attorney, petition the court having jurisdiction of the action on which the writ is based, for a hearing before it to determine the claim for priority, or the claim to priority is barred. If more than one attachment or execution is involved, the petition shall be filed in the court having jurisdiction over the senior attachment or execution. The hearing shall be held within 20 days from the filing of the petition, unless the court continues it for good cause. Ten days' notice of the hearing shall be given by the petitioner to the plaintiff, the defendant, and all parties claiming an interest in the property, or their attorneys. The notice may be informal and need specify only the name of the court, the names of the principal parties to the senior attachment or execution, and the name of the wage claimant or claimants on whose behalf it is filed but shall specify that the hearing is for the purpose of determining the claim for priority. The plaintiff, the defendant, or any other party claiming an interest may contest the amount or validity of the claim in spite of any confession of judgment or failure to appear or to contest the claim on the part of any other person.

(d) There shall be no cost for filing or hearing the petition. The hearing on the petition shall be informal but all parties testifying shall be sworn. Any claimant may appear on the claimant's own behalf at the hearing and may call and examine witnesses to substantiate his or her claim. An appeal may be taken from a judgment in a proceeding under this section in the manner provided for appeals from judgments of the court where the proceeding occurred, in an action of the same jurisdictional classification.

(e) The officer shall keep, until the determination of the claim for priority, any amount of the proceeds of the writ necessary to satisfy the claim. If the claim for priority is allowed, the officer shall pay the amount due, including the claimant's cost of suit, from those proceeds, immediately after the order allowing the claim becomes final.

  Ca. Civ. Proc. Code § 1206

Amended by Stats 2002 ch 664 (AB 3034),s 51, eff. 1/1/2003.
Amended by Stats 2001 ch 44 (SB 562), s 7, eff. 1/1/2002.

Section 1207 - Sworn statement denying that claim due

Within five days after receiving a copy of the statement provided for in the next preceding section, either the plaintiff or the defendant in the action in which the writ issued may file with the officer a sworn statement denying that any part of such claim is due for services rendered within ninety days next preceding the levy of the writ, or denying that any part of such claim, beyond a sum specified, is so due. Such sworn statement can not be made on information and belief unless the party swearing to same has actual information and belief that the wage claim, or the portion thereof that is contested, is not justly due, and in such case the nature and source of the information must be given. If a part of the claim is admitted to be due, and the claimant nevertheless files a petition for hearing and the court does not allow more than the amount so admitted, he can not recover costs but the costs must be adjudged against him, and the amount thereof deducted from the sum found due him.

  Ca. Civ. Proc. Code § 1207

Amended by Stats. 1935, Ch. 557.

Section 1208 - Distribution of proceeds of writ; right to proceed directly against money or property; notice of request to release original attachment or execution

If the claims presented under Section 1206 and not disputed, or, if disputed, established by judgment, exceed the proceeds of the writ not disposed of before their presentation, such proceeds shall be distributed among the claimants in proportion to the amount of their respective claims after the costs incurred by the senior attaching plaintiff or judgment creditor in such action have first been taken care of.

If sufficient money to pay in full all preferred labor claims filed under an attachment or execution does not become available immediately upon the expiration of the time for dispute of such claims under Section 1207, any of the claimants, or their assignees, have the right to proceed directly against the money or other property levied on in individual or joint actions by themselves or their assignees against the defendant, and the attachment or execution under which the preferred claims were filed shall be considered set aside as far as such claimants, or their assignees, are concerned so as to enable them, or any of them, or any of their assignees, to proceed directly against any or all of the money or other property in question by means of their own attachments or executions; provided, however, that any money collected on behalf of any such labor claimant, or his or her assignee, on the basis of such new attachment or execution shall be shared in by the other preferred labor claimants who have filed claims that have not been disputed, or, if disputed, established by judgment, in proportion to the amount of their respective claims, deducting only the costs in the action brought by the said labor claimant, or his or her assignee, and the costs in the original action brought by the senior attaching plaintiff or judgment creditor.

If such senior attaching plaintiff or judgment creditor requests a release of his or her original attachment or execution, and the preferred labor claims filed under same are not released, the officer who levied the writ must first mail notices of such request to release to each of the labor claimants who have filed claims, or their attorneys, which notices must specify that unless the claimants bring attachment actions of their own and levy on the money or property in question within five days from the date thereof the money or property will be released from the attachment or execution; provided, however, that such officer may instead collect sufficient money on the basis of the original writ to pay off the preferred labor claims in full and then release the attachment or execution, but in no case shall the officer release the attachment or execution without first taking care of the labor claims until the five-day period has expired, unless the officer's costs, keepers' fees or storage charges have not been immediately taken care of by some of the parties involved. In any case it shall be lawful for a garnishee to pay over to the officer levying the writ any money held by the garnishee without waiting for execution to be levied and the officer's receipt for the money shall be a sufficient quittance, and the officer shall collect such money and immediately pay off the established preferred labor claims in all cases where it is possible to do so without additional court proceedings on the officer's part.

Ca. Civ. Proc. Code § 1208

Amended by Stats. 1982, Ch. 497, Sec. 78. Operative July 1, 1983, by Sec. 185 of Ch. 497.

Chapter 4 - CERTAIN LIENS UPON ANIMALS

Section 1208.5 - Satisfaction of lien

A person having a lien upon an animal or animals under the provisions of Section 597a or 597.1 of the Penal Code may satisfy the lien in any of the following ways:

(a) If the lien is not discharged and satisfied, by the person responsible, within three days after the obligation becomes due, the person holding the lien may resort to the proper court to satisfy the claim.

(b) Three days after the charges against the property become due, sell the property, or an undivided fraction thereof as may become necessary, to defray the amount due and costs of sale, by giving three days' notice of the sale by advertising in some newspaper published in the county, or city and county, in which the lien has attached to the property.

(c) If there is no newspaper published in the county, by posting notices of the sale in three of the most public places in the town or county for three days previous to the sale. The notices shall contain an accurate description of the property to be sold, together with the terms of sale, which shall be for cash, payable on the consummation of the sale. The proceeds of the sale shall be applied to the discharge of the lien and the costs of sale; the remainder, if any, shall be paid over to the owner, if known, and if not known shall be paid into the treasury of the humane society of the county, or city and county, where the sale takes place. If there is no humane society in the county, then the remainder shall be paid into the county treasury.

Ca. Civ. Proc. Code § 1208.5
Amended by Stats 2019 ch 256 (SB 781),s 2, eff. 1/1/2020.
Amended by Stats 2003 ch 62 (SB 600),s 25, eff. 1/1/2004.
Amended by Stats 2002 ch 784 (SB 1316),s 81, eff. 1/1/2003.

Chapter 5 - LIENS ON AIRCRAFT

Section 1208.61 - Lien for making repairs, performing labor or furnishing supplies and materials

Subject to the limitations set forth in this chapter, every person has a lien dependent upon possession for the compensation to which he is legally entitled for making repairs or performing labor upon, and furnishing supplies or materials for, and for the storage, repair, or safekeeping of, any aircraft, also for reasonable charges for the use of any landing aid furnished such aircraft and reasonable landing fees.

Ca. Civ. Proc. Code § 1208.61
Added by Stats. 1953, Ch. 52.

Section 1208.62 - Notice and consent prior to commencing work or service

That portion of such lien in excess of two hundred fifty dollars ($250) for work or services rendered or performed at the request of any person other than the holder of the legal title is invalid, unless prior to commencing such work or service the person claiming the lien gives actual notice to the legal owner and the mortgagee, if any, of the aircraft, and the written consent of the legal owner and the mortgagee of the aircraft is obtained before such work or services are performed. For the purposes of this chapter the person named in the federal aircraft registration certificate issued by the Administrator of Civil Aeronautics shall be deemed to be the legal owner.

Ca. Civ. Proc. Code § 1208.62
Added by Stats. 1953, Ch. 52.

Section 1208.63 - Assignment of lien for labor and materials

Any lien for labor or materials provided for in this chapter may be assigned by written instrument accompanied by delivery of possession of the aircraft subject to the lien and the assignee may exercise the rights of a lienholder pursuant to this chapter. Any lienholder assigning a lien shall at the time of the assignment give written notice, either by personal delivery or by registered mail with return receipt requested, to the legal owner of the property covered by the lien, including the name and address of the person to whom the lien is assigned.

Ca. Civ. Proc. Code § 1208.63
Added by Stats. 1953, Ch. 52.

Section 1208.64 - Lien lost by reason of possession revived upon repossession by lienholder

Whenever the lien upon any aircraft is lost by reason of the loss of possession through trick, fraud, or device, the repossession of such aircraft by the lienholder revives the lien, but the lien so revived is subordinate to any right, title, or interest of any person under any sale, transfer, encumbrance, lien, or other interest acquired or secured in good faith and for value between the time of the loss of possession and the time of repossession.

Ca. Civ. Proc. Code § 1208.64
Added by Stats. 1953, Ch. 52.

Section 1208.65 - Sale of property to satisfy lien

If the lienholder is not paid the amount due within 10 days after it becomes due, the lienholder may proceed to sell the property, or so much thereof as is necessary to satisfy the lien and costs of sale, at public auction.

Ca. Civ. Proc. Code § 1208.65
Added by Stats. 1953, Ch. 52.

Section 1208.66 - Notice of sale

Prior to any such sale the lienholder shall publish a notice of the sale pursuant to Section 6062 of the Government Code in a newspaper published in the county in which the aircraft is situated, or if there is no such newspaper, by posting notice of sale in three of the most public places in the city or place where such aircraft is to be sold for 10 days previous to the date of the sale. Prior to the sale of any aircraft to satisfy any such lien, 20 days' notice by registered mail shall be given to the legal owner as it appears in the registration certificate.

Ca. Civ. Proc. Code § 1208.66
Amended by Stats. 1957, Ch. 452.

Section 1208.67 - Application of proceeds of sale

The proceeds of the sale must be applied to the discharge of the lien and the cost of keeping and selling the property. The remainder, if any, shall be paid to the legal owner.

Ca. Civ. Proc. Code § 1208.67
Added by Stats. 1953, Ch. 52.

Section 1208.68 - Redemption of sold aircraft

Within 20 days after the sale, the legal owner may redeem the aircraft so sold upon the payment of the amount of the lien, all costs and expenses of sale, and interest on such sum at the rate of 12 percent a year from the date it became due or the date when the amounts were advanced until the repayment.

Ca. Civ. Proc. Code § 1208.68
Added by Stats. 1953, Ch. 52.

Section 1208.69 - Obtaining possession of aircraft through trick, fraud or device perpetrated upon lienholder

It is a misdemeanor for any person to obtain possession of all or any part of any aircraft subject to a lien under this chapter through surreptitious removal or by trick, fraud, or device perpetrated upon the lienholder.

Ca. Civ. Proc. Code § 1208.69
Added by Stats. 1953, Ch. 52.

Section 1208.70 - Inapplicability to aircraft operated by air carrier or foreign aircraft

This chapter shall not apply to aircraft operated exclusively by an air carrier or a foreign air carrier, as defined in subdivisions (2) and (19) of Section 1 of Chapter 601 of the Statutes of the Seventy-fifth United States Congress, Second Session (1938), engaged in air transportation as defined in subdivision (10) of the same section while there is in force a certificate by, or a foreign air carrier permit of, the Civil Aeronautics Board of the United States, or its successor, authorizing such air carrier to engage in such transportation.

Ca. Civ. Proc. Code § 1208.70
Added by Stats. 1953, Ch. 52.

Title 5 - OF CONTEMPTS

Section 1209 - Acts or omissions deemed contempt upon authority of court

(a) The following acts or omissions in respect to a court of justice, or proceedings therein, are contempts of the authority of the court:

(1) Disorderly, contemptuous, or insolent behavior toward the judge while holding the court, tending to interrupt the due course of a trial or other judicial proceeding.

(2) A breach of the peace, boisterous conduct, or violent disturbance, tending to interrupt the due course of a trial or other judicial proceeding.

(3) Misbehavior in office, or other willful neglect or violation of duty by an attorney, counsel, clerk, sheriff, coroner, or other person, appointed or elected to perform a judicial or ministerial service.

(4) Abuse of the process or proceedings of the court, or falsely pretending to act under authority of an order or process of the court.

(5) Disobedience of any lawful judgment, order, or process of the court.

(6) Willful disobedience by a juror of a court admonishment related to the prohibition on any form of communication or research about the case, including all forms of electronic or wireless communication or research.

(7) Rescuing any person or property in the custody of an officer by virtue of an order or process of that court.

(8) Unlawfully detaining a witness or party to an action while going to, remaining at, or returning from the court where the action is on the calendar for trial.

(9) Any other unlawful interference with the process or proceedings of a court.

(10) Disobedience of a subpoena duly served, or refusing to be sworn or answer as a witness.

(11) When summoned as a juror in a court, neglecting to attend or serve as a juror, or improperly conversing with a party to an action to be tried at the court, or with any other person, in relation to the merits of the action, or receiving a communication from a party or other person in respect to the action, without immediately disclosing the communication to the court.

(12) Disobedience by an inferior tribunal or judicial officer of the lawful judgment, order, or process of a superior court, or proceeding in an action or special proceeding contrary to law, after the action or special proceeding is removed from the jurisdiction of the inferior tribunal or judicial officer.

(b) A speech or publication reflecting upon or concerning a court or an officer thereof shall not be treated or punished as a contempt of the court unless made in the immediate presence of the court while in session and in such a manner as to actually interfere with its proceedings.

(c) Notwithstanding Section 1211 or any other law, if an order of contempt is made affecting an attorney, his or her agent, investigator, or any person acting under the attorney's direction, in the preparation and conduct of an action or proceeding, the execution of any sentence shall be stayed pending the filing within three judicial days of a petition for extraordinary relief testing the lawfulness of the court's order, the violation of which is the basis of the contempt, except for conduct proscribed by subdivision (b) of Section 6068 of the Business and Professions Code, relating to an attorney's duty to maintain respect due to the courts and judicial officers.

(d) Notwithstanding Section 1211 or any other law, if an order of contempt is made affecting a public safety employee acting within the scope of employment for reason of the employee's failure to comply with a duly issued subpoena or subpoena duces tecum, the execution of any sentence shall be stayed pending the filing within three judicial days of a petition for extraordinary relief testing the lawfulness of the court's order, a violation of which is the basis for the contempt. As used in this subdivision, "public safety employee" includes any peace officer, firefighter, paramedic, or any other employee of a public law enforcement agency whose duty is either to maintain official records or to analyze or present evidence for investigative or prosecutorial purposes.

Ca. Civ. Proc. Code § 1209
Amended by Stats 2011 ch 181 (AB 141),s 3, eff. 1/1/2012.

Section 1209.5 - Parent not in compliance with order compelling parent to furnish support for child

When a court of competent jurisdiction makes an order compelling a parent to furnish support or necessary food, clothing, shelter, medical attendance, or other remedial care for his or her child, proof that the order was made, filed, and served on the parent or proof that the parent was present in court at the time the order was pronounced and proof that the parent did not comply with the order is prima facie evidence of a contempt of court.

Ca. Civ. Proc. Code § 1209.5

Amended by Stats. 1992, Ch. 163, Sec. 57. Effective January 1, 1993. Operative January 1, 1994, by Sec. 161 of Ch. 163.

Section 1210 - Reentry upon or taking possession of property after person dispossessed or ejected

Every person dispossessed or ejected from any real property by the judgment or process of any court of competent jurisdiction, who, not having right so to do, reenters into or upon or takes possession of the real property, or induces or procures any person not having right so to do, or aids or abets such a person therein, is guilty of a contempt of the court by which the judgment was rendered or from which the process issued. Upon a conviction for contempt the court must immediately issue an alias process, directed to the proper officer, and requiring the officer to restore possession to the party entitled under the original judgment or process, or to the party's lessee, grantee, or successor in interest. No appeal from the order directing the issuance of an alias writ of possession stays the execution of the writ, unless an undertaking is executed on the part of the appellant to the effect that the appellant will not commit or suffer to be committed any waste on the property, and if the order is affirmed, or the appeal dismissed, the appellant will pay the value of the use and occupation of the property from the time of the unlawful reentry until the delivery of the possession of the property, pursuant to the judgment or order, not exceeding a sum to be fixed by the judge of the court by which the order for the alias writ was made.

Ca. Civ. Proc. Code § 1210
Amended by Stats. 1982, Ch. 517, Sec. 179.

Section 1211 - Contempt committed in immediate view and presence of judge; contempt not committed in immediate view or presence of judge

(a) When a contempt is committed in the immediate view and presence of the court, or of the judge at chambers, it may be punished summarily; for which an order must be made, reciting the facts as occurring in such immediate view and presence, adjudging that the person proceeded against is thereby guilty of a contempt, and that he or she be punished as therein prescribed. When the contempt is not committed in the immediate view and presence of the court, or of the judge at chambers, an affidavit shall be presented to the court or judge of the facts constituting the contempt, or a statement of the facts by the referees or arbitrators, or other judicial officers.

(b) In family law matters, filing of the Judicial Council form entitled "Order to Show Cause and Affidavit for Contempt (Family Law)" shall constitute compliance with this section.

Ca. Civ. Proc. Code § 1211
Amended by Stats 2001 ch 754 (AB 1697), s 1, eff. 1/1/2002.

Section 1211.5 - Construction, amendment and review of affidavit or statement of facts

At all stages of all proceedings, the affidavit or statement of facts, as the case may be, required by Section 1211 shall be construed, amended, and reviewed according to the followings rules:
(a) If no objection is made to the sufficiency of such affidavit or statement during the hearing on the charges contained therein, jurisdiction of the subject matter shall not depend on the averments of such affidavit or statement, but may be established by the facts found by the trial court to have been proved at such hearing, and the court shall cause the affidavit or statement to be amended to conform to proof.

(b) The court may order or permit amendment of such affidavit or statement for any defect or insufficiency at any stage of the proceedings, and the trial of the person accused of contempt shall continue as if the affidavit or statement had been originally filed as amended, unless substantial rights of such person accused would be prejudiced thereby, in which event a reasonable postponement, not longer than the ends of justice require, may be granted.

(c) No such affidavit or statement is insufficient, nor can the trial, order, judgment, or other proceeding thereon be affected by reason of any defect or imperfection in matter of form which does not prejudice a substantial right of the person accused on the merits. No order or judgment of conviction of contempt shall be set aside, nor new trial granted, for any error as to any matter of pleading in such affidavit or statement, unless, after an examination of the entire cause, including the evidence, the court shall be of the opinion that the error complained of has resulted in a miscarriage of justice.

Ca. Civ. Proc. Code § 1211.5
Added by Stats. 1970, Ch. 1264.

Section 1212 - Issuance of warrant of attachment and warrant of commitment

When the contempt is not committed in the immediate view and presence of the court or judge, a warrant of attachment may be issued to bring the person charged to answer, or, without a previous arrest, a warrant of commitment may, upon notice, or upon an order to show cause, be granted; and no warrant of commitment can be issued without such previous attachment to answer, or such notice or order to show cause.

Ca. Civ. Proc. Code § 1212
Amended by Stats. 1951, Ch. 1737.

Section 1213 - Undertaking for person's appearance

Whenever a warrant of attachment is issued pursuant to this title the court or judge must direct, by an endorsement on the warrant, that the person charged may give an undertaking for the person's appearance in an amount to be specified in such endorsement.

Ca. Civ. Proc. Code § 1213

Amended by Stats. 1982, Ch. 517, Sec. 179.5.

Section 1214 - Execution of warrant of attachment

Upon executing the warrant of attachment, the officer executing the warrant must keep the person in custody, bring him before the court or judge, and detain him until an order be made in the premises, unless the person arrested entitle himself to be discharged, as provided in the next section.

Ca. Civ. Proc. Code § 1214

Amended by Stats. 1951, Ch. 1737.

Section 1215 - Discharge of person arrested upon executing and delivering undertaking

The person arrested must be discharged from the arrest upon executing and delivering to the officer, at any time before the return day of the warrant, an undertaking to the effect that the person arrested will appear on the return of the warrant and abide the order of the court or judge thereupon.

Ca. Civ. Proc. Code § 1215

Amended by Stats. 1982, Ch. 517, Sec. 180.

Section 1216 - Return of warrant and undertaking

The officer must return the warrant of arrest and undertaking, if any, received by him from the person arrested, by the return day specified therein.

Ca. Civ. Proc. Code § 1216

Enacted 1872.

Section 1217 - Investigation of charge and hearing on answer

When the person arrested has been brought up or appeared, the court or judge must proceed to investigate the charge, and must hear any answer which the person arrested may make to the same, and may examine witnesses for or against him, for which an adjournment may be had from time to time if necessary.

Ca. Civ. Proc. Code § 1217

Amended by Stats. 1951, Ch. 1737.

Section 1218 - Finding that person guilty of contempt

(a) Upon the answer and evidence taken, the court or judge shall determine whether the person proceeded against is guilty of the contempt charged, and if it be adjudged that the person is guilty of the contempt, a fine may be imposed on the person not exceeding one thousand dollars ($1,000), payable to the court, or the person may be imprisoned not exceeding five days, or both. In addition, a person who is subject to a court order as a party to the action, or any agent of this person, who is adjudged guilty of contempt for violating that court order may be ordered to pay to the party initiating the contempt proceeding the reasonable attorney's fees and costs incurred by this party in connection with the contempt proceeding.

(b) Any party, who is in contempt of a court order or judgment in a dissolution of marriage, dissolution of domestic partnership, or legal separation action, shall not be permitted to enforce such an order or judgment, by way of execution or otherwise, either in the same action or by way of a separate action, against the other party. This restriction shall not affect nor apply to the enforcement of child or spousal support orders.

(c)

(1) In any court action in which a party is found in contempt of court for failure to comply with a court order pursuant to the Family Code, the court shall, subject to the sentencing option provided in paragraph (2), order the following:

(A) Upon a first finding of contempt, the court shall order the contemner to perform community service of up to 120 hours, or to be imprisoned up to 120 hours, for each count of contempt.

(B) Upon the second finding of contempt, the court shall order the contemner to perform community service of up to 120 hours, in addition to ordering imprisonment of the contemner up to 120 hours, for each count of contempt.

(C) Upon the third or any subsequent finding of contempt, the court shall order that the contemner serve a term of imprisonment of up to 240 hours and perform community service of up to 240 hours, for each count of contempt. The court shall also order the contemner to pay an administrative fee, not to exceed the actual cost of the contemner's administration and supervision, while assigned to a community service program pursuant to this paragraph.

(D) The court shall take parties' employment schedules into consideration when ordering either community service or imprisonment, or both.

(2) In lieu of an order of imprisonment, community service, or both, as set forth in paragraph (1), the court may grant probation or a conditional sentence for a period not to exceed one year upon a first finding of contempt, a period not to exceed two years upon a second finding of contempt, and a period not to exceed three years upon a third or any subsequent finding of contempt.

(3) For purposes of this subdivision, "probation" and "conditional sentence" shall have the meanings set forth in subdivision (a) of Section 1203 of the Penal Code.
(d) Pursuant to Section 1211 and this section, a district attorney or city attorney may initiate and pursue a court action for contempt against a party for failing to comply with a court order entered pursuant to the Domestic Violence Protection Act (Division 10 (commencing with Section 6200) of the Family Code). Any attorney's fees and costs ordered by the court pursuant to subdivision (a) against a party who is adjudged guilty of contempt under this subdivision shall be paid to the Office of Emergency Services' account established for the purpose of funding domestic violence shelter service providers pursuant to subdivision (f) of Section 13823.15 of the Penal Code.

Ca. Civ. Proc. Code § 1218
Amended by Stats 2020 ch 283 (AB 2338),s 1, eff. 1/1/2021.
Amended by Stats 2013 ch 352 (AB 1317),s 56, eff. 9/26/2013, op.
7/1/2013.
Amended by Stats 2010 ch 618 (AB 2791),s 3, eff. 1/1/2011.
Amended by Stats 2005 ch 631 (SB 720),s 1, eff. 1/1/2006
Amended by Stats 2005 ch 75 (AB 145),s 44, eff. 7/19/2005, op.
1/1/2006
Amended by Stats 2000 ch 808 (AB 1358), s 20, eff. 9/28/2000.

Section 1218.5 - Contempt alleged for failure to pay support

(a) If the contempt alleged is for failure to pay child, family, or spousal support, each month for which payment has not been made in full may be alleged as a separate count of contempt and punishment imposed for each count proven.
(b) If the contempt alleged is the failure to pay child, family, or spousal support, the period of limitations for commencing a contempt action is three years from the date that the payment was due. If the action before the court is enforcement of another order under the Family Code, the period of limitations for commencing a contempt action is two years from the time that the alleged contempt occurred.
Ca. Civ. Proc. Code § 1218.5
Added by Stats. 1994, Ch. 1269, Sec. 3.5. Effective January 1, 1995.

Section 1219 - Imprisonment until person performs act; refusal of victim to testify concerning sexual assault or domestic violence

(a) Except as provided in subdivisions (b) and (c), if the contempt consists of the omission to perform an act which is yet in the power of the person to perform, he or she may be imprisoned until he or she has performed it, and in that case the act shall be specified in the warrant of commitment.
(b) Notwithstanding any other law, a court shall not imprison or otherwise confine or place in custody the victim of a sexual assault

or domestic violence crime for contempt if the contempt consists of refusing to testify concerning that sexual assault or domestic violence crime. Before finding a victim of a domestic violence crime in contempt as described in this section, the court may refer the victim for consultation with a domestic violence counselor. All communications between the victim and the domestic violence counselor that occur as a result of that referral shall remain confidential under Section 1037.2 of the Evidence Code.

(c) Notwithstanding any other law, a court shall not imprison, hold in physical confinement, or otherwise confine or place in custody a minor for contempt if the contempt consists of the minor's failure to comply with a court order pursuant to subdivision (b) of Section 601 of, or Section 727 of, the Welfare and Institutions Code, if the minor was adjudged a ward of the court on the ground that he or she is a person described in subdivision (b) of Section 601 of the Welfare and Institutions Code. Upon a finding of contempt of court, the court may issue any other lawful order, as necessary, to secure the minor's attendance at school.

(d) As used in this section, the following terms have the following meanings:

(1) "Sexual assault" means any act made punishable by Section 261, 262, 264.1, 285, 286, 287, 288, or 289 of, or former Section 288a of, the Penal Code.

(2) "Domestic violence" means "domestic violence" as defined in Section 6211 of the Family Code.

(3) "Domestic violence counselor" means "domestic violence counselor" as defined in subdivision (a) of Section 1037.1 of the Evidence Code.

(4) "Physical confinement" has the same meaning as defined in subdivision (d) of Section 726 of the Welfare and Institutions Code.

Ca. Civ. Proc. Code § 1219

Amended by Stats 2018 ch 423 (SB 1494),s 9, eff. 1/1/2019.
Amended by Stats 2014 ch 70 (SB 1296),s 1, eff. 1/1/2015.
Amended by Stats 2012 ch 510 (AB 2051),s 1, eff. 1/1/2013.

Amended by Stats 2009 ch 35 (SB 174),s 3, eff. 1/1/2010.
Amended by Stats 2008 ch 49 (SB 1356),s 1, eff. 1/1/2009.

Section 1219.5 - Refusal of minor 16 years of age to take oath and testify

(a) Except as provided in subdivision (d), in any case in which a contempt consists of the refusal of a minor under 16 years of age to take the oath or to testify, before imposing any sanction for the contempt, the court shall first refer the matter to the probation officer in charge of matters coming before the juvenile court for a report and recommendation as to the appropriateness of the imposition of a sanction. The probation officer shall prepare and file the report and recommendation within the time directed by the court. In making the report and recommendation, the probation officer shall consider factors such as the maturity of the minor, the reasons for the minor's refusal to take the oath or to testify, the probability that available sanctions will affect the decision of the minor not to take the oath or not to testify, the potential impact on the minor of his or her testimony, the potential impact on the pending litigation of the minor's unavailability as a witness, and the appropriateness of the various available sanctions in the minor's case. The court shall consider the report and recommendation in imposing a sanction in the case.

(b) A victim of a sex crime who is subject to subdivision (a) shall meet with a victim advocate, as defined in Section 679.04 of the Penal Code, unless the court, for good cause, finds that it is not in the best interest of the victim.

(c) In any case in which the court orders the minor to be placed outside of his or her home, the placement shall be in the least restrictive setting available. Except as provided in subdivision (e), the court shall not order the minor to be placed in a secure facility unless other placements have been made and the minor has fled the custody and control of the person under the control of whom he or she has been placed or has persistently refused to obey the reasonable and proper orders or directions of the person under the control of whom he or she has been placed.

(d) The court may impose a sanction for contempt prior to receipt of the report and recommendation required by subdivision (a) if the court enters a finding, supported by specific facts stated on the record, that the minor would be likely to flee if released before the receipt of the report and recommendation.

(e) The court may order the minor placed in a secure facility without first attempting the nonsecure placement required by subdivision (c) if the court enters a finding, supported by specific facts stated on the record, that the minor would be likely to flee if released to nonsecure placement as a prerequisite to secure confinement.

Ca. Civ. Proc. Code § 1219.5

Amended by Stats 2012 ch 223 (SB 1248),s 1, eff. 1/1/2013.

Section 1220 - Failure of person arrested to appear on return day

When the warrant of arrest has been returned served, if the person arrested does not appear on the return day, the court or judge may issue another warrant of arrest or may order the undertaking to be enforced, or both. If the undertaking is enforced, the measure of damages is the extent of the loss or injury sustained by the aggrieved party by reason of the misconduct for which the warrant was issued.

Ca. Civ. Proc. Code § 1220

Amended by Stats. 1982, Ch. 517, Sec. 181.

Section 1221 - Inability from illness or otherwise of officer to bring person confined before court or judge

Whenever, by the provisions of this title, an officer is required to keep a person arrested on a warrant of attachment in custody, and to bring him before a court or judge, the inability, from illness or otherwise, of the person to attend, is a sufficient excuse for not bringing him up; and the officer must not confine a person arrested upon the warrant in a prison, or otherwise restrain him of personal liberty, except so far as may be necessary to secure his personal attendance.

Ca. Civ. Proc. Code § 1221
Amended by Stats. 1951, Ch. 1737.

Section 1222 - Judgment or orders final and conclusive

The judgment and orders of the court or judge, made in cases of contempt, are final and conclusive.
Ca. Civ. Proc. Code § 1222
Amended by Stats. 1951, Ch. 1737.

Title 7 - EMINENT DOMAIN LAW

Chapter 1 - GENERAL PROVISIONS

Section 1230.010 - Title of law

This title shall be known and may be cited as the Eminent Domain Law.
Ca. Civ. Proc. Code § 1230.010
Added by Stats. 1975, Ch. 1275.

Section 1230.020 - Generally

Except as otherwise specifically provided by statute, the power of eminent domain may be exercised only as provided in this title.
Ca. Civ. Proc. Code § 1230.020
Added by Stats. 1975, Ch. 1275.

Section 1230.030 - Exercise of power not required by title; discretion of person authorized to acquire property

Nothing in this title requires that the power of eminent domain be exercised to acquire property necessary for public use. Whether property necessary for public use is to be acquired by purchase or other means or by eminent domain is a decision left to the discretion of the person authorized to acquire the property.
Ca. Civ. Proc. Code § 1230.030
Added by Stats. 1975, Ch. 1275.

Section 1230.040 - Applicability of rules of practice governing civil actions

Except as otherwise provided in this title, the rules of practice that govern civil actions generally are the rules of practice for eminent domain proceedings.

Ca. Civ. Proc. Code § 1230.040
Added by Stats. 1975, Ch. 1275.

Section 1230.050 - Power of court to determine right to possession and enforce orders for possession

The court in which a proceeding in eminent domain is brought has the power to:

(a) Determine the right to possession of the property, as between the plaintiff and the defendant, in accordance with this title.

(b) Enforce any of its orders for possession by appropriate process. The plaintiff is entitled to enforcement of an order for possession as a matter of right.

Ca. Civ. Proc. Code § 1230.050
Added by Stats. 1975, Ch. 1275.

Section 1230.060 - Title not to affect proceedings to Public Utilities Commission

Nothing in this title affects any other statute granting jurisdiction over any issue in eminent domain proceedings to the Public Utilities Commission.

Ca. Civ. Proc. Code § 1230.060
Added by Stats. 1975, Ch. 1275.

Section 1230.065 - Effective date

(a) This title becomes operative July 1, 1976.

(b) This title does not apply to an eminent domain proceeding commenced prior to January 1, 1976. Subject to subdivisions (c) and (d), in the case of an eminent domain proceeding which is commenced on or after January 1, 1976, but prior to the operative date, this title upon the operative date applies to the proceeding to the fullest extent practicable with respect to issues to be tried or retried.

(c) Chapter 3 (commencing with Section 1240.010), Chapter 4 (commencing with Section 1245.010), and Chapter 5 (commencing with Section 1250.010) do not apply to a proceeding commenced prior to the operative date.

(d) If, on the operative date, an appeal, motion to modify or vacate the verdict or judgment, or motion for new trial is pending, the law applicable thereto prior to the operative date governs the determination of the appeal or motion.

Ca. Civ. Proc. Code § 1230.065
Added by Stats. 1975, Ch. 1275.

Section 1230.070 - Judgments prior to operative date not affected

No judgment rendered prior to the operative date of this title in a proceeding to enforce the right of eminent domain is affected by the enactment of this title and the repeal of former Title 7 of this part.

Ca. Civ. Proc. Code § 1230.070
Added by Stats. 1975, Ch. 1275.

Chapter 2 - PRINCIPLES OF CONSTRUCTION; DEFINITIONS

Article 1 - CONSTRUCTION

Section 1235.010 - Generally

Unless the provision or context otherwise requires, these preliminary provisions and rules of construction shall govern the construction of this title.

Ca. Civ. Proc. Code § 1235.010
Added by Stats. 1975, Ch. 1275.

Section 1235.020 - Headings not to affect scope, meaning or intent

Chapter, article, and section headings do not in any manner affect the scope, meaning, or intent of the provisions of this title.

Ca. Civ. Proc. Code § 1235.020
Added by Stats. 1975, Ch. 1275.

Section 1235.030 - References to title applicable to amendments and additions

Whenever any reference is made to any portion of this title or to any other statute, such reference shall apply to all amendments and additions heretofore or hereafter made.

Ca. Civ. Proc. Code § 1235.030
Added by Stats. 1975, Ch. 1275.

Section 1235.040 - Definitions

Unless otherwise expressly stated:

(a) "Chapter" means a chapter of this title.

(b) "Article" means an article of the chapter in which that term occurs.

(c) "Section" means a section of this code.

(d) "Subdivision" means a subdivision of the section in which that term occurs.

(e) "Paragraph" means a paragraph of the subdivision in which that term occurs.

Ca. Civ. Proc. Code § 1235.040
Added by Stats. 1975, Ch. 1275.

Section 1235.050 - Present tense

The present tense includes the past and future tenses; and the future, the present.

Ca. Civ. Proc. Code § 1235.050
Added by Stats. 1975, Ch. 1275.

Section 1235.060 - Shall and may

"Shall" is mandatory and "may" is permissive.

Ca. Civ. Proc. Code § 1235.060
Added by Stats. 1975, Ch. 1275.

Section 1235.070 - Severability of provisions

If any provision or clause of this title or application thereof to any person or circumstances is held invalid, the invalidity does not affect other provisions or applications of the title that can be given effect without the invalid provision or application, and to this end the provisions of this title are severable.

Ca. Civ. Proc. Code § 1235.070
Added by Stats. 1975, Ch. 1275.

Article 2 - WORDS AND PHRASES DEFINED

Section 1235.110 - Generally

Unless the provision or context otherwise requires, these definitions govern the construction of this title.

Ca. Civ. Proc. Code § 1235.110
Added by Stats. 1975, Ch. 1275.

Section 1235.120 - Final judgment

"Final judgment" means a judgment with respect to which all possibility of direct attack by way of appeal, motion for a new trial, or motion under Section 663 to vacate the judgment has been exhausted.

Ca. Civ. Proc. Code § 1235.120
Added by Stats. 1975, Ch. 1275.

Section 1235.125 - Interest

When used with reference to property, "interest" includes any right, title, or estate in property.

Ca. Civ. Proc. Code § 1235.125
Added by Stats. 1975, Ch. 1275.

Section 1235.130 - Judgment

"Judgment" means the judgment determining the right to take the property by eminent domain and fixing the amount of compensation to be paid by the plaintiff.

Ca. Civ. Proc. Code § 1235.130
Added by Stats. 1975, Ch. 1275.

Section 1235.140 - Litigation expenses

"Litigation expenses" includes both of the following:

(a) All expenses reasonably and necessarily incurred in the proceeding in preparing for trial, during trial, and in any subsequent judicial proceedings.

(b) Reasonable attorney's fees, appraisal fees, and fees for the services of other experts where such fees were reasonably and necessarily incurred to protect the defendant's interests in the proceeding in preparing for trial, during trial, and in any subsequent judicial proceedings whether such fees were incurred for services rendered before or after the filing of the complaint.

Ca. Civ. Proc. Code § 1235.140
Added by Stats. 1975, Ch. 1275.

Section 1235.150 - Local public entity

"Local public entity" means any public entity other than the state.

Ca. Civ. Proc. Code § 1235.150
Added by Stats. 1975, Ch. 1275.

Section 1235.155 - Nonprofit special use property

"Nonprofit, special use property" means property which is operated for a special nonprofit, tax-exempt use such as a school, church, cemetery, hospital, or similar property. "Nonprofit, special use property" does not include property owned by a public entity.

Ca. Civ. Proc. Code § 1235.155
Added by Stats. 1992, Ch. 7, Sec. 1. Effective January 1, 1993.

Section 1235.160 - Person

"Person" includes any public entity, individual, association, organization, partnership, trust, limited liability company, or corporation.

Ca. Civ. Proc. Code § 1235.160

Amended by Stats. 1994, Ch. 1010, Sec. 63. Effective January 1, 1995.

Section 1235.165 - Proceeding

"Proceeding" means an eminent domain proceeding under this title.
  Ca. Civ. Proc. Code § 1235.165
Added by Stats. 1975, Ch. 1275.

Section 1235.170 - Property

"Property" includes real and personal property and any interest therein.
  Ca. Civ. Proc. Code § 1235.170
Added by Stats. 1975, Ch. 1275.

Section 1235.180 - Property appropriated to public use

"Property appropriated to public use" means property either already in use for a public purpose or set aside for a specific public purpose with the intention of using it for such purpose within a reasonable time.
  Ca. Civ. Proc. Code § 1235.180
Added by Stats. 1975, Ch. 1275.

Section 1235.190 - Public entity

"Public entity" includes the state, a county, city, district, public authority, public agency, and any other political subdivision in the state.
  Ca. Civ. Proc. Code § 1235.190
Added by Stats. 1975, Ch. 1275.

Section 1235.193 - Electric, gas or water utility property

"Electric, gas, or water public utility property" means property appropriated to a public use by a public utility, as defined in Section 218, 222, or 241 of the Public Utilities Code.

Ca. Civ. Proc. Code § 1235.193
Added by Stats. 1992, Ch. 812, Sec. 1. Effective January 1, 1993.

Section 1235.195 - Resolution
"Resolution" includes ordinance.
Ca. Civ. Proc. Code § 1235.195
Added by Stats. 1975, Ch. 1275.

Section 1235.200 - State
"State" means the State of California and includes the Regents of
the University of California.
Ca. Civ. Proc. Code § 1235.200
Added by Stats. 1975, Ch. 1275.

Section 1235.210 - Statute
"Statute" means a constitutional provision or statute, but does not
include a charter provision or ordinance.
Ca. Civ. Proc. Code § 1235.210
Added by Stats. 1975, Ch. 1275.

Chapter 3 - THE RIGHT TO TAKE

Article 1 - GENERAL LIMITATIONS ON EXERCISE OF POWER OF EMINENT DOMAIN

Section 1240.010 - Power exercised to acquire property for public use; legislative declaration as to public use
The power of eminent domain may be exercised to acquire property
only for a public use. Where the Legislature provides by statute that
a use, purpose, object, or function is one for which the power of
eminent domain may be exercised, such action is deemed to be a
declaration by the Legislature that such use, purpose, object, or
function is a public use.
Ca. Civ. Proc. Code § 1240.010
Added by Stats. 1975, Ch. 1275.

Section 1240.020 - Exercise of power to acquire property for particular use

The power of eminent domain may be exercised to acquire property for a particular use only by a person authorized by statute to exercise the power of eminent domain to acquire such property for that use.

Ca. Civ. Proc. Code § 1240.020
Added by Stats. 1975, Ch. 1275.

Section 1240.030 - Exercise of power to acquire property for proposed use

The power of eminent domain may be exercised to acquire property for a proposed project only if all of the following are established:
(a) The public interest and necessity require the project.
(b) The project is planned or located in the manner that will be most compatible with the greatest public good and the least private injury.
(c) The property sought to be acquired is necessary for the project.

Ca. Civ. Proc. Code § 1240.030
Added by Stats. 1975, Ch. 1275.

Section 1240.040 - Adoption of resolution by public entity required to exercise power

A public entity may exercise the power of eminent domain only if it has adopted a resolution of necessity that meets the requirements of Article 2 (commencing with Section 1245.210) of Chapter 4.

Ca. Civ. Proc. Code § 1240.040
Added by Stats. 1975, Ch. 1275.

Section 1240.050 - Acquisition of property within territorial limits, exception

A local public entity may acquire by eminent domain only property within its territorial limits except where the power to acquire by eminent domain property outside its limits is expressly granted by statute or necessarily implied as an incident of one of its other statutory powers.

Ca. Civ. Proc. Code § 1240.050
Added by Stats. 1975, Ch 1275.

Section 1240.055 - Acquisition of property subject to conservation easement

(a) As used in this section, the following terms have the following meanings:

(1) "Conservation easement" means a conservation easement as defined in Section 815.1 of the Civil Code and recorded as required by Section 815.5 of the Civil Code.

(2) "Holder of a conservation easement" means the entity or organization that holds the conservation easement on the property that is proposed for acquisition and that is authorized to acquire and hold conservation easements pursuant to Section 815.3 of the Civil Code.

(3) "Property appropriated to public use," as used in Article 6 (commencing with Section 1240.510) and Article 7 (commencing with Section 1240.610), includes a conservation easement if any of the following applies:

(A) The conservation easement is held by a public entity.

(B) A public entity provided funds, not including the value of a charitable contribution for federal or state income tax purposes but including the California Natural Heritage Preservation Tax Credit, for the acquisition of that easement.

(C) A public entity imposed conditions on approval or permitting of a project that were satisfied, in whole or in part, by the conservation easement.

(b) A person authorized to acquire property for public use by eminent domain shall exercise the power of eminent domain to acquire property that is subject to a conservation easement only as provided in this section.

(c) Not later than 105 days prior to the hearing held pursuant to Section 1245.235, or at the time of the offer made to the owner or owners of record pursuant to Section 7267.2 of the Government Code, whichever occurs earlier, the person seeking to acquire property subject to a conservation easement shall give notice to the holder of the conservation easement as provided in this subdivision. If the person is not required to hold a hearing pursuant to Section 1245.235, then the notice shall be given 105 days prior to the time of the offer made to the owner or owners of record pursuant to Section 7267.2 of the Government Code.

(1) The notice required by subdivision (c) shall be sent by first-class mail and shall state all of the following:

(A) A general description, in text or by diagram, of the property subject to a conservation easement that the person proposes to acquire by eminent domain.

(B) A description of the public use or improvement that the person is considering for the property subject to a conservation easement.

(C) That written comments on the acquisition may be submitted in accordance with paragraph (3) no later than 45 days from the date the person seeking to acquire the property mailed the notice to the holder of the conservation easement.

(D) That the holder of the conservation easement, within 15 days of receipt of the notice required by subdivision (c), is required, under certain circumstances, to do all of the following:

(i) Send a copy of the notice by first-class mail to each public entity that provided funds for the purchase of the easement or that imposed conditions on approval or permitting of a project that were satisfied, in whole or in part, by the creation of the conservation easement.

(ii) Inform the public entity that written comments on

the acquisition may be submitted in accordance with paragraph (3).

(iii) Notify the person seeking to acquire the property of the name and address of any public entity that was sent a copy of the notice pursuant to this paragraph.

(2)

(A) The holder of the conservation easement, within 15 days of receipt of the notice required by subdivision (c), shall do all of the following:

(i) Send a copy of the notice by first-class mail to each public entity that provided funds for the purchase of the easement or that imposed conditions on approval or permitting of a project that were satisfied, in whole or in part, by the creation of the conservation easement.

(ii) Inform the public entity that written comments on the acquisition may be submitted in accordance with paragraph (3).

(iii) Notify the person seeking to acquire the property of the name and address of any public entity that was sent a copy of the notice pursuant to this paragraph.

(B) Subparagraph (A) shall apply only if one of the following applies:

(i) The holder of the easement is the original grantee of the conservation easement and there is a public entity as described in subparagraph (A).

(ii) The holder of the easement has actual knowledge of a public entity as described in subparagraph (A).

(iii) Recorded documents evidence the identity of a public entity as described in subparagraph (A).

(3) The holder of the conservation easement or the public entity receiving notice, or both, may provide to the person seeking to acquire the property written comments on the acquisition, including identifying any potential conflict between the public use proposed for the property and the purposes and terms of the conservation easement. Written comments on the acquisition may be submitted no later than 45 days from the date the person seeking to acquire the property mailed the notice to the holder of the conservation easement.

(d) The person seeking to acquire the property subject to a conservation easement, within 30 days after receipt of written comments from the holder of the conservation easement or from a public entity described in paragraph (2) of subdivision (c), shall respond in writing to the comments. The response to the comments shall be mailed by first-class mail to each easement holder or public entity that filed comments.

(e) The notice of the hearing on the resolution of necessity, pursuant to Section 1245.235, shall be sent by first-class mail to the holder of any conservation easement and to any public entity whose name and address are provided as described in paragraph (2) of subdivision (c) and shall state that they have the right to appear and be heard on the matters referred to in Sections 1240.030, 1240.510, and 1240.610. The notice shall state that, pursuant to paragraph (3) of subdivision (b) of Section 1245.235, failure to file a written request to appear and be heard within 15 days after the notice was mailed will result in waiver of the right to appear and be heard. The resolution of necessity to acquire property subject to a conservation easement shall refer specifically either to Section 1240.510 or 1240.610 as authority for the acquisition of the property.

(f) In any eminent domain proceeding to acquire property subject to a conservation easement, the holder of the conservation easement:

(1) Shall be named as a defendant, as set forth in Section 1250.220.

(2) May appear in the proceedings, as set forth in Section 1250.230.

(3) Shall have all the same rights and obligations as any other defendant in the eminent domain proceeding.

(g)

(1) The holder of the conservation easement is an owner of property entitled to compensation determined pursuant to Section 1260.220 and Chapter 9 (commencing with Section 1263.010) and in accordance with all of the following:

(A) The total compensation for the acquisition of all interests in property encumbered by a conservation easement shall not be less than, and shall not exceed, the fair market value of the fee simple interest of the property as if it were not encumbered by the conservation easement.

(B) If the acquisition does not damage the conservation easement, the total compensation shall be assessed by determining the value of all interests in the property as encumbered by the conservation easement.

(C) If the acquisition damages the conservation easement in whole or in part, compensation shall be determined consistent with Section 1260.220 and the value of the fee simple interest of the property shall be assessed as if it were not encumbered by the conservation easement.

(2) This subdivision shall not apply if the requirements of Section 10261 of the Public Resources Code apply.

(h) This section shall not apply if the requirements of Section 1348.3 of the Fish and Game Code apply.

Ca. Civ. Proc. Code § 1240.055

Added by Stats 2011 ch 589 (SB 328),s 2, eff. 1/1/2012.

Article 2 - RIGHTS INCLUDED IN GRANT OF EMINENT DOMAIN AUTHORITY

Section 1240.110 - Acquisition of interest in property necessary for particular use

(a) Except to the extent limited by statute, any person authorized to acquire property for a particular use by eminent domain may exercise the power of eminent domain to acquire any interest in property necessary for that use including, but not limited to, submerged lands, rights of any nature in water, subsurface rights, airspace rights, flowage or flooding easements, aircraft noise or operation easements, right of temporary occupancy, public utility facilities and franchises, and franchises to collect tolls on a bridge or highway.

(b) Where a statute authorizes the acquisition by eminent domain only of specified interests in or types of property, this section does not expand the scope of the authority so granted.

Ca. Civ. Proc. Code § 1240.110
Added by Stats. 1975, Ch. 1275.

Section 1240.120 - Acquisition of property necessary to carry out and make effective principal purpose

(a) Subject to any other statute relating to the acquisition of property, any person authorized to acquire property for a particular use by eminent domain may exercise the power of eminent domain to acquire property necessary to carry out and make effective the principal purpose involved including but not limited to property to be used for the protection or preservation of the attractiveness, safety, and usefulness of the project.

(b) Subject to any applicable procedures governing the disposition of property, a person may acquire property under subdivision (a) with the intent to sell, lease, exchange, or otherwise dispose of the property, or an interest therein, subject to such reservations or restrictions as are necessary to protect or preserve the attractiveness, safety, and usefulness of the project.

Ca. Civ. Proc. Code § 1240.120
Added by Stats. 1975, Ch. 1275.

Section 1240.125 - Purposes for which local public entity may acquire property outside territorial limits

Except as otherwise expressly provided by statute and subject to any limitations imposed by statute, a local public entity may acquire property by eminent domain outside its territorial limits for water, gas, or electric supply purposes or for airports, drainage or sewer purposes if it is authorized to acquire property by eminent domain for the purposes for which the property is to be acquired.

Ca. Civ. Proc. Code § 1240.125
Added by Stats. 1975, Ch. 1275.

Section 1240.130 - Acquisition of property for particular use by purchase, lease, gift, etc.

Subject to any other statute relating to the acquisition of property, any public entity authorized to acquire property for a particular use by eminent domain may also acquire such property for such use by grant, purchase, lease, gift, devise, contract, or other means.

Ca. Civ. Proc. Code § 1240.130
Added by Stats. 1975, Ch. 1275.

Section 1240.140 - Agreement for joint exercise of power by two or more public agencies

(a) As used in this section, "public agencies" includes all those agencies included within the definition of "public agency" in Section 6500 of the Government Code.

(b) Two or more public agencies may enter into an agreement for the joint exercise of their respective powers of eminent domain, whether or not possessed in common, for the acquisition of property as a single parcel. Such agreement shall be entered into and performed pursuant to the provisions of Chapter 5 (commencing with Section 6500) of Division 7 of Title 1 of the Government Code.

Ca. Civ. Proc. Code § 1240.140
Added by Stats. 1975, Ch. 1275.

Section 1240.150 - Acquisition of remainder of property

Whenever a part of a larger parcel of property is to be acquired by a public entity for public use and the remainder, or a portion of the remainder, will be left in such size, shape, or condition as to be of little value to its owner or to give rise to a claim for severance or other damages, the public entity may acquire the remainder, or portion of the remainder, by any means (including eminent domain) expressly consented to by the owner.

Ca. Civ. Proc. Code § 1240.150
Added by Stats. 1975, Ch. 1275.

Section 1240.160 - Provisions distinct and separate authorization

(a) None of the provisions of this article is intended to limit, or shall limit, any other provision of this article, each of which is a distinct and separate authorization.

(b) None of the provisions of Article 2 (commencing with Section 1240.110), Article 3 (commencing with Section 1240.210), Article 4 (commencing with Section 1240.310), Article 5 (commencing with Section 1240.410), Article 6 (commencing with Section 1240.510), or Article 7 (commencing with Section 1240.610) is intended to limit, or shall limit, the provisions of any other of the articles, each of which articles is a distinct and separate authorization.

Ca. Civ. Proc. Code § 1240.160
Added by Stats. 1975, Ch. 1275.

Article 3 - FUTURE USE

Section 1240.210 - Date of use of property taken for public use

For the purposes of this article, the "date of use" of property taken for public use is the date when the property is devoted to that use or when construction is started on the project for which the property is taken with the intent to complete the project within a reasonable time. In determining the "date of use," periods of delay caused by extraordinary litigation or by failure to obtain from any public entity any agreement or permit necessary for construction shall not be included.

Ca. Civ. Proc. Code § 1240.210
Added by Stats. 1975, Ch. 1275.

Section 1240.220 - Generally

(a) Any person authorized to acquire property for a particular use by eminent domain may exercise the power of eminent domain to acquire property to be used in the future for that use, but property may be taken for future use only if there is a reasonable probability that its date of use will be within seven years from the date the complaint is filed or within such longer period as is reasonable.

(b) Unless the plaintiff plans that the date of use of property taken will be within seven years from the date the complaint is filed, the complaint, and the resolution of necessity if one is required, shall refer specifically to this section and shall state the estimated date of use.

Ca. Civ. Proc. Code § 1240.220
Added by Stats. 1975, Ch. 1275.

Section 1240.230 - Burden of proof if defendant objects to taking for future use

(a) If the defendant objects to a taking for future use, the burden of proof is as prescribed in this section.

(b) Unless the complaint states an estimated date of use that is not within seven years from the date the complaint is filed, the defendant has the burden of proof that there is no reasonable probability that the date of use will be within seven years from the date the complaint is filed.

(c) If the defendant proves that there is no reasonable probability that the date of use will be within seven years from the date the complaint is filed, or if the complaint states an estimated date of use that is not within seven years from the date the complaint is filed, the plaintiff has the burden of proof that a taking for future use satisfies the requirements of this article.

Ca. Civ. Proc. Code § 1240.230
Added by Stats. 1975, Ch. 1275.

Section 1240.240 - Acquisition of property by any means consented to by owner

Notwithstanding any other provision of this article, any public entity authorized to acquire property for a particular use by eminent domain may acquire property to be used in the future for that use by any means (including eminent domain) expressly consented to by its owner.

Ca. Civ. Proc. Code § 1240.240
Added by Stats. 1975, Ch. 1275.

Section 1240.250 - Property taken pursuant to Federal Aid Highway Act of 1973

Notwithstanding any other provision of this article, where property is taken pursuant to the Federal Aid Highway Act of 1973:

(a) A date of use within 10 years from the date the complaint is filed shall be deemed reasonable.

(b) The resolution of necessity and the complaint shall indicate that the taking is pursuant to the Federal Aid Highway Act of 1973 and shall state the estimated date of use.

(c) If the defendant objects to the taking, the defendant has the burden of proof that there is no reasonable probability that the date of use will be within 10 years from the date the complaint is filed. If the defendant proves that there is no reasonable probability that the date of use will be within 10 years from the date the complaint is filed, the plaintiff has the burden of proof that the taking satisfies the requirements of this article.

Ca. Civ. Proc. Code § 1240.250
Added by Stats. 1975, Ch. 1275.

Article 4 - SUBSTITUTE CONDEMNATION

Section 1240.310 - Definitions

As used in this article:

(a) "Necessary property" means property to be used for a public use for which the public entity is authorized to acquire property by eminent domain.

(b) "Substitute property" means property to be exchanged for necessary property.

Ca. Civ. Proc. Code § 1240.310
Added by Stats. 1975, Ch. 1275.

Section 1240.320 - Generally

(a) Any public entity authorized to exercise the power of eminent domain to acquire property for a particular use may exercise the power of eminent domain to acquire for that use substitute property if all of the following are established:

(1) The owner of the necessary property has agreed in writing to the exchange.

(2) The necessary property is devoted to or held for some public use and the substitute property will be devoted to or held for the same public use by the owner of the necessary property.

(3) The owner of the necessary property is authorized to exercise the power of eminent domain to acquire the substitute property for such use.

(b) Where property is sought to be acquired pursuant to this section, the resolution of necessity and the complaint filed pursuant to such resolution shall specifically refer to this section and shall include a statement that the property is necessary for the purpose specified in this section. The determination in the resolution that the taking of the substitute property is necessary has the effect prescribed in Section 1245.250.

Ca. Civ. Proc. Code § 1240.320
Added by Stats. 1975, Ch. 1275.

Section 1240.330 - Acquisition of substitute property relocation of public use to substitute property and conveyance of substitute property to owner of necessary property

(a) Where necessary property is devoted to public use, any public entity authorized to exercise the power of eminent domain to acquire such property for a particular use may exercise the power of eminent domain to acquire substitute property in its own name, relocate on such substitute property the public use to which necessary property is devoted, and thereafter convey the substitute property to the owner of the necessary property if all of the following are established:

(1) The public entity is required by court order or judgment in an eminent domain proceeding, or by agreement with the owner of the necessary property, to relocate the public use to which the necessary property is devoted and thereafter to convey the property upon which the public use has been relocated to the owner of the necessary property.

(2) The substitute property is necessary for compliance with the court order or judgment or agreement.

(3) The owner of the necessary property will devote the substitute property to the public use being displaced from the necessary property.

(b) Where property is sought to be acquired pursuant to this section, the resolution of necessity and the complaint filed pursuant to such resolution shall specifically refer to this section and shall include a statement that the property is necessary for the purpose specified in this section. The determination in the resolution that the taking of the substitute property is necessary has the effect prescribed in Section 1245.250.

Ca. Civ. Proc. Code § 1240.330
Added by Stats. 1975, Ch. 1275.

Section 1240.350 - Acquisition of additional property as appears necessary

(a) Whenever a public entity acquires property for a public use and exercises or could have exercised the power of eminent domain to acquire such property for such use, the public entity may exercise the power of eminent domain to acquire such additional property as appears reasonably necessary and appropriate (after taking into account any hardship to the owner of the additional property) to provide utility service to, or access to a public road from, any property that is not acquired for such public use but which is cut off from utility service or access to a public road as a result of the acquisition by the public entity.

(b) Where property is sought to be acquired pursuant to this section, the resolution of necessity and the complaint filed pursuant to such resolution shall specifically refer to this section and shall include a statement that the property is necessary for the purpose specified in this section. The determination in the resolution that the taking of the substitute property is necessary has the effect prescribed in Section 1245.250.

Ca. Civ. Proc. Code § 1240.350
Added by Stats. 1975, Ch. 1275.

Article 5 - EXCESS CONDEMNATION

Section 1240.410 - Acquisition of remnant

(a) As used in this section, "remnant" means a remainder or portion thereof that will be left in such size, shape, or condition as to be of little market value.

(b) Whenever the acquisition by a public entity by eminent domain of part of a larger parcel of property will leave a remnant, the public entity may exercise the power of eminent domain to acquire the remnant in accordance with this article.

(c) Property may not be acquired under this section if the defendant proves that the public entity has a reasonable, practicable, and economically sound means to prevent the property from becoming a remnant.

Ca. Civ. Proc. Code § 1240.410
Added by Stats. 1975, Ch. 1275.

Section 1240.420 - Resolution and complaint
When property is sought to be acquired pursuant to Section 1240.410, the resolution of necessity and the complaint filed pursuant to such resolution shall specifically refer to that section. It shall be presumed from the adoption of the resolution that the taking of the property is authorized under Section 1240.410. This presumption is a presumption affecting the burden of producing evidence.

Ca. Civ. Proc. Code § 1240.420
Added by Stats. 1975, Ch. 1275.

Section 1240.430 - Sale, lease or exchange of property taken
A public entity may sell, lease, exchange, or otherwise dispose of property taken under this article and may credit the proceeds to the fund or funds available for acquisition of the property being acquired for the public work or improvement. Nothing in this section relieves a public entity from complying with any applicable statutory procedures governing the disposition of property.

Ca. Civ. Proc. Code § 1240.430
Added by Stats. 1975, Ch. 1275.

Article 6 - CONDEMNATION FOR COMPATIBLE USE

Section 1240.510 - Acquisition of property appropriated to public use
Any person authorized to acquire property for a particular use by eminent domain may exercise the power of eminent domain to acquire for that use property appropriated to public use if the proposed use will not unreasonably interfere with or impair the

continuance of the public use as it then exists or may reasonably be expected to exist in the future. Where property is sought to be acquired pursuant to this section, the complaint, and the resolution of necessity if one is required, shall refer specifically to this section.

Ca. Civ. Proc. Code § 1240.510
Added by Stats. 1975, Ch. 1275.

Section 1240.520 - Burden proof

If the defendant objects to a taking under Section 1240.510, the defendant has the burden of proof that his property is appropriated to public use. If it is established that the property is appropriated to public use, the plaintiff has the burden of proof that its proposed use satisfies the requirements of Section 1240.510.

Ca. Civ. Proc. Code § 1240.520
Added by Stats. 1975, Ch. 1275.

Section 1240.530 - Agreement by parties determining terms and conditions; court fixing terms and conditions

(a) Where property is taken under Section 1240.510, the parties shall make an agreement determining the terms and conditions upon which the property is taken and the manner and extent of its use by each of the parties. Except as otherwise provided by statute, if the parties are unable to agree, the court shall fix the terms and conditions upon which the property is taken and the manner and extent of its use by each of the parties.

(b) If the court determines that the use in the manner proposed by the plaintiff would not satisfy the requirements of Section 1240.510, the court shall further determine whether the requirements of Section 1240.510 could be satisfied by fixing terms and conditions upon which the property may be taken. If the court determines that the requirements of Section 1240.510 could be so satisfied, the court shall permit the plaintiff to take the property upon such terms and conditions and shall prescribe the manner and extent of its use by each of the parties.

(c) Where property is taken under this article, the court may order any necessary removal or relocation of structures or improvements if such removal or relocation would not require any significant alteration of the use to which the property is appropriated. Unless otherwise provided by statute, all costs and damages that result from the relocation or removal shall be paid by the plaintiff.

Ca. Civ. Proc. Code § 1240.530
Added by Stats. 1975, Ch. 1275.

Article 7 - CONDEMNATION FOR MORE NECESSARY PUBLIC USE

Section 1240.610 - Generally

Any person authorized to acquire property for a particular use by eminent domain may exercise the power of eminent domain to acquire for that use property appropriated to public use if the use for which the property is sought to be taken is a more necessary public use than the use to which the property is appropriated. Where property is sought to be acquired pursuant to this section, the complaint, and the resolution of necessity if one is required, shall refer specifically to this section.

Ca. Civ. Proc. Code § 1240.610
Added by Stats. 1975, Ch. 1275.

Section 1240.620 - Burden of proof

If the defendant objects to a taking under Section 1240.610, the defendant has the burden of proof that his property is appropriated to public use. If it is established that the property is appropriated to public use, the plaintiff has the burden of proof that its use satisfies the requirements of Section 1240.610.

Ca. Civ. Proc. Code § 1240.620
Added by Stats. 1975, Ch. 1275.

Section 1240.630 - Defendant entitled to continue public use

(a) Where property is sought to be taken under Section 1240.610, the defendant is entitled to continue the public use to which the property is appropriated if the continuance of such use will not unreasonably interfere with or impair, or require a significant alteration of, the more necessary public use as it is then planned or exists or may reasonably be expected to exist in the future.

(b) If the defendant objects to a taking under this article on the ground that he is entitled under subdivision (a) to continue the public use to which the property is appropriated, upon motion of either party, the court shall determine whether the defendant is entitled under subdivision (a) to continue the use to which the property is appropriated; and, if the court determines that the defendant is so entitled, the parties shall make an agreement determining the terms and conditions upon which the defendant may continue the public use to which the property is appropriated, the terms and conditions upon which the property is taken by the plaintiff is acquired, and the manner and extent of the use of the property by each of the parties. Except as otherwise provided by statute, if the parties are unable to agree, the court shall fix such terms and conditions and the manner and extent of the use of the property by each of the parties.

Ca. Civ. Proc. Code § 1240.630
Added by Stats. 1975, Ch. 1275.

Section 1240.640 - Presumption that use by state more necessary use

(a) Where property has been appropriated to public use by any person other than the state, the use thereof by the state for the same use or any other public use is presumed to be a more necessary use than the use to which such property has already been appropriated.

(b) Where property has been appropriated to public use by the state, the use thereof by the state is presumed to be a more necessary use than any use to which such property might be put by any other person.

(c) The presumptions established by this section are presumptions affecting the burden of proof.

Ca. Civ. Proc. Code § 1240.640
Added by Stats. 1975, Ch. 1275.

Section 1240.650 - Use by public entity more necessary use

(a) Where property has been appropriated to public use by any person other than a public entity, the use thereof by a public entity for the same use or any other public use is a more necessary use than the use to which such property has already been appropriated.

(b) Where property has been appropriated to public use by a public entity, the use thereof by the public entity is a more necessary use than any use to which such property might be put by any person other than a public entity.

(c) Where property which has been appropriated to a public use is electric, gas, or water public utility property which the public entity intends to put to the same use, the presumption of a more necessary use established by subdivision (a) is a rebuttable presumption affecting the burden of proof, unless the acquiring public entity is a sanitary district exercising the powers of a county water district pursuant to Section 6512.7 of the Health and Safety Code.

Ca. Civ. Proc. Code § 1240.650

Amended by Stats. 1992, Ch. 812, Sec. 2. Effective January 1, 1993.

Section 1240.655 - Action by Golden State Energy to acquire PG&E

(a) If Golden State Energy commences an eminent domain action to acquire Pacific Gas and Electric Company property, including any franchise rights and stock, pursuant to Section 713 of the Public Utilities Code, that acquisition is for a more necessary public use pursuant to Section 1240.610. Golden State Energy may exclude from the acquisition only property not directly related to providing electrical or gas service.

(b) For purposes of this section, the following definitions apply:

(1) "Golden State Energy" has the same meaning as defined in Section 222.5 of the Public Utilities Code.

(2) "Pacific Gas and Electric Company" means Pacific Gas and Electric Company, PG&E Corporation, any subsidiary or affiliate of the foregoing holding any assets related to the provision of electrical or gas service within Pacific Gas and Electric Company's service territory, and any successor to any of the foregoing.

    Ca. Civ. Proc. Code § 1240.655

Added by Stats 2020 ch 27 (SB 350),s 3, eff. 1/1/2021.

Section 1240.660 - Presumption use by local public entity more necessary use

Where property has been appropriated to public use by a local public entity, the use thereof by the local public entity is presumed to be a more necessary use than any use to which such property might be put by any other local public entity. The presumption established by this section is a presumption affecting the burden of proof.

    Ca. Civ. Proc. Code § 1240.660

Added by Stats. 1975, Ch. 1275.

Section 1240.670 - Presumption property appropriated for best and most necessary public use

(a) Subject to Section 1240.690, notwithstanding any other provision of law, property is presumed to have been appropriated for the best and most necessary public use if all of the following are established:

    (1) The property is owned by a nonprofit organization contributions to which are deductible for state and federal income tax purposes under the laws of this state and of the United States and having the primary purpose of preserving areas in their natural condition.

    (2) The property is open to the public subject to reasonable restrictions and is appropriated, and used exclusively, for the preservation of native plants or native animals including, but not limited to, mammals, birds, and marine life, or biotic communities, or geological or geographical formations of scientific or educational interest.

(3) The property is irrevocably dedicated to such uses so that, upon liquidation, dissolution, or abandonment of or by the owner, such property will be distributed only to a fund, foundation, or corporation whose property is likewise irrevocably dedicated to such uses, or to a governmental agency holding land for such uses.
(b) The presumption established by this section is a presumption affecting the burden of proof.
Ca. Civ. Proc. Code § 1240.670
Added by Stats. 1975, Ch. 1275.

Section 1240.680 - Presumption property appropriated for best and most necessary public use
(a) Subject to Sections 1240.690 and 1240.700, notwithstanding any other provision of law, property is presumed to have been appropriated for the best and most necessary public use if the property is appropriated to public use as any of the following:

(1) A state, regional, county, or city park, open space, or recreation area.

(2) A wildlife or waterfowl management area established by the Department of Fish and Game pursuant to Section 1525 of the Fish and Game Code.

(3) A historic site included in the National Register of Historic Places or state-registered landmarks.

(4) An ecological reserve as provided for in Article 4 (commencing with Section 1580) of Chapter 5 of Division 2 of the Fish and Game Code.
(b) The presumption established by this section is a presumption affecting the burden of proof.
Ca. Civ. Proc. Code § 1240.680
Added by Stats. 1975, Ch. 1275, Sec. 3.

Section 1240.690 - Action for declaratory relief by public entity or nonprofit organization where property sought to be acquired for highway purposes

(a) When property described in Section 1240.670 or 1240.680 is sought to be acquired for state highway purposes, and the property was dedicated or devoted to a use described in those sections prior to the initiation of highway route location studies, an action for declaratory relief may be brought by the public entity or nonprofit organization owning the property in the superior court to determine the question of which public use is the best and most necessary public use for the property.

(b) The action for declaratory relief shall be filed and served within 120 days after the California Transportation Commission has published in a newspaper of general circulation pursuant to Section 6061 of the Government Code, and delivered to the public entity or nonprofit organization owning the property a written notice that a proposed route or an adopted route includes the property. In the case of nonprofit organizations, the written notice need only be given to nonprofit organizations that are on file with the Registrar of Charitable Trusts of this state.

(c) In the declaratory relief action, the resolution of the California Transportation Commission is not conclusive evidence of the matters set forth in Section 1240.030.

(d) With respect to property described in Section 1240.670 or 1240.680 which is sought to be acquired for state highway purposes:

(1) If an action for declaratory relief is not filed and served within the 120-day period established by subdivision (b), the right to bring the action is waived and Sections 1240.670 and 1240.680 do not apply.

(2) When a declaratory relief action may not be brought pursuant to this section, Sections 1240.670 and 1240.680 do not apply.

Ca. Civ. Proc. Code § 1240.690
Amended by Stats. 1982, Ch. 681, Sec. 2.

Section 1240.700 - Action for declaratory relief where property sought to be acquired for city or county road street or highway purposes

(a) When property described in Section 1240.680 is sought to be acquired for city or county road, street, or highway purposes, and such property was dedicated or devoted to regional park, recreational, or open-space purposes prior to the initiation of road, street, or highway route location studies, an action for declaratory relief may be brought in the superior court by the regional park district which operates the park, recreational, or open-space area to determine the question of which public use is the best and most necessary public use for such property.

(b) The action for declaratory relief shall be filed and served within 120 days after the city or county, as the case may be, has published in a newspaper of general circulation pursuant to Section 6061 of the Government Code, and delivered to the regional park district, a written notice that a proposed route or site or an adopted route includes such property.

(c) With respect to property dedicated or devoted to regionl park, recreational, or open-space purposes which is sought to be acquired for city or county road, street, or highway purposes:

(1) If an action for declaratory relief is not filed and served within the 120-day period established by subdivision (b), the right to bring such action is waived and the provisions of Section 1240.680 do not apply.

(2) When a declaratory relief action may not be brought pursuant to this section, the provisions of Section 1240.680 do not apply.

Ca. Civ. Proc. Code § 1240.700
Added by Stats. 1975, Ch. 1275.

Chapter 4 - PRECONDEMNATION ACTIVITIES

Article 1 - PRELIMINARY LOCATION, SURVEY, AND TESTS

Section 1245.010 - Right to enter property to make photographs, studies, surveys, etc.

Subject to requirements of this article, any person authorized to acquire property for a particular use by eminent domain may enter upon property to make photographs, studies, surveys, examinations, tests, soundings, borings, samplings, or appraisals or to engage in similar activities reasonably related to acquisition or use of the property for that use.

Ca. Civ. Proc. Code § 1245.010
Added by Stats. 1975, Ch. 1275.

Section 1245.020 - Duty to secure consent before entry

In any case in which the entry and activities mentioned in Section 1245.010 will subject the person having the power of eminent domain to liability under Section 1245.060, before making that entry and undertaking those activities, the person shall secure at least one of the following:

(a) The written consent of the owner to enter upon the owner's property and to undertake those activities.

(b) An order for entry from the superior court in accordance with Section 1245. 030.

Ca. Civ. Proc. Code § 1245.020
Amended by Stats 2021 ch 401 (AB 1578),s 3, eff. 1/1/2022.
Added by Stats. 1975, Ch. 1275.

Section 1245.030 - Petition seeking entry

(a) The person seeking to enter upon the property may petition the court for an order permitting the entry and shall give such prior notice to the owner of the property as the court determines is appropriate under the circumstances of the particular case.

(b) Upon such petition and after such notice has been given, the court shall determine the purpose for the entry, the nature and scope of the activities reasonably necessary to accomplish such purpose, and the probable amount of compensation to be paid to the owner of the property for the actual damage to the property and interference with its possession and use.

(c) After such determination, the court may issue its order permitting the entry. The order shall prescribe the purpose for the entry and the nature and scope of the activities to be undertaken and shall require the person seeking to enter to deposit with the court the probable amount of compensation.

Ca. Civ. Proc. Code § 1245.030
Added by Stats. 1975, Ch. 1275.

Section 1245.040 - Modification of order; amount of deposit increased by order of modification

(a) The court, after notice and hearing, may modify any of the provisions of an order made under Section 1245.030.

(b) If the amount required to be deposited is increased by an order of modification, the court shall specify the time within which the additional amount shall be deposited and may direct that any further entry or that specified activities under the order as modified be stayed until the additional amount has been deposited.

Ca. Civ. Proc. Code § 1245.040
Added by Stats. 1975, Ch. 1275.

Section 1245.050 - Period of retention of amount deposited; deposit made in Condemnation Deposits Fund

(a) Unless sooner disbursed by court order, the amount deposited under this article shall be retained on deposit for six months following the termination of the entry. The period of retention may be extended by the court for good cause.

(b) The deposit shall be made in the Condemnation Deposits Fund in the State Treasury or, upon written request of the plaintiff filed with the deposit, in the county treasury. If made in the State Treasury, the deposit shall be held, invested, deposited, and disbursed in accordance with Article 10 (commencing with Section

16429) of Chapter 2 of Part 2 of Division 4 of Title 2 of the Government Code.

Ca. Civ. Proc. Code § 1245.050
Added by Stats. 1975, Ch. 1275.

Section 1245.060 - Action for damage or interference with possession caused by entry and activities

(a) If the entry and activities upon property cause actual damage to or substantial interference with the possession or use of the property, whether or not a claim has been presented in compliance with Part 3 (commencing with Section 900) of Division 3.6 of Title 1 of the Government Code, the owner may recover for that damage or interference in a civil action, as a defendant in an eminent domain action affecting the property, or by application to the court under subdivision (c).

(b) The prevailing claimant in an action or proceeding under this section shall be awarded the claimant's costs and, if the court finds that any of the following occurred, the claimant's litigation expenses incurred in proceedings under this article:

(1) The entry was unlawful.

(2) The entry was lawful but the activities upon the property were abusive or lacking in due regard for the interests of the owner.

(3) There was a failure substantially to comply with the terms of an order made under Section 1245.030 or 1245.040.

(c) If funds are on deposit under this article, upon application of the owner, the court shall determine and award the amount the owner is entitled to recover under this section and shall order that amount paid out of the funds on deposit. If the funds on deposit are insufficient to pay the full amount of the award, the court shall enter judgment for the unpaid portion. In a proceeding under this subdivision, the owner has a right to a jury trial, unless waived, on the amount of compensation for actual damage or substantial interference with the possession or use of the property.

(d) Nothing in this section affects the availability of any other remedy the owner may have for the damaging of the owner's property.

Ca. Civ. Proc. Code § 1245.060

Amended by Stats 2021 ch 401 (AB 1578),s 4, eff. 1/1/2022. Added by Stats. 1975, Ch. 1275.

Article 2 - RESOLUTION OF NECESSITY

Section 1245.210 - "Governing body" defined

As used in this article, "governing body" means:

(a) In the case of a taking by a local public entity, the legislative body of the local public entity.

(b) In the case of a taking by the Sacramento and San Joaquin Drainage District, the Central Valley Flood Protection Board.

(c) In the case of a taking by the State Public Works Board pursuant to the Property Acquisition Law (Part 11 (commencing with Section 15850) of Division 3 of Title 2 of the Government Code), the State Public Works Board.

(d) In the case of a taking by the Department of Fish and Wildlife pursuant to Section 1348 of the Fish and Game Code, the Wildlife Conservation Board.

(e) In the case of a taking by the Department of Transportation (other than a taking pursuant to Section 21633 of the Public Utilities Code or Section 30100 of the Streets and Highways Code), the California Transportation Commission.

(f) In the case of a taking by the Department of Transportation pursuant to Section 21633 of the Public Utilities Code, the California Transportation Commission.

(g) In the case of a taking by the Department of Transportation pursuant to Section 30100 of the Streets and Highways Code, the California Transportation Commission.

(h) In the case of a taking by the Department of Water Resources, the California Water Commission.

(i) In the case of a taking by the University of California, the Regents of the University of California.

(j) In the case of a taking by the State Lands Commission, the State Lands Commission.

(k) In the case of a taking by the college named in Section 92200 of the Education Code, the board of directors of that college.
(l) In the case of a taking by the High-Speed Rail Authority, the State Public Works Board.

    Ca. Civ. Proc. Code § 1245.210
Amended by Stats 2022 ch 478 (AB 1936),s 3, eff. 1/1/2023.
Amended by Stats 2018 ch 790 (SB 1172),s 1, eff. 1/1/2019.

Section 1245.220 - Adoption of resolution required

A public entity may not commence an eminent domain proceeding until its governing body has adopted a resolution of necessity that meets the requirements of this article.

    Ca. Civ. Proc. Code § 1245.220
Added by Stats. 1975, Ch. 1275.

Section 1245.230 - Requirements of resolution

In addition to other requirements imposed by law, the resolution of necessity shall contain all of the following:
(a) A general statement of the public use for which the property is to be taken and a reference to the statute that authorizes the public entity to acquire the property by eminent domain.
(b) A description of the general location and extent of the property to be taken, with sufficient detail for reasonable identification.
(c) A declaration that the governing body of the public entity has found and determined each of the following:

    (1) The public interest and necessity require the proposed project.

    (2) The proposed project is planned or located in the manner that will be most compatible with the greatest public good and the least private injury.

    (3) The property described in the resolution is necessary for the proposed project.

(4) That either the offer required by Section 7267.2 of the Government Code has been made to the owner or owners of record, or the offer has not been made because the owner cannot be located with reasonable diligence. If at the time the governing body of a public entity is requested to adopt a resolution of necessity and the project for which the property is needed has been determined by the public entity to be an emergency project, which project is necessary either to protect or preserve health, safety, welfare, or property, the requirements of Section 7267.2 of the Government Code need not be a prerequisite to the adoption of an authorizing resolution at the time. However, in those cases the provisions of Section 7267.2 of the Government Code shall be implemented by the public entity within a reasonable time thereafter but in any event, not later than 90 days after adoption of the resolution of necessity.

Ca. Civ. Proc. Code § 1245.230
Amended by Stats. 1983, Ch. 1079, Sec. 1.

Section 1245.235 - Notice and hearing prior to adoption of resolution

(a) The governing body of the public entity may adopt a resolution of necessity only after the governing body has given each person whose property is to be acquired by eminent domain and whose name and address appears on the last equalized county assessment roll notice and a reasonable opportunity to appear and be heard on the matters referred to in Section 1240.030.

(b) The notice required by subdivision (a) shall be sent by first-class mail to each person described in subdivision (a) and shall state all of the following:

(1) The intent of the governing body to adopt the resolution.

(2) The right of such person to appear and be heard on the matters referred to in Section 1240.030.

(3) Failure to file a written request to appear and be heard within 15 days after the notice was mailed will result in waiver of the right to appear and be heard.

(c) The governing body, or a committee of not less than 11 members thereof designated by the governing body if the governing body has more than 40 members, shall hold a hearing at which all persons described in subdivision (a) who filed a written request within the time specified in the notice may appear and be heard on the matters referred to in Section 1240.030. Such a committee shall be reasonably representative of the various geographical areas within the public entity's jurisdiction. The governing body need not give an opportunity to appear and be heard to any person who fails to so file a written request within the time specified in the notice. If a committee is designated by the governing body pursuant to this subdivision to hold the hearing, the committee, subsequent to the hearing, shall provide the governing body and any person described in subdivision (a) who has appeared before the committee with a written summary of the hearing and a written recommendation as to whether to adopt the resolution of necessity. Any person described in subdivision (a) who has appeared before the committee shall also be given an opportunity to appear and be heard before the governing body on the matters referred to in Section 1240.030.

(d) Notwithstanding subdivision (b), the governing body may satisfy the requirements of this section through any other procedure that has given each person described in subdivision (a) reasonable written personal notice and a reasonable opportunity to appear and be heard on the matters referred to in Section 1240.030.

Ca. Civ. Proc. Code § 1245.235
Amended by Stats. 1986, Ch. 358, Sec. 1.

Section 1245.240 - Vote required to adopt resolution

Unless a greater vote is required by statute, charter, or ordinance, the resolution shall be adopted by a vote of two-thirds of all the members of the governing body of the public entity.

Ca. Civ. Proc. Code § 1245.240
Added by Stats. 1975, Ch. 1275.

Section 1245.245 - Property used for public use stated in resolution; sale of property not used for stated use; acquisition subject to requirements

(a) Property acquired by a public entity by any means set forth in subdivision (e) that is subject to a resolution of necessity adopted pursuant to this article shall only be used for the public use stated in the resolution unless the governing body of the public entity adopts a resolution authorizing a different use of the property by a vote of at least two-thirds of all members of the governing body of the public entity, or a greater vote as required by statute, charter, or ordinance. The resolution shall contain all of the following:

(1) A general statement of the new public use that is proposed for the property and a reference to the statute that would have authorized the public entity to acquire the property by eminent domain for that use.

(2) A description of the general location and extent of the property proposed to be used for the new use, with sufficient detail for reasonable identification.

(3) A declaration that the governing body has found and determined each of the following:

(A) The public interest and necessity require the proposed use.

(B) The proposed use is planned and located in the manner that will be most compatible with the greatest public good and least private injury.

(C) The property described in the resolution is necessary for the proposed use.

(b) Property acquired by a public entity by any means set forth in subdivision (e) that is subject to a resolution of necessity pursuant to this article, and is not used for the public use stated in the resolution of necessity within 10 years of the adoption of the resolution of necessity, shall be sold in accordance with the terms of subdivisions (f) and (g), unless the governing body adopts a resolution according to the terms of subdivision (a) or a resolution according to the terms of this subdivision reauthorizing the existing stated public use of the property by a vote of at least two-thirds of all members of the governing body of the public entity or a greater vote as required by statute, charter, or ordinance. A reauthorization resolution under this subdivision shall contain all of the following:

(1) A general statement of the public use that is proposed to be reauthorized for the property and a reference to the statute that authorized the public entity to acquire the property by eminent domain for that use.

(2) A description of the general location and extent of the property proposed to be used for the public use, but not yet in use for the public use, with sufficient detail for reasonable identification.

(3) A declaration that the governing body has found and determined each of the following:

(A) The public interest and necessity require the proposed use.

(B) The proposed use is planned and located in the manner that will be most compatible with the greatest public good and least private injury.

(C) The property described in the resolution is necessary for the proposed use.
(c) In addition to any notice required by law, the notice required for a new or reauthorization resolution sought pursuant to subdivision (a) or (b) shall comply with Section 1245.235 and shall be sent to each person who was given notice required by Section 1245.235 in connection with the original acquisition of the property by the public entity.
(d) Judicial review of an action pursuant to subdivision (a) or (b) may be obtained by a person who had an interest in the property

described in the resolution at the time that the property was acquired by the public entity, and shall be governed by Section 1085.

(e) The following property acquisitions are subject to the requirements of this section:

(1) Any acquisition by a public entity pursuant to eminent domain.

(2) Any acquisition by a public entity following adoption of a resolution of necessity pursuant to this article for the property.

(3) Any acquisition by a public entity prior to the adoption of a resolution of necessity pursuant to this article for the property, but subsequent to a written notice that the public entity may take the property by eminent domain.

(f) If the public entity fails to adopt either a new resolution pursuant to subdivision (a) or a reauthorization resolution pursuant to subdivision (b), as required by this section, and that property was not used for the public use stated in a resolution of necessity adopted pursuant to this article or a resolution adopted pursuant to subdivision (a) or (b) between the time of its acquisition and the time of the public entity's failure to adopt a resolution pursuant to subdivision (a) or (b), the public entity shall offer the person or persons from whom the property was acquired the right of first refusal to purchase the property pursuant to this section, as follows:

(1) At the present market value, as determined by independent licensed appraisers.

(2) For property that was a single-family residence at the time of acquisition, at an affordable price, which price shall not be greater than the price paid by the agency for the original acquisition, adjusted for inflation, and shall not be greater than fair market value, if the following requirements are met:

(A) The person or persons from whom the property was acquired certify their income to the public entity as persons or families of low or moderate income.

(B) If the single-family residence is offered at a price that is less than fair market value, the public entity may verify the certifications of income in accordance with procedures used for verification of incomes of purchasers and occupants of housing financed by the California Housing Finance Agency.

(C) If the single-family residence is offered at a price that is less than fair market value, the public entity shall impose terms, conditions, and restrictions to ensure that the residence will either:

(i) Remain owner-occupied by the person or persons from whom the property was acquired for at least five years.

(ii) Remain available to persons or families of low or moderate income and households with incomes no greater than the incomes of the present occupants in proportion to the area median income for the longest feasible time, but for not less than 55 years for rental units and 45 years for home ownership units.

(D) The Department of Housing and Community Development shall provide to the public entity recommendations of standards and criteria for those prices, terms, conditions, and restrictions.

(g) If after a diligent effort the public entity is unable to locate the person from whom the property was acquired, if the person from whom the property was acquired does not choose to purchase the property as provided in subdivision (f), or if the public entity fails to adopt a resolution as required pursuant to subdivision (a) or (b) but is not required to offer a right of first refusal pursuant to subdivision (f), the public entity shall sell the property as surplus property pursuant to Article 8 (commencing with Section 54220) of Chapter 5 of Part 1 of Division 2 of Title 5 of the Government Code.

(h) If residential property acquired by a public entity by any means set forth in subdivision (e) is sold as surplus property pursuant to subdivision (g), and that property was not used for the public use stated in a resolution of necessity adopted pursuant to this article or a resolution adopted pursuant to subdivision (a) or (b) between the time of its acquisition and the time of its sale as surplus property, the public entity shall pay to the person or persons from whom the public entity acquired the property the sum of any financial gain between the original acquisition price, adjusted for inflation, and the final sale price.

(i) Upon completion of any acquisition described in subdivision (e) or upon the adoption of a resolution of necessity pursuant to this section, whichever is later, the public entity shall give written notice to the person or persons from whom the property was acquired as described in subdivision (e) stating that the notice, right of first refusal, and return of financial gain rights discussed in this section may accrue.

(j) At least 60 days before selling the property pursuant to subdivision (g), the public entity shall make a diligent effort to locate the person from whom the property was acquired. At any time before the proposed sale, the person from whom the property was acquired may exercise the rights provided by this section. As used in this section, "diligent effort" means that the public entity has done all of the following:

(1) Mailed the notice of the proposed sale by certified mail, return receipt requested, to the last known address of the person from whom the property was acquired.

(2) Mailed the notice of the proposed sale by certified mail, return receipt requested, to each person with the same name as the person from whom the property was acquired at any other address on the last equalized assessment roll.

(3) Published the notice of the proposed sale pursuant to Section 6061 of the Government Code in at least one newspaper of general circulation within the city or county in which the property is located.

(4) Posted the notice of the proposed sale in at least three public places within the city or county in which the property is located.

(5) Posted the notice of the proposed sale on the property proposed to be sold.

(k) For purposes of this section, "adjusted for inflation" means the original acquisition price increased to reflect the proportional increase in the Consumer Price Index for all items for the State of California, as determined by the United States Bureau of Labor Statistics, for the period from the date of acquisition to the date the property is offered for sale.

Ca. Civ. Proc. Code § 1245.245
Amended by Stats 2007 ch 130 (AB 299),s 36, eff. 1/1/2008.
Added by Stats 2006 ch 602 (SB 1650),s 1, eff. 1/1/2007.

Section 1245.250 - Resolution conclusively establishes matters referred to in section 1240.030

(a) Except as otherwise provided by statute, a resolution of necessity adopted by the governing body of the public entity pursuant to this article conclusively establishes the matters referred to in Section 1240.030.

(b) If the taking is by a local public entity, other than a sanitary district exercising the powers of a county water district pursuant to Section 6512.7 of the Health and Safety Code, and the property is electric, gas, or water public utility property, the resolution of necessity creates a rebuttable presumption that the matters referred to in Section 1240.030 are true. This presumption is a presumption affecting the burden of proof.

(c) If the taking is by a local public entity and the property described in the resolution is not located entirely within the boundaries of the local public entity, the resolution of necessity creates a presumption that the matters referred to in Section 1240.030 are true. This presumption is a presumption affecting the burden of producing evidence.

(d) For the purposes of subdivision (b), a taking by the State Reclamation Board for the Sacramento and San Joaquin Drainage District is not a taking by a local public entity.

Ca. Civ. Proc. Code § 1245.250
Amended by Stats. 1992, Ch. 812, Sec. 3. Effective January 1, 1993.

Section 1245.255 - Judicial review of validity of resolution
(a) A person having an interest in the property described in a resolution of necessity adopted by the governing body of the public entity pursuant to this article may obtain judicial review of the validity of the resolution:

    (1) Before the commencement of the eminent domain proceeding, by petition for a writ of mandate pursuant to Section 1085. The court having jurisdiction of the writ of mandate action, upon motion of any party, shall order the writ of mandate action dismissed without prejudice upon commencement of the eminent domain proceeding unless the court determines that dismissal will not be in the interest of justice.

    (2) After the commencement of the eminent domain proceeding, by objection to the right to take pursuant to this title.
(b) A resolution of necessity does not have the effect prescribed in Section 1245.250 to the extent that its adoption or contents were influenced or affected by gross abuse of discretion by the governing body.
(c) Nothing in this section precludes a public entity from rescinding a resolution of necessity and adopting a new resolution as to the same property subject, after the commencement of an eminent domain proceeding, to the same consequences as a conditional dismissal of the proceeding under Section 1260.120.
    Ca. Civ. Proc. Code § 1245.255
Amended by Stats. 1978, Ch. 286.

Section 1245.260 - Inverse condemnation
(a) If a public entity has adopted a resolution of necessity but has not commenced an eminent domain proceeding to acquire the property within six months after the date of adoption of the resolution, or has commenced such proceeding but has not within six months after the commencement of such proceeding attempted diligently to serve the complaint and the summons relating to such proceeding, the property owner may, by an action in inverse condemnation, do either or both of the following:

(1) Require the public entity to take the property and pay compensation therefor.

(2) Recover damages from the public entity for any interference with the possession and use of the property resulting from adoption of the resolution. Service by mail pursuant to Section 415.30 shall constitute a diligent attempt at service within the meaning of this section.

(b) No claim need be presented against a public entity under Part 3 (commencing with Section 900) of Division 3.6 of Title 1 of the Government Code as a prerequisite to commencement or maintenance of an action under subdivision (a), but any such action shall be commenced within one year and six months after the date the public entity adopted the resolution of necessity.

(c) A public entity may commence an eminent domain proceeding or rescind a resolution of necessity as a matter of right at any time before the property owner commences an action under this section. If the public entity commences an eminent domain proceeding or rescinds the resolution of necessity before the property owner commences an action under this section, the property owner may not thereafter bring an action under this section.

(d) After a property owner has commenced an action under this section, the public entity may rescind the resolution of necessity and abandon the taking of the property only under the same circumstances and subject to the same conditions and consequences as abandonment of an eminent domain proceeding.

(e) Commencement of an action under this section does not affect any authority a public entity may have to commence an eminent domain proceeding, take possession of the property pursuant to Article 3 (commencing with Section 1255.410) of Chapter 6, or abandon the eminent domain proceeding.

(f) In lieu of bringing an action under subdivision (a) or if the limitations period provided in subdivision (b) has run, the property owner may obtain a writ of mandate to compel the public entity, within such time as the court deems appropriate, to rescind the resolution of necessity or to commence an eminent domain proceeding to acquire the property.

Ca. Civ. Proc. Code § 1245.260
Amended by Stats. 1978, Ch. 411.

Section 1245.270 - Member voting in favor of resolution receive or agreed to receive bribe

(a) A resolution of necessity does not meet the requirements of this article if the defendant establishes by a preponderance of the evidence both of the following:

(1) A member of the governing body who voted in favor of the resolution received or agreed to receive a bribe (as that term is defined in subdivision 6 of Section 7 of the Penal Code) involving adoption of the resolution.

(2) But for the conduct described in paragraph (1), the resolution would not otherwise have been adopted.
(b) Where there has been a prior criminal prosecution of the member for the conduct described in paragraph (1) of subdivision (a), proof of conviction shall be conclusive evidence that the requirement of paragraph (1) of subdivision (a) is satisfied, and proof of acquittal or other dismissal of the prosecution shall be conclusive evidence that the requirement of paragraph (1) of subdivision (a) is not satisfied. Where there is a pending criminal prosecution of the member for the conduct described in paragraph (1) of subdivision (a), the court may take such action as is just under the circumstances of the case.
(c) Nothing in this section precludes a public entity from rescinding a resolution of necessity and adopting a new resolution as to the same property, subject to the same consequences as a conditional dismissal of the proceeding under Section 1260.120.
Ca. Civ. Proc. Code § 1245.270
Added by Stats. 1975, Ch. 1275.

Article 3 - RESOLUTION CONSENTING TO EMINENT DOMAIN PROCEEDING BY QUASI-PUBLIC ENTITY

Section 1245.310 - Legislative body defined

As used in this article, "legislative body" means both of the following:

(a) The legislative body of each city within whose boundaries property sought to be taken by the quasi-public entity by eminent domain is located.

(b) If property sought to be taken by the quasi-public entity is not located within city boundaries, the legislative body of each county within whose boundaries such property is located.

Ca. Civ. Proc. Code § 1245.310

Added by Stats. 1975, Ch. 1275.

Section 1245.320 - Quasi-public entity

As used in this article, "quasi-public entity" means:

(a) An educational institution of collegiate grade not conducted for profit that seeks to take property by eminent domain under Section 94500 of the Education Code.

(b) A nonprofit hospital that seeks to take property by eminent domain under Section 1260 of the Health and Safety Code.

(c) A cemetery authority that seeks to take property by eminent domain under Section 8501 of the Health and Safety Code.

(d) A limited-dividend housing corporation that seeks to take property by eminent domain under Section 34874 of the Health and Safety Code.

(e) A land-chest corporation that seeks to take property by eminent domain under former Section 35167 of the Health and Safety Code.

(f) A mutual water company that seeks to take property by eminent domain under Section 2729 of the Public Utilities Code.

Ca. Civ. Proc. Code § 1245.320

Amended by Stats 2006 ch 538 (SB 1852),s 67, eff. 1/1/2007.

Section 1245.325 - Owner of property seeking to acquire appurtenant easement; requirements of resolution

Where an owner of real property seeks to acquire an appurtenant easement by eminent domain pursuant to Section 1001 of the Civil Code:

(a) The person seeking to exercise the power of eminent domain shall be deemed to be a "quasi-public entity" for the purposes of this article.

(b) In lieu of the requirements of subdivision (c) of Section 1245.340, the resolution required by this article shall contain a declaration that the legislative body has found and determined each of the following:

(1) There is a great necessity for the taking.

(2) The location of the easement affords the most reasonable service to the property to which it is appurtenant, consistent with the least damage to the burdened property.

(3) The hardship to the owner of the appurtenant property, if the taking is not permitted, clearly outweighs any hardship to the owner of the burdened property.

Ca. Civ. Proc. Code § 1245.325
Added by Stats. 1976, Ch. 994.

Section 1245.326 - Owner of property seeks to acquire temporary right of entry; requirements of resolution

Where an owner of real property seeks to acquire by eminent domain a temporary right of entry pursuant to Section 1002 of the Civil Code:

(a) The person seeking to exercise the power of eminent domain shall be deemed to be a "quasi-public entity" for the purposes of this article.

(b) In lieu of the requirements of subdivision (c) of Section 1245.340, the resolution required by this article shall contain a declaration that the legislative body has found and determined that each of the conditions required by Section 1002 of the Civil Code

appears to exist.
Ca. Civ. Proc. Code § 1245.326
Added by Stats. 1982, Ch. 1239, Sec. 2.

Section 1245.330 - Adoption of resolution required
Notwithstanding any other provision of law, a quasi-public entity may not commence an eminent domain proceeding to acquire any property until the legislative body has adopted a resolution consenting to the acquisition of such property by eminent domain.
Ca. Civ. Proc. Code § 1245.330
Added by Stats. 1975, Ch. 1275.

Section 1245.340 - Information required in resolution
The resolution required by this article shall contain all of the following:
(a) A general statement of the public use for which the property is to be taken and a reference to the statute that authorizes the quasi-public entity to acquire the property by eminent domain.
(b) A description of the general location and extent of the property to be taken, with sufficient detail for reasonable identification.
(c) A declaration that the legislative body has found and determined each of the following:

(1) The public interest and necessity require the proposed project.

(2) The proposed project is planned or located in the manner that will be most compatible with the greatest good and least private injury.

(3) The property described in the resolution is necessary for the proposed project.

(4) The hardship to the quasi-public entity if the acquisition of the property by eminent domain is not permitted outweighs any hardship to the owners of such property.

Ca. Civ. Proc. Code § 1245.340
Added by Stats. 1975, Ch. 1275.

Section 1245.350 - Hearing; notice

(a) The legislative body may refuse to consent to the acquisition with or without a hearing, but it may adopt the resolution required by this article only after the legislative body has held a hearing at which persons whose property is to be acquired by eminent domain have had a reasonable opportunity to appear and be heard.
(b) Notice of the hearing shall be sent by first-class mail to each person whose property is to be acquired by eminent domain if the name and address of the person appears on the last equalized county assessment roll (including the roll of state-assessed property). The notice shall state the time, place, and subject of the hearing and shall be mailed at least 15 days prior to the date of the hearing.

Ca. Civ. Proc. Code § 1245.350
Added by Stats. 1975, Ch. 1275.

Section 1245.360 - Vote required to adopt resolution

The resolution required by this article shall be adopted by a vote of two-thirds of all the members of the legislative body.

Ca. Civ. Proc. Code § 1245.360
Added by Stats. 1975, Ch. 1275.

Section 1245.370 - Payment of costs incurred by legislative body; deposit securing costs

The legislative body may require that the quasi-public entity pay all of the costs reasonably incurred by the legislative body under this article. The legislative body may require that such costs be secured by payment or deposit or other satisfactory security in advance of any action by the legislative body under this article.

Ca. Civ. Proc. Code § 1245.370
Added by Stats. 1975, Ch. 1275.

Section 1245.380 - Requirements in addition to other requirements

The requirement of this article is in addition to any other requirements imposed by law. Nothing in this article relieves the quasi-public entity from satisfying the requirements of Section 1240.030 or any other requirements imposed by law.

Ca. Civ. Proc. Code § 1245.380
Added by Stats. 1975, Ch. 1275.

Section 1245.390 - City or county not liable for damages caused by acquisition or by project

The adoption of a resolution pursuant to this article does not make the city or county liable for any damages caused by the acquisition of the property or by the project for which it is acquired.

Ca. Civ. Proc. Code § 1245.390
Added by Stats. 1975, Ch. 1275.

Chapter 5 - COMMENCEMENT OF PROCEEDING

Article 1 - JURISDICTION AND VENUE

Section 1250.010 - Superior court jurisdiction

Except as otherwise provided in Section 1230.060 and in Chapter 12 (commencing with Section 1273.010), all eminent domain proceedings shall be commenced and prosecuted in the superior court.

Ca. Civ. Proc. Code § 1250.010
Added by Stats. 1975, Ch. 1275.

Section 1250.020 - Venue

(a) Except as provided in subdivision (b), the proceeding shall be commenced in the county in which the property sought to be taken is located.

(b) When property sought to be taken is situated in more than one county, the plaintiff may commence the proceeding in any one of such counties.

Ca. Civ. Proc. Code § 1250.020
Added by Stats. 1975, Ch. 1275.

Section 1250.030 - Proper county

(a) Except as provided in subdivision (b), the county in which the proceeding is commenced pursuant to Section 1250.020 is the proper county for trial of the proceeding.

(b) Where the court changes the place of trial pursuant to Section 1250.040, the county to which the proceeding is transferred is the proper county for trial of the proceeding.

Ca. Civ. Proc. Code § 1250.030
Added by Stats. 1975, Ch. 1275.

Section 1250.040 - Change of place of trial

The provisions of the Code of Civil Procedure for the change of place of trial of actions apply to eminent domain proceedings.

Ca. Civ. Proc. Code § 1250.040
Added by Stats. 1975, Ch. 1275.

Article 2 - COMMENCEMENT OF PROCEEDING GENERALLY

Section 1250.110 - Commenced by filing complaint

An eminent domain proceeding is commenced by filing a complaint with the court.

Ca. Civ. Proc. Code § 1250.110
Added by Stats. 1975, Ch. 1275.

Section 1250.120 - Form and contents of summons; process served by publication

(a) Except as provided in subdivision (b), the form and contents of the summons shall be as in civil actions generally.

(b) Where process is served by publication, in addition to the summons, the publication shall describe the property sought to be taken in a manner reasonably calculated to give persons with an interest in the property actual notice of the pending proceeding.

Ca. Civ. Proc. Code § 1250.120
Added by Stats. 1975, Ch. 1275.

Section 1250.125 - Defendants named and property described in summons served by publication; failure to appear and answer

(a) Where summons is served by publication, the publication may name only the defendants to be served thereby and describe only the property in which the defendants to be served thereby have or claim interests.

(b) Judgment based on failure to appear and answer following service under this section shall be conclusive against the defendants named in respect only to property described in the publication.

(c) Notwithstanding subdivision (b), a defendant who did not receive the offer required by Section 7267.2 of the Government Code because the owner could not be located with reasonable diligence, who was served by publication, and who failed to appear, may contest the amount of compensation within one year of the judgment and for good cause shown, whereupon that issue shall be litigated according to the provisions of this title.

Ca. Civ. Proc. Code § 1250.125
Amended by Stats. 1983, Ch. 1079, Sec. 2.

Section 1250.130 - Plaintiff required to post copy of summons and record notice of pendency of proceeding

Where the court orders service by publication, it shall also order the plaintiff (1) to post a copy of the summons and complaint on the property sought to be taken and (2), if not already recorded, to record a notice of the pendency of the proceeding in the manner provided by Section 1250.150. Such posting and recording shall be done not later than 10 days after the date the order is made.

Ca. Civ. Proc. Code § 1250.130
Added by Stats. 1975, Ch. 1275.

Section 1250.140 - Service where state defendant

Where the state is a defendant, the summons and the complaint shall be served on the Attorney General.

Ca. Civ. Proc. Code § 1250.140

Added by Stats. 1975, Ch. 1275.

Section 1250.150 - Recording and serving notice of pendency of proceeding

The plaintiff, at the time of the commencement of the proceeding, shall record a notice of the pendency of the proceeding in the office of the county recorder of any county in which property described in the complaint is located. A copy of the notice shall be served with the summons and complaint.

Ca. Civ. Proc. Code § 1250.150

Amended by Stats. 1983, Ch. 78, Sec. 2.

Article 3 - PARTIES; JOINDER OF PROPERTY

Section 1250.210 - Persons named as plaintiffs

Each person seeking to take property by eminent domain shall be named as a plaintiff.

Ca. Civ. Proc. Code § 1250.210

Added by Stats. 1975, Ch. 1275.

Section 1250.220 - Persons named as defendants by plaintiff

(a) The plaintiff shall name as defendants, by their real names, those persons who appear of record or are known by the plaintiff to have or claim an interest in the property described in the complaint.

(b) If a person described in subdivision (a) is dead and the plaintiff knows of a duly qualified and acting personal representative of the estate of such person, the plaintiff shall name such personal representative as a defendant. If a person described in subdivision (a) is dead or is believed by the plaintiff to be dead and if plaintiff knows of no duly qualified and acting personal representative of the estate of such person and states these facts in an affidavit filed with the complaint, plaintiff may name as defendants "the heirs and devisees of _____ (naming such deceased person), deceased, and all persons claiming by, through, or under said decedent," naming them in that manner and, where it is stated in the affidavit that such person is believed by the plaintiff to be dead, such person also may be named as a defendant.

(c) In addition to those persons described in subdivision (a), the plaintiff may name as defendants "all persons unknown claiming an interest in the property," naming them in that manner.

(d) A judgment rendered in a proceeding under this title is binding and conclusive upon all persons named as defendants as provided in this section and properly served.

Ca. Civ. Proc. Code § 1250.220
Added by Stats. 1975, Ch. 1275.

Section 1250.230 - Appearance by persons claiming legal or equitable interest

Any person who claims a legal or equitable interest in the property described in the complaint may appear in the proceeding. Whether or not such person is named as a defendant in the complaint, he shall appear as a defendant.

Ca. Civ. Proc. Code § 1250.230
Added by Stats. 1975, Ch. 1275.

Section 1250.240 - Joinder of property in one complaint

The plaintiff may join in one complaint all property located within the same county which is sought to be acquired for the same project.

Ca. Civ. Proc. Code § 1250.240
Added by Stats. 1975, Ch. 1275.

Section 1250.250 - Naming holder of lien as defendant

(a) If the only interest of the county or other taxing agency in the property described in the complaint is a lien for ad valorem taxes, the county or other taxing agency need not be named as a defendant.

(b) The holder of a lien that secures a special assessment or a bond representing the special assessment shall be named as a defendant, regardless of the nature of the special assessment and the manner of collection of the special assessment. The holder of the lien may, instead of an answer, certify to the court within 30 days after service of the summons and complaint on the holder all of the following information:

(1) A complete description of the lien.

(2) A description of the property encumbered by the lien.

(3) The amount remaining due on the lien as of the date of the certificate.

(4) The date upon which each installment payable on the lien is due and the amount of each installment.

(c) A copy of the certification shall be sent by first-class mail to all parties to the proceeding at the time it is provided to the court. The filing of the certification or answer shall be considered as a general appearance.

Ca. Civ. Proc. Code § 1250.250
Amended by Stats. 1981, Ch. 139, Sec. 1.

Article 4 - PLEADINGS

Section 1250.310 - Requirements of complaint
The complaint shall contain all of the following:
(a) The names of all plaintiffs and defendants.
(b) A description of the property sought to be taken. The description may, but is not required to, indicate the nature or extent of the interest of the defendant in the property.
(c) If the plaintiff claims an interest in the property sought to be taken, the nature and extent of such interest.
(d) A statement of the right of the plaintiff to take by eminent domain the property described in the complaint. The statement shall include:

(1) A general statement of the public use for which the property is to be taken.

(2) An allegation of the necessity for the taking as required by Section 1240.030; where the plaintiff is a public entity, a reference to its resolution of necessity; where the plaintiff is a quasi-public entity within the meaning of Section 1245.320, a reference to the resolution adopted pursuant to Article 3 (commencing with Section 1245.310) of Chapter 4; where the plaintiff is a nonprofit hospital, a reference to the certificate required by Section 1260 of the Health and Safety Code; where the plaintiff is a public utility and relies on a certification of the State Energy Resources Conservation and Development Commission or a requirement of that commission that development rights be acquired, a reference to such certification or requirement.

(3) A reference to the statute that authorizes the plaintiff to acquire the property by eminent domain. Specification of the statutory authority may be in the alternative and may be inconsistent.

(e) A map or diagram portraying as far as practicable the property described in the complaint and showing its location in relation to the project for which it is to be taken.

Ca. Civ. Proc. Code § 1250.310
Amended by Stats. 1975, Ch. 1275.

Section 1250.320 - Answer
(a) The answer shall include a statement of the nature and extent of the interest the defendant claims in the property described in the complaint.
(b) If the defendant seeks compensation provided in Article 6 (commencing with Section 1263.510) (goodwill) of Chapter 9, the answer shall include a statement that the defendant claims compensation under Section 1263.510, but the answer need not specify the amount of that compensation.
(c) If the defendant seeks compensation as provided in Article 1 (commencing with Section 1245.010) of Chapter 4, the answer shall

include a statement that the defendant claims compensation under Section 1245.060, but need not specify the amount of that compensation.

(d) If the defendant seeks compensation for losses caused by the plaintiff's unreasonable conduct prior to commencing the eminent domain proceeding, the answer shall include a statement that the defendant claims compensation for that loss, but need not specify the amount of the compensation.

Ca. Civ. Proc. Code § 1250.320

Amended by Stats 2021 ch 401 (AB 1578),s 5, eff. 1/1/2022.

Added by Stats. 1975, Ch. 1275.

Section 1250.325 - Disclaimer

(a) A defendant may file a disclaimer at any time, whether or not he is in default, and the disclaimer supersedes an answer previously filed by the defendant. The disclaimer need not be in any particular form. It shall contain a statement that the defendant claims no interest in the property or in the compensation that may be awarded. Notwithstanding Section 1250.330, the disclaimer shall be signed by the defendant.

(b) Subject to subdivision (c), a defendant who has filed a disclaimer has no right to participate in further proceedings or to share in the compensation awarded.

(c) The court may implement the disclaimer by appropriate orders including, where justified, awarding costs and litigation expenses.

Ca. Civ. Proc. Code § 1250.325

Added by Stats. 1975, Ch. 1275.

Section 1250.330 - Pleadings signed by attorney representing party

Where a party is represented by an attorney, his pleading need not be verified but shall be signed by the attorney for the party. The signature of the attorney constitutes a certificate by him that he has read the pleading and that to the best of his knowledge, information, and belief there is ground to support it. If the pleading is not signed or is signed with intent to defeat the purposes of this

section, it may be stricken.
Ca. Civ. Proc. Code § 1250.330
Added by Stats. 1975, Ch. 1275.

Section 1250.340 - Amendment or supplement to pleading

(a) Subject to subdivisions (b) and (c), the court may allow upon such terms and conditions as may be just an amendment or supplement to any pleading. In the case of an amendment or supplement to the complaint, such terms and conditions may include a change in the applicable date of valuation for the proceeding and an award of costs and litigation expenses which would not have been incurred had the proceeding as originally commenced been the same as the proceeding following such amendment or supplement.

(b) A public entity may add to the property sought to be taken only if it has adopted a resolution of necessity that satisfies the requirements of Article 2 (commencing with Section 1245.210) of Chapter 4 for the property to be added.

(c) Property previously sought to be taken may be deleted from the complaint only if the plaintiff has followed the procedure for partial abandonment of the proceeding as to that property.

Ca. Civ. Proc. Code § 1250.340
Added by Stats. 1975, Ch. 1275.

Section 1250.345 - Waiver of objection to complaint

Subject to the power of the court to permit an amendment of the answer, if the defendant fails to object to the complaint, either by demurrer or answer, he is deemed to have waived the objection.

Ca. Civ. Proc. Code § 1250.345
Added by Stats. 1975, Ch. 1275.

Article 5 - OBJECTIONS TO RIGHT TO TAKE

Section 1250.350 - Demurrer or answer

A defendant may object to the plaintiff's right to take, by demurrer or answer as provided in Section 430.30, on any ground authorized by Section 1250.360 or Section 1250.370. The demurrer or answer shall state the specific ground upon which the objection is taken and, if the objection is taken by answer, the specific facts upon which the objection is based. An objection may be taken on more than one ground, and the grounds may be inconsistent.

Ca. Civ. Proc. Code § 1250.350
Added by Stats. 1975, Ch. 1275.

Section 1250.360 - Grounds regardless of whether plaintiff adopted resolution

Grounds for objection to the right to take, regardless of whether the plaintiff has adopted a resolution of necessity that satisfies the requirements of Article 2 (commencing with Section 1245.210) of Chapter 4, include:

(a) The plaintiff is not authorized by statute to exercise the power of eminent domain for the purpose stated in the complaint.

(b) The stated purpose is not a public use.

(c) The plaintiff does not intend to devote the property described in the complaint to the stated purpose.

(d) There is no reasonable probability that the plaintiff will devote the described property to the stated purpose within (1) seven years, or (2) 10 years where the property is taken pursuant to the Federal Aid Highway Act of 1973, or (3) such longer period as is reasonable.

(e) The described property is not subject to acquisition by the power of eminent domain for the stated purpose.

(f) The described property is sought to be acquired pursuant to Section 1240.410 (excess condemnation), 1240.510 (condemnation for compatible use), or 1240.610 (condemnation for more necessary public use), but the acquisition does not satisfy the requirements of those provisions.

(g) The described property is sought to be acquired pursuant to Section 1240.610 (condemnation for more necessary public use), but the defendant has the right under Section 1240.630 to continue the public use to which the property is appropriated as a joint use.

(h) Any other ground provided by law.

Ca. Civ. Proc. Code § 1250.360
Added by Stats. 1975, Ch. 1275.

Section 1250.370 - Grounds where plaintiff has not adopted resolution

In addition to the grounds listed in Section 1250.360, grounds for objection to the right to take where the plaintiff has not adopted a resolution of necessity that conclusively establishes the matters referred to in Section 1240.030 include:

(a) The plaintiff is a public entity and has not adopted a resolution of necessity that satisfies the requirements of Article 2 (commencing with Section 1245.210) of Chapter 4.

(b) The public interest and necessity do not require the proposed project.

(c) The proposed project is not planned or located in the manner that will be most compatible with the greatest public good and the least private injury.

(d) The property described in the complaint is not necessary for the proposed project.

(e) The plaintiff is a quasi-public entity within the meaning of Section 1245.320 and has not satisfied the requirements of Article 3 (commencing with Section 1245.310) of Chapter 4.

Ca. Civ. Proc. Code § 1250.370
Added by Stats. 1975, Ch. 1275.

Article 6 - SETTLEMENT OFFERS AND ALTERNATIVE DISPUTE RESOLUTION

Section 1250.410 - Offer of compensation served on defendant; demand for compensation served on plaintiff; litigation expenses

(a) At least 20 days prior to the date of the trial on issues relating to compensation, the plaintiff shall file with the court and serve on the defendant its final offer of compensation in the proceeding and the defendant shall file and serve on the plaintiff its final demand for compensation in the proceeding. The offer and the demand shall include all compensation required pursuant to this title, including compensation for loss of goodwill, if any, and shall state whether interest and costs are included. These offers and demands shall be the only offers and demands considered by the court in determining the entitlement, if any, to litigation expenses. Service shall be in the manner prescribed by Chapter 5 (commencing with Section 1010) of Title 14 of Part 2.

(b) If the court, on motion of the defendant made within 30 days after entry of judgment, finds that the offer of the plaintiff was unreasonable and that the demand of the defendant was reasonable viewed in the light of the evidence admitted and the compensation awarded in the proceeding, the costs allowed pursuant to Section 1268.710 shall include the defendant's litigation expenses.

(c) In determining the amount of litigation expenses allowed under this section, the court shall consider the offer required to be made by the plaintiff pursuant to Section 7267.2 of the Government Code, any deposit made by the plaintiff pursuant to Chapter 6 (commencing with Section 1255.010), and any other written offers and demands filed and served before or during the trial.

(d) If timely made, the offers and demands as provided in subdivision (a) shall be considered by the court on the issue of determining an entitlement to litigation expenses.

(e) As used in this section, "litigation expenses" means the party's reasonable attorney's fees and costs, including reasonable expert witness and appraiser fees.

    Ca. Civ. Proc. Code § 1250.410

Amended by Stats 2006 ch 594 (SB 1210),s 1, eff. 1/1/2007.
Amended by Stats 2002 ch 295 (AB 1770),s 1, eff. 1/1/2003.
Article heading amended by Stats 2001 ch 428 (AB 237), ss 1, 2eff. 1/1/2002.
Previously Amended July 13, 1999 (Bill Number: SB 634) (Chapter 102).

Section 1250.420 - Resolution of dispute by mediation or binding arbitration

The parties may by agreement refer a dispute that is the subject of an eminent domain proceeding for resolution by any of the following means:

(a) Mediation by a neutral mediator.

(b) Binding arbitration by a neutral arbitrator. The arbitration is subject to Chapter 12 (commencing with Section 1273.010).

(c) Nonbinding arbitration by a neutral arbitrator. The arbitrator's decision in a nonbinding arbitration is final unless within 30 days after service of the arbitrator's decision a party moves the court for a trial of the eminent domain proceeding. If the judgment in the eminent domain proceeding is not more favorable to the moving party, the court shall order that party to pay to the other parties the following nonrefundable costs and fees, unless the court finds in writing and on motion that the imposition of costs and fees would create such a substantial economic hardship as not to be in the interest of justice:

(1) All costs specified in Section 1033.5, limited to those incurred from the time of election of the trial de novo. Nothing in this subdivision affects the right of a defendant to recover costs otherwise allowable pursuant to Section 1268.710, incurred before election of a trial de novo, except that a defendant may recover the costs of determining the apportionment of the award made pursuant to subdivision (b) of Section 1260.220 whenever incurred.

(2) The reasonable costs of the services of expert witnesses who are not regular employees of any party, actually incurred and reasonably necessary in the preparation or trial of the case, limited to those incurred from the time of election of the trial de novo.

(3) The compensation paid by the parties to the arbitrator.
Ca. Civ. Proc. Code § 1250.420
Added by Stats 2001 ch 428 (AB 237), s 3, eff. 1/1/2002.

Section 1250.430 - Motion to postpone date of trial
Notwithstanding any other statute or rule of court governing the date of trial of an eminent domain proceeding, on motion of a party the court may postpone the date of trial for a period that appears adequate to enable resolution of a dispute pursuant to alternative resolution procedures, if it is demonstrated to the satisfaction of the court that all of the following conditions are satisfied:
(a) The parties are actively engaged in alternative resolution of the dispute pursuant to Section 1250.420.

(b) The parties appear to be making progress toward resolution of the dispute without the need for a trial of the matter.

(c) The parties agree that additional time for the purpose of alternative dispute resolution is desirable.

Ca. Civ. Proc. Code § 1250.430

Added by Stats 2001 ch 428 (AB 237), s 4, eff. 1/1/2002.

Chapter 6 - DEPOSIT AND WITHDRAWAL OF PROBABLE COMPENSATION; POSSESSION PRIOR TO JUDGMENT

Article 1 - DEPOSIT OF PROBABLE COMPENSATION

Section 1255.010 - Appraisal upon which deposit made; deposit without appraisal

(a) At any time before entry of judgment, the plaintiff may deposit with the State Treasury the probable amount of compensation, based on an appraisal, that will be awarded in the proceeding. The appraisal upon which the deposit is based shall be one that satisfies the requirements of subdivision (b). The deposit may be made whether or not the plaintiff applies for an order for possession or intends to do so.

(b) Before making a deposit under this section, the plaintiff shall have an expert qualified to express an opinion as to the value of the property (1) make an appraisal of the property and (2) prepare a written statement of, or summary of the basis for, the appraisal. The statement or summary shall contain detail sufficient to indicate clearly the basis for the appraisal, including, but not limited to, all of the following information:

(A) The date of valuation, highest and best use, and applicable zoning of the property.

(B) The principal transactions, reproduction or replacement cost analysis, or capitalization analysis, supporting the appraisal.

(C) If the appraisal includes compensation for damages to the remainder, the compensation for the property and for damages to the remainder separately stated, and the calculations and a narrative explanation supporting the compensation, including any offsetting benefits.

(c) On noticed motion, or upon ex parte application in an emergency, the court may permit the plaintiff to make a deposit without prior compliance with subdivision (b) if the plaintiff presents facts by affidavit showing that (1) good cause exists for permitting an immediate deposit to be made, (2) an adequate appraisal has not been completed and cannot reasonably be prepared before making the deposit, and (3) the amount of the deposit to be made is not less than the probable amount of compensation that the plaintiff, in good faith, estimates will be awarded in the proceeding. In its order, the court shall require that the plaintiff comply with subdivision (b) within a reasonable time, to be specified in the order, and also that any additional amount of compensation shown by the appraisal required by subdivision (b) be deposited within that time.

Ca. Civ. Proc. Code § 1255.010
Amended by Stats 2001 ch 428 (AB 237), s 5, eff. 1/1/2002.

Section 1255.020 - Notice of deposit; statement of summary of basis of appraisal

(a) On making a deposit pursuant to Section 1255.010, the plaintiff shall serve a notice of deposit on all parties who have appeared in the proceeding and file with the court a proof of service together with the notice of deposit. The plaintiff shall so serve parties who appear thereafter on their appearance. The notice of deposit shall state that a deposit has been made and the date and the amount of the deposit. Service of the notice of deposit shall be made in the manner provided in Section 1255.450 for service of an order for possession.

(b) The notice of deposit shall be accompanied by a written statement or summary of the basis for the appraisal referred to in Section 1255.010.

(c) If the plaintiff has obtained an order under Section 1255.010 deferring completion of the written statement or summary, the plaintiff:

(1) On making the deposit, shall comply with subdivision (a) and include with the notice a copy of all affidavits on which the order was based.

(2) Upon completion of the written statement or summary, shall comply with subdivision (b).
Ca. Civ. Proc. Code § 1255.020
Amended by Stats. 1990, Ch. 1491, Sec. 10.

Section 1255.030 - Whether deposit probable amount of compensation determination

(a) At any time after a deposit has been made pursuant to this article, the court shall, upon motion of the plaintiff or of any party having an interest in the property for which the deposit was made, determine or redetermine whether the amount deposited is the probable amount of compensation that will be awarded in the proceeding. The motion shall be supported with detail sufficient to indicate clearly the basis for the motion, including, but not limited to, the following information to the extent relevant to the motion:

(1) The date of valuation, highest and best use, and applicable zoning of the property.

(2) The principal transactions, reproduction or replacement cost analysis, or capitalization analysis, supporting the motion.

(3) The compensation for the property and for damages to the remainder separately stated, and the calculations and a narrative explanation supporting the compensation, including any offsetting benefits.

(b) If the plaintiff has not taken possession of the property and the court determines that the probable amount of compensation exceeds the amount deposited, the court may order the plaintiff to increase the deposit or may deny the plaintiff possession of the property until the amount deposited has been increased to the amount specified in the order.

(c) If the plaintiff has taken possession of the property and the court determines that the probable amount of compensation exceeds the amount deposited, the court shall order the amount deposited to be increased to the amount determined to be the probable amount of compensation. If the amount on deposit is not increased accordingly within 30 days from the date of the court's order, or any longer time as the court may have allowed at the time of making the order, the defendant may serve on the plaintiff a notice of election to treat that failure as an abandonment of the proceeding. If the plaintiff does not cure its failure within 10 days after receipt of such notice, the court shall, upon motion of the defendant, enter judgment dismissing the proceeding and awarding the defendant his or her litigation expenses and damages as provided in Sections 1268.610 and 1268.620.

(d) After any amount deposited pursuant to this article has been withdrawn by a defendant, the court may not determine or redetermine the probable amount of compensation to be less than the total amount already withdrawn. Nothing in this subdivision precludes the court from making a determination or redetermination that probable compensation is greater than the amount withdrawn.

(e) If the court determines that the amount deposited exceeds the probable amount of compensation, it may permit the plaintiff to withdraw the excess not already withdrawn by the defendant.

(f) The plaintiff may at any time increase the amount deposited without making a motion under this section. In that case, notice of the increase shall be served as provided in subdivision (a) of Section 1255.020.

Ca. Civ. Proc. Code § 1255.030
Amended by Stats 2001 ch 428 (AB 237), s 6, eff. 1/1/2002.

Section 1255.040 - Deposit where property includes dwelling occupied by defendant as residence

(a) If the plaintiff has not made a deposit that satisfies the requirements of this article and the property includes a dwelling containing not more than two residential units and the dwelling or one of its units is occupied as his or her residence by a defendant, the defendant may serve notice on the plaintiff requiring a deposit of the probable amount of compensation that will be awarded in the proceeding. The notice shall specify the date by which the defendant desires the deposit to be made. The date shall not be earlier than 30 days after the date of service of the notice and may be any later date.

(b) If the plaintiff deposits the probable amount of compensation, determined or redetermined as provided in this article, on or before the date specified by the defendant, the plaintiff may obtain an order for possession that authorizes the plaintiff to take possession of the property 30 days after the date for the deposit specified by the defendant or any later date as the plaintiff may request.

(c) Notwithstanding Section 1268.310, if the deposit is not made on or before the date specified by the defendant or such later date as the court specifies on motion and good cause shown by the plaintiff, the compensation awarded to the defendant in the proceeding shall draw legal interest from that date. The defendant is entitled to the full amount of such interest without offset for rents or other income received by him or her or the value of his or her continued possession of the property.

(d) If the proceeding is abandoned by the plaintiff, the interest under subdivision (c) may be recovered as costs in the proceeding in the manner provided for the recovery of litigation expenses under Section 1268.610. If, in the proceeding, the court or a jury verdict eventually determines the compensation that would have been awarded to the defendant, then the interest shall be computed on the amount of the award. If no determination is ever made, then the interest shall be computed on the probable amount of compensation as determined by the court.

(e) The serving of a notice pursuant to this section constitutes a waiver by operation of law, conditioned upon subsequent deposit by the plaintiff of the probable amount of compensation, of all claims and defenses in favor of the defendant except his or her claim for greater compensation.

(f) Notice of a deposit made under this section shall be served as provided by subdivision (a) of Section 1255.020. The defendant may withdraw the deposit as provided in Article 2 (commencing with Section 1255.210).

(g) No notice may be served by a defendant under subdivision (a) after entry of judgment unless the judgment is reversed, vacated, or set aside and no other judgment has been entered at the time the notice is served.

Ca. Civ. Proc. Code § 1255.040
Amended by Stats 2006 ch 594 (SB 1210),s 2, eff. 1/1/2007.

Section 1255.050 - Deposit where property to be taken subject to leasehold interest

If the property to be taken is subject to a leasehold interest and the plaintiff has not made a deposit that satisfies the requirements of this article, the lessor may serve notice on the plaintiff requiring a deposit of the probable amount of compensation that will be awarded in the proceeding in the same manner and subject to the same procedures and conditions as a motion pursuant to Section 1255.040 except that, if the plaintiff fails to make the deposit, the interest awarded shall be offset by the lessor's net rental profits on the property.

Ca. Civ. Proc. Code § 1255.050
Added by Stats. 1975, Ch. 1275.

Section 1255.060 - Trial of issue of compensation

(a) The amount deposited or withdrawn pursuant to this chapter may not be given in evidence or referred to in the trial of the issue of compensation.

(b) In the trial of the issue of compensation, an appraisal report, written statement and summary of an appraisal, or other statement made in connection with a deposit or withdrawal pursuant to this chapter may not be considered to be an admission of any party.

(c) Upon objection of the party at whose request an appraisal report, written statement and summary of the appraisal, or other statement was made in connection with a deposit or withdrawal pursuant to this chapter, the person who made the report or statement and summary or other statement may not be called at the trial on the issue of compensation by any other party to give an opinion as to compensation. If the person who prepared the report, statement and summary, or other statement is called at trial to give an opinion as to compensation, the report, statement and summary, or other statement may be used for impeachment of the witness.

Ca. Civ. Proc. Code § 1255.060

Amended by Stats 2002 ch 295 (AB 1770),s 2, eff. 1/1/2003.

Section 1255.070 - Deposit in county treasury in lieu of state treasury; investment of money deposited in state treasury

In lieu of depositing the money with the State Treasury as provided in Section 1255.010, upon written request of the plaintiff, the court shall order the money be deposited in the county treasury. If money is deposited in the State Treasury pursuant to Section 1255.010, it shall be held, invested, deposited, and disbursed in the manner specified in Article 10 (commencing with Section 16429) of Chapter 2 of Part 2 of Division 4 of Title 2 of the Government Code, and interest earned or other increment derived from its investment shall be apportioned and disbursed in the manner specified in that article. As between the parties to the proceeding, money deposited pursuant to this article shall remain at the risk of the plaintiff until paid or made payable to the defendant by order of the court.

Ca. Civ. Proc. Code § 1255.070

Amended by Stats. 1990, Ch. 1491, Sec. 11.

Section 1255.075 - Motion to invest deposit for benefit of defendants

(a) Prior to entry of judgment, a defendant who has an interest in the property for which a deposit has been made under this chapter may, upon notice to the other parties to the proceeding, move the court to have all of such deposit invested for the benefit of the defendants.

(b) At the hearing on the motion, the court shall consider the interests of the parties and the effect that investment would have upon them. The court may, in its discretion, if it finds that the interests of justice will be served, grant the motion subject to such terms and conditions as are appropriate under the circumstances of the case.

(c) An investment under this section shall be specified by the court and shall be limited to United States government obligations or interest-bearing accounts in an institution whose accounts are insured by an agency of the federal government.

(d) The investment of the deposit has the same consequences as if the deposit has been withdrawn under this chapter.

Ca. Civ. Proc. Code § 1255.075
Added by Stats. 1975, Ch. 1275.

Section 1255.080 - Rights not waived by plaintiff

By depositing the probable compensation pursuant to this article, the plaintiff does not waive the right to appeal from the judgment, the right to move to abandon, or the right to request a new trial.

Ca. Civ. Proc. Code § 1255.080
Added by Stats. 1975, Ch. 1275.

Article 2 - WITHDRAWAL OF DEPOSIT

Section 1255.210 - Application to court by defendant

Prior to entry of judgment, any defendant may apply to the court for the withdrawal of all or any portion of the amount deposited. The application shall be verified, set forth the applicant's interest in the property, and request withdrawal of a stated amount. The applicant shall serve a copy of the application on the plaintiff.

Ca. Civ. Proc. Code § 1255.210
Added by Stats. 1975, Ch. 1275.

Section 1255.220 - Court order for payment to applicant

Subject to the requirements of this article, the court shall order the amount requested in the application, or such portion of that amount as the applicant is entitled to receive, to be paid to the applicant.

Ca. Civ. Proc. Code § 1255.220
Added by Stats. 1975, Ch. 1275.

Section 1255.230 - Objections to withdrawal

(a) No withdrawal may be ordered until 20 days after service on the plaintiff of a copy of the application or until the time for all objections has expired, whichever is later.

(b) Within the 20-day period, the plaintiff may file objections to withdrawal on any one or more of the following grounds:

   (1) Other parties to the proceeding are known or believed to have interests in the property.

   (2) An undertaking should be filed by the applicant as provided in Section 1255.240 or 1255.250.

   (3) The amount of an undertaking filed by the applicant under this chapter or the sureties thereon are insufficient.

(c) If an objection is filed on the ground that other parties are known or believed to have interests in the property, the plaintiff shall serve or attempt to serve on such other parties a notice that they may appear within 10 days after such service and object to the withdrawal. The notice shall advise such parties that their failure to object will result in waiver of any rights against the plaintiff to the extent of the amount withdrawn. The notice shall be served in the manner provided in Section 1255.450 for service of an order for possession. The plaintiff shall file, and serve on the applicant, a report setting forth (1) the names of the parties upon whom the notice was served and the dates of service and (2) the names and last known addresses of the other parties who are known or believed to have interests in the property but who were not so served. The applicant may serve parties whom the plaintiff has been unable to serve. Parties served in the manner provided in Section 1255.450 shall have no claim against the plaintiff for compensation to the extent of the amount withdrawn by all applicants. The plaintiff shall remain liable to parties having an interest of record who are not so served but, if such liability is enforced, the plaintiff shall be subrogated to the rights of such parties under Section 1255.280.

(d) If any party objects to the withdrawal, or if the plaintiff so requests, the court shall determine, upon hearing, the amounts to be withdrawn, if any, and by whom.

Ca. Civ. Proc. Code § 1255.230
Added by Stats. 1975, Ch. 1275.

Section 1255.240 - Undertaking required of defendant prior to withdrawal

(a) If the court determines that an applicant is entitled to withdraw any portion of a deposit that another party claims or to which another person may be entitled, the court may require the applicant, before withdrawing such portion, to file an undertaking. The undertaking shall secure payment to such party or person of any amount withdrawn that exceeds the amount to which the applicant is entitled as finally determined in the proceeding, together with interest as provided in Section 1255.280. If withdrawal is permitted notwithstanding the lack of personal service of the application for withdrawal upon any party to the proceeding, the court may also require that the undertaking indemnify the plaintiff against any liability it may incur under Section 1255.230. The undertaking shall be in such amount as is fixed by the court, but if executed by an admitted surety insurer the amount shall not exceed the portion claimed by the adverse claimant or appearing to belong to another person. If executed by two or more sufficient sureties, the amount shall not exceed double such portion.

(b) If the undertaking is required primarily because of an issue as to title between the applicant and another party or person, the applicant filing the undertaking is not entitled to recover the premium reasonably paid for the undertaking as a part of the recoverable costs in the eminent domain proceeding.

Ca. Civ. Proc. Code § 1255.240
Amended by Stats. 1982, Ch. 517, Sec. 182.

Section 1255.250 - Undertaking if amount withdrawn exceeds amount of original deposit

(a) If the amount originally deposited is increased pursuant to Section 1255.030 and the total amount sought to be withdrawn exceeds the amount of the original deposit, the applicant, or each applicant if there are two or more, shall file an undertaking. The undertaking shall be in favor of the plaintiff and shall secure repayment of any amount withdrawn that exceeds the amount to which the applicant is entitled as finally determined in the eminent domain proceeding, together with interest as provided in Section 1255.280. If the undertaking is executed by an admitted surety insurer, the undertaking shall be in the amount by which the total amount to be withdrawn exceeds the amount originally deposited. If the undertaking is executed by two or more sufficient sureties, the undertaking shall be in double such amount, but the maximum amount that may be recovered from such sureties is the amount by which the total amount to be withdrawn exceeds the amount originally deposited.

(b) If there are two or more applicants, the applicants, in lieu of filing separate undertakings, may jointly file a single undertaking in the amount required by subdivision (a).

Ca. Civ. Proc. Code § 1255.250
Amended by Stats. 1982, Ch. 517, Sec. 183.

Section 1255.260 - Waiver of claims and defenses

If any portion of the money deposited pursuant to this chapter is withdrawn, the receipt of any such money shall constitute a waiver by operation of law of all claims and defenses in favor of the persons receiving such payment except a claim for greater compensation.

Ca. Civ. Proc. Code § 1255.260
Added by Stats. 1975, Ch. 1275.

Section 1255.280 - Withdrawal in amount in excess of amount party entitled

(a) Any amount withdrawn by a party pursuant to this article in excess of the amount to which he is entitled as finally determined in the eminent domain proceeding shall be paid to the parties entitled thereto. The court shall enter judgment accordingly.

(b) The judgment so entered shall not include interest except in the following cases:

(1) Any amount that is to be paid to a defendant shall include legal interest from the date of its withdrawal by another defendant.

(2) If the amount originally deposited by a plaintiff was increased pursuant to Section 1255.030 on motion of a party obligated to pay under this section, any amount that is attributable to such increase and that is to be repaid to the plaintiff shall include legal interest from the date of its withdrawal.

(c) If the judgment so entered is not paid within 30 days after its entry, the court may, on motion, enter judgment against the sureties, if any, for the amount of such judgment.

(d) The court may, in its discretion and with such security, if any, as it deems appropriate, grant a party obligated to pay under this section a stay of execution for any amount to be paid to a plaintiff. Such stay of execution shall not exceed one year following entry of judgment under this section.

Ca. Civ. Proc. Code § 1255.280

Added by Stats. 1975, Ch. 1275.

Article 3 - POSSESSION PRIOR TO JUDGMENT

Section 1255.410 - Motion for possession

(a) At the time of filing the complaint or at any time after filing the complaint and prior to entry of judgment, the plaintiff may move the court for an order for possession under this article, demonstrating that the plaintiff is entitled to take the property by eminent domain and has deposited pursuant to Article 1 (commencing with Section 1255.010) an amount that satisfies the requirements of that article. The motion shall describe the property of which the plaintiff is seeking to take possession, which description may be by reference to the complaint, and shall state the date after which the plaintiff is seeking to take possession of the property. The motion shall include a statement substantially in the following form: "You have the right to oppose this motion for an order of possession of your property. If you oppose this motion you must serve the plaintiff and file with the court a written opposition to the motion within 30 days from the date you were served with this motion." If the written opposition asserts a hardship, it shall be supported by a declaration signed under penalty of perjury stating facts supporting the hardship.

(b) The plaintiff shall serve a copy of the motion on the record owner of the property and on the occupants, if any. The plaintiff shall set the court hearing on the motion not less than 60 days after service of the notice of motion on the record owner of unoccupied property. If the property is lawfully occupied by a person dwelling thereon or by a farm or business operation, service of the notice of motion shall be made not less than 90 days prior to the hearing on the motion.

(c) Not later than 30 days after service of the plaintiff's motion seeking to take possession of the property, any defendant or occupant of the property may oppose the motion in writing by serving the plaintiff and filing with the court the opposition. If the written opposition asserts a hardship, it shall be supported by a declaration signed under penalty of perjury stating facts supporting the hardship. The plaintiff shall serve and file any reply to the opposition not less than 15 days before the hearing.

(d)

(1) If the motion is not opposed within 30 days of service on each defendant and occupant of the property, the court shall make an order for possession of the property if the court finds each of the following:

(A) The plaintiff is entitled to take the property by eminent domain.

(B) The plaintiff has deposited pursuant to Article 1 (commencing with Section 1255.010) an amount that satisfies the requirements of that article.

(2) If the motion is opposed by a defendant or occupant within 30 days of service, the court may make an order for possession of

the property upon consideration of the relevant facts and any opposition, and upon completion of a hearing on the motion, if the court finds each of the following:

(A) The plaintiff is entitled to take the property by eminent domain.

(B) The plaintiff has deposited pursuant to Article 1 (commencing with Section 1255.010) an amount that satisfies the requirements of that article.

(C) There is an overriding need for the plaintiff to possess the property prior to the issuance of final judgment in the case, and the plaintiff will suffer a substantial hardship if the application for possession is denied or limited.

(D) The hardship that the plaintiff will suffer if possession is denied or limited outweighs any hardship on the defendant or occupant that would be caused by the granting of the order of possession.

(e)

(1) Notwithstanding the time limits for notice prescribed by this section and Section 1255.450, a court may issue an order of possession upon an ex parte application by a water, wastewater, gas, electric, or telephone utility, as the court deems appropriate under the circumstances of the case, if the court finds each of the following:

(A) An emergency exists and as a consequence the utility has an urgent need for possession of the property. For purposes of this section, an emergency is defined to include, but is not limited to, a utility's urgent need to protect the public's health and safety or the reliability of utility service.

(B) An emergency order of possession will not displace or unreasonably affect any person in actual and lawful possession of the property to be taken or the larger parcel of which it is a part.

(2) Not later than 30 days after service of the order authorizing the plaintiff to take possession of the property, any defendant or occupant of the property may move for relief from an emergency order of possession that has been issued under this subdivision. The court may modify, stay, or vacate the order upon consideration of the relevant facts and any objections raised, and upon completion of a hearing if requested.

Ca. Civ. Proc. Code § 1255.410
Amended by Stats 2007 ch 436 (SB 698),s 1, eff. 1/1/2008.
Amended by Stats 2006 ch 594 (SB 1210),s 3, eff. 1/1/2007.

Section 1255.420 - [Repealed]
Ca. Civ. Proc. Code § 1255.420
Repealed by Stats 2006 ch 594 (SB 1210),s 4, eff. 1/1/2007.

Section 1255.430 - [Repealed]
Ca. Civ. Proc. Code § 1255.430
Repealed by Stats 2006 ch 594 (SB 1210),s 5, eff. 1/1/2007.

Section 1255.440 - Conditions specified in order not satisfied
If an order has been made under Section 1255.410 authorizing the plaintiff to take possession of property and the court subsequently determines that the conditions specified in Section 1255.410 for issuance of the order are not satisfied, the court shall vacate the order.

Ca. Civ. Proc. Code § 1255.440
Added by Stats. 1975, Ch. 1275.

Section 1255.450 - Service of copy of order
(a) As used in this section, "record owner" means the owner of the legal or equitable title to the fee or any lesser interest in property as shown by recorded deeds or other recorded instruments.
(b) The plaintiff shall serve a copy of the order for possession issued under Section 1255.410 on the record owner of the property

and on the occupants, if any. If the property is lawfully occupied by a person dwelling thereon or by a farm or business operation, service shall be made not less than 30 days prior to the time possession is to be taken pursuant to the order. In all other cases, service shall be made not less than 10 days prior to the time possession is to be taken pursuant to the order. Service may be made with or following service of summons.

(c) At least 30 days prior to the time possession is taken pursuant to an order for possession made pursuant to Section 1255.040, 1255.050, or 1255.460, the plaintiff shall serve a copy of the order on the record owner of the property and on the occupants, if any.

(d) Service of the order shall be made by personal service except that:

(1) If the person on whom service is to be made has previously appeared in the proceeding or been served with summons in the proceeding, service of the order may be made by mail upon that person and his or her attorney of record, if any.

(2) If the person on whom service is to be made resides out of the state, or has departed from the state or cannot with due diligence be found within the state, service of the order may be made by registered or certified mail addressed to that person at his or her last known address.

(e) When the record owner cannot be located, the court may, for good cause shown on ex parte application, authorize the plaintiff to take possession of unoccupied property without serving a copy of the order for possession upon a record owner.

(f) A single service upon or mailing to one of several persons having a common business or residence address is sufficient.

Ca. Civ. Proc. Code § 1255.450
Amended by Stats 2006 ch 594 (SB 1210),s 6, eff. 1/1/2007.

Section 1255.460 - Requirements of order of possession
An order for possession issued pursuant to Section 1255.410 shall:
(a) Recite that it has been made under this section.
(b) Describe the property to be acquired, which description may be

by reference to the complaint.

(c) State the date after which plaintiff is authorized to take possession of the property.

Ca. Civ. Proc. Code § 1255.460

Amended by Stats 2006 ch 594 (SB 1210),s 7, eff. 1/1/2007.

Section 1255.470 - Rights not waived

By taking possession pursuant to this chapter, the plaintiff does not waive the right to appeal from the judgment, the right to move to abandon, or the right to request a new trial.

Ca. Civ. Proc. Code § 1255.470

Added by Stats. 1975, Ch. 1275.

Section 1255.480 - Right of public entity to exercise police power

Nothing in this article limits the right of a public entity to exercise its police power in emergency situations.

Ca. Civ. Proc. Code § 1255.480

Added by Stats. 1975, Ch. 1275.

Chapter 7 - DISCOVERY; EXCHANGE OF VALUATION DATA

Article 1 - DISCOVERY

Section 1258.010 - Provisions supplemental

The provisions of this chapter supplement but do not replace, restrict, or prevent the use of discovery procedures or limit the matters that are discoverable in eminent domain proceedings.

Ca. Civ. Proc. Code § 1258.010

Added by Stats. 1975, Ch. 1275.

Section 1258.020 - Discovery after time of exchange; order to protect from annoyance, embarrassment or oppression

(a) Notwithstanding any other statute or any court rule relating to discovery, proceedings pursuant to subdivision (b) may be had without requirement of court order and may proceed until not later than 20 days prior to the day set for trial of the issue of compensation.

(b) A party to an exchange of lists of expert witnesses and statements of valuation data pursuant to Article 2 (commencing with Section 1258.210) or pursuant to court rule as provided in Section 1258.300 may after the time of the exchange obtain discovery from the other party to the exchange and from any person listed by him as an expert witness.

(c) The court, upon noticed motion by the person subjected to discovery pursuant to subdivision (b), may make any order that justice requires to protect such person from annoyance, embarrassment, or oppression.

Ca. Civ. Proc. Code § 1258.020

Amended by Stats. 1992, Ch. 876, Sec. 8. Effective January 1, 1993.

Section 1258.030 - Evidence not otherwise admissible not admissible

Nothing in this chapter makes admissible any evidence that is not otherwise admissible or permits a witness to base an opinion on any matter that is not a proper basis for such an opinion.

Ca. Civ. Proc. Code § 1258.030

Added by Stats. 1975, Ch. 1275.

Article 2 - EXCHANGE OF VALUATION DATA

Section 1258.210 - Demand to exchange lists of expert witnesses and statement of valuation data

(a) Not later than the 10th day after the trial date is selected, any party may file and serve on any other party a demand to exchange lists of expert witnesses and statements of valuation data. Thereafter, the court may, upon noticed motion and a showing of good cause, permit any party to serve such a demand upon any other party.

(b) The demand shall:

(1) Describe the property to which it relates, which description may be by reference to the complaint.

(2) Include a statement in substantially the following form: "You are required to serve and deposit with the clerk of court a list of expert witnesses and statements of valuation data in compliance with Article 2 (commencing with Section 1258.210) of Chapter 7 of Title 7 of Part 3 of the Code of Civil Procedure not later than the date of exchange to be set in accordance with that article. Except as otherwise provided in that article, your failure to do so will constitute a waiver of your right to call unlisted expert witnesses during your case in chief and of your right to introduce on direct examination during your case in chief any matter that is required to be, but is not, set forth in your statements of valuation data."

Ca. Civ. Proc. Code § 1258.210
Added by Stats. 1975, Ch. 1275.

Section 1258.220 - Date of exchange

(a) For the purposes of this article, the "date of exchange" is the date agreed to for the exchange of their lists of expert witnesses and statements of valuation data by the party who served a demand and the party on whom the demand was served or, failing agreement, a date 90 days prior to commencement of the trial on the issue of compensation or the date set by the court on noticed motion of either party establishing good cause therefor.

(b) Notwithstanding subdivision (a), unless otherwise agreed to by the parties, the date of exchange shall not be earlier than nine months after the date of commencement of the proceeding.

Ca. Civ. Proc. Code § 1258.220
Amended by Stats 2001 ch 428 (AB 237), s 7, eff. 1/1/2002.
Previously Amended July 13, 1999 (Bill Number: SB 634) (Chapter 102).

Section 1258.230 - Duties of parties not later than date of exchange

(a) Not later than the date of exchange:

(1) Each party who served a demand and each party upon whom a demand was served shall deposit with the clerk of the court a list of expert witnesses and statements of valuation data.

(2) A party who served a demand shall serve his list and statements upon each party on whom he served his demand.

(3) Each party on whom a demand was served shall serve his list and statements upon the party who served the demand.
(b) The clerk of the court shall make an entry in the register of actions for each list of expert witnesses and statement of valuation data deposited with him pursuant to this article. The lists and statements shall not be filed in the proceeding, but the clerk shall make them available to the court at the commencement of the trial for the limited purpose of enabling the court to apply the provisions of this article. Unless the court otherwise orders, the clerk shall, at the conclusion of the trial, return all lists and statements to the attorneys for the parties who deposited them. Lists or statements ordered by the court to be retained may thereafter be destroyed or otherwise disposed of in accordance with the provisions of law governing the destruction or disposition of exhibits introduced in the trial.

Ca. Civ. Proc. Code § 1258.230
Added by Stats. 1975, Ch. 1275.

Section 1258.240 - Information included in lists of expert witnesses

The list of expert witnesses shall include the name, business or residence address, and business, occupation, or profession of each person intended to be called as an expert witness by the party and a statement of the subject matter to which his testimony relates.

Ca. Civ. Proc. Code § 1258.240
Added by Stats. 1975, Ch. 1275.

Section 1258.250 - Statement of valuation data exchanged for each person party intents to call as witness

A statement of valuation data shall be exchanged for each person the party intends to call as a witness to testify to his opinion as to any of the following matters:

(a) The value of the property being taken.

(b) The amount of the damage, if any, to the remainder of the larger parcel from which such property is taken.

(c) The amount of the benefit, if any, to the remainder of the larger parcel from which such property is taken.

(d) The amount of any other compensation required to be paid by Chapter 9 (commencing with Section 1263.010) or Chapter 10 (commencing with Section 1265.010).

Ca. Civ. Proc. Code § 1258.250
Added by Stats. 1975, Ch. 1275.

Section 1258.260 - Information included in state of valuation data

(a) The statement of valuation data shall give the name and business or residence address of the witness and shall include a statement whether the witness will testify to an opinion as to any of the matters listed in Section 1258.250 and, as to each matter upon which the witness will give an opinion, what that opinion is and the following items to the extent that the opinion is based on them:

(1) The interest being valued.

(2) The date of valuation used by the witness.

(3) The highest and best use of the property.

(4) The applicable zoning and the opinion of the witness as to the probability of any change in zoning.

(5) The sales, contracts to sell and purchase, and leases supporting the opinion.

(6) The cost of reproduction or replacement of the existing improvements on the property, the depreciation or obsolescence the improvements have suffered, and the method of calculation used to determine depreciation.

(7) The gross income from the property, the deductions from gross income, and the resulting net income; the reasonable net rental value attributable to the land and existing improvements, and the estimated gross rental income and deductions upon which the reasonable net rental value is computed; the rate of capitalization used; and the value indicated by the capitalization.

(8) If the property is a portion of a larger parcel, a description of the larger parcel and its value.

(9) If the opinion concerns loss of goodwill, the method used to determine the loss, and a summary of the data supporting the opinion.

(b) With respect to each sale, contract, or lease listed under paragraph (5) of subdivision (a), the statement of valuation data shall give:

(1) The names and business or residence addresses, if known, of the parties to the transaction.

(2) The location of the property subject to the transaction.

(3) The date of the transaction.

(4) If recorded, the date of recording and the volume and page or other identification of the record of the transaction.

(5) The price and other terms and circumstances of the transaction. In lieu of stating the terms contained in any contract, lease, or other document, the statement may, if the document is available for inspection by the adverse party, state the place where and the times when it is available for inspection.

(6) The total area and shape of the property subject to the transaction.

(c) If any opinion referred to in Section 1258.250 is based in whole or in substantial part upon the opinion of another person, the statement of valuation data shall include the name and business or residence address of that other person, his business, occupation, or profession, and a statement as to the subject matter to which his or her opinion relates.

(d) Except when an appraisal report is used as a statement of valuation data as permitted by subdivision (e), the statement of valuation data shall include a statement, signed by the witness, that the witness has read the statement of valuation data and that it fairly and correctly states his or her opinions and knowledge as to the matters therein stated.

(e) An appraisal report that has been prepared by the witness which includes the information required to be included in a statement of valuation data may be used as a statement of valuation data under this article.

Ca. Civ. Proc. Code § 1258.260

Amended by Stats 2001 ch 428 (AB 237), s 8, eff. 1/1/2002.

Section 1258.270 - Notice to parties upon whom lists and statements served required

(a) A party who is required to exchange lists of expert witnesses and statements of valuation data shall diligently give notice to the parties upon whom his list and statements were served if, after service of his list and statements, he:

(1) Determines to call an expert witness not included in his list of expert witnesses to testify on direct examination during his case in chief;

(2) Determines to have a witness called by him testify on direct examination during his case in chief to any opinion or data required to be listed in the statement of valuation data for that witness but which was not so listed; or

(3) Discovers any data required to be listed in a statement of valuation data but which was not so listed.

(b) The notice required by subdivision (a) shall include the information specified in Sections 1258.240 and 1258.260 and shall be in writing; but such notice is not required to be in writing if it is given after the commencement of the trial.

Ca. Civ. Proc. Code § 1258.270
Added by Stats. 1975, Ch. 1275.

Section 1258.280 - Objection of party who has served list and statement

Except as provided in Section 1258.290, upon objection of a party who has served his list of expert witnesses and statements of valuation data in compliance with Section 1258.230:

(a) No party required to serve a list of expert witnesses on the objecting party may call an expert witness to testify on direct examination during his case in chief unless the information required by Section 1258.240 for such witness is included in the list served.

(b) No party required to serve statements of valuation data on the objecting party may call a witness to testify on direct examination during his case in chief to his opinion on any matter listed in Section 1258.250 unless a statement of valuation data for such witness was served.

(c) No witness called by a party required to serve statements of valuation data on the objecting party may testify on direct examination during the case in chief of the party who called him to any opinion or data required to be listed in the statement of valuation data for such witness unless such opinion or data is listed in the statement served except that testimony that is merely an explanation or elaboration of data so listed is not inadmissible under this subdivision.

Ca. Civ. Proc. Code § 1258.280
Added by Stats. 1975, Ch. 1275.

Section 1258.290 - Witness, opinion or data not included in party's list or statement

(a) The court may, upon such terms as may be just (including but not limited to continuing the trial for a reasonable period of time and awarding costs and litigation expenses), permit a party to call a witness, or permit a witness called by a party to testify to an opinion or data on direct examination, during the party's case in chief where such witness, opinion, or data is required to be, but is not, included in such party's list of expert witnesses or statements of valuation data if the court finds that such party has made a good faith effort to comply with Sections 1258.210 to 1258.260, inclusive, that he has complied with Section 1258.270, and that by the date of exchange he:

(1) Would not in the exercise of reasonable diligence have determined to call such witness or discovered or listed such opinion or data; or

(2) Failed to determine to call such witness or to discover or list such opinion or data through mistake, inadvertence, surprise, or excusable neglect.

(b) In making a determination under this section, the court shall take into account the extent to which the opposing party has relied upon the list of expert witnesses and statements of valuation data and will be prejudiced if the witness is called or the testimony concerning such opinion or data is given.

Ca. Civ. Proc. Code § 1258.290
Added by Stats. 1975, Ch. 1275.

Section 1258.300 - Court rule providing for exchange of valuation data in lieu of procedure provided for in article
The superior court in any county may provide by court rule a procedure for the exchange of valuation data which shall be used in lieu of the procedure provided by this article if the Judicial Council finds that such procedure serves the same purpose and is an adequate substitute for the procedure provided by this article.

Ca. Civ. Proc. Code § 1258.300
Added by Stats. 1975, Ch. 1275.

Chapter 8 - PROCEDURES FOR DETERMINING RIGHT TO TAKE AND COMPENSATION

Article 1 - GENERAL PROVISIONS

Section 1260.010 - Precedence over other civil actions

Proceedings under this title take precedence over all other civil actions in the matter of setting the same for hearing or trial in order that such proceedings shall be quickly heard and determined.

Ca. Civ. Proc. Code § 1260.010
Added by Stats. 1975, Ch. 1275.

Section 1260.020 - Determination whether public uses comparable if proceedings to acquire same property consolidated

(a) If proceedings to acquire the same property are consolidated, the court shall first determine whether the public uses for which the property is sought are compatible within the meaning of Article 6 (commencing with Section 1240.510) of Chapter 3. If the court determines that the uses are compatible, it shall permit the proceeding to continue with the plaintiffs acting jointly. The court shall apportion the obligation to pay any award in the proceeding in proportion to the use, damage, and benefits attributable to each plaintiff.

(b) If the court determines pursuant to subdivision (a) that the uses are not all compatible, it shall further determine which of the uses is the more necessary public use within the meaning of Article 7 (commencing with Section 1240.610) of Chapter 3. The court shall permit the plaintiff alleging the more necessary public use, along with any other plaintiffs alleging compatible public uses under subdivision (a), to continue the proceeding. The court shall dismiss the proceeding as to the other plaintiffs.

Ca. Civ. Proc. Code § 1260.020
Added by Stats. 1975, Ch. 1275.

Section 1260.030 - Determination as to whether property improvement pertaining to realty

(a) If there is a dispute between plaintiff and defendant whether particular property is an improvement pertaining to the realty, either party may, not later than 30 days prior to the date specified in an order for possession of the property, move the court for a determination whether the property is an improvement pertaining to the realty.

(b) A motion under this section shall be heard not sooner than 10 days and not later than 20 days after service of notice of the motion. At the hearing, the court may consider any relevant evidence, including a view of the premises and property, in making its determinations.

Ca. Civ. Proc. Code § 1260.030
Added by Stats. 1975, Ch. 1275.

Section 1260.040 - Motion for ruling on issue of compensation

(a) If there is a dispute between plaintiff and defendant over an evidentiary or other legal issue affecting the determination of compensation, either party may move the court for a ruling on the issue. The motion shall be made not later than 60 days before commencement of trial on the issue of compensation. The motion shall be heard by the judge assigned for trial of the case.

(b) Notwithstanding any other statute or rule of court governing the date of final offers and demands of the parties and the date of trial of an eminent domain proceeding, the court may postpone those dates for a period sufficient to enable the parties to engage in further proceedings before trial in response to its ruling on the motion.

(c) This section supplements, and does not replace any other pretrial or trial procedure otherwise available to resolve an evidentiary or other legal issue affecting the determination of compensation.

Ca. Civ. Proc. Code § 1260.040
Added by Stats 2001 ch 428 (AB 237), s 9, eff. 1/1/2002.

Article 2 - CONTESTING RIGHT TO TAKE

Section 1260.110 - Hearing objections

(a) Where objections to the right to take are raised, unless the court orders otherwise, they shall be heard and determined prior to the determination of the issue of compensation.

(b) The court may, on motion of any party, after notice and hearing, specially set such objections for trial.

Ca. Civ. Proc. Code § 1260.110

Added by Stats. 1975, Ch. 1275.

Section 1260.120 - Orders upon hearing and determining objections

(a) The court shall hear and determine all objections to the right to take.

(b) If the court determines that the plaintiff has the right to acquire by eminent domain the property described in the complaint, the court shall so order.

(c) If the court determines that the plaintiff does not have the right to acquire by eminent domain any property described in the complaint, it shall order either of the following:

(1) Immediate dismissal of the proceeding as to that property.

(2) Conditional dismissal of the proceeding as to that property unless such corrective and remedial action as the court may prescribe has been taken within the period prescribed by the court in the order. An order made under this paragraph may impose such limitations and conditions as the court determines to be just under the circumstances of the particular case including the requirement that the plaintiff pay to the defendant all or part of the reasonable litigation expenses necessarily incurred by the defendant because of the plaintiff's failure or omission which constituted the basis of the objection to the right to take.

Ca. Civ. Proc. Code § 1260.120

Added by Stats. 1975, Ch. 1275.

Article 3 - PROCEDURES RELATING TO DETERMINATION OF COMPENSATION

Section 1260.210 - Generally
(a) The defendant shall present his evidence on the issue of compensation first and shall commence and conclude the argument.
(b) Except as otherwise provided by statute, neither the plaintiff nor the defendant has the burden of proof on the issue of compensation.
   Ca. Civ. Proc. Code § 1260.210
Added by Stats. 1975, Ch. 1275.

Section 1260.220 - Divided interests in property acquired
(a) Except as provided in subdivision (b), where there are divided interests in property acquired by eminent domain, the value of each interest and the injury, if any, to the remainder of such interest shall be separately assessed and compensation awarded therefor.
(b) The plaintiff may require that the amount of compensation be first determined as between plaintiff and all defendants claiming an interest in the property. Thereafter, in the same proceeding, the trier of fact shall determine the respective rights of the defendants in and to the amount of compensation awarded and shall apportion the award accordingly. Nothing in this subdivision limits the right of a defendant to present during the first stage of the proceeding evidence of the value of, or injury to, the property or the defendant's interest in the property; and the right of a defendant to present evidence during the second stage of the proceeding is not affected by the failure to exercise the right to present evidence during the first stage of the proceeding.
   Ca. Civ. Proc. Code § 1260.220
Amended by Stats. 1978, Ch. 294.

Section 1260.230 - Issues separately assessed by trier of fact
As far as practicable, the trier of fact shall assess separately each of

the following:

(a) Compensation for the property taken as required by Article 4 (commencing with Section 1263.310) of Chapter 9.

(b) When the property acquired is part of a larger parcel:

(1) The amount of the damage, if any, to the remainder as required by Article 5 (commencing with Section 1263.410) of Chapter 9.

(2) The amount of the benefit, if any, to the remainder as required by Article 5 (commencing with Section 1263.410) of Chapter 9.

(c) Compensation for loss of goodwill, if any, as required by Article 6 (commencing with Section 1263.510) of Chapter 9.

(d) Compensation claimed under subdivision (c) of Section 1250.320.

(e) Compensation claimed under subdivision (d) of Section 1250.320.

Ca. Civ. Proc. Code § 1260.230

Amended by Stats 2021 ch 401 (AB 1578),s 6, eff. 1/1/2022.
Added by Stats. 1975, Ch. 1275.

Section 1260.240 - Determination when unknown persons or deceased persons properly joined as defendants

Where any persons unknown or any deceased persons or the heirs and devisees of any deceased persons have been properly joined as defendants but have not appeared either personally or by a personal representative, the court shall determine the extent of the interests of such defendants in the property taken or in the remainder if the property taken is part of a larger parcel and the compensation to be awarded for such interests. The court may determine the extent and value of the interests of all such defendants in the aggregate without apportionment between the respective defendants. In any event, in the case of deceased persons, the court shall determine only the extent and value of the interest of the decedent and shall not determine the extent and value of the separate interests of the heirs and devisees in such decedent's interest.

Ca. Civ. Proc. Code § 1260.240
Added by Stats. 1975, Ch. 1275.

Section 1260.250 - Court order directing county auditor and tax collector to certify information; information required to be certified

(a) In a county where both the auditor and the tax collector are elected officials, the court shall by order give the auditor or tax collector the legal description of the property sought to be taken and direct the auditor or tax collector to certify to the court the information required by subdivision (c), and the auditor or tax collector shall promptly certify the required information to the court. In all other counties, the court shall by order give the tax collector the legal description of the property sought to be taken and direct the tax collector to certify to the court the information required by subdivision (c), and the tax collector shall promptly certify the required information to the court.

(b) The court order shall be made on or before the earliest of the following dates:

(1) The date the court makes an order for possession.

(2) The date set for trial.

(3) The date of entry of judgment.

(c) The court order shall require certification of the following information:

(1) The current assessed value of the property together with its assessed identification number.

(2) All unpaid taxes on the property, and any penalties and costs that have accrued thereon while on the secured roll, levied for prior tax years that constitute a lien on the property.

(3) All unpaid taxes on the property, and any penalties and costs that have accrued thereon while on the secured roll, levied for the current tax year that constitute a lien on the property prorated to, but not including, the date of apportionment determined pursuant to Section 5082 of the Revenue and Taxation Code or the date of trial, whichever is earlier. If the amount of the current taxes is not ascertainable at the time of proration, the amount shall be estimated and computed based on the assessed value for the current assessment year and the tax rate levied on the property for the immediately prior tax year.

(4) The actual or estimated amount of taxes on the property that are or will become a lien on the property in the next succeeding tax year prorated to, but not including, the date of apportionment determined pursuant to Section 5082 of the Revenue and Taxation Code or the date of trial, whichever is earlier. Any estimated amount of taxes shall be computed based on the assessed value of the property for the current assessment year and the tax rate levied on the property for the current tax year.

(5) The amount of the taxes, penalties, and costs allocable to one day of the current tax year, and where applicable, the amount allocable to one day of the next succeeding tax year, hereinafter referred to as the "daily prorate."

(6) The total of paragraphs (2), (3), and (4).
(d) If the property sought to be taken does not have a separate valuation on the assessment roll, the information required by this section shall be for the larger parcel of which the property is a part.
(e) The court, as part of the judgment, shall separately state the amount certified pursuant to this section and order that the amount be paid to the tax collector from the award. If the amount so certified is prorated to the date of trial, the order shall include, in addition to the amount so certified, an amount equal to the applicable daily prorate multiplied by the number of days commencing on the date of trial and ending on and including the day before the date of apportionment determined pursuant to Section 5082 of the Revenue and Taxation Code.
(f) Notwithstanding any other provision of this section, if the board of supervisors provides the procedure set forth in Section 5087 of

the Revenue and Taxation Code, the court shall make no award of taxes in the judgment.

Ca. Civ. Proc. Code § 1260.250
Amended 10/10/1999 (Bill Number: AB 1672) (Chapter 892).

Chapter 9 - COMPENSATION

Article 1 - GENERAL PROVISIONS

Section 1263.010 - Owner of property acquired entitled to compensation

(a) The owner of property acquired by eminent domain is entitled to compensation as provided in this chapter.

(b) Nothing in this chapter affects any rights the owner of property acquired by eminent domain may have under any other statute. In any case where two or more statutes provide compensation for the same loss, the person entitled to compensation may be paid only once for that loss.

Ca. Civ. Proc. Code § 1263.010
Added by Stats. 1975, Ch. 1275.

Section 1263.015 - Agreement with owner specifying manner of payment

At the request of an owner of property acquired by eminent domain, the public entity may enter into an agreement with the owner specifying the manner of payment of compensation to which the owner is entitled as the result of the acquisition. The agreement may provide that the compensation shall be paid by the public entity to the owner over a period not to exceed 10 years from the date the owner's right to compensation accrues. The agreement may also provide for the payment of interest by the public entity; however, the rate of interest agreed upon may not exceed the maximum rate authorized by Section 16731 or 53531 of the Government Code, as applicable, in connection with the issuance of bonds.

Ca. Civ. Proc. Code § 1263.015
Added by Stats. 1982, Ch. 1368, Sec. 1.

Section 1263.020 - Date right to compensation deemed to have accrued

Except as otherwise provided by law, the right to compensation shall be deemed to have accrued at the date of filing the complaint.

Ca. Civ. Proc. Code § 1263.020

Added by Stats. 1975, Ch. 1275.

Section 1263.025 - Independent appraisal of property public entity offers to purchase under threat of eminent domain

(a) A public entity shall offer to pay the reasonable costs, not to exceed five thousand dollars ($5,000), of an independent appraisal ordered by the owner of a property that the public entity offers to purchase under a threat of eminent domain, at the time the public entity makes the offer to purchase the property. The independent appraisal shall be conducted by an appraiser licensed by the Office of Real Estate Appraisers.

(b) For purposes of this section, an offer to purchase a property "under a threat of eminent domain" is an offer to purchase a property pursuant to any of the following:

(1) Eminent domain.

(2) Following adoption of a resolution of necessity for the property pursuant to Section 1240.040.

(3) Following a statement that the public entity may take the property by eminent domain.

Ca. Civ. Proc. Code § 1263.025

Added by Stats 2006 ch 594 (SB 1210),s 8, eff. 1/1/2007.

Article 2 - DATE OF VALUATION

Section 1263.110 - Date on which deposit made; deposit not deemed to have been made

(a) Unless an earlier date of valuation is applicable under this article, if the plaintiff deposits the probable compensation in accordance with Article 1 (commencing with Section 1255.010) of Chapter 6 or the amount of the award in accordance with Article 2 (commencing with Section 1268.110) of Chapter 11, the date of valuation is the date on which the deposit is made.

(b) Whether or not the plaintiff has taken possession of the property or obtained an order for possession, if the court determines pursuant to Section 1255.030 that the probable amount of compensation exceeds the amount previously deposited pursuant to Article 1 (commencing with Section 1255.010) of Chapter 6 and the amount on deposit is not increased accordingly within the time allowed under Section 1255.030, no deposit shall be deemed to have been made for the purpose of this section.

Ca. Civ. Proc. Code § 1263.110
Added by Stats. 1975, Ch. 1275.

Section 1263.120 - Issued brought to trial within one year after commencement of proceeding

If the issue of compensation is brought to trial within one year after commencement of the proceeding, the date of valuation is the date of commencement of the proceeding.

Ca. Civ. Proc. Code § 1263.120
Added by Stats. 1975, Ch. 1275.

Section 1263.130 - Issue not brought to trial within one year after commencement of proceeding

Subject to Section 1263.110, if the issue of compensation is not brought to trial within one year after commencement of the proceeding, the date of valuation is the date of the commencement of the trial unless the delay is caused by the defendant, in which case the date of valuation is the date of commencement of the proceeding.

Ca. Civ. Proc. Code § 1263.130
Added by Stats. 1975, Ch. 1275.

Section 1263.140 - New trial order but not commenced within one year after commencement of proceeding
Subject to Section 1263.110, if a new trial is ordered by the trial or appellate court and the new trial is not commenced within one year after the commencement of the proceeding, the date of valuation is the date of the commencement of such new trial unless, in the interest of justice, the court ordering the new trial orders a different date of valuation.

Ca. Civ. Proc. Code § 1263.140
Added by Stats. 1975, Ch. 1275.

Section 1263.150 - Mistrial declared and retrial not commenced within one year after commencement of proceeding
Subject to Section 1263.110, if a mistrial is declared and the retrial is not commenced within one year after the commencement of the proceeding, the date of valuation is the date of the commencement of the retrial of the case unless, in the interest of justice, the court declaring the mistrial orders a different date of valuation.

Ca. Civ. Proc. Code § 1263.150
Added by Stats. 1975, Ch. 1275.

Article 3 - COMPENSATION FOR IMPROVEMENTS

Section 1263.205 - Improvements pertaining to the realty defined; determining whether property can be removed without substantial economic loss
(a) As used in this article, "improvements pertaining to the realty" include any machinery or equipment installed for use on property taken by eminent domain, or on the remainder if such property is part of a larger parcel, that cannot be removed without a substantial economic loss or without substantial damage to the property on which it is installed, regardless of the method of installation.
(b) In determining whether particular property can be removed "without a substantial economic loss" within the meaning of this section, the value of the property in place considered as a part of the

realty should be compared with its value if it were removed and sold.

Ca. Civ. Proc. Code § 1263.205
Added by Stats. 1975, Ch. 1275.

Section 1263.210 - All improvements taken into account in determining compensation

(a) Except as otherwise provided by statute, all improvements pertaining to the realty shall be taken into account in determining compensation.

(b) Subdivision (a) applies notwithstanding the right or obligation of a tenant, as against the owner of any other interest in real property, to remove such improvement at the expiration of his term.

Ca. Civ. Proc. Code § 1263.210
Added by Stats. 1975, Ch. 1275.

Section 1263.230 - Removed or destroyed improvements not taken into account

(a) Improvements pertaining to the realty shall not be taken into account in determining compensation to the extent that they are removed or destroyed before the earliest of the following times:

(1) The time the plaintiff takes title to the property.

(2) The time the plaintiff takes possession of the property.

(3) If the defendant moves from the property in compliance with an order for possession, the date specified in the order; except that, if the defendant so moves prior to such date and gives the plaintiff written notice thereof, the date 24 hours after such notice is received by the plaintiff.

(b) Where improvements pertaining to the realty are removed or destroyed by the defendant at any time, such improvements shall not be taken into account in determining compensation. Where such removal or destruction damages the remaining property, such damage shall be taken into account in determining compensation to the extent it reduces the value of the remaining property.

Ca. Civ. Proc. Code § 1263.230

Added by Stats. 1975, Ch. 1275.

Section 1263.240 - Improvement made subsequent to date of service of summons

Improvements pertaining to the realty made subsequent to the date of service of summons shall not be taken into account in determining compensation unless one of the following is established:

(a) The improvement is one required to be made by a public utility to its utility system.

(b) The improvement is one made with the written consent of the plaintiff.

(c) The improvement is one authorized to be made by a court order issued after a noticed hearing and upon a finding by the court that the hardship to the defendant of not permitting the improvement outweighs the hardship to the plaintiff of permitting the improvement. The court may, at the time it makes an order under this subdivision authorizing the improvement to be made, limit the extent to which the improvement shall be taken into account in determining compensation.

Ca. Civ. Proc. Code § 1263.240

Added by Stats. 1975, Ch. 1275.

Section 1263.250 - Defendant harvesting and marketing crops

(a) The acquisition of property by eminent domain shall not prevent the defendant from harvesting and marketing crops planted before or after the service of summons. If the plaintiff takes possession of the property at a time that prevents the defendant from harvesting and marketing the crops, the fair market value of the crops in place at the date the plaintiff is authorized to take possession of the property shall be included in the compensation awarded for the property taken.

(b) Notwithstanding subdivision (a), the plaintiff may obtain a court order precluding the defendant from planting crops after service of summons, in which case the compensation awarded for the property taken shall include an amount sufficient to compensate for loss caused by the limitation on the defendant's right to use the property.

Ca. Civ. Proc. Code § 1263.250
Added by Stats. 1975, Ch. 1275.

Section 1263.260 - Notice of election to remove improvements

Notwithstanding Section 1263.210, the owner of improvements pertaining to the realty may elect to remove any or all such improvements by serving on the plaintiff within 60 days after service of summons written notice of such election. If the plaintiff fails within 30 days thereafter to serve on the owner written notice of refusal to allow removal of such improvements, the owner may remove such improvements and shall be compensated for their reasonable removal and relocation cost not to exceed the market value of the improvements. Where such removal will cause damage to the structure in which the improvements are located, the defendant shall cause no more damage to the structure than is reasonably necessary in removing the improvements, and the structure shall be valued as if the removal had caused no damage to the structure.

Ca. Civ. Proc. Code § 1263.260
Added by Stats. 1975, Ch. 1275.

Section 1263.270 - Improvement located in part upon property taken and in part upon property not taken

Where an improvement pertaining to the realty is located in part upon property taken and in part upon property not taken, the court may, on motion of any party and a determination that justice so requires, direct the plaintiff to acquire the entire improvement, including the part located on property not taken, together with an easement or other interest reasonably necessary for the demolition, removal, or relocation of the improvement.

Ca. Civ. Proc. Code § 1263.270

Added by Stats. 1975, Ch. 1275.

Article 4 - MEASURE OF COMPENSATION FOR PROPERTY TAKEN

Section 1263.310 - Measure of compensation fair market value

Compensation shall be awarded for the property taken. The measure of this compensation is the fair market value of the property taken.

Ca. Civ. Proc. Code § 1263.310

Added by Stats. 1975, Ch. 1275.

Section 1263.320 - Fair market value defined; no relevant, comparable market

(a) The fair market value of the property taken is the highest price on the date of valuation that would be agreed to by a seller, being willing to sell but under no particular or urgent necessity for so doing, nor obliged to sell, and a buyer, being ready, willing, and able to buy but under no particular necessity for so doing, each dealing with the other with full knowledge of all the uses and purposes for which the property is reasonably adaptable and available.

(b) The fair market value of property taken for which there is no relevant, comparable market is its value on the date of valuation as determined by any method of valuation that is just and equitable.

Ca. Civ. Proc. Code § 1263.320

Amended by Stats. 1992, Ch. 7, Sec. 2. Effective January 1, 1993.

Section 1263.321 - Determining value of nonprofit special use property

A just and equitable method of determining the value of nonprofit, special use property for which there is no relevant, comparable market is as set forth in Section 824 of the Evidence Code, but subject to the exceptions set forth in subdivision (c) of Section 824 of the Evidence Code.

Ca. Civ. Proc. Code § 1263.321

Added by Stats. 1992, Ch. 7, Sec. 3. Effective January 1, 1993.

Section 1263.330 - Increase or decrease in value not included

The fair market value of the property taken shall not include any increase or decrease in the value of the property that is attributable to any of the following:

(a) The project for which the property is taken.

(b) The eminent domain proceeding in which the property is taken.

(c) Any preliminary actions of the plaintiff relating to the taking of the property.

Ca. Civ. Proc. Code § 1263.330

Added by Stats. 1975, Ch. 1275.

Article 5 - COMPENSATION FOR INJURY TO REMAINDER

Section 1263.410 - Generally

(a) Where the property acquired is part of a larger parcel, in addition to the compensation awarded pursuant to Article 4 (commencing with Section 1263.310) for the part taken, compensation shall be awarded for the injury, if any, to the remainder.

(b) Compensation for injury to the remainder is the amount of the damage to the remainder reduced by the amount of the benefit to the remainder. If the amount of the benefit to the remainder equals or exceeds the amount of the damage to the remainder, no compensation shall be awarded under this article. If the amount of the benefit to the remainder exceeds the amount of damage to the remainder, such excess shall be deducted from the compensation provided in Section 1263.510, if any, but shall not be deducted from the compensation required to be awarded for the property taken or from the other compensation required by this chapter.

Ca. Civ. Proc. Code § 1263.410

Added by Stats. 1975, Ch. 1275.

Section 1263.420 - Damage to remainder

Damage to the remainder is the damage, if any, caused to the remainder by either or both of the following:

(a) The severance of the remainder from the part taken.

(b) The construction and use of the project for which the property is taken in the manner proposed by the plaintiff whether or not the damage is caused by a portion of the project located on the part taken.

Ca. Civ. Proc. Code § 1263.420
Added by Stats. 1975, Ch. 1275.

Section 1263.430 - Benefit to remainder

Benefit to the remainder is the benefit, if any, caused by the construction and use of the project for which the property is taken in the manner proposed by the plaintiff whether or not the benefit is caused by a portion of the project located on the part taken.

Ca. Civ. Proc. Code § 1263.430
Added by Stats. 1975, Ch. 1275.

Section 1263.440 - Delay in time when damage or benefit actually realized; date of valuation base for determining amount of damage or benefit

(a) The amount of any damage to the remainder and any benefit to the remainder shall reflect any delay in the time when the damage or benefit caused by the construction and use of the project in the manner proposed by the plaintiff will actually be realized.

(b) The value of the remainder on the date of valuation, excluding prior changes in value as prescribed in Section 1263.330, shall serve as the base from which the amount of any damage and the amount of any benefit to the remainder shall be determined.

Ca. Civ. Proc. Code § 1263.440
Added by Stats. 1975, Ch. 1275.

Section 1263.450 - Features mitigating damage or providing benefit

Compensation for injury to the remainder shall be based on the project as proposed. Any features of the project which mitigate the damage or provide benefit to the remainder, including but not limited to easements, crossings, underpasses, access roads, fencing, drainage facilities, and cattle guards, shall be taken into account in determining the compensation for injury to the remainder.

Ca. Civ. Proc. Code § 1263.450
Added by Stats. 1975, Ch. 1275.

Article 6 - COMPENSATION FOR LOSS OF GOODWILL

Section 1263.510 - Proof required for compensation for loss; goodwill defined; leaseback agreement

(a) The owner of a business conducted on the property taken, or on the remainder if the property is part of a larger parcel, shall be compensated for loss of goodwill if the owner proves all of the following:

(1) The loss is caused by the taking of the property or the injury to the remainder.

(2) The loss cannot reasonably be prevented by a relocation of the business or by taking steps and adopting procedures that a reasonably prudent person would take and adopt in preserving the goodwill.

(3) Compensation for the loss will not be included in payments under Section 7262 of the Government Code.

(4) Compensation for the loss will not be duplicated in the compensation otherwise awarded to the owner.
(b) Within the meaning of this article, "goodwill" consists of the benefits that accrue to a business as a result of its location, reputation for dependability, skill or quality, and any other circumstances resulting in probable retention of old or acquisition of new patronage.
(c) If the public entity and the owner enter into a leaseback

agreement pursuant to Section 1263.615, the following shall apply:

(1) No additional goodwill shall accrue during the lease.

(2) The entering of a leaseback agreement shall not be a factor in determining goodwill. Any liability for goodwill shall be established and paid at the time of acquisition of the property by eminent domain or subsequent to notice that the property may be taken by eminent domain.

Ca. Civ. Proc. Code § 1263.510
Amended by Stats 2006 ch 602 (SB 1650),s 2, eff. 1/1/2007.

Section 1263.520 - State tax returns made available to plaintiff

The owner of a business who claims compensation under this article shall make available to the court, and the court shall, upon such terms and conditions as will preserve their confidentiality, make available to the plaintiff, the state tax returns of the business for audit for confidential use solely for the purpose of determining the amount of compensation under this article. Nothing in this section affects any right a party may otherwise have to discovery or to require the production of documents, papers, books, and accounts.

Ca. Civ. Proc. Code § 1263.520
Added by Stats. 1975, Ch. 1275.

Section 1263.530 - Temporary interference with or interruption of business

Nothing in this article is intended to deal with compensation for inverse condemnation claims for temporary interference with or interruption of business.

Ca. Civ. Proc. Code § 1263.530
Added by Stats. 1975, Ch. 1275.

Article 7 - MISCELLANEOUS PROVISIONS

Section 1263.610 - Agreement to relocate structure or carry work on property not taken

A public entity and the owner of property to be acquired for public use may make an agreement that the public entity will:

(a) Relocate for the owner any structure if such relocation is likely to reduce the amount of compensation otherwise payable to the owner by an amount equal to or greater than the cost of such relocation.

(b) Carry out for the owner any work on property not taken, including work on any structure, if the performance of the work is likely to reduce the amount of compensation otherwise payable to the owner by an amount equal to or greater than the cost of the work.

Ca. Civ. Proc. Code § 1263.610
Added by Stats. 1975, Ch. 1275.

Section 1263.615 - One-year leaseback agreement offered to owner

(a) A public entity shall offer a one-year leaseback agreement to the owner of a property to be acquired by any method set forth in subdivision (b) for that property owner's continued use of the property upon acquisition, subject to the property owner's payment of fair market rents and compliance with other conditions set forth in subdivision (c), unless the public entity states in writing that the development, redevelopment, or use of the property for its stated public use is scheduled to begin within two years of its acquisition. This section shall not apply if the public entity states in writing that a leaseback of the property would create or allow the continuation of a public nuisance to the surrounding community.

(b) The following property acquisitions are subject to the requirements of this section:

(1) Any acquisition by a public entity pursuant to eminent domain.

(2) Any acquisition by a public entity following adoption of a resolution of necessity pursuant to Article 2 (commencing with Section 1245.210) of Chapter 4 for the property.

(3) Any acquisition by a public entity prior to the adoption of a resolution of necessity pursuant to Article 2 (commencing with Section 1245.210) of Chapter 4 for the property, but subsequent to a written notice that the public entity may take the property by eminent domain.

(c) The following conditions shall apply to any leaseback offered pursuant to this section:

(1) The lessee shall be responsible for any additional waste or nuisance on the property, and for any other liability arising from the continued use of the property.

(2) The lessor may demand a security deposit to cover any potential liability arising from the leaseback. The security deposit shall be reasonable in light of the use of the leased property.

(3) The lessor shall be indemnified from any legal liability and attorney's fees resulting from any lawsuit against the lessee or lessor, arising from the operation of the lessee's business or use of the property.

(4) The lessor shall require the lessee to carry adequate insurance to cover potential liabilities arising from the lease and use of the property, and shall require that insurance to name the lessor as an additional insured.

(5) Additional goodwill shall not accrue during any lease.

(6) The lessee shall be subject to unlawful detainer proceedings as provided by law.

(d) A public entity shall offer to renew a leaseback agreement for one-year terms, subject to any rent adjustment to reflect inflation and upon compliance with other conditions set forth in subdivision (c), unless the public entity states in writing that the development, redevelopment, or use of the property for its stated public use is scheduled to begin within two years of the termination date of the lease. At least 60 days prior to the lease termination date, the public entity lessor shall either offer a one-year renewal of the lease or send a statement declaring that the lease will not be renewed because the development, redevelopment, or use of the property is scheduled to begin within two years of the lease termination date. The lessee shall either accept or reject a lease renewal offer at least 30 days prior to the lease termination date. The lessee's failure to accept a renewal offer in a timely manner shall constitute a rejection of the renewal offer. A lessor's failure to offer a renewal or give the notice as required shall extend the lease term for 60-day increments until an offer or notice is made, and if a notice of termination is given after the lease termination date, the lessee shall have no less than 60 days to vacate the property. A lessee's failure to accept within 30 days a renewal offer made subsequent to the lease termination date shall constitute a rejection of the offer.

(e) A party who holds over after expiration of the lease shall be subject to unlawful detainer proceedings and shall also be subject to the lessor for holdover damages.

(f) A leaseback entered into pursuant to this section shall not affect the amount of compensation otherwise payable to the property owner for the property to be acquired.

Ca. Civ. Proc. Code § 1263.615
Added by Stats 2006 ch 602 (SB 1650),s 3, eff. 1/1/2007.

Section 1263.620 - Cessation of construction of improvement or installation of machinery or equipment in response to service of summons

(a) Where summons is served during construction of an improvement or installation of machinery or equipment on the property taken or on the remainder if such property is part of a larger parcel, and the owner of the property ceases the construction or installation due to such service, the owner shall be compensated for his expenses reasonably incurred for work necessary for either of the following purposes:

(1) To protect against the risk of injury to persons or to other property created by the uncompleted improvement.

(2) To protect the partially installed machinery or equipment from damage, deterioration, or vandalism.
(b) The compensation provided in this section is recoverable only if the work was preceded by notice to the plaintiff except in the case of an emergency. The plaintiff may agree with the owner (1) that the plaintiff will perform work necessary for the purposes of this section or (2) as to the amount of compensation payable under this section.

Ca. Civ. Proc. Code § 1263.620
Added by Stats. 1975, Ch. 1275.

Article 8 - REMEDIATION OF HAZARDOUS MATERIALS ON PROPERTY TO BE ACQUIRED BY SCHOOL DISTRICTS

Section 1263.710 - Remedial action and removal defined; required action defined

(a) As used in this article, "remedial action" and "removal" shall have the meanings accorded to those terms in Sections 78125 and 78135, respectively, of the Health and Safety Code.
(b) As used in this article, "required action" means any removal or other remedial action with regard to hazardous materials that is necessary to comply with any requirement of federal, state, or local law.

Ca. Civ. Proc. Code § 1263.710
Amended by Stats 2022 ch 258 (AB 2327),s 10, eff. 1/1/2023, op. 1/1/2024.
Repealed and added by Stats. 1995, Ch. 247, Sec. 2. Effective January 1, 1996.

Section 1263.711 - Hazardous material defined

As used in this article, "hazardous material" shall have the same meaning as that term is defined in Section 25260 of the Health and Safety Code, except that under no circumstances shall petroleum which is naturally occurring on a site be considered a hazardous material.

Ca. Civ. Proc. Code § 1263.711

Added by Stats. 1995, Ch. 247, Sec. 2. Effective January 1, 1996.

Section 1263.720 - Duty of court upon determination that hazardous material present within property

(a) Upon petition of any party to the proceeding, the court in which the proceeding is brought shall specially set for hearing the issue of whether any hazardous material is present within the property to be taken.

(b) If the court determines that any hazardous material is present within the property to be taken, the court shall do all of the following:

(1) Identify those measures constituting the required action with regard to the hazardous material, the probable cost of the required action, and the party that shall be designated by the court to cause the required action to be performed.

(2) Designate a trustee to monitor the completion of the required action and to hold funds, deducted from amounts that are otherwise to be paid to the defendant pursuant to this title, to defray the probable cost of the required action.

(3) Transfer to the trustee funds necessary to defray the probable cost of the required action from amounts deposited with the court pursuant to Article 1 (commencing with Section 1255.010) of Chapter 6 or pursuant to Section 1268.110. In the case of any payment to be made directly to the defendant pursuant to Section 1268.010, the plaintiff shall first pay to the trustee the amount necessary to defray the probable cost of the required action, as identified by the court, and shall pay the remainder of the judgment to the defendant. The total amount transferred or paid to the trustee pursuant to this paragraph shall not exceed an amount equal to 75 percent of the following, as applicable:

(A) Prior to entry of judgment, the amount deposited as the probable amount of compensation pursuant to Article 1 (commencing with Section 1255.010) of Chapter 6.

(B) Subsequent to entry of judgment, the fair market value of the property taken, as determined pursuant to Article 4 (commencing with Section 1263.310). If the amount determined as fair market value pursuant to that article exceeds the amount deposited pursuant to Article 1 (commencing with Section 1255.010) of Chapter 6, that excess shall be available, subject to the 75 percent limit set forth in this paragraph, for transfer to the trustee for the purposes of this paragraph or for reimbursement of the plaintiff for payments made to the trustee pursuant to this paragraph. If the amount determined as fair market value pursuant to Article 4 (commencing with Section 1263.310) is less than the amount deposited pursuant to Article 1 (commencing with Section 1255.010) of Chapter 6, the plaintiff shall be entitled to a return of amounts thereby deposited, a judgment against the defendant, or both, as necessary to ensure that the total amount transferred or paid to the trustee pursuant to this paragraph not exceed an amount equal to 75 percent of the fair market value of the property taken, as determined pursuant to Article 4 (commencing with Section 1263.310).

(4) Establish a procedure by which the trustee shall make one or more payments from the funds it receives pursuant to paragraph (3) to the party causing the required action to be performed, upon completion of all or specified portions of the required action. Any amount of those funds that remains following the completion of all of the required action shall be applied in accordance with the provisions of this title that govern the disposition of the deposit amounts referred to in paragraph (3).

(c) The actual and reasonable costs of the trustee incurred pursuant to this section shall be paid by the plaintiff.

Ca. Civ. Proc. Code § 1263.720

Repealed and added by Stats. 1995, Ch. 247, Sec. 2. Effective January 1, 1996.

Section 1263.730 - Amount available to complete required action insufficient

Where the required action is caused to be performed by the plaintiff, and the amount available to the trustee under this article is insufficient to meet the actual cost incurred by the plaintiff to complete the required action, the plaintiff may either apply to the court for a new hearing regarding identification of the probable cost, or complete the required action at its own expense and bring an action against the defendant to recover the additional costs.

Ca. Civ. Proc. Code § 1263.730

Repealed and added by Stats. 1995, Ch. 247, Sec. 2. Effective January 1, 1996.

Section 1263.740 - Presence of hazardous material not considered in appraising property

The presence of any hazardous material within a property shall not be considered in appraising the property, for purposes of Section 1263.720, pursuant to Article 1 (commencing with Section 1255.010) of Chapter 6, or pursuant to Article 4 (commencing with Section 1263.310).

Ca. Civ. Proc. Code § 1263.740

Repealed and added by Stats. 1995, Ch. 247, Sec. 2. Effective January 1, 1996.

Section 1263.750 - Remedies available to plaintiff; plaintiff entitled to compensation for benefit if plaintiff abandons proceedings

(a) Notwithstanding any action taken pursuant to this article, the plaintiff shall have available all remedies in law that are available to a purchaser of real property with respect to any cost, loss, or liability for which the plaintiff is not reimbursed under this article.

(b) If the plaintiff abandons the proceeding at any time, the plaintiff shall be entitled to compensation for the benefit, if any, conferred on the property by reason of the remedial action performed pursuant to this article. That benefit shall be applied as an offset to the amount of any entitlement to damages on the part of the defendant pursuant to Section 1268.620 or, if it exceeds the amount of those damages, shall constitute a lien upon the property, to the extent of that excess, when recorded with the county recorder in the county in which the real property is located. The lien shall contain the legal description of the real property, the assessor's parcel number, and the name of the owner of record as shown on the latest equalized assessment roll. The lien shall be enforceable upon the transfer or sale of the property, and the priority of the lien shall be as of the date of recording. In determining the amount of the benefit, if any, neither party shall have the burden of proof. For the purposes of this subdivision, "benefit" means the extent to which the remedial action has enhanced the fair market value of the property.

Ca. Civ. Proc. Code § 1263.750
Repealed and added by Stats. 1995, Ch. 247, Sec. 2. Effective January 1, 1996.

Section 1263.760 - Satisfaction of requirements of section 7267.2, Government Code

An offer by the plaintiff to purchase the property subject to this article shall be deemed to satisfy the requirements of Section 7267.2 of the Government Code.

Ca. Civ. Proc. Code § 1263.760
Repealed and added by Stats. 1995, Ch. 247, Sec. 2. Effective January 1, 1996.

Section 1263.770 - Applicability of article to school districts

This article shall only apply to the acquisition of property by school districts.

Ca. Civ. Proc. Code § 1263.770
Repealed and added by Stats. 1995, Ch. 247, Sec. 2. Effective January 1, 1996.

Chapter 10 - DIVIDED INTERESTS

Article 1 - GENERAL PROVISIONS

Section 1265.010 - Compensation for other property interests not limited by chapter

Although this chapter provides rules governing compensation for particular interests in property, it does not otherwise limit or affect the right to compensation for any other interest in property.

Ca. Civ. Proc. Code § 1265.010
Added by Stats. 1975, Ch. 1275.

Article 2 - LEASES

Section 1265.110 - Termination of lease

Where all the property subject to a lease is acquired for public use, the lease terminates.

Ca. Civ. Proc. Code § 1265.110
Added by Stats. 1975, Ch. 1275.

Section 1265.120 - Termination of lease as to part of property taken

Except as provided in Section 1265.130, where part of the property subject to a lease is acquired for public use, the lease terminates as to the part taken and remains in force as to the remainder, and the rent reserved in the lease that is allocable to the part taken is extinguished.

Ca. Civ. Proc. Code § 1265.120
Added by Stats. 1975, Ch. 1275.

Section 1265.130 - Petition to terminate lease where part of property subject to lease taken

Where part of the property subject to a lease is acquired for public use, the court may, upon petition of any party to the lease, terminate the lease if the court determines that an essential part of the property subject to the lease is taken or that the remainder of the property subject to the lease is no longer suitable for the purposes of the lease.

Ca. Civ. Proc. Code § 1265.130
Added by Stats. 1975, Ch. 1275.

Section 1265.140 - Time of termination

The termination or partial termination of a lease pursuant to this article shall be at the earlier of the following times:

(a) The time title to the property is taken by the person who will put it to the public use.

(b) The time the plaintiff is authorized to take possession of the property as stated in an order for possession.

Ca. Civ. Proc. Code § 1265.140
Added by Stats. 1975, Ch. 1275.

Section 1265.150 - Right of lessee to compensation not affected

Nothing in this article affects or impairs any right a lessee may have to compensation for the taking of his lease in whole or in part or for the taking of any other property in which he has an interest.

Ca. Civ. Proc. Code § 1265.150
Added by Stats. 1975, Ch. 1275.

Section 1265.160 - Rights and obligations of parties to lease not affected

Nothing in this article affects or impairs the rights and obligations of the parties to a lease to the extent that the lease provides for such rights and obligations in the event of the acquisition of all or a portion of the property for public use.

Ca. Civ. Proc. Code § 1265.160
Added by Stats. 1975, Ch. 1275.

Article 3 - ENCUMBRANCES

Section 1265.210 - Lien defined
As used in this article, "lien" means a mortgage, deed of trust, or other security interest in property whether arising from contract, statute, common law, or equity.

Ca. Civ. Proc. Code § 1265.210
Added by Stats. 1975, Ch. 1275.

Section 1265.220 - Lien and indebtedness secured by lien not due at time of entry of judgment
Where property acquired by eminent domain is encumbered by a lien and the indebtedness secured thereby is not due at the time of the entry of judgment, the amount of such indebtedness may be, at the option of the plaintiff, deducted from the judgment and the lien shall be continued until such indebtedness is paid; but the amount for which, as between the plaintiff and the defendant, the plaintiff is liable under Article 5 (commencing with Section 1268.410) of Chapter 11 may not be deducted from the judgment.

Ca. Civ. Proc. Code § 1265.220
Added by Stats. 1975, Ch. 1275.

Section 1265.225 - Partial taking of property secured by lien
(a) Where there is a partial taking of property encumbered by a lien, the lienholder may share in the award only to the extent determined by the court to be necessary to prevent an impairment of the security, and the lien shall continue upon the part of the property not taken as security for the unpaid portion of the indebtedness.
(b) Notwithstanding subdivision (a), the lienholder and the property owner may at any time after commencement of the proceeding agree that some or all of the award shall be apportioned to the lienholder on the indebtedness.

Ca. Civ. Proc. Code § 1265.225
Added by Stats. 1975, Ch. 1275.

Section 1265.230 - Partial taking of property encumbered by lien and portion of property taken encumbered by junior lien

(a) This section applies only where there is a partial taking of property encumbered by a lien and the part taken or some portion of it is also encumbered by a junior lien that extends to only a portion of the property encumbered by the senior lien. This section provides only for allocation of the portion of the award, if any, that will be available for payment to the junior and senior lienholders and does not provide for determination of the amount of such portion.

(b) As used in this section, "impairment of security" means the security of the lienholder remaining after the taking, if any, is of less value in proportion to the remaining indebtedness than the value of the security before the taking was in proportion to the indebtedness secured thereby.

(c) The portion of the award that will be available for payment to the senior and junior lienholders shall be allocated first to the senior lien up to the full amount of the indebtedness secured thereby and the remainder, if any, to the junior lien.

(d) If the allocation under subdivision (c) would result in an impairment of the junior lienholder's security, the allocation to the junior lien shall be adjusted so as to preserve the junior lienholder's security to the extent that the remaining amount allocated to the senior lien, if paid to the senior lienholder, would not result in an impairment of the senior lienholder's security.

(e) The amounts allocated to the senior and junior liens by this section are the amounts of indebtedness owing to such senior and junior lienholders that are secured by their respective liens on the property taken, and any other indebtedness owing to the senior or junior lienholders shall not be considered as secured by the property taken. If the plaintiff makes the election provided in Section 1265.220, the indebtedness that is deducted from the judgment is the indebtedness so determined, and the lien shall continue until that amount of indebtedness is paid.

Ca. Civ. Proc. Code § 1265.230
Added by Stats. 1975, Ch. 1275.

Section 1265.240 - Prepayment penalty not included in amount payable to lienholder

Where the property acquired for public use is encumbered by a lien, the amount payable to the lienholder shall not include any penalty for prepayment.

Ca. Civ. Proc. Code § 1265.240
Added by Stats. 1975, Ch. 1275.

Section 1265.250 - Property acquired encumbered by lien of fixed lien special assessment

(a) As used in this section:

(1) "Fixed lien special assessment" means a nonrecurring assessment levied on property in a fixed amount by a local public entity for the capital expenditure for a specific improvement, whether collectible in a lump sum or in installments.

(2) "Special annual assessment" means a recurring assessment levied on property annually in an indeterminate amount by a local public entity, whether for the capital expenditure for a specific improvement or for other purposes.

(b) If property acquired by eminent domain is encumbered by the lien of a fixed lien special assessment or of a bond representing the fixed lien special assessment:

(1) The amount of the lien shall be paid to the lienholder from the award or withheld from the award for payment pursuant to Section 1265.220.

(2) Where there is a partial taking of the property, the amount of the lien prescribed in Section 1265.225 shall be paid to the lienholder from the award, or at the option of the lienholder the applicable statutory procedure, if any, for segregation and apportionment of the lien may be invoked and the amount apportioned to the part taken shall be paid to the lienholder from the award.

(c) If property acquired by eminent domain is encumbered by the lien of a special annual assessment:

(1) The amount of the lien prorated to, but not including, the date of apportionment determined pursuant to Section 5082 of the Revenue and Taxation Code, shall be paid to the lienholder from the award. As between the plaintiff and defendant, the plaintiff is liable for the amount of the lien prorated from and including the date of apportionment determined pursuant to Section 5082 of the Revenue and Taxation Code.

(2) Where there is a partial taking of the property, the amount of the lien, reduced by the amount for which the plaintiff is liable pursuant to this paragraph, shall be paid to the lienholder from the award. As between the plaintiff and defendant, the plaintiff is liable for the amount of the lien allocable to the part taken for the current assessment year, determined to the extent practicable in the same manner and by the same method as the amount of the assessment on the property for the current assessment year was determined, prorated from and including the date of apportionment determined pursuant to Section 5082 of the Revenue and Taxation Code.

Ca. Civ. Proc. Code § 1265.250
Added by Stats. 1980, Ch. 122, Sec. 2.

Article 4 - FUTURE INTERESTS

Section 1265.410 - Acquisition violates use restriction coupled with contingent future interest granting possession upon violation

(a) Where the acquisition of property for public use violates a use restriction coupled with a contingent future interest granting a right to possession of the property upon violation of the use restriction:

(1) If violation of the use restriction was otherwise reasonably imminent, the owner of the contingent future interest is entitled to compensation for its value, if any.

(2) If violation of the use restriction was not otherwise reasonably imminent but the benefit of the use restriction was appurtenant to other property, the owner of the contingent future interest is entitled to compensation to the extent that the failure to comply with the use restriction damages the dominant premises to which the restriction was appurtenant and of which he was the owner.

(b) Where the acquisition of property for public use violates a use restriction coupled with a contingent future interest granting a right to possession of the property upon violation of the use restriction but the contingent future interest is not compensable under subdivision (a), if the use restriction is that the property be devoted to a particular charitable or public use, the compensation for the property shall be devoted to the same or similar use coupled with the same contingent future interest.

Ca. Civ. Proc. Code § 1265.410
Added by Stats. 1975, Ch. 1275.

Section 1265.420 - Acquired property subject to life tenancy

Where property acquired for public use is subject to a life tenancy, upon petition of the life tenant or any other person having an interest in the property, the court may order any of the following:

(a) An apportionment and distribution of the award based on the value of the interest of life tenant and remainderman.

(b) The compensation to be used to purchase comparable property to be held subject to the life tenancy.

(c) The compensation to be held in trust and invested and the income (and, to the extent the instrument that created the life tenancy permits, principal) to be distributed to the life tenant for the remainder of the tenancy.

(d) Such other arrangement as will be equitable under the circumstances.

Ca. Civ. Proc. Code § 1265.420
Added by Stats. 1975, Ch. 1275.

Chapter 11 - POSTJUDGMENT PROCEDURE

Article 1 - PAYMENT OF JUDGMENT; FINAL ORDER OF CONDEMNATION

Section 1268.010 - Payment of full amount required by judgment

(a) Not later than 30 days after final judgment, or 30 days after the conclusion of any other court proceedings, including any federal court proceedings, commenced by the defendant challenging the judgment or any of the condemnation proceedings, whichever date is later, the plaintiff shall pay the full amount required by the judgment.

(b) Payment shall be made by either or both of the following methods:

(1) Payment of money directly to the defendant. Any amount which the defendant has previously withdrawn pursuant to Article 2 (commencing with Section 1255.210) of Chapter 6 shall be credited as a payment to him on the judgment.

(2) Deposit of money with the court pursuant to Section 1268.110. Upon entry of judgment, a deposit made pursuant to Article 1 (commencing with Section 1255.010) of Chapter 6 is deemed to be a deposit made pursuant to Section 1268.110 if the full amount required by the judgment is deposited or paid.

Ca. Civ. Proc. Code § 1268.010

Amended by Stats. 1981, Ch. 831, Sec. 1.

Section 1268.020 - Failure to timely pay full amount required by judgment

(a) If the plaintiff fails to pay the full amount required by the judgment within the time specified in Section 1268.010, the defendant may:

(1) If the plaintiff is a public entity, enforce the judgment as provided in Division 3.6 (commencing with Section 810) of Title 1 of the Government Code.

(2) If the plaintiff is not a public entity, enforce the judgment as in a civil case.

(b) Upon noticed motion of the defendant, the court shall enter judgment dismissing the eminent domain proceeding if all of the following are established:

(1) The plaintiff failed to pay the full amount required by the judgment within the time specified in Section 1268.010.

(2) The defendant has filed in court and served upon the plaintiff, by registered or certified mail, a written notice of the plaintiff's failure to pay the full amount required by the judgment within the time specified in Section 1268.010.

(3) The plaintiff has failed for 20 days after service of the notice under paragraph (2) to pay the full amount required by the judgment in the manner provided in subdivision (b) of Section 1268.010.

(c) The defendant may elect to exercise the remedy provided by subdivision (b) without attempting to use the remedy provided by subdivision (a).

(d) As used in this section, "public entity" does not include the Regents of the University of California.

Ca. Civ. Proc. Code § 1268.020
Amended by Stats. 1980, Ch. 215, Sec. 1.

Section 1268.030 - Final order if full amount paid

(a) Upon application of any party, the court shall make a final order of condemnation if the full amount of the judgment has been paid as required by Section 1268.010 or satisfied pursuant to Section 1268.020.

(b) The final order of condemnation shall describe the property taken and identify the judgment authorizing the taking.

(c) The party upon whose application the order was made shall serve notice of the making of the order on all other parties affected thereby. Any party affected by the order may thereafter record a certified copy of the order in the office of the recorder of the county in which the property is located and shall serve notice of recordation upon all other parties affected thereby. Title to the property vests in the plaintiff upon the date of recordation.

Ca. Civ. Proc. Code § 1268.030
Added by Stats. 1975, Ch. 1275.

Article 2 - DEPOSIT AND WITHDRAWAL OF AWARD

Section 1268.110 - Deposit of full amount of award with interest after entry of judgment

(a) Except as provided in subdivision (b), the plaintiff may, at any time after entry of judgment, deposit with the court for the persons entitled thereto the full amount of the award, together with interest then due thereon, less any amounts previously paid directly to the defendants or deposited pursuant to Article 1 (commencing with Section 1255.010) of Chapter 6.

(b) A deposit may be made under this section notwithstanding an appeal, a motion for a new trial, or a motion to vacate or set aside the judgment but may not be made after the judgment has been reversed, vacated, or set aside.

(c) Any amount deposited pursuant to this article on a judgment that is later reversed, vacated, or set aside shall be deemed to be an amount deposited pursuant to Article 1 (commencing with Section 1255.010) of Chapter 6.

Ca. Civ. Proc. Code § 1268.110
Added by Stats. 1975, Ch. 1275.

Section 1268.120 - Notice of deposit

If the deposit is made under Section 1268.110 prior to apportionment of the award, the plaintiff shall serve a notice that the deposit has been made on all of the parties who have appeared in the proceeding. If the deposit is made after apportionment of the award, the plaintiff shall serve a notice that the deposit has been made on all of the parties to the proceeding determined by the order apportioning the award to have an interest in the money deposited. The notice of deposit shall state that a deposit has been made and the date and the amount of the deposit. Service of the notice shall be made in the manner provided in Section 1268.220 for the service of an order for possession. Service of an order for possession under Section 1268.220 is sufficient compliance with this section.

Ca. Civ. Proc. Code § 1268.120
Added by Stats. 1975, Ch. 1275.

Section 1268.130 - Deposit of additional amount to secure further compensation, costs and interest

At any time after the plaintiff has made a deposit upon the award pursuant to Section 1268.110, the court may, upon motion of any defendant, order the plaintiff to deposit such additional amount as the court determines to be necessary to secure payment of any further compensation, costs, or interest that may be recovered in the proceeding. After the making of such an order, the court may, on motion of any party, order an increase or a decrease in such additional amount. A defendant may withdraw the amount deposited under this section or a portion thereof only if it is determined that he is entitled to recover such amount in the proceeding.

Ca. Civ. Proc. Code § 1268.130
Added by Stats. 1975, Ch. 1275.

Section 1268.140 - Application by defendant for payment from deposit

(a) After entry of judgment, any defendant who has an interest in the property for which a deposit has been made may apply for and obtain a court order that he be paid from the deposit the amount to which he is entitled upon his filing either of the following:

(1) A satisfaction of the judgment.

(2) A receipt for the money which shall constitute a waiver by operation of law of all claims and defenses except a claim for greater compensation.

(b) If the award has not been apportioned at the time the application is made, the applicant shall give notice of the application to all the other defendants who have appeared in the proceeding and who have an interest in the property. If the award has been apportioned at the time the application is made, the applicant shall give such notice to the other defendants as the court may require.

(c) Upon objection to the withdrawal made by any party to the proceeding, the court, in its discretion, may require the applicant to file an undertaking in the same manner and upon the conditions prescribed in Section 1255.240 for withdrawal of a deposit prior to entry of judgment.

(d) If the judgment is reversed, vacated, or set aside, a defendant may withdraw a deposit only pursuant to Article 2 (commencing with Section 1255.210) of Chapter 6.

Ca. Civ. Proc. Code § 1268.140
Added by Stats. 1975, Ch. 1275.

Section 1268.150 - Money ordered deposited in state treasury or upon request in county treasury

(a) Except as provided in subdivision (b), when money is deposited as provided in this article, the court shall order the money to be deposited in the State Treasury or, upon written request of the plaintiff filed with the deposit, in the county treasury. If the money is deposited in the State Treasury pursuant to this subdivision, it shall be held, invested, deposited, and disbursed in the manner specified in Article 10 (commencing with Section 16429) of Chapter 2 of Part 2 of Division 4 of Title 2 of the Government Code, and interest earned or other increment derived from its investment shall be apportioned and disbursed in the manner specified in that article. As between the parties to the proceeding, money deposited pursuant to this subdivision shall remain at the risk of the plaintiff until paid or made payable to the defendant by order of the court.

(b) If after entry of judgment but prior to apportionment of the award the defendants are unable to agree as to the withdrawal of all or a portion of any amount deposited, the court shall upon motion of any defendant order that the amount deposited be invested in United States government obligations or interest-bearing accounts in an institution whose accounts are insured by an agency of the federal government for the benefit of the defendants who shall be entitled to the interest earned on the investments in proportion to the amount of the award they receive when the award is apportioned.

Ca. Civ. Proc. Code § 1268.150
Added by Stats. 1975, Ch. 1275.

Section 1268.160 - Withdrawal in amount in excess of amount party entitled

(a) Any amount withdrawn by a party pursuant to this article in excess of the amount to which he is entitled as finally determined in the eminent domain proceeding shall be paid to the parties entitled thereto. The court shall enter judgment accordingly.

(b) The judgment so entered shall not include interest except that any amount that is to be paid to a defendant shall include legal interest from the date of its withdrawal by another defendant.

(c) If the judgment so entered is not paid within 30 days after its entry, the court may, on motion, enter judgment against the sureties, if any, for the amount of such judgment.

(d) The court may, in its discretion and with such security as it deems appropriate, grant a party obligated to pay under this section a stay of execution for any amount to be paid to a plaintiff. Such stay of execution shall not exceed one year following entry of judgment under this section.

Ca. Civ. Proc. Code § 1268.160
Added by Stats. 1975, Ch. 1275.

Section 1268.170 - Rights not waived by making deposit

By making a deposit pursuant to this article, the plaintiff does not waive the right to appeal from the judgment, the right to move to abandon, or the right to request a new trial.

Ca. Civ. Proc. Code § 1268.170
Added by Stats. 1975, Ch. 1275.

Article 3 - POSSESSION AFTER JUDGMENT

Section 1268.210 - Application for order of possession and authorization to take possession

(a) If the plaintiff is not in possession of the property to be taken, the plaintiff may, at any time after entry of judgment, apply ex parte to the court for an order for possession, and the court shall authorize the plaintiff to take possession of the property pending conclusion of the litigation if:

(1) The judgment determines that the plaintiff is entitled to take the property; and

(2) The plaintiff has paid to or deposited for the defendants, pursuant to Article 1 (commencing with Section 1255.010) of Chapter 6 or Article 2 (commencing with Section 1268.110), an amount not less than the amount of the award, together with the interest then due thereon.

(b) The court's order shall state the date after which the plaintiff is authorized to take possession of the property. Where deposit is made, the order shall state such fact and the date and the amount of the deposit.

(c) Where the judgment is reversed, vacated, or set aside, the plaintiff may obtain possession of the property only pursuant to Article 3 (commencing with Section 1255.410) of Chapter 6.

Ca. Civ. Proc. Code § 1268.210
Added by Stats. 1975, Ch. 1275.

Section 1268.220 - Service of copy of order of possession

(a) The plaintiff shall serve a copy of the order for possession upon each defendant and his attorney, either personally or by mail:

(1) At least 30 days prior to the date possession is to be taken of property lawfully occupied by a person dwelling thereon or by a farm or business operation.

(2) At least 10 days prior to the date possession is to be taken in any case not covered by paragraph (1).

(b) A single service upon or mailing to one of several persons having a common business or residence address is sufficient.

Ca. Civ. Proc. Code § 1268.220

Added by Stats. 1975, Ch. 1275.

Section 1268.230 - Rights not waived by taking possession

By taking possession pursuant to this article, the plaintiff does not waive the right to appeal from the judgment, the right to move to abandon, or the right to request a new trial.

Ca. Civ. Proc. Code § 1268.230

Added by Stats. 1975, Ch. 1275.

Section 1268.240 - Public entity's right to exercise police power not limited

Nothing in this article limits the right of a public entity to exercise its police power in emergency situations.

Ca. Civ. Proc. Code § 1268.240

Added by Stats. 1975, Ch. 1275.

Article 4 - INTEREST

Section 1268.310 - Dates from which interest computed

The compensation awarded in the proceeding shall draw interest, computed as prescribed by Section 1268.350, from the earliest of the following dates:

(a) The date of entry of judgment.

(b) The date the plaintiff takes possession of the property.

(c) The date after which the plaintiff is authorized to take possession of the property as stated in an order for possession.

Ca. Civ. Proc. Code § 1268.310

Amended by Stats. 1986, Ch. 1372, Sec. 1.

Section 1268.311 - Computation in inverse condemnation proceeding

In any inverse condemnation proceeding in which interest is awarded, the interest shall be computed as prescribed by Section 1268.350.

Ca. Civ. Proc. Code § 1268.311

Added by Stats. 1986, Ch. 1372, Sec. 2.

Section 1268.320 - Dates computation of interest ceases

The compensation awarded in the proceeding shall cease to draw interest at the earliest of the following dates:

(a) As to any amount deposited pursuant to Article 1 (commencing with Section 1255.010) of Chapter 6 (deposit of probable compensation prior to judgment), the date such amount is withdrawn by the person entitled thereto.

(b) As to the amount deposited in accordance with Article 2 (commencing with Section 1268.110) (deposit of amount of award), the date of such deposit.

(c) As to any amount paid to the person entitled thereto, the date of such payment.

Ca. Civ. Proc. Code § 1268.320

Added by Stats. 1975, Ch. 1275.

Section 1268.330 - Value of continued possession offset against interest; rents and other income received offset against interest

If, after the date that interest begins to accrue, the defendant:

(a) Continues in actual possession of the property, the value of that possession shall be offset against the interest. For the purpose of this section, the value of possession of the property shall be presumed to be the rate of interest calculated as prescribed by Section 1268.350 on the compensation awarded. This presumption is one affecting the burden of proof.

(b) Receives rents or other income from the property attributable to the period after interest begins to accrue, the net amount of these rents and other income shall be offset against the interest.

Ca. Civ. Proc. Code § 1268.330
Amended by Stats. 1986, Ch. 1372, Sec. 3.

Section 1268.340 - Interest assessed by court

Interest, including interest accrued due to possession of property by the plaintiff prior to judgment, and any offset against interest as provided in Section 1268.330, shall be assessed by the court rather than by jury.

Ca. Civ. Proc. Code § 1268.340
Added by Stats. 1975, Ch. 1275.

Section 1268.350 - Rate of interest payable for calendar quarter

(a) As used in this section, "apportionment rate" means the apportionment rate calculated by the Controller as the rate of earnings by the Surplus Money Investment Fund for each calendar quarter.

(b) The rate of interest payable under this article for each calendar quarter, or fraction thereof, for which interest is due, shall be the apportionment rate for the immediately preceding calendar quarter.

(c) Each district office of the Department of Transportation shall quote the apportionment rate to any person upon request.

Ca. Civ. Proc. Code § 1268.350
Amended by Stats 2006 ch 311 (SB 1586),s 1, eff. 1/1/2007.

Section 1268.360 - Computation of interest payable for calendar quarter

The interest payable for each calendar quarter shall draw interest, computed as prescribed by Section 1268.350, in each succeeding calendar quarter for which interest is due.

Ca. Civ. Proc. Code § 1268.360
Amended by Stats 2006 ch 311 (SB 1586),s 2, eff. 1/1/2007.

Article 5 - PRORATION OF PROPERTY TAXES

Section 1268.410 - Liability of plaintiff

As between the plaintiff and defendant, the plaintiff is liable for any ad valorem taxes, penalties, and costs upon property acquired by eminent domain prorated from and including the date of apportionment determined pursuant to Section 5082 of the Revenue and Taxation Code.

Ca. Civ. Proc. Code § 1268.410
Amended by Stats. 1979, Ch. 31.

Section 1268.420 - Acquisition makes property exempt from taxes

(a) Except as provided in subdivision (b):

(1) If the acquisition of property by eminent domain will make the property exempt property as defined in Section 5081 of the Revenue and Taxation Code, any ad valorem taxes, penalties, or costs on the property for which the plaintiff is liable pursuant to Section 1268.410 are not collectible.

(2) If the acquisition of property by eminent domain will not make the property exempt property as defined in Section 5081 of the Revenue and Taxation Code, the plaintiff shall be deemed to be the assessee for the purposes of collection of any ad valorem taxes, penalties, and costs on the property for which the plaintiff is liable pursuant to Section 1268.410.

(b) To the extent there is a dismissal or partial dismissal of the eminent domain proceeding, the amount of any unpaid ad valorem taxes, penalties, and costs on the property for which the plaintiff would be liable pursuant to Section 1268. 410 until the entry of judgment of dismissal shall be awarded to the defendant. The amount awarded shall be paid to the tax collector from the award or, if unpaid for any reason, are collectible from the defendant.

Ca. Civ. Proc. Code § 1268.420
Repealed and added by Stats. 1979, Ch. 31.

Section 1268.430 - Liability of plaintiff if defendant has paid

(a) If the defendant has paid any amount for which, as between the plaintiff and defendant, the plaintiff is liable under this article, the plaintiff shall pay to the defendant a sum equal to such amount.

(b) The amount the defendant is entitled to be paid under this section shall be claimed in the manner provided for claiming costs and at the following times:

(1) If the plaintiff took possession of the property prior to judgment, at the time provided for claiming costs.

(2) If the plaintiff did not take possession of the property prior to judgment, not later than 30 days after the plaintiff took title to the property.

Ca. Civ. Proc. Code § 1268.430
Added by Stats. 1975, Ch. 1275.

Section 1268.440 - Refund of taxes paid on exempt property

(a) If taxes have been paid on property that is exempt property as defined in Section 5081 of the Revenue and Taxation Code, the amount of the taxes that, if unpaid, would have been subject to cancellation under Article 5 (commencing with Section 5081) of Chapter 4 of Part 9 of Division 1 of the Revenue and Taxation Code shall be deemed to be erroneously collected and shall be refunded in the manner provided in Article 1 (commencing with Section 5096) of Chapter 5 of Part 9 of Division 1 of the Revenue and Taxation Code to the person who paid the taxes.

(b) The public entity shall be deemed to be the person who paid the taxes if the public entity reimbursed the defendant for the taxes under a cost bill filed in the eminent domain proceeding pursuant to Section 1268.430. A claim for refund of taxes filed by a public entity pursuant to this section shall contain a copy of the cost bill under which taxes were reimbursed or a declaration under penalty of perjury by the public entity that the taxes were reimbursed under a cost bill.

(c) Taxes paid on either the secured or unsecured roll may be refunded pursuant to this section.

Ca. Civ. Proc. Code § 1268.440
Added by Stats. 1979, Ch. 31.

Section 1268.450 - Separate valuation of property on assessment roll

If property acquired by eminent domain does not have a separate valuation on the assessment roll, any party to the eminent domain proceeding may, at any time after the taxes on the property are subject to cancellation under Article 5 (commencing with Section 5081) of Chapter 4 of Part 9 of Division 1 of the Revenue and Taxation Code, apply to the tax collector for a separate valuation of the property in accordance with Article 3 (commencing with Section 2821) of Chapter 3 of Part 5 of Division 1 of the Revenue and Taxation Code notwithstanding any provision in that article to the contrary.

Ca. Civ. Proc. Code § 1268.450
Added by Stats. 1979, Ch. 31.

Article 6 - ABANDONMENT

Section 1268.510 - Notice of abandonment; setting abandonment aside; dismissal of proceeding

(a) At any time after the filing of the complaint and before the expiration of 30 days after final judgment, the plaintiff may wholly or partially abandon the proceeding by serving on the defendant and filing in court a written notice of such abandonment.

(b) The court may, upon motion made within 30 days after the filing of such notice, set the abandonment aside if it determines that the position of the moving party has been substantially changed to his detriment in justifiable reliance upon the proceeding and such party cannot be restored to substantially the same position as if the proceeding had not been commenced.

(c) Upon denial of a motion to set aside such abandonment or, if no such motion is filed, upon the expiration of the time for filing such a motion, the court shall, on motion of any party, enter judgment

wholly or partially dismissing the proceeding.
    Ca. Civ. Proc. Code § 1268.510
Added by Stats. 1975, Ch. 1275.

Article 7 - LITIGATION EXPENSES AND DAMAGES UPON DISMISSAL OR DEFEAT OF RIGHT TO TAKE

Section 1268.610 - Award to defendant of litigation expenses

(a) Subject to subdivisions (b) and (c), the court shall award the defendant his or her litigation expenses whenever:

    (1) The proceeding is wholly or partly dismissed for any reason.

    (2) Final judgment in the proceeding is that the plaintiff cannot acquire property it sought to acquire in the proceeding.

(b) Where there is a partial dismissal or a final judgment that the plaintiff cannot acquire a portion of the property originally sought to be acquired, or a dismissal of one or more plaintiffs pursuant to Section 1260.020, the court shall award the defendant only those litigation expenses, or portion thereof, that would not have been incurred had the property sought to be acquired following the dismissal or judgment been the property originally sought to be acquired.

(c) If the plaintiff files a notice of abandonment as to a particular defendant, or a request for dismissal of a particular defendant, and the court determines that the defendant did not own or have any interest in the property that the plaintiff sought to acquire in the proceeding, the court shall award that defendant only those litigation expenses incurred up to the time of filing the notice of abandonment or request for dismissal.

(d) Litigation expenses under this section shall be claimed in and by a cost bill to be prepared, served, filed, and taxed as in a civil action. If the proceeding is dismissed upon motion of the plaintiff, the cost bill shall be filed within 30 days after notice of entry of judgment.

Ca. Civ. Proc. Code § 1268.610
Amended by Stats 2001 ch 192 (AB 1463), s 1, eff. 1/1/2002.

Section 1268.620 - Proceeding dismissed or judgment that plaintiff cannot acquire property

If, after the defendant moves from property in compliance with an order or agreement for possession or in reasonable contemplation of its taking by the plaintiff, the proceeding is dismissed with regard to that property for any reason or there is a final judgment that the plaintiff cannot acquire that property, the court shall:

(a) Order the plaintiff to deliver possession of the property to the persons entitled to it; and

(b) Make such provision as shall be just for the payment of all damages proximately caused by the proceeding and its dismissal as to that property.

Ca. Civ. Proc. Code § 1268.620
Added by Stats. 1975, Ch. 1275.

Article 8 - COSTS

Section 1268.710 - Defendants allowed costs

The defendants shall be allowed their costs, including the costs of determining the apportionment of the award made pursuant to subdivision (b) of Section 1260.220, except that the costs of determining any issue as to title between two or more defendants shall be borne by the defendants in such proportion as the court may direct.

Ca. Civ. Proc. Code § 1268.710
Added by Stats. 1975, Ch. 1275.

Section 1268.720 - Defendant allowed costs on appeal

Unless the court otherwise orders, whether or not he is the prevailing party, the defendant in the proceeding shall be allowed his costs on appeal. This section does not apply to an appeal involving issues between defendants.

Ca. Civ. Proc. Code § 1268.720
Added by Stats. 1975, Ch. 1275.

Chapter 12 - ARBITRATION OF COMPENSATION IN ACQUISITIONS OF PROPERTY FOR PUBLIC USE

Section 1273.010 - Agreement to arbitrate

(a) Any person authorized to acquire property for public use may enter into an agreement to arbitrate any controversy as to the compensation to be made in connection with the acquisition of the property.

(b) Where property is already appropriated to a public use, the person authorized to compromise or settle the claim arising from a taking or damaging of such property for another public use may enter into an agreement to arbitrate any controversy as to the compensation to be made in connection with such taking or damaging.

(c) For the purposes of this section, in the case of a public entity, "person" refers to the particular department, officer, commission, board, or governing body authorized to acquire property on behalf of the public entity or to compromise or settle a claim arising from the taking or damaging of the entity's property.

Ca. Civ. Proc. Code § 1273.010
Added by Stats. 1975, Ch. 1275.

Section 1273.020 - Payment of arbitrator's expenses and fees, witness fees and mileage and attorney's fees

(a) Notwithstanding Sections 1283.2 and 1284.2, the party acquiring the property shall pay all of the expenses and fees of the neutral arbitrator and the statutory fees and mileage of all witnesses subpoenaed in the arbitration, together with other expenses of the arbitration incurred or approved by the neutral arbitrator, not including attorney's fees or expert witness fees or other expenses incurred by other parties for their own benefit.

(b) An agreement authorized by this chapter may require that the party acquiring the property pay reasonable attorney's fees or expert witness fees, or both, to any other party to the arbitration. If the agreement requires the payment of such fees, the amount of the fees is a matter to be determined in the arbitration proceeding unless the agreement prescribes otherwise.

(c) The party acquiring the property may pay the expenses and fees referred to in subdivisions (a) and (b) from funds available for the acquisition of the property or other funds available for the purpose.

Ca. Civ. Proc. Code § 1273.020
Added by Stats. 1975, Ch. 1275.

Section 1273.030 - Rules applicable to agreements

(a) Except as specifically provided in this chapter, agreements authorized by this chapter are subject to Title 9 (commencing with Section 1280) of this part.

(b) An agreement authorized by this chapter may be made whether or not an eminent domain proceeding has been commenced to acquire the property. If a proceeding has been commenced or is commenced, any petition or response relating to the arbitration shall be filed and determined in the proceeding.

(c) Notwithstanding Section 1281.4, an agreement authorized by this chapter does not waive or restrict the power of any person to commence and prosecute an eminent domain proceeding, including the taking of possession prior to judgment, except that, upon motion of a party to the proceeding, the court shall stay the determination of compensation until any petition for an order to arbitrate is determined and, if arbitration is ordered, until arbitration is had in accordance with the order.

(d) The effect and enforceability of an agreement authorized by this chapter is not defeated or impaired by contention or proof by any party to the agreement that the party acquiring the property pursuant to the agreement lacks the power or capacity to take the property by eminent domain.

(e) Notwithstanding the rules as to venue provided by Sections 1292 and 1292.2, any petition relating to arbitration authorized by this chapter shall be filed in the superior court in the county in which the property, or any portion of the property, is located.

Ca. Civ. Proc. Code § 1273.030
Added by Stats. 1975, Ch. 1275.

Section 1273.040 - Terms and conditions specified in agreement; abandonment

(a) Except as provided in subdivision (b), an agreement authorized by this chapter may specify the terms and conditions under which the party acquiring the property may abandon the acquisition, the arbitration proceeding, and any eminent domain proceeding that may have been, or may be, filed. Unless the agreement provides that the acquisition may not be abandoned, the party acquiring the property may abandon the acquisition, the arbitration proceeding, and any eminent domain proceeding at any time not later than the time for filing and serving a petition or response to vacate an arbitration award under Sections 1288, 1288.2, and 1290.6.

(b) If the proceeding to acquire the property is abandoned after the arbitration agreement is executed, the party from whom the property was to be acquired is entitled to recover (1) all expenses reasonably and necessarily incurred (i) in preparing for the arbitration proceeding and for any judicial proceedings in connection with the acquisition of the property, (ii) during the arbitration proceeding and during any judicial proceedings in connection with the acquisition, and (iii) in any subsequent judicial proceedings in connection with the acquisition and (2) reasonable attorney's fees, appraisal fees, and fees for the services of other experts where such fees were reasonably and necessarily incurred to protect his interests in connection with the acquisition of the property. Unless the agreement otherwise provides, the amount of such expenses and fees shall be determined by arbitration in accordance with the agreement.

Ca. Civ. Proc. Code § 1273.040
Added by Stats. 1975, Ch. 1275.

Section 1273.050 - Acknowledgment and recording of agreement

(a) An agreement authorized by this chapter may be acknowledged and recorded, and rerecorded, in the same manner and with the same effect as a conveyance of real property except that two years after the date the agreement is recorded, or rerecorded, the record ceases to be notice to any person for any purpose.

(b) In lieu of recording the agreement, there may be recorded a memorandum thereof, executed by the parties to the agreement, containing at least the following information: the names of the parties to the agreement, a description of the property, and a statement that an arbitration agreement affecting such property has been entered into pursuant to this chapter. Such memorandum when acknowledged and recorded, or rerecorded, in the same manner as a conveyance of real property has the same effect as if the agreement itself were recorded or rerecorded.

Ca. Civ. Proc. Code § 1273.050
Added by Stats. 1975, Ch. 1275.

Title 8 - CHANGE OF NAMES

Section 1275 - Superior court jurisdiction
Applications for change of names must be determined by the Superior Courts.

Ca. Civ. Proc. Code § 1275
Amended by Stats. 1983, Ch. 486, Sec. 1.

Section 1276 - Applications generally
(a)

(1) All applications for change of names shall be made to the superior court of the county where the person whose name is proposed to be changed resides, except as specified in subdivision (e) or (g), either (A) by petition signed by the person or, if the person is under 18 years of age, by one of the person's parents, by any guardian of the person, or as specified in subdivision (e), or, if both parents are deceased and there is no guardian of the person, then by some near relative or friend of the person, or (B) as provided in Section 7638 of the Family Code.

(2) The petition or pleading shall specify the place of birth and residence of the person, the person's present name, the name proposed, and the reason for the change of name.

(b) In a proceeding for a change of name commenced by the filing of a petition, if the person whose name is to be changed is under 18 years of age, the petition shall, if neither parent of the person has signed the petition, name, as far as known to the person proposing the name change, the parents of the person and their place of residence, if living, or, if neither parent is living, near relatives of the person, and their place of residence.

(c) In a proceeding for a change of name commenced by the filing of a petition, if the person whose name is proposed to be changed is under 18 years of age and the petition is signed by only one parent, the petition shall specify the address, if known, of the other parent if living. If the petition is signed by a guardian, the petition shall specify the name and address, if known, of the parent or parents, if living, or the grandparents, if the addresses of both parents are unknown or if both parents are deceased, of the person whose name is proposed to be changed.

(d) In a proceeding for a change of name commenced by the filing of a petition, if the person whose name is proposed to be changed is 12 years of age or older, has been relinquished to an adoption agency by the person's parent or parents, and has not been legally adopted, the petition shall be signed by the person and the adoption agency to which the person was relinquished. The near relatives of the person and their place of residence shall not be included in the petition unless they are known to the person whose name is proposed to be changed.

(e) All petitions for the change of the name of a minor submitted by a guardian appointed by the juvenile court or the probate court, by a court-appointed dependency attorney appointed as guardian ad litem pursuant to rules adopted under Section 326.5 of the Welfare and Institutions Code, or by an attorney for a minor who is alleged or adjudged to be a person described in Section 601 or 602 of the Welfare and Institutions Code shall be made in the court having jurisdiction over the minor. All petitions for the change of name of a nonminor dependent may be made in the juvenile court.

(f) If the petition is signed by a guardian, the petition shall specify relevant information regarding the guardianship, the likelihood that the child will remain under the guardian's care until the child reaches the age of majority, and information suggesting that the child will not likely be returned to the custody of the child's parents.

(g)

(1) On or after January 1, 2023, an application for a change of name may be made to a superior court for a person whose name is proposed to be changed, even if the person does not reside within the State of California, if the person is seeking to change their name on at least one of the following documents:

(A) A birth certificate that was issued within this state to the person whose name is proposed to be changed.

(B) A birth certificate that was issued within this state to the legal child of the person whose name is proposed to be changed.

(C) A marriage license and certificate or a confidential marriage license and certificate that was issued within this state to the person whose name is proposed to be changed.

(2) For the purposes of this subdivision, the superior court in the county where the birth under subparagraph (A) or (B) of paragraph (1) occurred or marriage under subparagraph (C) of paragraph (1) was entered shall be a proper venue for the proceeding. The name change shall be adjudicated in accordance with California law.

Ca. Civ. Proc. Code § 1276
Amended by Stats 2021 ch 577 (AB 218),s 1.5, eff. 1/1/2022.
Amended by Stats 2021 ch 401 (AB 1578),s 7, eff. 1/1/2022.
Amended by Stats 2018 ch 776 (AB 3250),s 9, eff. 1/1/2019.
Amended by Stats 2006 ch 567 (AB 2303),s 10, eff. 1/1/2007.
Amended by Stats 2000 ch 111 (AB 2155), s 1, eff. 1/1/2001.

Section 1277 - Order to show cause; publication; participant in address confidentiality program; participant in state Witness Relocation and Assistance Program; application part of Uniform Parentage Act action; guardian files petition

(a)

(1) If a proceeding for a change of name is commenced by the filing of a petition, except as provided in subdivisions (b), (c), (d), and (f), or Section 1277.5, the court shall thereupon make an order reciting the filing of the petition, the name of the person by whom it is filed, and the name proposed. The order shall direct all persons interested in the matter to appear before the court at a time and place specified, which shall be not less than 6 weeks nor more than 12 weeks from the time of making the order, unless the court orders a different time, to show cause why the application for change of name should not be granted. The order shall direct all persons interested in the matter to make known any objection that they may have to the granting of the petition for change of name by filing a written objection, which includes the reasons for the objection, with the court at least two court days before the matter is scheduled to be heard and by appearing in court at the hearing to show cause why the petition for change of name should not be granted. The order shall state that, if no written objection is timely filed, the court may grant the petition without a hearing.

(2)

(A) A copy of the order to show cause shall be published pursuant to Section 6064 of the Government Code in a newspaper of general circulation to be designated in the order published in the county. If a newspaper of general circulation is not published in the county, a copy of the order to show cause shall be posted by the clerk of the court in three of the most public places in the county in which the court is located, for a like period. Proof shall be made to the satisfaction of the court of this publication or posting at the time of the hearing of the application.

(B)

(i) On or after January 1, 2023, if the person whose name is proposed to be changed does not live in the county where the petition is filed, pursuant to subdivision (g) of Section 1276, the copy of the order to show cause shall be published pursuant to Section 6064 of the Government Code in a newspaper of general circulation published in the county of the person's residence. If a newspaper of general circulation is not published in the county of the person's residence, a copy of the order to show cause shall be posted by the clerk of the court in the county of the person's residence or a similarly situated local official in three of the most public places in the county of the person's residence, for a like period. If the place where the person seeking the name change lives does not have counties, publication shall be made according to the requirements of this paragraph in the local subdivision or territory of the person's residence. Proof shall be made to the satisfaction of the court of this publication or posting at the time of the hearing of the application.

(ii) If the person is unable to publish or post a copy of the order to show cause pursuant to clause (i), the court may allow an alternate method of publication or posting or may waive this requirement after sufficient evidence of diligent efforts to publish or post a copy of the order has been submitted to the satisfaction of the court.

(3) Four weekly publications shall be sufficient publication of the order to show cause. If the order is published in a daily newspaper, publication once a week for four successive weeks shall be sufficient.

(4) If a petition has been filed for a minor by a parent and the other parent, if living, does not join in consenting thereto, the petitioner shall cause, not less than 30 days before the hearing, to be served notice of the time and place of the hearing or a copy of the order to show cause on the other parent pursuant to Section 413.10, 414.10, 415.10, or 415.40. If notice of the hearing cannot reasonably be accomplished pursuant to Section 415.10 or 415.40, the court may order that notice be given in a manner that the court determines is reasonably calculated to give actual notice to the nonconsenting parent. In that case, if the court determines that notice by publication is reasonably calculated to give actual notice to the nonconsenting parent, the court may determine that publication of the order to show cause pursuant to this subdivision is sufficient notice to the nonconsenting parent.

(b)

(1) If the petition for a change of name alleges a reason or circumstance described in paragraph (2), and the petitioner has established that the petitioner is an active participant in the address confidentiality program created pursuant to Chapter 3.1 (commencing with Section 6205) of Division 7 of Title 1 of the Government Code, and that the name the petitioner is seeking to acquire is on file with the Secretary of State, the action for a change of name is exempt from the requirement for publication of the order to show cause under subdivision (a), and the petition and the order of the court shall, in lieu of reciting the proposed name, indicate that the proposed name is confidential and is on file with the Secretary of State pursuant to the provisions of the address confidentiality program.

(2) The procedure described in paragraph (1) applies to petitions alleging any of the following reasons or circumstances:

(A) To avoid domestic violence, as defined in Section 6211 of the Family Code.

(B) To avoid stalking, as defined in Section 646.9 of the Penal Code.

(C) To avoid sexual assault, as defined in Section 1036.2 of the Evidence Code.

(D) To avoid human trafficking, as defined in Section 236.1 of the Penal Code.

(3) For any petition under this subdivision, the current legal name of the petitioner shall be kept confidential by the court and shall not be published or posted in the court's calendars, indexes, or register of actions, as required by Article 7 (commencing with Section 69840) of Chapter 5 of Title 8 of the Government Code, or by any means or in any public forum, including a hardcopy or an electronic copy, or any other type of public media or display.

(4) Notwithstanding paragraph (3), the court may, at the request of the petitioner, issue an order reciting the name of the petitioner at the time of the filing of the petition and the new legal name of the petitioner as a result of the court's granting of the petition.

(5) A petitioner may request that the court file the petition and any other papers associated with the proceeding under seal. The court may consider the request at the same time as the petition for name change, and may grant the request in any case in which the court finds that all of the following factors apply:

(A) There exists an overriding interest that overcomes the right of public access to the record.

(B) The overriding interest supports sealing the record.

(C) A substantial probability exists that the overriding interest will be prejudiced if the record is not sealed.

(D) The proposed order to seal the records is narrowly tailored.

(E) No less restrictive means exist to achieve the overriding interest.

(c) If the petition is filed for a minor or nonminor dependent who is under the jurisdiction of the juvenile court, the action for a change of name is exempt from the requirement for publication of the order to show cause under subdivision (a).

(d) A proceeding for a change of name for a witness participating in the state Witness Relocation and Assistance Program established by Title 7.5 (commencing with Section 14020) of Part 4 of the Penal Code who has been approved for the change of name by the program is exempt from the requirement for publication of the order to show cause under subdivision (a).

(e) If an application for change of name is brought as part of an action under the Uniform Parentage Act (Part 3 (commencing with Section 7600) of Division 12 of the Family Code), whether as part of a petition or cross-complaint or as a separate order to show cause in a pending action thereunder, service of the application shall be made upon all other parties to the action in a like manner as prescribed for the service of a summons, as set forth in Article 3 (commencing with Section 415.10) of Chapter 4 of Title 5 of Part 2. Upon the setting of a hearing on the issue, notice of the hearing shall be given to all parties in the action in a like manner and within the time limits prescribed generally for the type of hearing (whether trial or order to show cause) at which the issue of the change of name is to be decided.

(f) If a guardian files a petition to change the name of the guardian's minor ward pursuant to Section 1276:

(1) The guardian shall provide notice of the hearing to any living parent of the minor by personal service at least 30 days before the hearing.

(2) If either or both parents are deceased or cannot be located, the guardian shall cause, not less than 30 days before the hearing, to be served a notice of the time and place of the hearing or a copy of the order to show cause on the child's grandparents, if living, pursuant to Section 413.10, 414.10, 415.10, or 415.40.

Ca. Civ. Proc. Code § 1277

Amended by Stats 2021 ch 577 (AB 218),s 2.5, eff. 1/1/2022.
Amended by Stats 2021 ch 401 (AB 1578),s 8, eff. 1/1/2022.
Amended by Stats 2018 ch 818 (AB 2201),s 1, eff. 1/1/2019.
Amended by Stats 2018 ch 776 (AB 3250),s 10, eff. 1/1/2019.
Added by Stats 2017 ch 853 (SB 179),s 4, eff. 1/1/2018.

Section 1277.5 - Name change to conform to gender identity

(a)

(1) If a proceeding for a change of name to conform the petitioner's name to the petitioner's gender identity is commenced by the filing of a petition, the court shall thereupon make an order reciting the filing of the petition, the name of the person by whom it is filed, and the name proposed. The order shall direct all persons interested in the matter to make known any objection to the change of name by filing a written objection, which includes any reasons for the objection, within six weeks of the making of the order, and shall state that if no objection showing good cause to oppose the name change is timely filed, the court shall, without hearing, enter the order that the change of name is granted.

(2) If a petition is filed to change the name of a minor to conform to gender identity that does not include the signatures of both living parents, the petition and the order to show cause made in accordance with paragraph (1) shall be served on the parent who did not sign the petition, pursuant to Section 413.10, 414.10, 415.10, or 415.40, within 30 days from the date on which the order is made by the court. If service cannot reasonably be accomplished pursuant to Section 415.10 or 415.40, the court may order that service be accomplished in a manner that the court determines is reasonably calculated to give actual notice to the parent who did not sign the petition.

(b) The proceeding for a change of name to conform the petitioner's name to the petitioner's gender identity is exempt from any requirement for publication.

(c) A hearing date shall not be set in the proceeding unless an objection is timely filed and shows good cause for opposing the name change. Objections based solely on concerns that the proposed change is not the petitioner's actual gender identity or gender assigned at birth shall not constitute good cause. At the hearing, the court may examine under oath any of the petitioners, remonstrants, or other persons touching the petition or application, and may make an order changing the name or dismissing the

petition or application as the court may deem right and proper.
Ca. Civ. Proc. Code § 1277.5
Amended by Stats 2018 ch 776 (AB 3250),s 11, eff. 1/1/2019.
Added by Stats 2017 ch 853 (SB 179),s 5, eff. 1/1/2018.

Section 1278 - Hearing
(a)

(1) Except as provided in subdivisions (c) and (d), the petition or application shall be heard at the time designated by the court, only if objections are filed by a person who can, in those objections, show to the court good cause against the change of name. At the hearing, the court may examine on oath any of the petitioners, remonstrants, or other persons touching the petition or application, and may make an order changing the name, or dismissing the petition or application, as the court may deem right and proper.

(2) If no objection is filed at least two court days before the date set for hearing, the court may, without hearing, enter the order that the change of name is granted.
(b) If the provisions of subdivision (b) of Section 1277 apply, the court shall not disclose the proposed name unless the court finds by clear and convincing evidence that the allegations of domestic violence, stalking, or sexual assault in the petition are false.
(c) If the application for a change of name is brought as part of an action under the Uniform Parentage Act (Part 3 (commencing with Section 7600) of Division 12 of the Family Code), the hearing on the issue of the change of name shall be conducted pursuant to statutes and rules of court governing those proceedings, whether the hearing is conducted upon an order to show cause or upon trial.
(d) If the petition for a change of name is filed by a guardian on behalf of a minor ward, the court shall first find that the ward is likely to remain in the guardian's care until the age of majority and that the ward is not likely to be returned to the custody of the parents. Upon making those findings, the court shall consider the petition and may grant the petition only if it finds that the proposed name change is in the best interest of the child.

(e) This section shall become operative on September 1, 2018.

Ca. Civ. Proc. Code § 1278

Added by Stats 2017 ch 853 (SB 179),s 7, eff. 1/1/2018.

Section 1278.5 - Parents do not join in consent in proceeding to change minor's name

In any proceeding pursuant to this title in which a petition has been filed to change the name of a minor, and both parents, if living, do not join in consent, the court may deny the petition in whole or in part if it finds that any portion of the proposed name change is not in the best interest of the child.

Ca. Civ. Proc. Code § 1278.5

Amended by Stats 2006 ch 567 (AB 2303),s 13, eff. 1/1/2007.

Section 1279 - [Repealed]

Ca. Civ. Proc. Code § 1279

Repealed by Stats 2000 ch 506 (SB 1350), s 4, eff. 1/1/2001.

Section 1279.5 - Common law right not abrogated; petition by prisoners; petition by persons required to register as sex offenders

(a) Except as provided in subdivision (e) or (f), this title does not abrogate the common law right of a person to change his or her name.

(b) A person under the jurisdiction of the Department of Corrections and Rehabilitation or sentenced to county jail has the right to petition the court to obtain a name or gender change pursuant to this title or Article 7 (commencing with Section 103425) of Chapter 11 of Part 1 of Division 102 of the Health and Safety Code.

(c) A person under the jurisdiction of the Department of Corrections and Rehabilitation shall provide a copy of the petition for a name change to the department, in a manner prescribed by the department, at the time the petition is filed. A person sentenced to county jail shall provide a copy of the petition for name change to the sheriff's department, in a manner prescribed by the department, at the time the petition is filed.

(d) In all documentation of a person under the jurisdiction of the Department of Corrections and Rehabilitation or imprisoned within a county jail, the new name of a person who obtains a name change shall be used, and prior names shall be listed as an alias.

(e) Notwithstanding any other law, a court shall deny a petition for a name change pursuant to this title made by a person who is required to register as a sex offender under Section 290 of the Penal Code, unless the court determines that it is in the best interest of justice to grant the petition and that doing so will not adversely affect the public safety. If a petition for a name change is granted for an individual required to register as a sex offender, the individual shall, within five working days, notify the chief of police of the city in which he or she is domiciled, or the sheriff of the county if he or she is domiciled in an unincorporated area, and additionally with the chief of police of a campus of a University of California or California State University if he or she is domiciled upon the campus or in any of its facilities.

(f) For the purpose of this section, the court shall use the California Law Enforcement Telecommunications System (CLETS) and Criminal Justice Information System (CJIS) to determine whether or not an applicant for a name change is required to register as a sex offender pursuant to Section 290 of the Penal Code. Each person applying for a name change shall declare under penalty of perjury that he or she is not required to register as a sex offender pursuant to Section 290 of the Penal Code. If a court is not equipped with CLETS or CJIS, the clerk of the court shall contact an appropriate local law enforcement agency, which shall determine whether or not the petitioner is required to register as a sex offender pursuant to Section 290 of the Penal Code.

(g) This section shall become operative on September 1, 2018.

Ca. Civ. Proc. Code § 1279.5

Added by Stats 2017 ch 856 (SB 310),s 3, eff. 1/1/2018.

Section 1279.6 - Prohibited acts by trade or business

No person engaged in a trade or business of any kind or in the provision of a service of any kind shall do any of the following:

(a) Refuse to do business with a person, or refuse to provide the service to a person, regardless of the person's marital status, because he or she has chosen to use or regularly uses his or her birth name, former name, or name adopted upon solemnization of marriage or registration of domestic partnership.

(b) Impose, as a condition of doing business with a person, or as a condition of providing the service to a person, a requirement that the person, regardless of his or her marital status, use a name other than his or her birth name, former name, or name adopted upon solemnization of marriage or registration of domestic partnership, if the person has chosen to use or regularly uses that name.

Ca. Civ. Proc. Code § 1279.6

Amended by Stats 2007 ch 567 (AB 102),s 3, eff. 1/1/2008.

Title 9 - ARBITRATION

Chapter 1 - GENERAL PROVISIONS

Section 1280 - Definitions

As used in this title:

(a) "Agreement" includes, but is not limited to, agreements providing for valuations, appraisals, and similar proceedings and agreements between employers and employees or between their respective representatives.

(b) "Award" includes, but is not limited to, an award made pursuant to an agreement not in writing.

(c) "Consumer" means an individual who seeks, uses, or acquires, by purchase or lease, any goods or services for personal, family, or household purposes.

(d) "Controversy" means any question arising between parties to an agreement whether the question is one of law or of fact or both.

(e) "Drafting party" means the company or business that included a predispute arbitration provision in a contract with a consumer or employee. The term includes any third party relying upon, or otherwise subject to the arbitration provision, other than the employee or consumer.

(f) "Employee" means any current employee, former employee, or applicant for employment. The term includes any person who is, was, or who claims to have been misclassified as an independent contractor or otherwise improperly placed into a category other than employee or applicant for employment.

(g) "Neutral arbitrator" means an arbitrator who is (1) selected jointly by the parties or by the arbitrators selected by the parties, or (2) appointed by the court when the parties or the arbitrators selected by the parties fail to select an arbitrator who was to be selected jointly by the parties.

(h) "Party to the arbitration" means a party to the arbitration agreement, including any of the following:

(1) A party who seeks to arbitrate a controversy pursuant to the agreement.

(2) A party against whom such arbitration is sought pursuant to the agreement.

(3) A party who is made a party to the arbitration by order of the neutral arbitrator upon that party's application, upon the application of any other party to the arbitration, or upon the neutral arbitrator's own determination.

(i) "Written agreement" includes a written agreement that has been extended or renewed by an oral or implied agreement.

Ca. Civ. Proc. Code § 1280

Amended by Stats 2019 ch 870 (SB 707),s 2, eff. 1/1/2020.

Section 1280.2 - Reference to title applies to amendments and additions

Whenever reference is made in this title to any portion of the title or of any other law of this State, the reference applies to all amendments and additions thereto now or hereafter made.

Ca. Civ. Proc. Code § 1280.2

Repealed and added by Stats. 1961, Ch. 461.

Chapter 2 - ENFORCEMENT OF ARBITRATION AGREEMENTS

Section 1281 - Generally

A written agreement to submit to arbitration an existing controversy or a controversy thereafter arising is valid, enforceable and irrevocable, save upon such grounds as exist for the revocation of any contract.

Ca. Civ. Proc. Code § 1281

Repealed and added by Stats. 1961, Ch. 461.

Section 1281.1 - Request to arbitrate deemed made pursuant to written agreement

For the purposes of this article, any request to arbitrate made pursuant to subdivision (a) of Section 1299.4 shall be considered as made pursuant to a written agreement to submit a controversy to arbitration.

Ca. Civ. Proc. Code § 1281.1

Added by Stats 2000 ch 906 (SB 402), s 1, eff. 1/1/2001.

Section 1281.12 - Time limitations contained in agreement tolled by commencement of civil action by party to agreement

If an arbitration agreement requires that arbitration of a controversy be demanded or initiated by a party to the arbitration agreement within a period of time, the commencement of a civil action by that party based upon that controversy, within that period of time, shall toll the applicable time limitations contained in the arbitration agreement with respect to that controversy, from the date the civil action is commenced until 30 days after a final determination by the court that the party is required to arbitrate the controversy, or 30 days after the final termination of the civil action that was commenced and initiated the tolling, whichever date occurs first.

Ca. Civ. Proc. Code § 1281.12

Added by Stats 2006 ch 266 (AB 1553),s 1, eff. 1/1/2007.

Section 1281.2 - Grounds for not ordering parties to arbitrate controversy

On petition of a party to an arbitration agreement alleging the existence of a written agreement to arbitrate a controversy and that a party to the agreement refuses to arbitrate that controversy, the court shall order the petitioner and the respondent to arbitrate the controversy if it determines that an agreement to arbitrate the controversy exists, unless it determines that:

(a) The right to compel arbitration has been waived by the petitioner; or

(b) Grounds exist for rescission of the agreement.

(c) A party to the arbitration agreement is also a party to a pending court action or special proceeding with a third party, arising out of the same transaction or series of related transactions and there is a possibility of conflicting rulings on a common issue of law or fact. For purposes of this section, a pending court action or special proceeding includes an action or proceeding initiated by the party refusing to arbitrate after the petition to compel arbitration has been filed, but on or before the date of the hearing on the petition. This subdivision shall not be applicable to an agreement to arbitrate disputes as to the professional negligence of a health care provider made pursuant to Section 1295.

(d) The petitioner is a state or federally chartered depository institution that, on or after January 1, 2018, is seeking to apply a written agreement to arbitrate, contained in a contract consented to by a respondent consumer, to a purported contractual relationship with that respondent consumer that was created by the petitioner fraudulently without the respondent consumer's consent and by unlawfully using the respondent consumer's personal identifying information, as defined in Section 1798.92 of the Civil Code. If the court determines that a written agreement to arbitrate a controversy exists, an order to arbitrate that controversy may not be refused on the ground that the petitioner's contentions lack substantive merit.

If the court determines that there are other issues between the petitioner and the respondent which are not subject to arbitration and which are the subject of a pending action or special proceeding between the petitioner and the respondent and that a determination of such issues may make the arbitration unnecessary, the court may delay its order to arbitrate until the determination of such other issues or until such earlier time as the court specifies.

If the court determines that a party to the arbitration is also a party to litigation in a pending court action or special proceeding with a third party as set forth under subdivision (c), the court (1) may refuse to enforce the arbitration agreement and may order intervention or joinder of all parties in a single action or special proceeding; (2) may order intervention or joinder as to all or only certain issues; (3) may order arbitration among the parties who have agreed to arbitration and stay the pending court action or special proceeding pending the outcome of the arbitration proceeding; or (4) may stay arbitration pending the outcome of the court action or special proceeding.

Ca. Civ. Proc. Code § 1281.2
Amended by Stats 2018 ch 106 (AB 3247),s 1, eff. 1/1/2019.
Amended by Stats 2017 ch 480 (SB 33),s 1, eff. 1/1/2018.

Section 1281.3 - Consolidation of separate arbitration proceedings

A party to an arbitration agreement may petition the court to consolidate separate arbitration proceedings, and the court may order consolidation of separate arbitration proceedings when:
(1) Separate arbitration agreements or proceedings exist between the same parties; or one party is a party to a separate arbitration agreement or proceeding with a third party; and
(2) The disputes arise from the same transactions or series of related transactions; and
(3) There is common issue or issues of law or fact creating the possibility of conflicting rulings by more than one arbitrator or panel of arbitrators. If all of the applicable arbitration agreements name the same arbitrator, arbitration panel, or arbitration tribunal, the court, if it orders consolidation, shall order all matters to be heard before the arbitrator, panel, or tribunal agreed to by the parties. If the applicable arbitration agreements name separate

arbitrators, panels, or tribunals, the court, if it orders consolidation, shall, in the absence of an agreed method of selection by all parties to the consolidated arbitration, appoint an arbitrator in accord with the procedures set forth in Section 1281.6.

In the event that the arbitration agreements in consolidated proceedings contain inconsistent provisions, the court shall resolve such conflicts and determine the rights and duties of the various parties to achieve substantial justice under all the circumstances. The court may exercise its discretion under this section to deny consolidation of separate arbitration proceedings or to consolidate separate arbitration proceedings only as to certain issues, leaving other issues to be resolved in separate proceedings.

This section shall not be applicable to an agreement to arbitrate disputes as to the professional negligence of a health care provider made pursuant to Section 1295.

Ca. Civ. Proc. Code § 1281.3
Added by Stats. 1978, Ch. 260.

Section 1281.4 - Stay of action or proceeding until arbitration had in accordance with order or issue to arbitrate determined

If a court of competent jurisdiction, whether in this State or not, has ordered arbitration of a controversy which is an issue involved in an action or proceeding pending before a court of this State, the court in which such action or proceeding is pending shall, upon motion of a party to such action or proceeding, stay the action or proceeding until an arbitration is had in accordance with the order to arbitrate or until such earlier time as the court specifies.

If an application has been made to a court of competent jurisdiction, whether in this State or not, for an order to arbitrate a controversy which is an issue involved in an action or proceeding pending before a court of this State and such application is undetermined, the court in which such action or proceeding is pending shall, upon motion of a party to such action or proceeding, stay the action or proceeding until the application for an order to arbitrate is determined and, if arbitration of such controversy is ordered, until an arbitration is had in accordance with the order to arbitrate or until such earlier time as the court specifies.

If the issue which is the controversy subject to arbitration is severable, the stay may be with respect to that issue only.

Ca. Civ. Proc. Code § 1281.4
Added by Stats. 1961, Ch. 461.

Section 1281.5 - Arbitration by claimant to enforce lien

(a) Any person who proceeds to record and enforce a claim of lien by commencement of an action pursuant to Chapter 4 (commencing with Section 8400) of Title 2 of Part 6 of Division 4 of the Civil Code, does not thereby waive any right of arbitration the person may have pursuant to a written agreement to arbitrate, if, in filing an action to enforce the claim of lien, the claimant does either of the following:

(1) Includes an allegation in the complaint that the claimant does not intend to waive any right of arbitration, and intends to move the court, within 30 days after service of the summons and complaint, for an order to stay further proceedings in the action.

(2) At the same time that the complaint is filed, the claimant files an application that the action be stayed pending the arbitration of any issue, question, or dispute that is claimed to be arbitrable under the agreement and that is relevant to the action to enforce the claim of lien.

(b) Within 30 days after service of the summons and complaint, the claimant shall file and serve a motion and notice of motion pursuant to Section 1281.4 to stay the action pending the arbitration of any issue, question, or dispute that is claimed to be arbitrable under the agreement and that is relevant to the action to enforce the claim of lien. The failure of a claimant to comply with this subdivision is a waiver of the claimant's right to compel arbitration.

(c) The failure of a defendant to file a petition pursuant to Section 1281.2 at or before the time the defendant answers the complaint filed pursuant to subdivision (a) is a waiver of the defendant's right to compel arbitration.

Ca. Civ. Proc. Code § 1281.5

Amended by Stats 2010 ch 697 (SB 189),s 25, eff. 1/1/2011, op.
7/1/2012.

Amended by Stats 2003 ch 22 (SB 113), eff. 7/1/2003.

Amended by Stats 2002 ch 784 (SB 1316),s 82, eff. 1/1/2003.

Section 1281.6 - Method of appointing arbitrator; petition made to court to appoint neutral arbitrator

If the arbitration agreement provides a method of appointing an arbitrator, that method shall be followed. If the arbitration agreement does not provide a method for appointing an arbitrator, the parties to the agreement who seek arbitration and against whom arbitration is sought may agree on a method of appointing an arbitrator and that method shall be followed. In the absence of an agreed method, or if the agreed method fails or for any reason cannot be followed, or when an arbitrator appointed fails to act and his or her successor has not been appointed, the court, on petition of a party to the arbitration agreement, shall appoint the arbitrator. When a petition is made to the court to appoint a neutral arbitrator, the court shall nominate five persons from lists of persons supplied jointly by the parties to the arbitration or obtained from a governmental agency concerned with arbitration or private disinterested association concerned with arbitration. The parties to the agreement who seek arbitration and against whom arbitration is sought may within five days of receipt of notice of the nominees from the court jointly select the arbitrator whether or not the arbitrator is among the nominees. If the parties fail to select an arbitrator within the five-day period, the court shall appoint the arbitrator from the nominees.

Ca. Civ. Proc. Code § 1281.6

Amended by Stats 2001 ch 362 (SB 475), s 3, eff. 1/1/2002.

Section 1281.7 - Petition filed in lieu of answer to complaint

A petition pursuant to Section 1281.2 may be filed in lieu of filing an answer to a complaint. The petitioning defendant shall have 15 days after any denial of the petition to plead to the complaint.

Ca. Civ. Proc. Code § 1281.7

Added by Stats. 1987, Ch. 1080, Sec. 9.

Section 1281.8 - Application for provisional remedy in connection with arbitrable controversy

(a) As used in this section, "provisional remedy" includes the following:

(1) Attachments and temporary protective orders issued pursuant to Title 6.5 (commencing with Section 481.010) of Part 2.

(2) Writs of possession issued pursuant to Article 2 (commencing with Section 512.010) of Chapter 2 of Title 7 of Part 2.

(3) Preliminary injunctions and temporary restraining orders issued pursuant to Section 527.

(4) Receivers appointed pursuant to Section 564.

(b) A party to an arbitration agreement may file in the court in the county in which an arbitration proceeding is pending, or if an arbitration proceeding has not commenced, in any proper court, an application for a provisional remedy in connection with an arbitrable controversy, but only upon the ground that the award to which the applicant may be entitled may be rendered ineffectual without provisional relief. The application shall be accompanied by a complaint or by copies of the demand for arbitration and any response thereto. If accompanied by a complaint, the application shall also be accompanied by a statement stating whether the party is or is not reserving the party's right to arbitration.

(c) A claim by the party opposing issuance of a provisional remedy, that the controversy is not subject to arbitration, shall not be grounds for denial of any provisional remedy.

(d) An application for a provisional remedy under subdivision (b) shall not operate to waive any right of arbitration which the applicant may have pursuant to a written agreement to arbitrate, if, at the same time as the application for a provisional remedy is presented, the applicant also presents to the court an application that all other proceedings in the action be stayed pending the arbitration of any issue, question, or dispute which is claimed to be arbitrable under the agreement and which is relevant to the action pursuant to which the provisional remedy is sought.

Ca. Civ. Proc. Code § 1281.8
Added by Stats. 1989, Ch. 470, Sec. 2.

Section 1281.85 - Ethical standards for neutral arbitrators

(a) Beginning July 1, 2002, a person serving as a neutral arbitrator pursuant to an arbitration agreement shall comply with the ethics standards for arbitrators adopted by the Judicial Council pursuant to this section. The Judicial Council shall adopt ethical standards for all neutral arbitrators effective July 1, 2002. These standards shall be consistent with the standards established for arbitrators in the judicial arbitration program and may expand but may not limit the disclosure and disqualification requirements established by this chapter. The standards shall address the disclosure of interests, relationships, or affiliations that may constitute conflicts of interest, including prior service as an arbitrator or other dispute resolution neutral entity, disqualifications, acceptance of gifts, and establishment of future professional relationships.

(b) Subdivision (a) does not apply to an arbitration conducted pursuant to the terms of a public or private sector collective bargaining agreement.

(c) The ethics requirements and standards of this chapter are nonnegotiable and shall not be waived.

Ca. Civ. Proc. Code § 1281.85
Amended by Stats 2009 ch 133 (AB 1090),s 1, eff. 1/1/2010.
Amended by Stats 2002 ch 176 (SB 1707),s 1, eff. 1/1/2003.
Added by Stats 2001 ch 362 (SB 475), s 4, eff. 1/1/2002.

Section 1281.9 - Disclosures by neutral arbitrators

(a) In any arbitration pursuant to an arbitration agreement, when a person is to serve as a neutral arbitrator, the proposed neutral arbitrator shall disclose all matters that could cause a person aware of the facts to reasonably entertain a doubt that the proposed neutral arbitrator would be able to be impartial, including all of the following:

(1) The existence of any ground specified in Section 170.1 for disqualification of a judge. For purposes of paragraph (8) of subdivision (a) of Section 170.1, the proposed neutral arbitrator shall disclose whether or not he or she has a current arrangement concerning prospective employment or other compensated service as a dispute resolution neutral or is participating in, or, within the last two years, has participated in, discussions regarding such prospective employment or service with a party to the proceeding.

(2) Any matters required to be disclosed by the ethics standards for neutral arbitrators adopted by the Judicial Council pursuant to this chapter.

(3) The names of the parties to all prior or pending noncollective bargaining cases in which the proposed neutral arbitrator served or is serving as a party arbitrator for any party to the arbitration proceeding or for a lawyer for a party and the results of each case arbitrated to conclusion, including the date of the arbitration award, identification of the prevailing party, the names of the parties' attorneys and the amount of monetary damages awarded, if any. In order to preserve confidentiality, it shall be sufficient to give the name of any party who is not a party to the pending arbitration as "claimant" or "respondent" if the party is an individual and not a business or corporate entity.

(4) The names of the parties to all prior or pending noncollective bargaining cases involving any party to the arbitration or lawyer for a party for which the proposed neutral arbitrator served or is serving as neutral arbitrator, and the results of each case arbitrated to conclusion, including the date of the arbitration award, identification of the prevailing party, the names of the parties' attorneys and the amount of monetary damages awarded, if any. In order to preserve confidentiality, it shall be sufficient to give

the name of any party not a party to the pending arbitration as "claimant" or "respondent" if the party is an individual and not a business or corporate entity.

(5) Any attorney-client relationship the proposed neutral arbitrator has or had with any party or lawyer for a party to the arbitration proceeding.

(6) Any professional or significant personal relationship the proposed neutral arbitrator or his or her spouse or minor child living in the household has or has had with any party to the arbitration proceeding or lawyer for a party.

(b) Subject only to the disclosure requirements of law, the proposed neutral arbitrator shall disclose all matters required to be disclosed pursuant to this section to all parties in writing within 10 calendar days of service of notice of the proposed nomination or appointment.

(c) For purposes of this section, "lawyer for a party" includes any lawyer or law firm currently associated in the practice of law with the lawyer hired to represent a party.

(d) For purposes of this section, "prior cases" means noncollective bargaining cases in which an arbitration award was rendered within five years prior to the date of the proposed nomination or appointment.

(e) For purposes of this section, "any arbitration" does not include an arbitration conducted pursuant to the terms of a public or private sector collective bargaining agreement.

Ca. Civ. Proc. Code § 1281.9
Amended by Stats 2002 ch 1094 (AB 2504),s 2, eff. 1/1/2003.
Amended by Stats 2001 ch 362 (SB 475), s 5, eff. 1/1/2002.

Section 1281.91 - Disqualification of neutral arbitrators

(a) A proposed neutral arbitrator shall be disqualified if he or she fails to comply with Section 1281.9 and any party entitled to receive the disclosure serves a notice of disqualification within 15 calendar days after the proposed nominee or appointee fails to comply with Section 1281.9.

(b)

(1) If the proposed neutral arbitrator complies with Section 1281.9, the proposed neutral arbitrator shall be disqualified on the basis of the disclosure statement after any party entitled to receive the disclosure serves a notice of disqualification within 15 calendar days after service of the disclosure statement.

(2) A party shall have the right to disqualify one court-appointed arbitrator without cause in any single arbitration, and may petition the court to disqualify a subsequent appointee only upon a showing of cause.

(c) The right of a party to disqualify a proposed neutral arbitrator pursuant to this section shall be waived if the party fails to serve the notice pursuant to the times set forth in this section, unless the proposed nominee or appointee makes a material omission or material misrepresentation in his or her disclosure. Except as provided in subdivision (d), in no event may a notice of disqualification be given after a hearing of any contested issue of fact relating to the merits of the claim or after any ruling by the arbitrator regarding any contested matter. Nothing in this subdivision shall limit the right of a party to vacate an award pursuant to Section 1286.2, or to disqualify an arbitrator pursuant to any other law or statute.

(d) If any ground specified in Section 170.1 exists, a neutral arbitrator shall disqualify himself or herself upon the demand of any party made before the conclusion of the arbitration proceeding. However, this subdivision does not apply to arbitration proceedings conducted under a collective bargaining agreement between employers and employees or their respective representatives.

Ca. Civ. Proc. Code § 1281.91

Added by Stats 2001 ch 362 (SB 475), s 6, eff. 1/1/2002.

Section 1281.92 - Private arbitration company administering consumer arbitration

(a) No private arbitration company may administer a consumer arbitration, or provide any other services related to a consumer arbitration, if the company has, or within the preceding year has had, a financial interest, as defined in Section 170.5, in any party or attorney for a party.

(b) No private arbitration company may administer a consumer arbitration, or provide any other services related to a consumer arbitration, if any party or attorney for a party has, or within the preceding year has had, any type of financial interest in the private arbitration company.

(c) This section shall operate only prospectively so as not to prohibit the administration of consumer arbitrations on the basis of financial interests held prior to January 1, 2003.

(d) This section applies to all consumer arbitration agreements subject to this article, and to all consumer arbitration proceedings conducted in California.

(e) This section shall become operative on January 1, 2003.

    Ca. Civ. Proc. Code § 1281.92

Added by Stats 2002 ch 952 (AB 2574),s 1, eff. 1/1/2003.

Section 1281.95 - Declaration by arbitrator in arbitration pursuant to construction contract; disqualification

(a) In a binding arbitration of any claim for more than three thousand dollars ($3,000) pursuant to a contract for the construction or improvement of residential property consisting of one to four units, the arbitrator shall, within 10 days following his or her appointment, provide to each party a written declaration under penalty of perjury. This declaration shall disclose (1) whether the arbitrator or his or her employer or arbitration service had or has a personal or professional affiliation with either party, and (2) whether the arbitrator or his or her employer or arbitration service has been selected or designated as an arbitrator by either party in another transaction.

(b) If the arbitrator discloses an affiliation with either party, discloses that the arbitrator has been selected or designated as an arbitrator by either party in another arbitration, or fails to comply with this section, he or she may be disqualified from the arbitration by either party.

(c) A notice of disqualification shall be served within 15 days after the arbitrator makes the required disclosures or fails to comply. The right of a party to disqualify an arbitrator shall be waived if the party fails to serve the notice of disqualification pursuant to this subdivision unless the arbitration makes a material omission or material misrepresentation in his or her disclosure. Nothing in this section shall limit the right of a party to vacate an award pursuant to Section 1286.2, or to disqualify an arbitrator pursuant to any other law or statute.

Ca. Civ. Proc. Code § 1281.95
Amended by Stats 2002 ch 1008 (AB 3028),s 5, eff. 1/1/2003.

Section 1281.96 - Information required by private arbitration company administering consumer arbitration

(a) Except as provided in paragraph (2) of subdivision (c), a private arbitration company that administers or is otherwise involved in a consumer arbitration, shall collect, publish at least quarterly, and make available to the public on the internet website of the private arbitration company, if any, and on paper upon request, a single cumulative report that contains all of the following information regarding each consumer arbitration within the preceding five years:

(1) Whether arbitration was demanded pursuant to a pre-dispute arbitration clause and, if so, whether the pre-dispute arbitration clause designated the administering private arbitration company.

(2) The name of the nonconsumer party, if the nonconsumer party is a corporation or other business entity, and whether the nonconsumer party was the initiating party or the responding party, if known.

(3) The nature of the dispute involved as one of the following: goods; credit; other banking or finance; insurance; health care; construction; real estate; telecommunications, including software and Internet usage; debt collection; personal injury; employment; or other. If the dispute involved employment, the amount of the employee's annual wage divided into the following ranges: less than one hundred thousand dollars ($100,000), one hundred thousand dollars ($100,000) to two hundred fifty thousand dollars ($250,000), inclusive, and over two hundred fifty thousand dollars ($250,000). If the employee chooses not to provide wage information, it may be noted.

(4) Whether the consumer or nonconsumer party was the prevailing party. As used in this section, "prevailing party" includes the party with a net monetary recovery or an award of injunctive relief.

(5) The total number of occasions, if any, the nonconsumer party has previously been a party in an arbitration administered by the private arbitration company.

(6) The total number of occasions, if any, the nonconsumer party has previously been a party in a mediation administered by the private arbitration company.

(7) Whether the consumer party was represented by an attorney and, if so, the name of the attorney and the full name of the law firm that employs the attorney, if any.

(8) The date the private arbitration company received the demand for arbitration, the date the arbitrator was appointed, and the date of disposition by the arbitrator or private arbitration company.

(9) The type of disposition of the dispute, if known, identified as one of the following: withdrawal, abandonment, settlement, award after hearing, award without hearing, default, or dismissal without hearing. If a case was administered in a hearing, indicate whether the hearing was conducted in person, by telephone or video conference, or by documents only.

(10) The amount of the claim, whether equitable relief was requested or awarded, the amount of any monetary award, the

amount of any attorney's fees awarded, and any other relief granted, if any.

(11) The name of the arbitrator, the arbitrator's total fee for the case, the percentage of the arbitrator's fee allocated to each party, whether a waiver of any fees was granted, and, if so, the amount of the waiver.

(12) Demographic data, reported in the aggregate, relative to ethnicity, race, disability, veteran status, gender, gender identity, and sexual orientation of all arbitrators as self-reported by the arbitrators. Demographic data disclosed or released pursuant to this paragraph shall also indicate the percentage of respondents who declined to respond.

(b) The information required by this section shall be made available in a format that allows the public to search and sort the information using readily available software, and shall be directly accessible from a conspicuously displayed link on the internet website of the private arbitration company with the identifying description: "consumer case information."

(c)

(1) If the information required by subdivision (a) is provided by the private arbitration company in compliance with subdivision (b) and may be downloaded without a fee, the company may charge the actual cost of copying to any person who requests the information on paper. If the information required by subdivision (a) is not accessible by the internet in compliance with subdivision (b), the company shall provide that information without charge to any person who requests the information on paper.

(2) Notwithstanding paragraph (1), a private arbitration company that receives funding pursuant to Chapter 8 (commencing with Section 465) of Division 1 of the Business and Professions Code and that administers or conducts fewer than 50 consumer arbitrations per year may collect and publish the information required by subdivision (a) semiannually, provide the information only on paper, and charge the actual cost of copying.

(d) This section shall apply to any consumer arbitration commenced on or after January 1, 2003.

(e) A private arbitration company shall not have any liability for collecting, publishing, or distributing the information required by this section.

(f) It is the intent of the Legislature that private arbitration companies comply with all legal obligations of this section.

(g) The amendments to subdivision (a) made by the act adding this subdivision shall not apply to any consumer arbitration administered by a private arbitration company before January 1, 2015.

Ca. Civ. Proc. Code § 1281.96

Amended by Stats 2019 ch 870 (SB 707),s 3, eff. 1/1/2020.

Amended by Stats 2014 ch 870 (AB 802),s 1, eff. 1/1/2015.

Added by Stats 2002 ch 1158 (AB 2656),s 1, eff. 1/1/2003.

Section 1281.97 - Material breach for failure to pay fees before arbitration can proceed
(a)

(1) In an employment or consumer arbitration that requires, either expressly or through application of state or federal law or the rules of the arbitration provider, the drafting party to pay certain fees and costs before the arbitration can proceed, if the fees or costs to initiate an arbitration proceeding are not paid within 30 days after the due date the drafting party is in material breach of the arbitration agreement, is in default of the arbitration, and waives its right to compel arbitration under Section 1281.2.

(2) After an employee or consumer meets the filing requirements necessary to initiate an arbitration, the arbitration provider shall immediately provide an invoice for any fees and costs required before the arbitration can proceed to all of the parties to the arbitration. The invoice shall be provided in its entirety, shall state the full amount owed and the date that payment is due, and shall be sent to all parties by the same means on the same day. To avoid delay, absent an express provision in the arbitration

agreement stating the number of days in which the parties to the arbitration must pay any required fees or costs, the arbitration provider shall issue all invoices to the parties as due upon receipt.
(b) If the drafting party materially breaches the arbitration agreement and is in default under subdivision (a), the employee or consumer may do either of the following:

 (1) Withdraw the claim from arbitration and proceed in a court of appropriate jurisdiction.

 (2) Compel arbitration in which the drafting party shall pay reasonable attorney's fees and costs related to the arbitration.
(c) If the employee or consumer withdraws the claim from arbitration and proceeds with an action in a court of appropriate jurisdiction under paragraph (1) of subdivision (b), the statute of limitations with regard to all claims brought or that relate back to any claim brought in arbitration shall be tolled as of the date of the first filing of a claim in a court, arbitration forum, or other dispute resolution forum.
(d) If the employee or consumer proceeds with an action in a court of appropriate jurisdiction, the court shall impose sanctions on the drafting party in accordance with Section 1281.99.
 Ca. Civ. Proc. Code § 1281.97
Amended by Stats 2021 ch 222 (SB 762),s 2, eff. 1/1/2022.
Added by Stats 2019 ch 870 (SB 707),s 4, eff. 1/1/2020.

Section 1281.98 - Failure to pay fees and costs during pendency of proceeding
(a)

 (1) In an employment or consumer arbitration that requires, either expressly or through application of state or federal law or the rules of the arbitration provider, that the drafting party pay certain fees and costs during the pendency of an arbitration proceeding, if the fees or costs required to continue the arbitration proceeding are not paid within 30 days after the due date, the drafting party is in material breach of the arbitration agreement, is in default of the arbitration, and waives its right to compel the employee or consumer to proceed with that arbitration as a result of the material breach.

(2) The arbitration provider shall provide an invoice for any fees and costs required for the arbitration proceeding to continue to all of the parties to the arbitration. The invoice shall be provided in its entirety, shall state the full amount owed and the date that payment is due, and shall be sent to all parties by the same means on the same day. To avoid delay, absent an express provision in the arbitration agreement stating the number of days in which the parties to the arbitration must pay any required fees or costs, the arbitration provider shall issue all invoices to the parties as due upon receipt. Any extension of time for the due date shall be agreed upon by all parties. Once the invoice has been paid, the arbitration provider shall provide to all parties a document that reflects the date on which the invoice was paid.

(b) If the drafting party materially breaches the arbitration agreement and is in default under subdivision (a), the employee or consumer may unilaterally elect to do any of the following:

(1) Withdraw the claim from arbitration and proceed in a court of appropriate jurisdiction. If the employee or consumer withdraws the claim from arbitration and proceeds with an action in a court of appropriate jurisdiction, the statute of limitations with regard to all claims brought or that relate back to any claim brought in arbitration shall be tolled as of the date of the first filing of a claim in any court, arbitration forum, or other dispute resolution forum.

(2) Continue the arbitration proceeding, if the arbitration provider agrees to continue administering the proceeding, notwithstanding the drafting party's failure to pay fees or costs. The neutral arbitrator or arbitration provider may institute a collection action at the conclusion of the arbitration proceeding against the drafting party that is in default of the arbitration for payment of all fees associated with the employment or consumer arbitration proceeding, including the cost of administering any proceedings after the default.

(3) Petition the court for an order compelling the drafting party to pay all arbitration fees that the drafting party is obligated to pay under the arbitration agreement or the rules of the arbitration provider.

(4) Pay the drafting party's fees and proceed with the arbitration proceeding. As part of the award, the employee or consumer shall recover all arbitration fees paid on behalf of the drafting party without regard to any findings on the merits in the underlying arbitration.

(c) If the employee or consumer withdraws the claim from arbitration and proceeds in a court of appropriate jurisdiction pursuant to paragraph (1) of subdivision (b), both of the following apply:

(1) The employee or consumer may bring a motion, or a separate action, to recover all attorney's fees and all costs associated with the abandoned arbitration proceeding. The recovery of arbitration fees, interest, and related attorney's fees shall be without regard to any findings on the merits in the underlying action or arbitration.

(2) The court shall impose sanctions on the drafting party in accordance with Section 1281.99.

(d) If the employee or consumer continues in arbitration pursuant to paragraphs (2) through (4) of subdivision (b), inclusive, the arbitrator shall impose appropriate sanctions on the drafting party, including monetary sanctions, issue sanctions, evidence sanctions, or terminating sanctions.

   Ca. Civ. Proc. Code § 1281.98
Amended by Stats 2023 ch 478 (AB 1756),s 17, eff. 1/1/2024.
Amended by Stats 2021 ch 222 (SB 762),s 3, eff. 1/1/2022.
Added by Stats 2019 ch 870 (SB 707),s 5, eff. 1/1/2020.

Section 1281.99 - Sanctions

(a) The court shall impose a monetary sanction against a drafting party that materially breaches an arbitration agreement pursuant to subdivision (a) of Section 1281.97 or subdivision (a) of Section 1281.98, by ordering the drafting party to pay the reasonable expenses, including attorney's fees and costs, incurred by the employee or consumer as a result of the material breach.

(b) In addition to the monetary sanction described in subdivision (a), the court may order any of the following sanctions against a drafting party that materially breaches an arbitration agreement pursuant to subdivision (a) of Section 1281.97 or subdivision (a) of Section 1281.98, unless the court finds that the one subject to the sanction acted with substantial justification or that other circumstances make the imposition of the sanction unjust.

(1) An evidence sanction by an order prohibiting the drafting party from conducting discovery in the civil action.

(2) A terminating sanction by one of the following orders:

(A) An order striking out the pleadings or parts of the pleadings of the drafting party.

(B) An order rendering a judgment by default against the drafting party.

(3) A contempt sanction by an order treating the drafting party as in contempt of court.

Ca. Civ. Proc. Code § 1281.99
Added by Stats 2019 ch 870 (SB 707),s 6, eff. 1/1/2020.

Chapter 3 - CONDUCT OF ARBITRATION PROCEEDINGS

Section 1282 - Powers and duties of arbitrators
Unless the arbitration agreement otherwise provides, or unless the parties to the arbitration otherwise provide by an agreement which is not contrary to the arbitration agreement as made or as modified by all of the parties thereto:

(a) The arbitration shall be by a single neutral arbitrator.

(b) If there is more than one arbitrator, the powers and duties of the arbitrators, other than the powers and duties of a neutral arbitrator, may be exercised by a majority of them if reasonable notice of all proceedings has been given to all arbitrators.

(c) If there is more than one neutral arbitrator:

(1) The powers and duties of a neutral arbitrator may be exercised by a majority of the neutral arbitrators.

(2) By unanimous agreement of the neutral arbitrators, the powers and duties may be delegated to one of their number but the power to make or correct the award may not be so delegated.

(d) If there is no neutral arbitrator, the powers and duties of a neutral arbitrator may be exercised by a majority of the arbitrators.

Ca. Civ. Proc. Code § 1282

Amended by Stats. 1997, Ch. 445, Sec. 3. Effective January 1, 1998.

Section 1282.2 - Hearing

Unless the arbitration agreement otherwise provides, or unless the parties to the arbitration otherwise provide by an agreement which is not contrary to the arbitration agreement as made or as modified by all the parties thereto:

(a)

(1) The neutral arbitrator shall appoint a time and place for the hearing and cause notice thereof to be served personally or by registered or certified mail on the parties to the arbitration and on the other arbitrators not less than seven days before the hearing. Appearance at the hearing waives the right to notice.

(2) With the exception of matters arising out of collective-bargaining agreements, those described in Section 1283.05, actions involving personal injury or death, or as provided in the parties' agreement to arbitrate, in the event the aggregate amount in controversy exceeds fifty thousand dollars ($50,000) and the arbitrator is informed thereof by any party in writing by personal service, registered or certified mail, prior to designating a time and place of hearing pursuant to paragraph (1), the neutral arbitrator by the means prescribed in paragraph (1) shall appoint a time and place for hearing not less than 60 days before the hearing, and the following provisions shall apply:

(A) Either party shall within 15 days of receipt of the notice of hearing have the right to demand in writing, served personally or by registered or certified mail, that the other party provide a list of witnesses it intends to call designating which witnesses will be called as expert witnesses and a list of documents it intends to introduce at the hearing provided that the demanding party provides such lists at the time of its demand. A copy of such demand and the demanding party's lists shall be served on the arbitrator.

(B) Such lists shall be served personally or by registered or certified mail on the requesting party 15 days thereafter. Copies thereof shall be served on the arbitrator.

(C) Listed documents shall be made available for inspection and copying at reasonable times prior to the hearing.

(D) Time limits provided herein may be waived by mutual agreement of the parties if approved by the arbitrator.

(E) The failure to list a witness or a document shall not bar the testimony of an unlisted witness or the introduction of an undesignated document at the hearing, provided that good cause for omission from the requirements of subparagraph (A) is shown, as determined by the arbitrator.

(F) The authority of the arbitrator to administer and enforce this paragraph shall be as provided in subdivisions (b) to (e), inclusive, of Section 1283.05.

(b) The neutral arbitrator may adjourn the hearing from time to time as necessary. On request of a party to the arbitration for good cause, or upon his own determination, the neutral arbitrator may postpone the hearing to a time not later than the date fixed by the agreement for making the award, or to a later date if the parties to the arbitration consent thereto.

(c) The neutral arbitrator shall preside at the hearing, shall rule on the admission and exclusion of evidence and on questions of hearing procedure and shall exercise all powers relating to the conduct of the hearing.

(d) The parties to the arbitration are entitled to be heard, to present evidence and to cross-examine witnesses appearing at the hearing, but rules of evidence and rules of judicial procedure need not be observed. On request of any party to the arbitration, the testimony of witnesses shall be given under oath.

(e) If a court has ordered a person to arbitrate a controversy, the arbitrators may hear and determine the controversy upon the evidence produced notwithstanding the failure of a party ordered to arbitrate, who has been duly notified, to appear.

(f) If an arbitrator, who has been duly notified, for any reason fails to participate in the arbitration, the arbitration shall continue but only the remaining neutral arbitrator or neutral arbitrators may make the award.

(g) If a neutral arbitrator intends to base an award upon information not obtained at the hearing, he shall disclose the information to all parties to the arbitration and give the parties an opportunity to meet it.

Ca. Civ. Proc. Code § 1282.2

Amended by Stats. 1981, Ch. 714, Sec. 72.

Section 1282.4 - Representation by attorney

(a) A party to the arbitration has the right to be represented by an attorney at any proceeding or hearing in arbitration under this title. A waiver of this right may be revoked; but if a party revokes that waiver, the other party is entitled to a reasonable continuance for the purpose of procuring an attorney.

(b) Notwithstanding any other law, including Section 6125 of the Business and Professions Code, an attorney admitted to the bar of any other state may represent the parties in the course of, or in connection with, an arbitration proceeding in this state, provided that the attorney, if not admitted to the State Bar of California, satisfies all of the following:

(1) He or she timely serves the certificate described in subdivision (c).

(2) The attorney's appearance is approved in writing on that certificate by the arbitrator, the arbitrators, or the arbitral forum.

(3) The certificate bearing approval of the attorney's appearance is filed with the State Bar of California and served on the parties as described in this section.

(c) Within a reasonable period of time after the attorney described in subdivision (b) indicates an intention to appear in the arbitration, the attorney shall serve a certificate in a form prescribed by the State Bar of California on the arbitrator, arbitrators, or arbitral forum, the State Bar of California, and all other parties and counsel in the arbitration whose addresses are known to the attorney. The certificate shall state all of the following:

(1) The case name and number, and the name of the arbitrator, arbitrators, or arbitral forum assigned to the proceeding in which the attorney seeks to appear.

(2) The attorney's residence and office address.

(3) The courts before which the attorney has been admitted to practice and the dates of admission.

(4) That the attorney is currently a member in good standing of, and eligible to practice law before, the bar of those courts.

(5) That the attorney is not currently on suspension or disbarred from the practice of law before the bar of any court.

(6) That the attorney is not a resident of the State of California.

(7) That the attorney is not regularly employed in the State of California.

(8) That the attorney is not regularly engaged in substantial business, professional, or other activities in the State of California.

(9) That the attorney agrees to be subject to the jurisdiction of the courts of this state with respect to the law of this state governing the conduct of attorneys to the same extent as a member of the State Bar of California.

(10) The title of the court and the cause in which the attorney has filed an application to appear as counsel pro hac vice in this state or filed a certificate pursuant to this section in the preceding two years, the date of each application or certificate, and whether or not it was granted. If the attorney has made repeated appearances, the certificate shall reflect the special circumstances that warrant the approval of the attorney's appearance in the arbitration.

(11) The name, address, and telephone number of the active member of the State Bar of California who is the attorney of record.
(d) The arbitrator, arbitrators, or arbitral forum may approve the attorney's appearance if the attorney has complied with subdivision (c). Failure to timely file and serve the certificate described in subdivision (c) shall be grounds for disapproval of the appearance and disqualification from serving as an attorney in the arbitration in which the certificate was filed. In the absence of special circumstances, repeated appearances shall be grounds for disapproval of the appearance and disqualification from serving as an attorney in the arbitration in which the certificate was filed.
(e) Within a reasonable period of time after the arbitrator, arbitrators, or arbitral forum approves the certificate, the attorney shall file the certificate with the State Bar of California and serve the certificate as described in Section 1013a on all parties and counsel in the arbitration whose addresses are known to the attorney.
(f) An attorney who fails to file or serve the certificate required by this section or files or serves a certificate containing false information or who otherwise fails to comply with the standards of professional conduct required of members of the State Bar of California shall be subject to the disciplinary jurisdiction of the State Bar with respect to that certificate or any of his or her acts

occurring in the course of the arbitration.

(g) Notwithstanding any other law, including Section 6125 of the Business and Professions Code, an attorney who is a member in good standing of the bar of any state may represent the parties in connection with rendering legal services in this state in the course of and in connection with an arbitration pending in another state.

(h) Notwithstanding any other law, including Section 6125 of the Business and Professions Code, any party to an arbitration arising under collective bargaining agreements in industries and provisions subject to either state or federal law may be represented in the course of, and in connection with, those proceedings by any person, regardless of whether that person is licensed to practice law in this state.

(i) Nothing in this section shall apply to Division 4 (commencing with Section 3200) of the Labor Code.

(j)

(1) In enacting the amendments to this section made by Assembly Bill 2086 of the 1997-98 Regular Session, it is the intent of the Legislature to respond to the holding in Birbrower v. Superior Court (1998) 17 Cal.4th 119, to provide a procedure for nonresident attorneys who are not licensed in this state to appear in California arbitration proceedings.

(2) In enacting subdivision (h), it is the intent of the Legislature to make clear that any party to an arbitration arising under a collective bargaining agreement governed by the laws of this state may be represented in the course of and in connection with those proceedings by any person regardless of whether that person is licensed to practice law in this state.

(3) Except as otherwise specifically provided in this section, in enacting the amendments to this section made by Assembly Bill 2086 of the 1997-98 Regular Session, it is the Legislature's intent that nothing in this section is intended to expand or restrict the ability of a party prior to the decision in Birbrower to elect to be represented by any person in a nonjudicial arbitration proceeding, to the extent those rights or abilities existed prior to that decision.

To the extent that Birbrower is interpreted to expand or restrict that right or ability pursuant to the laws of this state, it is hereby abrogated except as specifically provided in this section.

(4) In enacting subdivision (i), it is the intent of the Legislature to make clear that nothing in this section shall affect those provisions of law governing the right of injured workers to elect to be represented by any person, regardless of whether that person is licensed to practice law in this state, as set forth in Division 4 (commencing with Section 3200) of the Labor Code.

Ca. Civ. Proc. Code § 1282.4

Amended by Stats 2014 ch 71 (SB 1304),s 20, eff. 1/1/2015.
Amended by Stats 2013 ch 76 (AB 383),s 24, eff. 1/1/2014.
Amended by Stats 2012 ch 53 (AB 1631),s 1, eff. 1/1/2013.
Amended by Stats 2010 ch 277 (SB 877),s 1, eff. 1/1/2011.
Amended by Stats 2006 ch 357 (AB 2482),s 1, eff. 1/1/2007.
Amended by Stats 2005 ch 607 (AB 415),s 1, eff. 10/6/2005.
Amended by Stats 2000 ch 1011 (SB 2153), s 2, eff. 1/1/2001.

Section 1282.5 - Transcription of arbitration proceedings

(a)

(1) A party to an arbitration has the right to have a certified shorthand reporter transcribe any deposition, proceeding, or hearing. The transcript shall be the official record of the deposition, proceeding, or hearing.

(2) A party requesting a certified shorthand reporter shall make his or her request in or at either of the following:

(A) A demand for arbitration, or a response, answer, or counterclaim to a demand for arbitration.

(B) A pre-hearing scheduling conference at which a deposition, proceeding, or hearing is being calendared.

(b) If an arbitration agreement does not provide for a certified shorthand reporter, the party requesting the transcript shall incur the expense of the certified shorthand reporter. However, in a consumer arbitration, a certified shorthand reporter shall be provided upon request of an indigent consumer, as defined in Section 1284.3, at the expense of the nonconsumer party.

(c) If an arbitrator refuses to allow a party to have a certified shorthand reporter transcribe any deposition, proceeding, or hearing pursuant to this section, the party may petition the court for an order to compel the arbitrator to grant the party's request. The petition may include a request for an order to stay any deposition, proceeding, or hearing related to the arbitration pending the court's determination of the petition.

(d) This section does not add grounds for vacating an arbitration award pursuant to subdivision (a) of Section 1286.2 or for correcting an arbitration award pursuant to Section 1286.6.

Ca. Civ. Proc. Code § 1282.5

Added by Stats 2016 ch 626 (SB 1007),s 1, eff. 1/1/2017.

Section 1282.6 - Subpoenas

(a)A subpoena requiring the attendance of witnesses, and a subpoena duces tecum for the production of books, records, documents and other evidence, at an arbitration proceeding or a deposition under Section 1283, and if Section 1283.05 is applicable, for the purposes of discovery, shall be issued as provided in this section. In addition, the neutral arbitrator upon their own determination may issue subpoenas for the attendance of witnesses and subpoenas duces tecum for the production of books, records, documents, and other evidence.

(b) Subpoenas shall be issued, as of course, signed but otherwise in blank, to the party requesting them, by a neutral association, organization, governmental agency, or office if the arbitration agreement provides for administration of the arbitration proceedings by, or under the rules of, a neutral association, organization, governmental agency or office, or by the neutral arbitrator.

(c) The party serving the subpoena shall fill it in before service. Subpoenas shall be served and enforced in accordance with Chapter 2 (commencing with Section 1985) of Title 3 of Part 4 of this code.

Ca. Civ. Proc. Code § 1282.6
Amended by Stats 2022 ch 420 (AB 2960),s 11, eff. 1/1/2023.
Amended by Stats. 1982, Ch. 108, Sec. 1.

Section 1282.8 - Oaths
The neutral arbitrator may administer oaths.
Ca. Civ. Proc. Code § 1282.8
Added by Stats. 1961, Ch. 461.

Section 1283 - Depositions
On application of a party to the arbitration, the neutral arbitrator
may order the deposition of a witness to be taken for use as
evidence and not for discovery if the witness cannot be compelled to
attend the hearing or if exceptional circumstances exist as to make
it desirable, in the interest of justice and with due regard to the
importance of presenting the testimony of witnesses orally at the
hearing, to allow the deposition to be taken. The deposition shall be
taken in the manner prescribed by law for the taking of depositions
in civil actions. If the neutral arbitrator orders the taking of the
deposition of a witness who resides outside the state, the party who
applied for the taking of the deposition shall obtain a commission,
letters rogatory, or a letter of request therefor from the superior
court in accordance with Chapter 10 (commencing with Section
2026.010) of Title 4 of Part 4.
Ca. Civ. Proc. Code § 1283
Amended by Stats 2005 ch 294 (AB 333),s 4, eff. 1/1/2006

Section 1283.05 - Procedure for taking depositions and discovery
To the extent provided in Section 1283.1 depositions may be taken
and discovery obtained in arbitration proceedings as follows:
(a) After the appointment of the arbitrator or arbitrators, the
parties to the arbitration shall have the right to take depositions
and to obtain discovery regarding the subject matter of the
arbitration, and, to that end, to use and exercise all of the same
rights, remedies, and procedures, and be subject to all of the same

duties, liabilities, and obligations in the arbitration with respect to the subject matter thereof, as provided in Chapter 2 (commencing with Section 1985) of Title 3 of Part 4, and in Title 4 (commencing with Section 2016.010) of Part 4, as if the subject matter of the arbitration were pending before a superior court of this state in a civil action other than a limited civil case, subject to the limitations as to depositions set forth in subdivision (e) of this section.

(b) The arbitrator or arbitrators themselves shall have power, in addition to the power of determining the merits of the arbitration, to enforce the rights, remedies, procedures, duties, liabilities, and obligations of discovery by the imposition of the same terms, conditions, consequences, liabilities, sanctions, and penalties as can be or may be imposed in like circumstances in a civil action by a superior court of this state under the provisions of this code, except the power to order the arrest or imprisonment of a person.

(c) The arbitrator or arbitrators may consider, determine, and make such orders imposing such terms, conditions, consequences, liabilities, sanctions, and penalties, whenever necessary or appropriate at any time or stage in the course of the arbitration, and such orders shall be as conclusive, final, and enforceable as an arbitration award on the merits, if the making of any such order that is equivalent to an award or correction of an award is subject to the same conditions, if any, as are applicable to the making of an award or correction of an award.

(d) For the purpose of enforcing the duty to make discovery, to produce evidence or information, including books and records, and to produce persons to testify at a deposition or at a hearing, and to impose terms, conditions, consequences, liabilities, sanctions, and penalties upon a party for violation of any such duty, such party shall be deemed to include every affiliate of such party as defined in this section. For such purpose:

(1) The personnel of every such affiliate shall be deemed to be the officers, directors, managing agents, agents, and employees of such party to the same degree as each of them, respectively, bears such status to such affiliate; and

(2) The files, books, and records of every such affiliate shall be deemed to be in the possession and control of, and capable of production by, such party. As used in this section, "affiliate" of the party to the arbitration means and includes any party or person for whose immediate benefit the action or proceeding is prosecuted or defended, or an officer, director, superintendent, member, agent, employee, or managing agent of such party or person.

(e) Depositions for discovery shall not be taken unless leave to do so is first granted by the arbitrator or arbitrators.

Ca. Civ. Proc. Code § 1283.05

Amended by Stats 2004 ch 182 (AB 3081),s 16, eff. 7/1/2005

Section 1283.1 - Provisions of section 1283.05 deemed incorporated into agreement

(a) All of the provisions of Section 1283.05 shall be conclusively deemed to be incorporated into, made a part of, and shall be applicable to, every agreement to arbitrate any dispute, controversy, or issue arising out of or resulting from any injury to, or death of, a person caused by the wrongful act or neglect of another.

(b) Only if the parties by their agreement so provide, may the provisions of Section 1283.05 be incorporated into, made a part of, or made applicable to, any other arbitration agreement.

Ca. Civ. Proc. Code § 1283.1

Amended by Stats. 1970, Ch. 1045.

Section 1283.2 - Witness fees and mileage

Except for the parties to the arbitration and their agents, officers and employees, all witnesses appearing pursuant to subpoena are entitled to receive fees and mileage in the same amount and under the same circumstances as prescribed by law for witnesses in civil actions in the superior court. The fee and mileage of a witness subpoenaed upon the application of a party to the arbitration shall be paid by such party. The fee and mileage of a witness subpoenaed soley upon the determination of the neutral arbitrator shall be paid in the manner provided for the payment of the neutral arbitrator's expenses.

Ca. Civ. Proc. Code § 1283.2
Added by Stats. 1961, Ch. 461.

Section 1283.4 - Award requirements
The award shall be in writing and signed by the arbitrators concurring therein. It shall include a determination of all the questions submitted to the arbitrators the decision of which is necessary in order to determine the controversy.
Ca. Civ. Proc. Code § 1283.4
Added by Stats. 1961, Ch. 461.

Section 1283.6 - Service of copy of award
The neutral arbitrator shall serve a signed copy of the award on each party to the arbitration personally or by registered or certified mail or as provided in the agreement.
Ca. Civ. Proc. Code § 1283.6
Added by Stats. 1961, Ch. 461.

Section 1283.8 - Time for making award
The award shall be made within the time fixed therefor by the agreement or, if not so fixed, within such time as the court orders on petition of a party to the arbitration. The parties to the arbitration may extend the time either before or after the expiration thereof. A party to the arbitration waives the objection that an award was not made within the time required unless he gives the arbitrators written notice of his objection prior to the service of a signed copy of the award on him.
Ca. Civ. Proc. Code § 1283.8
Added by Stats. 1961, Ch. 461.

Section 1284 - Application to correct award
The arbitrators, upon written application of a party to the arbitration, may correct the award upon any of the grounds set forth in subdivisions (a) and (c) of Section 1286.6 not later than 30 days after service of a signed copy of the award on the applicant.

Application for such correction shall be made not later than 10 days after service of a signed copy of the award on the applicant. Upon or before making such application, the applicant shall deliver or mail a copy of the application to all of the other parties to the arbitration. Any party to the arbitration may make written objection to such application. The objection shall be made not later than 10 days after the application is delivered or mailed to the objector. Upon or before making such objection, the objector shall deliver or mail a copy of the objection to the applicant and all the other parties to the arbitration.

The arbitrators shall either deny the application or correct the award. The denial of the application or the correction of the award shall be in writing and signed by the arbitrators concurring therein, and the neutral arbitrator shall serve a signed copy of such denial or correction on each party to the arbitration personally or by registered or certified mail or as provided in the agreement. If no denial of the application or correction of the award is served within the 30-day period provided in this section, the application for correction shall be deemed denied on the last day thereof.

Ca. Civ. Proc. Code § 1284
Repealed and added by Stats. 1961, Ch. 461.

Section 1284.2 - Payment of expenses and fees

Unless the arbitration agreement otherwise provides or the parties to the arbitration otherwise agree, each party to the arbitration shall pay his pro rata share of the expenses and fees of the neutral arbitrator, together with other expenses of the arbitration incurred or approved by the neutral arbitrator, not including counsel fees or witness fees or other expenses incurred by a party for his own benefit.

Ca. Civ. Proc. Code § 1284.2
Added by Stats. 1961, Ch. 461.

Section 1284.3 - Fees and costs assessed in consumer arbitration

(a) No neutral arbitrator or private arbitration company shall administer a consumer arbitration under any agreement or rule requiring that a consumer who is a party to the arbitration pay the fees and costs incurred by an opposing party if the consumer does not prevail in the arbitration, including, but not limited to, the fees and costs of the arbitrator, provider organization, attorney, or witnesses.

(b)

(1) All fees and costs charged to or assessed upon a consumer party by a private arbitration company in a consumer arbitration, exclusive of arbitrator fees, shall be waived for an indigent consumer. For the purposes of this section, "indigent consumer" means a person having a gross monthly income that is less than 300 percent of the federal poverty guidelines. Nothing in this section shall affect the ability of a private arbitration company to shift fees that would otherwise be charged or assessed upon a consumer party to a nonconsumer party.

(2) Prior to requesting or obtaining any fee, a private arbitration company shall provide written notice of the right to obtain a waiver of fees to a consumer or prospective consumer in a manner calculated to bring the matter to the attention of a reasonable consumer, including, but not limited to, prominently placing a notice in its first written communication to the consumer and in any invoice, bill, submission form, fee schedule, rules, or code of procedure.

(3) Any consumer requesting a waiver of fees or costs may establish his or her eligibility by making a declaration under oath on a form provided to the consumer by the private arbitration company for signature stating his or her monthly income and the number of persons living in his or her household. No private arbitration company may require a consumer to provide any further statement or evidence of indigence.

(4) Any information obtained by a private arbitration company about a consumer's identity, financial condition, income, wealth, or fee waiver request shall be kept confidential and may not be

disclosed to any adverse party or any nonparty to the arbitration, except a private arbitration company may not keep confidential the number of waiver requests received or granted, or the total amount of fees waived.

(c) This section applies to all consumer arbitration agreements subject to this article, and to all consumer arbitration proceedings conducted in California.

Ca. Civ. Proc. Code § 1284.3
Added by Stats 2002 ch 1101 (AB 2915),s 1, eff. 1/1/2003.

Chapter 4 - ENFORCEMENT OF THE AWARD

Article 1 - CONFIRMATION, CORRECTION OR VACATION OF THE AWARD

Section 1285 - Petition to confirm, correct or vacate award

Any party to an arbitration in which an award has been made may petition the court to confirm, correct or vacate the award. The petition shall name as respondents all parties to the arbitration and may name as respondents any other persons bound by the arbitration award.

Ca. Civ. Proc. Code § 1285
Repealed and added by Stats. 1961, Ch. 461.

Section 1285.2 - Response to petition

A response to a petition under this chapter may request the court to dismiss the petition or to confirm, correct or vacate the award.

Ca. Civ. Proc. Code § 1285.2
Added by Stats. 1961, Ch. 461.

Section 1285.4 - Petition requirements

A petition under this chapter shall:

(a) Set forth the substance of or have attached a copy of the agreement to arbitrate unless the petitioner denies the existence of such an agreement.

(b) Set forth names of the arbitrators.

(c) Set forth or have attached a copy of the award and the written opinion of the arbitrators, if any.

Ca. Civ. Proc. Code § 1285.4
Added by Stats. 1961, Ch. 461.

Section 1285.6 - Response requirements

Unless a copy thereof is set forth in or attached to the petition, a response to a petition under this chapter shall:

(a) Set forth the substance of or have attached a copy of the agreement to arbitrate unless the respondent denies the existence of such an agreement.

(b) Set forth the names of the arbitrators.

(c) Set forth or have attached a copy of the award and the written opinion of the arbitrators, if any.

Ca. Civ. Proc. Code § 1285.6
Added by Stats. 1961, Ch. 461.

Section 1285.8 - Petition or response to set forth grounds for correcting of vacating award

A petition to correct or vacate an award, or a response requesting such relief, shall set forth the grounds on which the request for such relief is based.

Ca. Civ. Proc. Code § 1285.8
Added by Stats. 1961, Ch. 461.

Section 1286 - Duty of court if petition and response duly served and filed

If a petition or response under this chapter is duly served and filed, the court shall confirm the award as made, whether rendered in this state or another state, unless in accordance with this chapter it corrects the award and confirms it as corrected, vacates the award or dismisses the proceedings.

Ca. Civ. Proc. Code § 1286
Amended by Stats. 1978, Ch. 260.

Section 1286.2 - Grounds for vacating award

(a) Subject to Section 1286.4, the court shall vacate the award if the court determines any of the following:

(1) The award was procured by corruption, fraud or other undue means.

(2) There was corruption in any of the arbitrators.

(3) The rights of the party were substantially prejudiced by misconduct of a neutral arbitrator.

(4) The arbitrators exceeded their powers and the award cannot be corrected without affecting the merits of the decision upon the controversy submitted.

(5) The rights of the party were substantially prejudiced by the refusal of the arbitrators to postpone the hearing upon sufficient cause being shown therefor or by the refusal of the arbitrators to hear evidence material to the controversy or by other conduct of the arbitrators contrary to the provisions of this title.

(6) An arbitrator making the award either:

(A) failed to disclose within the time required for disclosure a ground for disqualification of which the arbitrator was then aware; or

(B) was subject to disqualification upon grounds specified in Section 1281.91 but failed upon receipt of timely demand to disqualify himself or herself as required by that provision. However, this subdivision does not apply to arbitration proceedings conducted under a collective bargaining agreement between employers and employees or between their respective representatives.

(b) Petitions to vacate an arbitration award pursuant to Section 1285 are subject to the provisions of Section 128.7.

Ca. Civ. Proc. Code § 1286.2
Amended by Stats 2001 ch 362 (SB 475), s 7, eff. 1/1/2002.

Section 1286.4 - Petition or response required to be duly served and filed to vacate award

The court may not vacate an award unless:

(a) A petition or response requesting that the award be vacated has been duly served and filed; or

(b) A petition or response requesting that the award be corrected has been duly served and filed and;

(1) All petitioners and respondents are before the court; or

(2) All petitioners and respondents have been given reasonable notice that the court will be requested at the hearing to vacate the award or that the court on its own motion has determined to vacate the award and all petitioners and respondents have been given an opportunity to show why the award should not be vacated.

Ca. Civ. Proc. Code § 1286.4
Added by Stats. 1961, Ch. 461.

Section 1286.6 - Grounds for correcting award

Subject to Section 1286.8, the court, unless it vacates the award pursuant to Section 1286.2, shall correct the award and confirm it as corrected if the court determines that:

(a) There was an evident miscalculation of figures or an evident mistake in the description of any person, thing or property referred to in the award;

(b) The arbitrators exceeded their powers but the award may be corrected without affecting the merits of the decision upon the controversy submitted; or

(c) The award is imperfect in a matter of form, not affecting the merits of the controversy.

Ca. Civ. Proc. Code § 1286.6
Added by Stats. 1961, Ch. 461.

Section 1286.8 - Petition and response required to be duly served and filed to correct award

The court may not correct an award unless:

(a) A petition or response requesting that the award be corrected has been duly served and filed; or

(b) A petition or response requesting that the award be vacated has been duly served and filed and:

(1) All petitioners and respondents are before the court; or

(2) All petitioners and respondents have been given reasonable notice that the court will be requested at the hearing to correct the award or that the court on its own motion has determined to correct the award and all petitioners and respondents have been given an opportunity to show why the award should not be corrected.

Ca. Civ. Proc. Code § 1286.8

Added by Stats. 1961, Ch. 461.

Section 1287 - Rehearing if award vacated

If the award is vacated, the court may order a rehearing before new arbitrators. If the award is vacated on the grounds set forth in paragraph (4) or (5) of subdivision (a) of Section 1286.2, the court with the consent of the parties to the court proceeding may order a rehearing before the original arbitrators.

If the arbitration agreement requires that the award be made within a specified period of time, the rehearing may nevertheless be held and the award made within an equal period of time beginning with the date of the order for rehearing but only if the court determines that the purpose of the time limit agreed upon by the parties to the arbitration agreement will not be frustrated by the application of this provision.

Ca. Civ. Proc. Code § 1287

Amended by Stats 2012 ch 162 (SB 1171),s 15, eff. 1/1/2013.

Section 1287.2 - Dismissal of proceeding as to respondent

The court shall dismiss the proceeding under this chapter as to any person named as a respondent if the court determines that such person was not bound by the arbitration award and was not a party to the arbitration.

Ca. Civ. Proc. Code § 1287.2

Added by Stats. 1961, Ch. 461.

Section 1287.4 - Judgment confirming award

If an award is confirmed, judgment shall be entered in conformity therewith. The judgment so entered has the same force and effect as, and is subject to all the provisions of law relating to, a judgment in a civil action of the same jurisdictional classification; and it may be enforced like any other judgment of the court in which it is entered, in an action of the same jurisdictional classification.

Ca. Civ. Proc. Code § 1287.4

Amended by Stats. 1998, Ch. 931, Sec. 124. Effective September 28, 1998.

Section 1287.6 - Force and effect of judgment

An award that has not been confirmed or vacated has the same force and effect as a contract in writing between the parties to the arbitration.

Ca. Civ. Proc. Code § 1287.6

Added by Stats. 1961, Ch. 461.

Article 2 - LIMITATIONS OF TIME

Section 1288 - Time for serving and filing petitions

A petition to confirm an award shall be served and filed not later than four years after the date of service of a signed copy of the award on the petitioner. A petition to vacate an award or to correct an award shall be served and filed not later than 100 days after the date of the service of a signed copy of the award on the petitioner.

Ca. Civ. Proc. Code § 1288

Repealed and added by Stats. 1961, Ch. 461.

Section 1288.2 - Time for serving and filing response

A response requesting that an award be vacated or that an award be corrected shall be served and filed not later than 100 days after the date of service of a signed copy of the award upon:

(a) The respondent if he was a party to the arbitration; or

(b) The respondent's representative if the respondent was not a party to the arbitration.

Ca. Civ. Proc. Code § 1288.2

Added by Stats. 1961, Ch. 461.

Section 1288.4 - Time for serving and filing petition after service of award on petitioner

No petition may be served and filed under this chapter until at least 10 days after service of the signed copy of the award upon the petitioner.

Ca. Civ. Proc. Code § 1288.4

Added by Stats. 1961, Ch. 461.

Section 1288.6 - Service and filing petition after determination of application to arbitrators for correction

If an application is made to the arbitrators for correction of the award, a petition may not be served and filed under this chapter until the determination of that application.

Ca. Civ. Proc. Code § 1288.6

Added by Stats. 1961, Ch. 461.

Section 1288.8 - Date for service of award if application made to arbitrators for correction

If an application is made to the arbitrators for correction of the award, the date of the service of the award for the purposes of this article shall be deemed to be whichever of the following dates is the earlier:

(a) The date of service upon the petitioner of a signed copy of the correction of the award or of the denial of the application.

(b) The date that such application is deemed to be denied under Section 1284.

Ca. Civ. Proc. Code § 1288.8
Added by Stats. 1961, Ch. 461.

Chapter 5 - GENERAL PROVISIONS RELATING TO JUDICIAL PROCEEDINGS

Article 1 - PETITIONS AND RESPONSES

Section 1290 - Generally

A proceeding under this title in the courts of this State is commenced by filing a petition. Any person named as a respondent in a petition may file a response thereto. The allegations of a petition are deemed to be admitted by a respondent duly served therewith unless a response is duly served and filed. The allegations of a response are deemed controverted or avoided.

Ca. Civ. Proc. Code § 1290
Repealed and added by Stats. 1961, Ch. 461.

Section 1290.2 - Petition heard in manner for making and hearing motions

A petition under this title shall be heard in a summary way in the manner and upon the notice provided by law for the making and hearing of motions, except that not less than 10 days' notice of the date set for the hearing on the petition shall be given.

Ca. Civ. Proc. Code § 1290.2
Added by Stats. 1961, Ch. 461.

Section 1290.4 - Service of petition, notice of hearing and other papers

(a) A copy of the petition and a written notice of the time and place of the hearing thereof and any other papers upon which the petition is based shall be served in the manner provided in the arbitration agreement for the service of such petition and notice.

(b) If the arbitration agreement does not provide the manner in which such service shall be made and the person upon whom service is to be made has not previously appeared in the proceeding and has not previously been served in accordance with this subdivision:

(1) Service within this State shall be made in the manner provided by law for the service of summons in an action.

(2) Service outside this State shall be made by mailing the copy of the petition and notice and other papers by registered or certified mail. Personal service is the equivalent of such service by mail. Proof of service by mail shall be made by affidavit showing such mailing together with the return receipt of the United States Post Office bearing the signature of the person on whom service was made. Notwithstanding any other provision of this title, if service is made in the manner provided in this paragraph, the petition may not be heard until at least 30 days after the date of such service.

(c) If the arbitration agreement does not provide the manner in which such service shall be made and the person on whom service is to be made has previously appeared in the proceeding or has previously been served in accordance with subdivision (b) of this section, service shall be made in the manner provided in Chapter 5 (commencing with Section 1010) of Title 14 of Part 2 of this code.

Ca. Civ. Proc. Code § 1290.4
Added by Stats. 1961, Ch. 461.

Section 1290.6 - Time for serving and filing response

A response shall be served and filed within 10 days after service of the petition except that if the petition is served in the manner provided in paragraph (2) of subdivision (b) of Section 1290.4, the response shall be served and filed within 30 days after service of the petition. The time provided in this section for serving and filing a response may be extended by an agreement in writing between the parties to the court proceeding or, for good cause, by order of the court.

Ca. Civ. Proc. Code § 1290.6
Added by Stats. 1961, Ch. 461.

Section 1290.8 - Manner of serving response
A response shall be served as provided in Chapter 5 (commencing with Section 1010) of Title 14 of Part 2 of this code.
Ca. Civ. Proc. Code § 1290.8
Added by Stats. 1961, Ch. 461.

Section 1291 - Statement of decision
A statement of decision shall be made by the court, if requested pursuant to Section 632, whenever an order or judgment, except a special order after final judgment, is made that is appealable under this title.
Ca. Civ. Proc. Code § 1291
Amended by Stats. 1983, Ch. 302, Sec. 2.

Section 1291.2 - Preference of proceedings
In all proceedings brought under the provisions of this title, all courts wherein such proceedings are pending shall give such proceedings preference over all other civil actions or proceedings, except older matters of the same character and matters to which special precedence may be given by law, in the matter of setting the same for hearing and in hearing the same to the end that all such proceedings shall be quickly heard and determined.
Ca. Civ. Proc. Code § 1291.2
Added by Stats. 1961, Ch. 461.

Article 2 - VENUE, JURISDICTION AND COSTS

Section 1292 - Place for filing petition made prior to commencement of arbitration
Except as otherwise provided in this article, any petition made prior to the commencement of arbitration shall be filed in a court having jurisdiction in:
(a) The county where the agreement is to be performed or was made.
(b) If the agreement does not specify a county where the agreement is to be performed and the agreement was not made in any county

in this state, the county where any party to the court proceeding resides or has a place of business.

(c) In any case not covered by subdivision (a) or (b) of this section, in any county in this state.

Ca. Civ. Proc. Code § 1292

Amended by Stats. 1993, Ch. 1261, Sec. 2. Effective January 1, 1994.

Section 1292.2 - Place for filing petition made after commencement of arbitration

Except as otherwise provided in this article, any petition made after the commencement or completion of arbitration shall be filed in a court having jurisdiction in the county where the arbitration is being or has been held, or, if not held exclusively in any one county of this state, or if held outside of this state, then the petition shall be filed as provided in Section 1292.

Ca. Civ. Proc. Code § 1292.2

Amended by Stats. 1993, Ch. 1261, Sec. 3. Effective January 1, 1994.

Section 1292.4 - Petition for order to arbitrate filed in pending action or proceeding

If a controversy referable to arbitration under an alleged agreement is involved in an action or proceeding pending in a superior court, a petition for an order to arbitrate shall be filed in such action or proceeding.

Ca. Civ. Proc. Code § 1292.4

Added by Stats. 1961, Ch. 461.

Section 1292.6 - Retention of jurisdiction to determine subsequent petition involving same agreement and same controversy

After a petition has been filed under this title, the court in which such petition was filed retains jurisdiction to determine any subsequent petition involving the same agreement to arbitrate and the same controversy, and any such subsequent petition shall be filed in the same proceeding.

Ca. Civ. Proc. Code § 1292.6
Added by Stats. 1961, Ch. 461.

Section 1292.8 - Place for making motion for stay on ground issue subject to arbitration

A motion for a stay of an action on the ground that an issue therein is subject to arbitration shall be made in the court where the action is pending.

Ca. Civ. Proc. Code § 1292.8
Added by Stats. 1961, Ch. 461.

Section 1293 - Consent to jurisdiction of state courts to enforce agreement

The making of an agreement in this State providing for arbitration to be had within this State shall be deemed a consent of the parties thereto to the jurisdiction of the courts of this State to enforce such agreement by the making of any orders provided for in this title and by entering of judgment on an award under the agreement.

Ca. Civ. Proc. Code § 1293
Repealed and added by Stats. 1961, Ch. 461.

Section 1293.2 - Awarding costs upon judicial proceeding

The court shall award costs upon any judicial proceeding under this title as provided in Chapter 6 (commencing with Section 1021) of Title 14 of Part 2 of this code.

Ca. Civ. Proc. Code § 1293.2
Added by Stats. 1961, Ch. 461.

Article 3 - APPEALS

Section 1294 - Orders or judgments from which party may appeal

An aggrieved party may appeal from:

(a) An order dismissing or denying a petition to compel arbitration. Notwithstanding Section 916, the perfecting of such an appeal shall not automatically stay any proceedings in the trial court during the pendency of the appeal.

(b) An order dismissing a petition to confirm, correct or vacate an award.

(c) An order vacating an award unless a rehearing in arbitration is ordered.

(d) A judgment entered pursuant to this title.

(e) A special order after final judgment.

Ca. Civ. Proc. Code § 1294

Amended by Stats 2023 ch 710 (SB 365),s 1, eff. 1/1/2024.

Repealed and added by Stats. 1961, Ch. 461.

Section 1294.2 - Review by court upon appeal

The appeal shall be taken in the same manner as an appeal from an order or judgment in a civil action. Upon an appeal from any order or judgment under this title, the court may review the decision and any intermediate ruling, proceeding, order or decision which involves the merits or necessarily affects the order or judgment appealed from, or which substantially affects the rights of a party. The court may also on such appeal review any order on motion for a new trial. The respondent on the appeal, or party in whose favor the judgment or order was given may, without appealing from such judgment, request the court to and it may review any of the foregoing matters for the purpose of determining whether or not the appellant was prejudiced by the error or errors upon which he relies for reversal or modification of the judgment or order from which the appeal is taken. The provisions of this section do not authorize the court to review any decision or order from which an appeal might have been taken.

Ca. Civ. Proc. Code § 1294.2

Added by Stats. 1961, Ch. 461.

Section 1294.4 - Expedited appeal process for a person filing a claim arising under the Elder and Dependent Adult Civil Protection Act

(a) Except as provided in subdivision (b), in an appeal filed pursuant to subdivision (a) of Section 1294 involving a claim under the Elder and Dependent Adult Civil Protection Act (Chapter 11 (commencing with Section 15600) of Part 3 of Division 9 of the Welfare and Institutions Code) in which a party has been granted a preference pursuant to Section 36 of this code, the court of appeal shall issue its decision no later than 100 days after the notice of appeal is filed.

(b) The court of appeal may grant an extension of time in the appeal only if good cause is shown and the extension will promote the interests of justice.

(c) The Judicial Council shall, on or before July 1, 2017, adopt rules of court to do both of the following:

(1) Implement subdivisions (a) and (b).

(2) Establish a shortened notice of appeal period for the cases described in subdivision (a).

Ca. Civ. Proc. Code § 1294.4

Added by Stats 2016 ch 628 (SB 1065),s 2, eff. 1/1/2017.

Title 9.1 - ARBITRATION OF MEDICAL MALPRACTICE

Section 1295 - Form of provisions in medical services contract containing provisions for arbitration

(a) Any contract for medical services which contains a provision for arbitration of any dispute as to professional negligence of a health care provider shall have such provision as the first article of the contract and shall be expressed in the following language: "It is understood that any dispute as to medical malpractice, that is as to whether any medical services rendered under this contract were unnecessary or unauthorized or were improperly, negligently or incompetently rendered, will be determined by submission to arbitration as provided by California law, and not by a lawsuit or resort to court process except as California law provides for judicial review of arbitration proceedings. Both parties to this contract, by entering into it, are giving up their constitutional right to have any such dispute decided in a court of law before a jury, and instead are accepting the use of arbitration."

(b) Immediately before the signature line provided for the individual contracting for the medical services must appear the following in at least 10-point bold red type: "NOTICE: BY SIGNING THIS CONTRACT YOU ARE AGREEING TO HAVE ANY ISSUE OF MEDICAL MALPRACTICE DECIDED BY NEUTRAL ARBITRATION AND YOU ARE GIVING UP YOUR RIGHT TO A JURY OR COURT TRIAL. SEE ARTICLE 1 OF THIS CONTRACT."

(c) Once signed, such a contract governs all subsequent open-book account transactions for medical services for which the contract was signed until or unless rescinded by written notice within 30 days of signature. Written notice of such rescission may be given by a guardian or conservator of the patient if the patient is incapacitated or a minor.

(d) Where the contract is one for medical services to a minor, it shall not be subject to disaffirmance if signed by the minor's parent or legal guardian.

(e) Such a contract is not a contract of adhesion, nor unconscionable nor otherwise improper, where it complies with subdivisions (a), (b), and (c) of this section.

(f) Subdivisions (a), (b), and (c) shall not apply to any health care service plan contract offered by an organization registered pursuant to Article 2.5 (commencing with Section 12530) of Division 3 of Title 2 of the Government Code, or licensed pursuant to Chapter 2.2 (commencing with Section 1340) of Division 2 of the Health and Safety Code, which contains an arbitration agreement if the plan complies with paragraph (10) of subdivision (b) of Section 1363 of the Health and Safety Code, or otherwise has a procedure for notifying prospective subscribers of the fact that the plan has an arbitration provision, and the plan contracts conform to subdivision (h) of Section 1373 of the Health and Safety Code.

(g) For the purposes of this section:

(1) "Health care provider" means any person licensed or certified pursuant to Division 2 (commencing with Section 500) of the Business and Professions Code, or licensed pursuant to the

Osteopathic Initiative Act, or the Chiropractic Initiative Act, or licensed pursuant to Chapter 2.5 (commencing with Section 1440) of Division 2 of the Health and Safety Code; and any clinic, health dispensary, or health facility, licensed pursuant to Division 2 (commencing with Section 1200) of the Health and Safety Code. "Health care provider" includes the legal representatives of a health care provider;

(2) "Professional negligence" means a negligent act or omission to act by a health care provider in the rendering of professional services, which act or omission is the proximate cause of a personal injury or wrongful death, provided that such services are within the scope of services for which the provider is licensed and which are not within any restriction imposed by the licensing agency or licensed hospital.

Ca. Civ. Proc. Code § 1295
Amended by Stats 2023 ch 42 (AB 118),s 1, eff. 7/10/2023.
Amended by Stats. 1976, Ch. 1185.

Title 9.2 - PUBLIC CONSTRUCTION CONTRACT ARBITRATION

Section 1296 - Agreement that arbitrator's decision supported by law and substantial evidence

The parties to a construction contract with a public agency may expressly agree in writing that in any arbitration to resolve a dispute relating to the contract, the arbitrator's award shall be supported by law and substantial evidence. If the agreement so provides, a court shall, subject to Section 1286.4, vacate the award if after review of the award it determines either that the award is not supported by substantial evidence or that it is based on an error of law.

Ca. Civ. Proc. Code § 1296
Added by Stats. 1979, Ch. 46.

Title 9.3 - ARBITRATION AND CONCILIATION OF INTERNATIONAL COMMERCIAL DISPUTES

Chapter 1 - APPLICATION AND INTERPRETATION

Article 1 - SCOPE OF APPLICATION

Section 1297.11 - Applicability of title generally

This title applies to international commercial arbitration and conciliation, subject to any agreement which is in force between the United States and any other state or states.

Ca. Civ. Proc. Code § 1297.11
Added by Stats. 1988, Ch. 23, Sec. 1. Effective March 7, 1988.

Section 1297.12 - Applicability only if place of arbitration or conciliation in state

This title, except Article 2 (commencing with Section 1297.81) of Chapter 2 and Article 3 (commencing with Section 1297.91) of Chapter 2, applies only if the place of arbitration or conciliation is in the State of California.

Ca. Civ. Proc. Code § 1297.12
Added by Stats. 1988, Ch. 23, Sec. 1. Effective March 7, 1988.

Section 1297.13 - Conditions making agreement international

An arbitration or conciliation agreement is international if any of the following applies:

(a) The parties to an arbitration or conciliation agreement have, at the time of the conclusion of that agreement, their places of business in different states.

(b) One of the following places is situated outside the state in which the parties have their places of business:

(i) The place of arbitration or conciliation if determined in, or pursuant to, the arbitration or conciliation agreement.

(ii) Any place where a substantial part of the obligations of the commercial relationship is to be performed.

(iii) The place with which the subject matter of the dispute is most closely connected.

(c) The parties have expressly agreed that the subject matter of the arbitration or conciliation agreement relates to commercial interests in more than one state.

(d) The subject matter of the arbitration or conciliation agreement is otherwise related to commercial interests in more than one state.

Ca. Civ. Proc. Code § 1297.13

Added by Stats. 1988, Ch. 23, Sec. 1. Effective March 7, 1988.

Section 1297.14 - Place of business if party has more than one place of business

For the purposes of Section 1297.13, if a party has more than one place of business, the place of business is that which has the closest relationship to the arbitration agreement, and if a party does not have a place of business, reference is to be made to his habitual residence.

Ca. Civ. Proc. Code § 1297.14

Added by Stats. 1988, Ch. 23, Sec. 1. Effective March 7, 1988.

Section 1297.15 - States of United States considered one state

For the purposes of Section 1297.13, the states of the United States, including the District of Columbia, shall be considered one state.

Ca. Civ. Proc. Code § 1297.15

Added by Stats. 1988, Ch. 23, Sec. 1. Effective March 7, 1988.

Section 1297.16 - Relationships making agreement commercial

An arbitration or conciliation agreement is commercial if it arises out of a relationship of a commercial nature including, but not limited to, any of the following:

(a) A transaction for the supply or exchange of goods or services.

(b) A distribution agreement.

(c) A commercial representation or agency.

(d) An exploitation agreement or concession.

(e) A joint venture or other, related form of industrial or business cooperation.

(f) The carriage of goods or passengers by air, sea, rail, or road.

(g) Construction.

(h) Insurance.

(i) Licensing.

(j) Factoring.

(k) Leasing.

(l) Consulting.

(m) Engineering.

(n) Financing.

(o) Banking.

(p) The transfer of data or technology.

(q) Intellectual or industrial property, including trademarks, patents, copyrights and software programs.

(r) Professional services.

Ca. Civ. Proc. Code § 1297.16

Added by Stats. 1988, Ch. 23, Sec. 1. Effective March 7, 1988.

Section 1297.17 - Other state laws not affected

This title shall not affect any other law in force in California by virtue of which certain disputes may not be submitted to arbitration or may be submitted to arbitration only in accordance with provisions other than those of this title. Notwithstanding the foregoing, this title supersedes Sections 1280 to 1284.2, inclusive, with respect to international commercial arbitration and conciliation.

Ca. Civ. Proc. Code § 1297.17

Added by Stats. 1988, Ch. 23, Sec. 1. Effective March 7, 1988.

Article 2 - INTERPRETATION

Section 1297.21 - Definitions
For the purposes of this title:

(a) "Arbitral award" means any decision of the arbitral tribunal on the substance of the dispute submitted to it and includes an interim, interlocutory, or partial arbitral award.

(b) "Arbitral tribunal" means a sole arbitrator or a panel of arbitrators.

(c) "Arbitration" means any arbitration whether or not administered by a permanent arbitral institution.

(d) "Conciliation" means any conciliation whether or not administered by a permanent conciliation institution.

(e) "Chief Justice" means the Chief Justice of California or his or her designee.

(f) "Court" means a body or an organ of the judicial system of a state.

(g) "Party" means a party to an arbitration or conciliation agreement.

(h) "Superior court" means the superior court in the county in this state selected pursuant to Section 1297.61.

(i) "Supreme Court" means the Supreme Court of California.

Ca. Civ. Proc. Code § 1297.21

Added by Stats. 1988, Ch. 23, Sec. 1. Effective March 7, 1988.

Section 1297.22 - Right of parties to authorize third party to make determination
Where a provision of this title, except Article 1 (commencing with Section 1297.281) of Chapter 6, leaves the parties free to determine a certain issue, such freedom includes the right of the parties to authorize a third party, including an institution, to make that determination.

Ca. Civ. Proc. Code § 1297.22

Added by Stats. 1988, Ch. 23, Sec. 1. Effective March 7, 1988.

Section 1297.23 - Reference to agreement to include rules referred to in agreement

Where a provision of this title refers to the fact that the parties have agreed or that they may agree, or in any other way refers to an agreement of the parties, such agreement shall be deemed to include any arbitration or conciliation rules referred to in that agreement.

Ca. Civ. Proc. Code § 1297.23

Added by Stats. 1988, Ch. 23, Sec. 1. Effective March 7, 1988.

Section 1297.24 - Reference to claim applies to counterclaim

Where this title, other than Article 8 (commencing with Section 1297. 251) of Chapter 5, Article 5 (commencing with Section 1297.321) of Chapter 6, or subdivision (a) of Section 1297.322, refers to a claim, it also applies to a counterclaim, and where it refers to a defense, it also applies to a defense to that counterclaim.

Ca. Civ. Proc. Code § 1297.24

Added by Stats. 1988, Ch. 23, Sec. 1. Effective March 7, 1988.

Article 3 - RECEIPT OF WRITTEN COMMUNICATIONS

Section 1297.31 - When communication deemed received

Unless otherwise agreed by the parties, any written communication is deemed to have been received if it is delivered to the addressee personally or if it is delivered at his place of business, habitual residence, or mailing address, and the communication is deemed to have been received on the day it is so delivered.

Ca. Civ. Proc. Code § 1297.31

Added by Stats. 1988, Ch. 23, Sec. 1. Effective March 7, 1988.

Section 1297.32 - Communication sent to addresse's last known place of business, residence or mailing address

If none of the places referred to in Section 1297.31 can be found after making a reasonable inquiry, a written communication is

deemed to have been received if it is sent to the addressee's last
known place of business, habitual residence, or mailing address by
registered mail or by any other means which provides a record of
the attempt to deliver it.

Ca. Civ. Proc. Code § 1297.32

Added by Stats. 1988, Ch. 23, Sec. 1. Effective March 7, 1988.

Section 1297.33 - Inapplicable to communications in respect to court proceedings

This article does not apply to written communications in respect of
court proceedings.

Ca. Civ. Proc. Code § 1297.33

Added by Stats. 1988, Ch. 23, Sec. 1. Effective March 7, 1988.

Article 4 - WAIVER OF RIGHT TO OBJECT

Section 1297.41 - Proceeding to arbitration without timely stating objection

A party who knows that any provision of this title, or any
requirement under the arbitration agreement, has not been
complied with and yet proceeds with the arbitration without stating
his or her objection to noncompliance without undue delay or, if a
time limit is provided for stating that objection, within that period
of time, shall be deemed to have waived his right to object.

Ca. Civ. Proc. Code § 1297.41

Added by Stats. 1988, Ch. 23, Sec. 1. Effective March 7, 1988.

Section 1297.42 - Any provision of this title defined

For purposes of Section 1297.41, "any provision of this title" means
any provision of this title in respect of which the parties may
otherwise agree.

Ca. Civ. Proc. Code § 1297.42

Added by Stats. 1988, Ch. 23, Sec. 1. Effective March 7, 1988.

Article 5 - EXTENT OF JUDICIAL INTERVENTION

Section 1297.51 - Intervention by court

In matters governed by this title, no court shall intervene except
where so provided in this title, or applicable federal law.

Ca. Civ. Proc. Code § 1297.51

Added by Stats. 1988, Ch. 23, Sec. 1. Effective March 7, 1988.

Article 6 - FUNCTIONS

Section 1297.61 - Functions performed by superior courts

The functions referred to in Sections 1297.114, 1297.115, 1297.116,
1297.134, 1297.135, 1297.136, 1297.165, 1297.166, and 1297.167 shall
be performed by the superior court of the county in which the place
of arbitration is located. The functions referred to in Section
1297.81 shall be performed by the superior court selected pursuant
to Article 2 (commencing with Section 1292) of Chapter 5 of Title 9.

Ca. Civ. Proc. Code § 1297.61

Added by Stats. 1988, Ch. 23, Sec. 1. Effective March 7, 1988.

Chapter 2 - ARBITRATION AGREEMENTS AND JUDICIAL MEASURES IN AID OF ARBITRATION

Article 1 - DEFINITION AND FORM OF ARBITRATION AGREEMENTS

Section 1297.71 - Arbitration agreement defined

An "arbitration agreement" is an agreement by the parties to submit
to arbitration all or certain disputes which have arisen or which
may arise between them in respect of a defined legal relationship,
whether contractual or not. An arbitration agreement may be in the
form of an arbitration clause in a contract or in the form of a
separate agreement.

Ca. Civ. Proc. Code § 1297.71

Added by Stats. 1988, Ch. 23, Sec. 1. Effective March 7, 1988.

Section 1297.72 - Agreement to be in writing

An arbitration agreement shall be in writing. An agreement is in writing if it is contained in a document signed by the parties or in an exchange of letters, telex, telegrams, or other means of telecommunication which provide a record of this agreement, or in an exchange of statements of claim and defense in which the existence of an agreement is alleged by one party and not denied by another. The reference in a contract to a document containing an arbitration clause constitutes an arbitration agreement provided that the contract is in writing and the reference is such as to make that clause part of the contract.

Ca. Civ. Proc. Code § 1297.72

Added by Stats. 1988, Ch. 23, Sec. 1. Effective March 7, 1988.

Article 2 - STAY OF PROCEEDINGS

Section 1297.81 - Application for order to stay proceedings and compel arbitration

When a party to an international commercial arbitration agreement as defined in this title commences judicial proceedings seeking relief with respect to a matter covered by the agreement to arbitrate, any other party to the agreement may apply to the superior court for an order to stay the proceedings and to compel arbitration.

Ca. Civ. Proc. Code § 1297.81

Added by Stats. 1988, Ch. 23, Sec. 1. Effective March 7, 1988.

Section 1297.82 - Timely request granted

A timely request for a stay of judicial proceedings made under Section 1297.81 shall be granted.

Ca. Civ. Proc. Code § 1297.82

Added by Stats. 1988, Ch. 23, Sec. 1. Effective March 7, 1988.

Article 3 - INTERIM MEASURES

Section 1297.91 - Request for interim measures not incompatible with agreement

It is not incompatible with an arbitration agreement for a party to request from a superior court, before or during arbitral proceedings, an interim measure of protection, or for the court to grant such a measure.

Ca. Civ. Proc. Code § 1297.91

Added by Stats. 1988, Ch. 23, Sec. 1. Effective March 7, 1988.

Section 1297.92 - Request for enforcement of award of arbitral tribunal

Any party to an arbitration governed by this title may request from the superior court enforcement of an award of an arbitral tribunal to take any interim measure of protection of an arbitral tribunal pursuant to Article 2 (commencing with Section 1297.171) of Chapter 4. Enforcement shall be granted pursuant to the law applicable to the granting of the type of interim relief requested.

Ca. Civ. Proc. Code § 1297.92

Added by Stats. 1988, Ch. 23, Sec. 1. Effective March 7, 1988.

Section 1297.93 - Measures court may grant in connection with pending arbitration

Measures which the court may grant in connection with a pending arbitration include, but are not limited to:

(a) An order of attachment issued to assure that the award to which applicant may be entitled is not rendered ineffectual by the dissipation of party assets.

(b) A preliminary injunction granted in order to protect trade secrets or to conserve goods which are the subject matter of the arbitral dispute.

Ca. Civ. Proc. Code § 1297.93

Added by Stats. 1988, Ch. 23, Sec. 1. Effective March 7, 1988.

Section 1297.94 - Preclusive effect given to findings of fact of arbitral tribunal

In considering a request for interim relief, the court shall give preclusive effect to any and all findings of fact of the arbitral tribunal including the probable validity of the claim which is the subject of the award for interim relief and which the arbitral tribunal has previously granted in the proceeding in question, provided that such interim award is consistent with public policy.

Ca. Civ. Proc. Code § 1297.94
Added by Stats. 1988, Ch. 23, Sec. 1. Effective March 7, 1988.

Section 1297.95 - Preclusive effect to tribunal's findings given until court finding on jurisdiction

Where the arbitral tribunal has not ruled on an objection to its jurisdiction, the court shall not grant preclusive effect to the tribunal's findings until the court has made an independent finding as to the jurisdiction of the arbitral tribunal. If the court rules that the arbitral tribunal did not have jurisdiction, the application for interim measures of relief shall be denied. Such a ruling by the court that the arbitral tribunal lacks jurisdiction is not binding on the arbitral tribunal or subsequent judicial proceeding.

Ca. Civ. Proc. Code § 1297.95
Added by Stats. 1988, Ch. 23, Sec. 1. Effective March 7, 1988.

Chapter 3 - COMPOSITION OF ARBITRAL TRIBUNALS

Article 1 - NUMBER OF ARBITRATORS

Section 1297.101 - Generally

The parties may agree on the number of arbitrators. Otherwise, there shall be one arbitrator.

Ca. Civ. Proc. Code § 1297.101
Added by Stats. 1988, Ch. 23, Sec. 1. Effective March 7, 1988.

Article 2 - APPOINTMENT OF ARBITRATORS

Section 1297.111 - Person of any nationality

A person of any nationality may be an arbitrator.

Ca. Civ. Proc. Code § 1297.111

Added by Stats. 1988, Ch. 23, Sec. 1. Effective March 7, 1988.

Section 1297.112 - Parties may agree on procedure for appointing

Subject to Sections 1297.115 and 1297.116, the parties may agree on
a procedure for appointing the arbitral tribunal.

Ca. Civ. Proc. Code § 1297.112

Added by Stats. 1988, Ch. 23, Sec. 1. Effective March 7, 1988.

Section 1297.113 - Appointment in arbitration with three arbitrators and two parties

Failing such agreement referred to in Section 1297.112, in an
arbitration with three arbitrators and two parties, each party shall
appoint one arbitrator, and the two appointed arbitrators shall
appoint the third arbitrator.

Ca. Civ. Proc. Code § 1297.113

Added by Stats. 1988, Ch. 23, Sec. 1. Effective March 7, 1988.

Section 1297.114 - Failure to timely agree on appointment

If the appointment procedure in Section 1297.113 applies and either
a party fails to appoint an arbitrator within 30 days after receipt of a
request to do so from the other party, or the two appointed
arbitrators fail to agree on the third arbitrator within 30 days after
their appointment, the appointment shall be made, upon request of
a party, by the superior court.

Ca. Civ. Proc. Code § 1297.114

Added by Stats. 1988, Ch. 23, Sec. 1. Effective March 7, 1988.

Section 1297.115 - Appointment on failure to agree on sole arbitrator

Failing any agreement referred to in Section 1297.112, in an arbitration with a sole arbitrator, if the parties fail to agree on the arbitrator, the appointment shall be made, upon request of a party, by the superior court.

Ca. Civ. Proc. Code § 1297.115

Added by Stats. 1988, Ch. 23, Sec. 1. Effective March 7, 1988.

Section 1297.116 - Necessary measures taken by superior court

The superior court, upon the request of a party, may take the necessary measures, unless the agreement on the appointment procedure provides other means for securing the appointment, where, under an appointment procedure agreed upon by the parties, any of the following occurs:

(a) A party fails to act as required under that procedure.

(b) The parties, or two appointed arbitrators, fail to reach an agreement expected of them under that procedure.

(c) A third party, including an institution, fails to perform any function entrusted to it under that procedure.

Ca. Civ. Proc. Code § 1297.116

Added by Stats. 1988, Ch. 23, Sec. 1. Effective March 7, 1988.

Section 1297.117 - Decision of superior court final

A decision on a matter entrusted to the superior court pursuant to Sections 1297.114, 127.115, and 1297.116 is final and is not subject to appeal.

Ca. Civ. Proc. Code § 1297.117

Added by Stats. 1988, Ch. 23, Sec. 1. Effective March 7, 1988.

Section 1297.118 - Considerations by superior court in appointing arbitrator

The superior court, in appointing an arbitrator, shall have due regard to all of the following:

(a) Any qualifications required of the arbitrator by the agreement of the parties.

(b) Other considerations as are likely to secure the appointment of an independent and impartial arbitrator.

(c) In the case of a sole or third arbitrator, the advisability of appointing an arbitrator of a nationality other than those of the parties.

Ca. Civ. Proc. Code § 1297.118

Added by Stats. 1988, Ch. 23, Sec. 1. Effective March 7, 1988.

Section 1297.119 - Immunity of arbitrator

An arbitrator has the immunity of a judicial officer from civil liability when acting in the capacity of arbitrator under any statute or contract.

The immunity afforded by this section shall supplement, and not supplant, any otherwise applicable common law or statutory immunity.

Ca. Civ. Proc. Code § 1297.119

Added by Stats. 1994, Ch. 228, Sec. 1. Effective January 1, 1995.

Article 3 - GROUNDS FOR CHALLENGE

Section 1297.121 - Disclosure of information causing impartiality to be question

Except as otherwise provided in this title, all persons whose names have been submitted for consideration for appointment or designation as arbitrators or conciliators, or who have been appointed or designated as such, shall, within 15 days, make a disclosure to the parties of any information which might cause their impartiality to be questioned including, but not limited to, any of the following instances:

(a) The person has a personal bias or prejudice concerning a party, or personal knowledge of disputed evidentiary facts concerning the proceeding.

(b) The person served as a lawyer in the matter in controversy, or the person is or has been associated with another who has participated in the matter during such association, or he or she has been a material witness concerning it.

(c) The person served as an arbitrator or conciliator in another proceeding involving one or more of the parties to the proceeding.

(d) The person, individually or a fiduciary, or such person's spouse or minor child residing in such person's household, has a financial interest in the subject matter in controversy or in a party to the proceeding, or any other interest that could be substantially affected by the outcome of the proceeding.

(e) The person, his or her spouse, or a person within the third degree of relationship to either of them, or the spouse of such a person meets any of the following conditions:

(i) The person is or has been a party to the proceeding, or an officer, director, or trustee of a party.

(ii) The person is acting or has acted as a lawyer in the proceeding.

(iii) The person is known to have an interest that could be substantially affected by the outcome of the proceeding.

(iv) The person is likely to be a material witness in the proceeding.

(f) The person has a close personal or professional relationship with a person who meets any of the following conditions:

(i) The person is or has been a party to the proceeding, or an officer, director, or trustee of a party.

(ii) The person is acting or has acted as a lawyer or representative in the proceeding.

(iii) The person is or expects to be nominated as an arbitrator or conciliator in the proceedings.

(iv) The person is known to have an interest that could be substantially affected by the outcome of the proceeding.

(v) The person is likely to be a material witness in the proceeding.

Ca. Civ. Proc. Code § 1297.121

Added by Stats. 1988, Ch. 23, Sec. 1. Effective March 7, 1988.

Section 1297.122 - Waiver of disclosure

The obligation to disclose information set forth in Section 1297.121
is mandatory and cannot be waived as to the parties with respect to
persons serving either as the sole arbitrator or sole conciliator or as
the chief or prevailing arbitrator or conciliator. The parties may
otherwise agree to waive such disclosure.

Ca. Civ. Proc. Code § 1297.122

Added by Stats. 1988, Ch. 23, Sec. 1. Effective March 7, 1988.

Section 1297.123 - Continuation of duty to disclose

From the time of appointment and throughout the arbitral
proceedings, an arbitrator, shall, without delay, disclose to the
parties any circumstances referred to in Section 1297.121 which
were not previously disclosed.

Ca. Civ. Proc. Code § 1297.123

Added by Stats. 1988, Ch. 23, Sec. 1. Effective March 7, 1988.

Section 1297.124 - Justifiable doubts as to independence or impartiality or qualifications

Unless otherwise agreed by the parties or the rules governing the
arbitration, an arbitrator may be challenged only if circumstances
exist that give rise to justifiable doubts as to his or her
independence or impartiality, or as to his or her possession of the
qualifications upon which the parties have agreed.

Ca. Civ. Proc. Code § 1297.124

Added by Stats. 1988, Ch. 23, Sec. 1. Effective March 7, 1988.

Section 1297.125 - Challenge for reasons becoming apparent after appointment

A party may challenge an arbitrator appointed by it, or in whose
appointment it has participated, only for reasons of which it

becomes aware after the appointment has been made.

Ca. Civ. Proc. Code § 1297.125

Added by Stats. 1988, Ch. 23, Sec. 1. Effective March 7, 1988.

Article 4 - CHALLENGE PROCEDURE

Section 1297.131 - Parties may agree on procedure

The parties may agree on a procedure for challenging an arbitrator
and the decision reached pursuant to that procedure shall be final.

Ca. Civ. Proc. Code § 1297.131

Added by Stats. 1988, Ch. 23, Sec. 1. Effective March 7, 1988.

Section 1297.132 - Time for sending written statement of reasons for challenge

Failing any agreement referred to in Section 1297.131, a party which
intends to challenge an arbitrator shall, within 15 days after
becoming aware of the constitution of the arbitral tribunal or after
becoming aware of any circumstances referred to in Sections
1297.124 and 1297.125, whichever shall be later, send a written
statement of the reasons for the challenge to the arbitral tribunal.

Ca. Civ. Proc. Code § 1297.132

Added by Stats. 1988, Ch. 23, Sec. 1. Effective March 7, 1988.

Section 1297.133 - Arbitral tribunal to decide challenge

Unless the arbitrator challenged under Section 1297.132 withdraws
from his or her office or the other party agrees to the challenge, the
arbitral tribunal shall decide on the challenge.

Ca. Civ. Proc. Code § 1297.133

Added by Stats. 1988, Ch. 23, Sec. 1. Effective March 7, 1988.

Section 1297.134 - Requesting superior court to decide on challenge

If a challenge following the procedure under Section 1297.133 is not
successful, the challenging party may request the superior court,
within 30 days after having received notice of the decision rejecting

the challenge, to decide on the challenge. If a challenge is based upon the grounds set forth in Section 1297.121, and the superior court determines that the facts support a finding that such ground or grounds fairly exist, then the challenge should be sustained.

Ca. Civ. Proc. Code § 1297.134

Added by Stats. 1988, Ch. 23, Sec. 1. Effective March 7, 1988.

Section 1297.135 - Decision of superior court final

The decision of the superior court under Section 1297.134 is final and is not subject to appeal.

Ca. Civ. Proc. Code § 1297.135

Added by Stats. 1988, Ch. 23, Sec. 1. Effective March 7, 1988.

Section 1297.136 - Continuation with arbitral proceedings while request pending

While a request under Section 1297.134 is pending, the arbitral tribunal, including the challenged arbitrator, may continue with the arbitral proceedings and make an arbitral award.

Ca. Civ. Proc. Code § 1297.136

Added by Stats. 1988, Ch. 23, Sec. 1. Effective March 7, 1988.

Article 5 - FAILURE OR IMPOSSIBILITY TO ACT

Section 1297.141 - Termination of mandate of arbitrator

The mandate of an arbitrator terminates if he becomes de jure or de facto unable to perform his or her functions or for other reasons fails to act without undue delay, and he withdraws from his or her office or the parties agree to the termination of his or her mandate.

Ca. Civ. Proc. Code § 1297.141

Added by Stats. 1988, Ch. 23, Sec. 1. Effective March 7, 1988.

Section 1297.142 - Requesting superior court to decide remaining controversy

If a controversy remains concerning any of the grounds referred to in Section 1297.141, a party may request the superior court to decide on the termination of the mandate.

Ca. Civ. Proc. Code § 1297.142

Added by Stats. 1988, Ch. 23, Sec. 1. Effective March 7, 1988.

Section 1297.143 - Decision of superior court final

A decision of the superior court under Section 1297.142 is not subject to appeal.

Ca. Civ. Proc. Code § 1297.143

Added by Stats. 1988, Ch. 23, Sec. 1. Effective March 7, 1988.

Section 1297.144 - Acceptance of validity of ground referred to in section 1297.132 not implied

If, under this section or Section 1297.132, an arbitrator withdraws from office or a party agrees to the termination of the mandate of an arbitrator, this does not imply acceptance of the validity of any ground referred to in Section 1297.132.

Ca. Civ. Proc. Code § 1297.144

Added by Stats. 1988, Ch. 23, Sec. 1. Effective March 7, 1988.

Article 6 - TERMINATION OF MANDATE AND SUBSTITUTION OF ARBITRATORS

Section 1297.151 - Termination upon withdrawal of arbitrator

In addition to the circumstances referred to under Article 4 (commencing with Section 1297.131) and Article 5 (commencing with Section 1297.141) of this chapter, the mandate of an arbitrator terminates upon his or her withdrawal from office for any reason, or by or pursuant to agreement of the parties.

Ca. Civ. Proc. Code § 1297.151

Added by Stats. 1988, Ch. 23, Sec. 1. Effective March 7, 1988.

Section 1297.152 - Appointment of substitute arbitrator

Where the mandate of an arbitrator terminates, a substitute arbitrator shall be appointed according to the rules that were applicable to the appointment of the arbitrator being replaced.

Ca. Civ. Proc. Code § 1297.152
Added by Stats. 1988, Ch. 23, Sec. 1. Effective March 7, 1988.

Section 1297.153 - Hearings previously held repeated
Unless otherwise agreed by the parties:

(a) Where the sole or presiding arbitrator is replaced, any hearings previously held shall be repeated.

(b) Where an arbitrator other than the sole or presiding arbitrator is replaced, any hearings previously held may be repeated at the discretion of the arbitral tribunal.

Ca. Civ. Proc. Code § 1297.153
Added by Stats. 1988, Ch. 23, Sec. 1. Effective March 7, 1988.

Section 1297.154 - Order or ruling prior to replacement not invalid
Unless otherwise agreed by the parties, an order or ruling of the arbitral tribunal made prior to the replacement of an arbitrator under this section is not invalid because there has been a change in the composition of the tribunal.

Ca. Civ. Proc. Code § 1297.154
Added by Stats. 1988, Ch. 23, Sec. 1. Effective March 7, 1988.

Chapter 4 - JURISDICTION OF ARBITRAL TRIBUNALS

Article 1 - COMPETENCE OF AN ARBITRAL TRIBUNAL TO RULE ON ITS JURISDICTION

Section 1297.161 - Arbitration clause forming part of contract treated as agreement independent of other terms of contract
The arbitral tribunal may rule on its own jurisdiction, including ruling on any objections with respect to the existence or validity of the arbitration agreement, and for that purpose, an arbitration clause which forms part of a contract shall be treated as an

agreement independent of the other terms of the contract, and a
decision by the arbitral tribunal that the contract is null and void
shall not entail ipso jure the invalidity of the arbitration clause.

Ca. Civ. Proc. Code § 1297.161

Added by Stats. 1988, Ch. 23, Sec. 1. Effective March 7, 1988.

Section 1297.162 - Raising plea tribunal without jurisdiction

A plea that the arbitral tribunal does not have jurisdiction shall be
raised not later than the submission of the statement of defense.
However, a party is not precluded from raising such a plea by the
fact that he or she has appointed, or participated in the
appointment of, an arbitrator.

Ca. Civ. Proc. Code § 1297.162

Added by Stats. 1988, Ch. 23, Sec. 1. Effective March 7, 1988.

Section 1297.163 - Raising plea that tribunal exceeding jurisdiction

A plea that the arbitral tribunal is exceeding the scope of its
authority shall be raised as soon as the matter alleged to be beyond
the scope of its authority is raised during the arbitral proceedings.

Ca. Civ. Proc. Code § 1297.163

Added by Stats. 1988, Ch. 23, Sec. 1. Effective March 7, 1988.

Section 1297.164 - Admission of later plea if delay justified

The arbitral tribunal may, in either of the cases referred to in
Sections 1297.162 and 1297.163, admit a later plea if it considers the
delay justified.

Ca. Civ. Proc. Code § 1297.164

Added by Stats. 1988, Ch. 23, Sec. 1. Effective March 7, 1988.

Section 1297.165 - Plea rules on as preliminary question or award on merits

The arbitral tribunal may rule on a plea referred to in Sections
1297.162 and 1297.163 either as a preliminary question or in an

award on the merits.

Ca. Civ. Proc. Code § 1297.165

Added by Stats. 1988, Ch. 23, Sec. 1. Effective March 7, 1988.

Section 1297.166 - Time for requesting superior court to decide matter

If the arbitral tribunal rules as a preliminary question that it has jurisdiction, any party shall request the superior court, within 30 days after having received notice of that ruling, to decide the matter or shall be deemed to have waived objection to such finding.

Ca. Civ. Proc. Code § 1297.166

Added by Stats. 1988, Ch. 23, Sec. 1. Effective March 7, 1988.

Section 1297.167 - Continuation of proceedings while request pending

While a request under Section 1297.166 is pending, the arbitral tribunal may continue with the arbitral proceedings and make an arbitral award.

Ca. Civ. Proc. Code § 1297.167

Added by Stats. 1988, Ch. 23, Sec. 1. Effective March 7, 1988.

Article 2 - INTERIM MEASURES ORDERED BY ARBITRAL TRIBUNALS

Section 1297.171 - Authority to take measures of protection

Unless otherwise agreed by the parties, the arbitral tribunal may, at the request of a party, order a party to take any interim measure of protection as the arbitral tribunal may consider necessary in respect of the subject matter of the dispute.

Ca. Civ. Proc. Code § 1297.171

Added by Stats. 1988, Ch. 23, Sec. 1. Effective March 7, 1988.

Section 1297.172 - Appropriate security provided

The arbitral tribunal may require a party to provide appropriate

security in connection with a measure ordered under Section
1297.171.

Ca. Civ. Proc. Code § 1297.172

Added by Stats. 1988, Ch. 23, Sec. 1. Effective March 7, 1988.

Chapter 5 - MANNER AND CONDUCT OF ARBITRATION

Article 1 - EQUAL TREATMENT OF PARTIES

Section 1297.181 - Generally

The parties shall be treated with equality and each party shall be
given a full opportunity to present his or her case.

Ca. Civ. Proc. Code § 1297.181

Added by Stats. 1988, Ch. 23, Sec. 1. Effective March 7, 1988.

Article 1.5 - REPRESENTATION BY FOREIGN AND OUT-OF-STATE ATTORNEYS

Section 1297.185 - "Qualified attorney" defined

For purposes of this article, a "qualified attorney" means an
individual who is not admitted to practice law in this state but is all
of the following:

(a) Admitted to practice law in a state or territory of the United
States or the District of Columbia or a member of a recognized legal
profession in a foreign jurisdiction, the members of which are
admitted or otherwise authorized to practice as attorneys or
counselors at law or the equivalent.

(b) Subject to effective regulation and discipline by a duly
constituted professional body or public authority of that
jurisdiction.

(c) In good standing in every jurisdiction in which he or she is
admitted or otherwise authorized to practice.

Ca. Civ. Proc. Code § 1297.185

Added by Stats 2018 ch 134 (SB 766),s 1, eff. 1/1/2019.

Section 1297.186 - Provision of services in international commercial arbitration or related conciliation, mediation, or alternative dispute resolution proceeding

(a) Notwithstanding any other law, including Section 6125 of the Business and Professions Code, a qualified attorney may provide legal services in an international commercial arbitration or related conciliation, mediation, or alternative dispute resolution proceeding, if any of the following conditions is satisfied:

(1) The services are undertaken in association with an attorney who is admitted to practice in this state and who actively participates in the matter.

(2) The services arise out of or are reasonably related to the attorney's practice in a jurisdiction in which the attorney is admitted to practice.

(3) The services are performed for a client who resides in or has an office in the jurisdiction in which the attorney is admitted or otherwise authorized to practice.

(4) The services arise out of or are reasonably related to a matter that has a substantial connection to a jurisdiction in which the attorney is admitted or otherwise authorized to practice.

(5) The services arise out of a dispute governed primarily by international law or the law of a foreign or out-of-state jurisdiction.

(b) This section does not apply to a dispute or controversy concerning any of the following:

(1) An individual's acquisition or lease of goods or services primarily for personal, family, or household use.

(2) An individual's coverage under a health insurance plan or an interaction between an individual and a healthcare provider.

(3) An application for employment in California.

(4) The terms and conditions of, or right to, employment in California, unless the dispute or controversy primarily concerns intellectual property rights, including those involving trademarks, patents, copyright, and software programs.

(c) This section does not affect the right of an attorney admitted to practice law in this state to provide legal services in an international commercial arbitration or related conciliation, mediation, or alternative dispute resolution proceeding, or the right of representation established in Section 1297.351.

Ca. Civ. Proc. Code § 1297.186
Added by Stats 2018 ch 134 (SB 766),s 1, eff. 1/1/2019.

Section 1297.187 - Permission to appear pro hac vice

A qualified attorney rendering legal services pursuant to this article shall not appear in a court of this state unless he or she has applied for and received permission to appear as counsel pro hac vice pursuant to the California Rules of Court, as applicable.

Ca. Civ. Proc. Code § 1297.187
Added by Stats 2018 ch 134 (SB 766),s 1, eff. 1/1/2019.

Section 1297.188 - Disciplinary authority

(a) A qualified attorney rendering legal services pursuant to this article is subject to the jurisdiction of the courts and disciplinary authority of this state with respect to the California Rules of Professional Conduct and the laws governing the conduct of attorneys to the same extent as a member of the State Bar of California.

(b) The State Bar of California may report complaints and evidence of disciplinary violations against an attorney practicing pursuant to this article to the appropriate disciplinary authority of any jurisdiction in which the attorney is admitted or otherwise authorized to practice law. This section does not limit or affect the authority of the State Bar to report information about an attorney to authorities in any jurisdiction in which the attorney is admitted or otherwise authorized to practice law.

(c) On or before May 1 of each year, the State Bar shall submit a report to the Supreme Court that specifies the number and nature of any complaints that it has received during the prior calendar year against attorneys who provide legal services pursuant to this article and any actions it has taken in response to those complaints.

Ca. Civ. Proc. Code § 1297.188

Added by Stats 2018 ch 134 (SB 766),s 1, eff. 1/1/2019.

Section 1297.189 - Court rules

The Supreme Court may issue rules implementing this article.

Ca. Civ. Proc. Code § 1297.189

Added by Stats 2018 ch 134 (SB 766),s 1, eff. 1/1/2019.

Article 2 - DETERMINATION OF RULES OF PROCEDURE

Section 1297.191 - Parties may agree on procedure

Subject to this title, the parties may agree on the procedure to be followed by the arbitral tribunal in conducting the proceedings.

Ca. Civ. Proc. Code § 1297.191

Added by Stats. 1988, Ch. 23, Sec. 1. Effective March 7, 1988.

Section 1297.192 - Arbitration conducted in manner tribunal considers appropriate

Failing any agreement referred to in Section 1297.191, the arbitral tribunal may, subject to this title, conduct the arbitration in the manner it considers appropriate.

Ca. Civ. Proc. Code § 1297.192

Added by Stats. 1988, Ch. 23, Sec. 1. Effective March 7, 1988.

Section 1297.193 - Power of tribunal under section 1297.192

The power of the arbitral tribunal under Section 1297.192 includes the power to determine the admissibility, relevance, materiality, and weight of any evidence.

Ca. Civ. Proc. Code § 1297.193
Added by Stats. 1988, Ch. 23, Sec. 1. Effective March 7, 1988.

Article 3 - PLACE OF ARBITRATION

Section 1297.201 - Parties may agree
The parties may agree on the place of arbitration.
Ca. Civ. Proc. Code § 1297.201
Added by Stats. 1988, Ch. 23, Sec. 1. Effective March 7, 1988.

Section 1297.202 - Place determined by tribunal failing agreement
Failing any agreement referred to in Section 1297.201, the place of
arbitration shall be determined by the arbitral tribunal having
regard to the circumstances of the case, including the convenience
of the parties.
Ca. Civ. Proc. Code § 1297.202
Added by Stats. 1988, Ch. 23, Sec. 1. Effective March 7, 1988.

Section 1297.203 - Meeting at any place tribunal considers appropriate
Notwithstanding Section 1297.201, the arbitral tribunal may, unless
otherwise agreed by the parties, meet at any place it considers
appropriate for consultation among its members, for hearing
witnesses, experts, or the parties, or for inspection of documents,
goods, or other property.
Ca. Civ. Proc. Code § 1297.203
Added by Stats. 1988, Ch. 23, Sec. 1. Effective March 7, 1988.

Article 4 - COMMENCEMENT OF ARBITRAL PROCEEDINGS

Section 1297.211 - Generally
Unless otherwise agreed by the parties, the arbitral proceedings in
respect of a particular dispute commence on the date on which a

request for that dispute to be referred to arbitration is received by
the respondent.

Ca. Civ. Proc. Code § 1297.211

Added by Stats. 1988, Ch. 23, Sec. 1. Effective March 7, 1988.

Article 5 - LANGUAGE

Section 1297.221 - Parties may agree upon language used

The parties may agree upon the language or languages to be used in
the arbitral proceedings.

Ca. Civ. Proc. Code § 1297.221

Added by Stats. 1988, Ch. 23, Sec. 1. Effective March 7, 1988.

Section 1297.222 - Tribunal to determine language failing agreement

Failing any agreement referred to in Section 1297.221, the arbitral
tribunal shall determine the language or languages to be used in the
arbitral proceedings.

Ca. Civ. Proc. Code § 1297.222

Added by Stats. 1988, Ch. 23, Sec. 1. Effective March 7, 1988.

Section 1297.223 - Applicability of agreement or determination

The agreement or determination, unless otherwise specified, shall
apply to any written statement by a party, any hearing, and any
arbitral award, decision, or other communication by the arbitral
tribunal.

Ca. Civ. Proc. Code § 1297.223

Added by Stats. 1988, Ch. 23, Sec. 1. Effective March 7, 1988.

Section 1297.224 - Documentary evidence accompanied by translation

The arbitral tribunal may order that any documentary evidence
shall be accompanied by a translation into the language or
languages agreed upon by the parties or determined by the arbitral

tribunal.

Ca. Civ. Proc. Code § 1297.224

Added by Stats. 1988, Ch. 23, Sec. 1. Effective March 7, 1988.

Article 6 - STATEMENTS OF CLAIM AND DEFENSE

Section 1297.231 - Generally

Within the period of time agreed upon by the parties or determined by the arbitral tribunal, the claimant shall state the facts supporting his or her claim, the points at issue, and the relief or remedy sought, and the respondent shall state his or her defense in respect of these particulars, unless the parties have otherwise agreed as to the required elements of those statements.

Ca. Civ. Proc. Code § 1297.231

Added by Stats. 1988, Ch. 23, Sec. 1. Effective March 7, 1988.

Section 1297.232 - Submission of relevant documents with statements

The parties may submit with their statements all documents they consider to be relevant or may add a reference to the documents or other evidence they will submit.

Ca. Civ. Proc. Code § 1297.232

Added by Stats. 1988, Ch. 23, Sec. 1. Effective March 7, 1988.

Section 1297.233 - Amendment or supplementation of claim or defense

Unless otherwise agreed by the parties, either party may amend or supplement his or her claim or defense during the course of the arbitral proceedings, unless the arbitral tribunal considers it inappropriate to allow the amendment or supplement having regard to the delay in making it.

Ca. Civ. Proc. Code § 1297.233

Added by Stats. 1988, Ch. 23, Sec. 1. Effective March 7, 1988.

Article 7 - HEARINGS AND WRITTEN PROCEEDINGS

Section 1297.241 - Tribunal to decide

Unless otherwise agreed by the parties, the arbitral tribunal shall decide whether to hold oral hearings for the presentation of evidence or for oral argument, or whether the proceedings shall be conducted on the basis of documents and other materials.

Ca. Civ. Proc. Code § 1297.241

Added by Stats. 1988, Ch. 23, Sec. 1. Effective March 7, 1988.

Section 1297.242 - Holding oral hearings if requested

Unless the parties have agreed that no oral hearings shall be held, the arbitral tribunal shall hold oral hearings at an appropriate state of the proceedings, if so requested by a party.

Ca. Civ. Proc. Code § 1297.242

Added by Stats. 1988, Ch. 23, Sec. 1. Effective March 7, 1988.

Section 1297.243 - Notice of hearing or meeting

The parties shall be given sufficient advance notice of any hearing and of any meeting of the arbitral tribunal for the purpose of inspection of documents, goods, or other property.

Ca. Civ. Proc. Code § 1297.243

Added by Stats. 1988, Ch. 23, Sec. 1. Effective March 7, 1988.

Section 1297.244 - Information communicated to parties

All statements, documents, or other information supplied to, or applications made to, the arbitral tribunal by one party shall be communicated to the other party, and any expert report or evidentiary document on which the arbitral tribunal may rely in making its decision shall be communicated to the parties.

Ca. Civ. Proc. Code § 1297.244

Added by Stats. 1988, Ch. 23, Sec. 1. Effective March 7, 1988.

Section 1297.245 - Held in camera

Unless otherwise agreed by the parties, all oral hearings and
meetings in arbitral proceedings shall be held in camera.

Ca. Civ. Proc. Code § 1297.245

Added by Stats. 1988, Ch. 23, Sec. 1. Effective March 7, 1988.

Article 8 - DEFAULT OF A PARTY

Section 1297.251 - Failure of claimant to communicate statement of claim

Unless otherwise agreed by the parties, where, without showing
sufficient cause, the claimant fails to communicate his or her
statement of claim in accordance with Sections 1297.231 and
1297.232, the arbitral tribunal shall terminate the proceedings.

Ca. Civ. Proc. Code § 1297.251

Added by Stats. 1988, Ch. 23, Sec. 1. Effective March 7, 1988.

Section 1297.252 - Failure of respondent to communicate statement of defense

Unless otherwise agreed by the parties, where, without showing
sufficient cause, the respondent fails to communicate his or her
statement of defense in accordance with Sections 1297.231 and
1297.232, the arbitral tribunal shall continue the proceedings
without treating that failure in itself as an admission of the
claimant's allegations.

Ca. Civ. Proc. Code § 1297.252

Added by Stats. 1988, Ch. 23, Sec. 1. Effective March 7, 1988.

Section 1297.253 - Failure to appear at oral hearing or produce documentary evidence

Unless otherwise agreed by the parties, where, without showing
sufficient cause, a party fails to appear at an oral hearing or to
produce documentary evidence, the arbitral tribunal may continue
with the proceedings and make the arbitral award on the evidence
before it.

Ca. Civ. Proc. Code § 1297.253
Added by Stats. 1988, Ch. 23, Sec. 1. Effective March 7, 1988.

Article 9 - EXPERT APPOINTED BY ARBITRAL TRIBUNAL

Section 1297.261 - Generally

Unless otherwise agreed by the parties, the arbitral tribunal may appoint one or more experts to report to it on specific issues to be determined by the arbitral tribunal, and require a party to give the expert any relevant information or to produce, or to provide access to, any relevant documents, goods, or other property for his or her inspection.

Ca. Civ. Proc. Code § 1297.261
Added by Stats. 1988, Ch. 23, Sec. 1. Effective March 7, 1988.

Section 1297.262 - Participation of expert in oral hearing

Unless otherwise agreed by the parties, if a party so requests or if the arbitral tribunal considers it necessary, the expert shall, after delivery of his or her written or oral report, participate in an oral hearing where the parties have the opportunity to question the expert and to present expert witnesses on the points at issue.

Ca. Civ. Proc. Code § 1297.262
Added by Stats. 1988, Ch. 23, Sec. 1. Effective March 7, 1988.

Article 10 - COURT ASSISTANCE IN TAKING EVIDENCE AND CONSOLIDATING ARBITRATIONS

Section 1297.271 - Request for superior court assistance

The arbitral tribunal, or a party with the approval of the arbitral tribunal, may request from the superior court assistance in taking evidence and the court may execute the request within its competence and according to its rules on taking evidence. In addition, a subpoena may issue as provided in Section 1282.6, in which case the witness compensation provisions of Section 1283.2

shall apply.

Ca. Civ. Proc. Code § 1297.271
Added by Stats. 1988, Ch. 23, Sec. 1. Effective March 7, 1988.

Section 1297.272 - Power of court where consolidation of arbitrations agreed to by parties

Where the parties to two or more arbitration agreements have agreed, in their respective arbitration agreements or otherwise, to consolidate the arbitrations arising out of those arbitration agreements, the superior court may, on application by one party with the consent of all the other parties to those arbitration agreements, do one or more of the following:

(a) Order the arbitrations to be consolidated on terms the court considers just and necessary.

(b) Where all the parties cannot agree on an arbitral tribunal for the consolidated arbitration, appoint an arbitral tribunal in accordance with Section 1297.118.

(c) Where all the parties cannot agree on any other matter necessary to conduct the consolidated arbitration, make any other order it considers necessary.

Ca. Civ. Proc. Code § 1297.272
Added by Stats. 1988, Ch. 23, Sec. 1. Effective March 7, 1988.

Section 1297.273 - Authority of parties to agree to consolidation of arbitrations

Nothing in this article shall be construed to prevent the parties to two or more arbitrations from agreeing to consolidate those arbitrations and taking any steps that are necessary to effect that consolidation.

Ca. Civ. Proc. Code § 1297.273
Added by Stats. 1988, Ch. 23, Sec. 1. Effective March 7, 1988.

Chapter 6 - MAKING OF ARBITRAL AWARD AND TERMINATION OF PROCEEDINGS

Article 1 - RULES APPLICABLE TO SUBSTANCE OF DISPUTE

Section 1297.281 - Dispute decided by tribunal in accordance with rules of law designated by parties

The arbitral tribunal shall decide the dispute in accordance with the rules of law designated by the parties as applicable to the substance of the dispute.

Ca. Civ. Proc. Code § 1297.281
Added by Stats. 1988, Ch. 23, Sec. 1. Effective March 7, 1988.

Section 1297.282 - Construction of designation of law or legal system

Any designation by the parties of the law or legal system of a given state shall be construed, unless otherwise expressed, as directly referring to the substantive law of that state and not to its conflict of laws rules.

Ca. Civ. Proc. Code § 1297.282
Added by Stats. 1988, Ch. 23, Sec. 1. Effective March 7, 1988.

Section 1297.283 - Failure of designation

Failing any designation of the law under Section 1297.282 by the parties, the arbitral tribunal shall apply the rules of law it considers to be appropriate given all the circumstances surrounding the dispute.

Ca. Civ. Proc. Code § 1297.283
Added by Stats. 1988, Ch. 23, Sec. 1. Effective March 7, 1988.

Section 1297.284 - Decision ex aequo et bono or amiable compositeur

The arbitral tribunal shall decide ex aequo et bono or as amiable compositeur, if the parties have expressly authorized it to do so.

Ca. Civ. Proc. Code § 1297.284
Added by Stats. 1988, Ch. 23, Sec. 1. Effective March 7, 1988.

Section 1297.285 - Decision in accordance with contract terms taking into account usage of trade

In all cases, the arbitral tribunal shall decide in accordance with the terms of the contract and shall take into account the usages of the trade applicable to the transaction.

Ca. Civ. Proc. Code § 1297.285
Added by Stats. 1988, Ch. 23, Sec. 1. Effective March 7, 1988.

Article 2 - DECISIONMAKING BY PANEL OF ARBITRATORS

Section 1297.291 - Generally

Unless otherwise agreed by the parties, in arbitral proceedings with more than one arbitrator, any decision of the arbitral tribunal shall be made by a majority of all of its members.

Notwithstanding this section, if authorized by the parties or all the members of the arbitral tribunal, questions of procedure may be decided by a presiding arbitrator.

Ca. Civ. Proc. Code § 1297.291
Added by Stats. 1988, Ch. 23, Sec. 1. Effective March 7, 1988.

Article 3 - SETTLEMENT

Section 1297.301 - Generally

It is not incompatible with an arbitration agreement for an arbitral tribunal to encourage settlement of the dispute and, with the agreement of the parties, the arbitral tribunal may use mediation, conciliation, or other procedures at any time during the arbitral proceedings to encourage settlement.

Ca. Civ. Proc. Code § 1297.301
Added by Stats. 1988, Ch. 23, Sec. 1. Effective March 7, 1988.

Section 1297.302 - Termination of proceedings upon settlement during arbitral proceedings

If, during arbitral proceedings, the parties settle the dispute, the arbitral tribunal shall terminate the proceedings and, if requested by the parties and not objected to by the arbitral tribunal, record the settlement in the form of an arbitral award on agreed terms.

Ca. Civ. Proc. Code § 1297.302

Added by Stats. 1988, Ch. 23, Sec. 1. Effective March 7, 1988.

Section 1297.303 - Law governing award on agreed terms

An arbitral award on agreed terms shall be made in accordance with Article 4 (commencing with Section 1297.311) of this chapter and shall state that it is an arbitral award.

Ca. Civ. Proc. Code § 1297.303

Added by Stats. 1988, Ch. 23, Sec. 1. Effective March 7, 1988.

Section 1297.304 - Status and effect of award on agreed terms

An arbitral award on agreed terms has the same status and effect as any other arbitral award on the substance of the dispute.

Ca. Civ. Proc. Code § 1297.304

Added by Stats. 1988, Ch. 23, Sec. 1. Effective March 7, 1988.

Article 4 - FORM AND CONTENT OF ARBITRAL AWARD

Section 1297.311 - Award in writing and signed by tribunal members

An arbitral award shall be made in writing and shall be signed by the members of the arbitral tribunal.

Ca. Civ. Proc. Code § 1297.311

Added by Stats. 1988, Ch. 23, Sec. 1. Effective March 7, 1988.

Section 1297.312 - Signature of majority of tribunal members sufficient

For the purposes of Section 1297.311, in arbitral proceedings with more than one arbitrator, the signatures of the majority of all the members of the arbitral tribunal shall be sufficient so long as the reason for any omitted signature is stated.

Ca. Civ. Proc. Code § 1297.312

Added by Stats. 1988, Ch. 23, Sec. 1. Effective March 7, 1988.

Section 1297.313 - Award to state reasons upon which award based, exception

The arbitral award shall state the reasons upon which it is based, unless the parties have agreed that no reasons are to be given, or the award is an arbitral award on agreed terms under Article 3 (commencing with Section 1297.301) of this chapter.

Ca. Civ. Proc. Code § 1297.313

Added by Stats. 1988, Ch. 23, Sec. 1. Effective March 7, 1988.

Section 1297.314 - Award to state date and place of arbitration

The arbitral award shall state its date and the place of arbitration as determined in accordance with Article 3 (commencing with Section 1297.201) of Chapter 5 and the award shall be deemed to have been made at that place.

Ca. Civ. Proc. Code § 1297.314

Added by Stats. 1988, Ch. 23, Sec. 1. Effective March 7, 1988.

Section 1297.315 - Signed copy delivered to parties

After the arbitral award is made, a signed copy shall be delivered to each party.

Ca. Civ. Proc. Code § 1297.315

Added by Stats. 1988, Ch. 23, Sec. 1. Effective March 7, 1988.

Section 1297.316 - Interim award

The arbitral tribunal may, at any time during the arbitral

proceedings, make an interim arbitral award on any matter with
respect to which it may make a final arbitral award. The interim
award may be enforced in the same manner as a final arbitral
award.

Ca. Civ. Proc. Code § 1297.316
Added by Stats. 1988, Ch. 23, Sec. 1. Effective March 7, 1988.

Section 1297.317 - Interest
Unless otherwise agreed by the parties, the arbitral tribunal may
award interest.

Ca. Civ. Proc. Code § 1297.317
Added by Stats. 1988, Ch. 23, Sec. 1. Effective March 7, 1988.

Section 1297.318 - Costs
(a) Unless otherwise agreed by the parties, the costs of an
arbitration shall be at the discretion of the arbitral tribunal.
(b) In making an order for costs, the arbitral tribunal may include
as costs any of the following:

(1) The fees and expenses of the arbitrators and expert
witnesses.

(2) Legal fees and expenses.

(3) Any administration fees of the institution supervising the
arbitration, if any.

(4) Any other expenses incurred in connection with the arbitral
proceedings.
(c) In making an order for costs, the arbitral tribunal may specify
any of the following:

(1) The party entitled to costs.

(2) The party who shall pay the costs.

(3) The amount of costs or method of determining that amount.

(4) The manner in which the costs shall be paid.
Ca. Civ. Proc. Code § 1297.318
Added by Stats. 1988, Ch. 23, Sec. 1. Effective March 7, 1988.

Article 5 - TERMINATION OF PROCEEDINGS

Section 1297.321 - Generally; award final upon expiration of applicable periods

The arbitral proceedings are terminated by the final arbitral award or by an order of the arbitral tribunal under Section 1297.322. The award shall be final upon the expiration of the applicable periods in Article 6 (commencing with Section 1297.331) of this chapter.
Ca. Civ. Proc. Code § 1297.321
Added by Stats. 1988, Ch. 23, Sec. 1. Effective March 7, 1988.

Section 1297.322 - When order for termination issued

The arbitral tribunal shall issue an order for the termination of the arbitral proceedings where any of the following occurs:
(a) The claimant withdraws his or her claim, unless the respondent objects to the order and the arbitral tribunal recognizes a legitimate interest on the respondent's part in obtaining a final settlement of the dispute.
(b) The parties agree on the termination of the proceedings.
(c) The arbitral tribunal finds that the continuation of the proceedings has for any other reason become unnecessary or impossible.
Ca. Civ. Proc. Code § 1297.322
Added by Stats. 1988, Ch. 23, Sec. 1. Effective March 7, 1988.

Section 1297.323 - Termination of tribunal mandate

Subject to Article 6 (commencing with Section 1297.331) of this chapter, the mandate of the arbitral tribunal terminates with the termination of the arbitral proceedings.

Ca. Civ. Proc. Code § 1297.323
Added by Stats. 1988, Ch. 23, Sec. 1. Effective March 7, 1988.

Article 6 - CORRECTION AND INTERPRETATION OF AWARDS AND ADDITIONAL AWARDS

Section 1297.331 - Time for requesting correction or interpretation

Within 30 days after receipt of the arbitral award, unless another period of time has been agreed upon by the parties:

(a) A party may request the arbitral tribunal to correct in the arbitral award any computation errors, any clerical or typographical errors, or any other errors of a similar nature.

(b) A party may, if agreed by the parties, request the arbitral tribunal to give an interpretation of a specific point or part of the arbitral award.

Ca. Civ. Proc. Code § 1297.331
Added by Stats. 1988, Ch. 23, Sec. 1. Effective March 7, 1988.

Section 1297.332 - Time for making correction or interpretation

If the arbitral tribunal considers any request made under Section 1297.331 to be justified, it shall make the correction or give the interpretation within 30 days after receipt of the request and the interpretation shall form part of the arbitral award.

Ca. Civ. Proc. Code § 1297.332
Added by Stats. 1988, Ch. 23, Sec. 1. Effective March 7, 1988.

Section 1297.333 - Correction of error on tribunal's initiative, time period

The arbitral tribunal may correct any error of the type referred to in subdivision (a) of Section 1297.331, on its own initiative, within 30 days after the date of the arbitral award.

Ca. Civ. Proc. Code § 1297.333
Added by Stats. 1988, Ch. 23, Sec. 1. Effective March 7, 1988.

Section 1297.334 - Time for requesting additional award

Unless otherwise agreed by the parties, a party may request, within 30 days after receipt of the arbitral award, the arbitral tribunal to make an additional arbitral award as to the claims presented in the arbitral proceedings but omitted from the arbitral award.

Ca. Civ. Proc. Code § 1297.334

Added by Stats. 1988, Ch. 23, Sec. 1. Effective March 7, 1988.

Section 1297.335 - Time for making additional award

If the arbitral tribunal considers any request made under Section 1297.334 to be justified, it shall make the additional arbitral award within 60 days after receipt of the request.

Ca. Civ. Proc. Code § 1297.335

Added by Stats. 1988, Ch. 23, Sec. 1. Effective March 7, 1988.

Section 1297.336 - Extension of periods of time

The arbitral tribunal may extend, if necessary, the period of time within which it shall make a correction, give an interpretation, or make an additional arbitral award under Section 1297.331 or 1297.334.

Ca. Civ. Proc. Code § 1297.336

Added by Stats. 1988, Ch. 23, Sec. 1. Effective March 7, 1988.

Section 1297.337 - Applicability of Article 4

Article 4 (commencing with Section 1297.311) of this chapter applies to a correction or interpretation of the arbitral award or to an additional arbitral award made under this section.

Ca. Civ. Proc. Code § 1297.337

Added by Stats. 1988, Ch. 23, Sec. 1. Effective March 7, 1988.

Chapter 7 - CONCILIATION

Article 1 - APPOINTMENT OF CONCILIATORS

Section 1297.341 - Policy of state; selection of conciliators

It is the policy of the State of California to encourage parties to an international commercial agreement or transaction which qualifies for arbitration or conciliation pursuant to Section 1297.13, to resolve disputes arising from such agreements or transactions through conciliation. The parties may select or permit an arbitral tribunal or other third party to select one or more persons to serve as the conciliator or conciliators who shall assist the parties in an independent and impartial manner in their attempt to reach an amicable settlement of their dispute.

Ca. Civ. Proc. Code § 1297.341

Added by Stats. 1988, Ch. 23, Sec. 1. Effective March 7, 1988.

Section 1297.342 - Guided by principles of objectivity, fairness and justice

The conciliator or conciliators shall be guided by principles of objectivity, fairness, and justice, giving consideration to, among other things, the rights and obligations of the parties, the usages of the trade concerned and the circumstances surrounding the dispute, including any previous practices between the parties.

Ca. Civ. Proc. Code § 1297.342

Added by Stats. 1988, Ch. 23, Sec. 1. Effective March 7, 1988.

Section 1297.343 - Manner of conducting proceedings

The conciliator or conciliators may conduct the conciliation proceedings in such a manner as they consider appropriate, taking into account the circumstances of the case, the wishes of the parties, and the desirability of a speedy settlement of the dispute. Except as otherwise provided in this title, other provisions of this code, the Evidence Code, or the California Rules of Court, shall not apply to conciliation proceedings brought under this title.

Ca. Civ. Proc. Code § 1297.343
Added by Stats. 1988, Ch. 23, Sec. 1. Effective March 7, 1988.

Article 2 - REPRESENTATION AND ASSISTANCE

Section 1297.351 - Generally

The parties may appear in person or be represented or assisted by
any person of their choice. A person assisting or representing a
party need not be a member of the legal profession or licensed to
practice law in California.

Ca. Civ. Proc. Code § 1297.351
Added by Stats. 1988, Ch. 23, Sec. 1. Effective March 7, 1988.

Article 3 - REPORT OF CONCILIATORS

Section 1297.361 - Draft settlement

At any time during the proceedings, the conciliator or conciliators
may prepare a draft conciliation settlement which may include the
assessment and apportionment of costs between the parties, and
send copies to the parties, specifying the time within which they
must signify their approval.

Ca. Civ. Proc. Code § 1297.361
Added by Stats. 1988, Ch. 23, Sec. 1. Effective March 7, 1988.

Section 1297.362 - Authority to require party to accept settlement proposed

No party may be required to accept any settlement proposed by the
conciliator or conciliators.

Ca. Civ. Proc. Code § 1297.362
Added by Stats. 1988, Ch. 23, Sec. 1. Effective March 7, 1988.

Article 4 - CONFIDENTIALITY

Section 1297.371 - Generally

When persons agree to participate in conciliation under this title:

(a) Evidence of anything said or of any admission made in the course of the conciliation is not admissible in evidence, and disclosure of any such evidence shall not be compelled, in any civil action in which, pursuant to law, testimony may be compelled to be given. However, this subdivision does not limit the admissibility of evidence if all parties participating in conciliation consent to its disclosure.

(b) In the event that any such evidence is offered in contravention of this section, the arbitration tribunal or the court shall make any order which it considers to be appropriate to deal with the matter, including, without limitation, orders restricting the introduction of evidence, or dismissing the case without prejudice.

(c) Unless the document otherwise provides, no document prepared for the purpose of, or in the course of, or pursuant to, the conciliation, or any copy thereof, is admissible in evidence, and disclosure of any such document shall not be compelled, in any arbitration or civil action in which, pursuant to law, testimony may be compelled to be given.

Ca. Civ. Proc. Code § 1297.371
Added by Stats. 1988, Ch. 23, Sec. 1. Effective March 7, 1988.

Article 5 - STAY OF ARBITRATION AND RESORT TO OTHER PROCEEDINGS

Section 1297.381 - Agreement stay judicial or arbitration proceedings
The agreement of the parties to submit a dispute to conciliation shall be deemed an agreement between or among those parties to stay all judicial or arbitral proceedings from the commencement of conciliation until the termination of conciliation proceedings.

Ca. Civ. Proc. Code § 1297.381
Added by Stats. 1988, Ch. 23, Sec. 1. Effective March 7, 1988.

Section 1297.382 - Limitations periods tolled and periods of prescription extended
All applicable limitation periods including periods of prescription shall be tolled or extended upon the commencement of conciliation

proceedings to conciliate a dispute under this title and all limitation periods shall remain tolled and periods of prescription extended as to all parties to the conciliation proceedings until the 10th day following the termination of conciliation proceedings. For purposes of this article, conciliation proceedings are deemed to have commenced as soon as (a) a party has requested conciliation of a particular dispute or disputes, and (b) the other party or parties agree to participate in the conciliation proceeding.

Ca. Civ. Proc. Code § 1297.382

Added by Stats. 1988, Ch. 23, Sec. 1. Effective March 7, 1988.

Article 6 - TERMINATION

Section 1297.391 - Termination as to all parties by declaration of conciliator or parties or signing settlement

The conciliation proceedings may be terminated as to all parties by any of the following:

(a) A written declaration of the conciliator or conciliators, after consultation with the parties, to the effect that further efforts at conciliation are no longer justified, on the date of the declaration.

(b) A written declaration of the parties addressed to the conciliator or conciliators to the effect that the conciliation proceedings are terminated, on the date of the declaration.

(c) The signing of a settlement agreement by all of the parties, on the date of the agreement.

Ca. Civ. Proc. Code § 1297.391

Added by Stats. 1988, Ch. 23, Sec. 1. Effective March 7, 1988.

Section 1297.392 - Termination as to particular parties by declaration or signing settlement

The conciliation proceedings may be terminated as to particular parties by either of the following:

(a) A written declaration of a party to the other party and the conciliator or conciliators, if appointed, to the effect that the conciliation proceedings shall be terminated as to that particular party, on the date of the declaration.

(b) The signing of a settlement agreement by some of the parties, on the date of the agreement.

Ca. Civ. Proc. Code § 1297.392

Added by Stats. 1988, Ch. 23, Sec. 1. Effective March 7, 1988.

Section 1297.393 - Participation of conciliator in arbitral or judicial proceedings of same dispute

No person who has served as conciliator may be appointed as an arbitrator for, or take part in any arbitral or judicial proceedings in, the same dispute unless all parties manifest their consent to such participation or the rules adopted for conciliation or arbitration otherwise provide.

Ca. Civ. Proc. Code § 1297.393

Added by Stats. 1988, Ch. 23, Sec. 1. Effective March 7, 1988.

Section 1297.394 - Rights or remedies not waived by submitting to conciliation

By submitting to conciliation, no party shall be deemed to have waived any rights or remedies which that party would have had if conciliation had not been initiated, other than those set forth in any settlement agreement which results from the conciliation.

Ca. Civ. Proc. Code § 1297.394

Added by Stats. 1988, Ch. 23, Sec. 1. Effective March 7, 1988.

Article 7 - ENFORCEABILITY OF DECREE

Section 1297.401 - Generally

If the conciliation succeeds in settling the dispute, and the result of the conciliation is reduced to writing and signed by the conciliator or conciliators and the parties or their representatives, the written agreement shall be treated as an arbitral award rendered by an arbitral tribunal duly constituted in and pursuant to the laws of this state, and shall have the same force and effect as a final award in arbitration.

Ca. Civ. Proc. Code § 1297.401

Added by Stats. 1988, Ch. 23, Sec. 1. Effective March 7, 1988.

Article 8 - COSTS

Section 1297.411 - Conciliator to fix costs and give notice; included in costs

Upon termination of the conciliation proceedings, the conciliator shall fix the costs of the conciliation and give written notice thereof to the parties. As used in this article, "costs" includes only the following:

(a) A reasonable fee to be paid to the conciliator or conciliators.

(b) The travel and other reasonable expenses of the conciliator or conciliators.

(c) The travel and other reasonable expenses of witnesses requested by the conciliator or conciliators with the consent of the parties.

(d) The cost of any expert advice requested by the conciliator or conciliators with the consent of the parties.

(e) The cost of any court.

Ca. Civ. Proc. Code § 1297.411
Added by Stats. 1988, Ch. 23, Sec. 1. Effective March 7, 1988.

Section 1297.412 - Apportionment

These costs shall be borne equally by the parties unless the settlement agreement provides for a different apportionment. All other expenses incurred by a party shall be borne by that party.

Ca. Civ. Proc. Code § 1297.412
Added by Stats. 1988, Ch. 23, Sec. 1. Effective March 7, 1988.

Article 9 - EFFECT ON JURISDICTION

Section 1297.421 - Consent to participate not deemed consent to jurisdiction of court of state if conciliation fails

Neither the request for conciliation, the consent to participate in the conciliation proceedings, the participation in such proceedings, nor the entering into a conciliation agreement or settlement shall be deemed as consent to the jurisdiction of any court in this state in the event conciliation fails.

Ca. Civ. Proc. Code § 1297.421
Added by Stats. 1988, Ch. 23, Sec. 1. Effective March 7, 1988.

Article 10 - IMMUNITY OF CONCILIATORS AND PARTIES

Section 1297.431 - Immunity while present in state for conciliation purposes
Neither the conciliator or conciliators, the parties, nor their representatives shall be subject to service of process on any civil matter while they are present in this state for the purpose of arranging for or participating in conciliation pursuant to this title.
Ca. Civ. Proc. Code § 1297.431
Added by Stats. 1988, Ch. 23, Sec. 1. Effective March 7, 1988.

Section 1297.432 - Immunity of conciliator
No person who serves as a conciliator shall be held liable in an action for damages resulting from any act or omission in the performance of his or her role as a conciliator in any proceeding subject to this title.
Ca. Civ. Proc. Code § 1297.432
Added by Stats. 1988, Ch. 23, Sec. 1. Effective March 7, 1988.

Title 9.4 - REAL ESTATE CONTRACT ARBITRATION

Section 1298 - Provision in contracts; format
(a) Whenever any contract to convey real property, or contemplated to convey real property in the future, including marketing contracts, deposit receipts, real property sales contracts as defined in Section 2985 of the Civil Code, leases together with options to purchase, or ground leases coupled with improvements, but not including powers of sale contained in deeds of trust or mortgages, contains a provision for binding arbitration of any dispute between the principals in the transaction, the contract shall have that provision clearly titled "ARBITRATION OF DISPUTES."

Title 9.4 - REAL ESTATE CONTRACT ARBITRATION

If a provision for binding arbitration is included in a printed contract, it shall be set out in at least 8-point bold type or in contrasting red in at least 8-point type, and if the provision is included in a typed contract, it shall be set out in capital letters.

(b) Whenever any contract or agreement between principals and agents in real property sales transactions, including listing agreements, as defined in Section 1086 of the Civil Code, contains a provision requiring binding arbitration of any dispute between the principals and agents in the transaction, the contract or agreement shall have that provision clearly titled "ARBITRATION OF DISPUTES." If a provision for binding arbitration is included in a printed contract, it shall be set out in at least 8-point bold type or in contrasting red in at least 8-point type, and if the provision is included in a typed contract, it shall be set out in capital letters.

(c) Immediately before the line or space provided for the parties to indicate their assent or nonassent to the arbitration provision described in subdivision (a) or (b), and immediately following that arbitration provision, the following shall appear: "NOTICE: BY INITIALLING IN THE SPACE BELOW YOU ARE AGREEING TO HAVE ANY DISPUTE ARISING OUT OF THE MATTERS INCLUDED IN THE 'ARBITRATION OF DISPUTES' PROVISION DECIDED BY NEUTRAL ARBITRATION AS PROVIDED BY CALIFORNIA LAW AND YOU ARE GIVING UP ANY RIGHTS YOU MIGHT POSSESS TO HAVE THE DISPUTE LITIGATED IN A COURT OR JURY TRIAL. BY INITIALLING IN THE SPACE BELOW YOU ARE GIVING UP YOUR JUDICIAL RIGHTS TO DISCOVERY AND APPEAL, UNLESS THOSE RIGHTS ARE SPECIFICALLY INCLUDED IN THE 'ARBITRATION OF DISPUTES' PROVISION. IF YOU REFUSE TO SUBMIT TO ARBITRATION AFTER AGREEING TO THIS PROVISION, YOU MAY BE COMPELLED TO ARBITRATE UNDER THE AUTHORITY OF THE CALIFORNIA CODE OF CIVIL PROCEDURE. YOUR AGREEMENT TO THIS ARBITRATION PROVISION IS VOLUNTARY."
"WE HAVE READ AND UNDERSTAND THE FOREGOING AND AGREE TO SUBMIT DISPUTES ARISING OUT OF THE

MATTERS INCLUDED IN THE 'ARBITRATION OF DISPUTES'
PROVISION TO NEUTRAL ARBITRATION."
If the above provision is included in a printed contract, it shall be
set out either in at least 10-point bold type or in contrasting red
print in at least 8-point bold type, and if the provision is included in
a typed contract, it shall be set out in capital letters.

(d) Nothing in this section shall be construed to diminish the
authority of any court of competent jurisdiction with respect to real
property transactions in areas involving court supervision or
jurisdiction, including, but not limited to, probate, marital
dissolution, foreclosure of liens, unlawful detainer, or eminent
domain.
(e) In the event an arbitration provision is contained in an escrow
instruction, it shall not preclude the right of an escrowholder to
institute an interpleader action.

Ca. Civ. Proc. Code § 1298

Title head amended by Stats 2007 ch 130 (AB 299),s 38, eff.
1/1/2008.
Amended by Stats. 1989, Ch. 22, Sec. 1. Effective May 25, 1989.
Operative July 1, 1989, by Sec. 2 of Ch. 22.

Section 1298.5 - Recording notice of pending action not waiver of right to arbitration

Any party to an action who proceeds to record a notice of pending
action pursuant to Section 409 shall not thereby waive any right of
arbitration which that person may have pursuant to a written
agreement to arbitrate, nor any right to petition the court to compel
arbitration pursuant to Section 1281.2, if, in filing an action to
record that notice, the party at the same time presents to the court
an application that the action be stayed pending the arbitration of
any dispute which is claimed to be arbitrable and which is relevant
to the action.

Ca. Civ. Proc. Code § 1298.5

Added by Stats. 1988, Ch. 881, Sec. 1. Operative July 1, 1989, by
Section 1298.8.

Section 1298.7 - Rights of action not precluded by contract provision or agreement to arbitrate

In the event an arbitration provision is included in a contract or agreement covered by this title, it shall not preclude or limit any right of action for bodily injury or wrongful death, or any right of action to which Section 337.1 or 337.15 is applicable.

Ca. Civ. Proc. Code § 1298.7

Added by Stats. 1988, Ch. 881, Sec. 1. Operative July 1, 1989, by Section 1298.8.

Section 1298.8 - Effective date of title

This title shall become operative on July 1, 1989, and shall only apply to contracts or agreements entered into on or after that date.

Ca. Civ. Proc. Code § 1298.8

Added by Stats. 1988, Ch. 881, Sec. 1. Note: This section delayed the initial operation of Title 9.3 (now numbered 9.4), commencing with Section 1298.

Title 9.5 - ARBITRATION OF FIREFIGHTER AND LAW ENFORCEMENT OFFICER LABOR DISPUTES

Section 1299 - Legislative findings and declaration; legislative intent

The Legislature hereby finds and declares that strikes taken by firefighters and law enforcement officers against public employers are a matter of statewide concern, are a predictable consequence of labor strife and poor morale that is often the outgrowth of substandard wages and benefits, and are not in the public interest. The Legislature further finds and declares that the dispute resolution procedures contained in this title provide the appropriate method for resolving public sector labor disputes that could otherwise lead to strikes by firefighters or law enforcement officers. It is the intent of the Legislature to protect the health and welfare of the public by providing impasse remedies necessary to afford public employers the opportunity to safely alleviate the effects of labor strife that would otherwise lead to strikes by firefighters and law enforcement officers. It is further the intent of the Legislature that, in order to effectuate its predominant purpose, this title be construed to apply broadly to all public employers, including, but not limited to, charter cities, counties, and cities and counties in this state.

It is not the intent of the Legislature to alter the scope of issues subject to collective bargaining between public employers and employee organizations representing firefighters or law enforcement officers.

The provisions of this title are intended by the Legislature to govern the resolution of impasses reached in collective bargaining between public employers and employee organizations representing firefighters and law enforcement officers over economic issues that remain in dispute over their respective interests. However, the provisions of this title are not intended by the Legislature to be used as a procedure to determine the rights of any firefighter or law enforcement officer in any grievance initiated as a result of a disciplinary action taken by any public employer. The Legislature further intends that this title shall not apply to any law enforcement policy that pertains to how law enforcement officers interact with members of the public or pertains to police-community relations, such as policies on the use of police powers, enforcement priorities and practices, or supervision, oversight, and accountability covering officer behavior toward members of the public, to any community-oriented policing policy or to any process employed by an employer to investigate firefighter or law enforcement officer behavior that could lead to discipline against any firefighter or law enforcement officer, nor to contravene any provision of a charter that governs an employer that is a city, county, or city and county, which provision prescribes a procedure for the imposition of any disciplinary action taken against a firefighter or law enforcement officer.

Ca. Civ. Proc. Code § 1299

Added by Stats 2000 ch 906 (SB 402), s 2, eff. 1/1/2001.

Section 1299.2 - Applicability of title

This title shall apply to all employers of firefighters and law enforcement officers.

Ca. Civ. Proc. Code § 1299.2
Added by Stats 2000 ch 906 (SB 402), s 2, eff. 1/1/2001.

Section 1299.3 - Definitions

As used in this title:

(a) "Employee" means any firefighter or law enforcement officer represented by an employee organization, as defined in subdivision (b).

(b) "Employee organization" means any organization recognized by the employer for the purpose of representing firefighters or law enforcement officers in matters relating to wages, hours, and other terms and conditions of employment within the scope of arbitration.

(c) "Employer" means any local agency employing employees, as defined in subdivision (a), or any entity, except the State of California, acting as an agent of any local agency, either directly or indirectly.

(d) "Firefighter" means any person who is employed to perform firefighting, fire prevention, fire training, hazardous materials response, emergency medical services, fire or arson investigation, or any related duties, without respect to the rank, job title, or job assignment of that person.

(e) "Law enforcement officer" means any person who is a peace officer, as defined in Section 830.1 of, subdivisions (b) and (d) of Section 830.31 of, subdivisions (a), (b), and (c) of Section 830.32 of, subdivisions (a), (b), and (d) of Section 830.33 of, subdivisions (a) and (b) of Section 830.35 of, subdivision (a) of Section 830.5 of, and subdivision (a) of Section 830.55 of, the Penal Code, without respect to the rank, job title, or job assignment of that person.

(f) "Local agency" means any governmental subdivision, district, public and quasi-public corporation, joint powers agency, public agency or public service corporation, town, city, county, city and county, or municipal corporation, whether incorporated or not or whether chartered or not.

(g) "Scope of arbitration" means economic issues, including salaries, wages and overtime pay, health and pension benefits, vacation and other leave, reimbursements, incentives, differentials, and all other forms of remuneration. The scope of arbitration shall not include any issue that is protected by what is commonly referred to as the "management rights" clause contained in Section 3504 of the Government Code. Notwithstanding the foregoing, any employer that is not exempt under Section 1299.9 may supersede this subdivision by adoption of an ordinance that establishes a broader definition of "scope of arbitration."

Ca. Civ. Proc. Code § 1299.3

Amended by Stats 2002 ch 664 (AB 3034),s 52, eff. 1/1/2003.
Added by Stats 2000 ch 906 (SB 402), s 2, eff. 1/1/2001.

Section 1299.4 - Submission of differences to arbitration panel

(a) If an impasse has been declared after the parties have exhausted their mutual efforts to reach agreement over matters within the scope of arbitration, and the parties are unable to agree to the appointment of a mediator, or if a mediator agreed to by the parties is unable to effect settlement of a dispute between the parties after his or her appointment, the employee organization may, by written notification to the employer, request that their differences be submitted to an arbitration panel.

(b) Within three days after receipt of the written notification, each party shall designate a person to serve as its member of an arbitration panel. Within five days thereafter, or within additional periods to which they mutually agree, the two members of the arbitration panel appointed by the parties shall designate an impartial person with experience in labor and management dispute resolution to act as chairperson of the arbitration panel.

(c) In the event that the parties are unable or unwilling to agree upon a third person to serve as chairperson, the two members of the arbitration panel shall jointly request from the American Arbitration Association a list of seven impartial and experienced persons who are familiar with matters of employer-employee relations. The two panel members may as an alternative, jointly request a list of seven names from the California State Mediation and Conciliation Service, or a list from either entity containing more or less than seven names, so long as the number requested is an odd number. If after five days of receipt of the list, the two panel members cannot agree on which of the listed persons shall serve as chairperson, they shall, within two days, alternately strike names from the list, with the first panel member to strike names being determined by lot. The last person whose name remains on the list shall be chairperson.

(d) Employees as defined by this chapter shall not be permitted to engage in strikes that endanger public safety.

(e) No employer shall interfere with, intimidate, restrain, coerce, or discriminate against an employee organization or employee because of an exercise of rights under this title.

(f) No employer shall refuse to meet and confer or condition agreement upon a memorandum of understanding based upon an employee organization's exercise of rights under this title.

Ca. Civ. Proc. Code § 1299.4

Added by Stats 2000 ch 906 (SB 402), s 2, eff. 1/1/2001.

Section 1299.5 - inquiries and investigation, hearings and other action by panel

(a) The arbitration panel shall, within 10 days after its establishment or any additional periods to which the parties agree, meet with the parties or their representatives, either jointly or separately, make inquiries and investigations, hold hearings, and take any other action including further mediation, that the arbitration panel deems appropriate.

(b) For the purpose of its hearings, investigations, or inquiries, the arbitration panel may subpoena witnesses, administer oaths, take the testimony of any person, and issue subpoenas duces tecum to require the production and examination of any employer's or employee organization's records, books, or papers relating to any subject matter before the panel.

Ca. Civ. Proc. Code § 1299.5

Added by Stats 2000 ch 906 (SB 402), s 2, eff. 1/1/2001.

**Section 1299.6 - Submission of last best offer of settlement
by parties; decision of panel**

(a) The arbitration panel shall direct that five days prior to the
commencement of its hearings, each of the parties shall submit the
last best offer of settlement as to each of the issues within the scope
of arbitration, as defined in this title, made in bargaining as a
proposal or counterproposal and not previously agreed to by the
parties prior to any arbitration request made pursuant to
subdivision (a) of Section 1299.4. The arbitration panel, within 30
days after the conclusion of the hearing, or any additional period to
which the parties agree, shall separately decide on each of the
disputed issues submitted by selecting, without modification, the
last best offer that most nearly complies with the applicable factors
described in subdivision (c). This subdivision shall be applicable
except as otherwise provided in subdivision (b).

(b) Notwithstanding the terms of subdivision (a), the parties by
mutual agreement may elect to submit as a package the last best
offer of settlement made in bargaining as a proposal or
counterproposal on those issues within the scope of arbitration, as
defined in this title, not previously agreed to by the parties prior to
any arbitration request made pursuant to subdivision (a) of Section
1299.4. The arbitration panel, within 30 days after the conclusion of
the hearing, or any additional period to which the parties agree,
shall decide on the disputed issues submitted by selecting, without
modification, the last best offer package that most nearly complies
with the applicable factors described in subdivision (c).

(c) The arbitration panel, unless otherwise agreed to by the parties,
shall limit its findings to issues within the scope of arbitration and
shall base its findings, opinions, and decisions upon those factors
traditionally taken into consideration in the determination of those
matters within the scope of arbitration, including but not limited to
the following factors, as applicable:

  (1) The stipulations of the parties.

  (2) The interest and welfare of the public.

  (3) The financial condition of the employer and its ability to meet the costs of the award.

(4) The availability and sources of funds to defray the cost of
any changes in matters within the scope of arbitration.

(5) Comparison of matters within the scope of arbitration of
other employees performing similar services in corresponding fire
or law enforcement employment.

(6) The average consumer prices for goods and services,
commonly known as the Consumer Price Index.

(7) The peculiarity of requirements of employment, including,
but not limited to, mental, physical, and educational qualifications;
job training and skills; and hazards of employment.

(8) Changes in any of the foregoing that are traditionally taken
into consideration in the determination of matters within the scope
of arbitration.

Ca. Civ. Proc. Code § 1299.6
Added by Stats 2000 ch 906 (SB 402), s 2, eff. 1/1/2001.

**Section 1299.7 - Copy of decision delivered or mailed to
parties; decision not binding for period of five days after
service; disclosure and binding effect after five day
period; rejection by employer**
(a) The arbitration panel shall mail or otherwise deliver a copy of
the decision to the parties. However, the decision of the arbitration
panel shall not be publicly disclosed, and shall not be binding, for a
period of five days after service to the parties. During that five-day
period, the parties may meet privately, attempt to resolve their
differences and, by mutual agreement, amend or modify the
decision of the arbitration panel.
(b) At the conclusion of the five-day period, which may be extended
by the parties, the arbitration panel's decision, as may be amended
or modified by the parties pursuant to subdivision (a), shall be
publicly disclosed and, unless the governing body acts in

accordance with subdivision (c), shall be binding on all parties, and,
if specified by the arbitration panel, be incorporated into and made
a part of any existing memorandum of understanding as defined in
Section 3505.1 of the Government Code.

(c) The employer may by unanimous vote of all the members of the
governing body reject the decision of the arbitration panel, except
as specifically provided to the contrary in a city, county, or city and
county charter with respect to the rejection of an arbitration award.

Ca. Civ. Proc. Code § 1299.7

Amended by Stats 2003 ch 877 (SB 440),s 1, eff. 1/1/2004.
Added by Stats 2000 ch 906 (SB 402), s 2, eff. 1/1/2001.

Section 1299.8 - Applicability of Title 9

Unless otherwise provided in this title, Title 9 (commencing with
Section 1280) shall be applicable to any arbitration proceeding
undertaken pursuant to this title.

Ca. Civ. Proc. Code § 1299.8

Added by Stats 2000 ch 906 (SB 402), s 2, eff. 1/1/2001.

Section 1299.9 - Inapplicability to city, county or city and county with charter provisions for procedure for resolving disputes

(a) The provisions of this title shall not apply to any employer that
is a city, county, or city and county, governed by a charter that was
amended prior to January 1, 2004, to incorporate a procedure
requiring the submission of all unresolved disputes relating to
wages, hours, and other terms and conditions of employment
within the scope of arbitration to an impartial and experienced
neutral person or panel for final and binding determination,
provided however that the charter amendment is not subsequently
repealed or amended in a form that would no longer require the
submission of all unresolved disputes relating to wages, hours, and
other terms and conditions of employment within the scope of
arbitration to an impartial and experienced neutral person or panel,
for final and binding determination.

(b) Unless otherwise agreed to by the parties, the costs of the arbitration proceeding and the expenses of the arbitration panel, except those of the employer representative, shall be borne by the employee organization.

Ca. Civ. Proc. Code § 1299.9
Amended by Stats 2003 ch 877 (SB 440),s 2, eff. 1/1/2004.
Added by Stats 2000 ch 906 (SB 402), s 2, eff. 1/1/2001.

Title 10 - UNCLAIMED PROPERTY

Chapter 1 - GENERAL PROVISIONS

Article 1 - DEFINITIONS

Section 1300 - Definitions

For the purposes of this title, the following definitions shall apply:
(a) "Property," unless specifically qualified, includes all classes of property, real, personal and mixed.
(b) "Unclaimed property," unless specifically qualified, means all property (1) which is unclaimed, abandoned, escheated, permanently escheated, or distributed to the state, or (2) which, under any provision of law, will become unclaimed, abandoned, escheated, permanently escheated, or distributed to the state, or (3) to the possession of which the state is or will become entitled, if not claimed by the person or persons entitled thereto within the time allowed by law, whether or not there has been a judicial determination that such property is unclaimed, abandoned, escheated, permanently escheated, or distributed to the state.
(c) "Escheat," unless specifically qualified, means the vesting in the state of title to property the whereabouts of whose owner is unknown or whose owner is unknown or which a known owner has refused to accept, whether by judicial determination or by operation of law, subject to the right of claimants to appear and claim the escheated property or any portion thereof. When used in reference to the law of another state, "escheat" includes the transfer to the state of the right to the custody of such property.
(d) "Permanent escheat" means the absolute vesting in the state of title to property the whereabouts of whose owner is unknown or whose owner is unknown or which a known owner has refused to

accept, pursuant to judicial determination, pursuant to a proceeding of escheat as provided by Chapter 5 (commencing with Section 1410) of this title, or pursuant to operation of law, and the barring of all claims to the property by the former owner thereof or his successors.

(e) "Controller" means the State Controller.

(f) "Treasurer" means the State Treasurer.

(g) "Domicile," in the case of a corporation, refers to the place where the corporation is incorporated.

Ca. Civ. Proc. Code § 1300

Amended by Stats. 1968, Ch. 356.

Section 1301 - Construction of references to section, article or chapter

For the purposes of this title, unless otherwise specified, (1) a reference to a section refers to a section of this code; (2) a reference to an article refers to an article of the chapter of this title in which such reference is made; and (3) a reference to a chapter refers to a chapter of this title.

Ca. Civ. Proc. Code § 1301

Added by Stats. 1951, Ch. 1708.

Article 2 - PURPOSE AND SCOPE

Section 1305 - Purpose

It is the purpose of this title to provide for the receipt, custody, investment, management, disposal, escheat and permanent escheat of various classes of unclaimed property, to the possession of which the State is, or may become, entitled under the provisions of this title or under other provision of law.

Ca. Civ. Proc. Code § 1305

Added by Stats. 1951, Ch. 1708.

Section 1306 - Inapplicability to money or property held by state

The provisions of this title do not apply to money or other property held by the State or any officer thereof as trustee or bailee under the terms of an express contract to which the State or any officer thereof is a party.

Ca. Civ. Proc. Code § 1306
Added by Stats. 1951, Ch. 1708.

Chapter 2 - RECEIPT AND EXPENDITURE OF FUNDS

Article 1 - DEPOSIT OF UNCLAIMED PROPERTY

Section 1310 - Cash transmitted to Treasurer and person property transmitted to Controller for deposit

Whenever, under the provisions of this title or under any other provision of law, unclaimed money or other unclaimed property is payable into the State Treasury, the person responsible for making such payment shall, if it is cash, transmit it to the Treasurer, and if it is personal property other than cash, transmit it to the Controller for deposit in the State Treasury.

Ca. Civ. Proc. Code § 1310
Added by Stats. 1951, Ch. 1708.

Section 1311 - Notice to Controller of transmission of money or property to Treasurer or Controller

Any person transmitting money or other property to the Treasurer or Controller under the provisions of this title shall, at the time of such transmittal, furnish written notice thereof to the Controller, setting forth the amount of cash transmitted, the nature and description of the personal property other than cash transmitted, the name and last known address of the person entitled to such property or for whose benefit such property is transmitted, a reference to the specific statutory provision under which such property is transmitted, and if such property represents the proceeds of an estate of a decedent, or an unclaimed amount payable pursuant to an allowed and approved claim against such an estate, the name of the decedent, the county and court in which probate or escheat proceedings, if any, were held, the number of the action, if any; and, in the case of all classes of property so transmitted, such other identifying information available from the records of the person making such transmittal, as the Controller may require.

Ca. Civ. Proc. Code § 1311
Added by Stats. 1951, Ch. 1708.

Section 1312 - Order or decree of distribution in decedent's estate or vesting title in state

Whenever money or other property is paid to the State or any officer or employee thereof under the provisions of this title, and such money or other property has been covered by a decree of distribution in a decedent's estate, or by an order or decree of a court ordering such payment or adjudging that title to such property has vested in the State, the person transmitting such money or other property to the Treasurer or Controller shall, at the time of such transmittal, furnish to the Controller a certified copy of each court order or decree, and of each court order correcting or amending the same, covering such money or other property.

Ca. Civ. Proc. Code § 1312
Added by Stats. 1951, Ch. 1708.

Section 1313 - Unclaimed Property Fund

A fund is hereby created in the State Treasury, to be known as the Unclaimed Property Fund.

All money, except permanently escheated money, paid to the state or any officer or employee thereof for deposit in the State Treasury under the provisions of this title shall, on order of the Controller, be deposited in the Unclaimed Property Fund.

All property other than money, including the proceeds from the sale or other disposition thereof, except permanently escheated property received by, or coming into the possession of, the state or any officer or employee thereof under the provisions of this title shall, on order of the Controller, be deposited in the State Treasury to be held in the Unclaimed Property Fund.

Ca. Civ. Proc. Code § 1313
Amended by Stats. 1978, Ch. 1183.

Section 1314 - Account in Fund covering accountability for money deposited in Fund

The Controller shall maintain a separate account in the Unclaimed Property Fund covering the accountability for money deposited in the Unclaimed Property Fund under each article of Chapter 6. All real and personal property distributed to the State or delivered into the possession of the State or any officer or employee thereof under the provisions of this title, shall be accounted for by the Controller in the name of the account in the Unclaimed Property Fund to which the proceeds thereof, if converted into cash, would be credited under the provisions of this title. All personal property deposited in the State Treasury under the provisions of this title shall be held by the Treasurer in the name of the same account in the Unclaimed Property Fund for which such property is accounted by the Controller, as herein provided.

Ca. Civ. Proc. Code § 1314
Added by Stats. 1951, Ch. 1708.

Section 1315 - Recording unclaimed money or property of deceased person received by state

If unclaimed money or other property in an estate of a deceased person, or if any unclaimed amount payable pursuant to an allowed and approved claim against such an estate, is received by the State or any officer or employee thereof and deposited in the State Treasury under the provisions of this title, it shall be recorded on the books of the Controller to the credit, or in the name, of such estate, for the benefit of the person entitled thereto or his successors in interest.

Ca. Civ. Proc. Code § 1315
Added by Stats. 1951, Ch. 1708.

Section 1316 - Recording unclaimed money or property received by state for benefit of heirs, devisees, legatees, creditors, etc.

If unclaimed money or other property is received by the State or any officer or employee thereof and deposited in the State Treasury under the provisions of this title for the benefit of known heirs, devisees, legatees or creditors of an estate of a deceased person, or for the benefit of known claimants, payees, or other persons entitled thereto, it shall be recorded on the books of the Controller to the credit, or in the name, of such heirs, devisees, legatees, creditors, claimants, payees, or other persons entitled thereto.

Ca. Civ. Proc. Code § 1316
Added by Stats. 1951, Ch. 1708.

Section 1317 - Amount of canceled warrant credited to Fund transferred to General Fund

The amount of each canceled warrant credited to the Unclaimed Property Fund under the provisions of Section 17072 of the Government Code shall, on order of the Controller, be transferred to the General Fund.

Ca. Civ. Proc. Code § 1317
Amended by Stats. 1978, Ch. 1183.

Section 1318 - Deposit of interest and other income derived from investment of money in Fund

All interest received and other income derived from the investment of moneys in the Unclaimed Property Fund, as provided in Section 13470 of the Government Code, shall, on order of the Controller, be deposited in the General Fund.

Ca. Civ. Proc. Code § 1318
Amended by Stats. 1978, Ch. 1183.

Section 1319 - Deposit and credit of rents, interest, dividends or other income received and held by state

Except as otherwise provided in Section 1318, all rents, interest, dividends or other income or increment derived from real or personal property received and held by the State in the name of the Unclaimed Property Fund under the provisions of this title shall, on order of the Controller, be deposited in the Unclaimed Property Fund, and shall be credited by the Controller to the account maintained by him, in the name of which such property is accounted, as provided in Chapter 2. Any moneys deposited in the Unclaimed Property Fund under the provisions of this section shall be held for the benefit of the person or persons entitled to the property from which such moneys were derived, or their successors in interest; and shall be subject to claim in the same manner as such property may be claimed; but the period in which such moneys shall be available for claim by and payment to the person or persons entitled thereto shall not extend beyond the period in which the property from which such moneys were derived is available for claim and payment under the provisions of this title.

Ca. Civ. Proc. Code § 1319
Added by Stats. 1951, Ch. 1708.

Section 1320 - Deposit of rents, interest, dividends or other income or increment derived from property escheated to state

Except as otherwise provided in Section 1318, all rents, interest, dividends or other income or increment derived from real or personal property that has permanently escheated to the state, shall, on order of the Controller, be deposited in the General Fund. All moneys deposited in the General Fund under the provisions of this section shall be deemed to have permanently escheated to the state as of the date of permanent escheat of the property from which such moneys were derived.

Ca. Civ. Proc. Code § 1320
Amended by Stats. 1978, Ch. 1183.

Section 1321 - Immunity of person delivering money or property to state or holder of money or property

Any person delivering money or other property to the Treasurer or Controller under the provisions of this title shall, upon such delivery, be relieved and held harmless by the State from all or any claim or claims which exist at that time with reference to such money or other property, or which may thereafter be made, or which may come into existence, on account of, or in respect to, such money or other property.

No action shall be maintained against any person who is the holder of such money or other property, nor against any officer as agent thereof, for:

(a) The recovery of such money or other property delivered to the Treasurer or Controller pursuant to this title, or for interest thereon subsequent to the date of the report thereof, if any, to the Controller; or

(b) Damages alleged to have resulted from such delivery to the Treasurer or Controller. No owner of money or other property shall be entitled to receive interest thereon or with respect thereto from and after the date on which a report of such money or other property is made to the Controller pursuant to any provision of this title, whether or not he was entitled to such interest prior to such report.

As used in this section, "person" and "holder" have the respective meanings set forth in Section 1461 of this code.

Ca. Civ. Proc. Code § 1321
Added by Stats. 1953, Ch. 279.

Article 2 - APPROPRIATION

Section 1325 - Purposes for which money in Fund continuously appropriated to Controller for expenditure

Notwithstanding Section 13340 of the Government Code, all money in the Unclaimed Property Fund is hereby continuously appropriated to the Controller, without regard to fiscal years, for expenditure for any of the following purposes:

(a) For refund, to the person making such deposit, of amounts, including overpayments, deposited in error in such fund.

(b) For payment of the cost of title searches and appraisals incurred by the Controller covering real or personal property held in the name of an account in such fund.

(c) For payment of the cost incurred by the Controller covering indemnity bonds required in order to have duplicate certificates of ownership issued in order to replace lost certificates, covering personal property held in the name of an account in such fund.

(d) For payment of amounts required to be paid by the state as trustee, bailee, or successor in interest to the preceding owner, pursuant to the provisions of trust deeds, mortgages, or other liens on real property held in the name of an account in such fund.

(e) For payment of costs incurred by the Controller for the repair, maintenance and upkeep of real and personal property held in the name of an account in such fund.

(f) For payment of costs of official advertising in connection with the sale of real or personal property held in the name of an account in such fund.

(g) For payment to taxing agencies of the amounts deducted by the Controller from allowed and approved claims, in accordance with the provisions of subdivision (c) of Section 4986.5 of the Revenue and Taxation Code.

(h) For transfer to the Inheritance Tax Fund, on order of the Controller, of the amount of any inheritance taxes determined to be due and payable to the state by any claimant, with respect to any real or personal property, including cash, claimed by that person under the provisions of this title.

(i) For payment and delivery to claimants of money or other property held to the credit, or in the name, of an account in such fund, under the provisions of this title.

(j) For transfer to the General Fund, on order of the Controller, of any money or other property in the Unclaimed Property Fund which becomes permanently escheated to the state under the provisions of this title. Any expenditure made by the Controller pursuant to the provisions of this section shall be charged against any balance credited to the particular account in the Unclaimed Property Fund, in the name of which is held the real or personal property for which the expenditure is made; and if sufficient balance is not available in such account, the expenditure may be made from any appropriation from the General Fund for the support of the Controller, or, in the case of official advertising, from any appropriation available therefor, to be reimbursed from the proceeds of any subsequent sale of the property for which such expenditure is made.

Ca. Civ. Proc. Code § 1325
Amended by Stats. 1993, Ch. 692, Sec. 1. Effective January 1, 1994.

Chapter 3 - PAYMENT OF CLAIMS

Article 1 - GENERAL

Section 1335 - Immunity of state upon payment or delivering money or property to claimant
When payment or delivery of money or other property has been made to any claimant under the provisions of this chapter, no suit shall thereafter be maintained by any other claimant against the State or any officer thereof for or on account of such property.
Ca. Civ. Proc. Code § 1335
Added by Stats. 1951, Ch. 1708.

Article 2 - REFUND OF ERRONEOUS RECEIPTS

Section 1345 - Generally
If any person has erroneously delivered any unclaimed moneys or other unclaimed property to the state or any officer or employee thereof, and the moneys or other property is deposited in the Unclaimed Property Fund or is held by the Controller or Treasurer in the name of any account in that fund pursuant to this title, the moneys or other property delivered in error may be refunded or returned to that person on order of the Controller.
Ca. Civ. Proc. Code § 1345
Amended by Stats 2016 ch 31 (SB 836),s 11, eff. 6/27/2016.
Amended by Stats 2006 ch 538 (SB 1852),s 68, eff. 1/1/2007.

Section 1346 - Transfer of erroneously delivered cash to Unclaimed Property Fund or adjustment of records to show proper account if other than cash

If any person has erroneously delivered any unclaimed moneys or other unclaimed property to the state or any officer or employee thereof, and the moneys or other property is deposited in, or transferred to, the General Fund, or is held by the Controller or Treasurer in the name of that fund, pursuant to this title, the moneys or other property delivered in error, if cash, shall on order of the Controller, be transferred from the General Fund to the Unclaimed Property Fund, and, if other than cash, the records of the Controller and Treasurer shall be adjusted to show that it is held in the name of the proper account in the Unclaimed Property Fund; and the moneys or other property may be refunded or returned to that person on order of the Controller.

Ca. Civ. Proc. Code § 1346
Amended by Stats 2016 ch 31 (SB 836),s 12, eff. 6/27/2016.
Amended by Stats 2006 ch 538 (SB 1852),s 69, eff. 1/1/2007.

Section 1347 - Property held as permanently escheated subsequently determined not to be escheated

Whenever money deposited in the Unclaimed Property Fund is transferred to the General Fund under the provisions of this title, and whenever the records of the Controller and Treasurer covering property other than money held in the name of any account in the Unclaimed Property Fund are adjusted to record such property as held in the name of the General Fund, as permanently escheated property under the provisions of this title, if it is subsequently determined that such money or other property is not, in fact, permanently escheated, such money or other property, if cash, shall, on order of the Controller, be retransferred from the General Fund to the Unclaimed Property Fund; and, if the property is other than money, the records of the Controller and Treasurer shall be adjusted to show that it is held in the name and for the benefit of the proper account in the Unclaimed Property Fund.

Ca. Civ. Proc. Code § 1347
Amended by Stats. 1978, Ch. 1183.

Article 3 - CLAIMS

Section 1350 - Persons who may claim money or property

Unless otherwise provided in this title, all money or other property deposited in the State Treasury under the provisions of this title may be claimed by the person entitled thereto at any time prior to the date on which such money or other property has become permanently escheated, as provided by this title.

Ca. Civ. Proc. Code § 1350
Added by Stats. 1951, Ch. 1708.

Section 1351 - Money or property deposited becoming property of state by escheat

Unless otherwise provided in this title, all money or other property deposited in the State Treasury under the provisions of this title, if not claimed by the person entitled thereto within five years from the date of such deposit, shall become the property of the State by escheat; and upon request by the Controller, the Attorney General shall commence a proceeding under the provisions of Section 1410, or, in lieu of such proceeding, the Controller may take action as provided by Article 2 of Chapter 5, to have it adjudged, determined or established that the title to such money or other property has vested in the State.

Ca. Civ. Proc. Code § 1351
Added by Stats. 1951, Ch. 1708.

Section 1352 - Property held for third persons or title subject to rights of third persons

(a) Whenever unclaimed money or other property is deposited in the State Treasury under this title, and, except as otherwise provided by law, whenever there is in the possession of the state or its officers any money or other property which is held for third persons or the title to which has vested in the state subject to the rights of third persons, and the period during which it may be claimed by a person entitled thereto has not terminated, the period and person being prescribed by law, if the value of the money or other property to which the claimant is entitled is less than sixty thousand dollars ($60,000), any such person may present his or her claim for it to the Controller. The claim shall be made in the form prescribed by the Controller, which shall set forth the information required by Section 1355 or any other information that the Controller may deem necessary to establish right or title to the money or other property in the claimant.

(b) Property assigned or distributed to a name distributee may be claimed by the distributee himself or herself or his or her legal guardian or conservator, as provided in subdivision (a) regardless of the amount. This subdivision does not apply to the heirs or estate of a distributee, or to property distributed to the state for lack of known heirs.

(c) Any person aggrieved by a decision of the Controller may commence an action, naming the Controller as a defendant, to establish his or her claim in the superior court in any county or city and county in which the Attorney General has an office pursuant to Section 1541.

Ca. Civ. Proc. Code § 1352

Amended by Stats. 1990, Ch. 450, Sec. 1. Effective July 31, 1990.

Section 1353 - Superior court jurisdiction to determine title to money or property

Except as otherwise provided in Sections 401 or 1352, whenever money or other property is deposited in the State Treasury under the provisions of this title, and, except as otherwise provided by law, when there is in the possession of the State or its officers any money or other property which is to be held for third persons or the title to which has vested in the State subject to the rights of third persons, the Superior Court of the County of Sacramento shall have full and exclusive jurisdiction to determine the title to such money or other property and all claims thereto.

If the period in which such money or other property may be claimed by a person entitled thereto has not terminated, such period and person being prescribed by law, any such person may file a petition in the Superior Court of the County of Sacramento, or as provided in Section 401, showing his claim or right to the money or other property or the proceeds thereof, or any portion thereof.

The petition shall be verified, and, among other things, must, insofar as they are applicable or material to the matters at issue, state the facts required to be stated in a petition filed under Section 1355. If the money or other property at issue did not come into the possession of the State or its officers in connection with estates of deceased persons, the petition shall, in addition to the foregoing facts, state any material facts necessary to establish a prima facie right or title in the petitioner. Upon the filing of the petition, the same proceedings shall be had as are required in Section 1355.

If, upon trial of the issues, the court is satisfied of the claimant's right or title to the money or other property claimed, it shall grant him a certificate to that effect under its seal. Upon presentation of such certificate, the Controller shall draw his warrant on the Treasurer for the amount of money covered thereby; and if the certificate covers any property other than money, a certified copy of the certificate filed with the officer of the State having possession of the property shall serve as sufficient authority to the officer for the delivery of such property to the claimant.

Ca. Civ. Proc. Code § 1353
Added by Stats. 1951, Ch. 1708.

Section 1354 - Recovery on claim made or petition filed by representative of estate

Whenever any claim is made or petition filed by the representative of an estate or other person, under the provisions of this chapter, or under any other provision of law, to recover money or other property deposited in the State Treasury or held by the State or any officer thereof to the credit, or in the name, of any account in the Unclaimed Property Fund, no recovery will be allowed unless it affirmatively appears that there are heirs or legatees who will receive such money or other property or creditors of the deceased owner of the claim whose claims are valid and are not barred, and whose claims were in existence prior to the death of such deceased owner of the claim. Where only creditors exist, and there are no heirs or legatees, said claims shall be allowed only to the extent necessary to pay such claims and the reasonable costs of administration of the estate, including court costs, administrator's fees and attorney's fees. This section shall apply to all claims which are pending at the time that this section goes into effect as well as to claims arising hereafter.

Ca. Civ. Proc. Code § 1354
Added by Stats. 1951, Ch. 1708.

Section 1355 - Petition filed in Superior Court of Sacramento County showing claim or right to money or property

Within five years after date of entry of judgment in any proceeding had under the provisions of Chapter 5, or within five years after completion of notice by publication in an escheat action taken under the provisions of Section 1415, a person not a party or privy to such proceeding or action, if not otherwise barred, may file a petition in the Superior Court of the County of Sacramento, or as provided in Section 401, showing his claim or right to the money or other property, or the proceeds thereof.

Said petition shall be verified; and, in a proceeding for the recovery by the petitioner as heir, devisee, or legatee, or the successor in interest of an heir, devisee or legatee, of money or other property received by the State from the estate of a decedent under the provisions of Article 1 of Chapter 6, such petition, among other things must state:

The full name, and the place and date of birth of the decedent whose estate, or any part thereof, is claimed.

The full name of such decedent's father and the maiden name of his mother, the places and dates of their respective births, the place and date of their marriage, the full names of all children the issue of such marriage, with the date of birth of each, and the place and date of death of all children of such marriage who have died unmarried and without issue.

Whether or not such decedent was ever married, and if so, where, when and to whom.

How, when and where such marriage, if any, was dissolved.

Whether or not said decedent was ever remarried, and, if so, where, when and to whom.

The full names, and the dates and places of birth of all lineal descendants, if any, of said decedent; the dates and places of death of any thereof who died prior to the filing of such petition; and the places of residence of all who are then surviving, with the degree of relationship of each of such survivors to said decedent.

Whether any of the brothers or sisters of such decedent every married, and, if so, where, when and whom.

The full names, and the places and dates of birth of all children who are the issue of the marriage of any such brother or sister of the decedent, and the date and place of death of all deceased nephews and nieces of said decedent.

Whether or not said decedent, if of foreign birth, ever became a naturalized citizen of the United States, and, if so, when, where, and by what court citizenship was conferred.

The post-office names of the cities, towns or other places, each in its appropriate connection, wherein are preserved the records of the births, marriages and deaths hereinbefore enumerated, and, if known, the title of the public official or other person having custody of such records.

The nationality of each of the heirs of the decedent.

The street address of each of the heirs of the decedent.

If, for any reason, the petitioner is unable to set forth any of the matters or things hereinbefore required, he shall clearly state such reason in his petition.

At least 20 days before the hearing of the petition, a copy of the petition and notice of hearing must be served on the Attorney General and on the Controller, and the Attorney General may answer the same at his discretion.

If such claim includes a claim to real property or any interest therein, the petitioner shall record in the office of the county recorder of the county in which the real property is situated, a notice of the pendency of the petition containing the object of the action and a description of the property in the county affected thereby. From the time of filing such notice for record only, shall a purchaser or encumbrancer of the property be deemed to have constructive notice of the pendency of the action, and only of its pendency against parties designated by their real names.

The court must thereupon try the issue as issues are tried in civil actions; and if it is determined that such person is entitled to the money or other property or the proceeds thereof, it must order the property, if it has not been sold, to be delivered to him, or if it has been sold and the proceeds thereof paid into the State Treasury, it must order the Controller to draw his warrant on the Treasurer for the payment of the same, but without interest or cost to the State. A copy of such order, under the seal of the court, shall be a sufficient voucher for drawing such warrant.

All persons who fail to appear and file their petitions within the time limited are forever barred; saving, however, to infants and persons of unsound mind, the right to appear and file their petitions at any time within the time limited, or within one year after their respective disabilities cease.

Ca. Civ. Proc. Code § 1355
Amended by Stats. 1951, Ch. 1738.

Chapter 4 - MANAGEMENT OF UNCLAIMED PROPERTY

Article 1 - GENERAL PROVISIONS

Section 1360 - Definitions

For the purposes of this chapter, the following definitions shall apply:

(a) "Personal property" means personal property falling within the definition of "unclaimed property" under the provisions of this title;

(b) "Real property" means real property falling within the definition of "unclaimed property" under the provisions of this title;

(c) "Securities" includes stocks, bonds, notes, debentures, certificates of deposit, shares, and all other evidences of ownership or indebtedness, and all forms of chose in action and the interests in property represented thereby, falling within the definition of unclaimed property under the provisions of this title.

Ca. Civ. Proc. Code § 1360
Added by Stats. 1951, Ch. 1708.

Section 1361 - Care and custody of property assumed by state for benefit of those entitled

The care and custody of all property delivered to the Treasurer or Controller pursuant to this title is assumed by the State for the benefit of those entitled thereto, and the State is responsible for the payment of all claims established thereto pursuant to law, less any lawful deductions.

Ca. Civ. Proc. Code § 1361
Added by Stats. 1951, Ch. 1708.

Article 2 - POWERS OF THE CONTROLLER

Section 1365 - Generally

In connection with all unclaimed property, the Controller has all of the powers necessary in order to safeguard and conserve the interests of all parties, including the State, having any vested or expectant interest in such unclaimed property. His powers include, but are not limited to, the authority to incur obligations the payment of which is authorized by the provisions of Section 1325.

Ca. Civ. Proc. Code § 1365
Added by Stats. 1951, Ch. 1708.

Article 3 - SALE OR DISPOSAL OF PROPERTY

Section 1370 - Power of Controller to sell or lease personal property

The Controller may sell or lease personal property at any time, and in any manner, and may execute those leases on behalf and in the name of the State of California.

Ca. Civ. Proc. Code § 1370
Amended by Stats 2016 ch 31 (SB 836),s 13, eff. 6/27/2016.
Amended by Stats 2006 ch 538 (SB 1852),s 70, eff. 1/1/2007.

Section 1371 - Power of Controller as to securities, accounts, debts, contractual rights or other choses in action

The Controller may sell, cash, redeem, exchange, or otherwise dispose of any securities and all other classes of personal property, and may sell, cash, redeem, exchange, compromise, adjust, settle, or otherwise dispose of any accounts, debts, contractual rights, or other choses in action if, in his or her opinion, that action on his or her part is necessary or will tend to safeguard and conserve the interests of all parties, including the state, having any vested or expectant interest in the property.

   Ca. Civ. Proc. Code § 1371
Amended by Stats 2016 ch 31 (SB 836),s 14, eff. 6/27/2016.
Amended by Stats 2006 ch 538 (SB 1852),s 71, eff. 1/1/2007.

Section 1372 - Power of controller to sign, endorse or authenticate securities, bills of sale, documents or other instruments

The Controller may sign, endorse, or otherwise authenticate, in the name and on behalf of the State, subscribing his name, as Controller, under such writing, any securities, bills of sale, documents, or other instruments required, under customary business practice, for the consummation of the transactions authorized by this chapter. For all purposes, such endorsement is conclusive and binding against the State and the heirs, devisees, legatees, or other claimants of the property covered by such endorsement.

   Ca. Civ. Proc. Code § 1372
Added by Stats. 1951, Ch. 1708.

Section 1373 - Sale or lease at public auction; notice

The Controller may lease or sell any real property for cash at public auction to the highest bidder.

Before such sale or lease, notice thereof shall be published pursuant to Government Code Section 6063 in a newspaper published in the county in which the real property is situated, or in an adjoining

county, if there is no newspaper published in such county. The notice is sufficient for all the purposes of such lease or sale if the real property is described sufficiently to identify it. The cost of publication shall be a charge against the proceeds of the lease or sale, or, if the lease or sale is not consummated, such cost shall be a legal charge against the appropriation for official advertising.
If the value of the property to be sold does not appear to exceed one thousand dollars ($1,000) in the determination of the Controller, notice of sale thereof may be published pursuant to Government Code Section 6061.

Ca. Civ. Proc. Code § 1373
Amended by Stats. 1963, Ch. 752.

Section 1374 - Authority of Controller to reject bids

The Controller may reject any and all bids made at sales or public auctions held under the provisions of this chapter.

Ca. Civ. Proc. Code § 1374
Added by Stats. 1951, Ch. 1708.

Section 1375 - Power of Controller to sell or lease real property at private sale

Any real property may be sold or leased by the Controller at private sale without published notice.

Ca. Civ. Proc. Code § 1375
Amended by Stats 2016 ch 31 (SB 836),s 15, eff. 6/27/2016.
Amended by Stats 2006 ch 538 (SB 1852),s 72, eff. 1/1/2007.

Section 1376 - Execution of deed covering real property and bill of sale covering personal property

Upon receipt of the proceeds of any sale made pursuant to this chapter, the Controller shall execute, in the name and on behalf of the State of California, a deed covering the real property, and a bill of sale covering the personal property, sold. He may execute leases for real or personal property in the name and on behalf of the State of California.

Ca. Civ. Proc. Code § 1376
Added by Stats. 1951, Ch. 1708.

Section 1377 - Creating obligation not already obligation of owners, heirs, devisees, etc.

The Controller shall not enter into any transaction which shall create or impose upon the owners, heirs, devisees, legatees, or other claimants of the property involved, any obligation under an executory contract, the performance of which is not already an obligation of such owners, heirs, devisees, legatees, or other claimants prior to the consummation of the transactions authorized by this chapter.

Ca. Civ. Proc. Code § 1377
Added by Stats. 1951, Ch. 1708.

Section 1378 - Immunity of state on account of transaction entered into by Controller

No suit shall be maintained by any person against the State or any officer thereof, for or on account of any transaction entered into by the Controller pursuant to this chapter.

Ca. Civ. Proc. Code § 1378
Added by Stats. 1951, Ch. 1708.

Section 1379 - Power of Controller to destroy personal property other than cash deposited in Treasury

The Controller may destroy or otherwise dispose of any personal property other than cash deposited in the State Treasury under this title, if that property is determined by him or her to be valueless or of such little value that the costs of conducting a sale would probably exceed the amount that would be realized from the sale, and neither the Treasurer nor Controller shall be held to respond in damages at the suit of any person claiming loss by reason of that destruction or disposition.

Ca. Civ. Proc. Code § 1379
Amended by Stats 2016 ch 31 (SB 836),s 16, eff. 6/27/2016.
Amended by Stats 2006 ch 538 (SB 1852),s 73, eff. 1/1/2007.

Section 1380 - Transaction exempt from section 11009, Government Code

All sales, exchanges, or other transactions entered into by the Controller pursuant to this chapter are exempt from the provisions of Section 11009 of the Government Code.

Ca. Civ. Proc. Code § 1380
Added by Stats. 1951, Ch. 1708.

Section 1381 - Transactions conclusive against everyone except purchaser or encumbrancer for valuable consideration

All sales, leases or other transactions entered into by the Controller pursuant to this chapter shall be conclusive against everyone, except a purchaser or encumbrancer who in good faith and for a valuable consideration acquires a title or interest by an instrument in writing that is first duly recorded.

Ca. Civ. Proc. Code § 1381
Added by Stats. 1951, Ch. 1738.

Section 1382 - Real property to which article applies

Any provision of this article which authorizes the Controller to sell real property applies to any real property distributed or escheated to, or the title to which has vested in, the State of California by court order or decree of distribution, if such real property is held in the name of the Unclaimed Property Fund under the provision of this title, whether or not such real property has permanently escheated to the State.

This section does not apply to the disposition of tax-deeded lands under Chapter 7, 8 or 9 of Part 6 of Division 1 of the Revenue and Taxation Code.

Ca. Civ. Proc. Code § 1382
Added by Stats. 1953, Ch. 281.

Article 4 - DISPOSAL OF PROCEEDS OF SALE OR LEASE

Section 1390 - Proceeds deposited in Unclaimed Property Fund

The Controller shall deliver to the Treasurer the proceeds of any sale or lease of property, other than permanently escheated property, made pursuant to this chapter; and, on order of the Controller, the amount thereof shall be deposited in the Unclaimed Property Fund. Such amount shall be credited by the Controller to the account in said fund, in the name of which the property sold or leased was held. All moneys deposited in the Unclaimed Property Fund under the provisions of this section shall be held for the benefit of those entitled to claim the property sold or leased; but the period in which such moneys shall be available for claim by and payment to the persons entitled thereto shall not extend beyond the period in which such property is available for claim and payment under the provisions of this title.

Ca. Civ. Proc. Code § 1390
Added by Stats. 1951, Ch. 1708.

Section 1391 - Proceeds deposited in General Fund

The Controller shall deliver to the Treasurer the proceeds of any sale or lease of permanently escheated property made pursuant to this chapter; and, on order of the Controller, the amount thereof shall be deposited in the General Fund. All moneys deposited in the General Fund under the provisions of this section shall be deemed to have permanently escheated to the state as of the date of permanent escheat of the property from which such moneys were derived.

Ca. Civ. Proc. Code § 1391
Amended by Stats. 1978, Ch. 1183.

Section 1392 - Credit of proceeds to estate from which property affected by transaction received

The proceeds of any transaction by the Controller under the

provisions of this chapter in connection with property received and held by the state under the provisions of Article 1 (commencing with Section 1440) of Chapter 6 of this title shall be credited by the Controller to the estate from which the property affected by the transaction was received; or, if such property has permanently escheated to the state, to the account in the General Fund to which the permanently escheated cash derived from estates of deceased persons is credited.

Ca. Civ. Proc. Code § 1392
Amended by Stats. 1978, Ch. 1183.

Section 1393 - Credit of proceeds to unlocated heirs, devisees or legatees

The proceeds of any transaction by the Controller under the provisions of this chapter, in connection with property received and held by the state under the provisions of Article 1 (commencing with Section 1440) of Chapter 6 of this title, for the benefit of unlocated heirs, devisees or legatees of estates of deceased persons, shall be credited by the Controller to such heirs, devisees or legatees of the property affected by such transaction; or, if such property has permanently escheated to the state, to the account in the General Fund to which the permanently escheated cash derived from estates of deceased persons is credited.

Ca. Civ. Proc. Code § 1393
Amended by Stats. 1978, Ch. 1183.

Section 1394 - Credit of proceeds to persons entitled or to account in General Fund

The proceeds of any transaction by the Controller under the provisions of this chapter in connection with property received and held by the state under the provisions of this title, for the benefit of the persons entitled thereto, shall be credited by the Controller to such persons; or, if the property affected by such transaction has permanently escheated to the state, to the account in the General Fund in the name of which such permanently escheated property was recorded.

Ca. Civ. Proc. Code § 1394
Amended by Stats. 1978, Ch. 1183.

Chapter 5 - ESCHEAT PROCEEDINGS

Article 1 - ESCHEAT PROCEEDINGS ON UNCLAIMED PROPERTY

Section 1410 - Generally

The Attorney General shall, from time to time, commence actions on behalf of the state for the purpose of having it adjudged that title to unclaimed property to which the state has become entitled by escheat has vested in the state, and for the purpose of having it adjudged that property has been actually abandoned or that the owner thereof has died and there is no person entitled thereto and the same has escheated and vested in the state. Such actions shall be brought in the Superior Court for the County of Sacramento; except that if any real property covered by the petition is not situated in the County of Sacramento, an action respecting the real property shall be commenced in the superior court for the county in which such real property or any part thereof is situated. The Attorney General shall cause to be recorded in the office of the county recorder of the county in which the real property is situated, a notice of the pendency of the petition containing the names of the parties, and the object of the action and a description of the property in the county affected thereby. From the time of filing such notice for record only, shall a purchaser or encumbrancer of the property affected thereby be deemed to have constructive notice of the pendency of the action, and only of the pendency against parties designated by their real names.

Such action shall be commenced by filing a petition. The provisions of Section 1420, relating to the facts to be set forth in the petition, joinder of parties and causes of action, and the provisions of Section 1423, relating to appearances and pleadings, shall be applicable to any proceeding had under this section.

Upon the filing of the petition, the court shall make an order requiring all persons interested in the property or estate to appear on a day not more than 90 days nor less than 60 days from the date of the order and show cause, if any they have, why title to the property should not vest in the State of California.

Service of process in such actions shall be made by delivery of a copy of the order, together with a copy of the petition, to each person who claims title to any property covered by the petition and who is known to the Attorney General or the Controller or who has theretofore filed in the office of the Controller a written request for such service of process, stating his name and address, including street number, or post-office box number, if any, and by publishing the order at least once a week for two consecutive weeks in a newspaper published in the county in which the action is filed, the last publication to be at least 10 days prior to the date set for the hearing.

Upon completion of the service of process, as provided in this section, the court shall have full and complete jurisdiction over the estate, the property, and the person of everyone having or claiming any interest in the property, and shall have full and complete jursidiction to hear and determine the issues therein, and to render an appropriate judgment.

In addition to the foregoing publication of the order, a notice shall be given by publication, at least once a week for two successive weeks in a newspaper published in the county from which the property was forwarded to the State Treasury or is situated, of each estate and item of property from such county or situated in such county in excess of one thousand dollars ($1,000). Such notice shall state that a petition has been filed and an order made as hereinbefore provided and shall list each estate and item in excess of one thousand dollars ($1,000) and show the amount of the property, if money, or a description thereof, if other than money, and the name of the owner or claimant and his last known address. Any omission or defect in the giving of such additional notice shall not affect the jurisdiction of the court.

If it appears from the facts found or admitted that the state is entitled to the property or any part thereof mentioned in the petition, judgment shall be rendered that title to such property or part thereof, as the case may be, has vested in the state by escheat. No costs of suit shall be allowed against any party in any action or proceeding had under this section.

Ca. Civ. Proc. Code § 1410
Amended by Stats. 1984, Ch. 268, Sec. 1. Effective June 30, 1984.

Article 2 - ESCHEAT BY NOTICE AND PUBLICATION

Section 1415 - Generally

Whenever any money or other personal property of a value of one thousand dollars ($1,000) or less has heretofore been, or is hereafter, deposited in the State Treasury and the same is subject to being declared escheated to the state or being declared vested in the state as abandoned property, or otherwise, under any laws of this state, in lieu of the procedure provided for elsewhere in this chapter, the Controller may, from time to time, prepare a return listing such property and give notice thereof in the manner hereinafter provided. Such return shall list each item and show (1) the amount of the property, if money, or a description thereof if other than money; (2) the name of the owner or claimant and his last known address, if known; (3) the name and address of the person delivering the property to the State Treasury, if known but where the property is received from an estate, only the name of the decedent together with the name of the county and the number of the proceeding need be given; (4) the facts and circumstances by virtue of which it is claimed the property has escheated or vested in the state; and (5) such other information as the Controller may desire to include to assist in identifying each item.

When such return has been completed, the Controller shall prepare, date, and attach thereto a notice that the property listed in the return has escheated or vested in the state. Copies of such return and notice shall then be displayed and be open to public inspection during business hours in at least three offices of the Controller, one in the City of Sacramento, one in the City and County of San Francisco, and one in the City of Los Angeles.

The Controller shall then cause notice to be given by publication in one newspaper of general circulation published in the City of Sacramento, and also by publication in one newspaper of general circulation published in the City and County of San Francisco, and also by publication in one newspaper of general circulation published in the City of Los Angeles, at least once each calendar week for two consecutive weeks, that said return and notice that the property listed in the return has escheated or vested in the state has been prepared and is on display and open to public inspection during business hours, giving the addresses and room numbers of the locations where the same may be inspected.

Such publication shall be made within 90 days after attaching the notice to the return. Notice by such publication shall be deemed completed 120 days after attaching the notice to the return.

Within five years after such notice by publication is completed, any person entitled to such property may claim it in the manner provided in Chapter 3 of this title. All persons who fail to make such claim within the time limited are forever barred; saving, however, to infants and persons of unsound mind, the right to appear and claim such property at any time within the time limited, or within one year after their respective disabilities cease.

Ca. Civ. Proc. Code § 1415

Amended by Stats. 1984, Ch. 268, Sec. 2. Effective June 30, 1984.

Article 3 - ESCHEAT PROCEEDINGS IN DECEDENTS' ESTATES

Section 1420 - Generally

(a) At any time after two years after the death of any decedent who leaves property to which the state is entitled by reason of it having escheated to the state, the Attorney General shall commence a proceeding on behalf of the state in the Superior Court for the County of Sacramento to have it adjudged that the state is so entitled. The action shall be commenced by filing a petition, which shall be treated as the information elsewhere referred to in this title.

(b) The petition shall set forth a description of the property, the name of the person last in possession thereof, the name of the person, if any, claiming the property, or portion thereof, and the facts and circumstances by virtue of which it is claimed the property has escheated.

(c) Upon the filing of the petition, the court shall make an order requiring all persons interested in the estate to appear and show cause, if any, within 60 days from the date of the order, why the estate should not vest in the state. The order must be published at least once a week for four consecutive weeks in a newspaper published in the County of Sacramento, the last publication to be at least 10 days prior to the date set for the hearing. Upon the completion of the publication of the order, the court shall have full and complete jurisdiction over the estate, the property, and the person of everyone having or claiming any interest in the property, and shall have full and complete jurisdiction to hear and determine the issues therein, and render the appropriate judgment thereon.

(d) If proceedings for the administration of the estate have been instituted, a copy of the order must be filed with the papers in the estate. If proceedings for the administration of any estate of the decedent have been instituted and none of the persons entitled to succeed thereto have appeared and made claim to the property, or any portion thereof, before the decree of final distribution therein is made, or before the commencement of a proceeding by the Attorney General, or if the court shall find that the persons as have appeared are not entitled to the property of the estate, or any portion thereof, the court shall, upon final settlement of the proceedings for the administration of the estate, after the payment of all debts and expenses of administration, distribute all moneys and other property remaining to the State of California. In any proceeding brought by the Attorney General under this chapter, any two or more parties and any two or more causes of action may be joined in the same proceedings and in the same petition without being separately stated, and it shall be sufficient to allege in the petition that the decedent left no heirs to take the estate and the failure of heirs to appear and set up their claims in any proceeding, or in any proceedings for the administration of the estate, shall be sufficient proof upon which to base the judgment in any proceeding or decree of distribution.

(e) If proceedings for the administration of any estate have not been commenced within six months from the death of any decedent the Attorney General may direct the public administrator to commence the same forthwith.

Ca. Civ. Proc. Code § 1420
Amended by Stats 2003 ch 62 (SB 600),s 26, eff. 1/1/2004.
Amended by Stats 2002 ch 784 (SB 1316),s 83, eff. 1/1/2003.

Section 1421 - Action by Attorney General to determine state's rights to property or intervention in proceeding affecting estate and contesting claimants' rights

Whenever the Attorney General is informed that any estate has escheated or is about to escheat to the state, or that the property involved in any action or special proceeding has escheated or is about to escheat to the state, the Attorney General may commence an action on behalf of the state to determine its rights to the property or may intervene on its behalf in any action or special proceeding affecting the estate and contest the rights of any claimant or claimants thereto. The Attorney General may also apply to the superior court or any judge thereof for an order directing the county treasurer to deposit in the State Treasury all money, and to deliver to the Controller for deposit in the State Treasury, all other personal property, in the possession of the county treasurer, which may become payable to the State Treasury pursuant to Section 7643 of the Probate Code.

Ca. Civ. Proc. Code § 1421
Amended by Stats. 1988, Ch. 1199, Sec. 9. Operative July 1, 1989, by Sec. 119 of Ch. 1199.

Section 1422 - Appointment of receiver to take charge of estate

The court, upon the information being filed, and upon application of the Attorney General, either before or after answer, upon notice to the party claiming the estate, if known, may, upon sufficient cause therefor being shown, appoint a receiver to take charge of such estate, or any part thereof, or to receive the rents, income and profits of the same until the title of such estate is finally settled.

Ca. Civ. Proc. Code § 1422
Added by Stats. 1951, Ch. 1708.

Section 1423 - Appearance and answer by persons named in information

All persons named in the information may appear and answer, and may traverse or deny the facts stated therein at any time before the time for answering expires, and any other person claiming an interest in such estate may appear and be made a defendant, by motion for that purpose in open court within the time allowed for answering, and if no such person appears and answers within the time, then judgment must be rendered that the State is the owner of the property in such information claimed.

If any person appears and denies the title set up by the State, or traverses any material fact set forth in the information, the issue of fact must be tried as issues of fact are tried in civil actions.

If, after the issues are tried, it appears from the facts found or admitted that the State has good title to the property in the information mentioned, or any part thereof, judgment must be rendered that the State is the owner and entitled to the possession thereof, and that it recover costs of suit against the defendants who have appeared and answered.

In any judgment rendered, or that has heretofore been rendered by any court escheating property to the State, on motion of the Attorney General, the court must make an order that such property, unless it consists of money, be sold by the sheriff of the county where it is situate, at public sale, for cash, after giving notice of the time and place of sale, as may be prescribed by the court in such order; that the sheriff, within five days after such sale, make a report thereof to the court, and upon the hearing of such report, the court may examine the report and witnesses in relation thereto, and if the proceedings were unfair, or if the sum bid disproportionate to the value, or if it appears that a sum exceeding said bid, exclusive of the expense of a new sale, may be obtained, the court may vacate the sale, and direct another to be had, of which notice must be given, and the sale in all respects conducted as if no previous sale had taken place. If an offer greater in amount than that named in the report is made to the court in writing by a responsible person, the court may, in its discretion, accept such offer and confirm the sale to such person, or order a new sale.

If it appears to the court that the sale was legally made and fairly conducted and that the sum bid is not disproportionate to the value of the property sold, and that a sum exceeding such bid, exclusive of the expense of a new sale, cannot be obtained, or if the increased bid above mentioned is made and accepted by the court, the court must make an order confirming the sale and directing the sheriff, in the name of the State, to execute to the purchaser or purchasers a conveyance of said property sold; and said conveyance vests in the purchaser or purchasers all the right and title of the State therein. The sheriff shall, out of the proceeds of such sale, pay the cost of said proceedings incurred on behalf of the State, including the expenses of making such sale, and also an attorney's fee, if additional counsel was employed in said proceedings, to be fixed by the court, not exceeding 10 percent on the amount of such sale; and the residue thereof shall be paid by said sheriff into the State Treasury.

Ca. Civ. Proc. Code § 1423
Added by Stats. 1951, Ch. 1708.

Section 1424 - Distributing or vesting clause of judgment or decree creating trust in favor of unknown or unidentified persons

If, in any proceeding had under this title, the judgment or decree distributes or vests unclaimed property or any portion thereof to or in the State of California and the distributing or vesting clause contains words otherwise creating a trust in favor of certain unknown or unidentified persons as a class, such judgment or decree shall vest in the State of California both legal and equitable title to such property; saving, however, the right of claimants to appear and claim the property, as provided in this title.

Ca. Civ. Proc. Code § 1424
Added by Stats. 1951, Ch. 1708.

Article 4 - PERMANENT ESCHEAT

Section 1430 - Generally

(a) Upon the expiration of five years after the date of entry of judgment in any proceeding pursuant to this chapter, or upon the expiration of five years after completion of notice by publication in an escheat action taken pursuant to Section 1415, the property covered by that proceeding or action shall permanently escheat to the state, except as provided in subdivision (b).

(b) Infants and persons of unsound mind shall have the right to appear and claim such property as provided in this title if born before the expiration of the five-year period; but it shall be presumed that there are no infants nor persons of unsound mind who are or will be entitled to claim this property unless and until they appear and claim the property as provided in this title. This presumption shall be conclusive in favor of any purchaser in good faith and for a valuable consideration from the state and everyone subsequently claiming under him or her, saving however, to infants and persons of unsound mind the right of recourse to the proceeds of any sale or other disposition of any such property by the state and as herein provided.

(c) Except as otherwise provided in this subdivision, a named beneficiary of property that escheats pursuant to this title or, if the beneficiary is deceased or a court renders a judgment that the beneficiary is dead, a blood relative of the named beneficiary may claim property described in subdivision (a) at any time within five years after the date of entry of judgment in any proceeding under this chapter. The named beneficiary or, if a court has rendered a judgment that the named beneficiary is dead, the blood relative of the named beneficiary shall be entitled to immediate payment upon this claim. If a court has not rendered a judgment that the named beneficiary is dead, payment of the claim of a blood relative of the named beneficiary shall be made on the day before the expiration of the five-year period described in this section. This subdivision shall not apply to authorize a claim by any person, including any issue or blood relative of that person, whose interest or inheritance was specifically restricted or barred by a provision in the donating or transferring instrument.

Ca. Civ. Proc. Code § 1430
Amended by Stats. 1997, Ch. 671, Sec. 1. Effective January 1, 1998.

Section 1431 - Transfer of permanently escheated money to General Fund; adjustment of records of permanently escheated property

When money in the Unclaimed Property Fund has become permanently escheated to the state, the amount thereof shall, on order of the Controller, be transferred to the General Fund. When property other than money held by the Controller or Treasurer in the name of any account in the Unclaimed Property Fund has become permanently escheated to the state, the records of the Controller and Treasurer shall be adjusted to show that such property is held in the name of the General Fund.

Ca. Civ. Proc. Code § 1431
Amended by Stats. 1980, Ch. 676, Sec. 69.

Chapter 6 - DISPOSITION OF UNCLAIMED PROPERTY

Article 1 - ESTATES OF DECEASED PERSONS

Section 1440 - Money or property deemed paid under provisions of article

Whenever, under the provisions of this title or under any other provision of law, any unclaimed money or other property in an estate of a deceased person, or any unclaimed amount payable pursuant to an allowed and approved claim against such an estate, is paid to the State or any officer or employee thereof for deposit in the State Treasury, it shall be deemed to have been so paid under the provisions of this article.

Ca. Civ. Proc. Code § 1440
Added by Stats. 1951, Ch. 1708.

Section 1441 - Money or property permanently escheated without further proceeding

Money or other property distributed to the state under Chapter 6 (commencing with Section 11900) of Part 10 of Division 7 of the Probate Code, if not claimed within five years from the date of the order for distribution, as provided in Chapter 3, is permanently escheated to the state without further proceeding; saving, however, to infants and persons of unsound mind, the right to appear and file their claims within the time limited pursuant to Section 1430, or within one year after their respective disabilities cease; provided, however, that any such property shall be conclusively presumed to be permanently escheated to the state as to all persons in favor of a purchaser in good faith and for a valuable consideration from the state and anyone subsequently claiming under that purchaser, saving however, to infants and persons of unsound mind the right of recourse to the proceeds of any sale or other disposition of that property by the state and as herein provided.

Ca. Civ. Proc. Code § 1441

Amended by Stats. 1995, Ch. 105, Sec. 1. Effective January 1, 1996.

Section 1442 - Claim to money or other property by person entitled

Except as otherwise provided in Section 1441, any money or other property paid into the State Treasury under the provisions of this article may be claimed by the person entitled thereto, as provided in Chapter 3.

Ca. Civ. Proc. Code § 1442

Added by Stats. 1951, Ch. 1708.

Section 1443 - Money or property deemed paid or delivered for deposit in State Treasury

Notwithstanding any other provision of law, all money or other property paid or delivered to the state or any officer or employee thereof under the provisions of Section 7643 or 11428, Chapter 6 (commencing with Section 11900) of Part 10 of Division 7, or Section 6800, of the Probate Code, or under any other section of the Probate Code, or any amendment thereof adopted after the effective date of this section, shall be deemed to be paid or delivered for deposit in the State Treasury under the provisions of this article, and shall be transmitted, received, accounted for, and disposed of, as provided in this title.

Ca. Civ. Proc. Code § 1443

Amended by Stats. 1988, Ch. 1199, Sec. 11. Operative July 1, 1989, by Sec. 119 of Ch. 1199.

Section 1444 - Money or property deposited in county treasury paid to Treasurer or Controller

At the time of the next county settlement following the expiration of one year from the date of its deposit in the county treasury, all money or other property distributed in the administration of an estate of a deceased person and heretofore or hereafter deposited in the county treasury to the credit of known heirs, legatees, or devisees, and any money or other property remaining on deposit to the credit of an estate after final distribution to such known heirs, legatees or devisees, shall be paid to the Treasurer or Controller as provided in Chapter 2.

Ca. Civ. Proc. Code § 1444
Added by Stats. 1951, Ch. 1708.

Section 1444.5 - Money or property on deposit with county treasurer received from public administrator deemed permanently escheated to state

Notwithstanding any other provision of law, any money on deposit with the county treasurer of a county received from a public administrator of the county in trust and to the account of the estate of a deceased person or the creditor of a deceased person, in an amount of fifty dollars ($50) or less as to any one estate or creditor, and not covered by a decree of distribution, which was received or remained on hand after the final accounting in such deceased person's estate and the discharge of such public administrator as representative of the estate, and where the money has so remained on deposit in trust for a period of 15 years or more unclaimed by any heir, devisee or legatee of such deceased person, or by any creditor having an allowed and approved claim against the deceased person's estate remaining unpaid, shall be deemed permanently escheated to the State of California. The total of any such moneys so held in trust unclaimed for such period may be paid in a lump sum by the county treasurer, from such funds as he may have on hand for the purpose, to the State Treasurer, at the time of the next county settlement after the effective date of this section, or at any county settlement thereafter. Such lump sum payment may be made by designating it to have been made under this section, without the necessity of any further report or statement of the estates or claimants concerned, without the necessity of any order of court, and without being subject to the provisions of Section 1311 or 1312. Upon receipt by the State Treasurer, any permanently escheated money received by him under this section shall forthwith be deposited in the School Land Fund, subject only to the rights of minors and persons of unsound mind saved to them by Section 1430.

This section shall also apply in all respects to any money on deposit with a county treasurer received from the coroner of the county in trust and to the account of a deceased person, and any such money shall be held, deemed permanently escheated, reported and paid over in like manner as hereinabove set forth.

Ca. Civ. Proc. Code § 1444.5
Added by Stats. 1957, Ch. 1375.

Section 1445 - Petition by county treasurer for order directing payment of money or property into State Treasury

If money or other property is deposited in a county treasury, and if the deposits belong (1) to known decedents' estates on which letters testamentary or letters of administration have never been issued or (2) to known decedents' estates on which letters testamentary or letters of administration have been issued but no decree of distribution has been rendered, due to the absence of any parties interested in the estate or the failure of such parties diligently to protect their interests by taking reasonable steps for the purpose of securing a distribution of the estate, the county treasurer shall, within one year following the expiration of five years from the date of such deposit, file a petition in the superior court of the county in which the deposit is held, setting forth the fact that the money or other personal property has remained in the county treasury under such circumstances for such five-year period, and petitioning the court for an order directing him to pay such money or other property into the State Treasury.

At the time of the next county settlement following the date of the making of the order by the court, unless earlier payment is required by the Controller, the county treasurer shall pay such money or other property to the Treasurer or Controller as provided in Chapter 2.

Ca. Civ. Proc. Code § 1445
Added by Stats. 1951, Ch. 1708.

Section 1446 - Unclaimed money or other property belonging to person who dies while confined in state institution subject to jurisdiction of Director of Corrections

Notwithstanding any other provision of law, all unclaimed money or other property belonging to any person who dies while confined in any state institution subject to the jurisdiction of the Director of Corrections, which is paid or delivered to the State or any officer or employee thereof under the provisions of Section 5061 of the Penal Code, or under any amendment thereof adopted after the effective date of this section, shall be deemed to be paid or delivered for deposit in the State Treasury under the provisions of this article, and shall be transmitted, received, accounted for, and disposed of, as provided in this part.

Ca. Civ. Proc. Code § 1446
Added by Stats. 1951, Ch. 1708.

Section 1447 - Money or other property belonging to person who dies while confined in state institution subject to jurisdiction of State Department of State Hospitals

Notwithstanding any other law, all unclaimed money or other property belonging to a person who dies while confined in a state institution subject to the jurisdiction of the State Department of State Hospitals, which is paid or delivered to the state or an officer or employee thereof under the provisions of Section 166 of the Welfare and Institutions Code, or under any amendment thereof adopted after the effective date of Chapter 1708 of the Statutes of 1951 shall be deemed to be paid or delivered for deposit in the State Treasury under the provisions of this article, and shall be transmitted, received, accounted for, and disposed of, as provided in this part.

Ca. Civ. Proc. Code § 1447
Amended by Stats 2014 ch 144 (AB 1847),s 7, eff. 1/1/2015.

Section 1448 - Unclaimed money or property belonging to person who dies while confined in state institution subject to jurisdiction of Youth Authority

Notwithstanding any other provision of law, all unclaimed money or other property belonging to any person who dies while confined in any state institution subject to the jurisdiction of the Youth Authority, which is paid or delivered to the State or any officer thereof under the provisions of Section 1015 of the Welfare and Institutions Code or under any amendment thereof adopted after the effective date of this section, shall be deemed to be paid or delivered for deposit in the State Treasury under the provisions of this article, and shall be transmitted, received, accounted for, and disposed of, as provided in this part.

Ca. Civ. Proc. Code § 1448
Added by Stats. 1951, Ch. 1708.

Section 1449 - Presumptively abandoned money or property paid or delivered to Treasurer or Controller under section 7644, Probate Code

Notwithstanding any other provision of law, all presumptively abandoned money or other property paid or delivered to the Treasurer or Controller under the provisions of Section 7644 of the Probate Code shall be deemed to be paid or delivered for deposit in the State Treasury under the provisions of this article, and shall be transmitted, received, accounted for, and disposed of as provided in this title.

Ca. Civ. Proc. Code § 1449

Amended by Stats. 1988, Ch. 1199, Sec. 12. Operative July 1, 1989, by Sec. 119 of Ch. 1199.

Article 2 - ABANDONED PROPERTY

Section 1476 - Generally
The expiration of any period of time specified by law, during which an action or proceeding may be commenced or enforced to secure payment of a claim for money or recovery of property, shall not prevent any such money or other property from being deemed abandoned property, nor affect any duty to file a report required by this title or to deliver to the Treasurer or Controller any such abandoned property; and shall not serve as a defense in any action or proceeding brought under the provisions of this article to compel the filing of any report or the delivery of any abandoned property required by this article or to enforce or collect any penalty provided by this article.

Ca. Civ. Proc. Code § 1476
Added by Stats. 1951, Ch. 1708.

Chapter 7 - UNCLAIMED PROPERTY LAW

Article 1 - SHORT TITLE; DEFINITIONS; APPLICATION

Section 1500 - Title of law
This chapter may be cited as the Unclaimed Property Law.

Ca. Civ. Proc. Code § 1500
Amended by Stats. 1968, Ch. 356.

Section 1501 - Definitions
As used in this chapter, unless the context otherwise requires:
(a) "Apparent owner" means the person who appears from the records of the holder to be entitled to property held by the holder.
(b) "Banking organization" means any national or state bank, trust company, banking company, land bank, savings bank, safe-deposit

company, private banker, or any similar organization.

(c) "Business association" means any private corporation, joint stock company, business trust, partnership, or any association for business purposes of two or more individuals, whether or not for profit, including, but not by way of limitation, a banking organization, financial organization, life insurance corporation, and utility.

(d) "Financial organization" means any federal or state savings and loan association, building and loan association, credit union, investment company, or any similar organization.

(e) "Holder" means any person in possession of property subject to this chapter belonging to another, or who is trustee in case of a trust, or is indebted to another on an obligation subject to this chapter.

(f) "Life insurance corporation" means any association or corporation transacting the business of insurance on the lives of persons or insurance appertaining thereto, including, but not by way of limitation, endowments, and annuities.

(g) "Owner" means a depositor in case of a deposit, a beneficiary in case of a trust, or creditor, claimant, or payee in case of other choses in action, or any person having a legal or equitable interest in property subject to this chapter, or his or her legal representative.

(h) "Person" means any individual, business association, government or governmental subdivision or agency, two or more persons having a joint or common interest, or any other legal or commercial entity, whether that person is acting in his or her own right or in a representative or fiduciary capacity.

(i) "Employee benefit plan distribution" means any money, life insurance, endowment or annuity policy or proceeds thereof, securities or other intangible property, or any tangible property, distributable to a participant, former participant, or the beneficiary or estate or heirs of a participant or former participant or beneficiary, from a trust or custodial fund established under a plan to provide health and welfare, pension, vacation, severance, retirement benefit, death benefit, stock purchase, profit sharing, employee savings, supplemental unemployment insurance benefits or similar benefits, or which is established under a plan by a business association functioning as or in conjunction with a labor union which receives for distribution residuals on behalf of employees working under collective-bargaining agreements.

(j) "Residuals" means payments pursuant to a collective bargaining agreement of additional compensation for domestic and foreign uses of recorded materials.

Ca. Civ. Proc. Code § 1501

Amended by Stats. 1990, Ch. 450, Sec. 2. Effective July 31, 1990.

Section 1501.5 - Property received by state not to permanently escheat to state

(a) Notwithstanding any provision of law to the contrary, property received by the state under this chapter shall not permanently escheat to the state.

(b) The Legislature finds and declares that this section is declaratory of the existing law and sets forth the intent of the Legislature regarding the Uniform Disposition of Unclaimed Property Act (Chapter 1809, Statutes of 1959) and all amendments thereto and revisions thereof. Any opinions, rulings, orders, judgments, or other statements to the contrary by any court are erroneous and inconsistent with the intent of the Legislature.

(c) It is the intent of the Legislature that property owners be reunited with their property. In making changes to the unclaimed property program, the Legislature intends to adopt a more expansive notification program that will provide all of the following:

(1) Notification by the state to all owners of unclaimed property prior to escheatment.

(2) A more expansive postescheatment policy that takes action to identify those owners of unclaimed property.

(3) A waiting period of not less than seven years from delivery of property to the state prior to disposal of any unclaimed property deemed to have no commercial value.

Ca. Civ. Proc. Code § 1501.5

Amended by Stats 2014 ch 913 (AB 2747),s 10, eff. 1/1/2015.
Amended by Stats 2007 ch 179 (SB 86),s 1, eff. 8/24/2007.

Section 1502 - Inapplicability of chapter

(a) This chapter does not apply to any of the following:

(1) Any property in the official custody of a municipal utility district.

(2) Any property in the official custody of a local agency if such property may be transferred to the general fund of such agency under the provisions of Sections 50050- 50053 of the Government Code.

(3) Any property in the official custody of a court if the property may be transferred to the Trial Court Operations Fund under Section 68084.1 of the Government Code.
(b) None of the provisions of this chapter applies to any type of property received by the state under the provisions of Chapter 1 (commencing with Section 1300) to Chapter 6 (commencing with Section 1440), inclusive, of this title.
Ca. Civ. Proc. Code § 1502
Amended by Stats 2007 ch 738 (AB 1248),s 6, eff. 1/1/2008.
Amended by Stats 2004 ch 227 (SB 1102),s 13, eff. 8/16/2004.

Section 1503 - When holder not required to report under old act

(a) As used in this section:

(1) "Old act" means this chapter as it existed prior to January 1, 1969.

(2) "New act" means this chapter as it exists on and after January 1, 1969.

(3) "Property not subject to the old act" means property that was not presumed abandoned under the old act and would never have been presumed abandoned under the old act had the old act continued in existence on and after January 1, 1969, without change.

(b) The holder is not required to file a report concerning, or to pay or deliver to the Controller, any property not subject to the old act if an action by the owner against the holder to recover that property was barred by an applicable statute of limitations prior to January 1, 1969.

(c) The holder is not required to file a report concerning, or to pay or deliver to the Controller, any property not subject to the old act, or any property that was not required to be reported under the old act, unless on January 1, 1969, the property has been held by the holder for less than the escheat period. "Escheat period" means the period referred to in Sections 1513 to 1521, inclusive, of the new act, whichever is applicable to the particular property.

Ca. Civ. Proc. Code § 1503
Amended by Stats. 1990, Ch. 450, Sec. 3. Effective July 31, 1990.

Section 1504 - Property escheated under laws of another state

(a) As used in this section:

(1) "Old act" means this chapter as it existed prior to January 1, 1969.

(2) "New act" means this chapter as it exists on and after January 1, 1969.

(3) "Property not subject to the old act" means property that was not presumed abandoned under the old act and would never have been presumed abandoned under the old act had the old act continued in existence on and after January 1, 1969, without change.

(b) This chapter does not apply to any property that was escheated under the laws of another state prior to September 18, 1959.

(c) This chapter does not require the holder to pay or deliver any property not subject to the old act to this state if the property was escheated under the laws of another state prior to January 1, 1969, and was delivered to the custody of that state prior to January 1, 1970, in compliance with the laws of that state. Nothing in this subdivision affects or limits the right of the State Controller to recover such property from the other state.

Ca. Civ. Proc. Code § 1504
Added by Stats. 1968, Ch. 356.

Section 1505 - Duty to report or pay or deliver property arising prior to January 1, 1969

This chapter does not affect any duty to file a report with the State Controller or to pay or deliver any property to him that arose prior to January 1, 1969, under the provisions of this chapter as it existed prior to January 1, 1969. Such duties may be enforced by the State Controller, and the penalties for failure to perform such duties may be imposed, under the provisions of this chapter as it existed prior to January 1, 1969. The provisions of this chapter as it existed prior to January 1, 1969, are continued in existence for the purposes of this section.

Ca. Civ. Proc. Code § 1505
Repealed and added by Stats. 1968, Ch. 356.

Section 1506 - Construction of provisions as restatements and continuations

The provisions of this chapter as it exists on and after January 1, 1969, insofar as they are substantially the same as the provisions of this chapter as it existed prior to January 1, 1969, relating to the same subject matter, shall be construed as restatements and continuations thereof and not as new enactments.

Ca. Civ. Proc. Code § 1506
Added by Stats. 1968, Ch. 356.

Article 2 - ESCHEAT OF UNCLAIMED PERSONAL PROPERTY

Section 1510 - When intangible personal property escheats to state

Unless otherwise provided by statute of this state, intangible personal property escheats to this state under this chapter if the conditions for escheat stated in Sections 1513 through 1521 exist, and if:

(a) The last known address, as shown on the records of the holder, of the apparent owner is in this state.

(b) No address of the apparent owner appears on the records of the holder and:

(1) The last known address of the apparent owner is in this state; or

(2) The holder is domiciled in this state and has not previously paid the property to the state of the last known address of the apparent owner; or

(3) The holder is a government or governmental subdivision or agency of this state and has not previously paid the property to the state of the last known address of the apparent owner.

(c) The last known address, as shown on the records of the holder, of the apparent owner is in a state that does not provide by law for the escheat of such property and the holder is (1) domiciled in this state or (2) a government or governmental subdivision or agency of this state.

(d) The last known address, as shown on the records of the holder, of the apparent owner is in a foreign nation and the holder is (1) domiciled in this state or (2) a government or governmental subdivision or agency of this state.

Ca. Civ. Proc. Code § 1510
Amended by Stats. 1978, Ch. 1183.

Section 1511 - Money order, travelers check or similar written instrument

(a) Any sum payable on a money order, travelers check, or other similar written instrument (other than a third-party bank check) on which a business association is directly liable escheats to this state under this chapter if the conditions for escheat stated in Section 1513 exist and if:

(1) The books and records of such business association show that such money order, travelers check, or similar written instrument was purchased in this state;

(2) The business association has its principal place of business in this state and the books and records of the business association do not show the state in which such money order, travelers check, or similar written instrument was purchased; or

(3) The business association has its principal place of business in this state, the books and records of the business association show the state in which such money order, travelers check, or similar written instrument was purchased, and the laws of the state of purchase do not provide for the escheat of the sum payable on such instrument.

(b) Notwithstanding any other provision of this chapter, this section applies to sums payable on money orders, travelers checks, and similar written instruments deemed abandoned on or after February 1, 1965, except to the extent that such sums have been paid over to a state prior to January 1, 1974. For the purposes of this subdivision, the words "deemed abandoned" have the same meaning as those words have as used in Section 604 of Public Law Number 93-495 (October 28, 1974), 88th Statutes at Large 1500.

Ca. Civ. Proc. Code § 1511

Repealed and added by Stats. 1975, Ch. 25.

Section 1513 - Property held or owing by business association

(a) Subject to Sections 1510 and 1511, the following property held or owing by a business association escheats to this state:

(1)

(A) Except as provided in paragraph (6), any demand, savings, or matured time deposit, or account subject to a negotiable order of withdrawal, made with a banking organization, together with any interest or dividends thereon, excluding, from demand deposits and accounts subject to a negotiable order of withdrawal only, any reasonable service charges that may lawfully be withheld and that do not, where made in this state, exceed those set forth in schedules filed by the banking organization from time to time with the Controller, if the owner, for more than three years, has not done any of the following:

(i) Increased or decreased the amount of the deposit, cashed an interest check, or presented the passbook or other similar evidence of the deposit for the crediting of interest.

(ii) Corresponded electronically or in writing with the banking organization concerning the deposit.

(iii) Otherwise indicated an interest in the deposit as evidenced by a memorandum or other record on file with the banking organization.

(B) A deposit or account shall not, however, escheat to the state if, during the previous three years, the owner has owned another deposit or account with the banking organization or the owner has owned an individual retirement account or funds held by the banking organization under a retirement plan for self-employed individuals or a similar account or plan established pursuant to the internal revenue laws of the United States or the laws of this state, as described in paragraph (6), and, with respect to that deposit, account, or plan, the owner has done any of the acts described in clause (i), (ii), or (iii) of subparagraph (A), and the banking organization has communicated electronically or in writing with the owner, at the address to which communications regarding that deposit, account, or plan are regularly sent, with regard to the deposit or account that would otherwise escheat under subparagraph (A). For purposes of this subparagraph, "communications" includes account statements or statements required under the internal revenue laws of the United States.

(C) No banking organization may discontinue any interest or dividends on any savings deposit because of the inactivity contemplated by this section.

(2)

(A) Except as provided in paragraph (6), any demand, savings, or matured time deposit, or matured investment certificate, or account subject to a negotiable order of withdrawal, or other interest in a financial organization or any deposit made therewith, and any interest or dividends thereon, excluding, from demand deposits and accounts subject to a negotiable order of withdrawal only, any reasonable service charges that may lawfully be withheld and that do not, where made in this state, exceed those set forth in schedules filed by the financial organization from time to time with the Controller, if the owner, for more than three years, has not done any of the following:

(i) Increased or decreased the amount of the funds or deposit, cashed an interest check, or presented an appropriate record for the crediting of interest or dividends.

(ii) Corresponded electronically or in writing with the financial organization concerning the funds or deposit.

(iii) Otherwise indicated an interest in the funds or deposit as evidenced by a memorandum or other record on file with the financial organization.

(B) A deposit or account shall not, however, escheat to the state if, during the previous three years, the owner has owned another deposit or account with the financial organization or the owner has owned an individual retirement account or funds held by the financial organization under a retirement plan for self-employed individuals or a similar account or plan established pursuant to the internal revenue laws of the United States or the laws of this state, as described in paragraph (6), and, with respect to that deposit, account, or plan, the owner has done any of the acts described in clause (i), (ii), or (iii) of subparagraph (A), and the financial organization has communicated electronically or in writing with the owner, at the address to which communications regarding that deposit, account, or plan are regularly sent, with regard to the deposit or account that would otherwise escheat under subparagraph (A). For purposes of this subparagraph, "communications" includes account statements or statements required under the internal revenue laws of the United States.

(C) No financial organization may discontinue any interest or dividends on any funds paid toward purchase of shares or other interest, or on any deposit, because of the inactivity contemplated by this section.

(3) Any sum payable on a traveler's check issued by a business association that has been outstanding for more than 15 years from the date of its issuance, if the owner, for more than 15 years, has not corresponded in writing with the business association concerning it, or otherwise indicated an interest as evidenced by a memorandum or other record on file with the association.

(4) Any sum payable on any other written instrument on which a banking or financial organization is directly liable, including, by way of illustration but not of limitation, any draft, cashier's check, teller's check, or certified check, that has been outstanding for more than three years from the date it was payable, or from the date of its issuance if payable on demand, if the owner, for more than three years, has not corresponded electronically or in writing with the banking or financial organization concerning it, or otherwise indicated an interest as evidenced by a memorandum or other record on file with the banking or financial organization.

(5) Any sum payable on a money order issued by a business association, including a banking or financial organization, that has been outstanding for more than seven years from the date it was payable, or from the date of its issuance if payable on demand, excluding any reasonable service charges that may lawfully be withheld and that do not, when made in this state, exceed those set forth in schedules filed by the business association from time to time with the Controller, if the owner, for more than seven years,

has not corresponded electronically or in writing with the business association, banking, or financial organization concerning it, or otherwise indicated an interest as evidenced by a memorandum or other record on file with the business association. For the purposes of this subdivision, "reasonable service charge" means a service charge that meets all of the following requirements:

(A) It is uniformly applied to all of the issuer's money orders.

(B) It is clearly disclosed to the purchaser at the time of purchase and to the recipient of the money order.

(C) It does not begin to accrue until three years after the purchase date, and it stops accruing after the value of the money order escheats.

(D) It is permitted by contract between the issuer and the purchaser.

(E) It does not exceed 25 cents ($0.25) per month or the aggregate amount of twenty-one dollars ($21).

(6)

(A) Any funds held by a business association in an individual retirement account or under a retirement plan for self-employed individuals or similar account or plan established pursuant to the internal revenue laws of the United States or of this state, if the owner, for more than three years after the funds become payable or distributable, has not done any of the following:

(i) Increased or decreased the principal.

(ii) Accepted payment of principal or income.

(iii) Corresponded electronically or in writing concerning the property or otherwise indicated an interest.

(B) Funds held by a business association in an individual retirement account or under a retirement plan for self-employed individuals or a similar account or plan created pursuant to the internal revenue laws of the United States or the laws of this state shall not escheat to the state if, during the previous three years, the owner has owned another such account, plan, or any other deposit or account with the business association and, with respect to that deposit, account, or plan, the owner has done any of the acts described in clause (i), (ii), or (iii) of subparagraph (A), and the business association has communicated electronically or in writing with the owner, at the address to which communications regarding that deposit, account, or plan are regularly sent, with regard to the account or plan that would otherwise escheat under subparagraph (A). For purposes of this subparagraph, "communications" includes account statements or statements required under the internal revenue laws of the United States.

(C) These funds are not payable or distributable within the meaning of this subdivision unless either of the following is true:

(i) Under the terms of the account or plan, distribution of all or a part of the funds would then be mandatory.

(ii) For an account or plan not subject to mandatory distribution requirement under the internal revenue laws of the United States or the laws of this state, the owner has attained $70^1/_2$ years of age.

(7) Any wages or salaries that have remained unclaimed by the owner for more than one year after the wages or salaries become payable.

(b) For purposes of this section, "service charges" means service charges imposed because of the inactivity contemplated by this section.

(c) A holder shall, commencing on or before January 1, 2018, regard the following transactions that are initiated electronically and are reflected in the books and records of the banking or financial organization as evidence that an owner has increased or decreased the amount of the funds or deposit in an account, for purposes of paragraphs (1) and (2) of subdivision (a):

(1) A single or recurring debit transaction authorized by the owner.

(2) A single or recurring credit transaction authorized by the owner

(3) Recurring transactions authorized by the owner that represent payroll deposits or deductions.

(4) Recurring credits authorized by the owner or a responsible party that represent the deposit of any federal benefits, including social security benefits, veterans' benefits, and pension payments.

Ca. Civ. Proc. Code § 1513

Amended by Stats 2016 ch 463 (AB 2258),s 1, eff. 1/1/2017.
Amended by Stats 2011 ch 305 (SB 495),s 1, eff. 1/1/2012.
Amended by Stats 2009 ch 522 (AB 1291),s 1, eff. 1/1/2010.
Amended by Stats 2003 ch 304 (AB 378),s 1, eff. 1/1/2004.
Amended October 10, 1999 (Bill Number: AB 777) (Chapter 835).

Section 1513.5 - Notice by banking or financial organization that deposit, account, shares, etc. may escheat to state

(a) Except as provided in subdivision (c), if the holder has in its records an address for the apparent owner, which the holder's records do not disclose to be inaccurate, every banking or financial organization shall make reasonable efforts to notify any owner by mail or, if the owner has consented to electronic notice, electronically, that the owner's deposit, account, shares, or other interest in the banking or financial organization will escheat to the state pursuant to clause (i), (ii), or (iii) of subparagraph (A) of paragraph (1), (2), or (6) of subdivision (a) of Section 1513. The holder shall give notice either:

(1) Not less than two years nor more than two and one-half years after the date of last activity by, or communication with, the owner with respect to the account, deposit, shares, or other interest, as shown on the record of the banking or financial organization.

(2) Not less than 6 nor more than 12 months before the time the account, deposit, shares, or other interest becomes reportable to the Controller in accordance with this chapter.

(b) The notice required by this section shall specify the time that the deposit, account, shares, or other interest will escheat and the effects of escheat, including the necessity for filing a claim for the return of the deposit, account, shares, or other interest. The face of the notice shall contain a heading at the top that reads as follows: "THE STATE OF CALIFORNIA REQUIRES US TO NOTIFY YOU THAT YOUR UNCLAIMED PROPERTY MAY BE TRANSFERRED TO THE STATE IF YOU DO NOT CONTACT US," or substantially similar language. The notice required by this section shall, in boldface type or in a font a minimum of two points larger than the rest of the notice, exclusive of the heading, (1) specify that since the date of last activity, or for the last two years, there has been no owner activity on the deposit, account, shares, or other interest; (2) identify the deposit, account, shares, or other interest by number or identifier, which need not exceed four digits; (3) indicate that the deposit, account, shares, or other interest is in danger of escheating to the state; and (4) specify that the Unclaimed Property Law requires banking and financial organizations to transfer funds of a deposit, account, shares, or other interest if it has been inactive for three years. It shall also include a form, as prescribed by the Controller, by which the owner may declare an intention to maintain the deposit, account, shares, or other interest. If that form is filled out, signed by the owner, and returned to the banking or financial organization, it shall satisfy the requirement of clause (iii) of subparagraph (A) of paragraph (1), clause (iii) of subparagraph (A) of paragraph (2), or clause (iii) of subparagraph (A) of paragraph (6) of subdivision (a) of Section 1513. In lieu of returning the form, the banking or financial organization may provide a telephone number or other electronic means to enable the owner to contact that organization. The contact, as evidenced by a memorandum or other record on file with the banking or financial organization, shall satisfy the requirement of clause (iii) of subparagraph (A) of paragraph (1), clause (iii) of subparagraph (A) of paragraph (2), or clause (iii) of subparagraph (A) of paragraph (6) of subdivision (a) of Section 1513. If the deposit, account, shares, or other interest has a value greater than two dollars ($2), the banking or financial organization may impose a service charge on the deposit, account, shares, or other interest for this notice in an amount not to exceed the administrative cost of mailing or electronically sending the notice and form and in no case to exceed two dollars ($2).

(c) Notice as provided by subdivisions (a) and (b) shall not be required for deposits, accounts, shares, or other interests of less than fifty dollars ($50), and, except as provided in subdivision (b), no service charge may be made for notice on these items.

(d) In addition to the notices required pursuant to subdivision (a), the holder may give additional notice as described in subdivision (b) at any time between the date of last activity by, or communication with, the owner and the date the holder transfers the deposit, account, shares, or other interest to the Controller.

(e) At the time a new account is opened with a banking or financial organization, the organization shall provide a written notice to the person opening the account informing the person that his or her property may be transferred to the appropriate state if no activity occurs in the account within the time period specified by state law. If the person opening the account has consented to electronic notice, that notice may be provided electronically.

Ca. Civ. Proc. Code § 1513.5

Amended by Stats 2013 ch 362 (AB 212),s 1, eff. 1/1/2014.
Amended by Stats 2011 ch 305 (SB 495),s 2, eff. 1/1/2012.
Amended by Stats 2009 ch 522 (AB 1291),s 2, eff. 1/1/2010.
Amended by Stats 2002 ch 813 (AB 1772),s 1, eff. 1/1/2004

Section 1514 - Proceeds of contents of safe deposit box or other safekeeping repository

(a) The contents of, or the proceeds of sale of the contents of, any safe deposit box or any other safekeeping repository, held in this state by a business association, escheat to this state if unclaimed by the owner for more than three years from the date on which the lease or rental period on the box or other repository expired, or from the date of termination of any agreement because of which the box or other repository was furnished to the owner without cost, whichever last occurs.

(b) If a business association has in its records an address for an apparent owner of the contents of, or the proceeds of sale of the contents of, a safe deposit box or other safekeeping repository described in subdivision (a), and the records of the business association do not disclose the address to be inaccurate, the business association shall make reasonable efforts to notify the owner by mail, or, if the owner has consented to electronic notice, electronically, that the owner's contents, or the proceeds of the sale of the contents, will escheat to the state pursuant to this section. The business association shall give notice not less than 6 months and not more than 12 months before the time the contents, or the proceeds of the sale of the contents, become reportable to the Controller in accordance with this chapter.

(c) The face of the notice shall contain a heading at the top that reads as follows: "THE STATE OF CALIFORNIA REQUIRES US TO NOTIFY YOU THAT YOUR UNCLAIMED PROPERTY MAY BE TRANSFERRED TO THE STATE IF YOU DO NOT CONTACT US," or substantially similar language. The notice required by this subdivision shall specify the date that the property will escheat and the effects of escheat, including the necessity for filing a claim for the return of the property. The notice required by this section shall, in boldface type or in a font a minimum of two points larger than the rest of the notice, exclusive of the heading, do all of the following:

(**1**) Identify the safe deposit box or other safekeeping repository by number or identifier.

(**2**) State that the lease or rental period on the box or repository has expired or the agreement has terminated.

(**3**) Indicate that the contents of, or the proceeds of sale of the contents of, the safe deposit box or other safekeeping repository will escheat to the state unless the owner requests the contents or their proceeds.

(4) Specify that the Unclaimed Property Law requires business associations to transfer the contents of, or the proceeds of sale of the contents of, a safe deposit box or other safekeeping repository to the Controller if they remain unclaimed for more than three years.

(5) Advise the owner to make arrangements with the business association to either obtain possession of the contents of, or the proceeds of sale of the contents of, the safe deposit box or other safekeeping repository, or enter into a new agreement with the business association to establish a leasing or rental arrangement. If an owner fails to establish such an arrangement prior to the end of the period described in subdivision (a), the contents or proceeds shall escheat to this state.

(d) In addition to the notice required pursuant to subdivision (b), the business association may give additional notice in accordance with subdivision (c) at any time between the date on which the lease or rental period for the safe deposit box or repository expired, or from the date of the termination of any agreement, through which the box or other repository was furnished to the owner without cost, whichever is earlier, and the date the business association transfers the contents of, or the proceeds of sale of the contents of, the safe deposit box or other safekeeping repository to the Controller.

(e) The contents of, or the proceeds of sale of the contents of, a safe deposit box or other safekeeping repository shall not escheat to the state if, as of June 30 or the fiscal yearend next preceding the date on which a report is required to be filed under Section 1530, the owner has owned, with a banking organization providing the safe deposit box or other safekeeping repository, any demand, savings, or matured time deposit, or account subject to a negotiable order of withdrawal, which has not escheated under Section 1513 and is not reportable under subdivision (d) of Section 1530.

(f) The contents of, or the proceeds of sale of the contents of, a safe deposit box or other safekeeping repository shall not escheat to the state if, as of June 30 or the fiscal yearend next preceding the date on which a report is required to be filed under Section 1530, the owner has owned, with a financial organization providing the safe deposit box or other safekeeping repository, any demand, savings, or matured time deposit, or matured investment certificate, or account subject to a negotiable order of withdrawal, or other interest in a financial organization or any deposit made therewith, and any interest or dividends thereon, which has not escheated under Section 1513 and is not reportable under subdivision (d) of Section 1530.

(g) The contents of, or the proceeds of sale of the contents of, a safe deposit box or other safekeeping repository shall not escheat to the state if, as of June 30 or the fiscal yearend next preceding the date on which a report is required to be filed under Section 1530, the owner has owned, with a banking or financial organization providing the safe deposit box or other safekeeping repository, any funds in an individual retirement account or under a retirement plan for self-employed individuals or similar account or plan pursuant to the internal revenue laws of the United States or the income tax laws of this state, which has not escheated under Section 1513 and is not reportable under subdivision (d) of Section 1530.

(h) In the event the owner is in default under the safe deposit box or other safekeeping repository agreement and the owner has owned any demand, savings, or matured time deposit, account, or plan described in subdivision (e), (f), or (g), the banking or financial organization may pay or deliver the contents of, or the proceeds of sale of the contents of, the safe deposit box or other safekeeping repository to the owner after deducting any amount due and payable from those proceeds under that agreement. Upon making that payment or delivery under this subdivision, the banking or financial organization shall be relieved of all liability to the extent of the value of those contents or proceeds.

(i) For new accounts opened for a safe deposit box or other safekeeping repository with a business association on and after January 1, 2011, the business association shall provide a written notice to the person leasing the safe deposit box or safekeeping repository informing the person that his or her property, or the proceeds of sale of the property, may be transferred to the appropriate state upon running of the time period specified by state law from the date the lease or rental period on the safe deposit box or repository expired, or from the date of termination of any agreement because of which the box or other repository was furnished to the owner without cost, whichever is earlier.

(j) A business association may directly escheat the contents of a safe deposit box or other safekeeping repository without exercising its rights under Article 2 (commencing with Section 1630) of Chapter 17 of Division 1 of the Financial Code.

Ca. Civ. Proc. Code § 1514

Amended by Stats 2012 ch 162 (SB 1171),s 16, eff. 1/1/2013.
Amended by Stats 2011 ch 305 (SB 495),s 3, eff. 1/1/2012.
Amended by Stats 2009 ch 522 (AB 1291),s 3, eff. 1/1/2010.

Section 1515 - Funds held or owing by life insurance corporation under life or endowment insurance policy or annuity contract

(a) Subject to Section 1510, funds held or owing by a life insurance corporation under any life or endowment insurance policy or annuity contract which has matured or terminated escheat to this state if unclaimed and unpaid for more than three years after the funds became due and payable as established from the records of the corporation.

(b) If a person other than the insured or annuitant is entitled to the funds and no address of that person is known to the corporation or if it is not definite and certain from the records of the corporation what person is entitled to the funds, it is presumed that the last known address of the person entitled to the funds is the same as the last known address of the insured or annuitant according to the records of the corporation. This presumption is a presumption affecting the burden of proof.

(c) A life insurance policy not matured by actual proof of the death of the insured according to the records of the corporation is deemed to be matured and the proceeds due and payable if:

(1) The insured has attained, or would have attained if he or she were living, the limiting age under the mortality table on which the reserve is based.

(2) The policy was in force at the time the insured attained, or would have attained, the limiting age specified in paragraph (1).

(3) Neither the insured nor any other person appearing to have an interest in the policy has, within the preceding three years, according to the records of the corporation (i) assigned, readjusted, or paid premiums on the policy, (ii) subjected the policy to loan, or (iii) corresponded in writing with the life insurance corporation concerning the policy.

(d) Any funds otherwise payable according to the records of the corporation are deemed due and payable although the policy or contract has not been surrendered as required.

Ca. Civ. Proc. Code § 1515

Amended by Stats. 1993, Ch. 692, Sec. 3. Effective January 1, 1994.

Section 1515.5 - Property distributable in course of demutualization or reorganization of insurance company deemed abandoned

Property distributable in the course of a demutualization or related reorganization of an insurance company is deemed abandoned as follows:

(a) On the date of the demutualization or reorganization, if the instruments or statements reflecting the distribution are not mailed to the owner because the address on the books and records for the holder is known to be incorrect.

(b) Two years after the date of the demutualization or reorganization, if instruments or statements reflecting the distribution are mailed to the owner and returned by the post office as undeliverable and the owner has done neither of the following:

(1) Communicated in writing with the holder or its agent regarding the property.

(2) Otherwise communicated with the holder or its agent regarding the property as evidenced by a memorandum or other record on file with the holder or its agent.

(c) Three years after the date of the demutualization or reorganization, if instruments or statements reflecting the distribution are mailed to the owner and not returned by the post office as undeliverable and the owner has done neither of the following:

(1) Communicated in writing with the holder or its agent regarding the property.

(2) Otherwise communicated with the holder or its agent regarding the property as evidenced by a memorandum or other record on file with the holder or its agent.

Ca. Civ. Proc. Code § 1515.5
Added by Stats 2003 ch 304 (AB 378),s 2, eff. 1/1/2004.

Section 1516 - Dividend, profit, distribution, etc. held or owing by business organization for shareholder, certificate holder, member, etc.

(a) Subject to Section 1510, any dividend, profit, distribution, interest, payment on principal, or other sum held or owing by a business association for or to its shareholder, certificate holder, member, bondholder, or other security holder, or a participating patron of a cooperative, who has not claimed it, or corresponded in writing with the business association concerning it, within three years after the date prescribed for payment or delivery, escheats to this state.

(b) Subject to Section 1510, any intangible interest in a business association, as evidenced by the stock records or membership records of the association, escheats to this state if (1) the interest in the association is owned by a person who for more than three years has neither claimed a dividend or other sum referred to in subdivision (a) nor corresponded in writing with the association or otherwise indicated an interest as evidenced by a memorandum or other record on file with the association, and (2) the association does not know the location of the owner at the end of the three-year period. With respect to the interest, the business association shall be deemed the holder.

(c) Subject to Section 1510, any dividends or other distributions held for or owing to a person at the time the stock or other security to which they attach escheats to this state also escheat to this state as of the same time.

(d) If the business association has in its records an address for the apparent owner, which the business association's records do not disclose to be inaccurate, with respect to any interest that may escheat pursuant to subdivision (b), the business association shall make reasonable efforts to notify the owner by mail or, if the owner has consented to electronic notice, electronically, that the owner's interest in the business association will escheat to the state. The notice shall be given not less than 6 nor more than 12 months before the time the interest in the business association becomes reportable to the Controller in accordance with this chapter. The face of the notice shall contain a heading at the top that reads as follows: "THE STATE OF CALIFORNIA REQUIRES US TO NOTIFY YOU THAT YOUR UNCLAIMED PROPERTY MAY BE TRANSFERRED TO THE STATE IF YOU DO NOT CONTACT US," or substantially similar language. The notice required by this subdivision shall specify the time that the interest will escheat and the effects of escheat, including the necessity for filing a claim for the return of the interest. The notice required by this section shall, in boldface type or in a font a minimum of two points larger than the rest of the notice, exclusive of the heading, (1) specify that since the date of last activity, or for the last two years, there has been no owner activity on the deposit, account, shares, or other interest; (2) identify the deposit, account, shares, or other interest by number or identifier, which need not exceed four digits; (3) indicate that the deposit, account, shares, or other interest is in danger of escheating to the state; and (4) specify that the Unclaimed Property Law requires business associations to transfer funds of a deposit, account, shares, or other interest if it has been inactive for three years. It shall also include a form, as prescribed by the Controller, by which the owner may confirm the owner's current address. If that form is filled out, signed by the owner, and returned to the holder, it shall be deemed that the business association knows the location of the owner. In lieu of returning the form, the business association may provide a telephone number or other electronic means to enable the owner to contact the association. With that contact, as evidenced by a memorandum or other record on file with the business association, the business association shall be deemed to know the location of the owner. The business association may impose a service charge on the deposit, account, shares, or other interest for this notice and form in an amount not to exceed the administrative cost of mailing or electronically sending the notice and form, and in no case to exceed two dollars ($2).

(e) In addition to the notice required pursuant to subdivision (d), the holder may give additional notice as described in subdivision (d) at any time between the date of last activity by, or communication with, the owner and the date the holder transfers the deposit, shares, or other interest to the Controller.

(f) The interest that escheats pursuant to subdivision (b) shall not be reportable pursuant to Section 1530 unless and until the per share value, as set forth in Section 1172.80 of Title 2 of the California Code of Regulations, is equal to or greater than one cent ($0.01) or the aggregate value of the security held exceeds one thousand dollars ($1,000).

Ca. Civ. Proc. Code § 1516

Amended by Stats 2022 ch 420 (AB 2960),s 12, eff. 1/1/2023.
Amended by Stats 2011 ch 305 (SB 495),s 4, eff. 1/1/2012.
Amended by Stats 2009 ch 522 (AB 1291),s 4, eff. 1/1/2010.
Amended by Stats 2002 ch 813 (AB 1772),s 2, eff. 1/1/2004

Section 1517 - Property distributable in course of dissolution of business organization or insurer

(a) All property distributable in the course of a voluntary or involuntary dissolution or liquidation of a business association that is unclaimed by the owner within six months after the date of final distribution or liquidation escheats to this state.

(b) All property distributable in the course of voluntary or involuntary dissolution or liquidation of an insurer or other person brought under Article 14 (commencing with Section 1010) of Chapter 1 of Part 2 of Division 1 of the Insurance Code, that is unclaimed by the owner after six months of the date of final distribution, shall be transferred to the Department of Insurance, with any proceeds of sale of property and other funds to be deposited in the Insurance Fund for expenditure as provided in Section 12937 of the Insurance Code.

(c) This section applies to all tangible personal property located in this state and, subject to Section 1510, to all intangible personal property.

Ca. Civ. Proc. Code § 1517

Amended by Stats. 1996, Ch. 187, Sec. 1. Effective July 19, 1996.

Section 1518 - Personal property held in fiduciary capacity (a)

(1) All tangible personal property located in this state and, subject to Section 1510, all intangible personal property, including intangible personal property maintained in a deposit or account, and the income or increment on such tangible or intangible property, held in a fiduciary capacity for the benefit of another person escheats to this state if for more than three years after it becomes payable or distributable, the owner has not done any of the following:

(A) Increased or decreased the principal.

(B) Accepted payment of principal or income.

(C) Corresponded in writing concerning the property.

(D) Otherwise indicated an interest in the property as evidenced by a memorandum or other record on file with the fiduciary.

(2) Notwithstanding paragraph (1), tangible or intangible property, and the income or increment on the tangible or intangible property, held in a fiduciary capacity for another person shall not escheat to the state if the requirements of subparagraphs (A) and (B) are satisfied.

(A) During the previous three years, the fiduciary took one of the following actions:

(i) Held another deposit or account for the benefit of the owner.

(ii) Maintained a deposit or account on behalf of the owner in an individual retirement account.

(iii) Held funds or other property under a retirement plan for a self-employed individual, or similar account or plan, established pursuant to the internal revenue laws of the United States or the laws of this state.

(B) During the previous three years, the owner has done any of the acts described in subparagraph (A), (B), (C), or (D) of paragraph (1) with respect to the deposit, account, or plan described in subparagraph (A), and the fiduciary has communicated electronically or in writing with the owner at the address to which communications regarding that deposit, account, or plan are regularly sent, with regard to the deposit, account, or plan that would otherwise escheat under this subdivision. "Communications," for purposes of this subparagraph, includes account statements or statements required under the internal revenue laws of the United States.

(b) Funds in an individual retirement account or a retirement plan for self-employed individuals or similar account or plan established pursuant to the internal revenue laws of the United States or of this state are not payable or distributable within the meaning of subdivision (a) unless either of the following is true:

(1) Under the terms of the account or plan, distribution of all or part of the funds would then be mandatory.

(2) For an account or plan not subject to mandatory distribution requirement under the internal revenue laws of the United States or the laws of this state, the owner has attained $70^1/_2$ years of age.

(c) For the purpose of this section, when a person holds property as an agent for a business association, he or she is deemed to hold the property in a fiduciary capacity for the business association alone, unless the agreement between him or her and the business association clearly provides the contrary. For the purposes of this chapter, if a person holds property in a fiduciary capacity for a business association alone, he or she is the holder of the property only insofar as the interest of the business association in the property is concerned and the association is deemed to be the holder of the property insofar as the interest of any other person in the property is concerned.

Ca. Civ. Proc. Code § 1518
Amended by Stats 2011 ch 305 (SB 495),s 5, eff. 1/1/2012.

Section 1518.5 - Funds maintained in a preneed funeral trust or similar account; escheat

(a) Subject to Section 1510, funds maintained in a preneed funeral trust or similar account or plan escheat to the state if, for more than three years after the funds became payable and distributable pursuant to subdivision (b), as established from the records of the funeral establishment or trustee, the beneficiary or trustor has not corresponded electronically or in writing concerning the property or otherwise indicated an interest, as evidenced by a memorandum or other record on file with the funeral establishment or trustee.

(b) For the purposes of this section, the corpus of a preneed funeral trust or similar account or plan, together with any income accrued, less a revocation fee not to exceed the amount reserved pursuant to Section 7735 of the Business and Professions Code, becomes payable and distributable under any of the following circumstances:

(1) The beneficiary of the trust attained, or would have attained if living, 105 years of age.

(2) Forty-five years have passed since execution of the preneed funeral agreement.

(3) The holder received notification of the death or presumed death of the beneficiary and has not provided the contracted funeral merchandise or services.

(4) The preneed funeral trust is a preneed installment trust and the amount due to the funeral establishment from the trustor has not been paid during the three preceding years and neither the trustor nor the beneficiary has communicated with either the funeral establishment or the trustee about the preneed funeral installment trust during that three-year period.

(c) For purposes of this section, except subdivision (d), the funeral establishment obligated to provide preneed funeral services under the trust or similar account or plan is the holder. For purposes of subdivision (d), the trustee is the holder.

(d)

(1) All funds, including accrued income and revocation fees reserved pursuant to Section 7735 of the Business and Professions Code, maintained in a preneed funeral trust or similar account or plan held by a trustee for a funeral establishment that has been dissolved, closed, or had its license revoked shall escheat to the state if unclaimed by the funeral establishment, beneficiary, trustor, or legal representative of either the beneficiary or trustor within six months after the date of final distribution or liquidation.

(2) Notwithstanding paragraph (1), the revocation fee pursuant to Section 7735 of the Business and Professions Code shall not be retained by the funeral establishment.

(e) Escheatment of preneed funeral trust funds to the Controller shall release the funeral establishment from the obligation of furnishing the personal property, funeral merchandise, or services originally arranged in the preneed funeral agreement associated with the trust. However, if the funeral establishment provided personal property, or funeral merchandise or services to the beneficiary after funds have escheated, the funeral establishment shall be entitled to recover the escheated funds upon submission to the Controller of a death certificate and a statement detailing the personal property or funeral merchandise or services provided pursuant to Section 1560.

(f) Nothing in this section, or any other law or regulation, shall require escheatment of any funds received by a funeral establishment, cemetery, or other person from property or funeral merchandise or services provided under Chapter 4 (commencing with Section 8600) of Part 3 of Division 8 of the Health and Safety Code.

(g) A trustee or a funeral establishment shall not charge the trust, a trustor, or a beneficiary any fees or costs associated with a search or verification conducted pursuant to this section. However, a trustee or funeral establishment may incorporate fees or costs associated with a search or verification as part of the administration of the trust pursuant to Section 7735 of the Business and Professions Code.

(h) Delivery of the corpus of the trust, and the income accrued to the trust, to the funeral establishment, the trustor, the beneficiary, or the Controller pursuant to this article shall relieve the trustee of any further liability with regard to those funds.

(i) This section shall become operative on January 1, 2023.

Ca. Civ. Proc. Code § 1518.5

Added by Stats 2021 ch 514 (AB 293),s 5, eff. 1/1/2022.

Section 1519 - Personal property held for owner by government

All tangible personal property located in this state, and, subject to Section 1510, all intangible personal property, held for the owner by any government or governmental subdivision or agency, that has remained unclaimed by the owner for more than three years escheats to this state.

Ca. Civ. Proc. Code § 1519

Amended by Stats. 1990, Ch. 450, Sec. 10. Effective July 31, 1990.

Section 1519.5 - Sums held by business organization ordered refunded by court or administrative agency

Subject to Section 1510, any sums held by a business association that have been ordered to be refunded by a court or an administrative agency including, but not limited to, the Public Utilities Commission, which have remained unclaimed by the owner for more than one year after becoming payable in accordance with the final determination or order providing for the refund, whether or not the final determination or order requires any person entitled to a refund to make a claim for it, escheats to this state.

It is the intent of the Legislature that the provisions of this section shall apply retroactively to all funds held by business associations on or after January 1, 1977, and which remain undistributed by the business association as of the effective date of this act.

Further, it is the intent of the Legislature that nothing in this section shall be construed to change the authority of a court or administrative agency to order equitable remedies.

Ca. Civ. Proc. Code § 1519.5
Added by Stats. 1984, Ch. 1096, Sec. 1.

Section 1520 - Personal property held and owing in ordinary course of holder's business

(a) All tangible personal property located in this state and, subject to Section 1510, all intangible personal property, except property of the classes mentioned in Sections 1511, 1513, 1514, 1515, 1515.5, 1516, 1517, 1518, 1518.5, 1519, and 1521, including any income or increment thereon and deducting any lawful charges, that is held or owing in the ordinary course of the holder's business and has remained unclaimed by the owner for more than three years after it became payable or distributable escheats to this state.

(b) Except as provided in subdivision (a) of Section 1513.5, subdivision (b) of Section 1514, and subdivision (d) of Section 1516, if the holder has in its records an address for the apparent owner of property valued at fifty dollars ($50) or more, which the holder's records do not disclose to be inaccurate, the holder shall make reasonable efforts to notify the owner by mail or, if the owner has consented to electronic notice, electronically, that the owner's property will escheat to the state pursuant to this chapter. The notice shall be mailed not less than 6 nor more than 12 months before the time when the owner's property held by the business becomes reportable to the Controller in accordance with this chapter. The face of the notice shall contain a heading at the top that reads as follows: "THE STATE OF CALIFORNIA REQUIRES US TO NOTIFY YOU THAT YOUR UNCLAIMED PROPERTY MAY BE TRANSFERRED TO THE STATE IF YOU DO NOT CONTACT

US," or substantially similar language. The notice required by this subdivision shall specify the time when the property will escheat and the effects of escheat, including the need to file a claim in order for the owner's property to be returned to the owner. The notice required by this section shall, in boldface type or in a font a minimum of two points larger than the rest of the notice, exclusive of the heading, (1) specify that since the date of last activity, or for the last two years, there has been no owner activity on the deposit, account, shares, or other interest; (2) identify the deposit, account, shares, or other interest by number or identifier, which need not exceed four digits; (3) indicate that the deposit, account, shares, or other interest is in danger of escheating to the state; and (4) specify that the Unclaimed Property Law requires holders to transfer funds of a deposit, account, shares, or other interest if it has been inactive for three years. It shall also include a form, as prescribed by the Controller, by which the owner may confirm the owner's current address. If that form is filled out, signed by the owner, and returned to the holder, it shall be deemed that the account, or other device in which the owner's property is being held, remains currently active and recommences the escheat period. In lieu of returning the form, the holder may provide a telephone number or other electronic means to enable the owner to contact the holder. With that contact, as evidenced by a memorandum or other record on file with the holder, the account or other device in which the owner's property is being held shall be deemed to remain currently active and shall recommence the escheat period. The holder may impose a service charge on the deposit, account, shares, or other interest for this notice in an amount not to exceed the administrative cost of mailing or electronically sending the notice and form, and in no case to exceed two dollars ($2).

(c) In addition to the notice required pursuant to subdivision (b), the holder may give additional notice as described in subdivision (b) at any time between the date of last activity by, or communication with, the owner and the date the holder transfers the property to the Controller.

(d) For purposes of this section, "lawful charges" means charges that are specifically authorized by statute, other than the Unclaimed Property Law, or by a valid, enforceable contract.

(e) This section shall become operative on January 1, 2023.
Ca. Civ. Proc. Code § 1520
Added by Stats 2021 ch 514 (AB 293),s 7, eff. 1/1/2022.

Section 1520.5 - Gift certificates
Section 1520 does not apply to gift certificates subject to Title 1.4A (commencing with Section 1749.45) of Part 4 of Division 3 of the Civil Code. However, Section 1520 applies to any gift certificate that has an expiration date and that is given in exchange for money or any other thing of value.
Ca. Civ. Proc. Code § 1520.5
Amended by Stats 2003 ch 116 (AB 1092),s 3, eff. 1/1/2004.

Section 1521 - Employee benefit plan distributions
(a) Except as provided in subdivision (b), and subject to Section 1510, all employee benefit plan distributions and any income or other increment thereon escheats to the state if the owner has not, within three years after it becomes payable or distributable, accepted the distribution, corresponded in writing concerning the distribution, or otherwise indicated an interest as evidenced by a memorandum or other record on file with the fiduciary of the trust or custodial fund or administrator of the plan under which the trust or fund is established. As used in this section, "fiduciary" means any person exercising any power, authority, or responsibility of management or disposition with respect to any money or other property of a retirement system or plan, and "administrator" means the person specifically so designated by the plan, trust agreement, contract, or other instrument under which the retirement system or plan is operated, or if none is designated, the employer.
(b) Except as provided in subdivision (c), an employee benefit plan distribution and any income or other increment thereon shall not escheat to this state if, at the time the distribution shall become payable to a participant in an employee benefit plan, the plan contains a provision for forfeiture or expressly authorizes the administrator to declare a forfeiture of a distribution to a beneficiary thereof who cannot be found after a period of time

specified in the plan, and the trust or fund established under the plan has not terminated prior to the date on which the distribution would become forfeitable in accordance with the provision.

(c) A participant entitled to an employee benefit plan distribution in the form of residuals shall be relieved from a forfeiture declared under subdivision (b) upon the making of a claim therefor.

Ca. Civ. Proc. Code § 1521

Amended by Stats. 1990, Ch. 450, Sec. 12. Effective July 31, 1990.

Section 1522 - Charge or fee imposed because of inactive or unclaimed status

No service, handling, maintenance or other charge or fee of any kind which is imposed because of the inactive or unclaimed status contemplated by this chapter, may be deducted or withheld from any property subject to escheat under this chapter, unless specifically permitted by this chapter.

Even when specifically permitted by this chapter, such charges or fees may not be excluded, withheld or deducted from property subject to this chapter if, under its policy or procedure, the holder would not have excluded, withheld or deducted such charges or fees in the event the property had been claimed by the owner prior to being reported or remitted to the Controller.

Ca. Civ. Proc. Code § 1522

Amended by Stats. 1981, Ch. 831, Sec. 3.

Section 1523 - Policyholder entitled to Proposition 103 rebate not located

If an insurer, after a good faith effort to locate and deliver to a policyholder a Proposition 103 rebate ordered or negotiated pursuant to Section 1861.01 of the Insurance Code, determines that a policyholder cannot be located, all funds attributable to that rebate escheat to the state and shall be delivered to the Controller. The funds subject to escheat on or after July 1, 1997, shall be transferred by the Controller to the Department of Insurance for deposit in the Insurance Fund in the following amounts and for the following purposes:

(a) Up to the amount that will repay principal and interest on the General Fund loan authorized by Item 0845-001-0001 of the Budget Act of 1996 for expenditure as provided in Section 12936 of the Insurance Code.

(b) The sum of four million dollars ($4,000,000) for expenditure during the 1998-1999 fiscal year as provided in Section 12967 of the Insurance Code.

Ca. Civ. Proc. Code § 1523

Amended by Stats. 1998, Ch. 963, Sec. 1. Effective September 29, 1998.

Section 1528 - Unclaimed funds held by domestic fraternal benefit society

This chapter does not apply to unclaimed funds held by a life insurance corporation which is organized or admitted as a domestic fraternal benefit society under Chapter 10 (commencing with Section 10970) of Part 2 of Division 2 of the Insurance Code, so long as such funds are used for scholarship funds, exclusive of costs of administration thereof.

Ca. Civ. Proc. Code § 1528

Added by Stats. 1974, Ch. 1050.

Article 3 - IDENTIFICATION OF ESCHEATED PROPERTY

Section 1530 - Report required by persons holding funds or other property escheated to state

(a) Every person holding funds or other property escheated to this state under this chapter shall report to the Controller as provided in this section.

(b) The report shall be on a form prescribed or approved by the Controller and shall include:

(1) Except with respect to traveler's checks and money orders, the name, if known, and last known address, if any, of each person appearing from the records of the holder to be the owner of any property of value of at least fifty dollars ($50) escheated under this chapter. This paragraph shall become inoperative on July 1, 2014.

(2) Except with respect to traveler's checks and money orders, the name, if known, and last known address, if any, of each person appearing from the records of the holder to be the owner of any property of value of at least twenty-five dollars ($25) escheated under this chapter. This paragraph shall become operative on July 1, 2014.

(3) In the case of escheated funds of life insurance corporations, the full name of the insured or annuitant, and his or her last known address, according to the life insurance corporation's records.

(4) In the case of the contents of a safe deposit box or other safekeeping repository or in the case of other tangible property, a description of the property and the place where it is held and may be inspected by the Controller. The report shall set forth any amounts owing to the holder for unpaid rent or storage charges and for the cost of opening the safe deposit box or other safekeeping repository, if any, in which the property was contained.

(5) The nature and identifying number, if any, or description of any intangible property and the amount appearing from the records to be due, except that items of value under twenty-five dollars ($25) each may be reported in aggregate.

(6) Except for any property reported in the aggregate, the date when the property became payable, demandable, or returnable, and the date of the last transaction with the owner with respect to the property.

(7) Other information which the Controller prescribes by rule as necessary for the administration of this chapter.
(c) If the holder is a successor to other persons who previously held the property for the owner, or if the holder has changed his or her name while holding the property, he or she shall file with his or her report all prior known names and addresses of each holder of the property.

(d) The report shall be filed before November 1 of each year as of June 30 or fiscal yearend next preceding, but the report of life insurance corporations, and the report of all insurance corporation demutualization proceeds subject to Section 1515.5, shall be filed before May 1 of each year as of December 31 next preceding. The initial report for property subject to Section 1515.5 shall be filed on or before May 1, 2004, with respect to conditions in effect on December 31, 2003, and all property shall be determined to be reportable under Section 1515.5 as if that section were in effect on the date of the insurance company demutualization or related reorganization. The Controller may postpone the reporting date upon his or her own motion or upon written request by any person required to file a report.

(e) The report, if made by an individual, shall be verified by the individual; if made by a partnership, by a partner; if made by an unincorporated association or private corporation, by an officer; and if made by a public corporation, by its chief fiscal officer or other employee authorized by the holder.

Ca. Civ. Proc. Code § 1530

Amended by Stats 2014 ch 71 (SB 1304),s 21, eff. 1/1/2015.
Amended by Stats 2013 ch 362 (AB 212),s 2, eff. 1/1/2014.
Amended by Stats 2003 ch 304 (AB 378),s 4, eff. 1/1/2004.

Section 1531 - Notice within one year after payment or delivery of escheated property

(a) Within one year after payment or delivery of escheated property as required by Section 1532, the Controller shall cause a notice to be published in a manner that the Controller determines to be reasonable, which may include, but not be limited to, newspapers, Internet Web sites, radio, television, or other media. In carrying out this duty, the Controller shall not use any of the following:

(1) Money appropriated for the Controller's audit programs.

(2) More money than the Legislature appropriates for this subdivision's purpose.

(3) A photograph in a notice.

(4) An elected official's name in a notice.

(b) Within 165 days after the final date for filing the report required by Section 1530, the Controller shall mail a notice to each person having an address listed in the report who appears to be entitled to property of the value of fifty dollars ($50) or more escheated under this chapter. If the report filed pursuant to Section 1530 includes a social security number, the Controller shall request the Franchise Tax Board to provide a current address for the apparent owner on the basis of that number. The Controller shall mail the notice to the apparent owner for whom a current address is obtained if the address is different from the address previously reported to the Controller. If the Franchise Tax Board does not provide an address or a different address, then the Controller shall mail the notice to the address listed in the report required by Section 1530.

(c) The mailed notice shall contain all of the following:

(1) A statement that, according to a report filed with the Controller, property is being held to which the addressee appears entitled.

(2) The name and address of the person holding the property and any necessary information regarding changes of name and address of the holder.

(3) A statement that, if satisfactory proof of claim is not presented by the owner to the holder by the date specified in the notice, the property will be placed in the custody of the Controller and may be sold or destroyed pursuant to this chapter, and all further claims concerning the property or, if sold, the net proceeds of its sale, must be directed to the Controller.

(d) This section is intended to inform owners about the possible existence of unclaimed property identified pursuant to this chapter.

Ca. Civ. Proc. Code § 1531

Amended by Stats 2017 ch 200 (AB 772),s 1, eff. 1/1/2018.

Amended by Stats 2007 ch 179 (SB 86),s 2, eff. 8/24/2007.

Section 1531.5 - Notification program designed to inform owners about possible existence of unclaimed property

(a) The Controller shall establish and conduct a notification program designed to inform owners about the possible existence of unclaimed property received pursuant to this chapter.

(b) Any notice sent pursuant to this section shall not contain a photograph or likeness of an elected official.

(c)

(1) Notwithstanding any other law, upon the request of the Controller, a state or local governmental agency may furnish to the Controller from its records the address or other identification or location information that could reasonably be used to locate an owner of unclaimed property.

(2) If the address or other identification or location information requested by the Controller is deemed confidential under any laws or regulations of this state, it shall nevertheless be furnished to the Controller. However, neither the Controller nor any officer, agent, or employee of the Controller shall use or disclose that information except as may be necessary in attempting to locate the owner of unclaimed property.

(3) This subdivision shall not be construed to require disclosure of information in violation of federal law.

(4) If a fee or charge is customarily made for the information requested by the Controller, the Controller shall pay that customary fee or charge.

(d) Costs for administering this section shall be subject to the level of appropriation in the annual Budget Act.

Ca. Civ. Proc. Code § 1531.5

Added by Stats 2007 ch 179 (SB 86),s 3, eff. 8/24/2007.

Section 1531.6 - Notice to owners of savings bonds, war bond or military award

(a) In addition to the notices required pursuant to this chapter, the

Controller may mail a separate notice to an apparent owner of a United States savings bond, war bond, or military award whose name is shown on or can be associated with the contents of a safe deposit box or other safekeeping repository and is different from the reported owner of the safe deposit box or other safekeeping repository.

(b) A notice sent pursuant to this section shall not contain a photograph or likeness of an elected official.

(c)

(1) Notwithstanding any other law, upon request of the Controller, a state or local governmental agency may furnish to the Controller from its records the address or other identification or location information that could reasonably be used to locate an owner of unclaimed property.

(2) If the address or other identification or location information requested by the Controller is deemed confidential under any law or regulation of the state, it shall nevertheless be furnished to the Controller. However, neither the Controller nor any officer, agent, or employee of the Controller shall use or disclose that information, except as may be necessary in attempting to locate the owner of unclaimed property.

(3) This subdivision shall not be construed to require disclosure of information in violation of federal law.

(4) If a fee or charge is customarily made for the information requested by the Controller, the Controller shall pay the customary fee or charge.

(d) Costs for administering this section shall be subject to the level of appropriation in the annual Budget Act.

Ca. Civ. Proc. Code § 1531.6

Added by Stats 2015 ch 297 (AB 355),s 1, eff. 1/1/2016.

Section 1532 - Payment or delivery of escheated property by persons filing report

(a) Every person filing a report as provided by Section 1530 shall, no sooner than seven months and no later than seven months and 15 days after the final date for filing the report, pay or deliver to the Controller all escheated property specified in the report. Any payment of unclaimed cash in an amount of at least two thousand dollars ($2,000) shall be made by electronic funds transfer pursuant to regulations adopted by the Controller. The Controller may postpone the date for payment or delivery of the property, and the date for any report required by subdivision (b), upon the Controller's own motion or upon written request by any person required to pay or deliver the property or file a report as required by this section.

(b) If a person establishes their right to receive any property specified in the report to the satisfaction of the holder before that property has been delivered to the Controller, or it appears that, for any other reason, the property may not be subject to escheat under this chapter, the holder shall not pay or deliver the property to the Controller but shall instead file a report with the Controller, on a form and in a format prescribed or approved by the Controller, containing information pertaining to the property subject to escheat.

(c) Any property not paid or delivered pursuant to subdivision (b) that is later determined by the holder to be subject to escheat under this chapter shall not be subject to the interest provision of Section 1577.

(d) The holder of any interest under subdivision (b) of Section 1516 shall deliver a duplicate certificate to the Controller or shall register the securities in uncertificated form in the name of the Controller. Upon delivering a duplicate certificate or providing evidence of registration of the securities in uncertificated form to the Controller, the holder, any transfer agent, registrar, or other person acting for or on behalf of the holder in executing or delivering the duplicate certificate or registering the uncertificated securities, shall be relieved from all liability of every kind to any person including, but not limited to, any person acquiring the original certificate or the duplicate of the certificate issued to the Controller for any losses or damages resulting to that person by the issuance and delivery to the Controller of the duplicate certificate or the registration of the uncertificated securities to the Controller.

(e) Payment of any intangible property to the Controller shall be made at the office of the Controller in Sacramento or at another location as the Controller by regulation may designate. Except as otherwise agreed by the Controller and the holder, tangible personal property shall be delivered to the Controller at the place where it is held.

(f) Payment is deemed complete on the date the electronic funds transfer is initiated if the settlement to the state's demand account occurs on or before the banking day following the date the transfer is initiated. If the settlement to the state's demand account does not occur on or before the banking day following the date the transfer is initiated, payment is deemed to occur on the date settlement occurs.

(g) Any person required to pay cash by electronic funds transfer who makes the payment by means other than an authorized electronic funds transfer shall be liable for a civil penalty of 2 percent of the amount of the payment that is due pursuant to this section, in addition to any other penalty provided by law. Penalties are due at the time of payment. If the Controller finds that a holder's failure to make payment by an appropriate electronic funds transfer in accordance with the Controller's procedures is due to reasonable cause and circumstances beyond the holder's control, and occurred notwithstanding the exercise of ordinary care and in the absence of willful neglect, that holder shall be relieved of the penalties.

(h) An electronic funds transfer shall be accomplished by an automated clearinghouse debit, an automated clearinghouse credit, a Federal Reserve Wire Transfer (Fedwire), or by an international funds transfer. Banking costs incurred for the automated clearinghouse debit transaction by the holder shall be paid by the state. Banking costs incurred by the state for the automated clearinghouse credit transaction may be paid by the holder originating the credit. Banking costs incurred for the Fedwire transaction charged to the holder and the state shall be paid by the person originating the transaction. Banking costs charged to the holder and to the state for an international funds transfer may be charged to the holder.

(i) For purposes of this section:

(1) "Electronic funds transfer" means any transfer of funds, other than a transaction originated by check, draft, or similar paper instrument, that is initiated through an electronic terminal, telephonic instrument, modem, computer, or magnetic tape, so as to order, instruct, or authorize a financial institution to credit or debit an account.

(2) "Automated clearinghouse" means any federal reserve bank, or an organization established by agreement with the National Automated Clearing House Association or any similar organization, that operates as a clearinghouse for transmitting or receiving entries between banks or bank accounts and that authorizes an electronic transfer of funds between those banks or bank accounts.

(3) "Automated clearinghouse debit" means a transaction in which the state, through its designated depository bank, originates an automated clearinghouse transaction debiting the holder's bank account and crediting the state's bank account for the amount of payment.

(4) "Automated clearinghouse credit" means an automated clearinghouse transaction in which the holder, through its own bank, originates an entry crediting the state's bank account and debiting the holder's bank account.

(5) "Fedwire" means any transaction originated by the holder and utilizing the national electronic payment system to transfer funds through federal reserve banks, pursuant to which the holder debits its own bank account and credits the state's bank account.

(6) "International funds transfer" means any transaction originated by the holder and utilizing the international electronic payment system to transfer funds, pursuant to which the holder debits its own bank account, and credits the funds to a United

States bank that credits the Unclaimed Property Fund.

Ca. Civ. Proc. Code § 1532

Amended by Stats 2021 ch 103 (SB 308),s 1, eff. 1/1/2022.

Amended by Stats 2011 ch 305 (SB 495),s 7, eff. 1/1/2012.

Amended by Stats 2009 ch 522 (AB 1291),s 6, eff. 1/1/2010.

Amended by Stats 2007 ch 179 (SB 86),s 4, eff. 8/24/2007.

Amended by Stats 2004 ch 520 (AB 2530),s 2, eff. 1/1/2005

Section 1532.1 - Payment or delivery of property escheating to state pursuant to section 1514

Notwithstanding Sections 1531 and 1532, property that escheats to the state pursuant to Section 1514 shall not be paid or delivered to the state until the earlier of (a) the time when the holder is requested to do so by the Controller or (b) within one year after the final date for filing the report required by Section 1530 as specified in subdivision (d) of Section 1530. Within one year after receipt of property as provided by this section, the Controller shall cause a notice to be published as provided in Section 1531.

Ca. Civ. Proc. Code § 1532.1

Amended by Stats. 1996, Ch. 762, Sec. 8. Effective January 1, 1997.

Section 1533 - Not in interest of state to take custody of tangible personal property

Tangible personal property may be excluded from the notices required by Section 1531, shall not be delivered to the State Controller, and shall not escheat to the state, if the State Controller, in his discretion, determines that it is not in the interest of the state to take custody of the property and notifies the holder in writing, within 120 days from receipt of the report required by Section 1530, of his determination not to take custody of the property.

Ca. Civ. Proc. Code § 1533

Added by Stats. 1968, Ch. 356.

Article 4 - PAYMENT OF CLAIMS

Section 1540 - Generally

(a) Any person, excluding another state, who claims to have been the owner, as defined in subdivision (d), of property paid or delivered to the Controller under this chapter may file a claim to the property or to the net proceeds from its sale. The claim shall be on a form prescribed by the Controller and shall be verified by the claimant.

(b) The Controller shall consider each claim within 180 days after it is filed to determine if the claimant is the owner, as defined in subdivision (d), and may hold a hearing and receive evidence. The Controller shall give written notice to the claimant if the Controller denies the claim in whole or in part. The notice may be given by mailing it to the address, if any, stated in the claim as the address to which notices are to be sent. If no address is stated in the claim, the notice may be mailed to the address, if any, of the claimant as stated in the claim. A notice of denial need not be given if the claim fails to state either an address to which notices are to be sent or an address of the claimant.

(c) Interest shall not be payable on any claim paid under this chapter.

(d) Notwithstanding subdivision (g) of Section 1501, for purposes of filing a claim pursuant to this section, "owner" means the person who had legal right to the property before its escheat, the person's heirs or estate representative, the person's guardian or conservator, or a public administrator acting pursuant to the authority granted in Sections 7660 and 7661 of the Probate Code. An "owner" also means a nonprofit civic, charitable, or educational organization that granted a charter, sponsorship, or approval for the existence of the organization that had the legal right to the property before its escheat but that has dissolved or is no longer in existence, if the charter, sponsorship, approval, organization bylaws, or other governing documents provide that unclaimed or surplus property shall be conveyed to the granting organization upon dissolution or cessation to exist as a distinct legal entity. Only an owner, as defined in this subdivision, may file a claim with the Controller pursuant to this article.

(e) Following a public hearing, the Controller shall adopt guidelines and forms that shall provide specific instructions to assist owners in filing claims pursuant to this article.

(f) Notwithstanding any other provision, property reported to, and received by, the Controller pursuant to this chapter in the name of a state agency, including the University of California and the California State University, or a local agency, including a school district and community college district, may be transferred by the Controller directly to the state or local agency without the filing of a claim. Property transferred pursuant to this subdivision is immune from suit pursuant to Section 1566 in the same manner as if the state or local agency had filed a claim to the property. For purposes of this subdivision, "local agency" means a city, county, city and county, or district.

Ca. Civ. Proc. Code § 1540

Amended by Stats 2020 ch 36 (AB 3364),s 26, eff. 1/1/2021.
Amended by Stats 2019 ch 320 (AB 1637),s 1, eff. 1/1/2020.
Amended by Stats 2014 ch 330 (AB 1712),s 1, eff. 1/1/2015.
Amended by Stats 2013 ch 128 (AB 1275),s 1, eff. 1/1/2014.
Amended by Stats 2005 ch 706 (AB 1742),s 15, eff. 1/1/2006
Amended by Stats 2002 ch 1124 (AB 3000),s 3, eff. 9/30/2002.

Section 1541 - Action to establish claim

Any person aggrieved by a decision of the Controller or as to whose claim the Controller has failed to make a decision within 180 days after the filing of the claim, may commence an action, naming the Controller as a defendant, to establish his or her claim in the superior court in any county or city and county in which the Attorney General has an office. The action shall be brought within 90 days after the decision of the Controller or within 270 days from the filing of the claim if the Controller fails to make a decision. The summons and a copy of the complaint shall be served upon the Controller and the Attorney General and the Controller shall have 60 days within which to respond by answer. The action shall be tried without a jury.

Ca. Civ. Proc. Code § 1541
Amended by Stats. 2003, Ch. 228, Sec. 9. Effective August 11, 2003.

Section 1542 - Claim of another state
(a) At any time after property has been paid or delivered to the Controller under this chapter, another state is entitled to recover the property if:

(1) The property escheated to this state under subdivision (b) of Section 1510 because no address of the apparent owner of the property appeared on the records of the holder when the property was escheated under this chapter, the last known address of the apparent owner was in fact in that other state, and, under the laws of that state, the property escheated to that state.

(2) The last known address of the apparent owner of the property appearing on the records of the holder is in that other state and, under the laws of that state, the property has escheated to that state.

(3) The property is the sum payable on a travelers check, money order, or other similar instrument that escheated to this state under Section 1511, the travelers check, money order, or other similar instrument was in fact purchased in that other state, and, under the laws of that state, the property escheated to that state.

(4) The property is funds held or owing by a life insurance corporation that escheated to this state by application of the presumption provided by subdivision (b) of Section 1515, the last known address of the person entitled to the funds was in fact in that other state, and, under the laws of that state, the property escheated to that state.
(b) The claim of another state to recover escheated property under this section shall be presented in writing to the Controller, who shall consider the claim within 180 days after it is presented. The Controller may hold a hearing and receive evidence. The Controller shall allow the claim upon determination that the other state is

entitled to the escheated property.

(c) Paragraphs (1) and (2) of subdivision (a) do not apply to property described in paragraph (3) or (4) of that subdivision.

Ca. Civ. Proc. Code § 1542

Amended by Stats. 2003, Ch. 228, Sec. 10. Effective August 11, 2003.

Section 1543 - Unclaimed property; secure payment of claims

Notwithstanding Section 1540, the Controller may do any of the following to streamline the secure payment of claims:

(a) Minimize the number of documents a claimant is required to submit for property valued at less than five thousand dollars ($5,000).

(b) Allow electronic submission of documentation to the Controller's internet website for any claim deemed appropriate by the Controller.

(c) Authorize direct deposit by electronic fund transfer for the payment of an approved claim.

Ca. Civ. Proc. Code § 1543

Added by Stats 2022 ch 270 (AB 1208),s 1, eff. 1/1/2023.

Article 5 - ADMINISTRATION OF UNCLAIMED PROPERTY

Section 1560 - Generally

(a) Upon the payment or delivery of escheated property to the Controller, the state shall assume custody and shall be responsible for the safekeeping of the property. Any person who pays or delivers escheated property to the Controller under this chapter and who, prior to escheat, if the person's records contain an address for the apparent owner that the holder's records do not disclose to be inaccurate, has made reasonable efforts to notify the owner by mail or, if the owner has consented to electronic notice, electronically, in substantial compliance with Sections 1513.5, 1514, 1516, and 1520, that the owner's property, deposit, account, shares, or other interest will escheat to the state, is relieved of all liability to the extent of the value of the property so paid or delivered for any claim that then exists or that thereafter may arise or be made in respect to the property. Property removed from a safe-deposit box or other safekeeping repository shall be received by the Controller subject to any valid lien of the holder for rent and other charges, the rent and other charges to be paid out of the proceeds remaining after the Controller has deducted therefrom their selling cost.

(b) Any holder who has paid moneys to the Controller pursuant to this chapter may make payment to any person appearing to that holder to be entitled thereto, and upon filing proof of the payment and proof that the payee was entitled thereto, the Controller shall forthwith reimburse the holder for the payment without deduction of any fee or other charges. Where reimbursement is sought for a payment made on a negotiable instrument, including a traveler's check or money order, the holder shall be reimbursed under this subdivision upon filing proof that the instrument was duly presented to them and that payment was made thereon to a person who appeared to the holder to be entitled to payment.

(c) The holder shall be reimbursed under this section even if they made the payment to a person whose claim against them was barred because of the expiration of any period of time as those described in Section 1570.

(d) Any holder who has delivered personal property, including a certificate of any interest in a business association, to the Controller pursuant to this chapter may reclaim the personal property if still in the possession of the Controller without payment of any fee or other charges upon filing proof that the owner thereof has claimed such personal property from the holder. The Controller may, in their discretion, accept an affidavit of the holder stating the facts that entitle the holder to reimbursement under this subdivision as sufficient proof for the purposes of this subdivision.

(e) Any holder who has delivered funds maintained under a preneed funeral trust or similar account or plan to the Controller pursuant to this chapter and has fulfilled the services of the preneed funeral trust escheated to the Controller shall be reimbursed under this section upon submission of a death certificate for the beneficiary and a statement detailing the personal property or funeral merchandise or services provided.

(f) This section shall become operative on January 1, 2023.

Ca. Civ. Proc. Code § 1560

Added by Stats 2021 ch 514 (AB 293),s 9, eff. 1/1/2022.

Section 1561 - Claim of property paid or delivered to Controller by holder; payment or delivery of property because of mistake of law or fact

(a) If the holder pays or delivers escheated property to the State Controller in accordance with this chapter and thereafter any person claims the property from the holder or another state claims the property from the holder under that state's laws relating to escheat, the State Controller shall, upon written notice of such claim, defend the holder against the claim and indemnify him against any liability on the claim.

(b) If any holder, because of mistake of law or fact, pays or delivers any property to the State Controller that has not escheated under this chapter and thereafter claims the property from the State Controller, the State Controller shall, if he has not disposed of the property in accordance with this chapter, refund or redeliver the property to the holder without deduction for any fee or other charge.

(c) As used in this section, "escheated property" means property which this chapter provides escheats to this state, whether or not it is determined that another state had a superior right to escheat such property at the time it was paid or delivered to the State Controller or at some time thereafter.

Ca. Civ. Proc. Code § 1561

Added by Stats. 1968, Ch. 356.

Section 1562 - Dividends, interest or other increments realized or accruing prior to liquidation or conversion into money

When property other than money is delivered to the State Controller under this chapter, any dividends, interest or other increments realized or accruing on such property at or prior to liquidation or conversion thereof into money, shall upon receipt be credited to the owner's account by the State Conroller. Except for amounts so credited the owner is not entitled to receive income or other increments on money or other property paid or delivered to the State Controller under this chapter. All interest received and other income derived from the investment of moneys deposited in the Unclaimed Property Fund under the provisions of this chapter shall, on order of the State Controller, be transferred to the General Fund.

Ca. Civ. Proc. Code § 1562

Added by renumbering Section 1514 by Stats. 1968, Ch. 356.

Section 1563 - Sale of escheated property

(a) Except as provided in subdivisions (b) and (c), all escheated property delivered to the Controller under this chapter shall be sold by the Controller to the highest bidder at public sale in whatever city in the state affords in the Controller's judgment the most favorable market for the property involved, or the Controller may conduct the sale by electronic media, including, but not limited to, the internet, if in the Controller's judgment it is cost effective to conduct the sale of the property involved in that manner. However, no sale shall be made pursuant to this subdivision until 18 months after the final date for filing the report required by Section 1530. The Controller may decline the highest bid and reoffer the property for sale if the Controller considers the price bid insufficient. The Controller need not offer any property for sale if, in the Controller's opinion, the probable cost of sale exceeds the value of the property. Any sale of escheated property held under this section shall be preceded by a single publication of notice thereof, at least one week in advance of sale, in an English language newspaper of general circulation in the county where the property is to be sold.

(b) Securities listed on an established stock exchange shall be sold at the prevailing prices on that exchange. Other securities may be sold over the counter at prevailing prices or by any other method that the Controller may determine to be advisable. These securities shall be sold by the Controller no sooner than 18 months, but no later than 20 months, after the actual date of filing of the report required by Section 1530. If securities delivered to the Controller by a holder of the securities remain in the custody of the Controller, a person making a valid claim for those securities under this chapter shall be entitled to receive the securities from the Controller. If the securities have been sold, the person shall be entitled to receive the net proceeds received by the Controller from the sale of the securities. United States government savings bonds and United States war bonds shall be presented to the United States for payment. Subdivision (a) does not apply to the property described in this subdivision.

(c)

(1)All escheated property consisting of military awards, decorations, equipment, artifacts, memorabilia, documents, photographs, films, literature, and any other item relating to the military history of California and Californians that is delivered to the Controller is exempt from subdivision (a) and may, at the discretion of the Controller, be held in trust for the Controller at the California State Military Museum and Resource Center, or successor entity. All escheated property held in trust pursuant to this subdivision is subject to the applicable regulations of the United States Army governing Army museum activities as described in Section 179 of the Military and Veterans Code. A person claiming an interest in the escheated property may file a claim to the property pursuant to Article 4 (commencing with Section 1540).

(2)The California State Military Museum and Resource Center, or successor entity, shall be responsible for the costs of storage and maintenance of escheated property delivered by the Controller under this subdivision.

(d) The purchaser at any sale conducted by the Controller pursuant to this chapter shall receive title to the property purchased, free from all claims of the owner or prior holder thereof and of all persons claiming through or under them. The Controller shall execute all documents necessary to complete the transfer of title.

Ca. Civ. Proc. Code § 1563

Amended by Stats 2022 ch 420 (AB 2960),s 13, eff. 1/1/2023.
Amended by Stats 2016 ch 31 (SB 836),s 17, eff. 6/27/2016.

Amended by Stats 2015 ch 297 (AB 355),s 2, eff. 1/1/2016.
Amended by Stats 2007 ch 179 (SB 86),s 5, eff. 8/24/2007.
Amended by Stats 2003 ch 265 (AB 542),s 2, eff. 1/1/2004.
Amended by Stats 2000 ch 16 (AB 938), s 2, eff. 5/5/2000.
Amended by Stats 2000 ch 924 (AB 2935), s 2, eff. 1/1/2001.

Section 1564 - Money received deposited in Abandoned Property Account in Unclaimed Property Fund

(a) All money received under this chapter, including the proceeds from the sale of property under Section 1563, shall be deposited in the Unclaimed Property Fund in an account titled "Abandoned Property."

(b) Notwithstanding Section 13340 of the Government Code, all money in the Abandoned Property Account in the Unclaimed Property Fund is hereby continuously appropriated to the Controller, without regard to fiscal years, for expenditure in accordance with law in carrying out and enforcing the provisions of this chapter, including, but not limited to, the following purposes:

(1) For payment of claims allowed by the Controller under the provisions of this chapter.

(2) For refund, to the person making such deposit, of amounts, including overpayments, deposited in error in such fund.

(3) For payment of the cost of appraisals incurred by the Controller covering property held in the name of an account in such fund.

(4) For payment of the cost incurred by the Controller for the purchase of lost instrument indemnity bonds, or for payment to the person entitled thereto, for any unpaid lawful charges or costs which arose from holding any specific property or any specific funds which were delivered or paid to the Controller, or which arose from complying with this chapter with respect to such property or funds.

(5) For payment of amounts required to be paid by the state as trustee, bailee, or successor in interest to the preceding owner.

(6) For payment of costs incurred by the Controller for the repair, maintenance, and upkeep of property held in the name of an account in such fund.

(7) For payment of costs of official advertising in connection with the sale of property held in the name of an account in such fund.

(8) For transfer to the General Fund as provided in subdivision (c).

(9) For transfer to the Inheritance Tax Fund of the amount of any inheritance taxes determined to be due and payable to the state by any claimant with respect to any property claimed by him or her under the provisions of this chapter.

(c) At the end of each month, or more often if he or she deems it advisable, the Controller shall transfer all money in the Abandoned Property Account in excess of fifty thousand dollars ($50,000) to the General Fund. Before making this transfer, the Controller shall record the name and last known address of each person appearing from the holders' report to be entitled to the escheated property and the name and last known address of each insured person or annuitant, and with respect to each policy or contract listed in the report of a life insurance corporation, its number, and the name of the corporation. The record shall be available for public inspection at all reasonable business hours.

Ca. Civ. Proc. Code § 1564
Amended by Stats. 1993, Ch. 692, Sec. 7. Effective January 1, 1994.

Section 1564.5 - Abandoned IOLTA Property Account
(a) Notwithstanding any law, including, but not limited to, Section 1564, all money received under this chapter from funds held in an Interest on Lawyers' Trust Account (IOLTA) that escheat to the state shall be administered as set forth in this section. The money

shall be deposited into the Abandoned IOLTA Property Account, which is hereby established within the Unclaimed Property Fund. **(b)** Twenty-five percent of the money in the Abandoned IOLTA Property Account shall be deposited into the IOLTA Claims Reserve Subaccount, which is hereby established within the Abandoned IOLTA Property Account. Notwithstanding Section 13340 of the Government Code, funds in the subaccount are continuously appropriated to the Controller for the payment of all refunds and claims pursuant to this chapter related to escheated IOLTA funds. **(c)** The balance of the funds in the Abandoned IOLTA Property Account, excluding funds in the subaccount, shall be transferred on an annual basis to the Public Interest Attorney Loan Repayment Account established pursuant to Section 6032.5 of the Business and Professions Code. Before making this transfer, the Controller shall record the name and last known address of each person appearing from the holders' report to be entitled to the escheated property. The record shall be available for public inspection at all reasonable business hours.

Ca. Civ. Proc. Code § 1564.5
Amended by Stats 2018 ch 390 (AB 2350),s 1, eff. 1/1/2019.
Added by Stats 2015 ch 488 (SB 134),s 2, eff. 1/1/2016.

Section 1565 - Property of no apparent commercial value delivered to Controller

Any property delivered to the Controller pursuant to this chapter that has no apparent commercial value shall be retained by the Controller for a period of not less than seven years from the date the property is delivered to the Controller. If the Controller determines that any property delivered to him or her pursuant to this chapter has no apparent commercial value, he or she may at any time thereafter destroy or otherwise dispose of the property, and in that event no action or proceeding shall be brought or maintained against the state or any officer thereof, or against the holder for, or on account of any action taken by, the Controller pursuant to this chapter with respect to the property.

Ca. Civ. Proc. Code § 1565

Amended by Stats 2011 ch 305 (SB 495),s 8, eff. 1/1/2012.
Amended by Stats 2007 ch 179 (SB 86),s 6, eff. 8/24/2007.

Section 1566 - Immunity upon payment of delivery to claimant; transactions entered into by Controller

(a) When payment or delivery of money or other property has been made to any claimant under the provisions of this chapter, no suit shall thereafter be maintained by any other claimant against the state or any officer or employee thereof for or on account of such property.

(b) Except as provided in Section 1541, no suit shall be maintained by any person against the state or any officer or employee thereof for or on account of any transaction entered into by the State Controller pursuant to this chapter.

Ca. Civ. Proc. Code § 1566
Added by Stats. 1968, Ch. 356.

Section 1567 - Examination of property by Director of Parks and Recreation

The Director of Parks and Recreation may examine any tangible personal property delivered to the Controller under this chapter for purposes of determining whether such property would be useful under the provisions of Section 512 of the Public Resources Code. If the director makes such a determination with respect to the property, the Controller may deliver the property to the director for use in carrying out the purposes of Section 512 of the Public Resources Code. Upon the termination of any such use, the director shall return the property to the Controller.

Ca. Civ. Proc. Code § 1567
Amended by Stats. 1981, Ch. 714, Sec. 73.

Article 6 - COMPLIANCE AND ENFORCEMENT

Section 1570 - Expiration of period of time during which proceeding commenced or enforced to obtain payment

The expiration of any period of time specified by statute or court order, during which an action or proceeding may be commenced or enforced to obtain payment of a claim for money or recovery of property from the holder, does not prevent the money or property from being escheated, nor affect any duty to file a report required by this chapter or to pay or deliver escheated property to the State Controller.

Ca. Civ. Proc. Code § 1570
Added by renumbering Section 1515 by Stats. 1968, Ch. 356.

Section 1571 - Examination person believed to be holder who has failed to report property

(a) The Controller may at reasonable times and upon reasonable notice examine the records of any person if the Controller has reason to believe that the person is a holder who has failed to report property that should have been reported pursuant to this chapter.

(b) When requested by the Controller, the examination shall be conducted by any licensing or regulating agency otherwise empowered by the laws of this state to examine the records of the holder. For the purpose of determining compliance with this chapter, the Commissioner of Financial Protection and Innovation is vested with full authority to examine the records of any banking organization and any savings association doing business within this state but not organized under the laws of or created in this state.

(c) Following a public hearing, the Controller shall adopt guidelines as to the policies and procedures governing the activity of third-party auditors who are hired by the Controller.

(d) Following a public hearing, the Controller shall adopt guidelines, on or before July 1, 1999, establishing forms, policies, and procedures to enable a person to dispute or appeal the results of any record examination conducted pursuant to this section.

Ca. Civ. Proc. Code § 1571
Amended by Stats 2022 ch 452 (SB 1498),s 42, eff. 1/1/2023.
Amended by Stats 2014 ch 913 (AB 2747),s 11, eff. 1/1/2015.

Section 1572 - Actions by Controller

(a) The State Controller may bring an action in a court of appropriate jurisdiction, as specified in this section, for any of the following purposes:

(1) To enforce the duty of any person under this chapter to permit the examination of the records of such person.

(2) For a judicial determination that particular property is subject to escheat by this state pursuant to this chapter.

(3) To enforce the delivery of any property to the State Controller as required under this chapter.
(b) The State Controller may bring an action under this chapter in any court of this state of appropriate jurisdiction in any of the following cases:

(1) Where the holder is any person domiciled in this state, or is a government or governmental subdivision or agency of this state.

(2) Where the holder is any person engaged in or transacting business in this state, although not domiciled in this state.

(3) Where the property is tangible personal property and is held in this state.
(c) In any case where no court of this state can obtain jurisdiction over the holder, the State Controller may bring an action in any federal or state court with jurisdiction over the holder.
Ca. Civ. Proc. Code § 1572
Added by Stats. 1968, Ch. 356.

Section 1573 - Agreement to provide information to another state

The State Controller may enter into an agreement to provide information needed to enable another state to determine unclaimed property it may be entitled to escheat if such other state or an official thereof agrees to provide this state with information needed to enable this state to determine unclaimed property it may be entitled to escheat. The State Controller may, by regulation, require the reporting of information needed to enable him to comply with agreements made pursuant to this section and may, by regulation, prescribe the form, including verification, of the information to be reported and the times for filing the reports.

Ca. Civ. Proc. Code § 1573
Added by Stats. 1968, Ch. 356.

Section 1574 - Action by Attorney General in name of another state to enforce unclaimed property laws

At the request of another state, the Attorney General of this state may bring an action in the name of the other state, in any court of appropriate jurisdiction of this state or federal court within this state, to enforce the unclaimed property laws of the other state against a holder in this state of property subject to escheat by the other state, if:

(a) The courts of the other state cannot obtain jurisdiction over the holder;

(b) The other state has agreed to bring actions in the name of this state at the request of the Attorney General of this state to enforce the provisions of this chapter against any person in the other state believed by the State Controller to hold property subject to escheat under this chapter, where the courts of this state cannot obtain jurisdiction over such person; and

(c) The other state has agreed to pay reasonable costs incurred by the Attorney General in bringing the action.

Ca. Civ. Proc. Code § 1574
Added by Stats. 1968, Ch. 356.

Section 1575 - Request by Attorney General that another state bring action to enforce provisions of chapter

(a) If the State Controller believes that a person in another state holds property subject to escheat under this chapter and the courts of this state cannot obtain jurisdiction over that person, the Attorney General of this state may request an officer of the other state to bring an action in the name of this state to enforce the provisions of this chapter against such person.

(b) This state shall pay all reasonable costs incurred by the other state in any action brought under the authority of this section. The State Controller may agree to pay to any state bringing such an action a reward not to exceed fifteen percent of the value, after deducting reasonable costs, of any property recovered for this state as a direct or indirect result of such action. Any costs or rewards paid pursuant to this section shall be paid from the Abandoned Property Account in the Unclaimed Property Fund and shall not be deducted from the amount that is subject to be claimed by the owner in accordance with this chapter.

    Ca. Civ. Proc. Code § 1575
Added by Stats. 1968, Ch. 356.

Section 1576 - Willfully failing to render report; willfully refusing to pay or deliver escheated property

(a) Any person who willfully fails to render any report or perform other duties, including use of the report format described in Section 1530, required under this chapter shall be punished by a fine of one hundred dollars ($100) for each day such report is withheld or such duty is not performed, but not more than ten thousand dollars ($10,000).

(b) Any person who willfully refuses to pay or deliver escheated property to the Controller as required under this chapter shall be punished by a fine of not less than five thousand dollars ($5,000) nor more than fifty thousand dollars ($50,000).

(c) No person shall be considered to have willfully failed to report, pay, or deliver escheated property, or perform other duties unless he or she has failed to respond within a reasonable time after notification by certified mail by the Controller's office of his or her failure to act.

    Ca. Civ. Proc. Code § 1576
Amended by Stats. 1996, Ch. 762, Sec. 10. Effective January 1, 1997.

Section 1577 - Interest payable for failure to report, pay or deliver unclaimed property; waiver

(a) In addition to any damages, penalties, or fines for which a person may be liable under other provisions of law, any person who fails to report, pay, or deliver unclaimed property within the time prescribed by this chapter, unless that failure is due to reasonable cause, shall pay to the Controller interest at the rate of 12 percent per annum on that property or value thereof from the date the property should have been reported, paid, or delivered.

(b) If a holder reports and pays or delivers unclaimed property within the time prescribed by this chapter, but files a report that is not in substantial compliance with the requirements of Section 1530 or 1532, the interest payable on the unclaimed property that is paid or delivered in the time prescribed by this chapter shall not exceed ten thousand dollars ($10,000).

(c) The Controller may waive the interest payable under this section if the holder's failure to file a report that is in substantial compliance with the requirements of Section 1530 or 1532 is due to reasonable cause.

(d) The Controller shall waive the interest payable under this section if the holder participates in and completes all of the requirements of the California Voluntary Compliance Program under Section 1577.5, subject to the right to reinstate, as specified.

Ca. Civ. Proc. Code § 1577

Amended by Stats 2022 ch 282 (AB 2280),s 2, eff. 1/1/2023.
Amended by Stats 2009 ch 522 (AB 1291),s 8, eff. 1/1/2010.
Amended by Stats 2003 ch 304 (AB 378),s 5, eff. 1/1/2004.

Section 1577.5 - California Voluntary Compliance Program
(a) This section shall be known, and may be cited, as the "California Voluntary Compliance Program."

(b) The Controller may establish a program for the voluntary compliance of holders for the purpose of resolving unclaimed property that is due and owing to the state under this chapter.

(c)A holder that has not reported unclaimed property in accordance with Section 1530 may request to enroll in the program using a form prescribed by the Controller.

(d) The Controller, in their discretion, may enroll eligible holders in the program. A holder is ineligible to participate in the program if any of the following apply:

(1) At the time the holder's request to enroll is received by the Controller, the holder is the subject of an examination of records or has received notification from the Controller of an impending examination under Section 1571.

(2) At the time the holder's request to enroll is received by the Controller, the holder is the subject of a civil or criminal prosecution involving compliance with this chapter.

(3) The Controller has notified the holder of an interest assessment under Section 1577 within the previous five years, and the interest assessment remains unpaid at the time of the holder's request to enroll. A holder subject to an outstanding interest assessment may file or refile a request to enroll in the program after resolving the outstanding interest assessment.

(4) The Controller has waived interest assessed against the holder under this section within the previous five years. Notwithstanding the foregoing, if a holder acquired or merged with another entity within the five-year period, the holder may request to enroll in the program for the purpose of resolving unclaimed property that may be due and owing to the state as a result of the acquisition or merger.

(e) The Controller shall waive interest assessed under Section 1577 for a holder enrolled in the program if the holder does all the following within the prescribed timeframes and satisfies the other requirements of this section:

(1) Enrolls and participates in an unclaimed property educational training program provided by the Controller within three months after the date on which the Controller notified the holder of their enrollment in the program, unless the Controller sets a different date.

(2) Reviews their books and records for unclaimed property for at least the previous 10 years, starting from June 30 or the fiscal yearend preceding the date on which the report required by paragraph (4) is due.

(3) Makes reasonable efforts to notify owners of reportable property by mail or electronically, as applicable, pursuant to Sections 1513.5, 1514, 1516, or 1520, no less than 30 days prior to submitting the report required by paragraph (4).

(4) Reports to the Controller as required by subdivisions (b), (c), and (e) of Section 1530 within six months after the date on which the Controller notified the holder of their enrollment in the program. Upon written request by the enrolled holder, the Controller may postpone the reporting date for a period not to exceed 18 months after the date on which the Controller notified the holder of their enrollment in the program.

(5) Submits to the Controller an updated report and pays or delivers to the Controller all escheated property specified in the report as required by Section 1532, no sooner than seven months and no later than seven months and 15 days after the Controller received the report submitted pursuant to paragraph (4).
(f) The Controller may reinstate interest waived under subdivision (d) of Section 1577 if the holder does not pay or deliver all escheated property specified in the report submitted pursuant to and within the timeframe prescribed by paragraph (5) of subdivision (e).
(g) The Controller may adopt guidelines and forms that provide specific procedures for the administration of the program.
(h) This section shall become operative only upon an appropriation by the Legislature in the annual Budget Act for this purpose.
Ca. Civ. Proc. Code § 1577.5
Added by Stats 2022 ch 282 (AB 2280),s 4, eff. 1/1/2023.

Article 7 - MISCELLANEOUS

Section 1580 - Power of Controller to make rules and regulations
The State Controller is hereby authorized to make necessary rules and regulations to carry out the provisions of this chapter.
Ca. Civ. Proc. Code § 1580
Amended by Stats. 1978, Ch. 1183.

Section 1581 - Records required by business selling travelers checks, money orders or similar instruments in state

(a) Any business association that sells in this state its travelers checks, money orders, or other similar written instruments (other than third-party bank checks) on which such business association is directly liable, or that provides such travelers checks, money orders, or similar written instruments to others for sale in this state, shall maintain a record indicating those travelers checks, money orders, or similar written instruments that are purchased from it in this state.

(b) The record required by this section may be destroyed after it has been retained for such reasonable time as the State Controller shall designate by regulation.

(c) Any business association that willfully fails to comply with this section is liable to the state for a civil penalty of five hundred dollars ($500) for each day of such failure to comply, which penalty may be recovered in an action brought by the State Controller.

Ca. Civ. Proc. Code § 1581
Amended by Stats. 1975, Ch. 25.

Section 1582 - Validity of agreement to locate, deliver or recover property reported

(a)

(1)An agreement to locate, deliver, recover, or assist in the recovery of property reported under Section 1530 is invalid if either of the following apply:

(A)The agreement is entered into between the date a report is filed under subdivision (d) of Section 1530 and the date the property is paid or delivered under Section 1532.

(B)The agreement requires the owner to pay a fee or compensation prior to approval of the claim and payment of the recovered property to the owner by the Controller.

(2) An agreement to locate, deliver, recover, or assist in the recovery of property reported under Section 1530 made after payment or delivery under Section 1532 is valid if it meets all of the following requirements:

(A) The agreement is in writing and includes a disclosure of the nature and value of the property, that the Controller is in possession of the property, and the address where the owner can directly claim the property from the Controller.

(B) The agreement is signed by the owner after receipt of the disclosure described in subparagraph (A).

(C) The fee or compensation agreed upon is not in excess of 10 percent of the recovered property.

(3) This subdivision shall not be construed to prevent an owner from asserting, at any time, that an agreement to locate property is based upon an excessive or unjust consideration.
(b) Notwithstanding any other provision of law, records of the Controller's office pertaining to unclaimed property are not available for public inspection or copying until after publication of notice of the property or, if publication of notice of the property is not required, until one year after delivery of the property to the Controller.

Ca. Civ. Proc. Code § 1582
Amended by Stats 2022 ch 282 (AB 2280),s 5, eff. 1/1/2023.
Amended by Stats. 1990, Ch. 450, Sec. 16. Effective July 31, 1990.

Chapter 8 - PROPERTY IN CUSTODY OF FEDERAL OFFICERS, AGENCIES, AND DEPARTMENTS

Section 1600 - Policy of state to discover property in custody of United States

It is the policy of this State:

(a) To discover property in the custody of officers, departments, and agencies of the United States, which property is unclaimed by owners whose addresses are known or presumed to be in this State;

(b) To provide a procedure for judicial determination of the right of the State to receive custody of such unclaimed property; and

(c) To authorize expenditure of state funds to pay the proportionate cost of the State in discovering such unclaimed property and to hold the United States harmless against claims concerning such property when delivered to the custody of the State in accordance with this chapter.

Ca. Civ. Proc. Code § 1600
Added by Stats. 1959, Ch. 1801.

Section 1601 - Definitions

As used in this chapter:

(a) "Unclaimed property" means any tangible personal property or intangible personal property, including choses in action in amounts certain, and all debts owed or entrusted funds or other property held by any federal agency or any officer or employee thereof, whether occasioned by contract or operation of law or otherwise, except bonuses and gratuities, which has remained unclaimed by the owner for:

(1) Twenty years from the date of maturity or call for payment, if arising from transactions under the public debt; or

(2) Twenty years after the last transaction concerning principal or interest, if deposits in the postal savings system; or

(3) Five years after the property first became payable, demandable, or returnable, if arising from any other transaction.
(b) "Owner" means any person, including his or her legal representative, who has or had a legal or equitable interest in unclaimed property. The owner shall be conclusively presumed to be the person to whom unclaimed property was or is payable or returnable according to the records of the United States Government. If two or more persons are interested in the property, and the extent of their respective interests is unknown, it shall be presumed that their interests in such property are equal.
(c) "Person" includes any individual, partnership, corporation, limited liability company, unincorporated association, or other legal entity.

    Ca. Civ. Proc. Code § 1601
Amended by Stats. 1994, Ch. 1010, Sec. 64. Effective January 1, 1995.

Section 1602 - Agreement for payments of state's share of costs incurred by United States in examining records

The Controller is authorized to enter into agreements establishing the time and manner for payments of this State's proportionate share of the actual and necessary cost incurred by the United States in examining records and reporting information to this State as such share of such cost shall be determined pursuant to federal law. Said agreements may provide for single payments at stated times over a period of years. The State Controller shall make all payments at the time and in the manner provided in said agreements.

    Ca. Civ. Proc. Code § 1602
Added by Stats. 1959, Ch. 1801.

Section 1603 - United States held harmless against claim concerning property delivered to state

The State hereby undertakes to hold the United States harmless against any claim concerning property delivered to the custody of the State in accordance with the provisions of this chapter. In the event an action or proceeding on such claim is brought against the

United States the Attorney General shall intervene therein. The State consents to suit by such claimant in such contingency and any defense in favor of the United States shall be available to and urged by the State.

Ca. Civ. Proc. Code § 1603
Added by Stats. 1959, Ch. 1801.

Section 1604 - Property subject to delivery to state if last known address of owner in state

(a) All unclaimed intangible property, together with all interest and other increments accruing thereto, is subject to delivery to this state if the last known address of the owner is in this state. If the last known address of an owner is in this state, any other owner's address which is unknown shall be presumed to be in this state. If the last known addresses of owners are in this state and in one or more other states, the addresses of other owners whose addresses are unknown shall be presumed to be within this state if the federal agency having custody of the unclaimed property initially acquired possession in this state. If the records of the United States do not disclose the address of any owner of unclaimed property, such address shall be presumed to be within this state if the federal agency having custody of such property initially acquired possession in this state. All addresses presumed to be within this state are presumed to be within the County of Sacramento. For the purposes of this chapter, it shall be presumed that the situs of unclaimed intangible property is in this state if the last known or presumed address of the owner is in this state.

(b) All unclaimed tangible property is subject to delivery to this state if the federal agency having custody of the unclaimed property initially acquired possession in this state.

Ca. Civ. Proc. Code § 1604
Amended by Stats. 1968, Ch. 356.

Section 1605 - Certification by Governor that United States will be compensated for cost of examining records

The Governor shall certify to the Comptroller General or other proper officer of the United States that the law of this State provides effective means whereby the United States shall be compensated at reasonable times for this State's proportionate share of the actual and necessary cost of examining records and for reporting information and whereby the United States shall be held harmless in the event of claim for property delivered to this State in accordance with the provisions of this chapter.

Such certification shall be made on the thirtieth day of June next following the effective date of any federal statute requiring such certification.

Ca. Civ. Proc. Code § 1605
Added by Stats. 1959, Ch. 1801.

Section 1606 - Request that Comptroller General report previously unreported information

On the thirtieth day of June next following the date of certification by the Governor, and annually thereafter, the Controller shall request the Comptroller General or other proper officer of the United States to report all previously unreported information relating to unclaimed property as determined by that officer pursuant to federal law.

Ca. Civ. Proc. Code § 1606
Added by Stats. 1959, Ch. 1801.

Section 1607 - Copy of report posted at superior court courthouses; claim against United States by person asserting interest in property

When a report is received from the Comptroller General or other proper officer of the United States, the Controller shall prepare and forward a copy thereof to the clerk of the superior court of each county within this state and the clerk shall post a copy at the courthouse for a period of 60 days. Any person asserting an interest in property mentioned in the report may elect to claim against the United States under the laws of the United States, in which event and within 90 days following the date of initial posting by the clerk the person shall notify the Controller of the asserted interest and intention to so claim. The Controller shall omit the property from any claim by the state until such time as the asserted interest may be finally determined against the claimant. The interest may not thereafter be asserted against the state.

Ca. Civ. Proc. Code § 1607

Amended by Stats 2003 ch 62 (SB 600),s 27, eff. 1/1/2004.
Amended by Stats 2002 ch 784 (SB 1316),s 84, eff. 1/1/2003.

Section 1608 - Expiration of period of time for commencing proceeding not to affect state's right to acquire possession of property

The expiration of any period of time specified by statute or court order, during which an action or proceeding may be commenced or enforced to obtain payment of a claim for funds or delivery of property shall not affect the right of this State to acquire possession of unclaimed property in accordance with the provisions of this chapter.

Ca. Civ. Proc. Code § 1608

Added by Stats. 1959, Ch. 1801.

Section 1609 - Proceeding commenced by Attorney General to determine state's right to custody of property

Within 120 days following the date of initial posting by the clerk of the superior court, the Attorney General shall commence a proceeding by filing a petition to determine the state's right to custody of all property mentioned in such report and unclaimed within the time and in the manner provided by Section 1607. The proceeding shall be commenced and heard in the superior court in the County of Sacramento and venue shall not be affected by the provisions of Section 401, Code of Civil Procedure.

The petition shall name as respondents all persons known to have been interested and "all persons unknown claiming any title or interest in or to the property described or referred to in the petition." If the records of the United States fail to disclose with reasonable certainty the identity or number of owners or claimants of specific funds or other personal property, or the extent of their interests therein, such persons may be designated and described as a class, to wit, as "all unknown owners or claimants to the funds or property mentioned in or affected by _____," and, as the case may be, the petition shall identify and set forth the court actions or proceedings to the credit of which such funds or other property are held, or the accounts or other identifying references under which they are carried upon the records of the United States. The petition shall describe or refer to the property, and may include one or more items, as the Attorney General may be advised, without prejudice to his right to commence subsequent proceedings relating to other items not included. The petition shall also state the name of the owner and his last address as known or as presumed under this chapter, and shall set forth the facts and circumstances by virtue of which it is claimed that such funds or property are subject to custody by the state. Any number of respondents may be joined whether they reside in the same or different counties, and any number of causes of action may be joined and need not be separately stated.

Ca. Civ. Proc. Code § 1609
Amended by Stats 2002 ch 784 (SB 1316),s 85, eff. 1/1/2003.

Section 1610 - Notice of proceeding

No summons or other process shall issue to direct the appearance and answer of a respondent. Commencing within five days after filing petition, notice of the proceeding shall be published once each week for three consecutive weeks in a newspaper of general circulation published within the County of Sacramento. At the time the notice is first published, a copy of the petition and notice shall be posted at the courthouse in the county where each defendant was last known or presumed to have had an address. Such petition and such notice shall remain posted for 45 days. The notice of proceeding shall advise that the State seeks custody of unclaimed property held by the United States. The names but not the addresses of the respondents shall be contained in the notice with a statement that such persons are believed to live or to have lived within the State and are believed to be or to have been owners of the unclaimed property. The notice shall not contain a description of the unclaimed property but shall advise that such description together with the last known or presumed addresses of owners may be determined by examining the petition filed in the proceeding. The petition and its place of filing shall be sufficiently identified and described. The notice shall advise that persons claiming an interest must answer the petition within the time prescribed by law, which time shall be stated, if they elect to pursue their claims against the United States, otherwise their rights to property shall be preserved subject to delayed delivery as provided by law. The notice shall advise that Section 1611, Code of Civil Procedure, should be consulted for the time, form, and costs of an answer.

The notice shall be deemed completed 45 days after the date of first publication, whereupon the court shall have full and complete jurisdiction over the property described in the petition and not claimed within the time or in the manner provided in Section 1611, and shall have full and complete jurisdiction to determine the right of the State to custody and to render an appropriate judgment therefor.

Ca. Civ. Proc. Code § 1610
Added by Stats. 1959, Ch. 1801.

Section 1611 - Response to petition

Any person, whether or not named in the petition, may within 15 days after completion of notice respond to the petition by answer describing the property, asserting an interest as owner or successor, and declaring an intention to claim the same from the United States under the laws of the United States. Such answer shall not be filed unless accompanied by the sum of ten dollars ($10) for deposit in court, and no other answer or response shall be filed by or on behalf of a claimant. The court shall strike from the petition and dismiss from the proceeding all property described in the answer. The funds on deposit shall be transmitted by the court to the Controller and shall be received for deposit in the abandoned property account in the Unclaimed Property Fund as total reimbursement for costs and services expended on behalf of the claimant. Such dismissal shall be without prejudice to a subsequent petition should it appear that the claimant is not entitled to the property, and the interest asserted in

said answer shall not thereafter be asserted against the State.
Ca. Civ. Proc. Code § 1611
Added by Stats. 1959, Ch. 1801.

Section 1612 - Application for judgment, findings and declaration by court

Within 20 days following expiration of time for filing answer under Section 1611, the Attorney General shall apply to the court for a judgment relating to all property set forth in the petition and not claimed by answer. The court shall find that such property appears to be or to have been owned by persons residing within this State and remains unclaimed by such persons. The court shall declare that the property, which shall be described, is subject to custody of the State and shall be delivered to and received by the State of California to be retained until such time as it may be claimed pursuant to law.
Ca. Civ. Proc. Code § 1612
Added by Stats. 1959, Ch. 1801.

Section 1613 - Request for delivery or payment of property described in judgment

The Controller shall request delivery or payment of all unclaimed property described in the judgment declaring the right of the State to receive custody of such property. The request shall be accompanied by a certified copy of said judgment and shall be directed to such officer, agency, or department of the United States as may be designated for such purposes by federal law. The Controller shall furnish receipts for all property delivered or paid.
Ca. Civ. Proc. Code § 1613
Added by Stats. 1959, Ch. 1801.

Section 1614 - Deposit or sale of property received

Property received under this chapter shall be deposited or sold by the State Controller as though received under Chapter 7 (commencing with Section 1500) of this title. Property received under this chapter shall not be subject to claim within two years following the date upon which it is paid to or received by the state. Thereafter, claims shall be made in the manner provided in Chapter 7 (commencing with Section 1500) of this title.

Ca. Civ. Proc. Code § 1614
Amended by Stats. 1968, Ch. 356.

Section 1615 - Money in abandoned property account appropriated for expenditure by Controller

All money in the abandoned property account in the Unclaimed Property Fund is hereby continuously appropriated to the State Controller without regard to fiscal years, for expenditure in accordance with this chapter for the following purposes:

(a) For payment of the proportionate costs of this State pursuant to the terms of any contract entered with the United States;

(b) For payment of sums necessary to indemnify the United States for losses occasioned by claims to property delivered to the custody of this State.

Ca. Civ. Proc. Code § 1615
Added by Stats. 1959, Ch. 1801.

Title 11 - MONEY JUDGMENTS OF OTHER JURISDICTIONS

Chapter 1 - SISTER STATE MONEY JUDGMENTS

Section 1710.10 - Definitions

As used in this chapter:

(a) "Judgment creditor" means the person or persons who can bring an action to enforce a sister state judgment.

(b) "Judgment debtor" means the person or persons against whom an action to enforce a sister state judgment can be brought.

(c) "Sister state judgment" means that part of any judgment, decree, or order of a court of a state of the United States, other than California, which requires the payment of money, but does not include a support order as defined in Section 155 of the Family Code.

Ca. Civ. Proc. Code § 1710.10

Title heading amended by Stats 2017 ch 168 (AB 905),s 1, eff. 1/1/2018.
Chapter heading amended by Stats 2017 ch 168 (AB 905),s 2, eff. 1/1/2018.
Amended by Stats. 1992, Ch. 163, Sec. 64. Effective January 1, 1993. Operative January 1, 1994, by Sec. 161 of Ch. 163.

Section 1710.15 - Application by judgment creditor for entry of judgment based on sister state judgment

(a) A judgment creditor may apply for the entry of a judgment based on a sister state judgment by filing an application pursuant to Section 1710.20.

(b) The application shall be executed under oath and shall include all of the following:

(1) A statement that an action in this state on the sister state judgment is not barred by the applicable statute of limitations.

(2) A statement, based on the applicant's information and belief, that no stay of enforcement of the sister state judgment is currently in effect in the sister state.

(3) A statement of the amount remaining unpaid under the sister state judgment and, if accrued interest on the sister state judgment is to be included in the California judgment, a statement of the amount of interest accrued on the sister state judgment (computed at the rate of interest applicable to the judgment under the law of the sister state), a statement of the rate of interest applicable to the judgment under the law of the sister state, and a citation to the law of the sister state establishing the rate of interest.

(4) A statement that no action based on the sister state judgment is currently pending in any court in this state and that no judgment based on the sister state judgment has previously been entered in any proceeding in this state.

(5) Where the judgment debtor is an individual, a statement

setting forth the name and last known residence address of the judgment debtor. Where the judgment debtor is a corporation, a statement of the corporation's name, place of incorporation, and whether the corporation, if foreign, has qualified to do business in this state under the provisions of Chapter 21 (commencing with Section 2100) of Division 1 of Title 1 of the Corporations Code. Where the judgment debtor is a partnership, a statement of the name of the partnership, whether it is a foreign partnership, and, if it is a foreign partnership, whether it has filed a statement pursuant to Section 15800 of the Corporations Code designating an agent for service of process. Except for facts which are matters of public record in this state, the statements required by this paragraph may be made on the basis of the judgment creditor's information and belief.

(6) A statement setting forth the name and address of the judgment creditor.

(c) A properly authenticated copy of the sister state judgment shall be attached to the application.

Ca. Civ. Proc. Code § 1710.15
Amended by Stats. 1985, Ch. 106, Sec. 11.

Section 1710.20 - Filing application; proper county
(a) An application for entry of a judgment based on a sister state judgment shall be filed in a superior court.
(b) Subject to the power of the court to transfer proceedings under this chapter pursuant to Title 4 (commencing with Section 392) of Part 2, the proper county for the filing of an application is any of the following:

(1) The county in which any judgment debtor resides.

(2) If no judgment debtor is a resident, any county in this state.
(c) A case in which the sister state judgment amounts to thirty-five thousand dollars ($35,000) or less is a limited civil case.

Ca. Civ. Proc. Code § 1710.20

Amended by Stats 2023 ch 861 (SB 71),s 7, eff. 1/1/2024.
Amended by Stats 2002 ch 784 (SB 1316),s 86, eff. 1/1/2003.

Section 1710.25 - Amounts of judgment entered
(a) Upon the filing of the application, the clerk shall enter a judgment based upon the application for the total of the following amounts as shown therein:

    (1) The amount remaining unpaid under the sister state judgment.

    (2) The amount of interest accrued on the sister state judgment (computed at the rate of interest applicable to the judgment under the law of the sister state).

    (3) The amount of the fee for filing the application for entry of the sister state judgment.
(b) Entry shall be made in the same manner as entry of an original judgment of the court. From the time of entry, interest shall accrue on the judgment so entered at the rate of interest applicable to a judgment entered in this state.
    Ca. Civ. Proc. Code § 1710.25
Amended by Stats. 1984, Ch. 311, Sec. 4.

Section 1710.30 - Service of notice of entry of judgment
(a) Notice of entry of judgment shall be served promptly by the judgment creditor upon the judgment debtor in the manner provided for service of summons by Article 3 (commencing with Section 415.10) of Chapter 4 of Title 5 of Part 2. Notice shall be in a form prescribed by the Judicial Council and shall inform the judgment debtor that the judgment debtor has 30 days within which to make a motion to vacate the judgment.
(b) The fee for service of the notice of entry of judgment under this section is an item of costs recoverable in the same manner as statutory fees for service of a writ as provided in Chapter 5 (commencing with Section 685.010) of Division 1 of Title 9 of Part

2, but such fee may not exceed the amount allowed to a public officer or employee in this state for such service.

Ca. Civ. Proc. Code § 1710.30

Amended by Stats. 1982, Ch. 497, Sec. 79. Operative July 1, 1983, by Sec. 185 of Ch. 497.

Section 1710.35 - Effect of judgment

Except as otherwise provided in this chapter, a judgment entered pursuant to this chapter shall have the same effect as an original money judgment of the court and may be enforced or satisfied in like manner.

Ca. Civ. Proc. Code § 1710.35

Amended by Stats. 1984, Ch. 311, Sec. 5.

Section 1710.40 - Vacation of judgment

(a) A judgment entered pursuant to this chapter may be vacated on any ground which would be a defense to an action in this state on the sister state judgment, including the ground that the amount of interest accrued on the sister state judgment and included in the judgment entered pursuant to this chapter is incorrect.

(b) Not later than 30 days after service of notice of entry of judgment pursuant to Section 1710.30, proof of which has been made in the manner provided by Article 5 (commencing with Section 417.10) of Chapter 4 of Title 5 of Part 2, the judgment debtor, on written notice to the judgment creditor, may make a motion to vacate the judgment under this section.

(c) Upon the hearing of the motion to vacate the judgment under this section, the judgment may be vacated upon any ground provided in subdivision (a) and another and different judgment entered, including, but not limited to, another and different judgment for the judgment creditor if the decision of the court is that the judgment creditor is entitled to such different judgment. The decision of the court on the motion to vacate the judgment shall be given and filed with the clerk of court in the manner provided in Sections 632, 634, and 635, except that the court is not required to make any written findings and conclusions if the amount of the judgment as entered under Section 1710.25 does not exceed one thousand dollars ($1,000).

Ca. Civ. Proc. Code § 1710.40
Amended by Stats. 1977, Ch. 232.

Section 1710.45 - Writ of execution or enforcement on judgment

(a) Except as otherwise provided in this section, a writ of execution on a judgment entered pursuant to this chapter shall not issue, nor may the judgment be enforced by other means, until at least 30 days after the judgment creditor serves notice of entry of the judgment upon the judgment debtor, proof of which has been made in the manner provided by Article 5 (commencing with Section 417.10) of Chapter 4 of Title 5 of Part 2.

(b) A writ of execution may be issued, or other enforcement sought, before service of the notice of entry of judgment if the judgment debtor is any of the following:

(1) An individual who does not reside in this state.

(2) A foreign corporation not qualified to do business in this state under the provisions of Chapter 21 (commencing with Section 2100) of Division 1 of Title 1 of the Corporations Code.

(3) A foreign partnership which has not filed a statement pursuant to Section 15700 of the Corporations Code designating an agent for service of process.

(c) The court may order that a writ of execution be issued, or may permit enforcement by other means, before service of the notice of entry of judgment if the court finds upon an ex parte showing that great or irreparable injury would result to the judgment creditor if issuance of the writ or enforcement were delayed as provided in subdivision (a).

(d) Property levied upon pursuant to a writ issued under subdivision (b) or (c) or otherwise sought to be applied to the satisfaction of the judgment shall not be sold or distributed before 30 days after the judgment creditor serves notice of entry of the judgment upon the judgment debtor, proof of which has been made in the manner provided by Article 5 (commencing with Section 417.10) of Chapter 4 of Title 5 of Part 2. However, if property levied upon is perishable, it may be sold in order to prevent its destruction or loss of value, but the proceeds of the sale shall not be distributed to the judgment creditor before the date sale of nonperishable property is permissible.

Ca. Civ. Proc. Code § 1710.45
Amended by Stats. 1982, Ch. 497, Sec. 80. Operative July 1, 1983, by Sec. 185 of Ch. 497.

Section 1710.50 - Stay of enforcement
(a) The court shall grant a stay of enforcement where:

(1) An appeal from the sister state judgment is pending or may be taken in the state which originally rendered the judgment. Under this paragraph, enforcement shall be stayed until the proceedings on appeal have been concluded or the time for appeal has expired.

(2) A stay of enforcement of the sister state judgment has been granted in the sister state. Under this paragraph, enforcement shall be stayed until the sister state stay of enforcement expires or is vacated.

(3) The judgment debtor has made a motion to vacate pursuant to Section 1710.40. Under this paragraph, enforcement shall be stayed until the judgment debtor's motion to vacate is determined.

(4) A money judgment or lien on real property was obtained against a person or entity for exercising a right guaranteed under the United States Constitution or a right guaranteed under the California Constitution, or against a person or entity for aiding and abetting the exercise of said rights. The stay of enforcement shall remain in place until such time as the statute of limitations in Section 1798.303 of the Civil Code has elapsed or an action prosecuted under Section 1798.303 has concluded, whichever is later.

(5) Any other circumstance exists where the interests of justice require a stay of enforcement.

(b) The court may grant a stay of enforcement under this section on its own motion, on ex parte motion, or on noticed motion.

(c) The court shall grant a stay of enforcement under this section on such terms and conditions as are just including but not limited to the following:

(1) The court may require an undertaking in an amount it determines to be just, but the amount of the undertaking shall not exceed double the amount of the judgment creditor's claim.

(2) If a writ of execution has been issued, the court may order that it remain in effect.

(3) If property of the judgment debtor has been levied upon under a writ of execution, the court may order the levying officer to retain possession of the property capable of physical possession and to maintain the levy on other property.

Ca. Civ. Proc. Code § 1710.50
Amended by Stats 2023 ch 260 (SB 345),s 9, eff. 1/1/2024.
Added by Stats. 1974, Ch. 211.

Section 1710.55 - Entry of judgment based on sister state judgment prohibited

No judgment based on a sister state judgment may be entered pursuant to this chapter in any of the following cases:

(a) A stay of enforcement of the sister state judgment is currently in effect in the sister state.

(b) An action based on the sister state judgment is currently pending in any court in this state.

(c) A judgment based on the sister state judgment has previously been entered in any proceeding in this state.

Ca. Civ. Proc. Code § 1710.55
Added by Stats. 1974, Ch. 211.

Section 1710.60 - Action to enforce sister state judgment

(a) Except as provided in subdivision (b), nothing in this chapter affects any right a judgment creditor may have to bring an action to enforce a sister state judgment.

(b) No action to enforce a sister state judgment may be brought where a judgment based on such sister state judgment has previously been entered pursuant to this chapter.

Ca. Civ. Proc. Code § 1710.60
Added by Stats. 1974, Ch. 211.

Section 1710.65 - Action by judgment creditor based on part of judgment not requiring payment of money

The entry of a judgment based on a sister state judgment pursuant to this chapter does not limit the right of the judgment creditor to bring an action based on the part of a judgment of a sister state which does not require the payment of money, nor does the bringing of such an action limit the right of the judgment creditor to obtain entry of judgment based on the sister state judgment pursuant to this chapter.

Ca. Civ. Proc. Code § 1710.65
Added by Stats. 1974, Ch. 211.

Chapter 2 - FOREIGN-COUNTRY MONEY JUDGMENTS

Section 1713 - Title of act

This chapter may be cited as the Uniform Foreign-Country Money Judgments Recognition Act.

Ca. Civ. Proc. Code § 1713
Added by Stats 2007 ch 212 (SB 639),s 2, eff. 1/1/2008.

Section 1714 - Definitions

As used in this chapter:

(a) "Foreign country" means a government other than any of the following:

(1) The United States.

(2) A state, district, commonwealth, territory, or insular possession of the United States.

(3) A federally recognized Indian nation, tribe, pueblo, band, or Alaska Native village.

(4) Any other government with regard to which the decision in this state as to whether to recognize a judgment of that government's courts is initially subject to determination under the Full Faith and Credit Clause of the United States Constitution.
(b) "Foreign-country judgment" means a judgment of a court of a foreign country.
Ca. Civ. Proc. Code § 1714
Amended by Stats 2017 ch 168 (AB 905),s 3, eff. 1/1/2018.
Amended by Stats 2014 ch 243 (SB 406),s 2, eff. 1/1/2015.
Added by Stats 2007 ch 212 (SB 639),s 2, eff. 1/1/2008.

Section 1715 - Applicability of chapter
(a) Except as otherwise provided in subdivision (b), this chapter applies to a foreign-country judgment to the extent that the judgment both:

(1) Grants or denies recovery of a sum of money.

(2) Under the law of the foreign country where rendered, is final, conclusive, and enforceable.
(b) This chapter does not apply to a foreign-country judgment, even if the judgment grants or denies recovery of a sum of money, to the extent that the judgment is any of the following:

(1) A judgment for taxes.

(2) A fine or other penalty.

(3)

(A) A judgment for divorce, support, or maintenance, or other judgment rendered in connection with domestic relations.

(B) A judgment for divorce, support, or maintenance, or other judgment rendered in connection with domestic relations may be recognized by a court of this state pursuant to Section 1723.
(c) A party seeking recognition of a foreign-country judgment has the burden of establishing that the foreign-country judgment is entitled to recognition under this chapter.
   Ca. Civ. Proc. Code § 1715
Added by Stats 2007 ch 212 (SB 639),s 2, eff. 1/1/2008.

Section 1716 - State required to recognize judgments to which chapter applies; judgments state shall not to recognize; judgments state not required to recognize

(a) Except as otherwise provided in subdivisions (b), (c), (d), and (f), a court of this state shall recognize a foreign-country judgment to which this chapter applies.
(b) A court of this state shall not recognize a foreign-country judgment if any of the following apply:

(1) The judgment was rendered under a judicial system that does not provide impartial tribunals or procedures compatible with the requirements of due process of law.

(2) The foreign court did not have personal jurisdiction over the defendant.

(3) The foreign court did not have jurisdiction over the subject matter.
(c)

(1) A court of this state shall not recognize a foreign-country judgment if any of the following apply:

(A) The defendant in the proceeding in the foreign court did not receive notice of the proceeding in sufficient time to enable the defendant to defend.

(B) The judgment was obtained by fraud that deprived the losing party of an adequate opportunity to present its case.

(C) The judgment or the cause of action or claim for relief on which the judgment is based is repugnant to the public policy of this state or of the United States.

(D) The proceeding in the foreign court was contrary to an agreement between the parties under which the dispute in question was to be determined otherwise than by proceedings in that foreign court.

(E) In the case of jurisdiction based only on personal service, the foreign court was a seriously inconvenient forum for the trial of the action.

(F) The judgment was rendered in circumstances that raise substantial doubt about the integrity of the rendering court with respect to the judgment.

(G) The specific proceeding in the foreign court leading to the judgment was not compatible with the requirements of due process of law.

(2) Notwithstanding an applicable ground for nonrecognition under paragraph (1), the court may nonetheless recognize a foreign-country judgment if the party seeking recognition of the judgment demonstrates good reason to recognize the judgment that outweighs the ground for nonrecognition.

(d) A court of this state is not required to recognize a foreign-country judgment if the judgment conflicts with another final and conclusive judgment.

(e) If the party seeking recognition of a foreign-country judgment has met its burden of establishing recognition of the foreign-country judgment pursuant to subdivision (c) of Section 1715, a party resisting recognition of a foreign-country judgment has the burden of establishing that a ground for nonrecognition stated in subdivision (b), (c), or (d) exists.

(f) A court of this state shall not recognize a foreign-country judgment for defamation if that judgment is not recognizable under Section 4102 of Title 28 of the United States Code.

Ca. Civ. Proc. Code § 1716

Amended by Stats 2017 ch 168 (AB 905),s 5, eff. 1/1/2018.
Amended by Stats 2009 ch 579 (SB 320),s 1, eff. 1/1/2010.
Added by Stats 2007 ch 212 (SB 639),s 2, eff. 1/1/2008.

Section 1717 - Bases for personal jurisdiction

(a) For the purpose of paragraph (2) of subdivision (b) of Section 1716, a foreign court lacks personal jurisdiction over a defendant if either of the following conditions is met:

(1) The foreign court lacks a basis for exercising personal jurisdiction that would be sufficient according to the standards governing personal jurisdiction in this state.

(2) The foreign court lacks personal jurisdiction under its own law.

(b) A foreign-country judgment shall not be refused recognition for lack of personal jurisdiction under paragraph (1) of subdivision (a) if any of the following apply:

(1) The defendant was served with process personally in the foreign country.

(2) The defendant voluntarily appeared in the proceeding, other than for the purpose of protecting property seized or threatened with seizure in the proceeding or of contesting the jurisdiction of the court over the defendant.

(3) The defendant, before the commencement of the proceeding, had agreed to submit to the jurisdiction of the foreign court with respect to the subject matter involved.

(4) The defendant was domiciled in the foreign country when the proceeding was instituted or was a corporation or other form of business organization that had its principal place of business in, or was organized under the laws of, the foreign country.

(5) The defendant had a business office in the foreign country and the proceeding in the foreign court involved a cause of action or claim for relief arising out of business done by the defendant through that office in the foreign country.

(6) The defendant operated a motor vehicle or airplane in the foreign country and the proceeding involved a cause of action or claim for relief arising out of that operation.

(c) The list of bases for personal jurisdiction in subdivision (b) is not exclusive. The courts of this state may recognize bases of personal jurisdiction other than those listed in subdivision (b) as sufficient for the purposes of paragraph (1) of subdivision (a).

Ca. Civ. Proc. Code § 1717

Amended by Stats 2017 ch 168 (AB 905),s 6, eff. 1/1/2018.

Amended by Stats 2009 ch 579 (SB 320),s 2, eff. 1/1/2010.

Added by Stats 2007 ch 212 (SB 639),s 2, eff. 1/1/2008.

Section 1718 - Recognition issue raise by filing action; raised by filing counterclaim, cross-claim or affirmative defense

(a) If recognition of a foreign-country judgment is sought as an original matter, the issue of recognition shall be raised by filing an action seeking recognition of the foreign-country judgment.

(b) If recognition of a foreign-country judgment is sought in a pending action, the issue of recognition may be raised by counterclaim, cross-claim, or affirmative defense.

Ca. Civ. Proc. Code § 1718

Added by Stats 2007 ch 212 (SB 639),s 2, eff. 1/1/2008.

Section 1719 - Conclusive effect of judgment; enforcement

If the court in a proceeding under Section 1718 finds that the foreign-country judgment is entitled to recognition under this chapter then, to the extent that the foreign-country judgment grants or denies recovery of a sum of money, the foreign-country judgment is both of the following:

(a) Conclusive between the parties to the same extent as the judgment of a sister state entitled to full faith and credit in this state would be conclusive.

(b) Enforceable in the same manner and to the same extent as a judgment rendered in this state.

Ca. Civ. Proc. Code § 1719

Added by Stats 2007 ch 212 (SB 639),s 2, eff. 1/1/2008.

Section 1720 - Stay if appeal pending or will be taken

If a party establishes that an appeal from a foreign-country judgment is pending or will be taken in the foreign country, the court may stay any proceedings with regard to the foreign-country judgment until the appeal is concluded, the time for appeal expires, or the appellant has had sufficient time to prosecute the appeal and has failed to do so.

Ca. Civ. Proc. Code § 1720

Added by Stats 2007 ch 212 (SB 639),s 2, eff. 1/1/2008.

Section 1721 - Time for commencing action to recognize judgment

An action to recognize a foreign-country judgment shall be commenced within the earlier of the time during which the foreign-country judgment is effective in the foreign country or 10 years from the date that the foreign-country judgment became effective in the foreign country.

Ca. Civ. Proc. Code § 1721

Added by Stats 2007 ch 212 (SB 639),s 2, eff. 1/1/2008.

Section 1722 - Need to promote uniformity of law

In applying and construing this uniform act, consideration shall be given to the need to promote uniformity of the law with respect to its subject matter among states that enact it.

Ca. Civ. Proc. Code § 1722

Added by Stats 2007 ch 212 (SB 639),s 2, eff. 1/1/2008.

Section 1723 - Recognition under principles of comity or otherwise

This chapter does not prevent the recognition under principles of comity or otherwise of a foreign-country judgment not within the scope of this chapter.

Ca. Civ. Proc. Code § 1723

Added by Stats 2007 ch 212 (SB 639),s 2, eff. 1/1/2008.

Section 1724 - Effective date

(a) This chapter applies to all actions commenced on or after the effective date of this chapter in which the issue of recognition of a foreign-country judgment is raised.

(b) The former Uniform Foreign Money-Judgments Recognition Act (Chapter 2 (commencing with Section 1713) of Title 11 of Part 3) applies to all actions commenced before the effective date of this chapter in which the issue of recognition of a foreign-country judgment is raised.

Ca. Civ. Proc. Code § 1724

Added by Stats 2007 ch 212 (SB 639),s 2, eff. 1/1/2008.

Section 1725 - Declaratory relief

(a) If all of the following conditions are satisfied, a person against whom a foreign-country defamation judgment was rendered may seek declaratory relief with respect to liability for the judgment or a determination that the judgment is not recognizable under section 1716:

(1) The person is a resident or other person or entity amendable to jurisdiction in this state.

(2) The person either has assets in this state that may be subject to an enforcement proceeding to satisfy the foreign-country defamation judgment or may have to take actions in this state to comply with the foreign-country defamation judgment.

(3) The publication at issue was published in this state.
(b) A court of this state has jurisdiction to determine a declaratory relief action or issue a determination pursuant to this section and has personal jurisdiction over the person or entity who obtained the foreign-country defamation judgment.
(c) This section shall apply to a foreign-country defamation judgment regardless of when it was rendered.

Ca. Civ. Proc. Code § 1725
Added by Stats 2017 ch 168 (AB 905),s 7, eff. 1/1/2018.

Chapter 3 - TRIBAL COURT CIVIL MONEY JUDGMENT ACT

Section 1730 - Short title
This chapter shall be known and may be cited as the Tribal Court Civil Money Judgment Act.

Ca. Civ. Proc. Code § 1730
Amended by Stats 2017 ch 168 (AB 905),s 10, eff. 1/1/2018.
Chapter heading added by Stats 2017 ch 168 (AB 905),s 9, eff. 1/1/2018.
Title heading repealed by Stats 2017 ch 168 (AB 905),s 8, eff. 1/1/2018.
Added by Stats 2014 ch 243 (SB 406),s 4, eff. 1/1/2015.

Section 1731 - Scope
(a) This chapter governs the procedures by which the superior courts of the State of California recognize and enter tribal court money judgments of any federally recognized Indian tribe. Determinations regarding recognition and entry of a tribal court money judgment pursuant to state law shall have no effect upon the independent authority of that judgment. To the extent not inconsistent with this chapter, the Code of Civil Procedure shall apply.

(b) This chapter does not apply to any of the following tribal court money judgments:

(1) For taxes, fines, or other penalties, except for tribal taxes as described in clause 3 of subparagraph (B) of paragraph (3) of subdivision (d) of Section 1616 of Article 10 of Chapter 4 of Division 2 of Title 18 of the California Code of Regulations, and related interest or penalties.

(2) For which federal law requires that states grant full faith and credit recognition, including child support orders under the Full Faith and Credit for Child Support Orders Act (28 U.S.C. Sec. 1738B), except for the purposes of recognizing a tribal court order establishing the right of a child or other dependent of a participant in a retirement plan or other plan of deferred compensation to an assignment of all or a portion of the benefits payable.

(3) For which state law provides for recognition, including child support orders recognized under the Uniform Child Custody Jurisdiction and Enforcement Act (Part 3 (commencing with Section 3400) of Division 8 of the Family Code), other forms of family support orders under the Uniform Interstate Family Support Act (Part 6 (commencing with Section 5700.101) of Division 9 of the Family Code), except for the purposes of recognizing a tribal court order establishing the right of a spouse, former spouse, child, or other dependent of a participant in a retirement plan or other plan of deferred compensation to an assignment of all or a portion of the benefits payable.

(4) For decedents' estates, guardianships, conservatorships, internal affairs of trusts, powers of attorney, or other tribal court money judgments that arise in proceedings that are or would be governed by the Probate Code.
(c) Nothing in this chapter shall be deemed or construed to expand or limit the jurisdiction of either the state or any Indian tribe.

Ca. Civ. Proc. Code § 1731
Amended by Stats 2023 ch 138 (AB 1139),s 1, eff. 1/1/2024.
Amended by Stats 2021 ch 58 (AB 627),s 1, eff. 1/1/2022.

Amended by Stats 2017 ch 168 (AB 905),s 11, eff. 1/1/2018.
Amended by Stats 2015 ch 493 (SB 646),s 1, eff. 1/1/2016.
Added by Stats 2014 ch 243 (SB 406),s 4, eff. 1/1/2015.

Section 1732 - Definitions

For purposes of this chapter:

(a) "Applicant" means the person or persons who can bring an action to enforce a tribal court money judgment.

(b) "Civil action or proceeding" means any action or proceeding that is not criminal, except for those actions or proceedings expressly excluded by subdivision (b) of Section 1731.

(c) "Due process" includes, but is not limited to, the right to be represented by legal counsel, to receive reasonable notice and an opportunity for a hearing, to call and cross-examine witnesses, and to present evidence and argument to an impartial decisionmaker.

(d) "Good cause" means a substantial reason, taking into account the prejudice or irreparable harm a party will suffer if a hearing is not held on an objection or not held within the time periods established by this chapter.

(e) "Respondent" means the person or persons against whom an action to enforce a tribal court money judgment can be brought.

(f) "Tribal court" means any court or other tribunal of any federally recognized Indian nation, tribe, pueblo, band, or Alaska Native village, duly established under tribal or federal law, including Courts of Indian Offenses organized pursuant to Part 11 of Title 25 of the Code of Federal Regulations.

(g) "Tribal court money judgment" means any written judgment, decree, or order of a tribal court for a specified amount of money that was issued in a civil action or proceeding that is final, conclusive, and enforceable by the tribal court in which it was issued and is duly authenticated in accordance with the laws and procedures of the tribe or tribal court.

Ca. Civ. Proc. Code § 1732

Amended by Stats 2017 ch 168 (AB 905),s 12, eff. 1/1/2018.
Added by Stats 2014 ch 243 (SB 406),s 4, eff. 1/1/2015.

Section 1733 - Application for entry of judgment

(a) An application for entry of a judgment under this chapter shall be filed in a superior court.

(b) Subject to the power of the court to transfer proceedings under this chapter pursuant to Title 4 (commencing with Section 392) of Part 2, and except as provided in Section 1733.1, the proper county for the filing of an application is either of the following:

(1) The county in which any respondent resides or owns property.

(2) If no respondent is a resident, any county in this state.

(c) A case in which the tribal court money judgment amounts to thirty-five thousand dollars ($35,000) or less is a limited civil case.

Ca. Civ. Proc. Code § 1733

Amended by Stats 2023 ch 861 (SB 71),s 8, eff. 1/1/2024.
Amended by Stats 2021 ch 58 (AB 627),s 2, eff. 1/1/2022.
Amended by Stats 2017 ch 168 (AB 905),s 13, eff. 1/1/2018.
Added by Stats 2014 ch 243 (SB 406),s 4, eff. 1/1/2015.

Section 1733.1 - Joint application for the recognition of a tribal court order

(a)

(1) If the parties to the underlying tribal court proceeding agree, the parties may file a joint application for the recognition of a tribal court order that establishes a right to child support, spousal support payments, or marital property rights to such spouse, former spouse, child, or other dependent of a participant in a retirement plan or other plan of deferred compensation, which order assigns all or a portion of the benefits payable with respect to the participant to an alternate payee.

(2)If one of the parties to a tribal court order described in paragraph (1) does not agree to join in the application, the other party may proceed by having the tribal court execute a certificate in lieu of the signature of the other party. The Judicial Council shall adopt a format for the certificate.

(3) The application shall be on a form adopted by the Judicial Council, executed under penalty of perjury by parties to the proceeding submitting the application.

(4) The application shall include the name, current address, telephone number, and email address of each party, the name and mailing address of the issuing tribal court, and a certified copy of the order to be recognized.

(b) The filing fee for an application filed under this section is one hundred dollars ($100).

(c) An application filed pursuant to this section may be filed in the county in which either one of the parties resides.

(d) Entry of the tribal court order under this section does not confer any jurisdiction on a court of this state to modify or enforce the tribal court order.

Ca. Civ. Proc. Code § 1733.1

Amended by Stats 2022 ch 420 (AB 2960),s 14, eff. 1/1/2023.

Amended by Stats 2022 ch 28 (SB 1380),s 29, eff. 1/1/2023. Not implemented per s 168.

Added by Stats 2021 ch 58 (AB 627),s 3, eff. 1/1/2022.

Section 1734 - Form of application

(a) An applicant may apply for recognition and entry of a judgment based on a tribal court money judgment by filing an application in superior court pursuant to Section 1733.

(b) The application shall be executed under penalty of perjury and include all of the following information:

(1) The name and address of the tribal court that issued the judgment to be enforced and the date of the tribal court money judgment or any renewal thereof.

(2) The name and address of the party seeking recognition.

(3)

    (A) Any of the following statements, as applicable:

        (i) If the respondent is an individual, the name and last known residence address of the respondent.

        (ii) If the respondent is a corporation, the corporation's name, place of incorporation, and whether the corporation, if foreign, has qualified to do business in this state under the provisions of Chapter 21 (commencing with Section 2100) of Division 1 of Title 1 of the Corporations Code.

        (iii) If the respondent is a partnership, the name of the partnership, whether it is a foreign partnership, and if it is a foreign partnership, whether it has filed a statement pursuant to Section 15800 of the Corporations Code designating an agent for service of process.

        (iv) If the respondent is a limited liability company, the company's name, whether it is a foreign company, and if so, whether it has filed a statement pursuant to Section 17060 of the Corporations Code.

    (B) Except for facts that are matters of public record in this state, the statements required by this paragraph may be made on the basis of the applicant's information and belief.

    (4) A statement that an action in this state to enforce the tribal court money judgment is not barred by the applicable statute of limitations.

    (5) A statement, based on the applicant's information and belief, that the tribal court money judgment is final and that no stay of enforcement of the tribal court money judgment is currently in effect.

    (6) A statement that includes all of the following:

(A) The amount of the award granted in the tribal court money judgment that remains unpaid.

(B) If accrued interest on the tribal court money judgment is to be included in the California judgment, the amount of interest accrued on the tribal court money judgment, computed at the rate of interest applicable to the judgment under the law of the tribal jurisdiction in which the tribal court money judgment was issued.

(C) The rate of interest applicable to the money judgment under the law of the jurisdiction in which the tribal court money judgment was issued.

(D) A citation to the supporting authority.

(7) A statement that no action based on the tribal court money judgment is currently pending in any state court and that no judgment based on the tribal court money judgment has previously been entered in any proceeding in this state.

(c) All of the following items shall be attached to the application:

(1) An authenticated copy of the tribal court money judgment, certified by the judge or clerk of the tribal court.

(2) A copy of the tribal court rules of procedure pursuant to which the tribal court money judgment was entered.

(3) A declaration under penalty of perjury by the tribal court clerk, applicant, or applicant's attorney stating, based on personal knowledge, that the case that resulted in the entry of the judgment was conducted in compliance with the tribal court's rules of procedure.

Ca. Civ. Proc. Code § 1734
Added by Stats 2014 ch 243 (SB 406),s 4, eff. 1/1/2015.

Section 1735 - Service; notice

(a) Promptly upon the filing of an application pursuant to Section

1734, the applicant shall serve upon the respondent a notice of filing of the application to recognize and enter the tribal court money judgment, together with a copy of the application and any documents filed with the application. The notice of filing shall be in a form that shall be prescribed by the Judicial Council, and shall inform the respondent that the respondent has 30 days from service of the notice of filing to file objections to the enforcement of the tribal court money judgment. The notice shall include the name and address of the applicant and the applicant's attorney, if any, and the text of Sections 1736 and 1737.

(b) Except as provided in subdivision (c), service shall be made in the manner provided for service of summons by Article 3 (commencing with Section 415.10) of Chapter 4 of Title 5 of Part 2.

(c) If a respondent is the State of California or any of its officers, employees, departments, agencies, boards, or commissions, service of the notice of filing on that respondent may be by mail to the office of the Attorney General.

(d) The fee for service of the notice of filing under this section is an item of costs recoverable in the same manner as statutory fees for service of a writ as provided in Chapter 5 (commencing with Section 685.010) of Division 1 of Title 9 of Part 2, but the recoverable amount for that fee shall not exceed the amount allowed to a public officer or employee of this state for that service.

(e) The applicant shall file a proof of service of the notice promptly following service.

Ca. Civ. Proc. Code § 1735

Amended by Stats 2021 ch 58 (AB 627),s 4, eff. 1/1/2022.
Added by Stats 2014 ch 243 (SB 406),s 4, eff. 1/1/2015.

Section 1736 - Entry of judgment

(a) If no objections are timely filed in accordance with Section 1737, the clerk shall certify that no objections were timely filed, and a judgment shall be entered.

(b) The judgment entered by the superior court shall be based on and contain the provisions and terms of the tribal court money judgment. The judgment shall be entered in the same manner, have the same effect, and be enforceable in the same manner as any civil judgment, order, or decree of a court of this state, except as provided in Section 1733.1.

Ca. Civ. Proc. Code § 1736

Amended by Stats 2021 ch 58 (AB 627),s 5, eff. 1/1/2022.

Added by Stats 2014 ch 243 (SB 406),s 4, eff. 1/1/2015.

Section 1737 - Objections

(a) Any objection to the recognition and entry of the tribal court money judgment sought under Section 1734 shall be served and filed within 30 days of service of the notice of filing. If any objection is filed within this time period, the superior court shall set a time period for replies and set the matter for a hearing. The hearing shall be held by the superior court within 45 days from the date the objection is filed unless good cause exists for a later hearing. The only grounds for objecting to the recognition or enforcement of a tribal court money judgment are the grounds set forth in subdivisions (b), (c), and (d).

(b) A tribal court money judgment shall not be recognized and entered if the respondent demonstrates to the superior court that at least one of the following occurred:

(1) The tribal court did not have personal jurisdiction over the respondent.

(2) The tribal court did not have jurisdiction over the subject matter.

(3) The judgment was rendered under a judicial system that does not provide impartial tribunals or procedures compatible with the requirements of due process of law.

(c)

(1) The superior court shall decline to recognize and enter a tribal court money judgment if any one of the following grounds applies:

(A) The defendant in the proceeding in the tribal court did not receive notice of the proceeding in sufficient time to enable the defendant to defend.

(B) The judgment was obtained by fraud that deprived the losing party of an adequate opportunity to present its case.

(C) The judgment or the cause of action or claim for relief on which the judgment is based is repugnant to the public policy of the state or of the United States.

(D) The proceeding in the tribal court was contrary to an agreement between the parties under which the dispute in question was to be determined otherwise than by proceedings in that tribal court.

(E) In the case of jurisdiction based on personal service only, the tribal court was a seriously inconvenient forum for the trial of the action.

(F) The judgment was rendered under circumstances that raise substantial doubt about the integrity of the rendering court with respect to the judgment.

(G) The specific proceeding in the tribal court leading to the judgment was not compatible with the requirements of due process of law.

(H) The judgment includes recovery for a claim of defamation, unless the court determines that the defamation law applied by the tribal court provided at least as much protection for freedom of speech and the press as provided by both the United States and California Constitutions.

(2) Notwithstanding an applicable ground for nonrecognition under paragraph (1), the court may nonetheless recognize a tribal court money judgment if the applicant demonstrates good reason to recognize the judgment that outweighs the ground for nonrecognition.

(d) The superior court may, in its discretion, decline to recognize and enter a tribal court money judgment if the judgment conflicts with another final and conclusive judgment.

(e) If objections have been timely filed, the applicant has the burden of establishing that the tribal court money judgment is entitled to recognition. If the applicant has met its burden, a party resisting recognition of the tribal court money judgment has the burden of establishing that a ground for nonrecognition exists pursuant to subdivision (b), (c), or (d).

Ca. Civ. Proc. Code § 1737
Amended by Stats 2021 ch 58 (AB 627),s 6, eff. 1/1/2022.
Amended by Stats 2017 ch 168 (AB 905),s 14, eff. 1/1/2018.
Added by Stats 2014 ch 243 (SB 406),s 4, eff. 1/1/2015.

Section 1738 - Stay

The superior court shall grant a stay of enforcement if the respondent establishes one of the following to the superior court:

(a) An appeal from the tribal court money judgment is pending or may be taken in the tribal court, in which case the superior court shall stay state execution of the tribal court money judgment until the proceeding on appeal has been concluded or the time for appeal has expired.

(b) A stay of enforcement of the tribal court money judgment has been granted by the tribal court, in which case the superior court shall stay enforcement of the tribal court money judgment until the stay of execution expires or is vacated.

(c) Any other circumstance exists where the interests of justice require a stay of enforcement.

Ca. Civ. Proc. Code § 1738
Added by Stats 2014 ch 243 (SB 406),s 4, eff. 1/1/2015.

Section 1739 - Action to recognize judgment

An action to recognize a tribal court money judgment or any renewal thereof shall be commenced within the earlier of the following periods:

(a) The time during which the tribal court money judgment is effective within the territorial jurisdiction of the tribal court.

(b) Ten years from the date that the tribal court money judgment became effective in the tribal jurisdiction.

Ca. Civ. Proc. Code § 1739

Added by Stats 2014 ch 243 (SB 406),s 4, eff. 1/1/2015.

Section 1740 - Resolution of issues with tribal court judge

(a) The superior court may, after notice to all parties, attempt to resolve any issues raised regarding a tribal court money judgment by contacting the tribal court judge who issued the judgment.

(b) The superior court shall allow the parties to participate in, and shall prepare a record of, any communication made with the tribal court judge pursuant to this section.

Ca. Civ. Proc. Code § 1740

Added by Stats 2014 ch 243 (SB 406),s 4, eff. 1/1/2015.

Section 1741 - Construction with other law

(a) The Uniform Foreign-Country Money Judgments Recognition Act (Chapter 2 (commencing with Section 1713)) applies to all actions commenced in superior court before January 1, 2015, in which the issue of recognition of a tribal court money judgment is raised.

(b) This chapter applies to all actions to enforce tribal court money judgments as defined herein commenced in superior court on or after January 1, 2015. A judgment entered under this chapter shall not limit the right of a party to seek enforcement of any part of a judgment, order, or decree entered by a tribal court that is not encompassed by the judgment entered under this chapter.

Ca. Civ. Proc. Code § 1741

Amended by Stats 2017 ch 168 (AB 905),s 15, eff. 1/1/2018.

Added by Stats 2014 ch 243 (SB 406),s 4, eff. 1/1/2015.

Section 1742 - [Repealed]

Ca. Civ. Proc. Code § 1742

Repealed by Stats 2017 ch 168 (AB 905),s 16, eff. 1/1/2018.

Added by Stats 2014 ch 243 (SB 406),s 4, eff. 1/1/2015.

Title 11.6 - CIVIL ACTION MEDIATION

Section 1775 - Legislative findings and declaration
The Legislature finds and declares that:

(a) The peaceful resolution of disputes in a fair, timely, appropriate, and cost-effective manner is an essential function of the judicial branch of state government under Article VI of the California Constitution.

(b) In the case of many disputes, litigation culminating in a trial is costly, time consuming, and stressful for the parties involved. Many disputes can be resolved in a fair and equitable manner through less formal processes.

(c) Alternative processes for reducing the cost, time, and stress of dispute resolution, such as mediation, have been effectively used in California and elsewhere. In appropriate cases mediation provides parties with a simplified and economical procedure for obtaining prompt and equitable resolution of their disputes and a greater opportunity to participate directly in resolving these disputes. Mediation may also assist to reduce the backlog of cases burdening the judicial system. It is in the public interest for mediation to be encouraged and used where appropriate by the courts.

(d) Mediation and similar alternative processes can have the greatest benefit for the parties in a civil action when used early, before substantial discovery and other litigation costs have been incurred. Where appropriate, participants in disputes should be encouraged to utilize mediation and other alternatives to trial for resolving their differences in the early stages of a civil action.

(e) As a pilot project in Los Angeles County and in other counties which elect to apply this title, courts should be able to refer cases to appropriate dispute resolution processes such as judicial arbitration and mediation as an alternative to trial, consistent with the parties' right to obtain a trial if a dispute is not resolved through an alternative process.

(f) The purpose of this title is to encourage the use of court-annexed alternative dispute resolution methods in general, and mediation in particular. It is estimated that the average cost to the court for processing a civil case of the kind described in Section

1775.3 through judgment is three thousand nine hundred forty-three dollars ($3,943) for each judge day, and that a substantial portion of this cost can be saved if these cases are resolved before trial. The Judicial Council, through the Administrative Office of the Courts, shall conduct a survey to determine the number of cases resolved by alternative dispute resolution authorized by this title, and shall estimate the resulting savings realized by the courts and the parties. The results of the survey shall be included in the report submitted pursuant to Section 1775.14. The programs authorized by this title shall be deemed successful if they result in estimated savings of at least two hundred fifty thousand dollars ($250,000) to the courts and corresponding savings to the parties.

Ca. Civ. Proc. Code § 1775
Added by Stats. 1993, Ch. 1261, Sec. 4. Effective January 1, 1994.

Section 1775.1 - Mediation defined; act performed by party may also be performed by counsel

(a) As used in this title, "mediation" means a process in which a neutral person or persons facilitate communication between the disputants to assist them in reaching a mutually acceptable agreement.
(b) Unless otherwise specified in this title or ordered by the court, any act to be performed by a party may also be performed by his or her counsel of record.
Ca. Civ. Proc. Code § 1775.1
Amended by Stats 2002 ch 784 (SB 1316),s 87, eff. 1/1/2003.

Section 1775.2 - Title applicable to Los Angeles County courts; election by other county courts to apply title; effective date

(a) This title shall apply to the courts of the County of Los Angeles.
(b) A court of any county, at the option of the presiding judge, may elect whether or not to apply this title to eligible actions filed in that court, and this title shall not apply in any court which has not so elected. An election under this subdivision may be revoked by the

court at any time.

(c) Courts are authorized to apply this title to all civil actions pending or commenced on or after January 1, 1994.

Ca. Civ. Proc. Code § 1775.2

Added by Stats. 1993, Ch. 1261, Sec. 4. Effective January 1, 1994.

Section 1775.3 - Civil actions which may be submitted to mediation by presiding judge or designate

(a) In the courts of the County of Los Angeles and in other courts that elect to apply this title, all at-issue civil actions in which arbitration is otherwise required pursuant to Section 1141.11, whether or not the action includes a prayer for equitable relief, may be submitted to mediation by the presiding judge or the judge designated under this title as an alternative to judicial arbitration pursuant to Chapter 2.5 (commencing with Section 1141.10) of Title 3.

(b) Any civil action otherwise within the scope of this title in which a party to the action is a public agency or public entity may be submitted to mediation pursuant to subdivision (a).

Ca. Civ. Proc. Code § 1775.3

Added by Stats. 1993, Ch. 1261, Sec. 4. Effective January 1, 1994.

Section 1775.4 - Action ordered into arbitration not order into mediation; action ordered into mediation not ordered into arbitration

An action that has been ordered into arbitration pursuant to Section 1141.11 or 1141.12 may not be ordered into mediation under this title, and an action that has been ordered into mediation pursuant to Section 1775.3 may not be ordered into arbitration pursuant to Section 1141.11.

Ca. Civ. Proc. Code § 1775.4

Added by Stats. 1993, Ch. 1261, Sec. 4. Effective January 1, 1994.

Section 1775.5 - Amount in controversy

The court shall not order a case into mediation where the amount in controversy exceeds fifty thousand dollars ($50,000). The determination of the amount in controversy shall be made in the same manner as provided in Section 1141.16 and, in making this determination, the court shall not consider the merits of questions of liability, defenses, or comparative negligence.

Ca. Civ. Proc. Code § 1775.5

Added by Stats. 1993, Ch. 1261, Sec. 4. Effective January 1, 1994.

Section 1775.6 - Time for selection of mediator; method of selection and qualification

In actions submitted to mediation pursuant to Section 1775.3, a mediator shall be selected for the action within 30 days of its submission to mediation. The method of selection and qualification of the mediator shall be as the parties determine. If the parties are unable to agree on a mediator within 15 days of the date of submission of the action to mediation, the court may select a mediator pursuant to standards adopted by the Judicial Council.

Ca. Civ. Proc. Code § 1775.6

Added by Stats. 1993, Ch. 1261, Sec. 4. Effective January 1, 1994.

Section 1775.7 - Time periods specified in Chapter 1.5 not suspended; computing five-year period specified in section 583.310

(a) Submission of an action to mediation pursuant to this title shall not suspend the running of the time periods specified in Chapter 1.5 (commencing with Section 583.110) of Title 8 of Part 2, except as provided in this section.

(b) If an action is or remains submitted to mediation pursuant to this title more than four years and six months after the plaintiff has filed the action, then the time beginning on the date four years and six months after the plaintiff has filed the action and ending on the date on which a statement of nonagreement is filed pursuant to Section 1775.9 shall not be included in computing the five-year period specified in Section 583.310.

Ca. Civ. Proc. Code § 1775.7

Added by Stats. 1993, Ch. 1261, Sec. 4. Effective January 1, 1994.

Section 1775.8 - Compensation of court-appointed mediators; payment of administrative costs

(a) The compensation of court-appointed mediators shall be the same as the compensation of arbitrators pursuant to Section 1141.18, except that no compensation shall be paid prior to the filing of a statement of nonagreement by the mediator pursuant to Section 1775.9 or prior to settlement of the action by the parties.

(b) All administrative costs of mediation, including compensation of mediators, shall be paid in the same manner as for arbitration pursuant to Section 1141.28. Funds allocated for the payment of arbitrators under the judicial arbitration program shall be equally available for the payment of mediators under this title.

Ca. Civ. Proc. Code § 1775.8
Added by Stats. 1993, Ch. 1261, Sec. 4. Effective January 1, 1994.

Section 1775.9 - Statement of nonagreement filed by mediator

(a) In the event that the parties to mediation are unable to reach a mutually acceptable agreement and any party to the mediation wishes to terminate the mediation, then the mediator shall file a statement of nonagreement. This statement shall be in a form to be developed by the Judicial Council.

(b) Upon the filing of a statement of nonagreement, the matter shall be calendared for trial, by court or jury, both as to law and fact, insofar as possible, so that the trial shall be given the same place on the active list as it had prior to mediation, or shall receive civil priority on the next setting calendar.

Ca. Civ. Proc. Code § 1775.9
Added by Stats. 1993, Ch. 1261, Sec. 4. Effective January 1, 1994.

Section 1775.10 - Confidentiality of statements made by parties

All statements made by the parties during the mediation shall be subject to Sections 703.5 and 1152, and Chapter 2 (commencing with Section 1115) of Division 9, of the Evidence Code.

Ca. Civ. Proc. Code § 1775.10
Amended by Stats. 1997, Ch. 772, Sec. 2. Effective January 1, 1998.

Section 1775.11 - Discovery
Any party who participates in mediation pursuant to Section 1775.3 shall retain the right to obtain discovery to the extent available under the Civil Discovery Act, Title 4 (commencing with Section 2016.010) of Part 4.
Ca. Civ. Proc. Code § 1775.11
Amended by Stats 2004 ch 182 (AB 3081),s 17, eff. 7/1/2005

Section 1775.12 - Reference to mediation or statement of nonagreement in subsequent trial irregularity
Any reference to the mediation or the statement of nonagreement filed pursuant to Section 1775.9 during any subsequent trial shall constitute an irregularity in the proceedings of the trial for the purposes of Section 657.
Ca. Civ. Proc. Code § 1775.12
Added by Stats. 1993, Ch. 1261, Sec. 4. Effective January 1, 1994.

Section 1775.13 - Other alternative dispute resolution programs not preempted
It is the intent of the Legislature that nothing in this title be construed to preempt other current or future alternative dispute resolution programs operating in the trial courts.
Ca. Civ. Proc. Code § 1775.13
Added by Stats. 1993, Ch. 1261, Sec. 4. Effective January 1, 1994.

Section 1775.14 - Report by Judicial Council to Legislature
(a) On or before January 1, 1998, the Judicial Council shall submit a report to the Legislature concerning court alternative dispute resolution programs. This report shall include, but not be limited to, a review of programs operated in Los Angeles County and other courts that have elected to apply this title, and shall examine, among other things, the effect of this title on the judicial arbitration

programs of courts that have participated in that program.

(b) The Judicial Council shall, by rule, require that each court applying this title file with the Judicial Council data that will enable the Judicial Council to submit the report required by subdivision (a).

Ca. Civ. Proc. Code § 1775.14

Amended by Stats 2006 ch 538 (SB 1852),s 74, eff. 1/1/2007.

Section 1775.15 - Rules

Notwithstanding any other provision of law except the provisions of this title, the Judicial Council shall provide by rule for all of the following:

(a) The procedures to be followed in submitting actions to mediation under this act.

(b) Coordination of the procedures and processes under this act with those under the trial Court Delay Reduction Act, Article 5 (commencing with Section 68600) of Chapter 2 of Title 8 of the Government Code.

(c) Exceptions for cause from provisions of this title. In providing for exceptions, the Judicial Council shall take into consideration whether the civil action might not be amenable to mediation.

Ca. Civ. Proc. Code § 1775.15

Added by Stats. 1993, Ch. 1261, Sec. 4. Effective January 1, 1994.

Title 11.7 - RECOVERY OF PREFERENCES AND EXEMPT PROPERTY IN AN ASSIGNMENT FOR THE BENEFIT OF CREDITORS

Section 1800 - Definitions

(a) As used in this section, the following terms have the following meanings:

(1) "Insolvent" means:

(A) With reference to a person other than a partnership, a financial condition such that the sum of the person's debts is greater than all of the person's property, at a fair valuation, exclusive of both of the following:

(i) Property transferred, concealed, or removed with intent to hinder, delay, or defraud the person's creditors.

(ii) Property that is exempt from property of the estate pursuant to the election of the person made pursuant to Section 1801.

(B) With reference to a partnership, financial condition such that the sum of the partnership's debts are greater than the aggregate of, at a fair valuation, both of the following:

(i) All of the partnership's property, exclusive of property of the kind specified in clause (i) of subparagraph (A).

(ii) The sum of the excess of the value of each general partner's separate property, exclusive of property of the kind specified in clause (ii) of subparagraph (A), over the partner's separate debts.

(2) "Inventory" means personal property leased or furnished, held for sale or lease, or to be furnished under a contract for service, raw materials, work in process, or materials used or consumed in a business, including farm products such as crops or livestock, held for sale or lease.

(3) "Insider" means:

(A) If the assignor is an individual, any of the following:

(i) A relative of the assignor or of a general partner of the assignor.

(ii) A partnership in which the assignor is a general partner.

(iii) A general partner of the assignor.

(iv) A corporation of which the assignor is a director, officer, or person in control.

(B) If the assignor is a corporation, any of the following:

(i) A director of the assignor.

(ii) An officer of the assignor.

(iii) A person in control of the assignor.

(iv) A partnership in which the assignor is a general partner.

(v) A general partner of the assignor.

(vi) A relative of a general partner, director, officer, or person in control of the assignor.

(C) If the assignor is a partnership, any of the following:

(i) A general partner in the assignor.

(ii) A relative of a general partner in, general partner of, or person in control of the assignor.

(iii) A partnership in which the assignor is a general partner.

(iv) A general partner of the assignor.

(v) A person in control of the assignor.

(D) An affiliate of the assignor or an insider of an affiliate as if the affiliate were the assignor.

(E) A managing agent of the assignor. As used in this paragraph, the following terms have the following meanings: "Relative" means an individual related by affinity or consanguinity within the third degree as determined by the common law, or an individual in a step or adoptive relationship within the third degree. An "affiliate" means a person that directly or indirectly owns, controls, or holds, with power to vote, 20 percent or more of the outstanding voting securities of the assignor, or 20 percent or more of whose outstanding voting securities are directly or indirectly owned, controlled, or held with power to vote by the assignor, excluding securities held in a fiduciary or agency capacity without sole discretionary power to vote, or held solely to secure a debt if the holder has not in fact exercised the power to vote, or a person who operates the business of the assignor under a lease or operating agreement or whose business is operated by the assignor under a lease or operating agreement.

(4) "Judicial lien" means a lien obtained by judgment, levy, sequestration, or other legal or equitable process or proceeding.

(5) "New value" means money or money's worth in goods, services, or new credit, or release by a transferee of property previously transferred to the transferee in a transaction that is neither void nor voidable by the assignor or the assignee under any applicable law, but does not include an obligation substituted for an existing obligation.

(6) "Receivable" means a right to payment, whether or not the right has been earned by performance.

(7) "Security agreement" means an agreement that creates or provides for a security interest.

(8) "Security interest" means a lien created by an agreement.

(9) "Statutory lien" means a lien arising solely by force of a statute on specified circumstances or conditions, or lien of distress for rent, whether or not statutory, but does not include a security interest or judicial lien, whether or not the interest or lien is provided by or is dependent on a statute and whether or not the interest or lien is made fully effective by statute.

(10) "Transfer" means every mode, direct or indirect, absolute or conditional, voluntary or involuntary, or disposing of or parting with property or with an interest in property, including retention of title as a security interest.

(b) Except as provided in subdivision (c), the assignee of any general assignment for the benefit of creditors, as defined in Section 493.010, may recover any transfer of property of the assignor that is all of the following:

(1) To or for the benefit of a creditor.

(2) For or on account of an antecedent debt owed by the assignor before the transfer was made.

(3) Made while the assignor was insolvent.

(4) Made on or within 90 days before the date of the making of the assignment or made between 90 days and one year before the date of making the assignment if the creditor, at the time of the transfer, was an insider and had reasonable cause to believe the debtor was insolvent at the time of the transfer.

(5) Enables the creditor to receive more than another creditor of the same class.

(c) The assignee may not recover under this section a transfer as follows:

(1) To the extent that the transfer was both of the following:

(A) Intended by the assignor and the creditor to or for whose benefit the transfer was made to be a contemporaneous exchange for new value given to the assignor.

553

(B) In fact a substantially contemporaneous exchange.

(2) To the extent that the transfer was all of the following:

(A) In payment of a debt incurred in the ordinary course of business or financial affairs of the assignor and the transferee.

(B) Made in the ordinary course of business or financial affairs of the assignor and the transferee.

(C) Made according to ordinary business terms.

(3) Of a security interest in property acquired by the assignor that meets both of the following:

(A) To the extent the security interest secures new value that was all of the following:

(i) Given at or after the signing of a security agreement that contains a description of the property as collateral.

(ii) Given by or on behalf of the secured party under the agreement.

(iii) Given to enable the assignor to acquire the property.

(iv) In fact used by the assignor to acquire the property.

(B) That is perfected within 20 days after the security interest attaches.

(4) To or for the benefit of a creditor, to the extent that, after the transfer, the creditor gave new value to or for the benefit of the assignor that meets both of the following:

(A) Not secured by an otherwise unavoidable security interest.

(B) On account of which new value the assignor did not make an otherwise unavoidable transfer to or for the benefit of the creditor.

(5) Of a perfected security interest in inventory or a receivable or the proceeds of either, except to the extent that the aggregate of all the transfers to the transferee caused a reduction, as of the date of the making of the assignment and to the prejudice of other creditors holding unsecured claims, of any amount by which the debt secured by the security interest exceeded the value of all security interest for the debt on the later of the following:

(A) Ninety days before the date of the making of the assignment.

(B) The date on which new value was first given under the security agreement creating the security interest.

(6) That is the fixing of a statutory lien.

(7) That is payment to a claimant, as defined in Section 8004 of the Civil Code, in exchange for the claimant's waiver or release of any potential or asserted claim of lien, stop payment notice, or right to recover on a payment bond, or any combination thereof.

(8) To the extent that the transfer was a bona fide payment of a debt to a spouse, former spouse, or child of the debtor, for alimony to, maintenance for, or support of, the spouse or child, in connection with a separation agreement, divorce decree, or other order of a court of record, or a determination made in accordance with state or territorial law by a governmental unit, or property settlement agreement; but not to the extent that either of the following occurs:

(A) The debt is assigned to another entity voluntarily, by operation of law or otherwise, in which case the assignee may not recover that portion of the transfer that is assigned to the state or any political subdivision of the state pursuant to Part D of Title IV

of the Social Security Act (42 U.S.C. Sec. 601 et seq.) and passed on
to the spouse, former spouse, or child of the debtor.

(B) The debt includes a liability designated as alimony,
maintenance, or support, unless the liability is actually in the
nature of alimony, maintenance, or support.

(d) An assignee of any general assignment for the benefit of
creditors, as defined in Section 493.010, may avoid a transfer of
property of the assignor transferred to secure reimbursement of a
surety that furnished a bond or other obligation to dissolve a
judicial lien that would have been avoidable by the assignee under
subdivision (b). The liability of the surety under the bond or
obligation shall be discharged to the extent of the value of the
property recovered by the assignee or the amount paid to the
assignee.

(e)

(1) For the purposes of this section:

(A) A transfer of real property other than fixtures, but
including the interest of a seller or purchaser under a contract for
the sale of real property, is perfected when a bona fide purchaser of
the property from the debtor, against whom applicable law permits
the transfer to be perfected, cannot acquire an interest that is
superior to the interest of the transferee.

(B) A transfer of a fixture or property other than real
property is perfected when a creditor on a simple contract cannot
acquire a judicial lien that is superior to the interest of the
transferee.

(2) For the purposes of this section, except as provided in
paragraph (3), a transfer is made at any of the following times:

(A) At the time the transfer takes effect between the
transferor and the transferee, if the transfer is perfected at, or
within 10 days after, the time, except as provided in subparagraph
(B) of paragraph (3) of subdivision (c).

(B) At the time the transfer is perfected, if the transfer is perfected after the 10 days.

(C) Immediately before the date of making the assignment if the transfer is not perfected at the later of:

(i) The making of the assignment.

(ii) Ten days after the transfer takes effect between the transferor and the transferee.

(3) For the purposes of this section, a transfer is not made until the assignor has acquired rights in the property transferred.
(f) For the purposes of this section, the assignor is presumed to have been insolvent on and during the 90 days immediately preceding the date of making the assignment.
(g) An action by an assignee under this section must be commenced within one year after making the assignment.

Ca. Civ. Proc. Code § 1800

Amended by Stats 2010 ch 697 (SB 189),s 26, eff. 1/1/2011, op. 7/1/2012.
Amended by Stats 2006 ch 538 (SB 1852),s 75, eff. 1/1/2007.
EFFECTIVE 1/1/2000. Amended July 28, 1999 (Bill Number: SB 219) (Chapter 202).

Section 1801 - Exempt property
In any general assignment for the benefit of creditors (as defined in Section 493.010), the assignor, if an individual, may choose to retain as exempt property either the property which is otherwise exempt under Chapter 4 (commencing with Section 703.010) of Division 2 of Title 9 of Part 2 or, in the alternative, the following property:
(a) The assignor's aggregate interest, not to exceed seven thousand five hundred dollars ($7,500) in value, in real property or personal property that the assignor or a dependent of the assignor uses as a residence, in a cooperative that owns property that the assignor or a dependent of the assignor uses as a residence, or in a burial plot for

the assignor or a dependent of the assignor.

(b) The assignor's interest, not to exceed one thousand two hundred dollars ($1,200) in value, in one motor vehicle.

(c) The assignor's interest, not to exceed two hundred dollars ($200) in value in any particular item, in household furnishings, household goods, wearing apparel, appliances, books, animals, crops, or musical instruments, that are held primarily for the personal, family, or household use of the assignor or a dependent of the assignor.

(d) The assignor's aggregate interest, not to exceed five hundred dollars ($500) in value, in jewelry held primarily for the personal, family, or household use of the assignor or a dependent of the assignor.

(e) The assignor's aggregate interest, not to exceed in value four hundred dollars ($400) plus any unused amount of the exemption provided under subdivision (a), in any property.

(f) The assignor's aggregate interest, not to exceed seven hundred fifty dollars ($750) in value, in any implements, professional books, or tools, of the trade of the assignor or the trade of a dependent of the assignor.

(g) Any unmatured life insurance contract owned by the assignor, other than a credit life insurance contract.

(h) The assignor's aggregate interest, not to exceed in value four thousand dollars ($4,000) in any accrued dividend or interest under, or loan value of, any unmatured life insurance contract owned by the assignor under which the insured is the assignor or an individual of whom the assignor is a dependent.

(i) Professionally prescribed health aids for the assignor or a dependent of the assignor.

(j) The assignor's right to receive any of the following:

(1) A social security benefit, unemployment compensation, or a local public assistance benefit except that this paragraph does not preclude the application of Section 1255.7 of the Unemployment Insurance Code.

(2) A veterans' benefit.

(3) A disability, illness, or unemployment benefit except that this paragraph does not preclude the application of Section 1255.7 of the Unemployment Insurance Code.

(4) Alimony, support, or separate maintenance, to the extent reasonably necessary for the support of the assignor and any dependent of the assignor.

(5) A payment under a stock bonus, pension, profit sharing, annuity, or similar plan or contract on account of illness, disability, death, age, or length of service, to the extent reasonably necessary for the support of the assignor and any dependent of the assignor, unless:

   (i) The plan or contract was established by or under the auspices of an employer of which the assignor was a partner, officer, director or controlling person at the time the assignor's rights under the plan or contract arose;

   (ii) The payment is on account of age or length of service; and

   (iii) Such plan or contract does not qualify under Section 401(a), 403(a), 403(b), 408, or 409 of the Internal Revenue Code of 1954 (26 U.S.C. 401(a), 403(a), 403(b), 408, or 409).
(k) The assignor's right to receive, or property that is traceable to any of the following:

   (1) An award under a crime victim's reparation law.

   (2) A payment on account of the wrongful death of an individual of whom the assignor was a dependent, to the extent reasonably necessary for the support of the assignor and any dependent of the assignor.

   (3) A payment under a life insurance contract that insured the life of an individual of whom the assignor was a dependent on the date of such individual's death, to the extent reasonably necessary for the support of the assignor and any dependent of the assignor.

(4) A payment, not to exceed seven thousand five hundred dollars ($7,500), on account of personal bodily injury, as compensation for pain and suffering or actual pecuniary loss (other than loss of future earnings), of the assignor or an individual of whom the assignor is a dependent.

(5) A payment in compensation of loss of future earnings of the assignor or an individual of whom the assignor is or was a dependent, to the extent reasonably necessary for the support of the assignor and any dependent of the assignor. In this section, "dependent" includes spouse, whether or not actually dependent, "assignor" means each spouse, if the assignment is made by a married couple, and "value" means fair market value as of the date of the making of the assignment.

Ca. Civ. Proc. Code § 1801
Amended by Stats. 1983, Ch. 155, Sec. 23. Effective June 30, 1983. Operative July 1, 1983, by Sec. 32 of Ch. 155.

Section 1802 - Notice of assignment given by assignee
(a) In any general assignment for the benefit of creditors, as defined in Section 493.010, the assignee shall, within 30 days after the assignment has been accepted in writing, give written notice of the assignment to the assignor's creditors, equityholders, and other parties in interest as set forth on the list provided by the assignor pursuant to subdivision (c).
(b) In the notice given pursuant to subdivision (a), the assignee shall establish a date by which creditors must file their claims to be able to share in the distribution of proceeds of the liquidation of the assignor's assets. That date shall be not less than 150 days and not greater than 180 days after the date of the first giving of the written notice to creditors and parties in interest.
(c) The assignor shall provide to the assignee at the time of the making of the assignment a list of creditors, equityholders, and other parties in interest, signed under penalty of perjury, which

shall include the names, addresses, cities, states, and ZIP Codes for each person together with the amount of that person's anticipated claim in the assignment proceedings.

Ca. Civ. Proc. Code § 1802
Added by Stats. 1992, Ch. 1348, Sec. 8. Effective January 1, 1993.

Title 12 - TRIBAL INJUNCTIONS

Section 1811 - Injunction against gaming or authorization of gaming

(a) Following the issuance of the bonds as specified in Section 63048.65 of the Government Code and during the term of the bonds, if it reasonably appears that the exclusive right of an Indian tribe with a designated tribal compact, as defined in subdivision (b) of Section 63048.6 of the Government Code, pursuant to Section 3.2(a) of that compact has been violated, the tribe may seek a preliminary and permanent injunction against that gaming or the authorization of that gaming as a substantial impairment of the rights specified in Section 3.2(a), in order to afford the tribe stability in its gaming operation and to maintain the bargained-for source of payment and security of the bonds. However, no remedy other than an injunction shall be available against the state or any of its political subdivisions for a violation of Section 3.2(a). The Legislature hereby finds and declares that any such violation of the exclusive right to gaming under Section 3.2(a) is a substantial impairment of the rights specified in that section and will cause irreparable harm that cannot be adequately remedied by damages. No undertaking shall be required on the part of the tribes in connection with any action to seek the preliminary or permanent injunction.

(b) Notwithstanding any other provision of law, the parties to an action brought pursuant to subdivision (a) may petition the Supreme Court for a writ of mandate from any order granting or denying a preliminary injunction. Any such petition shall be filed within 15 days following the notice of entry of the superior court order, and no extension of that period shall be allowed. In any case in which a petition has been filed within the time allowed therefor, the Supreme Court shall make any orders, as it may deem proper in the circumstances.

Ca. Civ. Proc. Code § 1811
Added by Stats 2004 ch 91 (AB 687), s 2, eff. 6/30/2004.

Title 13 - INSPECTION WARRANTS

Section 1822.50 - Defined
An inspection warrant is an order, in writing, in the name of the people, signed by a judge of a court of record, directed to a state or local official, commanding him to conduct any inspection required or authorized by state or local law or regulation relating to building, fire, safety, plumbing, electrical, health, labor, or zoning.

Ca. Civ. Proc. Code § 1822.50
Amended by Stats. 1980, Ch. 230, Sec. 1.

Section 1822.51 - Issued upon cause; supported by affidavit
An inspection warrant shall be issued upon cause, unless some other provision of state or federal law makes another standard applicable. An inspection warrant shall be supported by an affidavit, particularly describing the place, dwelling, structure, premises, or vehicle to be inspected and the purpose for which the inspection is made. In addition, the affidavit shall contain either a statement that consent to inspect has been sought and refused or facts or circumstances reasonably justifying the failure to seek such consent.

Ca. Civ. Proc. Code § 1822.51
Amended by Stats. 1984, Ch. 476, Sec. 2.

Section 1822.52 - Cause deemed to exist
Cause shall be deemed to exist if either reasonable legislative or administrative standards for conducting a routine or area inspection are satisfied with respect to the particular place, dwelling, structure, premises, or vehicle, or there is reason to believe that a condition of nonconformity exists with respect to the

particular place, dwelling, structure, premises, or vehicle.
Ca. Civ. Proc. Code § 1822.52
Added by Stats. 1968, Ch. 1097.

Section 1822.53 - Examination of applicant and other witnesses by judge

Before issuing an inspection warrant, the judge may examine on oath the applicant and any other witness, and shall satisfy himself of the existence of grounds for granting such application.
Ca. Civ. Proc. Code § 1822.53
Added by Stats. 1968, Ch. 1097.

Section 1822.54 - Issuance of warrant

If the judge is satisfied that the proper standard for issuance of the warrant has been met, he or she shall issue the warrant particularly describing each place, dwelling, structure, premises, or vehicle to be inspected and designating on the warrant the purpose and limitations of the inspection, including the limitations required by this title.
Ca. Civ. Proc. Code § 1822.54
Amended by Stats. 1984, Ch. 476, Sec. 3.

Section 1822.55 - Time period warrant effective; execution and return; void after expiration of time

An inspection warrant shall be effective for the time specified therein, but not for a period of more than 14 days, unless extended or renewed by the judge who signed and issued the original warrant, upon satisfying himself that such extension or renewal is in the public interest. Such inspection warrant must be executed and returned to the judge by whom it was issued within the time specified in the warrant or within the extended or renewed time. After the expiration of such time, the warrant, unless executed, is void.
Ca. Civ. Proc. Code § 1822.55
Added by Stats. 1968, Ch. 1097.

Section 1822.56 - Inspection pursuant to warrant

An inspection pursuant to this warrant may not be made between 6:00 p.m. of any day and 8:00 a.m. of the succeeding day, nor in the absence of an owner or occupant of the particular place, dwelling, structure, premises, or vehicle unless specifically authorized by the judge upon a showing that such authority is reasonably necessary to effectuate the purpose of the regulation being enforced. An inspection pursuant to a warrant shall not be made by means of forcible entry, except that the judge may expressly authorize a forcible entry where facts are shown sufficient to create a reasonable suspicion of a violation of a state or local law or regulation relating to building, fire, safety, plumbing, electrical, health, labor, or zoning, which, if such violation existed, would be an immediate threat to health or safety, or where facts are shown establishing that reasonable attempts to serve a previous warrant have been unsuccessful. Where prior consent has been sought and refused, notice that a warrant has been issued must be given at least 24 hours before the warrant is executed, unless the judge finds that immediate execution is reasonably necessary in the circumstances shown.

Ca. Civ. Proc. Code § 1822.56
Amended by Stats. 1980, Ch. 230, Sec. 2.

Section 1822.57 - Willfully refusing to permit inspection

Any person who willfully refuses to permit an inspection lawfully authorized by warrant issued pursuant to this title is guilty of a misdemeanor.

Ca. Civ. Proc. Code § 1822.57
Added by Stats. 1968, Ch. 1097.

Section 1822.58 - Inspections by Department of Fish and Game of places fish or aquatic plants held or stored

A warrant may be issued under the requirements of this title to authorize personnel of the Department of Fish and Game to conduct inspections of locations where fish, amphibia, or aquatic plants are held or stored under Division 12 (commencing with

Section 15000) of the Fish and Game Code.
Ca. Civ. Proc. Code § 1822.58
Added by Stats. 1982, Ch. 1486, Sec. 1.

Section 1822.59 - Inspection by Department of Food and Agriculture for purposes of animal or plant disease eradication

(a) Notwithstanding the provisions of Section 1822.54, for purposes of an animal or plant pest or disease eradication effort pursuant to Division 4 (commencing with Section 5001) or Division 5 (commencing with Section 9101) of the Food and Agricultural Code, the judge may issue a warrant under the requirements of this title describing a specified geographic area to be inspected by authorized personnel of the Department of Food and Agriculture.

(b) A warrant issued pursuant to this section may only authorize the inspection of the exterior of places, dwellings, structures, premises or vehicles, and only in areas urban in character. The warrant shall state the geographical area which it covers and the purpose of and limitations on the inspection.

(c) A warrant may be issued pursuant to this section whether or not the property owners in the area have refused to consent to the inspection. A peace officer may use reasonable force to enter a property to be inspected if so authorized by the warrant.

Ca. Civ. Proc. Code § 1822.59
Added by Stats. 1984, Ch. 476, Sec. 4.

Section 1822.60 - Department of Justice inspections conducted under section 19827(a), Business and Professions Code

A warrant may be issued under the requirements of this title to authorize personnel of the Department of Justice to conduct inspections as provided in subdivision (a) of Section 19827 of the Business and Professions Code.

Ca. Civ. Proc. Code § 1822.60
Amended by Stats 2007 ch 176 (SB 82),s 51, eff. 8/24/2007.

Part 4 - MISCELLANEOUS PROVISIONS

Title 1 - OF THE GENERAL PRINCIPLES OF EVIDENCE

Section 1855 - Copy of map injured, destroyed, lost or stolen offered for record in place of original map

When any map which has been recorded in the office of the recorder of any county is injured, destroyed, lost, or stolen, any person interested may file in the superior court of the county in which the map was originally filed or recorded a verified petition in writing alleging that the map has been injured, destroyed, lost, or stolen without fault of the person making the application, and that the petitioner has a true and correct copy of the original map which he or she offers for record in the place of the original map. The petition shall be accompanied by a copy of the true copy offered for recording.

Upon the filing of the petition the clerk shall set it for hearing by the court, and give notice of the hearing by causing notice of the time and place of the hearing to be posted at the courthouse in the county where the court is held at least 10 days prior to the hearing. A copy of the petition and a copy of the true copy offered for record shall be served upon the recorder of the county in which the proceedings are brought at least 10 days prior to the hearing. The court may order any further notice to be given as it deems proper.

At the time set for the hearing the court shall take evidence for and against the petition, and if it appears to the court from the evidence presented that the copy of the map submitted is a true copy of the original map, it shall decree that the copy is a true copy of the original map, and order the copy placed of record in the office of the recorder in the place of the original map.

A certified copy of the decree shall accompany the true copy of the map for record. When presented to the county recorder for record, he or she shall place of record the copy of the map in the place of the original map.

When placed of record the copy shall have the same effect as the original map, and conveyances of property referring to the original map shall have the same effect as though the original map had not been injured, destroyed, lost, or stolen, and conveyances thereafter made referring to the copy of the original map shall be deemed to refer also to the original map.

Ca. Civ. Proc. Code § 1855

Added by renumbering Section 1855b by Stats. 1987, Ch. 56, Sec. 23.

Section 1856 - Contradiction of terms of agreement by evidence of prior agreement or contemporaneous oral agreement; evidence explaining or supplementing terms

(a) Terms set forth in a writing intended by the parties as a final expression of their agreement with respect to the terms included therein may not be contradicted by evidence of a prior agreement or of a contemporaneous oral agreement.

(b) The terms set forth in a writing described in subdivision (a) may be explained or supplemented by evidence of consistent additional terms unless the writing is intended also as a complete and exclusive statement of the terms of the agreement.

(c) The terms set forth in a writing described in subdivision (a) may be explained or supplemented by course of dealing or usage of trade or by course of performance.

(d) The court shall determine whether the writing is intended by the parties as a final expression of their agreement with respect to the terms included therein and whether the writing is intended also as a complete and exclusive statement of the terms of the agreement.

(e) Where a mistake or imperfection of the writing is put in issue by the pleadings, this section does not exclude evidence relevant to that issue.

(f) Where the validity of the agreement is the fact in dispute, this section does not exclude evidence relevant to that issue.

(g) This section does not exclude other evidence of the circumstances under which the agreement was made or to which it relates, as defined in Section 1860, or to explain an extrinsic ambiguity or otherwise interpret the terms of the agreement, or to establish illegality or fraud.

(h) As used in this section, "agreement" includes trust instruments,

deeds, wills, and contracts between parties.
Ca. Civ. Proc. Code § 1856
Amended by Stats 2013 ch 81 (AB 824),s 1, eff. 1/1/2014.

Section 1857 - Interpretation of language of writing

The language of a writing is to be interpreted according to the meaning it bears in the place of its execution, unless the parties have reference to a different place.
Ca. Civ. Proc. Code § 1857
Enacted 1872.

Section 1858 - Office of judge in construction of statute or instrument

In the construction of a statute or instrument, the office of the Judge is simply to ascertain and declare what is in terms or in substance contained therein, not to insert what has been omitted, or to omit what has been inserted; and where there are several provisions or particulars, such a construction is, if possible, to be adopted as will give effect to all.
Ca. Civ. Proc. Code § 1858
Enacted 1872.

Section 1859 - Intention of Legislature or intention of parties in construction of statute or instrument

In the construction of a statute the intention of the Legislature, and in the construction of the instrument the intention of the parties, is to be pursued, if possible; and when a general and particular provision are inconsistent, the latter is paramount to the former. So a particular intent will control a general one that is inconsistent with it.
Ca. Civ. Proc. Code § 1859
Enacted 1872.

Section 1860 - Circumstances under which instrument made

For the proper construction of an instrument, the circumstances under which it was made, including the situation of the subject of the instrument, and of the parties to it, may also be shown, so that the Judge be placed in the position of those whose language he is to interpret.

Ca. Civ. Proc. Code § 1860
Enacted 1872.

Section 1861 - Presumption terms of writing used in primary and general acceptation; evidence of local, technical or peculiar signification

The terms of a writing are presumed to have been used in their primary and general acceptation, but evidence is nevertheless admissible that they have a local, technical, or otherwise peculiar signification, and were so used and understood in the particular instance, in which case the agreement must be construed accordingly.

Ca. Civ. Proc. Code § 1861
Enacted 1872.

Section 1862 - Words of instrument partly in writing and partly in printed form inconsistent

When an instrument consists partly of written words and partly of a printed form, and the two are inconsistent, the former controls the latter.

Ca. Civ. Proc. Code § 1862
Enacted 1872.

Section 1864 - Terms of agreement intended in different sense by different parties

When the terms of an agreement have been intended in a different sense by the different parties to it, that sense is to prevail against either party in which he supposed the other understood it, and when different constructions of a provision are otherwise equally proper, that is to be taken which is most favorable to the party in whose favor the provision was made.

Ca. Civ. Proc. Code § 1864
Enacted 1872.

Section 1865 - Construction of written notice
A written notice, as well as every other writing, is to be construed according to the ordinary acceptation of its terms. Thus a notice to the drawers or indorsers of a bill of exchange or promissory note, that it has been protested for want of acceptance or payment, must be held to import that the same has been duly presented for acceptance or payment and the same refused, and that the holder looks for payment to the person to whom the notice is given.

Ca. Civ. Proc. Code § 1865
Enacted 1872.

Section 1866 - Statute or instrument susceptible to two interpretations
When a statute or instrument is equally susceptible of two interpretations, one in favor of natural right, and the other against it, the former is to be adopted.

Ca. Civ. Proc. Code § 1866
Enacted 1872.

Title 2 - OF THE KINDS AND DEGREES OF EVIDENCE

Chapter 2 - WITNESSES

Section 1878 - Witness defined
A witness is a person whose declaration under oath is received as evidence for any purpose, whether such declaration be made on oral examination, or by deposition or affidavit.

Ca. Civ. Proc. Code § 1878
Enacted 1872.

Chapter 3 - WRITINGS

Article 2 - PUBLIC WRITINGS

Section 1895 - Law either written or unwritten

Laws, whether organic or ordinary, are either written or unwritten.

Ca. Civ. Proc. Code § 1895

Enacted 1872.

Section 1896 - Written law defined

A written law is that which is promulgated in writing, and of which a record is in existence.

Ca. Civ. Proc. Code § 1896

Enacted 1872.

Section 1897 - Organic laws; statutes; written laws contained in constitution and statutes

The organic law is the Constitution of Government, and is altogether written. Other written laws are denominated statutes. The written law of this State is therefore contained in its Constitution and statutes, and in the Constitution and statutes of the United States.

Ca. Civ. Proc. Code § 1897

Enacted 1872.

Section 1898 - Public or private statutes

Statutes are public or private. A private statute is one which concerns only certain designated individuals, and affects only their private rights. All other statutes are public, in which are included statutes creating or affecting corporations.

Ca. Civ. Proc. Code § 1898

Enacted 1872.

Section 1899 - Unwritten law defined

Unwritten law is the law not promulgated and recorded, as mentioned in Section 1896, but which is, nevertheless, observed and administered in the Courts of the country. It has no certain repository, but is collected from the reports of the decisions of the Courts, and the treatises of learned men.

Ca. Civ. Proc. Code § 1899

Enacted 1872.

Section 1904 - Judicial record defined

A judicial record is the record or official entry of the proceedings in a Court of justice, or of the official act of a judicial officer, in an action or special proceeding.

Ca. Civ. Proc. Code § 1904

Enacted 1872.

Section 1908 - Effect of judgment or final order

(a) The effect of a judgment or final order in an action or special proceeding before a court or judge of this state, or of the United States, having jurisdiction to pronounce the judgment or order, is as follows:

(1) In case of a judgment or order against a specific thing, or in respect to the probate of a will, or the administration of the estate of a decedent, or in respect to the personal, political, or legal condition or relation of a particular person, the judgment or order is conclusive upon the title to the thing, the will, or administration, or the condition or relation of the person.

(2) In other cases, the judgment or order is, in respect to the matter directly adjudged, conclusive between the parties and their successors in interest by title subsequent to the commencement of the action or special proceeding, litigating for the same thing under the same title and in the same capacity, provided they have notice, actual or constructive, of the pendency of the action or proceeding.
(b) A person who is not a party but who controls an action,

individually or in cooperation with others, is bound by the adjudications of litigated matters as if he were a party if he has a proprietary or financial interest in the judgment or in the determination of a question of fact or of a question of law with reference to the same subject matter or transaction; if the other party has notice of his participation, the other party is equally bound. At any time prior to a final judgment, as defined in Section 577, a determination of whether the judgment, verdict upon which it was entered, or a finding upon which it was entered is to be binding upon a nonparty pursuant to this subdivision or whether such nonparty is entitled to the benefit of this subdivision may, on the noticed motion of any party or any nonparty that may be affected by this subdivision, be made in the court in which the action was tried or in which the action is pending on appeal. If no such motion is made before the judgment becomes final, the determination may be made in a separate action. If appropriate, a judgment may be entered or ordered to be entered pursuant to such determination.

Ca. Civ. Proc. Code § 1908
Amended by Stats. 1975, Ch. 225.

Section 1908.5 - Alleging conclusive judgment or order in pleadings

When a judgment or order of a court is conclusive, the judgment or order must be alleged in the pleadings if there be an opportunity to do so; if there be no such opportunity, the judgment or order may be used as evidence.

Ca. Civ. Proc. Code § 1908.5
Added by Stats. 1965, Ch. 299.

Section 1909 - Disputable presumption created by judicial orders

Other judicial orders of a Court or Judge of this State, or of the United States, create a disputable presumption, according to the matter directly determined, between the same parties and their representatives and successors in interest by title subsequent to the commencement of the action or special proceeding, litigating for the same thing under the same title and in the same capacity.

Ca. Civ. Proc. Code § 1909
Enacted 1872.

Section 1910 - Parties deemed same

The parties are deemed to be the same when those between whom the evidence is offered were on opposite sides in the former case, and a judgment or other determination could in that case have been made between them alone, though other parties were joined with both or either.

Ca. Civ. Proc. Code § 1910
Enacted 1872.

Section 1911 - That deemed adjudged in former judgment

That only is deemed to have been adjudged in a former judgment which appears upon its face to have been so adjudged, or which was actually and necessarily included therein or necessary thereto.

Ca. Civ. Proc. Code § 1911
Enacted 1872.

Section 1912 - Party bound by record and party stands in relation to surety

Whenever, pursuant to the last four sections, a party is bound by a record, and such party stands in the relation of a surety for another, the latter is also bound from the time that he has notice of the action or proceeding, and an opportunity at the surety's request to join in the defense.

Ca. Civ. Proc. Code § 1912
Enacted 1872.

Section 1913 - Effect of judicial record on sister state

(a) Subject to subdivision (b), the effect of a judicial record of a sister state is the same in this state as in the state where it was made, except that it can only be enforced in this state by an action or special proceeding.

(b) The authority of a guardian, conservator, or committee, or of a personal representative, does not extend beyond the jurisdiction of the government under which that person was invested with authority, except to the extent expressly authorized by Article 4 (commencing with Section 2011) of Chapter 8 of Part 3 of Division 4 of the Probate Code or another statute.

Ca. Civ. Proc. Code § 1913

Amended by Stats 2014 ch 553 (SB 940),s 1, eff. 1/1/2015, op. 1/1/2016.

Section 1914 - Effect of judicial record of court of admiralty of foreign country

The effect of the judicial record of a Court of admiralty of a foreign country is the same as if it were the record of a Court of admiralty of the United States.

Ca. Civ. Proc. Code § 1914

Enacted 1872.

Section 1916 - Grounds for impeaching judicial record

Any judicial record may be impeached by evidence of a want of jurisdiction in the Court or judicial officer, of collusion between the parties, or of fraud in the party offering the record, in respect to the proceedings.

Ca. Civ. Proc. Code § 1916

Enacted 1872.

Section 1917 - Jurisdiction to sustain record

The jurisdiction sufficient to sustain a record is jurisdiction over the cause, over the parties, and over the thing, when a specific thing is the subject of the judgment.

Ca. Civ. Proc. Code § 1917

Enacted 1872.

Article 3 - PRIVATE WRITINGS

Section 1929 - Either sealed or unsealed
Private writings are either:
1. Sealed; or,
2. Unsealed.
   Ca. Civ. Proc. Code § 1929
Enacted 1872.

Section 1930 - Seal defined
A seal is a particular sign, made to attest, in the most formal manner, the execution of an instrument.
   Ca. Civ. Proc. Code § 1930
Enacted 1872.

Section 1931 - Public seal of state; private seal; seal of sister state or foreign country regarded in state
Section Nineteen Hundred and Thirty-one. A public seal in this State is a stamp or impression made by a public officer with an instrument provided by law, to attest the execution of an official or public document, upon the paper, or upon any substance attached to the paper, which is capable of receiving a visible impression. A private seal may be made in the same manner by any instrument, or it may be made by the scroll of a pen, or by writing the word "seal" against the signature of the writer. A scroll or other sign, made in a sister State or foreign country, and there recognized as a seal, must be so regarded in this State.
   Ca. Civ. Proc. Code § 1931
Amended by Code Amendments 1873-74, Ch. 383.

Section 1932 - No difference between sealed and unsealed writings
Section Nineteen Hundred and Thirty-two. There shall be no difference hereafter, in this State, between sealed and unsealed writings. A writing under seal may therefore be changed, or

altogether discharged by a writing not under seal.

Ca. Civ. Proc. Code § 1932
Amended by Code Amendments 1873-74, Ch. 383.

Section 1933 - Execution of instrument
The execution of an instrument is the subscribing and delivering it, with or without affixing a seal.

Ca. Civ. Proc. Code § 1933
Enacted 1872.

Section 1934 - Agreement in writing without seal for compromise or settlement of debt
An agreement, in writing, without a seal, for the compromise or settlement of a debt, is as obligatory as if a seal were affixed.

Ca. Civ. Proc. Code § 1934
Enacted 1872.

Section 1935 - Subscribing witness
A subscribing witness is one who sees a writing executed or hears it acknowledged, and at the request of the party thereupon signs his name as a witness.

Ca. Civ. Proc. Code § 1935
Enacted 1872.

Section 1950 - Removal of record from office where kept
Section Nineteen Hundred and Fifty. The record of a conveyance of real property, or any other record, a transcript of which is admissible in evidence, must not be removed from the office where it is kept, except upon the order of a Court, in cases where the inspection of the record is shown to be essential to the just determination of the cause or proceeding pending, or where the Court is held in the same building with such office.

Ca. Civ. Proc. Code § 1950
Amended by Code Amendments 1873-74, Ch. 383.

Section 1952 - Exhibits, depositions or administrative record introduced at trial of civil action or proceeding

(a) The clerk shall retain in his or her custody any exhibit, deposition, or administrative record introduced in the trial of a civil action or proceeding or filed in the action or proceeding until the final determination thereof or the dismissal of the action or proceeding, except that the court may order the exhibit, deposition, or administrative record returned to the respective party or parties at any time upon oral stipulation in open court or by written stipulation by the parties or for good cause shown.

(b) No exhibit or deposition shall be ordered destroyed or otherwise disposed of pursuant to this section where a party to the action or proceeding files a written notice with the court requesting the preservation of any exhibit, deposition, or administrative record for a stated time, but not to exceed one year.

(c) Upon the conclusion of the trial of a civil action or proceeding at which any exhibit or deposition has been introduced, the court shall order that the exhibit or deposition be destroyed or otherwise disposed of by the clerk. The operative destruction or disposition date shall be 60 days following final determination of the action or proceeding. Final determination includes final determination on appeal. Written notice of the order shall be sent by first-class mail to the parties by the clerk.

(d) Upon the conclusion of any posttrial hearing at which any exhibit, deposition, or administrative record has been introduced, the court shall order that the exhibit or deposition be destroyed or otherwise disposed of by the clerk. The operative date of destruction or disposition shall be 60 days following the conclusion of the hearing, or if an appeal is taken, upon final determination of the appeal. Written notice of the order shall be sent by first-class mail to the parties by the clerk.

Ca. Civ. Proc. Code § 1952
Amended by Stats. 1991, Ch. 1090, Sec. 7.

Section 1952.2 - Return of exhibits, depositions and administrative records

Notwithstanding any other provisions of law, upon a judgment becoming final, at the expiration of the appeal period, unless an appeal is pending, the court, in its discretion, and on its own motion by a written order signed by the judge, filed in the action, and an entry thereof made in the register of actions, may order the clerk to return all of the exhibits, depositions, and administrative records introduced or filed in the trial of a civil action or proceeding to the attorneys for the parties introducing or filing the same.

Ca. Civ. Proc. Code § 1952.2
Amended by Stats. 1991, Ch. 1090, Sec. 8.

Section 1952.3 - Destruction of exhibit, deposition or administrative record

Notwithstanding any other provision of the law, the court, on its own motion, may order the destruction or other disposition of any exhibit, deposition, or administrative record introduced in the trial or posttrial hearing of a civil action or proceeding or filed in the action or proceeding that, if appeal has not been taken from the decision of the court in the action or proceeding, remains in the custody of the court or clerk five years after time for appeal has expired, or, if appeal has been taken, remains in the custody of the court or clerk five years after final determination thereof, or that remains in the custody of the court or clerk for a period of five years after any of the following:

(a) A motion for a new trial has been granted and a memorandum to set the case for trial has not been filed, or a motion to set for trial has not been made within five years.

(b) The dismissal of the action or proceeding. In addition, the court on its own motion, may order the destruction or other disposition of any exhibit, deposition, or administrative record that remains in the custody of the court or clerk for a period of 10 years after the introduction or filing of the action or proceeding if, in the discretion of the court, the exhibit, deposition, or administrative record should be disposed of or destroyed.

The order shall be entered in the register of actions of each case in which the order is made.

No exhibit, deposition, or administrative record shall be ordered destroyed or otherwise disposed of pursuant to this section if a party to the action or proceeding files a written notice with the court requesting the preservation of any exhibit, deposition, or administrative record for a stated time, but not to exceed one year. Any sealed file shall be retained for at least two years after the date on which destruction would otherwise be authorized pursuant to this section.

Ca. Civ. Proc. Code § 1952.3
Amended by Stats. 1991, Ch. 1090, Sec. 9.

Article 4 - RECORDS DESTROYED IN FIRE OR CALAMITY

Section 1953 - Record includes
As used in this article "record" includes all or any part of any judgment, decree, order, document, paper, process, or file.
Ca. Civ. Proc. Code § 1953
Added by Stats. 1953, Ch. 52.

Section 1953.01 - Application for order authorizing record be supplied by copy of original
Whenever in any action or special proceeding, civil or criminal, in any court of this State any record is lost, injured, or destroyed by reason of conflagration or other public calamity, any person interested therein may apply by a duly verified petition in writing to the court for an order authorizing such defect to be supplied by a duly certified copy of the original, where such copy can be obtained.
Ca. Civ. Proc. Code § 1953.01
Added by Stats. 1953, Ch. 52.

Section 1953.02 - Court order that copy of record have same effect as original
Upon notice given pursuant to Sections 1010 to 1020, inclusive, of this code, and its being shown to the satisfaction of the court that the record has been so lost, injured, or destroyed, the court shall make an order that the certified copy shall thereafter have the same

effect in all respects as the original would have had.

Ca. Civ. Proc. Code § 1953.02
Added by Stats. 1953, Ch. 52.

Section 1953.03 - Application that copy of record cannot be obtained and unless supplied or remedied damage to applicant may result

Whenever in any action or special proceeding, civil or criminal, in any court of this State any record is lost, injured, or destroyed by reason of conflagration or other public calamity, and a certified copy of the original cannot be supplied, any person interested therein may make written application to the court, verified by affidavit, showing such loss, injury, or destruction, and that a certified copy of the record cannot be obtained by the person making the application, and that such loss, injury, or destruction occurred by conflagration, or other calamity, without the fault or neglect of the person making the application, and that such loss, injury, or destruction, unless supplied or remedied may result in damage to the person making the application. Thereupon the court shall cause notice of the application to be given pursuant to Sections 1010 to 1020, inclusive, of this code.

Ca. Civ. Proc. Code § 1953.03
Added by Stats. 1953, Ch. 52.

Section 1953.04 - Order reciting substance of lost, injured or destroyed record

Upon the hearing if the court is satisfied that the statements contained in the written application are true, it shall make an order reciting the substance and effect of the lost, injured, or destroyed record. The order shall have the same effect that the original would have had if it had not been lost, injured, or destroyed, so far as concerns the person making the application, and the persons who have been notified, pursuant to Section 1953.03.

Ca. Civ. Proc. Code § 1953.04
Added by Stats. 1953, Ch. 52.

Section 1953.05 - Restored record in proceeding in rem

The record in all cases where the proceeding is in rem, including probate, guardianship, conservatorship, and insolvency proceedings, may be supplied in like manner upon like notice to all persons who have appeared therein, and upon notice by publication or postings for not less than 10 days, as the court may order, to all persons who have not appeared. When restored the record shall have the same effect as the original upon all persons who have been personally served with notice of the application, and as to all other persons it shall be prima facie evidence of the contents of the original.

Ca. Civ. Proc. Code § 1953.05
Amended by Stats. 1979, Ch. 730.

Section 1953.06 - Certified copy of transcript of record filed in reviewing court

If an appeal to a reviewing court has been taken in any action or special proceeding in any trial court in which the record has been subsequently lost or destroyed by conflagration or other public calamity and a transcript of such record has been filed in the reviewing court, any person interested in the action or special proceeding may obtain a certified copy of all or any portion of the transcript from the clerk of the reviewing court and may file such certified copy in the office of the clerk of the court from which the appeal was taken. Thereupon the certified copy may be made the basis of any further proceedings or processes in the trial court in such action or special proceeding to all intents and purposes as if the original record were on file.

Ca. Civ. Proc. Code § 1953.06
Amended by Stats. 1967, Ch. 17.

Article 4.5 - PRIVATE RECORDS DESTROYED IN DISASTER OR CALAMITY

Section 1953.10 - Application for order establishing record

Any person, corporation, copartnership, organization, institution, business, member of profession or calling interested in establishing the existence, substance, genuineness, or authenticity of any memorandum, book, map, chart, manuscript, writing, account, entry, record, print, document, representation, or combination thereof that has been damaged, rendered wholly or partially illegible, destroyed in whole or in part or lost by explosion, conflagration, earthquake, disaster or other public calamity, may apply by duly verified petition to the court for an order establishing, reciting, or declaring the existence, substance, genuineness or authenticity of the same.

Ca. Civ. Proc. Code § 1953.10
Added by Stats. 1961, Ch. 1311.

Section 1953.11 - Notice of petition and hearing
Notice of the filing of the petition and of the time and place of the hearing thereof shall be given to such persons, if any, as the court shall designate by its order. Such order shall specify how such notice shall be given and may be by publication, posting, personal service or otherwise as the court shall direct. Upon the hearing of the petition proof shall be submitted to the court that notice has been given as prescribed in such order.

Ca. Civ. Proc. Code § 1953.11
Added by Stats. 1961, Ch. 1311.

Section 1953.12 - Order reciting existence of record
Upon the hearing the court shall receive such evidence as may be required and if the court is satisfied that the statements contained in the petition are true, it shall make an order reciting the existence, substance, genuineness or authenticity of the destroyed or lost memorandum, book, map, chart, manuscript, writing, account, entry, print, document, representation or combination thereof.

Ca. Civ. Proc. Code § 1953.12
Added by Stats. 1961, Ch. 1311.

Section 1953.13 - Order deemed in lieu of original and of same effect as original
The order of court made upon such hearing shall refer to the

memorandum, book, map, chart, manuscript, writing, account, entry, record, print, document, representation or combination thereof which is the subject of said petition and such court order shall be deemed in lieu of the original and have the same effect as if the original had not been damaged, destroyed or otherwise rendered wholly or partially illegible.

Ca. Civ. Proc. Code § 1953.13
Added by Stats. 1961, Ch. 1311.

Chapter 6 - INDISPENSABLE EVIDENCE

Section 1971 - Creating, granting, assigning, surrendering or declaring estate or interest in real property

No estate or interest in real property, other than for leases for a term not exceeding one year, nor any power over or concerning it, or in any manner relating thereto, can be created, granted, assigned, surrendered, or declared, otherwise than by operation of law, or a conveyance or other instrument in writing, subscribed by the party creating, granting, assigning, surrendering, or declaring the same, or by the party's lawful agent thereunto authorized by writing.

Ca. Civ. Proc. Code § 1971
Amended by Stats. 1986, Ch. 820, Sec. 19. Operative July 1, 1987, by Sec. 43 of Ch. 820.

Section 1972 - Power to compel specific performance; trust not prevented from arising or being extinguished

(a) Section 1971 shall not be construed to abridge the power of any court to compel the specific performance of an agreement, in case of part performance thereof.

(b) Section 1971 does not affect the creation of a trust under Division 9 (commencing with Section 15000) of the Probate Code nor prevent any trust from arising or being extinguished by implication or operation of law.

Ca. Civ. Proc. Code § 1972
Amended by Stats. 1986, Ch. 820, Sec. 20. Operative July 1, 1987, by Sec. 43 of Ch. 820.

Section 1974 - Charging person upon representation as to credit of third person

No evidence is admissible to charge a person upon a representation as to the credit of a third person, unless such representation, or some memorandum thereof, be in writing, and either subscribed by or in the handwriting of the party to be charged. This section is a Statute of Frauds provision and is to be applied in a manner that is consistent with the manner in which subdivision 2 of Section 1624 of the Civil Code is applied.

Ca. Civ. Proc. Code § 1974

Amended by Stats. 1970, Ch. 720.

Title 3 - OF THE PRODUCTION OF EVIDENCE

Chapter 2 - MEANS OF PRODUCTION

Section 1985 - Subpoenas or subpoenas duces tecum

(a) The process by which the attendance of a witness is required is the subpoena. It is a writ or order directed to a person and requiring the person's attendance at a particular time and place to testify as a witness. It may also require a witness to bring any books, documents, electronically stored information, or other things under the witness's control which the witness is bound by law to produce in evidence. When a county recorder is using the microfilm system for recording, and a witness is subpoenaed to present a record, the witness shall be deemed to have complied with the subpoena if the witness produces a certified copy thereof.

(b) A copy of an affidavit shall be served with a subpoena duces tecum issued before trial, showing good cause for the production of the matters and things described in the subpoena, specifying the exact matters or things desired to be produced, setting forth in full detail the materiality thereof to the issues involved in the case, and stating that the witness has the desired matters or things in his or her possession or under his or her control.

(c) The clerk, or a judge, shall issue a subpoena or subpoena duces tecum signed and sealed but otherwise in blank to a party requesting it, who shall fill it in before service. An attorney at law who is the attorney of record in an action or proceeding, may sign and issue a subpoena to require attendance before the court in which the action or proceeding is pending or at the trial of an issue therein, or upon the taking of a deposition in an action or proceeding pending therein; the subpoena in such a case need not be sealed. An attorney at law who is the attorney of record in an action or proceeding, may sign and issue a subpoena duces tecum to require production of the matters or things described in the subpoena.

Ca. Civ. Proc. Code § 1985
Amended by Stats 2012 ch 72 (SB 1574),s 1, eff. 1/1/2013.

Section 1985.1 - Agreement to appear at time other than time specified in subpoena; failure to appear pursuant to agreement

Any person who is subpoenaed to appear at a session of court, or at the trial of an issue therein, may, in lieu of appearance at the time specified in the subpoena, agree with the party at whose request the subpoena was issued to appear at another time or upon such notice as may be agreed upon. Any failure to appear pursuant to such agreement may be punished as a contempt by the court issuing the subpoena. The facts establishing or disproving such agreement and the failure to appear may be proved by an affidavit of any person having personal knowledge of the facts.

Ca. Civ. Proc. Code § 1985.1
Added by Stats. 1969, Ch. 140.

Section 1985.2 - Notice contained in subpoena requiring attendance of witness

Any subpoena which requires the attendance of a witness at any civil trial shall contain the following notice in a type face designed to call attention to the notice:

Contact the attorney requesting this subpoena, listed above, before the date on which you are required to be in court, if you have any question about the time or date for you to appear, or if you want to be certain that your presence in court is required.

Ca. Civ. Proc. Code § 1985.2
Added by Stats. 1978, Ch. 431.

Section 1985.3 - Service on consumer whose records are being sought

(a) For purposes of this section, the following definitions apply:

(1) "Personal records" means the original, any copy of books, documents, other writings, or electronically stored information pertaining to a consumer and which are maintained by any "witness" which is a physician, dentist, ophthalmologist, optometrist, chiropractor, physical therapist, acupuncturist, podiatrist, veterinarian, veterinary hospital, veterinary clinic, pharmacist, pharmacy, hospital, medical center, clinic, radiology or MRI center, clinical or diagnostic laboratory, state or national bank, state or federal association (as defined in Section 5102 of the Financial Code), state or federal credit union, trust company, anyone authorized by this state to make or arrange loans that are secured by real property, security brokerage firm, insurance company, title insurance company, underwritten title company, escrow agent licensed pursuant to Division 6 (commencing with Section 17000) of the Financial Code or exempt from licensure pursuant to Section 17006 of the Financial Code, attorney, accountant, institution of the Farm Credit System, as specified in Section 2002 of Title 12 of the United States Code, or telephone corporation which is a public utility, as defined in Section 216 of the Public Utilities Code, or psychotherapist, as defined in Section 1010 of the Evidence Code, or a private or public preschool, elementary school, secondary school, or postsecondary school as described in Section 76244 of the Education Code.

(2) "Consumer" means any individual, partnership of five or fewer persons, association, or trust which has transacted business with, or has used the services of, the witness or for whom the witness has acted as agent or fiduciary.

(3) "Subpoenaing party" means the person or persons causing a subpoena duces tecum to be issued or served in connection with any civil action or proceeding pursuant to this code, but shall not include the state or local agencies described in Section 7465 of the Government Code, or any entity provided for under Article VI of the California Constitution in any proceeding maintained before an adjudicative body of that entity pursuant to Chapter 4 (commencing with Section 6000) of Division 3 of the Business and Professions Code.

(4) "Deposition officer" means a person who meets the qualifications specified in Section 2020.420.

(b) Prior to the date called for in the subpoena duces tecum for the production of personal records, the subpoenaing party shall serve or cause to be served on the consumer whose records are being sought a copy of the subpoena duces tecum, of the affidavit supporting the issuance of the subpoena, if any, and of the notice described in subdivision (e), and proof of service as indicated in paragraph (1) of subdivision (c). This service shall be made as follows:

(1) To the consumer personally, or at his or her last known address, or in accordance with Chapter 5 (commencing with Section 1010) of Title 14 of Part 3, or, if he or she is a party, to his or her attorney of record. If the consumer is a minor, service shall be made on the minor's parent, guardian, conservator, or similar fiduciary, or if one of them cannot be located with reasonable diligence, then service shall be made on any person having the care or control of the minor or with whom the minor resides or by whom the minor is employed, and on the minor if the minor is at least 12 years of age.

(2) Not less than 10 days prior to the date for production specified in the subpoena duces tecum, plus the additional time provided by Section 1013 if service is by mail.

(3) At least five days prior to service upon the custodian of the records, plus the additional time provided by Section 1013 if service is by mail.

(c) Prior to the production of the records, the subpoenaing party shall do either of the following:

(1) Serve or cause to be served upon the witness a proof of personal service or of service by mail attesting to compliance with subdivision (b).

(2) Furnish the witness a written authorization to release the records signed by the consumer or by his or her attorney of record. The witness may presume that any attorney purporting to sign the authorization on behalf of the consumer acted with the consent of the consumer, and that any objection to release of records is waived.

(d) A subpoena duces tecum for the production of personal records shall be served in sufficient time to allow the witness a reasonable time, as provided in Section 2020.410, to locate and produce the records or copies thereof.

(e) Every copy of the subpoena duces tecum and affidavit, if any, served on a consumer or his or her attorney in accordance with subdivision (b) shall be accompanied by a notice, in a typeface designed to call attention to the notice, indicating that (1) records about the consumer are being sought from the witness named on the subpoena; (2) if the consumer objects to the witness furnishing the records to the party seeking the records, the consumer must file papers with the court or serve a written objection as provided in subdivision (g) prior to the date specified for production on the subpoena; and (3) if the party who is seeking the records will not agree in writing to cancel or limit the subpoena, an attorney should be consulted about the consumer's interest in protecting his or her rights of privacy. If a notice of taking of deposition is also served, that other notice may be set forth in a single document with the notice required by this subdivision.

(f) A subpoena duces tecum for personal records maintained by a telephone corporation which is a public utility, as defined in Section 216 of the Public Utilities Code, shall not be valid or effective unless it includes a consent to release, signed by the consumer whose records are requested, as required by Section 2891 of the Public Utilities Code.

(g) Any consumer whose personal records are sought by a

subpoena duces tecum and who is a party to the civil action in which this subpoena duces tecum is served may, prior to the date for production, bring a motion under Section 1987.1 to quash or modify the subpoena duces tecum. Notice of the bringing of that motion shall be given to the witness and deposition officer at least five days prior to production. The failure to provide notice to the deposition officer shall not invalidate the motion to quash or modify the subpoena duces tecum but may be raised by the deposition officer as an affirmative defense in any action for liability for improper release of records. Any other consumer or nonparty whose personal records are sought by a subpoena duces tecum may, prior to the date of production, serve on the subpoenaing party, the witness, and the deposition officer, a written objection that cites the specific grounds on which production of the personal records should be prohibited.

No witness or deposition officer shall be required to produce personal records after receipt of notice that the motion has been brought by a consumer, or after receipt of a written objection from a nonparty consumer, except upon order of the court in which the action is pending or by agreement of the parties, witnesses, and consumers affected.

The party requesting a consumer's personal records may bring a motion under Section 1987.1 to enforce the subpoena within 20 days of service of the written objection. The motion shall be accompanied by a declaration showing a reasonable and good faith attempt at informal resolution of the dispute between the party requesting the personal records and the consumer or the consumer's attorney.

(h) Upon good cause shown and provided that the rights of witnesses and consumers are preserved, a subpoenaing party shall be entitled to obtain an order shortening the time for service of a subpoena duces tecum or waiving the requirements of subdivision (b) where due diligence by the subpoenaing party has been shown. **(i)** Nothing contained in this section shall be construed to apply to any subpoena duces tecum which does not request the records of any particular consumer or consumers and which requires a custodian of records to delete all information which would in any way identify any consumer whose records are to be produced.

(j) This section shall not apply to proceedings conducted under Division 1 (commencing with Section 50), Division 4 (commencing with Section 3200), Division 4.5 (commencing with Section 6100), or Division 4.7 (commencing with Section 6200), of the Labor Code.

(k) Failure to comply with this section shall be sufficient basis for the witness to refuse to produce the personal records sought by a subpoena duces tecum.

(l) If the subpoenaing party is the consumer, and the consumer is the only subject of the subpoenaed records, notice to the consumer, and delivery of the other documents specified in subdivision (b) to the consumer, is not required under this section.

Ca. Civ. Proc. Code § 1985.3

Amended by Stats 2012 ch 72 (SB 1574),s 2, eff. 1/1/2013.
Amended by Stats 2005 ch 300 (AB 496),s 6, eff. 1/1/2006
Amended by Stats 2004 ch 182 (AB 3081),s 18, eff. 1/1/2005
Amended September 21, 1999 (Bill Number: AB 794) (Chapter 444).

Section 1985.4 - Procedure applicable to records containing personal information

The procedures set forth in Section 1985.3 are applicable to a subpoena duces tecum for records containing "personal information," as defined in Section 1798.3 of the Civil Code that are otherwise exempt from public disclosure under a provision listed in Section 7920.505 of the Government Code that are maintained by a state or local agency as defined in Section 7920.510 or 7920.540 of the Government Code. For the purposes of this section, "witness" means a state or local agency as defined in Section 7920.510 or 7920.540 of the Government Code and "consumer" means any employee of any state or local agency as defined in Section 7920.510 or 7920.540 of the Government Code, or any other natural person. Nothing in this section shall pertain to personnel records as defined in Section 832.8 of the Penal Code.

Ca. Civ. Proc. Code § 1985.4

Amended by Stats 2021 ch 615 (AB 474),s 57, eff. 1/1/2022, op.

1/1/2023.
Amended by Stats. 1988, Ch. 441, Sec. 1.

Section 1985.5 - Subpoena requiring attendance before officer or commissioner out of court

If a subpena requires the attendance of a witness before an officer or commissioner out of court, it shall, for a refusal to be sworn, or to answer as a witness, or to subscribe an affidavit or deposition when required, also require the witness to attend a session of the court issuing the subpena at a time and place thereof to be fixed by said officer or commissioner.

Ca. Civ. Proc. Code § 1985.5
Added by Stats. 1941, Ch. 405.

Section 1985.6 - Service on employee whose records are being sought

(a) For purposes of this section, the following terms have the following meanings:

(1) "Deposition officer" means a person who meets the qualifications specified in Section 2020.420.

(2) "Employee" means any individual who is or has been employed by a witness subject to a subpoena duces tecum. "Employee" also means any individual who is or has been represented by a labor organization that is a witness subject to a subpoena duces tecum.

(3) "Employment records" means the original or any copy of books, documents, other writings, or electronically stored information pertaining to the employment of any employee maintained by the current or former employer of the employee, or by any labor organization that has represented or currently represents the employee.

(4) "Labor organization" has the meaning set forth in Section

1117 of the Labor Code.

(5) "Subpoenaing party" means the person or persons causing a subpoena duces tecum to be issued or served in connection with any civil action or proceeding, but does not include the state or local agencies described in Section 7465 of the Government Code, or any entity provided for under Article VI of the California Constitution in any proceeding maintained before an adjudicative body of that entity pursuant to Chapter 4 (commencing with Section 6000) of Division 3 of the Business and Professions Code.

(b) Prior to the date called for in the subpoena duces tecum of the production of employment records, the subpoenaing party shall serve or cause to be served on the employee whose records are being sought a copy of: the subpoena duces tecum; the affidavit supporting the issuance of the subpoena, if any; the notice described in subdivision (e); and proof of service as provided in paragraph (1) of subdivision (c). This service shall be made as follows:

(1) To the employee personally, or at his or her last known address, or in accordance with Chapter 5 (commencing with Section 1010) of Title 14 of Part 2, or, if he or she is a party, to his or her attorney of record. If the employee is a minor, service shall be made on the minor's parent, guardian, conservator, or similar fiduciary, or if one of them cannot be located with reasonable diligence, then service shall be made on any person having the care or control of the minor, or with whom the minor resides, and on the minor if the minor is at least 12 years of age.

(2) Not less than 10 days prior to the date for production specified in the subpoena duces tecum, plus the additional time provided by Section 1013 if service is by mail.

(3) At least five days prior to service upon the custodian of the employment records, plus the additional time provided by Section 1013 if service is by mail.

(c) Prior to the production of the records, the subpoenaing party shall either:

(1) Serve or cause to be served upon the witness a proof of personal service or of service by mail attesting to compliance with subdivision (b).

(2) Furnish the witness a written authorization to release the records signed by the employee or by his or her attorney of record. The witness may presume that the attorney purporting to sign the authorization on behalf of the employee acted with the consent of the employee, and that any objection to the release of records is waived.

(d) A subpoena duces tecum for the production of employment records shall be served in sufficient time to allow the witness a reasonable time, as provided in Section 2020.410, to locate and produce the records or copies thereof.

(e) Every copy of the subpoena duces tecum and affidavit served on an employee or his or her attorney in accordance with subdivision (b) shall be accompanied by a notice, in a typeface designed to call attention to the notice, indicating that (1) employment records about the employee are being sought from the witness named on the subpoena; (2) the employment records may be protected by a right of privacy; (3) if the employee objects to the witness furnishing the records to the party seeking the records, the employee shall file papers with the court prior to the date specified for production on the subpoena; and (4) if the subpoenaing party does not agree in writing to cancel or limit the subpoena, an attorney should be consulted about the employee's interest in protecting his or her rights of privacy. If a notice of taking of deposition is also served, that other notice may be set forth in a single document with the notice required by this subdivision.

(f)

(1) Any employee whose employment records are sought by a subpoena duces tecum may, prior to the date for production, bring a motion under Section 1987.1 to quash or modify the subpoena duces tecum. Notice of the bringing of that motion shall be given to the witness and the deposition officer at least five days prior to production. The failure to provide notice to the deposition officer does not invalidate the motion to quash or modify the subpoena duces tecum but may be raised by the deposition officer as an affirmative defense in any action for liability for improper release of records.

(2) Any nonparty employee whose employment records are sought by a subpoena duces tecum may, prior to the date of production, serve on the subpoenaing party, the deposition officer, and the witness a written objection that cites the specific grounds on which production of the employment records should be prohibited.

(3) No witness or deposition officer shall be required to produce employment records after receipt of notice that the motion has been brought by an employee, or after receipt of a written objection from a nonparty employee, except upon order of the court in which the action is pending or by agreement of the parties, witnesses, and employees affected.

(4) The party requesting an employee's employment records may bring a motion under subdivision (c) of Section 1987 to enforce the subpoena within 20 days of service of the written objection. The motion shall be accompanied by a declaration showing a reasonable and good faith attempt at informal resolution of the dispute between the party requesting the employment records and the employee or the employee's attorney.

(g) Upon good cause shown and provided that the rights of witnesses and employees are preserved, a subpoenaing party shall be entitled to obtain an order shortening the time for service of a subpoena duces tecum or waiving the requirements of subdivision (b) if due diligence by the subpoenaing party has been shown.

(h) This section may not be construed to apply to any subpoena duces tecum that does not request the records of any particular employee or employees and that requires a custodian of records to delete all information that would in any way identify any employee whose records are to be produced.

(i) This section does not apply to proceedings conducted under Division 1 (commencing with Section 50), Division 4 (commencing with Section 3200), Division 4.5 (commencing with Section 6100), or Division 4.7 (commencing with Section 6200), of the Labor Code.

(j) Failure to comply with this section shall be sufficient basis for the witness to refuse to produce the employment records sought by subpoena duces tecum.

(k) If the subpoenaing party is the employee, and the employee is the only subject of the subpoenaed records, notice to the employee, and delivery of the other documents specified in subdivision (b) to the employee, are not required under this section.

Ca. Civ. Proc. Code § 1985.6
Amended by Stats 2012 ch 72 (SB 1574),s 3, eff. 1/1/2013.
Amended by Stats 2006 ch 538 (SB 1852),s 76, eff. 1/1/2007.
Amended by Stats 2005 ch 300 (AB 496),s 7.5, eff. 1/1/2006
Amended by Stats 2005 ch 294 (AB 333),s 5, eff. 1/1/2006
Amended by Stats 2004 ch 101 (SB 1465), s 1, eff. 7/1/2005.
Amended September 21, 1999 (Bill Number: AB 794) (Chapter 444).

Section 1985.7 - Order to show cause why medical provider's records should not be produced

When a medical provider fails to comply with Section 1158 of the Evidence Code, in addition to any other available remedy, the demanding party may apply to the court for an order to show cause why the records should not be produced.

Any order to show cause issued pursuant to this section shall be served upon respondent in the same manner as a summons. It shall be returnable no sooner than 20 days after issuance unless ordered otherwise upon a showing of substantial hardship. The court shall impose monetary sanctions pursuant to Section 1158 of the Evidence Code unless it finds that the person subject to the sanction acted with substantial justification or that other circumstances make the imposition of the sanction unjust.

Ca. Civ. Proc. Code § 1985.7
Added by Stats. 1996, Ch. 1159, Sec. 12. Effective January 1, 1997.

Section 1985.8 - Production of electronically stored information

(a)

(1) A subpoena in a civil proceeding may require that electronically stored information, as defined in Section 2016.020, be produced and that the party serving the subpoena, or someone acting on the party's request, be permitted to inspect, copy, test, or sample the information.

(2) Any subpoena seeking electronically stored information shall comply with the requirements of this chapter.

(b) A party serving a subpoena requiring production of electronically stored information may specify the form or forms in which each type of information is to be produced.

(c) If a person responding to a subpoena for production of electronically stored information objects to the specified form or forms for producing the information, the subpoenaed person may provide an objection stating the form or forms in which it intends to produce each type of information.

(d) Unless the subpoenaing party and the subpoenaed person otherwise agree or the court otherwise orders, the following shall apply:

(1) If a subpoena requiring production of electronically stored information does not specify a form or forms for producing a type of electronically stored information, the person subpoenaed shall produce the information in the form or forms in which it is ordinarily maintained or in a form that is reasonably usable.

(2) A subpoenaed person need not produce the same electronically stored information in more than one form.

(e) The subpoenaed person opposing the production, inspection, copying, testing, or sampling of electronically stored information on the basis that information is from a source that is not reasonably accessible because of undue burden or expense shall bear the burden of demonstrating that the information is from a source that is not reasonably accessible because of undue burden or expense.

(f) If the person from whom discovery of electronically stored information is subpoenaed establishes that the information is from a source that is not reasonably accessible because of undue burden or expense, the court may nonetheless order discovery if the subpoenaing party shows good cause, subject to any limitations imposed under subdivision (i).

(g) If the court finds good cause for the production of electronically stored information from a source that is not reasonably accessible, the court may set conditions for the discovery of the electronically stored information, including allocation of the expense of discovery.

(h) If necessary, the subpoenaed person, at the reasonable expense of the subpoenaing party, shall, through detection devices, translate any data compilations included in the subpoena into a reasonably usable form.

(i) The court shall limit the frequency or extent of discovery of electronically stored information, even from a source that is reasonably accessible, if the court determines that any of the following conditions exists:

(1) It is possible to obtain the information from some other source that is more convenient, less burdensome, or less expensive.

(2) The discovery sought is unreasonably cumulative or duplicative.

(3) The party seeking discovery has had ample opportunity by discovery in the action to obtain the information sought.

(4) The likely burden or expense of the proposed discovery outweighs the likely benefit, taking into account the amount in controversy, the resources of the parties, the importance of the issues in the litigation, and the importance of the requested discovery in resolving the issues.

(j) If a subpoenaed person notifies the subpoenaing party that electronically stored information produced pursuant to a subpoena is subject to a claim of privilege or of protection as attorney work product, as described in Section 2031.285, the provisions of Section 2031.285 shall apply.

(k) A party serving a subpoena requiring the production of electronically stored information shall take reasonable steps to avoid imposing undue burden or expense on a person subject to the subpoena.

(l) An order of the court requiring compliance with a subpoena issued under this section shall protect a person who is neither a party nor a party's officer from undue burden or expense resulting from compliance.

(m)

    (1) Absent exceptional circumstances, the court shall not impose sanctions on a subpoenaed person or any attorney of a subpoenaed person for failure to provide electronically stored information that has been lost, damaged, altered, or overwritten as the result of the routine, good faith operation of an electronic information system.

    (2) This subdivision shall not be construed to alter any obligation to preserve discoverable information.

    Ca. Civ. Proc. Code § 1985.8

Amended by Stats 2012 ch 72 (SB 1574),s 4, eff. 1/1/2013.
Added by Stats 2009 ch 5 (AB 5),s 2, eff. 6/29/2009.

Section 1986 - When subpoena obtainable
A subpoena is obtainable as follows:

(a) To require attendance before a court, or at the trial of an issue therein, or upon the taking of a deposition in an action or proceeding pending therein, it is obtainable from the clerk of the court in which the action or proceeding is pending.

(b) To require attendance before a commissioner appointed to take testimony by a court of a foreign country, or of the United States, or of any other state in the United States, or before any officer or officers empowered by the laws of the United States to take testimony, it may be obtained from the clerk of the superior court of the county in which the witness is to be examined.

(c) To require attendance out of court, in cases not provided for in subdivision (a), before a judge, justice, or other officer authorized to administer oaths or take testimony in any matter under the laws of this state, it is obtainable from the judge, justice, or other officer before whom the attendance is required. If the subpoena is to require attendance before a court, or at the trial of an issue therein, it is obtainable from the clerk, as of course, upon the application of the party desiring it. If it is obtained to require attendance before a commissioner or other officer upon the taking of a deposition, it must be obtained, as of course, from the clerk of the superior court of the county wherein the attendance is required upon the application of the party requiring it.

Ca. Civ. Proc. Code § 1986
Amended by Stats 2007 ch 263 (AB 310),s 14, eff. 1/1/2008.

Section 1986.1 - Testimony or other evidence given by journalist

(a) No testimony or other evidence given by a journalist under subpoena in a civil or criminal proceeding may be construed as a waiver of the immunity rights provided by subdivision (b) of Section 2 of Article I of the California Constitution.

(b)

(1) Because important constitutional rights of a third-party witness are adjudicated when rights under subdivision (b) of Section 2 of Article I of the California Constitution are asserted, except in circumstances that pose a clear and substantial threat to the integrity of the criminal investigation or present an imminent risk of death or serious bodily harm, a journalist who is subpoenaed in any civil or criminal proceeding shall be given at least five days' notice by the party issuing the subpoena that his or her appearance will be required.

(2) To protect against the inadvertent disclosure by a third party of information protected by Section 2 of Article I of the California Constitution, a party issuing a subpoena in any civil or criminal proceeding to a third party that seeks the records of a journalist shall, except in circumstances that pose a clear and substantial threat to the integrity of the criminal investigation or present an imminent risk of death or serious bodily harm, provide notice of the subpoena to the journalist and the publisher of the newspaper, magazine, or other publication or station operations manager of the broadcast station that employs or contracts with the journalist, as applicable, at least five days prior to issuing the subpoena. The party issuing the subpoena shall include in the notice, at a minimum, an explanation of why the requested records will be of material assistance to the party seeking them and why alternate sources of information are not sufficient to avoid the need for the subpoena.

(c) If a trial court holds a journalist in contempt of court in a criminal proceeding notwithstanding subdivision (b) of Section 2 of Article I of the California Constitution, the court shall set forth findings, either in writing or on the record, stating at a minimum, why the information will be of material assistance to the party seeking the evidence, and why alternate sources of the information are not sufficient to satisfy the defendant's right to a fair trial under the Sixth Amendment to the United States Constitution and Section 15 of Article I of the California Constitution.

(d) As used in this section, "journalist" means the persons specified in subdivision (b) of Section 2 of Article I of the California Constitution.

Ca. Civ. Proc. Code § 1986.1
Amended by Stats 2013 ch 519 (SB 558),s 1, eff. 1/1/2014.
Added by Stats 2000 ch 377 (AB 1860), s 1, eff. 1/1/2001.

Section 1986.5 - Fees and mileage of person subpoenaed and required to give deposition

Any person who is subpoenaed and required to give a deposition shall be entitled to receive the same witness fees and mileage as if the subpoena required him or her to attend and testify before a court in which the action or proceeding is pending.

Notwithstanding this requirement, the only fees owed to a witness who is required to produce business records under Section 1560 of the Evidence Code pursuant to a subpoena duces tecum, but who is not required to personally attend a deposition away from his or her place of business, shall be those prescribed in Section 1563 of the

Evidence Code.
Ca. Civ. Proc. Code § 1986.5
Amended by Stats. 1986, Ch. 603, Sec. 4.

Section 1987 - Service of subpoena

(a) Except as provided in Sections 68097.1 to 68097.8, inclusive, of the Government Code, the service of a subpoena is made by delivering a copy, or a ticket containing its substance, to the witness personally, giving or offering to the witness at the same time, if demanded by him or her, the fees to which he or she is entitled for travel to and from the place designated, and one day's attendance there. The service shall be made so as to allow the witness a reasonable time for preparation and travel to the place of attendance. The service may be made by any person. If service is to be made on a minor, service shall be made on the minor's parent, guardian, conservator, or similar fiduciary, or if one of those persons cannot be located with reasonable diligence, service shall be made on any person having the care or control of the minor or with whom the minor resides or by whom the minor is employed, and on the minor if the minor is 12 years of age or older. If the minor is alleged to come within the description of Section 300, 601, or 602 of the Welfare and Institutions Code and the minor is not in the custody of a parent or guardian, regardless of the age of the minor, service also shall be made upon the designated agent for service of process at the county child welfare department or the probation department under whose jurisdiction the minor has been placed.

(b) In the case of the production of a party to the record of any civil action or proceeding or of a person for whose immediate benefit an action or proceeding is prosecuted or defended or of anyone who is an officer, director, or managing agent of any such party or person, the service of a subpoena upon any such witness is not required if written notice requesting the witness to attend before a court, or at a trial of an issue therein, with the time and place thereof, is served upon the attorney of that party or person. The notice shall be served at least 10 days before the time required for attendance unless the court prescribes a shorter time. If entitled thereto, the witness, upon demand, shall be paid witness fees and mileage before being required to testify. The giving of the notice shall have the same effect as service of a subpoena on the witness, and the parties shall have those rights and the court may make those orders, including the imposition of sanctions, as in the case of a subpoena for attendance before the court.

(c) If the notice specified in subdivision (b) is served at least 20 days before the time required for attendance, or within any shorter period of time as the court may order, it may include a request that the party or person bring with him or her books, documents, electronically stored information, or other things. The notice shall state the exact materials or things desired and that the party or person has them in his or her possession or under his or her control. Within five days thereafter, or any other time period as the court may allow, the party or person of whom the request is made may serve written objections to the request or any part thereof, with a statement of grounds. Thereafter, upon noticed motion of the requesting party, accompanied by a showing of good cause and of materiality of the items to the issues, the court may order production of items to which objection was made, unless the objecting party or person establishes good cause for nonproduction or production under limitations or conditions. The procedure of this subdivision is alternative to the procedure provided by Sections 1985 and 1987.5 in the cases herein provided for, and no subpoena duces tecum shall be required. Subject to this subdivision, the notice provided in this subdivision shall have the same effect as is provided in subdivision (b) as to a notice for attendance of that party or person.

Ca. Civ. Proc. Code § 1987
Amended by Stats 2012 ch 72 (SB 1574),s 5, eff. 1/1/2013.
Amended by Stats 2002 ch 1008 (AB 3028),s 6, eff. 1/1/2003.

Section 1987.1 - Motion for order quashing, modifying or directing compliance with subpoena including protective orders

(a) If a subpoena requires the attendance of a witness or the production of books, documents, electronically stored information, or other things before a court, or at the trial of an issue therein, or at the taking of a deposition, the court, upon motion reasonably made by any person described in subdivision (b), or upon the court's own motion after giving counsel notice and an opportunity to be heard, may make an order quashing the subpoena entirely, modifying it, or directing compliance with it upon those terms or conditions as the court shall declare, including protective orders. In addition, the court may make any other order as may be appropriate to protect the person from unreasonable or oppressive demands, including unreasonable violations of the right of privacy of the person.

(b) The following persons may make a motion pursuant to subdivision (a):

(1) A party.

(2) A witness.

(3) A consumer described in Section 1985.3.

(4) An employee described in Section 1985.6.

(5) A person whose personally identifying information, as defined in subdivision (b) of Section 1798.79.8 of the Civil Code, is sought in connection with an underlying action involving that person's exercise of free speech rights.

(c) Nothing in this section shall require any person to move to quash, modify, or condition any subpoena duces tecum of personal records of any consumer served under paragraph (1) of subdivision (b) of Section 1985.3 or employment records of any employee served under paragraph (1) of subdivision (b) of Section 1985.6.

Ca. Civ. Proc. Code § 1987.1

Amended by Stats 2012 ch 72 (SB 1574),s 6, eff. 1/1/2013.
Amended by Stats 2008 ch 742 (AB 2433),s 1, eff. 1/1/2009.
Amended by Stats 2007 ch 113 (AB 1126),s 3, eff. 1/1/2008.

Section 1987.2 - Reasonable expenses in making or opposing motions

(a) Except as specified in subdivision (c), in making an order pursuant to motion made under subdivision (c) of Section 1987 or under Section 1987.1, the court may in its discretion award the amount of the reasonable expenses incurred in making or opposing the motion, including reasonable attorney's fees, if the court finds the motion was made or opposed in bad faith or without substantial justification or that one or more of the requirements of the subpoena was oppressive.

(b)

(1) Notwithstanding subdivision (a), absent exceptional circumstances, the court shall not impose sanctions on a subpoenaed person or the attorney of a subpoenaed person for failure to provide electronically stored information that has been lost, damaged, altered, or overwritten as the result of the routine, good faith operation of an electronic information system.

(2) This subdivision shall not be construed to alter any obligation to preserve discoverable information.

(c) If a motion is filed under Section 1987.1 for an order to quash or modify a subpoena from a court of this state for personally identifying information, as defined in subdivision (b) of Section 1798.79.8 of the Civil Code, for use in an action pending in another state, territory, or district of the United States, or in a foreign nation, and that subpoena has been served on any Internet service provider, or on the provider of any other interactive computer service, as defined in Section 230(f)(2) of Title 47 of the United States Code, if the moving party prevails, and if the underlying action arises from the moving party's exercise of free speech rights on the Internet and the respondent has failed to make a prima facie showing of a cause of action, the court shall award the amount of the reasonable expenses incurred in making the motion, including reasonable attorney's fees.

Ca. Civ. Proc. Code § 1987.2

Amended by Stats 2012 ch 72 (SB 1574),s 7, eff. 1/1/2013.
Amended by Stats 2008 ch 742 (AB 2433),s 2, eff. 1/1/2009.

Section 1987.3 - Subpoena served on custodian of records and personal appearance not required

When a subpoena duces tecum is served upon a custodian of records or other qualified witness as provided in Article 4 (commencing with Section 1560) of Chapter 2 of Division 11 of the Evidence Code, and his personal attendance is not required by the terms of the subpoena, Section 1989 shall not apply.

Ca. Civ. Proc. Code § 1987.3
Added by Stats. 1970, Ch. 590.

Section 1987.5 - Service of copy of affidavit upon which subpoena based

The service of a subpoena duces tecum is invalid unless at the time of such service a copy of the affidavit upon which the subpoena is based is served on the person served with the subpoena. In the case of a subpoena duces tecum which requires appearance and the production of matters and things at the taking of a deposition, the subpoena shall not be valid unless a copy of the affidavit upon which the subpoena is based and the designation of the materials to be produced, as set forth in the subpoena, is attached to the notice of taking the deposition served upon each party or its attorney as provided in Chapter 3 (commencing with Section 2002) and in Title 4 (commencing with Section 2016.010). If matters and things are produced pursuant to a subpoena duces tecum in violation of this section, any other party to the action may file a motion for, and the court may grant, an order providing appropriate relief, including, but not limited to, exclusion of the evidence affected by the violation, a retaking of the deposition notwithstanding any other limitation on discovery proceedings, or a continuance. The party causing the subpoena to be served shall retain the original affidavit until final judgment in the action, and shall file the affidavit with the court only upon reasonable request by any party or witness affected thereby. This section does not apply to deposition subpoenas commanding only the production of business records for copying under Article 4 (commencing with Section 2020.410) of Chapter 6 of Title 4.

Ca. Civ. Proc. Code § 1987.5
Amended by Stats 2004 ch 182 (AB 3081),s 20, eff. 7/1/2005

Section 1988 - Witness concealed so as to prevent service

If a witness is concealed in a building or vessel, so as to prevent the service of subpoena upon him, any Court or Judge, or any officer issuing the subpoena, may, upon proof by affidavit of the concealment, and of the materiality of the witness, make an order that the Sheriff of the county serve the subpoena; and the Sheriff must serve it accordingly, and for that purpose may break into the building or vessel where the witness is concealed.

Ca. Civ. Proc. Code § 1988
Enacted 1872.

Section 1989 - Witness not obliged to attend unless resident within state at time of service

A witness, including a witness specified in subdivision (b) of Section 1987, is not obliged to attend as a witness before any court, judge, justice or any other officer, unless the witness is a resident within the state at the time of service.

Ca. Civ. Proc. Code § 1989
Amended by Stats. 1981, Ch. 184, Sec. 3.

Section 1990 - Requiring person present in court or before judicial officer to testify

A person present in Court, or before a judicial officer, may be required to testify in the same manner as if he were in attendance upon a subpoena issued by such Court or officer.

Ca. Civ. Proc. Code § 1990
Enacted 1872.

Section 1991 - Disobedience to subpoena, refusal to be sworn or to answer as witness or to subscribe affidavit or deposition

Disobedience to a subpoena, or a refusal to be sworn, or to answer as a witness, or to subscribe an affidavit or deposition when required, may be punished as a contempt by the court issuing the subpoena.

When the subpoena, in any such case, requires the attendance of the witness before an officer or commissioner out of court, it is the duty of the officer or commissioner to report any disobedience or refusal to be sworn or to answer a question or to subscribe an affidavit or deposition when required, to the court issuing the subpoena. The witness shall not be punished for any refusal to be sworn or to answer a question or to subscribe an affidavit or deposition, unless, after a hearing upon notice, the court orders the witness to be sworn, or to so answer or subscribe and then only for disobedience to the order.

Any judge, justice, or other officer mentioned in subdivision (c) of Section 1986, may report any disobedience or refusal to be sworn or to answer a question or to subscribe an affidavit or deposition when required to the superior court of the county in which attendance was required; and the court thereupon has power, upon notice, to order the witness to perform the omitted act, and any refusal or neglect to comply with the order may be punished as a contempt of court.

In lieu of the reporting of the refusal as hereinabove provided, the party seeking to obtain the deposition or to have the deposition or affidavit signed, at the time of the refusal may request the officer or commissioner to notify the witness that at a time stated, not less than five days nor more than 20 days from the date of the refusal, he or she will report the refusal of the witness to the court and that the party will, at that time, or as soon thereafter as he or she may be heard, apply to the court for an order directing the witness to be sworn, or to answer as a witness, or subscribe the deposition or affidavit, as the case may be, and that the witness is required to attend that session of the court.

The officer or commissioner shall enter in the record of the proceedings an exact transcription of the request made of him or her that he or she notify the witness that the party will apply for an order directing the witness to be sworn or to answer as a witness or subscribe the deposition or affidavit, and of his or her notice to the witness, and the transcription shall be attached to his or her report to the court of the refusal of the witness. The report shall be filed by the officer with the clerk of the court issuing the subpoena, and the witness shall attend that session of the court, and for failure or refusal to do so may be punished for contempt.

At the time so specified by the officer, or at a subsequent time to which the court may have continued the matter, if the officer has theretofore filed a report showing the refusal of the witness, the court shall hear the matter, and without further notice to the witness, may order the witness to be sworn or to answer as a witness or subscribe the deposition or affidavit, as the case may be, and may in the order specify the time and place at which compliance shall be made or to which the taking of the deposition is continued. Thereafter if the witness refuses to comply with the order he or she may be punished for contempt.

Ca. Civ. Proc. Code § 1991
Amended by Stats. 1987, Ch. 56, Sec. 24.

Section 1991.1 - Disobedience to subpoena requiring attendance before officer out of court

Disobedience to a subpoena requiring attendance of a witness before an officer out of court in a deposition taken pursuant to Title 4 (commencing with Section 2016.010), or refusal to be sworn as a witness at that deposition, may be punished as contempt, as provided in subdivision (e) of Section 2023.030, without the necessity of a prior order of court directing compliance by the witness.

Ca. Civ. Proc. Code § 1991.1
Amended by Stats 2004 ch 182 (AB 3081),s 21, eff. 7/1/2005

Section 1991.2 - Inapplicability of section 1991 to act or omission occurring in deposition pursuant to Title 4

The provisions of Section 1991 do not apply to any act or omission occurring in a deposition taken pursuant to Title 4 (commencing with Section 2016.010). The provisions of Chapter 7 (commencing with Section 2023.010) of Title 4 are exclusively applicable.

Ca. Civ. Proc. Code § 1991.2
Amended by Stats 2005 ch 294 (AB 333),s 6, eff. 1/1/2006

Section 1992 - Amount forfeited to aggrieved party and damages for failure to appear

A person failing to appear pursuant to a subpoena or a court order also forfeits to the party aggrieved the sum of five hundred dollars ($500), and all damages that he or she may sustain by the failure of the person to appear pursuant to the subpoena or court order, which forfeiture and damages may be recovered in a civil action.

Ca. Civ. Proc. Code § 1992
Amended by Stats 2005 ch 474 (AB 1150),s 1, eff. 1/1/2006

Section 1993 - Warrant for arrest of person as alternative to warrant for contempt

(a)

(1) As an alternative to issuing a warrant for contempt pursuant to paragraph (5) or (9) of subdivision (a) of Section 1209, the court may issue a warrant for the arrest of a witness who failed to appear pursuant to a subpoena or a person who failed to appear pursuant to a court order. The court, upon proof of the service of the subpoena or order, may issue a warrant to the sheriff of the county in which the witness or person may be located and the sheriff shall, upon payment of fees as provided in Section 26744.5 of the Government Code, arrest the witness or person and bring him or her before the court.

(2) Before issuing a warrant for a failure to appear pursuant to a subpoena pursuant to this section, the court shall issue a "failure to appear" notice informing the person subject to the subpoena that a failure to appear in response to the notice may result in the issuance of a warrant. This notice requirement may be omitted only upon a showing that the appearance of the person subject to the subpoena is material to the case and that urgency dictates the person's immediate appearance.

(b) The warrant shall contain all of the following:

(1) The title and case number of the action.

(2) The name and physical description of the person to be arrested.

(3) The last known address of the person to be arrested.

(4) The date of issuance and county in which it is issued.

(5) The signature or name of the judicial officer issuing the warrant, the title of his or her office, and the name of the court.

(6) A command to arrest the person for failing to appear pursuant to the subpoena or court order, and specifying the date of service of the subpoena or court order.

(7) A command to bring the person to be arrested before the issuing court, or the nearest court if in session, for the setting of bail in the amount of the warrant or to release on the person's own recognizance. Any person so arrested shall be released from custody if he or she cannot be brought before the court within 12 hours of arrest, and the person shall not be arrested if the court will not be in session during the 12-hour period following the arrest.

(8) A statement indicating the expiration date of the warrant as determined by the court.

(9) The amount of bail.

(10) An endorsement for nighttime service if good cause is shown, as provided in Section 840 of the Penal Code.

(11) A statement indicating whether the person may be released upon a promise to appear, as provided by Section 1993.1. The court shall permit release upon a promise to appear, unless it makes a written finding that the urgency and materiality of the person's appearance in court precludes use of the promise to appear process.

(12) The date and time to appear in court if arrested and released pursuant to paragraph (11).

Ca. Civ. Proc. Code § 1993

Amended by Stats 2010 ch 680 (AB 2394),s 15, eff. 1/1/2011.

Amended by Stats 2006 ch 277 (AB 2369),s 3, eff. 1/1/2007.

Added by Stats 2005 ch 474 (AB 1150),s 3, eff. 1/1/2006.

Repealed by Stats 2005 ch 474 (AB 1150),s 2, eff. 1/1/2006.

Section 1993.1 - Release of person arrested upon promise to appear; notice to appear

(a) If authorized by the court as provided by paragraph (11) of subdivision (b) of Section 1993, the sheriff may release the person arrested upon his or her promise to appear as provided in this section.

(b) The sheriff shall prepare in duplicate a written notice to appear in court, containing the title of the case, case number, name and address of the person, the offense charged, and the time when, and place where, the person shall appear in court. In addition, the notice shall advise the person arrested of the provisions of Section 1992.

(c) The date and time specified in the notice to appear in court shall be that determined by the issuing court pursuant to paragraph (12) of subdivision (b) of Section 1993.

(d) The sheriff shall deliver one copy of the notice to appear to the arrested person, and the arrested person, in order to secure release, shall give his or her written promise to appear in court as specified in the notice by signing the duplicate notice, which shall be retained by the sheriff, and the sheriff may require the arrested person, if he or she has no satisfactory identification, to place a right thumbprint, or a left thumbprint or fingerprint if the person has a missing or disfigured right thumb, on the notice to appear. Except for law enforcement purposes relating to the identity of the arrestee, no person or entity may sell, give away, allow the distribution of, include in a database, or create a database with, this print. Upon the signing of the duplicate notice, the arresting officer shall immediately release the person arrested from custody.

(e) The sheriff shall, as soon as practicable, file the original notice with the issuing court. The notice may be electronically transmitted to the court.

(f) The person arrested shall be released unless one of the following is a reason for nonrelease, in which case the arresting officer either may release the person or shall indicate, on a form to be established by his or her employing law enforcement agency, which of the following was a reason for the nonrelease:

(1) The person arrested was so intoxicated that he or she could have been a danger to himself or herself or to others.

(2) The person arrested required medical examination or medical care or was otherwise unable to care for his or her own safety.

(3) There were one or more additional outstanding arrest warrants for the person.

(4) The person arrested demanded to be taken before a magistrate or refused to sign the notice to appear.

Ca. Civ. Proc. Code § 1993.1

Added by Stats 2005 ch 474 (AB 1150),s 4, eff. 1/1/2006.

Section 1993.2 - Failure to appear after being released on promise to appear

If a person arrested on a civil bench warrant issued pursuant to Section 1993 fails to appear after being released on a promise to appear, the court may issue another warrant to bring the person before the court or assess a civil assessment in the amount of not more than one thousand dollars ($1,000), which shall be collected as follows:

(a) The assessment shall not become effective until at least 10 calendar days after the court mails a warning notice to the person by first-class mail to the address shown on the promise to appear or to the person's last known address. If the person appears within the time specified in the notice and shows good cause for the failure to appear or for the failure to pay a fine, the court shall vacate the assessment.

(b) The assessment imposed under subdivision (a) may be enforced in the same manner as a money judgment in a limited civil case, and shall be subject to the due process requirements governing defense of actions and collection of civil money judgments generally.

Ca. Civ. Proc. Code § 1993.2
Added by Stats 2005 ch 474 (AB 1150),s 5, eff. 1/1/2006.

Section 1994 - Cause of commitment and question refused specified in warrant of commitment

Every warrant of commitment, issued by a court or officer pursuant to this chapter, shall specify therein, particularly, the cause of the commitment, and if it be for refusing to answer a question, that question shall be stated in the warrant.

Ca. Civ. Proc. Code § 1994
Amended by Stats 2005 ch 474 (AB 1150),s 6, eff. 1/1/2006

Section 1995 - Order for examination if witness confined in jail

If the witness be a prisoner, confined in a jail within this state, an order for his examination in the jail upon deposition, or for his temporary removal and production before a court or officer may be made as follows:

1.By the court itself in which the action or special proceeding is pending, unless it be a small claims court.

2.By a justice of the Supreme Court, or a judge of the superior court of the county where the action or proceeding is pending, if pending before a small claims court, or before a judge or other person out of court.

Ca. Civ. Proc. Code § 1995
Amended by Stats. 1977, Ch. 1257.

Section 1996 - Order made upon motion

Such order can only be made on the motion of a party, upon affidavit showing the nature of the action or proceeding, the testimony expected from the witness, and its materiality.

Ca. Civ. Proc. Code § 1996

Enacted 1872.

Section 1997 - Production required if witness confined in jail in county where action pending; otherwise examination upon deposition

If the witness be imprisoned in a jail in the county where the action or proceeding is pending, his production may be required. In all other cases his examination, when allowed, must be taken upon deposition.

Ca. Civ. Proc. Code § 1997

Amended by Stats. 1941, Ch. 802.

Chapter 3 - MANNER OF PRODUCTION

Article 1 - MODE OF TAKING THE TESTIMONY OF WITNESSES

Section 2002 - Three modes

The testimony of witnesses is taken in three modes:

1. By affidavit;

2. By deposition;

3. By oral examination.

Ca. Civ. Proc. Code § 2002

Enacted 1872.

Section 2003 - Affidavit

An affidavit is a written declaration under oath, made without notice to the adverse party.

Ca. Civ. Proc. Code § 2003

Enacted 1872.

Section 2004 - Deposition

A deposition is a written declaration, under oath, made upon notice to the adverse party, for the purpose of enabling him to attend and cross-examine. In all actions and proceedings where the default of the defendant has been duly entered, and in all proceedings to obtain letters of administration, or for the probate of wills and the issuance of letters testamentary thereon, where, after due and legal notice, those entitled to contest the application have failed to appear, the entry of said defaults, and the failure of said persons to appear after notice, shall be deemed to be a waiver of the right to any further notice of any application or proceeding to take testimony by deposition in such action or proceeding.

Ca. Civ. Proc. Code § 2004
Amended by Stats. 1907, Ch. 527.

Section 2005 - Oral examination

An oral examination is an examination in presence of the jury or tribunal which is to decide the fact or act upon it, the testimony being heard by the jury or tribunal from the lips of the witness.

Ca. Civ. Proc. Code § 2005
Enacted 1872.

Article 2 - AFFIDAVITS

Section 2009 - Use of affidavit

An affidavit may be used to verify a pleading or a paper in a special proceeding, to prove the service of a summons, notice, or other paper in an action or special proceeding, to obtain a provisional remedy, the examination of a witness, or a stay of proceedings, and in uncontested proceedings to establish a record of birth, or upon a motion, and in any other case expressly permitted by statute.

Ca. Civ. Proc. Code § 2009
Amended by Stats. 1965, Ch. 299.

Section 2010 - Evidence of publication given by affidavit

Evidence of the publication of a document or notice required by law, or by an order of a Court or Judge, to be published in a newspaper, may be given by the affidavit of the printer of the newspaper, or his foreman or principal clerk, annexed to a copy of the document or notice, specifying the times when, and the paper in which, the publication was made.

Ca. Civ. Proc. Code § 2010

Enacted 1872.

Section 2011 - Place of filing; prima facie evidence of facts stated

Section Two Thousand and Eleven. If such affidavit be made in an action or special proceeding pending in a Court, it may be filed with the Court or a Clerk thereof. If not so made, it may be filed with the Clerk of the county where the newspaper is printed. In either case the original affidavit, or a copy thereof, certified by the Judge of the Court or Clerk having it in custody, is prima facie evidence of the facts stated therein.

Ca. Civ. Proc. Code § 2011

Amended by Code Amendments 1873-74, Ch. 383.

Section 2012 - Taken before officer authorized to administer oaths

An affidavit to be used before any court, judge, or officer of this state may be taken before any officer authorized to administer oaths.

Ca. Civ. Proc. Code § 2012

Amended by Stats. 1907, Ch. 393.

Section 2013 - Affidavit taken in another state to be used in state

Section Two Thousand and Thirteen. An affidavit taken in another State of the United States, to be used in this State, may be taken before a Commissioner appointed by the Governor of this State to take affidavits and depositions in such other State, or before any Notary Public in another State, or before any Judge or Clerk of a Court of record having a seal.

Ca. Civ. Proc. Code § 2013
Amended by Code Amendments 1873-74, Ch. 383.

Section 2014 - Affidavit taken in foreign county to be used in state

Section Two Thousand and Fourteen. An affidavit taken in a foreign country to be used in this State, may be taken before an Embassador, Minister, Consul, Vice Consul, or Consular Agent of the United States, or before any Judge of a Court of record having a seal in such foreign country.

Ca. Civ. Proc. Code § 2014
Amended by Code Amendments 1873-74, Ch. 383.

Section 2015 - Certification required when affidavit before judge or court in another state or foreign country

When an affidavit is taken before a Judge or a Court in another State, or in a foreign country, the genuineness of the signature of the Judge, the existence of the Court, and the fact that such Judge is a member thereof, must be certified by the Clerk of the Court, under the seal thereof.

Ca. Civ. Proc. Code § 2015
Enacted 1872.

Section 2015.3 - Force and effect of certificate of sheriff, marshal or clerk of superior court

The certificate of a sheriff, marshal, or the clerk of the superior court, has the same force and effect as his or her affidavit.

Ca. Civ. Proc. Code § 2015.3
Amended by Stats 2002 ch 784 (SB 1316),s 88, eff. 1/1/2003.

Section 2015.5 - Certificate or declaration under penalty of perjury of truth and correctness of matter

Whenever, under any law of this state or under any rule, regulation, order or requirement made pursuant to the law of this state, any matter is required or permitted to be supported, evidenced, established, or proved by the sworn statement, declaration, verification, certificate, oath, or affidavit, in writing of the person making the same (other than a deposition, or an oath of office, or an oath required to be taken before a specified official other than a notary public), such matter may with like force and effect be supported, evidenced, established or proved by the unsworn statement, declaration, verification, or certificate, in writing of such person which recites that it is certified or declared by him or her to be true under penalty of perjury, is subscribed by him or her, and (1), if executed within this state, states the date and place of execution, or (2), if executed at any place, within or without this state, states the date of execution and that it is so certified or declared under the laws of the State of California. The certification or declaration may be in substantially the following form:

(a) If executed within this state: "I certify (or declare) under penalty of perjury that the foregoing is true and correct":

_____ _____(Date and Place)(Signature)

(b) If executed at any place, within or without this state: "I certify (or declare) under penalty of perjury under the laws of the State of California that the foregoing is true and correct":

_____ _____

(Date)   (Signature)

Ca. Civ. Proc. Code § 2015.5
Amended by Stats. 1980, Ch. 889, Sec. 1. Operative July 1, 1981, by Sec. 6 of Ch. 889.

Section 2015.6 - Affirmation in lieu of oath
Whenever, under any law of this State or under any rule, regulation, order or requirement made pursuant to law, an oath is required to be taken by a person appointed to discharge specific duties in a particular action, proceeding or matter, whether or not pending in court, including but not limited to a person appointed as executor, administrator, guardian, conservator, appraiser, receiver, or elisor, an unsworn written affirmation may be made and executed, in lieu of such oath. Such affirmation shall commence "I solemnly affirm,"

shall state the substance of the other matter required by the oath, the date and place of execution and shall be subscribed by him.

Ca. Civ. Proc. Code § 2015.6

Added by Stats. 1961, Ch. 1364.

Title 4 - CIVIL DISCOVERY ACT

Chapter 1 - GENERAL PROVISIONS

Section 2016.010 - Title of act

This title may be cited as the "Civil Discovery Act."

Ca. Civ. Proc. Code § 2016.010

Added by Stats 2004 ch 182 (AB 3081),s 23, eff. 7/1/2005.

Section 2016.020 - Definitions

As used in this title:

(a) "Action" includes a civil action and a special proceeding of a civil nature.

(b) "Court" means the trial court in which the action is pending, unless otherwise specified.

(c) "Document" and "writing" mean a writing, as defined in Section 250 of the Evidence Code.

(d) "Electronic" means relating to technology having electrical, digital, magnetic, wireless, optical, electromagnetic, or similar capabilities.

(e) "Electronically stored information" means information that is stored in an electronic medium.

Ca. Civ. Proc. Code § 2016.020

Amended by Stats 2009 ch 5 (AB 5),s 3, eff. 6/29/2009.

Added by Stats 2004 ch 182 (AB 3081),s 23, eff. 7/1/2005.

Section 2016.030 - Modification of procedures by stipulation

Unless the court orders otherwise, the parties may by written stipulation modify the procedures provided by this title for any method of discovery permitted under Section 2019.010.

Ca. Civ. Proc. Code § 2016.030
Added by Stats 2004 ch 182 (AB 3081),s 23, eff. 7/1/2005.

Section 2016.040 - Meet and confer declaration in support of motion

A meet and confer declaration in support of a motion shall state facts showing a reasonable and good faith attempt at an informal resolution of each issue presented by the motion.

Ca. Civ. Proc. Code § 2016.040
Added by Stats 2004 ch 182 (AB 3081),s 23, eff. 7/1/2005.

Section 2016.050 - Applicability of sections 1011 and 1013

Sections 1011 and 1013 apply to any method of discovery or service of a motion provided for in this title.

Ca. Civ. Proc. Code § 2016.050
Amended by Stats 2017 ch 64 (SB 543),s 2, eff. 1/1/2018.
Added by Stats 2004 ch 182 (AB 3081),s 23, eff. 7/1/2005.

Section 2016.060 - Last day to perform act falls on Saturday, Sunday or holiday

When the last day to perform or complete any act provided for in this title falls on a Saturday, Sunday, or holiday as specified in Section 10, the time limit is extended until the next court day closer to the trial date.

Ca. Civ. Proc. Code § 2016.060
Added by Stats 2004 ch 171 (AB 3078),s 4, eff. 7/1/2005.
Added by Stats 2004 ch 182 (AB 3081),, 23.5eff. 7/1/2005.

See Stats 2004 ch 171 (AB 3078), s 7.
See Stats 2004 ch 182 (AB 3081), s 62.

Section 2016.070 - Applicability to discovery in aid of enforcement of money judgment

This title applies to discovery in aid of enforcement of a money judgment only to the extent provided in Article 1 (commencing with Section 708.010) of Chapter 6 of Title 9 of Part 2.

Ca. Civ. Proc. Code § 2016.070
Added by Stats 2004 ch 182 (AB 3081),s 23, eff. 7/1/2005.

Section 2016.080 - Court conducted informal discovery conference; request by party; timing

(a) If an informal resolution is not reached by the parties, as described in Section 2016.040, the court may conduct an informal discovery conference upon request by a party or on the court's own motion for the purpose of discussing discovery matters in dispute between the parties.

(b) If a party requests an informal discovery conference, the party shall file a declaration described in Section 2016.040 with the court. Any party may file a response to a declaration filed pursuant to this subdivision. If a court is in session and does not grant, deny, or schedule the party's request within 10 calendar days after the initial request, the request shall be deemed denied.

(c)

(1) If a court grants or orders an informal discovery conference, the court may schedule and hold the conference no later than 30 calendar days after the court granted the request or issued its order, and before the discovery cutoff date.

(2) If an informal discovery conference is granted or ordered, the court may toll the deadline for filing a discovery motion or make any other appropriate discovery order.

(d) If an informal discovery conference is not held within 30 calendar days from the date the court granted the request, the request for an informal discovery conference shall be deemed denied, and any tolling period previously ordered by the court shall continue to apply to that action.

(e) The outcome of an informal discovery conference does not bar a party from filing a discovery motion or prejudice the disposition of a discovery motion.

(f) This section does not prevent the parties from stipulating to the timing of discovery proceedings as described in Section 2024.060.

(g) This section shall remain in effect only until January 1, 2023, and as of that date is repealed, unless a later enacted statute that is enacted before January 1, 2023, deletes or extends that date.

Ca. Civ. Proc. Code § 2016.080

Amended by Stats 2018 ch 92 (SB 1289),s 44, eff. 1/1/2019.
Added by Stats 2017 ch 189 (AB 383),s 1, eff. 1/1/2018.

Section 2016.090 - [Effective until 1/1/2027] Initial disclosures

(a) The following shall apply in a civil action unless modified by stipulation by all parties to the action:

(1) Within 60 days of a demand by any party to the action, each party that has appeared in the action, including the party that made the demand, shall provide to the other parties an initial disclosure that includes all of the following information:

(A) The names, addresses, telephone numbers, and email addresses of all persons likely to have discoverable information, along with the subjects of that information, that the disclosing party may use to support its claims or defenses, or that is relevant to the subject matter of the action or the order on any motion made in that action, unless the use would be solely for impeachment. The disclosure required by this subparagraph is not required to include persons who are expert trial witnesses or are retained as consultants who may later be designated as expert trial witnesses, as that term is described in Chapter 18 (commencing with Section 2034.010) of Title 4 of Part 4.

(B) A copy, or a description by category and location, of all documents, electronically stored information, and tangible things that the disclosing party has in its possession, custody, or control and may use to support its claims or defenses, or that is relevant to the subject matter of the action or the order on any motion made in that action, unless the use would be solely for impeachment.

(C) Any contractual agreement and any insurance policy under which an insurance company may be liable to satisfy, in whole or in part, a judgment entered in the action or to indemnify or reimburse for payments made to satisfy the judgment.

(D) Any and all contractual agreements and any and all insurance policies under which a person, as defined in Section 175 of the Evidence Code, may be liable to satisfy, in whole or in part, a judgment entered in the action or to indemnify or reimburse for payments made to satisfy the judgment. Only those provisions of an agreement that are material to the terms of the insurance, indemnification, or reimbursement are required to be included in the initial disclosure. Material provisions include, but are not limited to, the identities of parties to the agreement, the nature and limits of the coverage, and any and all documents regarding whether any insurance carrier is disputing the agreement's or policy's coverage of the claim involved in the action.

(2) A party shall make its initial disclosures based on the information then reasonably available to it. A party is not excused from making its initial disclosures because it has not fully investigated the case, because it challenges the sufficiency of another party's disclosures, or because another party has not made its disclosures.

(3)

(A) A party that has made, or responded to, a demand for an initial disclosure pursuant to paragraph (1) may propound a supplemental demand on any other party to elicit any later-acquired information bearing on all disclosures previously made by any party.

(B) A party may propound a supplemental demand twice before the initial setting of a trial date, and, subject to the time limits on discovery proceedings and motions provided in Chapter 8 (commencing with Section 2024.010) of Title 4 of Part 4, once after the initial setting of a trial date.

(C) Notwithstanding subparagraphs (A) and (B), on motion, for good cause shown, the court may grant leave to a party to propound one additional supplemental demand.

(4) A party's obligations under this section may be enforced by a court on its own motion or the motion of a party to compel disclosure.

(5) A party's disclosures under this section shall be verified either in a written declaration by the party or the party's authorized representative, or signed by the party's counsel.
(b) Notwithstanding subdivision (a), this section does not apply to the following actions:

(1) An unlawful detainer action, as defined in Section 1161.

(2) An action in the small claims division of a court, as defined in Section 116.210.

(3) An action or proceeding commenced in whole or in part under the Family Code.

(4) An action or proceeding commenced in whole or in part under the Probate Code.

(5) An action in which a party has been granted preference pursuant to Section 36.
(c) This section does not apply to any party in the action who is not represented by counsel.
(d) The changes made to this section by the act adding this subdivision apply only to civil actions filed on or after January 1, 2024.
(e) This section shall remain in effect until January 1, 2027, and as of that date is repealed.
   Ca. Civ. Proc. Code § 2016.090
Amended by Stats 2023 ch 284 (SB 235),s 1, eff. 1/1/2024.
Added by Stats 2019 ch 836 (SB 17),s 1, eff. 1/1/2020.
   This section is set out more than once due to postponed, multiple, or conflicting amendments.

Section 2016.090 - [Operative 1/1/2027] Initial disclosures
(a) The following shall apply only to a civil action upon an order of the court following stipulation by all parties to the action:

(1) Within 45 days of the order of the court, a party shall, without awaiting a discovery request, provide to the other parties an initial disclosure that includes all of the following information:

(A) The names, addresses, telephone numbers, and email addresses of all persons likely to have discoverable information, along with the subjects of that information, that the disclosing party may use to support its claims or defenses, unless the use would be solely for impeachment.

(B) A copy, or a description by category and location, of all documents, electronically stored information, and tangible things that the disclosing party has in its possession, custody, or control and may use to support its claims or defenses, unless the use would be solely for impeachment.

(C) Any agreement under which an insurance company may be liable to satisfy, in whole or in part, a judgment entered in the action or to indemnify or reimburse for payments made to satisfy the judgment.

(D) Any agreement under which a person, as defined in Section 175 of the Evidence Code, may be liable to satisfy, in whole or in part, a judgment entered in the action or to indemnify or reimburse for payments made to satisfy the judgment. Only those provisions of an agreement that are material to the terms of the insurance, indemnification, or reimbursement are required to be included in the initial disclosure. Material provisions include, but are not limited to, the identities of parties to the agreement and the nature and limits of the coverage.

(2) A party shall make its initial disclosures based on the information then reasonably available to it. A party is not excused from making its initial disclosures because it has not fully investigated the case, because it challenges the sufficiency of another party's disclosures, or because another party has not made its disclosures.

(3) A party that has made its initial disclosures, as described in paragraph (1), or that has responded to another party's discovery request, shall supplement or correct a disclosure or response in the following situations:

(A) In a timely manner if the party learns that in some material respect the disclosure or response is incomplete or incorrect and the additional or corrective information has not otherwise been made known to the other parties during the disclosure or discovery process.

(B) As ordered by the court.

(4) A party's obligations under this section may be enforced by a court on its own motion or the motion of a party to compel disclosure.

(5) A party's disclosures under this section shall be verified under penalty of perjury as being true and correct to the best of the party's knowledge.
(b) Notwithstanding subdivision (a), this section does not apply to the following actions:

(1) An unlawful detainer action, as defined in Section 1161.

(2) An action in the small claims division of a court, as defined in Section 116.210.
(c) This section shall become operative on January 1, 2027.
Ca. Civ. Proc. Code § 2016.090
Added by Stats 2023 ch 284 (SB 235),s 2, eff. 1/1/2024.
Amended by Stats 2023 ch 284 (SB 235),s 1, eff. 1/1/2024.
Added by Stats 2019 ch 836 (SB 17),s 1, eff. 1/1/2020.

Chapter 2 - SCOPE OF DISCOVERY

Article 1 - GENERAL PROVISIONS

Section 2017.010 - Generally

Unless otherwise limited by order of the court in accordance with this title, any party may obtain discovery regarding any matter, not privileged, that is relevant to the subject matter involved in the pending action or to the determination of any motion made in that action, if the matter either is itself admissible in evidence or appears reasonably calculated to lead to the discovery of admissible evidence. Discovery may relate to the claim or defense of the party seeking discovery or of any other party to the action. Discovery may be obtained of the identity and location of persons having knowledge of any discoverable matter, as well as of the existence, description, nature, custody, condition, and location of any document, electronically stored information, tangible thing, or land or other property.

Ca. Civ. Proc. Code § 2017.010
Amended by Stats 2012 ch 72 (SB 1574),s 8, eff. 1/1/2013.
Added by Stats 2004 ch 182 (AB 3081),s 23, eff. 7/1/2005.

Section 2017.020 - Limiting scope of discovery by motion for protective order

(a) The court shall limit the scope of discovery if it determines that the burden, expense, or intrusiveness of that discovery clearly outweighs the likelihood that the information sought will lead to the discovery of admissible evidence. The court may make this determination pursuant to a motion for protective order by a party or other affected person. This motion shall be accompanied by a meet and confer declaration under Section 2016.040.

(b) The court shall impose a monetary sanction under Chapter 7 (commencing with Section 2023.010) against any party, person, or attorney who unsuccessfully makes or opposes a motion for a protective order, unless it finds that the one subject to the sanction acted with substantial justification or that other circumstances make the imposition of the sanction unjust.

(c)

(1) Notwithstanding subdivision (b), or any other section of this title, absent exceptional circumstances, the court shall not impose sanctions on a party or any attorney of a party for failure to provide electronically stored information that has been lost, damaged, altered, or overwritten as the result of the routine, good faith operation of an electronic information system.

(2) This subdivision shall not be construed to alter any obligation to preserve discoverable information.

Ca. Civ. Proc. Code § 2017.020

Amended by Stats 2012 ch 72 (SB 1574),s 9, eff. 1/1/2013.

Added by Stats 2004 ch 182 (AB 3081),s 23, eff. 7/1/2005.

Article 2 - SCOPE OF DISCOVERY IN SPECIFIC CONTEXTS

Section 2017.210 - Existence and contents of agreement under which insurance carrier may be liable

A party may obtain discovery of the existence and contents of any agreement under which any insurance carrier may be liable to satisfy in whole or in part a judgment that may be entered in the action or to indemnify or reimburse for payments made to satisfy the judgment. This discovery may include the identity of the carrier and the nature and limits of the coverage. A party may also obtain discovery as to whether that insurance carrier is disputing the agreement's coverage of the claim involved in the action, but not as to the nature and substance of that dispute. Information concerning the insurance agreement is not by reason of disclosure admissible in evidence at trial.

Ca. Civ. Proc. Code § 2017.210

Added by Stats 2004 ch 182 (AB 3081),s 23, eff. 7/1/2005.

Section 2017.220 - Civil action alleging sexual harassment, sexual assault or sexual battery

(a) In any civil action alleging conduct that constitutes sexual harassment, sexual assault, or sexual battery, any party seeking discovery concerning the plaintiff's sexual conduct with individuals other than the alleged perpetrator shall establish specific facts showing that there is good cause for that discovery, and that the matter sought to be discovered is relevant to the subject matter of the action and reasonably calculated to lead to the discovery of admissible evidence. This showing shall be made by a noticed motion, accompanied by a meet and confer declaration under Section 2016.040, and shall not be made or considered by the court at an ex parte hearing.

(b) The court shall impose a monetary sanction under Chapter 7 (commencing with Section 2023.010) against any party, person, or attorney who unsuccessfully makes or opposes a motion for discovery under subdivision (a), unless it finds that the one subject to the sanction acted with substantial justification or that other circumstances make the imposition of the sanction unjust.

Ca. Civ. Proc. Code § 2017.220
Added by Stats 2004 ch 182 (AB 3081),s 23, eff. 7/1/2005.

Article 3 - VIOLATION OF THE ELDER ABUSE AND DEPENDENT ADULT CIVIL PROTECTION ACT

Section 2017.310 - Confidential settlement agreement

(a) Notwithstanding any other provision of law, it is the policy of the State of California that confidential settlement agreements are disfavored in any civil action the factual foundation for which establishes a cause of action for a violation of the Elder Abuse and Dependent Adult Civil Protection Act (Chapter 11(commencing with Section 15600) of Part 3 of Division 9 of the Welfare and Institutions Code).

(b) Provisions of a confidential settlement agreement described in subdivision (a) may not be recognized or enforced by the court absent a showing of any of the following:

(1) The information is privileged under existing law.

(2) The information is not evidence of abuse of an elder or dependent adult, as described in Sections 15610.30, 15610.57, and 15610.63 of the Welfare and Institutions Code.

(3) The party seeking to uphold the confidentiality of the information has demonstrated that there is a substantial probability that prejudice will result from the disclosure and that the party's interest in the information cannot be adequately protected through redaction.

(c) Nothing in paragraph (1), (2), or (3) of subdivision (b) permits the sealing or redacting of a defendant's name in any information made available to the public.

(d) Except as expressly provided in this section, nothing in this section is intended to alter, modify, or amend existing law.

(e) Nothing in this section may be deemed to prohibit the entry or enforcement of that part of a confidentiality agreement, settlement agreement, or stipulated agreement between the parties that requires the nondisclosure of the amount of any money paid in a settlement of a claim.

(f) Nothing in this section applies to or affects an action for professional negligence against a health care provider.

Ca. Civ. Proc. Code § 2017.310
Added by Stats 2004 ch 182 (AB 3081),s 23, eff. 7/1/2005.

Section 2017.320 - Information protected from disclosure by stipulated protective order

(a) In any civil action the factual foundation for which establishes a cause of action for a violation of the Elder Abuse and Dependent Adult Civil Protection Act (Chapter 11 (commencing with Section 15600) of Part 3 of Division 9 of the Welfare and Institutions Code), any information that is acquired through discovery and is protected from disclosure by a stipulated protective order shall remain subject to the protective order, except for information that is evidence of abuse of an elder or dependent adult as described in Sections 15610.30, 15610.57, and 15610.63 of the Welfare and Institutions Code.

(b) In that instance, after redacting information in the document that is not evidence of abuse of an elder or dependent adult as described in Sections 15610.30, 15610.57, and 15610.63 of the Welfare and Institutions Code, a party may file that particularized information with the court. The party proposing to file the information shall offer to meet and confer with the party from whom the information was obtained at least one week prior to filing that information with the court.

(c) The filing party shall give concurrent notice of the filing with the court and its basis to the party from whom the information was obtained.

(d) Any filed information submitted to the court shall remain confidential under any protective order for 30 days after the filing and shall be part of the public court record thereafter, unless an affected party petitions the court and shows good cause for a court protective order.

(e) The burden of showing good cause shall be on the party seeking the court protective order.

(f) A stipulated protective order may not be recognized or enforced by the court to prevent disclosure of information filed with the court pursuant to subdivision (b), absent a showing of any of the following:

(1) The information is privileged under existing law.

(2) The information is not evidence of abuse of an elder or dependent adult as described in Sections 15610.30, 15610.57, and 15610.63 of the Welfare and Institutions Code.

(3) The party seeking to uphold the confidentiality of the information has demonstrated that there is a substantial probability that prejudice will result from the disclosure and that the party's interest in the information cannot be adequately protected through redaction.

(g) If the court denies the petition for a court protective order, it shall redact any part of the filed information it finds is not evidence of abuse of an elder or dependent adult, as described in Sections 15610.30, 15610.57, and 15610.63 of the Welfare and Institutions Code. Nothing in this subdivision or in paragraph (1), (2), or (3) of subdivision (f) permits the sealing or redacting of a defendant's name in any information made available to the public.

(h) Nothing in this section applies to or affects an action for professional negligence against a health care provider.

Ca. Civ. Proc. Code § 2017.320

Added by Stats 2004 ch 182 (AB 3081),s 23, eff. 7/1/2005.

Chapter 3 - USE OF TECHNOLOGY IN CONDUCTING DISCOVERY IN A COMPLEX CASE

Section 2017.710 - [Repealed]

Ca. Civ. Proc. Code § 2017.710

Repealed by Stats 2012 ch 72 (SB 1574),s 10, eff. 1/1/2013.

Added by Stats 2004 ch 182 (AB 3081),s 23, eff. 7/1/2005.

Section 2017.720 - [Repealed]

Ca. Civ. Proc. Code § 2017.720

Repealed by Stats 2012 ch 72 (SB 1574),s 11, eff. 1/1/2013.

Added by Stats 2004 ch 182 (AB 3081),s 23, eff. 7/1/2005.

Section 2017.730 - [Repealed]

Ca. Civ. Proc. Code § 2017.730

Repealed by Stats 2012 ch 72 (SB 1574),s 12, eff. 1/1/2013.

Added by Stats 2004 ch 182 (AB 3081),s 23, eff. 7/1/2005.

Section 2017.740 - [Repealed]

Ca. Civ. Proc. Code § 2017.740

Repealed by Stats 2012 ch 72 (SB 1574),s 13, eff. 1/1/2013.

Added by Stats 2004 ch 182 (AB 3081),s 23, eff. 7/1/2005.

Chapter 4 - ATTORNEY WORK PRODUCT

Section 2018.010 - Client defined

For purposes of this chapter, "client" means a "client" as defined in

Section 951 of the Evidence Code.
Ca. Civ. Proc. Code § 2018.010
Added by Stats 2004 ch 182 (AB 3081),s 23, eff. 7/1/2005.

Section 2018.020 - Policy of state
It is the policy of the state to do both of the following:
(a) Preserve the rights of attorneys to prepare cases for trial with that degree of privacy necessary to encourage them to prepare their cases thoroughly and to investigate not only the favorable but the unfavorable aspects of those cases.
(b) Prevent attorneys from taking undue advantage of their adversary's industry and efforts.
Ca. Civ. Proc. Code § 2018.020
Added by Stats 2004 ch 182 (AB 3081),s 23, eff. 7/1/2005.

Section 2018.030 - Generally
(a) A writing that reflects an attorney's impressions, conclusions, opinions, or legal research or theories is not discoverable under any circumstances.
(b) The work product of an attorney, other than a writing described in subdivision (a), is not discoverable unless the court determines that denial of discovery will unfairly prejudice the party seeking discovery in preparing that party's claim or defense or will result in an injustice.
Ca. Civ. Proc. Code § 2018.030
Added by Stats 2004 ch 182 (AB 3081),s 23, eff. 7/1/2005.

Section 2018.040 - Restatement of existing law
This chapter is intended to be a restatement of existing law relating to protection of work product. It is not intended to expand or reduce the extent to which work product is discoverable under existing law in any action.
Ca. Civ. Proc. Code § 2018.040
Added by Stats 2004 ch 182 (AB 3081),s 23, eff. 7/1/2005.

Section 2018.050 - Lawyer suspected of participating in crime of fraud

Notwithstanding Section 2018.040, when a lawyer is suspected of knowingly participating in a crime or fraud, there is no protection of work product under this chapter in any official investigation by a law enforcement agency or proceeding or action brought by a public prosecutor in the name of the people of the State of California if the services of the lawyer were sought or obtained to enable or aid anyone to commit or plan to commit a crime or fraud.

Ca. Civ. Proc. Code § 2018.050
Added by Stats 2004 ch 182 (AB 3081),s 23, eff. 7/1/2005.

Section 2018.060 - In camera hearing

Nothing in this chapter is intended to limit an attorney's ability to request an in camera hearing as provided for in People v. Superior Court (Laff) (2001) 25 Cal.4th 703.

Ca. Civ. Proc. Code § 2018.060
Added by Stats 2004 ch 182 (AB 3081),s 23, eff. 7/1/2005.

Section 2018.070 - Discovery by State Bar

(a) The State Bar may discover the work product of an attorney against whom disciplinary charges are pending when it is relevant to issues of breach of duty by the lawyer and requisite client approval has been granted.

(b) Where requested and for good cause, discovery under this section shall be subject to a protective order to ensure the confidentiality of the work product except for its use by the State Bar in disciplinary investigations and its consideration under seal in State Bar Court proceedings.

(c) For purposes of this chapter, whenever a client has initiated a complaint against an attorney, the requisite client approval shall be deemed to have been granted.

Ca. Civ. Proc. Code § 2018.070
Added by Stats 2004 ch 182 (AB 3081),s 23, eff. 7/1/2005.

Section 2018.080 - Action between attorney and client or former client

In an action between an attorney and a client or a former client of the attorney, no work product privilege under this chapter exists if the work product is relevant to an issue of breach by the attorney of a duty to the client arising out of the attorney-client relationship.

Ca. Civ. Proc. Code § 2018.080

Added by Stats 2004 ch 182 (AB 3081),s 23, eff. 7/1/2005.

Chapter 5 - METHODS AND SEQUENCE OF DISCOVERY

Article 1 - GENERAL PROVISIONS

Section 2019.010 - Methods of discovery

Any party may obtain discovery by one or more of the following methods:

(a) Oral and written depositions.

(b) Interrogatories to a party.

(c) Inspections of documents, things, and places.

(d) Physical and mental examinations.

(e) Requests for admissions.

(f) Simultaneous exchanges of expert trial witness information.

Ca. Civ. Proc. Code § 2019.010

Added by Stats 2004 ch 182 (AB 3081),s 23, eff. 7/1/2005.

Section 2019.020 - Methods used in sequence

(a) Except as otherwise provided by a rule of the Judicial Council, a local court rule, or a local uniform written policy, the methods of discovery may be used in any sequence, and the fact that a party is conducting discovery, whether by deposition or another method, shall not operate to delay the discovery of any other party.

(b) Notwithstanding subdivision (a), on motion and for good cause shown, the court may establish the sequence and timing of discovery for the convenience of parties and witnesses and in the interests of justice.

Ca. Civ. Proc. Code § 2019.020
Added by Stats 2004 ch 182 (AB 3081),s 23, eff. 7/1/2005.

Section 2019.030 - Restricting frequency or extent of use of discovery

(a) The court shall restrict the frequency or extent of use of a discovery method provided in Section 2019.010 if it determines either of the following:

(1) The discovery sought is unreasonably cumulative or duplicative, or is obtainable from some other source that is more convenient, less burdensome, or less expensive.

(2) The selected method of discovery is unduly burdensome or expensive, taking into account the needs of the case, the amount in controversy, and the importance of the issues at stake in the litigation.

(b) The court may make these determinations pursuant to a motion for a protective order by a party or other affected person. This motion shall be accompanied by a meet and confer declaration under Section 2016.040.

(c) The court shall impose a monetary sanction under Chapter 7 (commencing with Section 2023.010) against any party, person, or attorney who unsuccessfully makes or opposes a motion for a protective order, unless it finds that the one subject to the sanction acted with substantial justification or that other circumstances make the imposition of the sanction unjust.

Ca. Civ. Proc. Code § 2019.030
Added by Stats 2004 ch 182 (AB 3081), 23eff. 7/1/2005.

Section 2019.040 - Electronically stored information

(a) When any method of discovery permits the production, inspection, copying, testing, or sampling of documents or tangible things, that method shall also permit the production, inspection, copying, testing, or sampling of electronically stored information.

(b) All procedures available under this title to compel, prevent, or limit the production, inspection, copying, testing, or sampling of documents or tangible things shall be available to compel, prevent, or limit the production, inspection, copying, testing, or sampling of electronically stored information.

Ca. Civ. Proc. Code § 2019.040
Added by Stats 2012 ch 72 (SB 1574),s 14, eff. 1/1/2013.

Article 2 - METHODS AND SEQUENCE OF DISCOVERY IN SPECIFIC CONTEXTS

Section 2019.210 - Action alleging misappropriation of trade secret

In any action alleging the misappropriation of a trade secret under the Uniform Trade Secrets Act (Title 5 (commencing with Section 3426) of Part 1 of Division 4 of the Civil Code), before commencing discovery relating to the trade secret, the party alleging the misappropriation shall identify the trade secret with reasonable particularity subject to any orders that may be appropriate under Section 3426.5 of the Civil Code.

Ca. Civ. Proc. Code § 2019.210
Added by Stats. 2004, Ch. 182, Sec. 23. Effective January 1, 2005. Operative July 1, 2005, by Sec. 64 of Ch. 182.

Chapter 6 - NONPARTY DISCOVERY

Article 1 - GENERAL PROVISIONS

Section 2020.010 - Methods to obtain discovery

(a) Any of the following methods may be used to obtain discovery within the state from a person who is not a party to the action in which the discovery is sought:

(1) An oral deposition under Chapter 9 (commencing with Section 2025.010).

(2) A written deposition under Chapter 11 (commencing with Section 2028.010).

(3) A deposition for production of business records and things under Article 4 (commencing with Section 2020.410) or Article 5 (commencing with Section 2020.510).

(b) Except as provided in subdivision (a) of Section 2025.280, the process by which a nonparty is required to provide discovery is a deposition subpoena.

Ca. Civ. Proc. Code § 2020.010

Added by Stats 2004 ch 182 (AB 3081),s 23, eff. 7/1/2005.

Section 2020.020 - Demand of deposition subpoena

A deposition subpoena may command any of the following:

(a) Only the attendance and the testimony of the deponent, under Article 3 (commencing with Section 2020.310).

(b) Only the production of business records for copying, under Article 4 (commencing with Section 2020.410).

(c) The attendance and the testimony of the deponent, as well as the production of business records, other documents, electronically stored information, and tangible things, under Article 5 (commencing with Section 2020.510).

Ca. Civ. Proc. Code § 2020.020

Amended by Stats 2012 ch 72 (SB 1574),s 15, eff. 1/1/2013.

Added by Stats 2004 ch 182 (AB 3081),s 23, eff. 7/1/2005.

Section 2020.030 - Provisions applicable to deposition subpoena

Except as modified in this chapter, the provisions of Chapter 2 (commencing with Section 1985) of Title 3 of Part 4 of this code, and of Article 4 (commencing with Section 1560) of Chapter 2 of Division 11 of the Evidence Code, apply to a deposition subpoena.

Ca. Civ. Proc. Code § 2020.030

Added by Stats 2004 ch 182 (AB 3081),s 23, eff. 7/1/2005.

Article 2 - PROCEDURES APPLICABLE TO ALL TYPES OF DEPOSITION SUBPOENAS

Section 2020.210 - Court-issued subpoena; attorney issued subpoena

(a) The clerk of the court in which the action is pending shall issue a deposition subpoena signed and sealed, but otherwise in blank, to a party requesting it, who shall fill it in before service.

(b) Instead of a court-issued deposition subpoena, an attorney of record for any party may sign and issue a deposition subpoena. A deposition subpoena issued under this subdivision need not be sealed. A copy may be served on the nonparty, and the attorney may retain the original.

Ca. Civ. Proc. Code § 2020.210

Added by Stats 2004 ch 182 (AB 3081),ss 23, 23 eff. 7/1/2005.

Section 2020.220 - Service of subpoena

(a) Subject to subdivision (c) of Section 2020.410, service of a deposition subpoena shall be effected a sufficient time in advance of the deposition to provide the deponent a reasonable opportunity to locate and produce any designated business records, documents, electronically stored information, and tangible things, as described in Article 4 (commencing with Section 2020.410), and, where personal attendance is commanded, a reasonable time to travel to the place of deposition.

(b) Any person may serve the subpoena by personal delivery of a copy of it as follows:

(1) If the deponent is a natural person, to that person.

(2) If the deponent is an organization, to any officer, director, custodian of records, or to any agent or employee authorized by the organization to accept service of a subpoena.

(c) Personal service of any deposition subpoena is effective to require all of the following of any deponent who is a resident of California at the time of service:

(1) Personal attendance and testimony, if the subpoena so specifies.

(2) Any specified production, inspection, testing, and sampling.

(3) The deponent's attendance at a court session to consider any issue arising out of the deponent's refusal to be sworn, or to answer any question, or to produce specified items, or to permit inspection or photocopying, if the subpoena so specifies, or specified testing and sampling of the items produced.

(d) Unless the subpoenaing party and the subpoenaed person otherwise agree or the court otherwise orders, the following shall apply:

(1) If a subpoena requiring production of electronically stored information does not specify a form or forms for producing a type of electronically stored information, the person subpoenaed shall produce the information in the form or forms in which it is ordinarily maintained or in a form that is reasonably usable.

(2) A subpoenaed person need not produce the same electronically stored information in more than one form.

(e) The subpoenaed person opposing the production, inspection, copying, testing, or sampling of electronically stored information on the basis that the information is from a source that is not reasonably accessible because of undue burden or expense shall bear the burden of demonstrating that the information is from a source that is not reasonably accessible because of undue burden or expense.

(f) If the person from whom discovery of electronically stored information is subpoenaed establishes that the information is from a source that is not reasonably accessible because of undue burden or expense, the court may nonetheless order discovery if the subpoenaing party shows good cause, subject to any limitations imposed under subdivision (i).

(g) If the court finds good cause for the production of electronically stored information from a source that is not reasonably accessible, the court may set conditions for the discovery of the electronically

stored information, including allocation of the expense of discovery.
(h) If necessary, the subpoenaed person, at the reasonable expense of the subpoenaing party, shall, through detection devices, translate any data compilations included in the subpoena into a reasonably usable form.

(i) The court shall limit the frequency or extent of discovery of electronically stored information, even from a source that is reasonably accessible, if the court determines that any of the following conditions exists:

(1) It is possible to obtain the information from some other source that is more convenient, less burdensome, or less expensive.

(2) The discovery sought is unreasonably cumulative or duplicative.

(3) The party seeking discovery has had ample opportunity by discovery in the action to obtain the information sought.

(4) The likely burden or expense of the proposed discovery outweighs the likely benefit, taking into account the amount in controversy, the resources of the parties, the importance of the issues in the litigation, and the importance of the requested discovery in resolving the issues.

(j) If a subpoenaed person notifies the subpoenaing party that electronically stored information produced pursuant to a subpoena is subject to a claim of privilege or of protection as attorney work product, as described in Section 2031.285, the provisions of Section 2031.285 shall apply.

(k) A party serving a subpoena requiring the production of electronically stored information shall take reasonable steps to avoid imposing undue burden or expense on a person subject to the subpoena.

(l) An order of the court requiring compliance with a subpoena issued under this section shall protect a person who is neither a party nor a party's officer from undue burden or expense resulting from compliance.

(m)

(1) Absent exceptional circumstances, the court shall not impose sanctions on a subpoenaed person or any attorney of a subpoenaed person for failure to provide electronically stored information that has been lost, damaged, altered, or overwritten as the result of the routine, good faith operation of an electronic information system.

(2) The subdivision shall not be construed to alter any obligation to preserve discoverable information.

Ca. Civ. Proc. Code § 2020.220

Amended by Stats 2012 ch 72 (SB 1574),s 16, eff. 1/1/2013.

Added by Stats 2004 ch 182 (AB 3081),s 23, eff. 7/1/2005.

Section 2020.230 - Witness fee and mileage if personal appearance of deponent required

(a) If a deposition subpoena requires the personal attendance of the deponent, under Article 3 (commencing with Section 2020.310) or Article 5 (commencing with Section 2020.510), the party noticing the deposition shall pay to the deponent in cash or by check the same witness fee and mileage required by Chapter 1 (commencing with Section 68070) of Title 8 of the Government Code for attendance and testimony before the court in which the action is pending. This payment, whether or not demanded by the deponent, shall be made, at the option of the party noticing the deposition, either at the time of service of the deposition subpoena, or at the time the deponent attends for the taking of testimony.

(b) Service of a deposition subpoena that does not require the personal attendance of a custodian of records or other qualified person, under Article 4 (commencing with Section 2020.410), shall be accompanied, whether or not demanded by the deponent, by a payment in cash or by check of the witness fee required by paragraph (6) of subdivision (b) of Section 1563 of the Evidence Code.

Ca. Civ. Proc. Code § 2020.230

Added by Stats 2004 ch 182 (AB 3081),s 23, eff. 7/1/2005.

Section 2020.240 - Disobedience of subpoena by deponent
A deponent who disobeys a deposition subpoena in any manner described in subdivision (c) of Section 2020.220 may be punished for contempt under Chapter 7 (commencing with Section 2023.010) without the necessity of a prior order of court directing compliance by the witness. The deponent is also subject to the forfeiture and the payment of damages set forth in Section 1992.
Ca. Civ. Proc. Code § 2020.240
Added by Stats 2004 ch 182 (AB 3081),s 23, eff. 7/1/2005.

Article 3 - SUBPOENA COMMANDING ONLY ATTENDANCE AND TESTIMONY OF THE DEPONENT

Section 2020.310 - Rules applicable
The following rules apply to a deposition subpoena that commands only the attendance and the testimony of the deponent:
(a) The subpoena shall specify the time when and the place where the deponent is commanded to attend the deposition.
(b) The subpoena shall set forth a summary of all of the following:

(1) The nature of a deposition.

(2) The rights and duties of the deponent.

(3) The penalties for disobedience of a deposition subpoena, as described in Section 2020.240.
(c) If the deposition will be recorded using audio or video technology by, or at the direction of, the noticing party under Section 2025.340, the subpoena shall state that it will be recorded in that manner.
(d) If the deposition testimony will be conducted using instant visual display, the subpoena shall state that it will be conducted in that manner.
(e) If the deponent is an organization, the subpoena shall describe with reasonable particularity the matters on which examination is requested. The subpoena shall also advise the organization of its

duty to make the designation of employees or agents who will attend the deposition, as described in Section 2025.230.

Ca. Civ. Proc. Code § 2020.310
Added by Stats 2004 ch 182 (AB 3081),s 23, eff. 7/1/2005.

Article 4 - SUBPOENA COMMANDING ONLY PRODUCTION OF BUSINESS RECORDS FOR COPYING 2020.410

Section 2020.410 - Generally

(a) A deposition subpoena that commands only the production of business records for copying shall designate the business records to be produced either by specifically describing each individual item or by reasonably particularizing each category of item, and shall specify the form in which any electronically stored information is to be produced, if a particular form is desired.

(b) Notwithstanding subdivision (a), specific information identifiable only to the deponent's records system, like a policy number or the date when a consumer interacted with the witness, is not required.

(c) A deposition subpoena that commands only the production of business records for copying need not be accompanied by an affidavit or declaration showing good cause for the production of the business records designated in it. It shall be directed to the custodian of those records or another person qualified to certify the records. It shall command compliance in accordance with Section 2020.430 on a date that is no earlier than 20 days after the issuance, or 15 days after the service, of the deposition subpoena, whichever date is later.

(d) If, under Section 1985.3 or 1985.6, the one to whom the deposition subpoena is directed is a witness, and the business records described in the deposition subpoena are personal records pertaining to a consumer, the service of the deposition subpoena shall be accompanied either by a copy of the proof of service of the notice to the consumer described in subdivision (e) of Section 1985.3, or subdivision (b) of Section 1985.6, as applicable, or by the consumer's written authorization to release personal records

described in paragraph (2) of subdivision (c) of Section 1985.3, or
paragraph (2) of subdivision (c) of Section 1985.6, as applicable.

Ca. Civ. Proc. Code § 2020.410
Amended by Stats 2012 ch 72 (SB 1574),s 17, eff. 1/1/2013.
Added by Stats 2004 ch 182 (AB 3081),s 23, eff. 7/1/2005.

Section 2020.420 - Deposition officer

The officer for a deposition seeking discovery only of business
records for copying under this article shall be a professional
photocopier registered under Chapter 20 (commencing with
Section 22450) of Division 8 of the Business and Professions Code,
or a person exempted from the registration requirements of that
chapter under Section 22451 of the Business and Professions Code.
This deposition officer shall not be financially interested in the
action, or a relative or employee of any attorney of the parties. Any
objection to the qualifications of the deposition officer is waived
unless made before the date of production or as soon thereafter as
the ground for that objection becomes known or could be
discovered by reasonable diligence.

Ca. Civ. Proc. Code § 2020.420
Added by Stats 2004 ch 182 (AB 3081),s 23, eff. 7/1/2005.

Section 2020.430 - Delivery required by custodian of records to deposition officer

(a) Except as provided in subdivision (e), if a deposition subpoena
commands only the production of business records for copying, the
custodian of the records or other qualified person shall, in person,
by messenger, or by mail, deliver both of the following only to the
deposition officer specified in the subpoena:

(1) A true, legible, and durable copy of the records.

(2) An affidavit in compliance with Section 1561 of the Evidence
Code.

(b) If the delivery required by subdivision (a) is made to the office
of the deposition officer, the records shall be enclosed, sealed, and

directed as described in subdivision (c) of Section 1560 of the Evidence Code.

(c) If the delivery required by subdivision (a) is made at the office of the business whose records are the subject of the deposition subpoena, the custodian of those records or other qualified person shall do one of the following:

(1) Permit the deposition officer specified in the deposition subpoena to make a copy of the originals of the designated business records during normal business hours, as defined in subdivision (e) of Section 1560 of the Evidence Code.

(2) Deliver to the deposition officer a true, legible, and durable copy of the records on receipt of payment in cash or by check, by or on behalf of the party serving the deposition subpoena, of the reasonable costs of preparing that copy, together with an itemized statement of the cost of preparation, as determined under subdivision (b) of Section 1563 of the Evidence Code. This copy need not be delivered in a sealed envelope.

(d) Unless the parties, and if the records are those of a consumer as defined in Section 1985.3 or 1985.6, the consumer, stipulate to an earlier date, the custodian of the records shall not deliver to the deposition officer the records that are the subject of the deposition subpoena prior to the date and time specified in the deposition subpoena. The following legend shall appear in boldface type on the deposition subpoena immediately following the date and time specified for production: "Do not release the requested records to the deposition officer prior to the date and time stated above."

(e) This section does not apply if the subpoena directs the deponent to make the records available for inspection or copying by the subpoenaing party's attorney or a representative of that attorney at the witness' business address under subdivision (e) of Section 1560 of the Evidence Code.

(f) The provisions of Section 1562 of the Evidence Code concerning the admissibility of the affidavit of the custodian or other qualified person apply to a deposition subpoena served under this article.

Ca. Civ. Proc. Code § 2020.430

Added by Stats 2004 ch 182 (AB 3081),s 23, eff. 7/1/2005.

Section 2020.440 - Copy of records provided by deposition officer

Promptly on or after the deposition date and after the receipt or the making of a copy of business records under this article, the deposition officer shall provide that copy to the party at whose instance the deposition subpoena was served, and a copy of those records to any other party to the action who then or subsequently, within a period of six months following the settlement of the case, notifies the deposition officer that the party desires to purchase a copy of those records.

Ca. Civ. Proc. Code § 2020.440
Added by Stats 2004 ch 182 (AB 3081),s 23, eff. 7/1/2005.

Article 5 - SUBPOENA COMMANDING BOTH PRODUCTION OF BUSINESS RECORDS AND ATTENDANCE AND TESTIMONY OF THE DEPONENT 2020.510

Section 2020.510 - Generally

(a) A deposition subpoena that commands the attendance and the testimony of the deponent, as well as the production of business records, documents, electronically stored information, and tangible things, shall:

(1) Comply with the requirements of Section 2020.310.

(2) Designate the business records, documents, electronically stored information, and tangible things to be produced either by specifically describing each individual item or by reasonably particularizing each category of item.

(3) Specify any testing or sampling that is being sought.

(4) Specify the form in which any electronically stored information is to be produced, if a particular form is desired.
(b) A deposition subpoena under subdivision (a) need not be accompanied by an affidavit or declaration showing good cause for

the production of the documents and things designated.

(c) If, as described in Section 1985.3, the person to whom the deposition subpoena is directed is a witness, and the business records described in the deposition subpoena are personal records pertaining to a consumer, the service of the deposition subpoena shall be accompanied either by a copy of the proof of service of the notice to the consumer described in subdivision (e) of Section 1985.3, or by the consumer's written authorization to release personal records described in paragraph (2) of subdivision (c) of Section 1985.3.

(d) If, as described in Section 1985.6, the person to whom the deposition subpoena is directed is a witness and the business records described in the deposition subpoena are employment records pertaining to an employee, the service of the deposition subpoena shall be accompanied either by a copy of the proof of service of the notice to the employee described in subdivision (e) of Section 1985.6, or by the employee's written authorization to release personal records described in paragraph (2) of subdivision (c) of Section 1985.6.

Ca. Civ. Proc. Code § 2020.510

Amended by Stats 2012 ch 72 (SB 1574),s 18, eff. 1/1/2013.
Amended by Stats 2007 ch 113 (AB 1126),s 4, eff. 1/1/2008.
Added by Stats 2004 ch 182 (AB 3081),s 23, eff. 7/1/2005.

Chapter 7 - SANCTIONS

Section 2023.010 - Misuses of discovery process

Misuses of the discovery process include, but are not limited to, the following:

(a) Persisting, over objection and without substantial justification, in an attempt to obtain information or materials that are outside the scope of permissible discovery.

(b) Using a discovery method in a manner that does not comply with its specified procedures.

(c) Employing a discovery method in a manner or to an extent that causes unwarranted annoyance, embarrassment, or oppression, or undue burden and expense.

(d) Failing to respond or to submit to an authorized method of discovery.

(e) Making, without substantial justification, an unmeritorious objection to discovery.

(f) Making an evasive response to discovery.

(g) Disobeying a court order to provide discovery.

(h) Making or opposing, unsuccessfully and without substantial justification, a motion to compel or to limit discovery.

(i) Failing to confer in person, by telephone, or by letter with an opposing party or attorney in a reasonable and good faith attempt to resolve informally any dispute concerning discovery, if the section governing a particular discovery motion requires the filing of a declaration stating facts showing that an attempt at informal resolution has been made.

Ca. Civ. Proc. Code § 2023.010

Added by Stats 2004 ch 182 (AB 3081),s 23, eff. 7/1/2005.

Section 2023.020 - Monetary sanction

Notwithstanding the outcome of the particular discovery motion, the court shall impose a monetary sanction ordering that any party or attorney who fails to confer as required pay the reasonable expenses, including attorney's fees, incurred by anyone as a result of that conduct.

Ca. Civ. Proc. Code § 2023.020

Added by Stats 2004 ch 182 (AB 3081),s 23, eff. 7/1/2005.

Section 2023.030 - Sanctions for misuse of discovery process

To the extent authorized by the chapter governing any particular discovery method or any other provision of this title, the court, after notice to any affected party, person, or attorney, and after opportunity for hearing, may impose the following sanctions against anyone engaging in conduct that is a misuse of the discovery process:

(a) The court may impose a monetary sanction ordering that one engaging in the misuse of the discovery process, or any attorney advising that conduct, or both pay the reasonable expenses, including attorney's fees, incurred by anyone as a result of that conduct. The court may also impose this sanction on one unsuccessfully asserting that another has engaged in the misuse of the discovery process, or on any attorney who advised that assertion, or on both. If a monetary sanction is authorized by any provision of this title, the court shall impose that sanction unless it finds that the one subject to the sanction acted with substantial justification or that other circumstances make the imposition of the sanction unjust.

(b) The court may impose an issue sanction ordering that designated facts shall be taken as established in the action in accordance with the claim of the party adversely affected by the misuse of the discovery process. The court may also impose an issue sanction by an order prohibiting any party engaging in the misuse of the discovery process from supporting or opposing designated claims or defenses.

(c) The court may impose an evidence sanction by an order prohibiting any party engaging in the misuse of the discovery process from introducing designated matters in evidence.

(d) The court may impose a terminating sanction by one of the following orders:

(1) An order striking out the pleadings or parts of the pleadings of any party engaging in the misuse of the discovery process.

(2) An order staying further proceedings by that party until an order for discovery is obeyed.

(3) An order dismissing the action, or any part of the action, of that party.

(4) An order rendering a judgment by default against that party.

(e) The court may impose a contempt sanction by an order treating the misuse of the discovery process as a contempt of court.

(f)

(1) Notwithstanding subdivision (a), or any other section of this title, absent exceptional circumstances, the court shall not impose sanctions on a party or any attorney of a party for failure to provide electronically stored information that has been lost, damaged, altered, or overwritten as the result of the routine, good faith operation of an electronic information system.

(2) This subdivision shall not be construed to alter any obligation to preserve discoverable information.

Ca. Civ. Proc. Code § 2023.030

Amended by Stats 2012 ch 72 (SB 1574),s 19, eff. 1/1/2013.

Added by Stats 2004 ch 182 (AB 3081),s 23, eff. 7/1/2005.

Section 2023.040 - Request for sanction

A request for a sanction shall, in the notice of motion, identify every person, party, and attorney against whom the sanction is sought, and specify the type of sanction sought. The notice of motion shall be supported by a memorandum of points and authorities, and accompanied by a declaration setting forth facts supporting the amount of any monetary sanction sought.

Ca. Civ. Proc. Code § 2023.040

Added by Stats 2004 ch 182 (AB 3081),s 23, eff. 7/1/2005.

Section 2023.050 - Court-imposed sanctions

(a) Notwithstanding any other law, and in addition to any other sanctions imposed pursuant to this chapter, a court shall impose a one-thousand-dollar ($1,000) sanction, payable to the requesting party, upon a party, person, or attorney if, upon reviewing a request for a sanction made pursuant to Section 2023.040, the court finds any of the following:

(1) The party, person, or attorney did not respond in good faith to a request for the production of documents made pursuant to Section 2020.010, 2020.410, 2020.510, or 2025.210, or to an inspection demand made pursuant to Section 2031.010.

(2) The party, person, or attorney produced requested

documents within seven days before the court was scheduled to hear a motion to compel production of the records pursuant to Section 2025.450, 2025.480, or 2031.320 that is filed by the requesting party as a result of the other party's, person's, or attorney's failure to respond in good faith.

(3) The party, person, or attorney failed to confer in person, by telephone, letter, or other means of communication in writing, as defined in Section 250 of the Evidence Code, with the party or attorney requesting the documents in a reasonable and good faith attempt to resolve informally any dispute concerning the request.
(b) Notwithstanding paragraph (3) of subdivision (o) of Section 6068 of the Business and Professions Code, the court may, in its discretion, require an attorney who is sanctioned pursuant to subdivision (a) to report the sanction, in writing, to the State Bar within 30 days of the imposition of the sanction.
(c) The court may excuse the imposition of the sanction required by subdivision (a) if the court makes written findings that the one subject to the sanction acted with substantial justification or that other circumstances make the imposition of the sanction unjust.
(d) Sanctions pursuant to this section shall be imposed only after notice to the party, person, or attorney against whom the sanction is proposed to be imposed and opportunity for that party, person, or attorney to be heard.
(e) For purposes of this section, there is a rebuttable presumption that a natural person acted in good faith if that person was not represented by an attorney in the action at the time the conduct that is sanctionable under subdivision (a) occurred. This presumption may only be overcome by clear and convincing evidence.
  Ca. Civ. Proc. Code § 2023.050
Amended by Stats 2023 ch 284 (SB 235),s 3, eff. 1/1/2024.
Added by Stats 2019 ch 836 (SB 17),s 2, eff. 1/1/2020.

Chapter 8 - TIME FOR COMPLETION OF DISCOVERY

Section 2024.010 - Motion for leave to complete discovery proceedings or motion concerning discovery heard closer to initial trial date or to reopen discovery after new trial date set

As used in this chapter, discovery is considered completed on the day a response is due or on the day a deposition begins.

Ca. Civ. Proc. Code § 2024.010

Added by Stats 2004 ch 182 (AB 3081),s 23, eff. 1/1/2005, op. 7/1/2005.

Section 2024.020 - Time to complete proceedings or have motions heard

(a) Except as otherwise provided in this chapter, any party shall be entitled as a matter of right to complete discovery proceedings on or before the 30th day, and to have motions concerning discovery heard on or before the 15th day, before the date initially set for the trial of the action.

(b) Except as provided in Section 2024.050, a continuance or postponement of the trial date does not operate to reopen discovery proceedings.

Ca. Civ. Proc. Code § 2024.020

Added by Stats 2004 ch 182 (AB 3081),s 23, eff. 7/1/2005.

Section 2024.030 - Time for completion of proceedings concerning witnesses and have motion heard

Any party shall be entitled as a matter of right to complete discovery proceedings pertaining to a witness identified under Chapter 18 (commencing with Section 2034.010) on or before the 15th day, and to have motions concerning that discovery heard on or before the 10th day, before the date initially set for the trial of the action.

Ca. Civ. Proc. Code § 2024.030

Added by Stats 2004 ch 182 (AB 3081),s 23, eff. 7/1/2005.

Section 2024.040 - Time limit on completing discovery in action to arbitrate; inapplicability to summary proceedings to obtain possession of real property and eminent domain

(a) The time limit on completing discovery in an action to be arbitrated under Chapter 2.5 (commencing with Section 1141.10) of Title 3 of Part 3 is subject to Judicial Council Rule. After an award in a case ordered to judicial arbitration, completion of discovery is limited by Section 1141.24.

(b) This chapter does not apply to either of the following:

(1) Summary proceedings for obtaining possession of real property governed by Chapter 4 (commencing with Section 1159) of Title 3 of Part 3. Except as provided in Sections 2024.050 and 2024.060, discovery in these proceedings shall be completed on or before the fifth day before the date set for trial.

(2) Eminent domain proceedings governed by Title 7 (commencing with Section 1230.010) of Part 3.

Ca. Civ. Proc. Code § 2024.040

Amended by Stats 2012 ch 162 (SB 1171),s 17, eff. 1/1/2013.
Added by Stats 2004 ch 182 (AB 3081),s 23, eff. 7/1/2005.

Section 2024.050 - Motion to grant leave to complete proceedings and have motion heard closer to initial trial date or after new trial date set

(a) On motion of any party, the court may grant leave to complete discovery proceedings, or to have a motion concerning discovery heard, closer to the initial trial date, or to reopen discovery after a new trial date has been set. This motion shall be accompanied by a meet and confer declaration under Section 2016.040.

(b) In exercising its discretion to grant or deny this motion, the court shall take into consideration any matter relevant to the leave requested, including, but not limited to, the following:

(1) The necessity and the reasons for the discovery.

(2) The diligence or lack of diligence of the party seeking the discovery or the hearing of a discovery motion, and the reasons that the discovery was not completed or that the discovery motion was not heard earlier.

(3) Any likelihood that permitting the discovery or hearing the discovery motion will prevent the case from going to trial on the date set, or otherwise interfere with the trial calendar, or result in prejudice to any other party.

(4) The length of time that has elapsed between any date previously set, and the date presently set, for the trial of the action. **(c)** The court shall impose a monetary sanction under Chapter 7 (commencing with Section 2023.010) against any party, person, or attorney who unsuccessfully makes or opposes a motion to extend or to reopen discovery, unless it finds that the one subject to the sanction acted with substantial justification or that other circumstances make the imposition of the sanction unjust.

Ca. Civ. Proc. Code § 2024.050
Added by Stats 2004 ch 182 (AB 3081),s 23, eff. 7/1/2005.

Section 2024.060 - Agreement to extend time for completion of proceedings and hearing motions
Parties to an action may, with the consent of any party affected by it, enter into an agreement to extend the time for the completion of discovery proceedings or for the hearing of motions concerning discovery, or to reopen discovery after a new date for trial of the action has been set. This agreement may be informal, but it shall be confirmed in a writing that specifies the extended date. In no event shall this agreement require a court to grant a continuance or postponement of the trial of the action.

Ca. Civ. Proc. Code § 2024.060
Added by Stats 2004 ch 182 (AB 3081),s 23, eff. 7/1/2005.

Chapter 9 - ORAL DEPOSITION INSIDE CALIFORNIA

Article 1 - GENERAL PROVISIONS

Section 2025.010 - Generally

Any party may obtain discovery within the scope delimited by Chapter 2 (commencing with Section 2017.010), and subject to the restrictions set forth in Chapter 5 (commencing with Section 2019.010), by taking in California the oral deposition of any person, including any party to the action. The person deposed may be a natural person, an organization such as a public or private corporation, a partnership, an association, or a governmental agency.

Ca. Civ. Proc. Code § 2025.010
Amended by Stats 2016 ch 86 (SB 1171),s 41, eff. 1/1/2017.
Added by Stats 2004 ch 182 (AB 3081),s 23, eff. 7/1/2005.

Article 2 - DEPOSITION NOTICE

Section 2025.210 - Service of notice

Subject to Sections 2025.270 and 2025.610, an oral deposition may be taken as follows:

(a) The defendant may serve a deposition notice without leave of court at any time after that defendant has been served or has appeared in the action, whichever occurs first.

(b) The plaintiff may serve a deposition notice without leave of court on any date that is 20 days after the service of the summons on, or appearance by, any defendant. On motion with or without notice, the court, for good cause shown, may grant to a plaintiff leave to serve a deposition notice on an earlier date.

Ca. Civ. Proc. Code § 2025.210
Added by Stats 2004 ch 182 (AB 3081),s 23, eff. 7/1/2005.

Section 2025.220 - Notice requirements

(a) A party desiring to take the oral deposition of any person shall give notice in writing. The deposition notice shall state all of the following, in at least 12-point type:

(1) The address where the deposition will be taken.

(2) The date of the deposition, selected under Section 2025.270, and the time it will commence.

(3) The name of each deponent, and the address and telephone number, if known, of any deponent who is not a party to the action. If the name of the deponent is not known, the deposition notice shall set forth instead a general description sufficient to identify the person or particular class to which the person belongs.

(4) The specification with reasonable particularity of any materials or category of materials, including any electronically stored information, to be produced by the deponent.

(5) Any intention by the party noticing the deposition to record the testimony by audio or video technology, in addition to recording the testimony by the stenographic method as required by Section 2025.330 and any intention to record the testimony by stenographic method through the instant visual display of the testimony. If the deposition will be conducted using instant visual display, a copy of the deposition notice shall also be given to the deposition officer. Any offer to provide the instant visual display of the testimony or to provide rough draft transcripts to any party which is accepted prior to, or offered at, the deposition shall also be made by the deposition officer at the deposition to all parties in attendance. Any party or attorney requesting the provision of the instant visual display of the testimony, or rough draft transcripts, shall pay the reasonable cost of those services, which may be no greater than the costs charged to any other party or attorney.

(6) Any intention to reserve the right to use at trial a video recording of the deposition testimony of a treating or consulting physician or of an expert witness under subdivision (d) of Section 2025.620. In this event, the operator of the video camera shall be a person who is authorized to administer an oath, and shall not be financially interested in the action or be a relative or employee of any attorney of any of the parties.

(7) The form in which any electronically stored information is to be produced, if a particular form is desired.

(8)

(A) A statement disclosing the existence of a contract, if any is known to the noticing party, between the noticing party or a third party who is financing all or part of the action and either of the following for any service beyond the noticed deposition:

(i) The deposition officer.

(ii) The entity providing the services of the deposition officer.

(B) A statement disclosing that the party noticing the deposition, or a third party financing all or part of the action, directed his or her attorney to use a particular officer or entity to provide services for the deposition, if applicable.

(b) Notwithstanding subdivision (a), where under Article 4 (commencing with Section 2020.410) only the production by a nonparty of business records for copying is desired, a copy of the deposition subpoena shall serve as the notice of deposition.

Ca. Civ. Proc. Code § 2025.220

Amended by Stats 2018 ch 268 (AB 3019),s 1, eff. 1/1/2019.
Amended by Stats 2015 ch 346 (AB 1197),s 2, eff. 1/1/2016.
Amended by Stats 2012 ch 72 (SB 1574),s 20, eff. 1/1/2013.
Added by Stats 2004 ch 182 (AB 3081),s 23, eff. 7/1/2005.

Section 2025.230 - Designation of persons to testify if deponent named not natural person

If the deponent named is not a natural person, the deposition notice shall describe with reasonable particularity the matters on which examination is requested. In that event, the deponent shall designate and produce at the deposition those of its officers, directors, managing agents, employees, or agents who are most qualified to testify on its behalf as to those matters to the extent of any information known or reasonably available to the deponent.

Ca. Civ. Proc. Code § 2025.230

Added by Stats 2004 ch 182 (AB 3081),s 23, eff. 7/1/2005.

Section 2025.240 - Notice given to every party appearing in action; service on consumer or employee

(a) The party who prepares a notice of deposition shall give the notice to every other party who has appeared in the action. The deposition notice, or the accompanying proof of service, shall list all the parties or attorneys for parties on whom it is served.

(b) If, as defined in subdivision (a) of Section 1985.3 or subdivision (a) of Section 1985.6, the party giving notice of the deposition is a subpoenaing party, and the deponent is a witness commanded by a deposition subpoena to produce personal records of a consumer or employment records of an employee, the subpoenaing party shall serve on that consumer or employee all of the following:

(1) A notice of the deposition.

(2) The notice of privacy rights specified in subdivision (e) of Section 1985.3 or in subdivision (e) of Section 1985.6.

(3) A copy of the deposition subpoena.

(c) If the attendance of the deponent is to be compelled by service of a deposition subpoena under Chapter 6 (commencing with Section 2020.010), an identical copy of that subpoena shall be served with the deposition notice.

Ca. Civ. Proc. Code § 2025.240

Amended by Stats 2007 ch 113 (AB 1126),s 5, eff. 1/1/2008.

Added by Stats 2004 ch 182 (AB 3081),s 23, eff. 7/1/2005.

Section 2025.250 - Place for taking deposition

(a) Unless the court orders otherwise under Section 2025.260, the deposition of a natural person, whether or not a party to the action, shall be taken at a place that is, at the option of the party giving notice of the deposition, either within 75 miles of the deponent's residence, or within the county where the action is pending and within 150 miles of the deponent's residence.

(b) The deposition of an organization that is a party to the action shall be taken at a place that is, at the option of the party giving notice of the deposition, either within 75 miles of the organization's principal executive or business office in California, or within the county where the action is pending and within 150 miles of that office.

(c) Unless the organization consents to a more distant place, the deposition of any other organization shall be taken within 75 miles of the organization's principal executive or business office in California.

(d) If an organization has not designated a principal executive or business office in California, the deposition shall be taken at a place that is, at the option of the party giving notice of the deposition, either within the county where the action is pending, or within 75 miles of any executive or business office in California of the organization.

Ca. Civ. Proc. Code § 2025.250
Amended by Stats 2005 ch 294 (AB 333),s 7, eff. 1/1/2006
Added by Stats 2004 ch 182 (AB 3081),s 23, eff. 7/1/2005.

Section 2025.260 - Motion that deponent attend deposition at place more distant than permitted

(a) A party desiring to take the deposition of a natural person who is a party to the action or an officer, director, managing agent, or employee of a party may make a motion for an order that the deponent attend for deposition at a place that is more distant than that permitted under Section 2025.250. This motion shall be accompanied by a meet and confer declaration under Section 2016.040.

(b) In exercising its discretion to grant or deny this motion, the court shall take into consideration any factor tending to show whether the interests of justice will be served by requiring the deponent's attendance at that more distant place, including, but not limited to, the following:

(1) Whether the moving party selected the forum.

(2) Whether the deponent will be present to testify at the trial of the action.

(3) The convenience of the deponent.

(4) The feasibility of conducting the deposition by written questions under Chapter 11 (commencing with Section 2028.010), or of using a discovery method other than a deposition.

(5) The number of depositions sought to be taken at a place more distant than that permitted under Section 2025.250.

(6) The expense to the parties of requiring the deposition to be taken within the distance permitted under Section 2025.250.

(7) The whereabouts of the deponent at the time for which the deposition is scheduled.
(c) The order may be conditioned on the advancement by the moving party of the reasonable expenses and costs to the deponent for travel to the place of deposition.
(d) The court shall impose a monetary sanction under Chapter 7 (commencing with Section 2023.010) against any party, person, or attorney who unsuccessfully makes or opposes a motion to increase the travel limits for a party deponent, unless it finds that the one subject to the sanction acted with substantial justification or that other circumstances make the imposition of the sanction unjust.
    Ca. Civ. Proc. Code § 2025.260
Added by Stats 2004 ch 182 (AB 3081),s 23, eff. 7/1/2005.

Section 2025.270 - Scheduling

(a) An oral deposition shall be scheduled for a date at least 10 days after service of the deposition notice.

(b) Notwithstanding subdivision (a), in an unlawful detainer action or other proceeding under Chapter 4 (commencing with Section 1159) of Title 3 of Part 3, an oral deposition shall be scheduled for a date at least five days after service of the deposition notice, but not later than five days before trial.

(c) Notwithstanding subdivisions (a) and (b), if, as defined in Section 1985.3 or 1985.6, the party giving notice of the deposition is a subpoenaing party, and the deponent is a witness commanded by a deposition subpoena to produce personal records of a consumer or employment records of an employee, the deposition shall be scheduled for a date at least 20 days after issuance of that subpoena.

(d) On motion or ex parte application of any party or deponent, for good cause shown, the court may shorten or extend the time for scheduling a deposition, or may stay its taking until the determination of a motion for a protective order under Section 2025.420.

Ca. Civ. Proc. Code § 2025.270

Amended by Stats 2007 ch 113 (AB 1126),s 6, eff. 1/1/2008.
Added by Stats 2004 ch 182 (AB 3081),s 23, eff. 7/1/2005.

Section 2025.280 - Force and effect of notice

(a) The service of a deposition notice under Section 2025.240 is effective to require any deponent who is a party to the action or an officer, director, managing agent, or employee of a party to attend and to testify, as well as to produce any document, electronically stored information, or tangible thing for inspection and copying.

(b) The attendance and testimony of any other deponent, as well as the production by the deponent of any document, electronically stored information, or tangible thing for inspection and copying, requires the service on the deponent of a deposition subpoena under Chapter 6 (commencing with Section 2020.010).

(c) A deponent required by notice or subpoena to produce electronically stored information shall provide a means of gaining direct access to, or a translation into a reasonably usable form of, any electronically stored information that is password protected or otherwise inaccessible.

Ca. Civ. Proc. Code § 2025.280
Amended by Stats 2016 ch 467 (AB 2427),s 2, eff. 1/1/2017.
Amended by Stats 2012 ch 72 (SB 1574),s 21, eff. 1/1/2013.
Added by Stats 2004 ch 182 (AB 3081),s 23, eff. 7/1/2005.

Section 2025.290 - Time limits on examination by other than witness' counsel of record

(a) Except as provided in subdivision (b), or by any court order, including a case management order, a deposition examination of the witness by all counsel, other than the witness' counsel of record, shall be limited to seven hours of total testimony. The court shall allow additional time, beyond any limits imposed by this section, if needed to fairly examine the deponent or if the deponent, another person, or any other circumstance impedes or delays the examination.

(b) This section shall not apply under any of the following circumstances:

(1) If the parties have stipulated that this section will not apply to a specific deposition or to the entire proceeding.

(2) To any deposition of a witness designated as an expert pursuant to Sections 2034.210 to 2034.310, inclusive.

(3) To any case designated as complex by the court pursuant to Rule 3.400 of the California Rules of Court, unless a licensed physician attests in a declaration served on the parties that the deponent suffers from an illness or condition that raises substantial medical doubt of survival of the deponent beyond six months, in which case the deposition examination of the witness by all counsel, other than the witness' counsel of record, shall be limited to two days of no more than seven hours of total testimony each day, or 14 hours of total testimony.

(4) To any case brought by an employee or applicant for employment against an employer for acts or omissions arising out of or relating to the employment relationship.

(5) To any deposition of a person who is designated as the most qualified person to be deposed under Section 2025.230.

(6) To any party who appeared in the action after the deposition has concluded, in which case the new party may notice another deposition subject to the requirements of this section.
(c) It is the intent of the Legislature that any exclusions made by this section shall not be construed to create any presumption or any substantive change to existing law relating to the appropriate time limit for depositions falling within the exclusion. Nothing in this section shall be construed to affect the existing right of any party to move for a protective order or the court's discretion to make any order that justice requires to limit a deposition in order to protect any party, deponent, or other natural person or organization from unwarranted annoyance, embarrassment, oppression, undue burden, or expense.
Ca. Civ. Proc. Code § 2025.290
Added by Stats 2012 ch 346 (AB 1875),s 1, eff. 1/1/2013.

Section 2025.295 - Duration of deposition examination of plaintiff suffering from mesothelioma or silicosis

(a) Notwithstanding Section 2025.290, in any civil action for injury or illness that results in mesothelioma or silicosis, a deposition examination of the plaintiff by all counsel, other than the plaintiff's counsel of record, shall be limited to seven hours of total testimony if a licensed physician attests in a declaration served on the parties that the deponent suffers from mesothelioma or silicosis, raising substantial medical doubt of the survival of the deponent beyond six months.
(b) Notwithstanding the presumptive time limit in subdivision (a), upon request by a defendant, a court may, in its discretion, grant one of the following up to:

(1) An additional three hours of deposition testimony for no more than 10 hours of total deposition conducted by the defendants if there are more than 10 defendants appearing at the deposition.

(2) An additional seven hours of deposition testimony for no more than 14 hours of total deposition conducted by the defendants if there are more than 20 defendants appearing at the deposition.
(c) The court may grant the additional time provided for in paragraphs (1) and (2) of subdivision (b) only if it finds that an extension, in the instant case, is in the interest of fairness, which includes consideration of the number of defendants appearing at the deposition, and determines that the health of the deponent does not appear to be endangered by the grant of additional time.

Ca. Civ. Proc. Code § 2025.295
Added by Stats 2019 ch 212 (SB 645),s 1, eff. 1/1/2020.

Article 3 - CONDUCT OF DEPOSITION

Section 2025.310 - Physical presence

(a) At the election of the deponent or the deposing party, the deposition officer may attend the deposition at a different location than the deponent via remote means. A deponent is not required to be physically present with the deposition officer when being sworn in at the time of the deposition.
(b) Subject to Section 2025.420, any party or attorney of record may, but is not required to, be physically present at the deposition at the location of the deponent. If a party or attorney of record elects to be physically present at the location of the deponent, all physically present participants in the deposition shall comply with local health and safety ordinances, rules, and orders.
(c) The procedures to implement this section shall be established by court order in the specific action or proceeding or by the California Rules of Court.
(d) An exercise of the authority granted by subdivision (a) or (b) does not waive any other provision of this title, including, but not limited to, provisions regarding the time, place, or manner in which a deposition shall be conducted.

(e) This section does not alter or amend who may lawfully serve as a deposition officer pursuant to this title or who otherwise may administer oaths pursuant to Sections 2093 and 2094 of this code or Section 8201 of the Government Code.

    Ca. Civ. Proc. Code § 2025.310
Amended by Stats 2022 ch 92 (SB 1037),s 1, eff. 1/1/2023.
Amended by Stats 2020 ch 112 (SB 1146),s 3, eff. 9/18/2020.
Added by Stats 2004 ch 182 (AB 3081),s 23, eff. 7/1/2005.

Section 2025.320 - Conducted under supervision of deposition officer

Except as provided in Section 2020.420, the deposition shall be conducted under the supervision of an officer who is authorized to administer an oath and is subject to all of the following requirements:

(a) The officer shall not be financially interested in the action and shall not be a relative or employee of any attorney of the parties, or of any of the parties.

(b) Services and products offered or provided by the deposition officer or the entity providing the services of the deposition officer to any party or to any party's attorney or third party who is financing all or part of the action shall be offered to all parties or their attorneys attending the deposition. No service or product may be offered or provided by the deposition officer or by the entity providing the services of the deposition officer to any party or any party's attorney or third party who is financing all or part of the action unless the service or product is offered or provided to all parties or their attorneys attending the deposition. All services and products offered or provided shall be made available at the same time to all parties or their attorneys.

(c) The deposition officer or the entity providing the services of the deposition officer shall not provide to any party or any party's attorney or third party who is financing all or part of the action any service or product consisting of the deposition officer's notations or comments regarding the demeanor of any witness, attorney, or party present at the deposition. The deposition officer or entity providing the services of the deposition officer shall not collect any personal identifying information about the witness as a service or product to be provided to any party or third party who is financing all or part of the action.

(d) Upon the request of any party or any party's attorney attending a deposition, any party or any party's attorney attending the deposition shall enter in the record of the deposition all services and products made available to that party or party's attorney or third party who is financing all or part of the action by the deposition officer or by the entity providing the services of the deposition officer. A party in the action who is not represented by an attorney shall be informed by the noticing party or the party's attorney that the unrepresented party may request this statement.

(e) Any objection to the qualifications of the deposition officer is waived unless made before the deposition begins or as soon thereafter as the ground for that objection becomes known or could be discovered by reasonable diligence.

(f) Violation of this section by any person may result in a civil penalty of up to five thousand dollars ($5,000) imposed by a court of competent jurisdiction.

Ca. Civ. Proc. Code § 2025.320
Added by Stats 2004 ch 182 (AB 3081),s 23, eff. 7/1/2005.

Section 2025.330 - Taking testimony
(a) The deposition officer shall put the deponent under oath or affirmation.

(b) Unless the parties agree or the court orders otherwise, the testimony, as well as any stated objections, shall be taken stenographically. If taken stenographically, it shall be by a person certified pursuant to Article 3 (commencing with Section 8020) of Chapter 13 of Division 3 of the Business and Professions Code.

(c) The party noticing the deposition may also record the testimony by audio or video technology if the notice of deposition stated an intention also to record the testimony by either of those methods, or if all the parties agree that the testimony may also be recorded by either of those methods. Any other party, at that party's expense, may make an audio or video record of the deposition, provided that the other party promptly, and in no event less than three calendar days before the date for which the deposition is scheduled, serves a written notice of this intention to make an audio or video record of the deposition testimony on the party or attorney who noticed the deposition, on all other parties or attorneys on whom the deposition notice was served under Section 2025.240, and on any deponent whose attendance is being compelled by a deposition subpoena under Chapter 6 (commencing with Section 2020.010). If this notice is given three calendar days before the deposition date, it shall be made by personal service under Section 1011.

(d) Examination and cross-examination of the deponent shall proceed as permitted at trial under the provisions of the Evidence Code.

(e) In lieu of participating in the oral examination, parties may transmit written questions in a sealed envelope to the party taking the deposition for delivery to the deposition officer, who shall unseal the envelope and propound them to the deponent after the oral examination has been completed.

Ca. Civ. Proc. Code § 2025.330

Amended by Stats 2005 ch 294 (AB 333),s 8, eff. 1/1/2006

Added by Stats 2004 ch 182 (AB 3081),s 23, eff. 7/1/2005.

Section 2025.340 - Deposition recorded by means of audio or video technology

If a deposition is being recorded by means of audio or video technology by, or at the direction of, any party, the following procedure shall be observed:

(a) The area used for recording the deponent's oral testimony shall be suitably large, adequately lighted, and reasonably quiet.

(b) The operator of the recording equipment shall be competent to set up, operate, and monitor the equipment in the manner prescribed in this section. Except as provided in subdivision (c), the operator may be an employee of the attorney taking the deposition unless the operator is also the deposition officer.

(c) If a video recording of deposition testimony is to be used under subdivision (d) of Section 2025.620, the operator of the recording equipment shall be a person who is authorized to administer an oath, and shall not be financially interested in the action or be a relative or employee of any attorney of any of the parties, unless all parties attending the deposition agree on the record to waive these qualifications and restrictions.

(d) Services and products offered or provided by the deposition officer or the entity providing the services of the deposition officer to any party or to any party's attorney or third party who is financing all or part of the action shall be offered or provided to all parties or their attorneys attending the deposition. No service or product may be offered or provided by the deposition officer or by the entity providing the services of the deposition officer to any party or any party's attorney or third party who is financing all or part of the action unless the service or product is offered or provided to all parties or their attorneys attending the deposition. All services and products offered or provided shall be made available at the same time to all parties or their attorneys.

(e) The deposition officer or the entity providing the services of the deposition officer shall not provide to any party or any other person or entity any service or product consisting of the deposition officer's notations or comments regarding the demeanor of any witness, attorney, or party present at the deposition. The deposition officer or the entity providing the services of the deposition officer shall not collect any personal identifying information about the witness as a service or product to be provided to any party or third party who is financing all or part of the action.

(f) Upon the request of any party or any party's attorney attending a deposition, any party or any party's attorney attending the deposition shall enter in the record of the deposition all services and products made available to that party or party's attorney or third party who is financing all or part of the action by the deposition officer or by the entity providing the services of the deposition officer. A party in the action who is not represented by an attorney shall be informed by the noticing party that the unrepresented party may request this statement.

(g) The operator shall not distort the appearance or the demeanor of participants in the deposition by the use of camera or sound recording techniques.

(h) The deposition shall begin with an oral or written statement on camera or on the audio recording that includes the operator's name and business address, the name and business address of the operator's employer, the date, time, and place of the deposition, the caption of the case, the name of the deponent, a specification of the party on whose behalf the deposition is being taken, and any stipulations by the parties.

(i) Counsel for the parties shall identify themselves on camera or on the audio recording.

(j) The oath shall be administered to the deponent on camera or on the audio recording.

(k) If the length of a deposition requires the use of more than one unit of tape or electronic storage, the end of each unit and the beginning of each succeeding unit shall be announced on camera or on the audio recording.

(l) At the conclusion of a deposition, a statement shall be made on camera or on the audio recording that the deposition is ended and shall set forth any stipulations made by counsel concerning the custody of the audio or video recording and the exhibits, or concerning other pertinent matters.

(m) A party intending to offer an audio or video recording of a deposition in evidence under Section 2025.620 shall notify the court and all parties in writing of that intent and of the parts of the deposition to be offered. That notice shall be given within sufficient time for objections to be made and ruled on by the judge to whom the case is assigned for trial or hearing, and for any editing of the recording. Objections to all or part of the deposition shall be made in writing. The court may permit further designations of testimony and objections as justice may require. With respect to those portions of an audio or video record of deposition testimony that are not designated by any party or that are ruled to be objectionable, the court may order that the party offering the recording of the deposition at the trial or hearing suppress those portions, or that an edited version of the deposition recording be prepared for use at the trial or hearing. The original audio or video record of the deposition shall be preserved unaltered. If no stenographic record of the deposition testimony has previously been made, the party offering an audio or video recording of that testimony under Section 2025.620 shall accompany that offer with a stenographic transcript prepared from that recording.

Ca. Civ. Proc. Code § 2025.340
Added by Stats 2004 ch 182 (AB 3081),s 23, eff. 7/1/2005.

Article 4 - OBJECTIONS, SANCTIONS, PROTECTIVE ORDERS, MOTIONS TO COMPEL, AND SUSPENSION OF DEPOSITIONS

Section 2025.410 - Generally

(a) Any party served with a deposition notice that does not comply with Article 2 (commencing with Section 2025.210) waives any error or irregularity unless that party promptly serves a written objection specifying that error or irregularity at least three calendar days prior to the date for which the deposition is scheduled, on the party seeking to take the deposition and any other attorney or party on whom the deposition notice was served.

(b) If an objection is made three calendar days before the deposition date, the objecting party shall make personal service of that objection pursuant to Section 1011 on the party who gave notice of the deposition. Any deposition taken after the service of a written objection shall not be used against the objecting party under Section 2025.620 if the party did not attend the deposition and if the court determines that the objection was a valid one.

(c) In addition to serving this written objection, a party may also move for an order staying the taking of the deposition and quashing the deposition notice. This motion shall be accompanied by a meet and confer declaration under Section 2016.040. The taking of the deposition is stayed pending the determination of this motion.

(d) The court shall impose a monetary sanction under Chapter 7 (commencing with Section 2023.010) against any party, person, or attorney who unsuccessfully makes or opposes a motion to quash a deposition notice, unless it finds that the one subject to the sanction acted with substantial justification or that other circumstances make the imposition of the sanction unjust.

(e)

(1) Notwithstanding subdivision (d), absent exceptional circumstances, the court shall not impose sanctions on any party,

person, or attorney for failure to provide electronically stored information that has been lost, damaged, altered, or overwritten as the result of the routine, good faith operation of an electronic information system.

(2) This subdivision shall not be construed to alter any obligation to preserve discoverable information.
Ca. Civ. Proc. Code § 2025.410
Amended by Stats 2012 ch 72 (SB 1574),s 22, eff. 1/1/2013.
Added by Stats 2004 ch 182 (AB 3081),s 23, eff. 7/1/2005.

Section 2025.420 - Motion for protective order

(a) Before, during, or after a deposition, any party, any deponent, or any other affected natural person or organization may promptly move for a protective order. The motion shall be accompanied by a meet and confer declaration under Section 2016.040.

(b) The court, for good cause shown, may make any order that justice requires to protect any party, deponent, or other natural person or organization from unwarranted annoyance, embarrassment, or oppression, or undue burden and expense. This protective order may include, but is not limited to, one or more of the following directions:

(1) That the deposition not be taken at all.

(2) That the deposition be taken at a different time.

(3) That a video recording of the deposition testimony of a treating or consulting physician or of any expert witness, intended for possible use at trial under subdivision (d) of Section 2025.620, be postponed until the moving party has had an adequate opportunity to prepare, by discovery deposition of the deponent, or other means, for cross-examination.

(4) That the deposition be taken at a place other than that specified in the deposition notice, if it is within a distance permitted by Sections 2025.250 and 2025.260.

(5) That the deposition be taken only on certain specified terms and conditions.

(6) That the deponent's testimony be taken by written, instead of oral, examination.

(7) That the method of discovery be interrogatories to a party instead of an oral deposition.

(8) That the testimony be recorded in a manner different from that specified in the deposition notice.

(9) That certain matters not be inquired into.

(10) That the scope of the examination be limited to certain matters.

(11) That all or certain of the writings or tangible things designated in the deposition notice not be produced, inspected, copied, tested, or sampled, or that conditions be set for the production of electronically stored information designated in the deposition notice.

(12) That designated persons, other than the parties to the action and their officers and counsel, be excluded from attending the deposition.

(13) That a trade secret or other confidential research, development, or commercial information not be disclosed or be disclosed only to specified persons or only in a specified way.

(14) That the parties simultaneously file specified documents enclosed in sealed envelopes to be opened as directed by the court.

(15) That the deposition be sealed and thereafter opened only on order of the court.

(16) That examination of the deponent be terminated. If an order terminates the examination, the deposition shall not thereafter be resumed, except on order of the court.

(c) The party, deponent, or any other affected natural person or organization that seeks a protective order regarding the production, inspection, copying, testing, or sampling of electronically stored information on the basis that the information is from a source that is not reasonably accessible because of undue burden or expense shall bear the burden of demonstrating that the information is from a source that is not reasonably accessible because of undue burden or expense.

(d) If the party or affected person from whom discovery of electronically stored information is sought establishes that the information is from a source that is not reasonably accessible because of undue burden or expense, the court may nonetheless order discovery if the demanding party shows good cause, subject to any limitations imposed under subdivision (f).

(e) If the court finds good cause for the production of electronically stored information from a source that is not reasonably accessible, the court may set conditions for the discovery of the electronically stored information, including allocation of the expense of discovery.

(f) The court shall limit the frequency or extent of discovery of electronically stored information, even from a source that is reasonably accessible, if the court determines that any of the following conditions exist:

(1) It is possible to obtain the information from some other source that is more convenient, less burdensome, or less expensive.

(2) The discovery sought is unreasonably cumulative or duplicative.

(3) The party seeking discovery has had ample opportunity by discovery in the action to obtain the information sought.

(4) The likely burden or expense of the proposed discovery outweighs the likely benefit, taking into account the amount in controversy, the resources of the parties, the importance of the issues in the litigation, and the importance of the requested discovery in resolving the issues.

(g) If the motion for a protective order is denied in whole or in part, the court may order that the deponent provide or permit the discovery against which protection was sought on those terms and conditions that are just.

(h) The court shall impose a monetary sanction under Chapter 7 (commencing with Section 2023.010) against any party, person, or attorney who unsuccessfully makes or opposes a motion for a protective order, unless it finds that the one subject to the sanction acted with substantial justification or that other circumstances make the imposition of the sanction unjust.

(i)

(1) Notwithstanding subdivision (h), absent exceptional circumstances, the court shall not impose sanctions on any party, deponent, or other affected natural person or organization or any of their attorneys for failure to provide electronically stored information that has been lost, damaged, altered, or overwritten as the result of the routine, good faith operation of an electronic information system.

(2) This subdivision shall not be construed to alter any obligation to preserve discoverable information.

Ca. Civ. Proc. Code § 2025.420

Amended by Stats 2012 ch 72 (SB 1574),s 23, eff. 1/1/2013.

Added by Stats 2004 ch 182 (AB 3081),s 23, eff. 7/1/2005.

Section 2025.430 - Failure of party giving notice of deposition to attend or proceed

If the party giving notice of a deposition fails to attend or proceed with it, the court shall impose a monetary sanction under Chapter 7 (commencing with Section 2023.010) against that party, or the attorney for that party, or both, and in favor of any party attending in person or by attorney, unless it finds that the one subject to the sanction acted with substantial justification or that other circumstances make the imposition of the sanction unjust.

Ca. Civ. Proc. Code § 2025.430
Added by Stats 2004 ch 182 (AB 3081),s 23, eff. 7/1/2005.

Section 2025.440 - Failure of deponent to attend because party giving notice failed to serve deposition subpoena

(a) If a deponent does not appear for a deposition because the party giving notice of the deposition failed to serve a required deposition subpoena, the court shall impose a monetary sanction under Chapter 7 (commencing with Section 2023.010) against that party, or the attorney for that party, or both, in favor of any other party who, in person or by attorney, attended at the time and place specified in the deposition notice in the expectation that the deponent's testimony would be taken, unless the court finds that the one subject to the sanction acted with substantial justification or that other circumstances make the imposition of the sanction unjust.

(b) If a deponent on whom a deposition subpoena has been served fails to attend a deposition or refuses to be sworn as a witness, the court may impose on the deponent the sanctions described in Section 2020.240.

Ca. Civ. Proc. Code § 2025.440
Added by Stats 2004 ch 182 (AB 3081),s 23, eff. 7/1/2005.

Section 2025.450 - Motion to compel deponent testimony and production

(a) If, after service of a deposition notice, a party to the action or an officer, director, managing agent, or employee of a party, or a person designated by an organization that is a party under Section 2025.230, without having served a valid objection under Section 2025.410, fails to appear for examination, or to proceed with it, or to produce for inspection any document, electronically stored information, or tangible thing described in the deposition notice, the party giving the notice may move for an order compelling the deponent's attendance and testimony, and the production for inspection of any document, electronically stored information, or tangible thing described in the deposition notice.

(b) A motion under subdivision (a) shall comply with both of the following:

(1) The motion shall set forth specific facts showing good cause justifying the production for inspection of any document, electronically stored information, or tangible thing described in the deposition notice.

(2) The motion shall be accompanied by a meet and confer declaration under Section 2016.040, or, when the deponent fails to attend the deposition and produce the documents, electronically stored information, or things described in the deposition notice, by a declaration stating that the petitioner has contacted the deponent to inquire about the nonappearance.

(c) In a motion under subdivision (a) relating to the production of electronically stored information, the party or party-affiliated deponent objecting to or opposing the production, inspection, copying, testing, or sampling of electronically stored information on the basis that the information is from a source that is not reasonably accessible because of the undue burden or expense shall bear the burden of demonstrating that the information is from a source that is not reasonably accessible because of undue burden or expense.

(d) If the party or party-affiliated deponent from whom discovery of electronically stored information is sought establishes that the information is from a source that is not reasonably accessible because of the undue burden or expense, the court may nonetheless order discovery if the demanding party shows good cause, subject to any limitations imposed under subdivision (f).

(e) If the court finds good cause for the production of electronically stored information from a source that is not reasonably accessible, the court may set conditions for the discovery of the electronically stored information, including allocation of the expense of discovery.

(f) The court shall limit the frequency or extent of discovery of electronically stored information, even from a source that is reasonably accessible, if the court determines that any of the following conditions exists:

(1) It is possible to obtain the information from some other source that is more convenient, less burdensome, or less expensive.

(2) The discovery sought is unreasonably cumulative or duplicative.

(3) The party seeking discovery has had ample opportunity by discovery in the action to obtain the information sought.

(4) The likely burden or expense of the proposed discovery outweighs the likely benefit, taking into account the amount in controversy, the resources of the parties, the importance of the issues in the litigation, and the importance of the requested discovery in resolving the issues.

(g)

(1) If a motion under subdivision (a) is granted, the court shall impose a monetary sanction under Chapter 7 (commencing with Section 2023.010) in favor of the party who noticed the deposition and against the deponent or the party with whom the deponent is affiliated, unless the court finds that the one subject to the sanction acted with substantial justification or that other circumstances make the imposition of the sanction unjust.

(2) On motion of any other party who, in person or by attorney, attended at the time and place specified in the deposition notice in the expectation that the deponent's testimony would be taken, the court shall impose a monetary sanction under Chapter 7 (commencing with Section 2023.010) in favor of that party and against the deponent or the party with whom the deponent is affiliated, unless the court finds that the one subject to the sanction acted with substantial justification or that other circumstances make the imposition of the sanction unjust.

(h) If that party or party-affiliated deponent then fails to obey an order compelling attendance, testimony, and production, the court may make those orders that are just, including the imposition of an issue sanction, an evidence sanction, or a terminating sanction under Chapter 7 (commencing with Section 2023.010) against that party deponent or against the party with whom the deponent is affiliated. In lieu of, or in addition to, this sanction, the court may impose a monetary sanction under Chapter 7 (commencing with Section 2023.010) against that deponent or against the party with whom that party deponent is affiliated, and in favor of any party who, in person or by attorney, attended in the expectation that the deponent's testimony would be taken pursuant to that order.

(i)

(1) Notwithstanding subdivisions (g) and (h), absent exceptional circumstances, the court shall not impose sanctions on a party or any attorney of a party for failure to provide electronically stored information that has been lost, damaged, altered, or overwritten as the result of the routine, good faith operation of an electronic information system.

(2) This subdivision shall not be construed to alter any obligation to preserve discoverable information.

Ca. Civ. Proc. Code § 2025.450
Amended by Stats 2012 ch 72 (SB 1574),s 24, eff. 1/1/2013.
Added by Stats 2004 ch 182 (AB 3081),s 23, eff. 7/1/2005.

Section 2025.460 - Waiver unless objection made
(a) The protection of information from discovery on the ground that it is privileged or that it is a protected work product under Chapter 4 (commencing with Section 2018.010) is waived unless a specific objection to its disclosure is timely made during the deposition.
(b) Errors and irregularities of any kind occurring at the oral examination that might be cured if promptly presented are waived unless a specific objection to them is timely made during the deposition. These errors and irregularities include, but are not limited to, those relating to the manner of taking the deposition, to the oath or affirmation administered, to the conduct of a party, attorney, deponent, or deposition officer, or to the form of any question or answer. Unless the objecting party demands that the taking of the deposition be suspended to permit a motion for a

protective order under Sections 2025.420 and 2025.470, the deposition shall proceed subject to the objection.

(c) Objections to the competency of the deponent, or to the relevancy, materiality, or admissibility at trial of the testimony or of the materials produced are unnecessary and are not waived by failure to make them before or during the deposition.

(d) If a deponent objects to the production of electronically stored information on the grounds that it is from a source that is not reasonably accessible because of undue burden or expense and that the deponent will not search the source in the absence of an agreement with the deposing party or court order, the deponent shall identify in its objection the types or categories of sources of electronically stored information that it asserts are not reasonably accessible. By objecting and identifying information of a type or category of source or sources that are not reasonably accessible, the deponent preserves any objections it may have relating to that electronically stored information.

(e) If a deponent fails to answer any question or to produce any document, electronically stored information, or tangible thing under the deponent's control that is specified in the deposition notice or a deposition subpoena, the party seeking that answer or production may adjourn the deposition or complete the examination on other matters without waiving the right at a later time to move for an order compelling that answer or production under Section 2025.480.

(f) Notwithstanding subdivision (a), if a deponent notifies the party that took a deposition that electronically stored information produced pursuant to the deposition notice or subpoena is subject to a claim of privilege or of protection as attorney work product, as described in Section 2031.285, the provisions of Section 2031.285 shall apply.

Ca. Civ. Proc. Code § 2025.460
Amended by Stats 2012 ch 72 (SB 1574),s 25, eff. 1/1/2013.
Added by Stats 2004 ch 182 (AB 3081),s 23, eff. 7/1/2005.

Section 2025.470 - Suspension of taking of testimony

The deposition officer may not suspend the taking of testimony without the stipulation of all parties present unless any party attending the deposition, including the deponent, demands that the deposition officer suspend taking the testimony to enable that party or deponent to move for a protective order under Section 2025.420 on the ground that the examination is being conducted in bad faith or in a manner that unreasonably annoys, embarrasses, or oppresses that deponent or party.

Ca. Civ. Proc. Code § 2025.470
Added by Stats 2004 ch 182 (AB 3081),s 23, eff. 7/1/2005.

Section 2025.480 - Motion to compel answer or production

(a) If a deponent fails to answer any question or to produce any document, electronically stored information, or tangible thing under the deponent's control that is specified in the deposition notice or a deposition subpoena, the party seeking discovery may move the court for an order compelling that answer or production.

(b) This motion shall be made no later than 60 days after the completion of the record of the deposition, and shall be accompanied by a meet and confer declaration under Section 2016.040.

(c) Notice of this motion shall be given to all parties and to the deponent either orally at the examination, or by subsequent service in writing. If the notice of the motion is given orally, the deposition officer shall direct the deponent to attend a session of the court at the time specified in the notice.

(d) In a motion under subdivision (a) relating to the production of electronically stored information, the deponent objecting to or opposing the production, inspection, copying, testing, or sampling of electronically stored information on the basis that the information is from a source that is not reasonably accessible because of the undue burden or expense shall bear the burden of demonstrating that the information is from a source that is not reasonably accessible because of undue burden or expense.

(e) If the deponent from whom discovery of electronically stored information is sought establishes that the information is from a source that is not reasonably accessible because of the undue burden or expense, the court may nonetheless order discovery if the deposing party shows good cause, subject to any limitations imposed under subdivision (g).

(f) If the court finds good cause for the production of electronically stored information from a source that is not reasonably accessible, the court may set conditions for the discovery of the electronically stored information, including allocation of the expense of discovery.

(g) The court shall limit the frequency or extent of discovery of electronically stored information, even from a source that is reasonably accessible, if the court determines that any of the following conditions exists:

(1) It is possible to obtain the information from some other source that is more convenient, less burdensome, or less expensive.

(2) The discovery sought is unreasonably cumulative or duplicative.

(3) The party seeking discovery has had ample opportunity by discovery in the action to obtain the information sought.

(4) The likely burden or expense of the proposed discovery outweighs the likely benefit, taking into account the amount in controversy, the resources of the parties, the importance of the issues in the litigation, and the importance of the requested discovery in resolving the issues.

(h) Not less than five days prior to the hearing on this motion, the moving party shall lodge with the court a certified copy of any parts of the stenographic transcript of the deposition that are relevant to the motion. If a deposition is recorded by audio or video technology, the moving party is required to lodge a certified copy of a transcript of any parts of the deposition that are relevant to the motion.

(i) If the court determines that the answer or production sought is subject to discovery, it shall order that the answer be given or the production be made on the resumption of the deposition.

(j) The court shall impose a monetary sanction under Chapter 7 (commencing with Section 2023.010) against any party, person, or attorney who unsuccessfully makes or opposes a motion to compel an answer or production, unless it finds that the one subject to the sanction acted with substantial justification or that other circumstances make the imposition of the sanction unjust.

(k) If a deponent fails to obey an order entered under this section, the failure may be considered a contempt of court. In addition, if the disobedient deponent is a party to the action or an officer, director, managing agent, or employee of a party, the court may make those orders that are just against the disobedient party, or against the party with whom the disobedient deponent is affiliated, including the imposition of an issue sanction, an evidence sanction, or a terminating sanction under Chapter 7 (commencing with Section 2023.010). In lieu of or in addition to this sanction, the court may impose a monetary sanction under Chapter 7 (commencing with Section 2023.010) against that party deponent or against any party with whom the deponent is affiliated.

(l)

(1) Notwithstanding subdivisions (j) and (k), absent exceptional circumstances, the court shall not impose sanctions on a deponent or any attorney of a deponent for failure to provide electronically stored information that has been lost, damaged, altered, or overwritten as the result of the routine, good faith operation of an electronic information system.

(2) This subdivision shall not be construed to alter any obligation to preserve discoverable information.

Ca. Civ. Proc. Code § 2025.480
Amended by Stats 2012 ch 72 (SB 1574),s 26, eff. 1/1/2013.
Amended by Stats 2005 ch 22 (SB 1108),s 21, eff. 1/1/2006
Added by Stats 2004 ch 182 (AB 3081),s 23, eff. 7/1/2005.

Article 5 - TRANSCRIPT OR RECORDING

Section 2025.510 - Generally

(a) Unless the parties agree otherwise, the testimony at a deposition recorded by stenographic means shall be transcribed.

(b) The party noticing the deposition shall bear the cost of the transcription, unless the court, on motion and for good cause shown, orders that the cost be borne or shared by another party.

(c) Notwithstanding subdivision (b) of Section 2025.320, any other party or the deponent, at the expense of that party or deponent, may obtain a copy of the transcript.

(d) If the deposition officer receives a request from a party for an original or a copy of the deposition transcript, or any portion thereof, and the full or partial transcript will be available to that party prior to the time the original or copy would be available to any other party, the deposition officer shall immediately notify all other parties attending the deposition of the request, and shall, upon request by any party other than the party making the original request, make that copy of the full or partial deposition transcript available to all parties at the same time.

(e) Stenographic notes of depositions shall be retained by the reporter for a period of not less than eight years from the date of the deposition, where no transcript is produced, and not less than one year from the date on which the transcript is produced. The notes may be either on paper or electronic media, as long as it allows for satisfactory production of a transcript at any time during the periods specified.

(f) At the request of any other party to the action, including a party who did not attend the taking of the deposition testimony, any party who records or causes the recording of that testimony by means of audio or video technology shall promptly do both of the following:

(1) Permit that other party to hear the audio recording or to view the video recording.

(2) Furnish a copy of the audio or video recording to that other party on receipt of payment of the reasonable cost of making that copy of the recording.

(g) If the testimony at the deposition is recorded both stenographically and by audio or video technology, the stenographic transcript shall be the official record of that testimony for the purpose of the trial and any subsequent hearing or appeal.

(h)

(1) The requesting attorney or party appearing in propria persona shall timely pay the deposition officer or the entity providing the services of the deposition officer for the transcription or copy of the transcription described in subdivision (b) or (c), and any other deposition product or service that is requested either orally or in writing.

(2) This subdivision shall apply unless responsibility for the payment is otherwise provided by law or unless the deposition officer or entity is notified in writing at the time the services or products are requested that the party or another identified person will be responsible for payment.

(3) This subdivision does not prohibit or supersede an agreement between an attorney and a party allocating responsibility for the payment of deposition costs to the party.

(4) Nothing in the case of Serrano v. Stefan Merli Plastering Co., Inc. (2008) 162 Cal.App.4th 1014 shall be construed to alter the standards by which a court acquires personal jurisdiction over a nonparty to an action.

(5) The requesting attorney or party appearing in propria persona, upon the written request of a deposition officer who has obtained a final judgment for payment of services provided pursuant to this subdivision, shall provide to the deposition officer an address that can be used to effectuate service for the purpose of Section 708.110 in the manner specified in Section 415.10.
(i) For purposes of this section, "deposition product or service" means any product or service provided in connection with a deposition that qualifies as shorthand reporting, as described in Section 8017 of the Business and Professions Code, and any product or service derived from that shorthand reporting.

Ca. Civ. Proc. Code § 2025.510
Amended by Stats 2014 ch 913 (AB 2747),s 12, eff. 1/1/2015.
Amended by Stats 2012 ch 125 (AB 2372),s 1, eff. 1/1/2013.

Amended by Stats 2007 ch 115 (AB 1211),s 1, eff. 1/1/2008.
Added by Stats 2004 ch 182 (AB 3081),s 23, eff. 7/1/2005.

Section 2025.520 - Notice that transcript of testimony available; changing form or substance of answer or approving or disapproving transcript

(a) If the deposition testimony is stenographically recorded, the deposition officer shall send written notice to the deponent and to all parties attending the deposition when the original transcript of the testimony for each session of the deposition is available for reading, correcting, and signing, unless the deponent and the attending parties agree on the record that the reading, correcting, and signing of the transcript of the testimony will be waived or that the reading, correcting, and signing of a transcript of the testimony will take place after the entire deposition has been concluded or at some other specific time.

(b) For 30 days following each notice under subdivision (a), unless the attending parties and the deponent agree on the record or otherwise in writing to a longer or shorter time period, the deponent may change the form or the substance of the answer to a question, and may either approve the transcript of the deposition by signing it, or refuse to approve the transcript by not signing it.

(c) Alternatively, within this same period, the deponent may change the form or the substance of the answer to any question and may approve or refuse to approve the transcript by means of a letter to the deposition officer signed by the deponent which is mailed by certified or registered mail with return receipt requested. A copy of that letter shall be sent by first-class mail to all parties attending the deposition.

(d) For good cause shown, the court may shorten the 30-day period for making changes, approving, or refusing to approve the transcript.

(e) The deposition officer shall indicate on the original of the transcript, if the deponent has not already done so at the office of the deposition officer, any action taken by the deponent and indicate on the original of the transcript, the deponent's approval of, or failure or refusal to approve, the transcript. The deposition officer shall also notify in writing the parties attending the deposition of any changes which the deponent timely made in person.

(f) If the deponent fails or refuses to approve the transcript within the allotted period, the deposition shall be given the same effect as though it had been approved, subject to any changes timely made by the deponent.

(g) Notwithstanding subdivision (f), on a seasonable motion to suppress the deposition, accompanied by a meet and confer declaration under Section 2016.040, the court may determine that the reasons given for the failure or refusal to approve the transcript require rejection of the deposition in whole or in part.

(h) The court shall impose a monetary sanction under Chapter 7 (commencing with Section 2023.010) against any party, person, or attorney who unsuccessfully makes or opposes a motion to suppress a deposition under this section, unless the court finds that the one subject to the sanction acted with substantial justification or that other circumstances make the imposition of the sanction unjust.

Ca. Civ. Proc. Code § 2025.520
Added by Stats 2004 ch 182 (AB 3081),s 23, eff. 7/1/2005.

Section 2025.530 - Notice that audio or video recording available; changing substance of answer; signing deposition or statement refusing to sign

(a) If there is no stenographic transcription of the deposition, the deposition officer shall send written notice to the deponent and to all parties attending the deposition that the audio or video recording made by, or at the direction of, any party, is available for review, unless the deponent and all these parties agree on the record to waive the hearing or viewing of the audio or video recording of the testimony.

(b) For 30 days following a notice under subdivision (a), the deponent, either in person or by signed letter to the deposition officer, may change the substance of the answer to any question.

(c) The deposition officer shall set forth in a writing to accompany the recording any changes made by the deponent, as well as either the deponent's signature identifying the deposition as the deponent's own, or a statement of the deponent's failure to supply the signature, or to contact the officer within the period prescribed by subdivision (b).

(d) When a deponent fails to contact the officer within the period prescribed by subdivision (b), or expressly refuses by a signature to identify the deposition as the deponent's own, the deposition shall be given the same effect as though signed.

(e) Notwithstanding subdivision (d), on a reasonable motion to suppress the deposition, accompanied by a meet and confer declaration under Section 2016.040, the court may determine that the reasons given for the refusal to sign require rejection of the deposition in whole or in part.

(f) The court shall impose a monetary sanction under Chapter 7 (commencing with Section 2023.010) against any party, person, or attorney who unsuccessfully makes or opposes a motion to suppress a deposition under this section, unless it finds that the one subject to the sanction acted with substantial justification or that other circumstances make the imposition of the sanction unjust.

Ca. Civ. Proc. Code § 2025.530
Added by Stats 2004 ch 182 (AB 3081),s 23, eff. 7/1/2005.

Section 2025.540 - Certification by deposition officer

(a) The deposition officer shall certify on the transcript of the deposition, or in a writing accompanying an audio or video record of deposition testimony, as described in Section 2025.530, that the deponent was duly sworn and that the transcript or recording is a true record of the testimony given.

(b) When prepared as a rough draft transcript, the transcript of the deposition may not be certified and may not be used, cited, or transcribed as the certified transcript of the deposition proceedings. The rough draft transcript may not be cited or used in any way or at any time to rebut or contradict the certified transcript of deposition proceedings as provided by the deposition officer.

Ca. Civ. Proc. Code § 2025.540
Added by Stats 2004 ch 182 (AB 3081),s 23, eff. 7/1/2005.

Section 2025.550 - Transcript of deposition transmitted to attorney for party who noticed deposition

(a) The certified transcript of a deposition shall not be filed with the court. Instead, the deposition officer shall securely seal that transcript in an envelope or package endorsed with the title of the action and marked: "Deposition of (here insert name of deponent)," and shall promptly transmit it to the attorney for the party who noticed the deposition. This attorney shall store it under conditions that will protect it against loss, destruction, or tampering.

(b) The attorney to whom the transcript of a deposition is transmitted shall retain custody of it until six months after final disposition of the action. At that time, the transcript may be destroyed, unless the court, on motion of any party and for good cause shown, orders that the transcript be preserved for a longer period.

Ca. Civ. Proc. Code § 2025.550

Added by Stats 2004 ch 182 (AB 3081),s 23, eff. 7/1/2005.

Section 2025.560 - Retention of audio or video recording of deposition by operator

(a) An audio or video recording of deposition testimony made by, or at the direction of, any party, including a certified recording made by an operator qualified under subdivisions (b) to (f), inclusive, of Section 2025.340, shall not be filed with the court. Instead, the operator shall retain custody of that recording and shall store it under conditions that will protect it against loss, destruction, or tampering, and preserve as far as practicable the quality of the recording and the integrity of the testimony and images it contains.

(b) At the request of any party to the action, including a party who did not attend the taking of the deposition testimony, or at the request of the deponent, that operator shall promptly do both of the following:

(1) Permit the one making the request to hear or to view the recording on receipt of payment of a reasonable charge for providing the facilities for hearing or viewing the recording.

(2) Furnish a copy of the audio or video recording to the one making the request on receipt of payment of the reasonable cost of making that copy of the recording.

(c) The attorney or operator who has custody of an audio or video recording of deposition testimony made by, or at the direction of, any party, shall retain custody of it until six months after final disposition of the action. At that time, the audio or video recording may be destroyed or erased, unless the court, on motion of any party and for good cause shown, orders that the recording be preserved for a longer period.

Ca. Civ. Proc. Code § 2025.560
Amended by Stats 2009 ch 88 (AB 176),s 18, eff. 1/1/2010.
Added by Stats 2004 ch 182 (AB 3081),s 23, eff. 7/1/2005.

Section 2025.570 - Copy of transcript or recording made available by deposition officer

(a) Notwithstanding subdivision (b) of Section 2025.320, unless the court issues an order to the contrary, a copy of the transcript of the deposition testimony made by, or at the direction of, any party, or an audio or video recording of the deposition testimony, if still in the possession of the deposition officer, shall be made available by the deposition officer to any person requesting a copy, on payment of a reasonable charge set by the deposition officer.

(b) If a copy is requested from the deposition officer, the deposition officer shall mail a notice to all parties attending the deposition and to the deponent at the deponent's last known address advising them of all of the following:

(1) The copy is being sought.

(2) The name of the person requesting the copy.

(3) The right to seek a protective order under Section 2025.420.

(c) If a protective order is not served on the deposition officer within 30 days of the mailing of the notice, the deposition officer shall make the copy available to the person requesting the copy.

(d) This section shall apply only to recorded testimony taken at

depositions occurring on or after January 1, 1998.
Ca. Civ. Proc. Code § 2025.570
Added by Stats 2004 ch 182 (AB 3081),s 23, eff. 7/1/2005.

Article 6 - POST-DEPOSITION PROCEDURES 2025.610

Section 2025.610 - Leave to take subsequent deposition

(a) Once any party has taken the deposition of any natural person, including that of a party to the action, neither the party who gave, nor any other party who has been served with a deposition notice pursuant to Section 2025.240 may take a subsequent deposition of that deponent.

(b) Notwithstanding subdivision (a), for good cause shown, the court may grant leave to take a subsequent deposition, and the parties, with the consent of any deponent who is not a party, may stipulate that a subsequent deposition be taken.

(c) This section does not preclude taking one subsequent deposition of a natural person who has previously been examined under either or both of the following circumstances:

(1) The person was examined as a result of that person's designation to testify on behalf of an organization under Section 2025.230.

(2) The person was examined pursuant to a court order under Section 485.230, for the limited purpose of discovering pursuant to Section 485.230 the identity, location, and value of property in which the deponent has an interest.

(d) This section does not authorize the taking of more than one subsequent deposition for the limited purpose of Section 485.230.
Ca. Civ. Proc. Code § 2025.610
Added by Stats 2004 ch 182 (AB 3081),s 23, eff. 7/1/2005.

Section 2025.620 - Use of deposition at trial or other hearing

At the trial or any other hearing in the action, any part or all of a deposition may be used against any party who was present or represented at the taking of the deposition, or who had due notice of the deposition and did not serve a valid objection under Section 2025.410, so far as admissible under the rules of evidence applied as though the deponent were then present and testifying as a witness, in accordance with the following provisions:

(a) Any party may use a deposition for the purpose of contradicting or impeaching the testimony of the deponent as a witness, or for any other purpose permitted by the Evidence Code.

(b) An adverse party may use for any purpose, a deposition of a party to the action, or of anyone who at the time of taking the deposition was an officer, director, managing agent, employee, agent, or designee under Section 2025.230 of a party. It is not ground for objection to the use of a deposition of a party under this subdivision by an adverse party that the deponent is available to testify, has testified, or will testify at the trial or other hearing.

(c) Any party may use for any purpose the deposition of any person or organization, including that of any party to the action, if the court finds any of the following:

(1) The deponent resides more than 150 miles from the place of the trial or other hearing.

(2) The deponent, without the procurement or wrongdoing of the proponent of the deposition for the purpose of preventing testimony in open court, is any of the following:

(A) Exempted or precluded on the ground of privilege from testifying concerning the matter to which the deponent's testimony is relevant.

(B) Disqualified from testifying.

(C) Dead or unable to attend or testify because of existing physical or mental illness or infirmity.

(D) Absent from the trial or other hearing and the court is unable to compel the deponent's attendance by its process.

(E) Absent from the trial or other hearing and the proponent of the deposition has exercised reasonable diligence but has been unable to procure the deponent's attendance by the court's process.

(3) Exceptional circumstances exist that make it desirable to allow the use of any deposition in the interests of justice and with due regard to the importance of presenting the testimony of witnesses orally in open court.

(d) Any party may use a video recording of the deposition testimony of a treating or consulting physician or of any expert witness even though the deponent is available to testify if the deposition notice under Section 2025.220 reserved the right to use the deposition at trial, and if that party has complied with subdivision (m) of Section 2025.340.

(e) Subject to the requirements of this chapter, a party may offer in evidence all or any part of a deposition, and if the party introduces only part of the deposition, any other party may introduce any other parts that are relevant to the parts introduced.

(f) Substitution of parties does not affect the right to use depositions previously taken.

(g) When an action has been brought in any court of the United States or of any state, and another action involving the same subject matter is subsequently brought between the same parties or their representatives or successors in interest, all depositions lawfully taken and duly filed in the initial action may be used in the subsequent action as if originally taken in that subsequent action. A deposition previously taken may also be used as permitted by the Evidence Code.

Ca. Civ. Proc. Code § 2025.620
Added by Stats 2004 ch 182 (AB 3081),s 23, eff. 7/1/2005.

Chapter 10 - ORAL DEPOSITION OUTSIDE CALIFORNIA

Section 2026.010 - Generally
(a) Any party may obtain discovery by taking an oral deposition, as described in Section 2025.010, in another state of the United States,

or in a territory or an insular possession subject to its jurisdiction. Except as modified in this section, the procedures for taking oral depositions in California set forth in Chapter 9 (commencing with Section 2025.010) apply to an oral deposition taken in another state of the United States, or in a territory or an insular possession subject to its jurisdiction.

(b) If a deponent is a party to the action or an officer, director, managing agent, or employee of a party, the service of the deposition notice is effective to compel that deponent to attend and to testify, as well as to produce any document, electronically stored information, or tangible thing for inspection, copying, testing, or sampling. The deposition notice shall specify a place in the state, territory, or insular possession of the United States that is within 75 miles of the residence or a business office of a deponent.

(c) If the deponent is not a party to the action or an officer, director, managing agent, or employee of a party, a party serving a deposition notice under this section shall use any process and procedures required and available under the laws of the state, territory, or insular possession where the deposition is to be taken to compel the deponent to attend and to testify, as well as to produce any document, electronically stored information, or tangible thing for inspection, copying, testing, sampling, and any related activity.

(d) A deposition taken under this section shall be conducted in either of the following ways:

(1) Under the supervision of a person who is authorized to administer oaths by the laws of the United States or those of the place where the examination is to be held, and who is not otherwise disqualified under Section 2025.320 and subdivisions (b) to (f), inclusive, of Section 2025.340.

(2) Before a person appointed by the court.

(e) An appointment under subdivision (d) is effective to authorize that person to administer oaths and to take testimony.

(f) On request, the clerk of the court shall issue a commission authorizing the deposition in another state or place. The commission shall request that process issue in the place where the examination is to be held, requiring attendance and enforcing the obligations of the deponents to produce documents and electronically stored information and answer questions. The commission shall be issued by the clerk to any party in any action pending in its venue without a noticed motion or court order. The commission may contain terms that are required by the foreign jurisdiction to initiate the process. If a court order is required by the foreign jurisdiction, an order for a commission may be obtained by ex parte application.

Ca. Civ. Proc. Code § 2026.010

Amended by Stats 2012 ch 72 (SB 1574),s 27, eff. 1/1/2013.
Added by Stats 2004 ch 182 (AB 3081),s 23, eff. 7/1/2005.

Section 2027.010 - Taking deposition in foreign country
(a) Any party may obtain discovery by taking an oral deposition, as described in Section 2025.010, in a foreign nation. Except as modified in this section, the procedures for taking oral depositions in California set forth in Chapter 9 (commencing with Section 2025.010) apply to an oral deposition taken in a foreign nation.
(b) If a deponent is a party to the action or an officer, director, managing agent, or employee of a party, the service of the deposition notice is effective to compel the deponent to attend and to testify, as well as to produce any document, electronically stored information, or tangible thing for inspection, copying, testing, or sampling.
(c) If a deponent is not a party to the action or an officer, director, managing agent or employee of a party, a party serving a deposition notice under this section shall use any process and procedures required and available under the laws of the foreign nation where the deposition is to be taken to compel the deponent to attend and to testify, as well as to produce any document, electronically stored information, or tangible thing for inspection, copying, testing, sampling, and any related activity.
(d) A deposition taken under this section shall be conducted under the supervision of any of the following:

(1) A person who is authorized to administer oaths or their equivalent by the laws of the United States or of the foreign nation, and who is not otherwise disqualified under Section 2025.320 and subdivisions (b) to (f), inclusive, of Section 2025.340.

(2) A person or officer appointed by commission or under letters rogatory.

(3) Any person agreed to by all the parties.
(e) On motion of the party seeking to take an oral deposition in a foreign nation, the court in which the action is pending shall issue a commission, letters rogatory, or a letter of request, if it determines that one is necessary or convenient. The commission, letters rogatory, or letter of request may include any terms and directions that are just and appropriate. The deposition officer may be designated by name or by descriptive title in the deposition notice and in the commission. Letters rogatory or a letter of request may be addressed: "To the Appropriate Judicial Authority in [name of foreign nation]."

Ca. Civ. Proc. Code § 2027.010
Amended by Stats 2012 ch 72 (SB 1574),s 28, eff. 1/1/2013.
Added by Stats 2004 ch 182 (AB 3081),s 23, eff. 7/1/2005.

Chapter 11 - DEPOSITION BY WRITTEN QUESTIONS

Section 2028.010 - Generally
Any party may obtain discovery by taking a deposition by written questions instead of by oral examination. Except as modified in this chapter, the procedures for taking oral depositions set forth in Chapters 9 (commencing with Section 2025.010) and 10 (commencing with Section 2026.010) apply to written depositions.

Ca. Civ. Proc. Code § 2028.010
Added by Stats 2004 ch 182 (AB 3081),s 23, eff. 7/1/2005.

Section 2028.020 - Notice
The notice of a written deposition shall comply with Sections 2025.220 and 2025.230, and with subdivision (c) of Section

2020.240, except as follows:

(a) The name or descriptive title, as well as the address, of the deposition officer shall be stated.

(b) The date, time, and place for commencement of the deposition may be left to future determination by the deposition officer.

Ca. Civ. Proc. Code § 2028.020
Added by Stats 2004 ch 182 (AB 3081),s 23, eff. 7/1/2005.

Section 2028.030 - Service of questions with notice; time for serving cross questions; redirect questions; recross questions; extension of time

(a) The questions to be propounded to the deponent by direct examination shall accompany the notice of a written deposition.

(b) Within 30 days after the deposition notice and questions are served, a party shall serve any cross questions on all other parties entitled to notice of the deposition.

(c) Within 15 days after being served with cross questions, a party shall serve any redirect questions on all other parties entitled to notice of the deposition.

(d) Within 15 days after being served with redirect questions, a party shall serve any recross questions on all other parties entitled to notice of the deposition.

(e) The court may, for good cause shown, extend or shorten the time periods for the interchange of cross, redirect, and recross questions.

Ca. Civ. Proc. Code § 2028.030
Added by Stats 2004 ch 182 (AB 3081),s 23, eff. 7/1/2005.

Section 2028.040 - Objection to form of question

(a) A party who objects to the form of any question shall serve a specific objection to that question on all parties entitled to notice of the deposition within 15 days after service of the question. A party who fails to timely serve an objection to the form of a question waives it.

(b) The objecting party shall promptly move the court to sustain the objection. This motion shall be accompanied by a meet and confer declaration under Section 2016.040. Unless the court has sustained that objection, the deposition officer shall propound to the deponent that question subject to that objection as to its form.

(c) The court shall impose a monetary sanction under Chapter 7 (commencing with Section 2023.010) against any party, person, or attorney who unsuccessfully makes or opposes a motion to sustain an objection, unless it finds that the one subject to the sanction acted with substantial justification or that other circumstances make the imposition of the sanction unjust.

Ca. Civ. Proc. Code § 2028.040
Added by Stats 2004 ch 182 (AB 3081),s 23, eff. 7/1/2005.

Section 2028.050 - Objection to question on ground that it calls for privileged information or protected work product

(a) A party who objects to any question on the ground that it calls for information that is privileged or is protected work product under Chapter 4 (commencing with Section 2018.010) shall serve a specific objection to that question on all parties entitled to notice of the deposition within 15 days after service of the question. A party who fails to timely serve that objection waives it.

(b) The party propounding any question to which an objection is made on those grounds may then move the court for an order overruling that objection. This motion shall be accompanied by a meet and confer declaration under Section 2016.040. The deposition officer shall not propound to the deponent any question to which a written objection on those grounds has been served unless the court has overruled that objection.

(c) The court shall impose a monetary sanction under Chapter 7 (commencing with Section 2023.010) against any party, person, or attorney who unsuccessfully makes or opposes a motion to overrule an objection, unless it finds that the one subject to the sanction acted with substantial justification or that other circumstances make the imposition of the sanction unjust.

Ca. Civ. Proc. Code § 2028.050
Added by Stats 2004 ch 182 (AB 3081),s 23, eff. 7/1/2005.

Section 2028.060 - Forwarding copy of questions on direct examination to deponent for study prior to deposition

(a) The party taking a written deposition may forward to the deponent a copy of the questions on direct examination for study prior to the deposition.

(b) No party or attorney shall permit the deponent to preview the form or the substance of any cross, redirect, or recross questions.

Ca. Civ. Proc. Code § 2028.060

Added by Stats 2004 ch 182 (AB 3081),s 23, eff. 7/1/2005.

Section 2028.070 - Court orders

In addition to any appropriate order listed in Section 2025.420, the court may order any of the following:

(a) That the deponent's testimony be taken by oral, instead of written, examination.

(b) That one or more of the parties receiving notice of the written deposition be permitted to attend in person or by attorney and to propound questions to the deponent by oral examination.

(c) That objections under Sections 2028.040 and 2028.050 be sustained or overruled.

(d) That the deposition be taken before an officer other than the one named or described in the deposition notice.

Ca. Civ. Proc. Code § 2028.070

Added by Stats 2004 ch 182 (AB 3081),s 23, eff. 7/1/2005.

Section 2028.080 - Delivery of copy of notice and questions served to deposition officer

The party taking a written deposition shall deliver to the officer designated in the deposition notice a copy of that notice and of all questions served under Section 2028.030. The deposition officer shall proceed promptly to propound the questions and to take and record the testimony of the deponent in response to the questions.

Ca. Civ. Proc. Code § 2028.080

Added by Stats 2004 ch 182 (AB 3081),s 23, eff. 7/1/2005.

Chapter 12 - DISCOVERY IN ACTION PENDING OUTSIDE CALIFORNIA

Section 2029.010 - [Repealed]

Ca. Civ. Proc. Code § 2029.010

Repealed by Stats 2008 ch 231 (AB 2193),s 2, eff. 1/1/2009.

Chapter heading amended by Stats 2008 ch 231 (AB 2193),s 1, eff. 1/1/2009.

Amended by Stats 2005 ch 294 (AB 333),s 9, eff. 1/1/2006.

Added by Stats 2004 ch 182 (AB 3081),s 23, eff. 7/1/2005.

Article 1 - INTERSTATE AND INTERNATIONAL DEPOSITIONS AND DISCOVERY ACT

Section 2029.100 - Title of act

This article may be cited as the Interstate and International Depositions and Discovery Act.

Ca. Civ. Proc. Code § 2029.100

Added by Stats 2008 ch 231 (AB 2193),s 3, eff. 1/1/2009.

Section 2029.200 - Definitions

In this article:

(a)"Foreign jurisdiction" means either of the following:

(1)A state other than this state.

(2)A foreign nation.

(b)"Foreign penal civil action" means a civil action authorized by the law of a state other than this state in which the sole purpose is to punish an offense against the public justice of that state.

(c)"Foreign subpoena" means a subpoena issued under authority of a court of record of a foreign jurisdiction.

(d)"Person" means an individual, corporation, business trust, estate, trust, partnership, limited liability company, association, joint venture, public corporation, government, or governmental subdivision, agency, or instrumentality, or any other legal or commercial entity.

(e)"State" means a state of the United States, the District of Columbia, Puerto Rico, the Virgin Islands, a federally recognized Indian tribe, or any territory or insular possession subject to the jurisdiction of the United States.

(f)"Subpoena" means a document, however denominated, issued under authority of a court of record requiring a person to do any of the following:

(1)Attend and give testimony at a deposition.

(2)Produce and permit inspection, copying, testing, or sampling of designated books, documents, records, electronically stored information, or tangible things in the possession, custody, or control of the person.

(3)Permit inspection of premises under the control of the person.

Ca. Civ. Proc. Code § 2029.200
Amended by Stats 2022 ch 628 (AB 2091),s 3, eff. 9/27/2022.
Amended by Stats 2012 ch 72 (SB 1574),s 29, eff. 1/1/2013.
Added by Stats 2008 ch 231 (AB 2193),s 3, eff. 1/1/2009.

Section 2029.300 - Request for issuance of subpoena

(a) To request issuance of a subpoena under this section, a party shall submit the original or a true and correct copy of a foreign subpoena to the clerk of the superior court in the county in which discovery is sought to be conducted in this state. A request for the issuance of a subpoena under this section does not constitute making an appearance in the courts of this state.

(b) In addition to submitting a foreign subpoena under subdivision (a), a party seeking discovery shall do both of the following:

(1) Submit an application requesting that the superior court issue a subpoena with the same terms as the foreign subpoena. The application shall be on a form prescribed by the Judicial Council pursuant to Section 2029.390. No civil case cover sheet is required.

(2) Pay the fee specified in Section 70626 of the Government Code.

(c) When a party submits a foreign subpoena to the clerk of the superior court in accordance with subdivision (a), and satisfies the requirements of subdivision (b), the clerk shall promptly issue a subpoena for service upon the person to which the foreign subpoena is directed.

(d) A subpoena issued under this section shall satisfy all of the following conditions:

(1) It shall incorporate the terms used in the foreign subpoena.

(2) It shall contain or be accompanied by the names, addresses, and telephone numbers of all counsel of record in the proceeding to which the subpoena relates and of any party not represented by counsel.

(3) It shall bear the caption and case number of the out-of-state case to which it relates.

(4) It shall state the name of the court that issues it.

(5) It shall be on a form prescribed by the Judicial Council pursuant to Section 2029.390.

(e) Notwithstanding subdivision (a), a subpoena shall not be issued pursuant to this section in any of the following circumstances:

(1) If the foreign subpoena is based on a violation of another state's laws that interfere with a person's right to allow a child to receive gender-affirming health care or gender-affirming mental health care. For the purpose of this paragraph, "gender-affirming health care" and "gender-affirming mental health care" shall have the same meaning as provided in Section 16010.2 of the Welfare and Institutions Code.

(2) If the submitted foreign subpoena relates to a foreign penal civil action and would require disclosure of information related to sensitive services. For purposes of this paragraph, "sensitive services" has the same meaning as defined in Section 791.02 of the Insurance Code.

Ca. Civ. Proc. Code § 2029.300

Amended by Stats 2022 ch 810 (SB 107),s 2.5, eff. 1/1/2023.

Amended by Stats 2022 ch 628 (AB 2091),s 4, eff. 9/27/2022.

Added by Stats 2008 ch 231 (AB 2193),s 3, eff. 1/1/2009.

Section 2029.350 - Subpoena issued by attorney

(a) Notwithstanding Sections 1986 and 2029.300, if a party to a proceeding pending in a foreign jurisdiction retains an attorney licensed to practice in this state, who is an active member of the State Bar, and that attorney receives the original or a true and correct copy of a foreign subpoena, the attorney may issue a subpoena under this article.

(b)

(1) Notwithstanding subdivision (a), an authorized attorney shall not issue a subpoena pursuant to subdivision (a) if the foreign subpoena is based on a violation of another state's laws that interfere with a person's right to allow a child to receive gender-affirming health care or gender-affirming mental health care.

(2) For the purpose of this subdivision, "gender-affirming health care" and "gender-affirming mental health care" shall have the same meaning as provided in Section 16010.2 of the Welfare and Institutions Code.

(c) Notwithstanding subdivision (a), an attorney shall not issue a subpoena under this article based on a foreign subpoena that relates to a foreign penal civil action and that would require disclosure of information related to sensitive services. For purposes of this subdivision, "sensitive services" has the same meaning as defined in Section 791.02 of the Insurance Code.

(d) A subpoena issued under this section shall satisfy all of the following conditions:

(1) It shall incorporate the terms used in the foreign subpoena.

(2) It shall contain or be accompanied by the names, addresses, and telephone numbers of all counsel of record in the proceeding to which the subpoena relates and of any party not represented by counsel.

(3) It shall bear the caption and case number of the out-of-state case to which it relates.

(4) It shall state the name of the superior court of the county in which the discovery is to be conducted.

(5) It shall be on a form prescribed by the Judicial Council pursuant to Section 2029.390.

Ca. Civ. Proc. Code § 2029.350

Amended by Stats 2022 ch 810 (SB 107),s 3.5, eff. 1/1/2023.

Amended by Stats 2022 ch 628 (AB 2091),s 5, eff. 9/27/2022.

Added by Stats 2008 ch 231 (AB 2193),s 3, eff. 1/1/2009.

Section 2029.390 - Preparation of application form and new subpoena forms

On or before January 1, 2010, the Judicial Council shall do all of the following:

(a) Prepare an application form to be used for purposes of Section 2029.300.

(b) Prepare one or more new subpoena forms that include clear instructions for use in issuance of a subpoena under Section 2029.300 or 2029.350. Alternatively, the Judicial Council may modify one or more existing subpoena forms to include clear instructions for use in issuance of a subpoena under Section 2029.300 or 2029.350.

Ca. Civ. Proc. Code § 2029.390

Added by Stats 2008 ch 231 (AB 2193),s 3, eff. 1/1/2009.

Section 2029.400 - Personal service of subpoena

A subpoena issued under this article shall be personally served in compliance with the law of this state, including, without limitation,

Section 1985.
Ca. Civ. Proc. Code § 2029.400
Added by Stats 2008 ch 231 (AB 2193),s 3, eff. 1/1/2009.

Section 2029.500 - Applicability of laws or rules governing depositions, production or inspection

Titles 3 (commencing with Section 1985) and 4 (commencing with Section 2016.010) of Part 4, and any other law or court rule of this state governing a deposition, a production of documents or other tangible items, or an inspection of premises, including any law or court rule governing payment of court costs or sanctions, apply to discovery under this article.
Ca. Civ. Proc. Code § 2029.500
Added by Stats 2008 ch 231 (AB 2193),s 3, eff. 1/1/2009.

Section 2029.600 - Request for relief

(a) If a dispute arises relating to discovery under this article, any request for a protective order or to enforce, quash, or modify a subpoena, or for other relief may be filed in the superior court in the county in which discovery is to be conducted and, if so filed, shall comply with the applicable rules or statutes of this state.
(b) A request for relief pursuant to this section shall be referred to as a petition notwithstanding any statute under which a request for the same relief would be referred to as a motion or by another term if it was brought in a proceeding pending in this state.
(c) A petition for relief pursuant to this section shall be accompanied by a civil case cover sheet.
Ca. Civ. Proc. Code § 2029.600
Added by Stats 2008 ch 231 (AB 2193),s 3, eff. 1/1/2009.

Section 2029.610 - First appearance fee; requirements of petition, response, other document filed

(a) On filing a petition under Section 2029.600, a petitioner who is a party to the out-of-state proceeding shall pay a first appearance fee as specified in Section 70611 of the Government Code. A petitioner who is not a party to the out-of-state proceeding shall pay the fee specified in subdivision (c) of Section 70626 of the Government Code.

(b) The court in which the petition is filed shall assign it a case number.

(c) On responding to a petition under Section 2029.600, a party to the out-of-state proceeding shall pay a first appearance fee as specified in Section 70612 of the Government Code. A person who is not a party to the out-of-state proceeding may file a response without paying a fee.

(d) Any petition, response, or other document filed under this section shall satisfy all of the following conditions:

(1) It shall bear the caption and case number of the out-of-state case to which it relates.

(2) The first page shall state the name of the court in which the document is filed.

(3) The first page shall state the case number assigned by the court under subdivision (b).

(4) The first page shall state whether or not the person filing the document is a party to the out-of-state case.

Ca. Civ. Proc. Code § 2029.610

Amended by Stats 2011 ch 308 (SB 647),s 4, eff. 1/1/2012.
Added by Stats 2008 ch 231 (AB 2193),s 3, eff. 1/1/2009.

Section 2029.620 - Petition for relief if another dispute later arises relating to discovery in same case

(a) If a petition has been filed under Section 2029.600 and another dispute later arises relating to discovery being conducted in the same county for purposes of the same out-of-state proceeding, the deponent or other disputant may file a petition for appropriate relief in the same superior court as the previous petition.

(b) The first page of the petition shall clearly indicate that it is not the first petition filed in that court that relates to the out-of-state case.

(c)

(1) If the petitioner in the new dispute is a party to the out-of-state case who previously paid a first appearance fee under this article, the petitioner shall pay a motion fee as specified in subdivision (a) of Section 70617 of the Government Code. If the petitioner in the new dispute is a party to the out-of-state case but has not previously paid a first appearance fee under this article, the petitioner shall pay a first appearance fee as specified in Section 70611 of the Government Code.

(2) If the petitioner in the new dispute is not a party to the out-of-state case, the petitioner shall pay the fee specified in subdivision (c) of Section 70626 of the Government Code, unless the petitioner previously paid that fee. If the petitioner previously paid the fee specified in subdivision (c) of Section 70626 of the Government Code, the petitioner shall pay a motion fee as specified in subdivision (a) of Section 70617 of the Government Code.

(d) If a person responding to the new petition is not a party to the out-of-state case, or is a party who previously paid a first appearance fee under this article, that person does not have to pay a fee for responding. If a person responding to the new petition is a party to the out-of-state case but has not previously paid a first appearance fee under this article, that person shall pay a first appearance fee as specified in Section 70612 of the Government Code.

(e) Any petition, response, or other document filed under this section shall satisfy all of the following conditions:

(1) It shall bear the caption and case number of the out-of-state case to which it relates.

(2) The first page shall state the name of the court in which the document is filed.

(3) The first page shall state the same case number that the court assigned to the first petition relating to the out-of-state case.

(4) The first page shall state whether or not the person filing the document is a party to the out-of-state case.

(f) A petition for relief pursuant to this section shall be accompanied by a civil case cover sheet.

Ca. Civ. Proc. Code § 2029.620

Amended by Stats 2011 ch 308 (SB 647),s 5, eff. 1/1/2012.

Added by Stats 2008 ch 231 (AB 2193),s 3, eff. 1/1/2009.

Section 2029.630 - Petition requirements

A petition under Section 2029.600 or Section 2029.620 is subject to the requirements of Section 1005 relating to notice and to filing and service of papers.

Ca. Civ. Proc. Code § 2029.630

Added by Stats 2008 ch 231 (AB 2193),s 3, eff. 1/1/2009.

Section 2029.640 - Relief without obtaining subpoena or being subpoenaed

If a party to a proceeding pending in a foreign jurisdiction seeks discovery from a witness in this state by properly issued notice or by agreement, it is not necessary for that party to obtain a subpoena under this article to be able to seek relief under Section 2029.600 or 2029.620. The deponent or any other party may also seek relief under Section 2029.600 or 2029.620 in those circumstances, regardless of whether the deponent was subpoenaed under this article.

Ca. Civ. Proc. Code § 2029.640

Added by Stats 2008 ch 231 (AB 2193),s 3, eff. 1/1/2009.

Section 2029.650 - Petition for extraordinary writ

(a) If a superior court issues an order granting, denying, or otherwise resolving a petition under Section 2029.600 or 2029.620, a person aggrieved by the order may petition the appropriate court of appeal for an extraordinary writ. No order or other action of a court under this article is appealable in this state.

(b) Pending its decision on the writ petition, the court of appeal may stay the order of the superior court, the discovery that is the subject of that order, or both.

Ca. Civ. Proc. Code § 2029.650

Added by Stats 2008 ch 231 (AB 2193),s 3, eff. 1/1/2009.

Section 2029.700 - Sections referred to as California version of Uniform Interstate Depositions and Discovery Act

(a) Sections 2029.100, 2029.200, 2029.300, 2029.400, 2029.500, 2029.600, 2029.800, 2029.900, and this section, collectively, constitute and may be referred to as the "California version of the Uniform Interstate Depositions and Discovery Act."

(b) In applying and construing this uniform act, consideration shall be given to the need to promote uniformity of the law with respect to its subject matter among the states that enact it.

Ca. Civ. Proc. Code § 2029.700

Added by Stats 2008 ch 231 (AB 2193),s 3, eff. 1/1/2009.

Section 2029.800 - Applicability to cases pending on operative date

This article applies to requests for discovery in cases pending on or after the operative date of this section.

Ca. Civ. Proc. Code § 2029.800

Added by Stats 2008 ch 231 (AB 2193),s 3, eff. 1/1/2009.

Section 2029.900 - Operative date

Section 2029.390 is operative on January 1, 2009. The remainder of this article is operative on January 1, 2010.

Ca. Civ. Proc. Code § 2029.900

Added by Stats 2008 ch 231 (AB 2193),s 3, eff. 1/1/2009.

Chapter 13 - WRITTEN INTERROGATORIES

Article 1 - PROPOUNDING INTERROGATORIES

Section 2030.010 - Generally

(a) Any party may obtain discovery within the scope delimited by Chapter 2 (commencing with Section 2017.010), and subject to the restrictions set forth in Chapter 5 (commencing with Section 2019.010), by propounding to any other party to the action written interrogatories to be answered under oath.

(b) An interrogatory may relate to whether another party is making a certain contention, or to the facts, witnesses, and writings on which a contention is based. An interrogatory is not objectionable because an answer to it involves an opinion or contention that relates to fact or the application of law to fact, or would be based on information obtained or legal theories developed in anticipation of litigation or in preparation for trial.

Ca. Civ. Proc. Code § 2030.010

Amended by Stats 2015 ch 303 (AB 731),s 42, eff. 1/1/2016.

Added by Stats 2004 ch 182 (AB 3081),s 23, op. 7/1/2005.

Section 2030.020 - Propounding interrogatories without leave of court

(a) A defendant may propound interrogatories to a party to the action without leave of court at any time.

(b) A plaintiff may propound interrogatories to a party without leave of court at any time that is 10 days after the service of the summons on, or appearance by, that party, whichever occurs first.

(c) Notwithstanding subdivision (b), in an unlawful detainer action or other proceeding under Chapter 4 (commencing with Section 1159) of Title 3 of Part 3, a plaintiff may propound interrogatories to a party without leave of court at any time that is five days after service of the summons on, or appearance by, that party, whichever occurs first.

(d) Notwithstanding subdivisions (b) and (c), on motion with or without notice, the court, for good cause shown, may grant leave to a plaintiff to propound interrogatories at an earlier time.

Ca. Civ. Proc. Code § 2030.020
Amended by Stats 2007 ch 113 (AB 1126),s 7, eff. 1/1/2008.
Added by Stats 2004 ch 182 (AB 3081),s 23, eff. 7/1/2005.

Section 2030.030 - Number of interrogatories

(a) A party may propound to another party either or both of the following:

(1) Thirty-five specially prepared interrogatories that are relevant to the subject matter of the pending action.

(2) Any additional number of official form interrogatories, as described in Chapter 17 (commencing with Section 2033.710), that are relevant to the subject matter of the pending action.
(b) Except as provided in Section 2030.070, no party shall, as a matter of right, propound to any other party more than 35 specially prepared interrogatories. If the initial set of interrogatories does not exhaust this limit, the balance may be propounded in subsequent sets.
(c) Unless a declaration as described in Section 2030.050 has been made, a party need only respond to the first 35 specially prepared interrogatories served, if that party states an objection to the balance, under Section 2030.240, on the ground that the limit has been exceeded.
Ca. Civ. Proc. Code § 2030.030
Added by Stats 2004 ch 182 (AB 3081),s 23, eff. 7/1/2005.

Section 2030.040 - Propounding greater number of interrogatories

(a) Subject to the right of the responding party to seek a protective order under Section 2030.090, any party who attaches a supporting declaration as described in Section 2030.050 may propound a greater number of specially prepared interrogatories to another party if this greater number is warranted because of any of the following:

(1) The complexity or the quantity of the existing and potential issues in the particular case.

(2) The financial burden on a party entailed in conducting the discovery by oral deposition.

(3) The expedience of using this method of discovery to provide to the responding party the opportunity to conduct an inquiry, investigation, or search of files or records to supply the information sought.

(b) If the responding party seeks a protective order on the ground that the number of specially prepared interrogatories is unwarranted, the propounding party shall have the burden of justifying the number of these interrogatories.

Ca. Civ. Proc. Code § 2030.040

Added by Stats 2004 ch 182 (AB 3081),s 23, eff. 7/1/2005.

Section 2030.050 - Declaration for additional discovery

Any party who is propounding or has propounded more than 35 specially prepared interrogatories to any other party shall attach to each set of those interrogatories a declaration containing substantially the following:

DECLARATION FOR ADDITIONAL DISCOVERY

I, _____, declare:

1. I am (a party to this action or proceeding appearing in propria persona) (presently the attorney for _____, a party to this action or proceeding).

2. I am propounding to _____ the attached set of interrogatories.

3. This set of interrogatories will cause the total number of specially prepared interrogatories propounded to the party to whom they are directed to exceed the number of specially prepared interrogatories permitted by Section 2030.030 of the Code of Civil Procedure.

4. I have previously propounded a total of _____ interrogatories to this party, of which _____ interrogatories were not official form interrogatories.

5. This set of interrogatories contains a total of _____ specially prepared interrogatories.

6. I am familiar with the issues and the previous discovery conducted by all of the parties in the case.

7. I have personally examined each of the questions in this set of interrogatories.

8. This number of questions is warranted under Section 2030.040 of the Code of Civil Procedure because _____. (Here state each factor described in Section 2030.040 that is relied on, as well as the reasons why any factor relied on is applicable to the instant lawsuit.)

9. None of the questions in this set of interrogatories is being propounded for any improper purpose, such as to harass the party, or the attorney for the party, to whom it is directed, or to cause unnecessary delay or needless increase in the cost of litigation. I declare under penalty of perjury under the laws of California that the foregoing is true and correct, and that this declaration was executed on _____.

_____ (Signature) _____

Attorney for

Ca. Civ. Proc. Code § 2030.050
Amended by Stats 2005 ch 22 (SB 1108),s 22, eff. 1/1/2006
Added by Stats 2004 ch 182 (AB 3081),s 23, eff. 7/1/2005.

Section 2030.060 - Requirements of interrogatories

(a) A party propounding interrogatories shall number each set of interrogatories consecutively.

(b) In the first paragraph immediately below the title of the case, there shall appear the identity of the propounding party, the set number, and the identity of the responding party.

(c) Each interrogatory in a set shall be separately set forth and identified by number or letter.

(d) Each interrogatory shall be full and complete in and of itself. No preface or instruction shall be included with a set of interrogatories unless it has been approved under Chapter 17 (commencing with Section 2033.710).

(e) Any term specially defined in a set of interrogatories shall be typed with all letters capitalized wherever that term appears.

(f) No specially prepared interrogatory shall contain subparts, or a compound, conjunctive, or disjunctive question.

(g) An interrogatory may not be made a continuing one so as to impose on the party responding to it a duty to supplement an answer to it that was initially correct and complete with later acquired information.

Ca. Civ. Proc. Code § 2030.060
Added by Stats 2004 ch 182 (AB 3081),s 23, eff. 7/1/2005.

Section 2030.070 - Supplemental interrogatory

(a) In addition to the number of interrogatories permitted by Sections 2030.030 and 2030.040, a party may propound a supplemental interrogatory to elicit any later acquired information bearing on all answers previously made by any party in response to interrogatories.

(b) A party may propound a supplemental interrogatory twice before the initial setting of a trial date, and, subject to the time limits on discovery proceedings and motions provided in Chapter 8 (commencing with Section 2024.010), once after the initial setting of a trial date.

(c) Notwithstanding subdivisions (a) and (b), on motion, for good cause shown, the court may grant leave to a party to propound an additional number of supplemental interrogatories.

Ca. Civ. Proc. Code § 2030.070
Added by Stats 2004 ch 182 (AB 3081),s 23, eff. 7/1/2005.

Section 2030.080 - Service of copies of interrogatories

(a) The party propounding interrogatories shall serve a copy of them on the party to whom the interrogatories are directed.

(b) The propounding party shall also serve a copy of the interrogatories on all other parties who have appeared in the action.

On motion, with or without notice, the court may relieve the party from this requirement on its determination that service on all other parties would be unduly expensive or burdensome.

Ca. Civ. Proc. Code § 2030.080
Added by Stats 2004 ch 182 (AB 3081),s 23, eff. 7/1/2005.

Section 2030.090 - Motion for protective order

(a) When interrogatories have been propounded, the responding party, and any other party or affected natural person or organization may promptly move for a protective order. This motion shall be accompanied by a meet and confer declaration under Section 2016.040.

(b) The court, for good cause shown, may make any order that justice requires to protect any party or other natural person or organization from unwarranted annoyance, embarrassment, or oppression, or undue burden and expense. This protective order may include, but is not limited to, one or more of the following directions:

(1) That the set of interrogatories, or particular interrogatories in the set, need not be answered.

(2) That, contrary to the representations made in a declaration submitted under Section 2030.050, the number of specially prepared interrogatories is unwarranted.

(3) That the time specified in Section 2030.260 to respond to the set of interrogatories, or to particular interrogatories in the set, be extended.

(4) That the response be made only on specified terms and conditions.

(5) That the method of discovery be an oral deposition instead of interrogatories to a party.

(6) That a trade secret or other confidential research,

development, or commercial information not be disclosed or be disclosed only in a certain way.

(7) That some or all of the answers to interrogatories be sealed and thereafter opened only on order of the court.

(c) If the motion for a protective order is denied in whole or in part, the court may order that the party provide or permit the discovery against which protection was sought on terms and conditions that are just.

(d) The court shall impose a monetary sanction under Chapter 7 (commencing with Section 2023.010) against any party, person, or attorney who unsuccessfully makes or opposes a motion for a protective order under this section, unless it finds that the one subject to the sanction acted with substantial justification or that other circumstances make the imposition of the sanction unjust.

Ca. Civ. Proc. Code § 2030.090
Added by Stats 2004 ch 182 (AB 3081),s 23, eff. 7/1/2005.

Article 2 - RESPONSE TO INTERROGATORIES

Section 2030.210 - Methods of responding; requirements
(a) The party to whom interrogatories have been propounded shall respond in writing under oath separately to each interrogatory by any of the following:

(1) An answer containing the information sought to be discovered.

(2) An exercise of the party's option to produce writings.

(3) An objection to the particular interrogatory.
(b) In the first paragraph of the response immediately below the title of the case, there shall appear the identity of the responding party, the set number, and the identity of the propounding party.
(c) Each answer, exercise of option, or objection in the response shall bear the same identifying number or letter and be in the same sequence as the corresponding interrogatory. The text of that

interrogatory need not be repeated, except as provided in paragraph (6) of subdivision (d).

(d) In order to facilitate the discovery process:

(1) Except as provided in paragraph (5), upon request by the responding party, the propounding party shall provide the interrogatories in an electronic format to the responding party within three court days of the request.

(2) Except as provided in paragraph (5), upon request by the propounding party after receipt of the responses to the interrogatories, the responding party shall provide the responses in an electronic format to the propounding party within three court days of the request.

(3) A party may provide the interrogatories or responses to the interrogatories requested pursuant to paragraphs (1) and (2) in any format agreed upon by the parties. If the parties are unable to agree on a format, the interrogatories or responses to interrogatories shall be provided in plain text format.

(4) A party may transmit the interrogatories or responses to the interrogatories requested pursuant to paragraphs (1) and (2) by any method agreed upon by the parties. If the parties are unable to agree on a method of transmission, the interrogatories or responses to interrogatories shall be transmitted by electronic mail to an email address provided by the requesting party.

(5) If the interrogatories or responses to interrogatories were not created in an electronic format, a party is not required to create the interrogatories or response to interrogatories in an electronic format for the purpose of transmission to the requesting party.

(6) A responding party who has requested and received the interrogatories in an electronic format pursuant to paragraph (1) shall include the text of the interrogatory immediately preceding the response.

Ca. Civ. Proc. Code § 2030.210

Amended by Stats 2019 ch 190 (AB 1349),s 1, eff. 1/1/2020.
Added by Stats 2004 ch 182 (AB 3081),s 23, eff. 7/1/2005.

Section 2030.220 - Answers

(a) Each answer in a response to interrogatories shall be as complete and straightforward as the information reasonably available to the responding party permits.

(b) If an interrogatory cannot be answered completely, it shall be answered to the extent possible.

(c) If the responding party does not have personal knowledge sufficient to respond fully to an interrogatory, that party shall so state, but shall make a reasonable and good faith effort to obtain the information by inquiry to other natural persons or organizations, except where the information is equally available to the propounding party.

Ca. Civ. Proc. Code § 2030.220
Added by Stats 2004 ch 182 (AB 3081),s 23, eff. 7/1/2005.

Section 2030.230 - Specification of writings from which answer may be derived or ascertained

If the answer to an interrogatory would necessitate the preparation or the making of a compilation, abstract, audit, or summary of or from the documents of the party to whom the interrogatory is directed, and if the burden or expense of preparing or making it would be substantially the same for the party propounding the interrogatory as for the responding party, it is a sufficient answer to that interrogatory to refer to this section and to specify the writings from which the answer may be derived or ascertained. This specification shall be in sufficient detail to permit the propounding party to locate and to identify, as readily as the responding party can, the documents from which the answer may be ascertained. The responding party shall then afford to the propounding party a reasonable opportunity to examine, audit, or inspect these documents and to make copies, compilations, abstracts, or summaries of them.

Ca. Civ. Proc. Code § 2030.230
Added by Stats 2004 ch 182 (AB 3081),s 23, eff. 7/1/2005.

Section 2030.240 - Objection

(a) If only a part of an interrogatory is objectionable, the remainder of the interrogatory shall be answered.

(b) If an objection is made to an interrogatory or to a part of an interrogatory, the specific ground for the objection shall be set forth clearly in the response. If an objection is based on a claim of privilege, the particular privilege invoked shall be clearly stated. If an objection is based on a claim that the information sought is protected work product under Chapter 4 (commencing with Section 2018.010), that claim shall be expressly asserted.

Ca. Civ. Proc. Code § 2030.240
Added by Stats 2004 ch 182 (AB 3081),s 23, eff. 7/1/2005.

Section 2030.250 - Signing responses under oath

(a) The party to whom the interrogatories are directed shall sign the response under oath unless the response contains only objections.

(b) If that party is a public or private corporation, or a partnership, association, or governmental agency, one of its officers or agents shall sign the response under oath on behalf of that party. If the officer or agent signing the response on behalf of that party is an attorney acting in that capacity for the party, that party waives any lawyer-client privilege and any protection for work product under Chapter 4 (commencing with Section 2018.010) during any subsequent discovery from that attorney concerning the identity of the sources of the information contained in the response.

(c) The attorney for the responding party shall sign any responses that contain an objection.

Ca. Civ. Proc. Code § 2030.250
Added by Stats 2004 ch 182 (AB 3081),s 23, eff. 7/1/2005.

Section 2030.260 - Time for service of original response on propounding party; time from date of service to respond; service of copy of responses on other parties

(a) Within 30 days after service of interrogatories, the party to whom the interrogatories are propounded shall serve the original of the response to them on the propounding party, unless on motion of the propounding party the court has shortened the time for response, or unless on motion of the responding party the court has extended the time for response.

(b) Notwithstanding subdivision (a), in an unlawful detainer action or other proceeding under Chapter 4 (commencing with Section 1159) of Title 3 of Part 3, the party to whom the interrogatories are propounded shall have five days from the date of service to respond, unless on motion of the propounding party the court has shortened the time for response, or unless on motion of the responding party the court has extended the time for response.

(c) The party to whom the interrogatories are propounded shall also serve a copy of the response on all other parties who have appeared in the action. On motion, with or without notice, the court may relieve the party from this requirement on its determination that service on all other parties would be unduly expensive or burdensome.

Ca. Civ. Proc. Code § 2030.260
Amended by Stats 2007 ch 113 (AB 1126),s 8, eff. 1/1/2008.
Added by Stats 2004 ch 182 (AB 3081),s 23, eff. 7/1/2005.

Section 2030.270 - Agreement to extend time for service of response

(a) The party propounding interrogatories and the responding party may agree to extend the time for service of a response to a set of interrogatories, or to particular interrogatories in a set, to a date beyond that provided in Section 2030.260.

(b) This agreement may be informal, but it shall be confirmed in a writing that specifies the extended date for service of a response.

(c) Unless this agreement expressly states otherwise, it is effective to preserve to the responding party the right to respond to any interrogatory to which the agreement applies in any manner specified in Sections 2030.210, 2030.220, 2030.230, and 2030.240.

Ca. Civ. Proc. Code § 2030.270

Added by Stats 2004 ch 182 (AB 3081),s 23, eff. 7/1/2005.

Section 2030.280 - Filing with court; retention of originals by propounding party

(a) The interrogatories and the response thereto shall not be filed with the court.

(b) The propounding party shall retain both the original of the interrogatories, with the original proof of service affixed to them, and the original of the sworn response until six months after final disposition of the action. At that time, both originals may be destroyed, unless the court on motion of any party and for good cause shown orders that the originals be preserved for a longer period.

Ca. Civ. Proc. Code § 2030.280

Added by Stats 2004 ch 182 (AB 3081),s 23, eff. 7/1/2005.

Section 2030.290 - Failure to serve timely response; motion for order compelling response

If a party to whom interrogatories are directed fails to serve a timely response, the following rules apply:

(a) The party to whom the interrogatories are directed waives any right to exercise the option to produce writings under Section 2030.230, as well as any objection to the interrogatories, including one based on privilege or on the protection for work product under Chapter 4 (commencing with Section 2018.010). The court, on motion, may relieve that party from this waiver on its determination that both of the following conditions are satisfied:

(1) The party has subsequently served a response that is in substantial compliance with Sections 2030.210, 2030.220, 2030.230, and 2030.240.

(2) The party's failure to serve a timely response was the result of mistake, inadvertence, or excusable neglect.

(b) The party propounding the interrogatories may move for an order compelling response to the interrogatories.

(c) The court shall impose a monetary sanction under Chapter 7 (commencing with Section 2023.010) against any party, person, or attorney who unsuccessfully makes or opposes a motion to compel a response to interrogatories, unless it finds that the one subject to the sanction acted with substantial justification or that other circumstances make the imposition of the sanction unjust. If a party then fails to obey an order compelling answers, the court may make those orders that are just, including the imposition of an issue sanction, an evidence sanction, or a terminating sanction under Chapter 7 (commencing with Section 2023.010). In lieu of or in addition to that sanction, the court may impose a monetary sanction under Chapter 7 (commencing with Section 2023.010).

Ca. Civ. Proc. Code § 2030.290
Added by Stats 2004 ch 182 (AB 3081),s 23, eff. 7/1/2005.

Section 2030.300 - Motion for order compelling further response

(a) On receipt of a response to interrogatories, the propounding party may move for an order compelling a further response if the propounding party deems that any of the following apply:

(1) An answer to a particular interrogatory is evasive or incomplete.

(2) An exercise of the option to produce documents under Section 2030.230 is unwarranted or the required specification of those documents is inadequate.

(3) An objection to an interrogatory is without merit or too general.

(b)

(1) A motion under subdivision (a) shall be accompanied by a meet and confer declaration under Section 2016.040.

(2) In lieu of a separate statement required under the California Rules of Court, the court may allow the moving party to submit a concise outline of the discovery request and each response in dispute.

(c) Unless notice of this motion is given within 45 days of the service of the verified response, or any supplemental verified response, or on or before any specific later date to which the propounding party and the responding party have agreed in writing, the propounding party waives any right to compel a further response to the interrogatories.

(d) The court shall impose a monetary sanction under Chapter 7 (commencing with Section 2023.010) against any party, person, or attorney who unsuccessfully makes or opposes a motion to compel a further response to interrogatories, unless it finds that the one subject to the sanction acted with substantial justification or that other circumstances make the imposition of the sanction unjust.

(e) If a party then fails to obey an order compelling further response to interrogatories, the court may make those orders that are just, including the imposition of an issue sanction, an evidence sanction, or a terminating sanction under Chapter 7 (commencing with Section 2023.010). In lieu of, or in addition to, that sanction, the court may impose a monetary sanction under Chapter 7 (commencing with Section 2023.010).

Ca. Civ. Proc. Code § 2030.300
Amended by Stats 2018 ch 317 (AB 2230),s 3, eff. 1/1/2019, op. 1/1/2020.
Amended by Stats 2013 ch 18 (AB 1183),s 1, eff. 1/1/2014.
Added by Stats 2004 ch 182 (AB 3081),s 23, eff. 7/1/2005.

Section 2030.310 - Amended answer to response; motion that initial answer binding on responding party

(a) Without leave of court, a party may serve an amended answer to any interrogatory that contains information subsequently discovered, inadvertently omitted, or mistakenly stated in the initial interrogatory. At the trial of the action, the propounding party or any other party may use the initial answer under Section 2030.410, and the responding party may then use the amended answer.

(b) The party who propounded an interrogatory to which an amended answer has been served may move for an order that the initial answer to that interrogatory be deemed binding on the responding party for the purpose of the pending action. This motion shall be accompanied by a meet and confer declaration under Section 2016.040.

(c) The court shall grant a motion under subdivision (b) if it determines that all of the following conditions are satisfied:

(1) The initial failure of the responding party to answer the interrogatory correctly has substantially prejudiced the party who propounded the interrogatory.

(2) The responding party has failed to show substantial justification for the initial answer to that interrogatory.

(3) The prejudice to the propounding party cannot be cured either by a continuance to permit further discovery or by the use of the initial answer under Section 2030.410.

(d) The court shall impose a monetary sanction under Chapter 7 (commencing with Section 2023.010) against any party, person, or attorney who unsuccessfully makes or opposes a motion to deem binding an initial answer to an interrogatory, unless it finds that the one subject to the sanction acted with substantial justification or that other circumstances make the imposition of the sanction unjust.

Ca. Civ. Proc. Code § 2030.310
Added by Stats 2004 ch 182 (AB 3081),s 23, eff. 7/1/2005.

Article 3 - USE OF INTERROGATORY ANSWER

Section 2030.410 - Generally

At the trial or any other hearing in the action, so far as admissible under the rules of evidence, the propounding party or any party other than the responding party may use any answer or part of an answer to an interrogatory only against the responding party. It is not ground for objection to the use of an answer to an interrogatory that the responding party is available to testify, has testified, or will testify at the trial or other hearing.

Ca. Civ. Proc. Code § 2030.410

Added by Stats 2004 ch 182 (AB 3081),s 23, eff. 7/1/2005.

Chapter 14 - INSPECTION, COPYING, TESTING, SAMPLING, AND PRODUCTION OF DOCUMENTS, ELECTRONICALLY STORED INFORMATION, TANGIBLE THINGS, LAND, AND OTHER PROPERTY

Article 1 - INSPECTION DEMAND

Section 2031.010 - Generally

(a) Any party may obtain discovery within the scope delimited by Chapter 2 (commencing with Section 2017.010), and subject to the restrictions set forth in Chapter 5 (commencing with Section 2019.010), by inspecting, copying, testing, or sampling documents, tangible things, land or other property, and electronically stored information in the possession, custody, or control of any other party to the action.

(b) A party may demand that any other party produce and permit the party making the demand, or someone acting on the demanding party's behalf, to inspect and to copy a document that is in the possession, custody, or control of the party on whom the demand is made.

(c) A party may demand that any other party produce and permit the party making the demand, or someone acting on the demanding party's behalf, to inspect and to photograph, test, or sample any tangible things that are in the possession, custody, or control of the party on whom the demand is made.

(d) A party may demand that any other party allow the party making the demand, or someone acting on the demanding party's behalf, to enter on any land or other property that is in the possession, custody, or control of the party on whom the demand is made, and to inspect and to measure, survey, photograph, test, or sample the land or other property, or any designated object or operation on it.

(e) A party may demand that any other party produce and permit the party making the demand, or someone acting on the demanding party's behalf, to inspect, copy, test, or sample electronically stored information in the possession, custody, or control of the party on whom demand is made.

Ca. Civ. Proc. Code § 2031.010

Amended by Stats 2016 ch 86 (SB 1171),s 42, eff. 1/1/2017.

Chapter heading amended by Stats 2012 ch 72 (SB 1574),s 30, eff. 1/1/2013.

Amended by Stats 2009 ch 5 (AB 5),s 4, eff. 6/29/2009.

Added by Stats 2004 ch 182 (AB 3081),s 23, eff. 7/1/2005.

Section 2031.020 - Demand for inspection without leave of court

(a) A defendant may make a demand for inspection, copying, testing, or sampling without leave of court at any time.

(b) A plaintiff may make a demand for inspection, copying, testing, or sampling without leave of court at any time that is 10 days after the service of the summons on, or appearance by, the party to whom the demand is directed, whichever occurs first.

(c) Notwithstanding subdivision (b), in an unlawful detainer action or other proceeding under Chapter 4 (commencing with Section 1159) of Title 3 of Part 3, a plaintiff may make a demand for inspection, copying, testing, or sampling without leave of court at any time that is five days after service of the summons on, or appearance by, the party to whom the demand is directed, whichever occurs first.

(d) Notwithstanding subdivisions (b) and (c), on motion with or without notice, the court, for good cause shown, may grant leave to a plaintiff to make a demand for inspection, copying, testing, or sampling at an earlier time.

Ca. Civ. Proc. Code § 2031.020

Amended by Stats 2009 ch 5 (AB 5),s 5, eff. 6/29/2009.

Amended by Stats 2007 ch 113 (AB 1126),s 9, eff. 1/1/2008.

Added by Stats 2004 ch 182 (AB 3081),s 23, eff. 7/1/2005.

Section 2031.030 - Requirements of demand

(a)

(1) A party demanding inspection, copying, testing, or sampling shall number each set of demands consecutively.

(2) A party demanding inspection, copying, testing, or sampling of electronically stored information may specify the form or forms in which each type of electronically stored information is to be produced.

(b) In the first paragraph immediately below the title of the case, there shall appear the identity of the demanding party, the set number, and the identity of the responding party.

(c) Each demand in a set shall be separately set forth, identified by number or letter, and shall do all of the following:

(1) Designate the documents, tangible things, land or other property, or electronically stored information to be inspected, copied, tested, or sampled either by specifically describing each individual item or by reasonably particularizing each category of item.

(2) Specify a reasonable time for the inspection, copying, testing, or sampling that is at least 30 days after service of the demand, unless the court for good cause shown has granted leave to specify an earlier date. In an unlawful detainer action or other proceeding under Chapter 4 (commencing with Section 1159) of Title 3 of Part 3, the demand shall specify a reasonable time for the inspection, copying, testing, or sampling that is at least five days after service of the demand, unless the court, for good cause shown, has granted leave to specify an earlier date.

(3) Specify a reasonable place for making the inspection, copying, testing, or sampling, and performing any related activity.

(4) Specify any inspection, copying, testing, sampling, or related activity that is being demanded, as well as the manner in which that activity will be performed, and whether that activity will permanently alter or destroy the item involved.

Ca. Civ. Proc. Code § 2031.030

Amended by Stats 2009 ch 5 (AB 5),s 6, eff. 6/29/2009.

Amended by Stats 2007 ch 113 (AB 1126),s 10, eff. 1/1/2008.

Added by Stats 2004 ch 182 (AB 3081),s 23, eff. 7/1/2005.

Section 2031.040 - Service of copy of demand

 The party making a demand for inspection, copying, testing, or sampling shall serve a copy of the demand on the party to whom it is directed and on all other parties who have appeared in the action.

Ca. Civ. Proc. Code § 2031.040

Amended by Stats 2009 ch 5 (AB 5),s 7, eff. 6/29/2009.

Added by Stats 2004 ch 182 (AB 3081),s 23, eff. 7/1/2005.

Section 2031.050 - Supplemental demand

(a) In addition to the demands for inspection, copying, testing, or sampling permitted by this chapter, a party may propound a supplemental demand to inspect, copy, test, or sample any later acquired or discovered documents, tangible things, land or other property, or electronically stored information in the possession, custody, or control of the party on whom the demand is made.

(b) A party may propound a supplemental demand for inspection, copying, testing, or sampling twice before the initial setting of a trial date, and, subject to the time limits on discovery proceedings and motions provided in Chapter 8 (commencing with Section 2024.010), once after the initial setting of a trial date.

(c) Notwithstanding subdivisions (a) and (b), on motion, for good cause shown, the court may grant leave to a party to propound an additional number of supplemental demands for inspection, copying, testing, or sampling.

Ca. Civ. Proc. Code § 2031.050

Amended by Stats 2009 ch 5 (AB 5),s 8, eff. 6/29/2009.

Added by Stats 2004 ch 182 (AB 3081),s 23, eff. 7/1/2005.

Section 2031.060 - Motion for protective order

(a) When an inspection, copying, testing, or sampling of documents, tangible things, places, or electronically stored information has been demanded, the party to whom the demand has been directed, and any other party or affected person, may promptly move for a protective order. This motion shall be accompanied by a meet and confer declaration under Section 2016.040.

(b) The court, for good cause shown, may make any order that justice requires to protect any party or other person from unwarranted annoyance, embarrassment, or oppression, or undue burden and expense. This protective order may include, but is not limited to, one or more of the following directions:

(1) That all or some of the items or categories of items in the demand need not be produced or made available at all.

(2) That the time specified in Section 2031.260 to respond to the set of demands, or to a particular item or category in the set, be extended.

(3) That the place of production be other than that specified in the demand.

(4) That the inspection, copying, testing, or sampling be made only on specified terms and conditions.

(5) That a trade secret or other confidential research, development, or commercial information not be disclosed, or be disclosed only to specified persons or only in a specified way.

(6) That the items produced be sealed and thereafter opened only on order of the court.

(c) The party or affected person who seeks a protective order regarding the production, inspection, copying, testing, or sampling of electronically stored information on the basis that the information is from a source that is not reasonably accessible because of undue burden or expense shall bear the burden of demonstrating that the information is from a source that is not reasonably accessible because of undue burden or expense.

(d) If the party or affected person from whom discovery of electronically stored information is sought establishes that the information is from a source that is not reasonably accessible because of undue burden or expense, the court may nonetheless order discovery if the demanding party shows good cause, subject to any limitations imposed under subdivision (f).

(e) If the court finds good cause for the production of electronically stored information from a source that is not reasonably accessible, the court may set conditions for the discovery of the electronically stored information, including allocation of the expense of discovery.

(f) The court shall limit the frequency or extent of discovery of electronically stored information, even from a source that is reasonably accessible, if the court determines that any of the following conditions exist:

(1) It is possible to obtain the information from some other source that is more convenient, less burdensome, or less expensive.

(2) The discovery sought is unreasonably cumulative or duplicative.

(3) The party seeking discovery has had ample opportunity by discovery in the action to obtain the information sought.

(4) The likely burden or expense of the proposed discovery outweighs the likely benefit, taking into account the amount in controversy, the resources of the parties, the importance of the issues in the litigation, and the importance of the requested discovery in resolving the issues.

(g) If the motion for a protective order is denied in whole or in part, the court may order that the party to whom the demand was directed provide or permit the discovery against which protection was sought on terms and conditions that are just.

(h) Except as provided in subdivision (i), the court shall impose a monetary sanction under Chapter 7 (commencing with Section 2023.010) against any party, person, or attorney who unsuccessfully makes or opposes a motion for a protective order, unless it finds that the one subject to the sanction acted with substantial justification or that other circumstances make the imposition of the sanction unjust.

(i)

(1) Notwithstanding subdivision (h), absent exceptional circumstances, the court shall not impose sanctions on a party or any attorney of a party for failure to provide electronically stored information that has been lost, damaged, altered, or overwritten as the result of the routine, good faith operation of an electronic information system.

(2) This subdivision shall not be construed to alter any obligation to preserve discoverable information.

Ca. Civ. Proc. Code § 2031.060

Amended by Stats 2021 ch 124 (AB 938),s 15, eff. 1/1/2022.

Amended by Stats 2009 ch 5 (AB 5),s 9, eff. 6/29/2009.

Added by Stats 2004 ch 182 (AB 3081),s 23, eff. 7/1/2005.

Article 2 - RESPONSE TO INSPECTION DEMAND

Section 2031.210 - Requirements of response

(a) The party to whom a demand for inspection, copying, testing, or sampling has been directed shall respond separately to each item or category of item by any of the following:

(1) A statement that the party will comply with the particular demand for inspection, copying, testing, or sampling by the date set for the inspection, copying, testing, or sampling pursuant to paragraph (2) of subdivision (c) of Section 2031.030 and any related activities.

(2) A representation that the party lacks the ability to comply with the demand for inspection, copying, testing, or sampling of a particular item or category of item.

(3) An objection to the particular demand for inspection, copying, testing, or sampling.

(b) In the first paragraph of the response immediately below the title of the case, there shall appear the identity of the responding party, the set number, and the identity of the demanding party.

(c) Each statement of compliance, each representation, and each objection in the response shall bear the same number and be in the same sequence as the corresponding item or category in the demand, but the text of that item or category need not be repeated.

(d) If a party objects to the discovery of electronically stored information on the grounds that it is from a source that is not reasonably accessible because of undue burden or expense and that the responding party will not search the source in the absence of an agreement with the demanding party or court order, the responding party shall identify in its response the types or categories of sources of electronically stored information that it asserts are not reasonably accessible. By objecting and identifying information of a type or category of source or sources that are not reasonably accessible, the responding party preserves any objections it may have relating to that electronically stored information.

Ca. Civ. Proc. Code § 2031.210
Amended by Stats 2009 ch 5 (AB 5),s 10, eff. 6/29/2009.
Amended by Stats 2007 ch 738 (AB 1248),s 7, eff. 1/1/2008.
Added by Stats 2004 ch 182 (AB 3081),s 23, eff. 7/1/2005.

Section 2031.220 - Statement that party to whom demand directed will comply demand

A statement that the party to whom a demand for inspection, copying, testing, or sampling has been directed will comply with the particular demand shall state that the production, inspection, copying, testing, or sampling, and related activity demanded, will be allowed either in whole or in part, and that all documents or things in the demanded category that are in the possession, custody, or control of that party and to which no objection is being made will be included in the production.

Ca. Civ. Proc. Code § 2031.220
Amended by Stats 2009 ch 5 (AB 5),s 11, eff. 6/29/2009.
Added by Stats 2004 ch 182 (AB 3081),s 23, eff. 7/1/2005.

Section 2031.230 - Statement of inability to comply with demand

A representation of inability to comply with the particular demand for inspection, copying, testing, or sampling shall affirm that a diligent search and a reasonable inquiry has been made in an effort to comply with that demand. This statement shall also specify whether the inability to comply is because the particular item or category has never existed, has been destroyed, has been lost, misplaced, or stolen, or has never been, or is no longer, in the possession, custody, or control of the responding party. The statement shall set forth the name and address of any natural person or organization known or believed by that party to have possession, custody, or control of that item or category of item.

Ca. Civ. Proc. Code § 2031.230

Amended by Stats 2009 ch 5 (AB 5),s 12, eff. 6/29/2009.
Added by Stats 2004 ch 182 (AB 3081),s 23, eff. 7/1/2005.

Section 2031.240 - Objections

(a) If only part of an item or category of item in a demand for inspection, copying, testing, or sampling is objectionable, the response shall contain a statement of compliance, or a representation of inability to comply with respect to the remainder of that item or category.

(b) If the responding party objects to the demand for inspection, copying, testing, or sampling of an item or category of item, the response shall do both of the following:

(1) Identify with particularity any document, tangible thing, land, or electronically stored information falling within any category of item in the demand to which an objection is being made.

(2) Set forth clearly the extent of, and the specific ground for, the objection. If an objection is based on a claim of privilege, the particular privilege invoked shall be stated. If an objection is based on a claim that the information sought is protected work product under Chapter 4 (commencing with Section 2018.010), that claim shall be expressly asserted.

(c)

(1) If an objection is based on a claim of privilege or a claim that the information sought is protected work product, the response shall provide sufficient factual information for other parties to evaluate the merits of that claim, including, if necessary, a privilege log.

(2) It is the intent of the Legislature to codify the concept of a privilege log as that term is used in California case law. Nothing in this subdivision shall be construed to constitute a substantive change in case law.

Ca. Civ. Proc. Code § 2031.240
Amended by Stats 2012 ch 232 (AB 1354),s 1, eff. 1/1/2013.
Amended by Stats 2009 ch 5 (AB 5),s 13, eff. 6/29/2009.
Added by Stats 2004 ch 182 (AB 3081),s 23, eff. 7/1/2005.

Section 2031.250 - Signing response under oath

(a) The party to whom the demand for inspection, copying, testing, or sampling is directed shall sign the response under oath unless the response contains only objections.

(b) If that party is a public or private corporation or a partnership or association or governmental agency, one of its officers or agents shall sign the response under oath on behalf of that party. If the officer or agent signing the response on behalf of that party is an attorney acting in that capacity for a party, that party waives any lawyer-client privilege and any protection for work product under Chapter 4 (commencing with Section 2018.010) during any subsequent discovery from that attorney concerning the identity of the sources of the information contained in the response.

(c) The attorney for the responding party shall sign any responses that contain an objection.

Ca. Civ. Proc. Code § 2031.250
Amended by Stats 2009 ch 5 (AB 5),s 14, eff. 6/29/2009.
Added by Stats 2004 ch 182 (AB 3081),s 23, eff. 7/1/2005.

Section 2031.260 - Time for service of original of response; time from date of service to respond

(a) Within 30 days after service of a demand for inspection, copying, testing, or sampling, the party to whom the demand is directed shall serve the original of the response to it on the party making the demand, and a copy of the response on all other parties who have appeared in the action, unless on motion of the party making the demand, the court has shortened the time for response, or unless on motion of the party to whom the demand has been directed, the court has extended the time for response.

(b) Notwithstanding subdivision (a), in an unlawful detainer action or other proceeding under Chapter 4 (commencing with Section 1159) of Title 3 of Part 3, the party to whom a demand for inspection, copying, testing, or sampling is directed shall have at least five days from the date of service of the demand to respond, unless on motion of the party making the demand, the court has shortened the time for the response, or unless on motion of the party to whom the demand has been directed, the court has extended the time for response.

Ca. Civ. Proc. Code § 2031.260

Amended by Stats 2009 ch 5 (AB 5),s 15, eff. 6/29/2009.

Amended by Stats 2007 ch 113 (AB 1126),s 11, eff. 1/1/2008.

Added by Stats 2004 ch 182 (AB 3081),s 23, eff. 7/1/2005.

Section 2031.270 - Agreement to extend date of inspection or time of service of response

(a) The party demanding inspection, copying, testing, or sampling and the responding party may agree to extend the date for the inspection, copying, testing, or sampling or the time for service of a response to a set of demands, or to particular items or categories of items in a set, to a date or dates beyond those provided in Sections 2031.030, 2031.210, 2031.260, and 2031.280.

(b) This agreement may be informal, but it shall be confirmed in a writing that specifies the extended date for inspection, copying, testing, or sampling, or for the service of a response.

(c) Unless this agreement expressly states otherwise, it is effective to preserve to the responding party the right to respond to any item or category of item in the demand to which the agreement applies in any manner specified in Sections 2031.210, 2031.220, 2031.230, 2031.240, and 2031.280.

Ca. Civ. Proc. Code § 2031.270
Amended by Stats 2009 ch 5 (AB 5),s 16, eff. 6/29/2009.
Amended by Stats 2007 ch 738 (AB 1248),s 8, eff. 1/1/2008.
Added by Stats 2004 ch 182 (AB 3081),s 23, eff. 7/1/2005.

Section 2031.280 - Production of documents in response to demand

(a) Any documents or category of documents produced in response to a demand for inspection, copying, testing, or sampling shall be identified with the specific request number to which the documents respond.

(b) The documents shall be produced on the date specified in the demand pursuant to paragraph (2) of subdivision (c) of Section 2031.030, unless an objection has been made to that date. If the date for inspection has been extended pursuant to Section 2031.270, the documents shall be produced on the date agreed to pursuant to that section.

(c) If a party responding to a demand for production of electronically stored information objects to a specified form for producing the information, or if no form is specified in the demand, the responding party shall state in its response the form in which it intends to produce each type of information.

(d) Unless the parties otherwise agree or the court otherwise orders, the following shall apply:

(1) If a demand for production does not specify a form or forms for producing a type of electronically stored information, the responding party shall produce the information in the form or forms in which it is ordinarily maintained or in a form that is reasonably usable.

(2) A party need not produce the same electronically stored information in more than one form.

(e) If necessary, the responding party at the reasonable expense of the demanding party shall, through detection devices, translate any data compilations included in the demand into reasonably usable form.

Ca. Civ. Proc. Code § 2031.280

Amended by Stats 2019 ch 208 (SB 370),s 1, eff. 1/1/2020.
Amended by Stats 2009 ch 5 (AB 5),s 17, eff. 6/29/2009.
Amended by Stats 2007 ch 738 (AB 1248),s 9, eff. 1/1/2008.
Added by Stats 2004 ch 182 (AB 3081),s 23, eff. 7/1/2005.

Section 2031.285 - Electronically stored information produced subject to claim of privilege or protection as attorney work product

(a) If electronically stored information produced in discovery is subject to a claim of privilege or of protection as attorney work product, the party making the claim may notify any party that received the information of the claim and the basis for the claim.

(b) After being notified of a claim of privilege or of protection under subdivision (a), a party that received the information shall immediately sequester the information and either return the specified information and any copies that may exist or present the information to the court conditionally under seal for a determination of the claim.

(c)

(1) Prior to the resolution of the motion brought under subdivision (d), a party shall be precluded from using or disclosing the specified information until the claim of privilege is resolved.

(2) A party who received and disclosed the information before being notified of a claim of privilege or of protection under subdivision (a) shall, after that notification, immediately take reasonable steps to retrieve the information.

(d)

(1) If the receiving party contests the legitimacy of a claim of privilege or protection, he or she may seek a determination of the claim from the court by making a motion within 30 days of receiving the claim and presenting the information to the court conditionally under seal.

(2) Until the legitimacy of the claim of privilege or protection is resolved, the receiving party shall preserve the information and keep it confidential and shall be precluded from using the information in any manner.

Ca. Civ. Proc. Code § 2031.285
Added by Stats 2009 ch 5 (AB 5),s 18, eff. 6/29/2009.

Section 2031.290 - Demand and response filed with court; retention by demanding party until final disposition

(a) The demand for inspection, copying, testing, or sampling, and the response to it, shall not be filed with the court.

(b) The party demanding an inspection, copying, testing, or sampling shall retain both the original of the demand, with the original proof of service affixed to it, and the original of the sworn response until six months after final disposition of the action. At that time, both originals may be destroyed, unless the court, on motion of any party and for good cause shown, orders that the originals be preserved for a longer period.

Ca. Civ. Proc. Code § 2031.290
Amended by Stats 2009 ch 5 (AB 5),s 19, eff. 6/29/2009.
Added by Stats 2004 ch 182 (AB 3081),s 23, eff. 7/1/2005.

Section 2031.300 - Failure to serve timely response; motion to compel response

If a party to whom a demand for inspection, copying, testing, or sampling is directed fails to serve a timely response to it, the following rules shall apply:

(a) The party to whom the demand for inspection, copying, testing, or sampling is directed waives any objection to the demand, including one based on privilege or on the protection for work product under Chapter 4 (commencing with Section 2018.010). The court, on motion, may relieve that party from this waiver on its determination that both of the following conditions are satisfied:

(1) The party has subsequently served a response that is in substantial compliance with Sections 2031.210, 2031.220, 2031.230, 2031.240, and 2031.280.

(2) The party's failure to serve a timely response was the result of mistake, inadvertence, or excusable neglect.

(b) The party making the demand may move for an order compelling response to the demand.

(c) Except as provided in subdivision (d), the court shall impose a monetary sanction under Chapter 7 (commencing with Section 2023.010) against any party, person, or attorney who unsuccessfully makes or opposes a motion to compel a response to a demand for inspection, copying, testing, or sampling, unless it finds that the one subject to the sanction acted with substantial justification or that other circumstances make the imposition of the sanction unjust. If a party then fails to obey the order compelling a response, the court may make those orders that are just, including the imposition of an issue sanction, an evidence sanction, or a terminating sanction under Chapter 7 (commencing with Section 2023.010). In lieu of or in addition to this sanction, the court may impose a monetary sanction under Chapter 7 (commencing with Section 2023.010).

(d)

(1) Notwithstanding subdivision (c), absent exceptional circumstances, the court shall not impose sanctions on a party or any attorney of a party for failure to provide electronically stored information that has been lost, damaged, altered, or overwritten as a result of the routine, good faith operation of an electronic information system.

(2) This subdivision shall not be construed to alter any obligation to preserve discoverable information.

Ca. Civ. Proc. Code § 2031.300

Amended by Stats 2009 ch 5 (AB 5),s 20, eff. 6/29/2009.
Amended by Stats 2005 ch 22 (SB 1108),s 23, eff. 1/1/2006
Added by Stats 2004 ch 182 (AB 3081),s 23, eff. 7/1/2005.

Section 2031.310 - Motion for order compelling further response

(a) On receipt of a response to a demand for inspection, copying, testing, or sampling, the demanding party may move for an order compelling further response to the demand if the demanding party deems that any of the following apply:

(1) A statement of compliance with the demand is incomplete.

(2) A representation of inability to comply is inadequate, incomplete, or evasive.

(3) An objection in the response is without merit or too general.
(b) A motion under subdivision (a) shall comply with each of the following:

(1) The motion shall set forth specific facts showing good cause justifying the discovery sought by the demand.

(2) The motion shall be accompanied by a meet and confer declaration under Section 2016.040.

(3) In lieu of a separate statement required under the California Rules of Court, the court may allow the moving party to submit a concise outline of the discovery request and each response in dispute.
(c) Unless notice of this motion is given within 45 days of the service of the verified response, or any supplemental verified response, or on or before any specific later date to which the demanding party and the responding party have agreed in writing, the demanding party waives any right to compel a further response to the demand.
(d) In a motion under subdivision (a) relating to the production of electronically stored information, the party or affected person objecting to or opposing the production, inspection, copying, testing, or sampling of electronically stored information on the basis that the information is from a source that is not reasonably accessible because of the undue burden or expense shall bear the

burden of demonstrating that the information is from a source that is not reasonably accessible because of undue burden or expense.

(e) If the party or affected person from whom discovery of electronically stored information is sought establishes that the information is from a source that is not reasonably accessible because of the undue burden or expense, the court may nonetheless order discovery if the demanding party shows good cause, subject to any limitations imposed under subdivision (g).

(f) If the court finds good cause for the production of electronically stored information from a source that is not reasonably accessible, the court may set conditions for the discovery of the electronically stored information, including allocation of the expense of discovery.

(g) The court shall limit the frequency or extent of discovery of electronically stored information, even from a source that is reasonably accessible, if the court determines that any of the following conditions exists:

(1) It is possible to obtain the information from some other source that is more convenient, less burdensome, or less expensive.

(2) The discovery sought is unreasonably cumulative or duplicative.

(3) The party seeking discovery has had ample opportunity by discovery in the action to obtain the information sought.

(4) The likely burden or expense of the proposed discovery outweighs the likely benefit, taking into account the amount in controversy, the resources of the parties, the importance of the issues in the litigation, and the importance of the requested discovery in resolving the issues.

(h) Except as provided in subdivision (j), the court shall impose a monetary sanction under Chapter 7 (commencing with Section 2023.010) against any party, person, or attorney who unsuccessfully makes or opposes a motion to compel further response to a demand, unless it finds that the one subject to the sanction acted with substantial justification or that other circumstances make the imposition of the sanction unjust.

(i) Except as provided in subdivision (j), if a party fails to obey an order compelling further response, the court may make those orders that are just, including the imposition of an issue sanction, an evidence sanction, or a terminating sanction under Chapter 7 (commencing with Section 2023.010). In lieu of, or in addition to, that sanction, the court may impose a monetary sanction under Chapter 7 (commencing with Section 2023.010).

(j)

(1) Notwithstanding subdivisions (h) and (i), absent exceptional circumstances, the court shall not impose sanctions on a party or any attorney of a party for failure to provide electronically stored information that has been lost, damaged, altered, or overwritten as the result of the routine, good faith operation of an electronic information system.

(2) This subdivision shall not be construed to alter any obligation to preserve discoverable information.

Ca. Civ. Proc. Code § 2031.310

Amended by Stats 2018 ch 317 (AB 2230),s 4, eff. 1/1/2019, op. 1/1/2020.

Amended by Stats 2013 ch 18 (AB 1183),s 2, eff. 1/1/2014.

Amended by Stats 2009 ch 5 (AB 5),s 21, eff. 6/29/2009.

Added by Stats 2004 ch 182 (AB 3081),s 23, eff. 7/1/2005.

Section 2031.320 - Motion to compel compliance with demand; failure to obey order compelling inspection

(a) If a party filing a response to a demand for inspection, copying, testing, or sampling under Sections 2031.210, 2031.220, 2031.230, 2031.240, and 2031.280 thereafter fails to permit the inspection, copying, testing, or sampling in accordance with that party's statement of compliance, the demanding party may move for an order compelling compliance.

(b) Except as provided in subdivision (d), the court shall impose a monetary sanction under Chapter 7 (commencing with Section 2023.010) against any party, person, or attorney who unsuccessfully makes or opposes a motion to compel compliance with a demand, unless it finds that the one subject to the sanction acted with substantial justification or that other circumstances make the imposition of the sanction unjust.

(c) Except as provided in subdivision (d), if a party then fails to obey an order compelling inspection, copying, testing, or sampling, the court may make those orders that are just, including the imposition of an issue sanction, an evidence sanction, or a terminating sanction under Chapter 7 (commencing with Section 2023.010). In lieu of or in addition to that sanction, the court may impose a monetary sanction under Chapter 7 (commencing with Section 2023.010).

(d)

(1) Notwithstanding subdivisions (b) and (c), absent exceptional circumstances, the court shall not impose sanctions on a party or any attorney of a party for failure to provide electronically stored information that has been lost, damaged, altered, or overwritten as the result of the routine, good faith operation of an electronic information system.

(2) This subdivision shall not be construed to alter any obligation to preserve discoverable information.

Ca. Civ. Proc. Code § 2031.320
Amended by Stats 2009 ch 5 (AB 5),s 22, eff. 6/29/2009.
Added by Stats 2004 ch 182 (AB 3081),s 23, eff. 7/1/2005.

Article 3 - INSPECTION AND PRODUCTION OF DOCUMENTS AND OTHER PROPERTY IN SPECIFIC CONTEXTS

Section 2031.510 - Boundary of land patented in dispute or validity of state patent or grant

(a) In any action, regardless of who is the moving party, where the boundary of land patented or otherwise granted by the state is in dispute, or the validity of any state patent or grant dated before 1950 is in dispute, all parties shall have the duty to disclose to all opposing parties all nonprivileged relevant written evidence then known and available, including evidence against interest, relating to the above issues.

(b) This evidence shall be disclosed within 120 days after the filing with the court of proof of service upon all named defendants. Thereafter, the parties shall have the continuing duty to make all subsequently discovered relevant and nonprivileged written evidence available to the opposing parties.

Ca. Civ. Proc. Code § 2031.510

Added by Stats 2004 ch 182 (AB 3081),s 23, eff. 7/1/2005.

Chapter 15 - PHYSICAL OR MENTAL EXAMINATION

Article 1 - GENERAL PROVISIONS

Section 2032.010 - Construction

(a) This chapter does not affect genetic testing under Chapter 2 (commencing with Section 7550) of Part 2 of Division 12 of the Family Code.

(b) This chapter does not require the disclosure of the identity of an expert consulted by an attorney in order to make the certification required in an action for professional negligence under Section 411.35.

Ca. Civ. Proc. Code § 2032.010

Amended by Stats 2018 ch 876 (AB 2684),s 2, eff. 1/1/2019.

Added by Stats 2004 ch 182 (AB 3081),s 23, eff. 7/1/2005.

Section 2032.020 - Generally

(a) Any party may obtain discovery, subject to the restrictions set forth in Chapter 5 (commencing with Section 2019.010), by means of a physical or mental examination of (1) a party to the action, (2) an agent of any party, or (3) a natural person in the custody or under the legal control of a party, in any action in which the mental or physical condition (including the blood group) of that party or other person is in controversy in the action.

(b) A physical examination conducted under this chapter shall be performed only by a licensed physician or other appropriate licensed health care practitioner.

(c)

(1) A mental examination conducted under this chapter shall be performed only by a licensed physician, or by a licensed clinical psychologist who holds a doctoral degree in psychology and has had at least five years of postgraduate experience in the diagnosis of emotional and mental disorders.

(2) If an action involves allegations of sexual abuse of a minor, including any act listed in paragraphs (1) to (3), inclusive, of subdivision (a) of Section 1002, and the examinee is less than 15 years of age, the licensed physician or clinical psychologist shall have expertise in child abuse and trauma.

Ca. Civ. Proc. Code § 2032.020

Amended by Stats 2017 ch 133 (SB 755),s 1, eff. 1/1/2018.

Added by Stats 2004 ch 182 (AB 3081),s 23, eff. 7/1/2005.

Article 2 - PHYSICAL EXAMINATION OF PERSONAL INJURY PLAINTIFF

Section 2032.210 - Plaintiff includes

As used in this article, "plaintiff" includes a cross-complainant, and "defendant" includes a cross-defendant.

Ca. Civ. Proc. Code § 2032.210

Added by Stats 2004 ch 182 (AB 3081),s 23, eff. 7/1/2005.

Section 2032.220 - Demand by defendant in case in which plaintiff seeking recovery for person injuries

(a) In any case in which a plaintiff is seeking recovery for personal injuries, any defendant may demand one physical examination of the plaintiff, if both of the following conditions are satisfied:

(1) The examination does not include any diagnostic test or procedure that is painful, protracted, or intrusive.

(2) The examination is conducted at a location within 75 miles of the residence of the examinee.

(b) A defendant may make a demand under this article without leave of court after that defendant has been served or has appeared in the action, whichever occurs first.

(c) A demand under subdivision (a) shall specify the time, place, manner, conditions, scope, and nature of the examination, as well as the identity and the specialty, if any, of the physician who will perform the examination.

(d) A physical examination demanded under subdivision (a) shall be scheduled for a date that is at least 30 days after service of the demand. On motion of the party demanding the examination, the court may shorten this time.

(e) The defendant shall serve a copy of the demand under subdivision (a) on the plaintiff and on all other parties who have appeared in the action.

Ca. Civ. Proc. Code § 2032.220
Added by Stats 2004 ch 182 (AB 3081),s 23, eff. 7/1/2005.

Section 2032.230 - Response by plaintiff by written statement; time for service of response by plaintiff; extension of time

(a) The plaintiff to whom a demand for a physical examination under this article is directed shall respond to the demand by a written statement that the examinee will comply with the demand as stated, will comply with the demand as specifically modified by the plaintiff, or will refuse, for reasons specified in the response, to submit to the demanded physical examination.

(b) Within 20 days after service of the demand the plaintiff to whom the demand is directed shall serve the original of the response to it on the defendant making the demand, and a copy of the response on all other parties who have appeared in the action. On motion of the defendant making the demand, the court may shorten the time for response. On motion of the plaintiff to whom the demand is directed, the court may extend the time for response.

Ca. Civ. Proc. Code § 2032.230
Added by Stats 2004 ch 182 (AB 3081),s 23, eff. 7/1/2005.

Section 2032.240 - Waiver of objection to demand if response not timely served; motion for order compelling response and compliance

(a) If a plaintiff to whom a demand for a physical examination under this article is directed fails to serve a timely response to it, that plaintiff waives any objection to the demand. The court, on motion, may relieve that plaintiff from this waiver on its determination that both of the following conditions are satisfied:

(1) The plaintiff has subsequently served a response that is in substantial compliance with Section 2032.230.

(2) The plaintiff's failure to serve a timely response was the result of mistake, inadvertence, or excusable neglect.

(b) The defendant may move for an order compelling response and compliance with a demand for a physical examination.

(c) The court shall impose a monetary sanction under Chapter 7 (commencing with Section 2023.010) against any party, person, or attorney who unsuccessfully makes or opposes a motion to compel response and compliance with a demand for a physical examination, unless it finds that the one subject to the sanction acted with substantial justification or that other circumstances make the imposition of the sanction unjust.

(d) If a plaintiff then fails to obey the order compelling response and compliance, the court may make those orders that are just, including the imposition of an issue sanction, an evidence sanction, or a terminating sanction under Chapter 7 (commencing with Section 2023.010). In lieu of or in addition to that sanction the court may impose a monetary sanction under Chapter 7 (commencing with Section 2023.010).

Ca. Civ. Proc. Code § 2032.240
Added by Stats 2004 ch 182 (AB 3081),s 23, eff. 7/1/2005.

Section 2032.250 - Motion for order compelling compliance with demand

(a) If a defendant who has demanded a physical examination under this article, on receipt of the plaintiff's response to that demand, deems that any modification of the demand, or any refusal to submit to the physical examination is unwarranted, that defendant may move for an order compelling compliance with the demand. This motion shall be accompanied by a meet and confer declaration under Section 2016.040.

(b) The court shall impose a monetary sanction under Chapter 7 (commencing with Section 2023.010) against any party, person, or attorney who unsuccessfully makes or opposes a motion to compel compliance with a demand for a physical examination, unless it finds that the one subject to the sanction acted with substantial justification or that other circumstances make the imposition of the sanction unjust.

Ca. Civ. Proc. Code § 2032.250
Added by Stats 2004 ch 182 (AB 3081),s 23, eff. 7/1/2005.

Section 2032.260 - Demand and response filed with court; retention by defendant of originals until final disposition

(a) The demand for a physical examination under this article and the response to it shall not be filed with the court.

(b) The defendant shall retain both the original of the demand, with the original proof of service affixed to it, and the original response until six months after final disposition of the action. At that time, the original may be destroyed, unless the court, on motion of any party and for good cause shown, orders that the originals be preserved for a longer period.

Ca. Civ. Proc. Code § 2032.260
Added by Stats 2004 ch 182 (AB 3081),s 23, eff. 7/1/2005.

Article 3 - MOTION FOR PHYSICAL OR MENTAL EXAMINATION

Section 2032.310 - Leave of court required; motion for examination; service of notice of motion

(a) If any party desires to obtain discovery by a physical examination other than that described in Article 2 (commencing with Section 2032.210), or by a mental examination, the party shall obtain leave of court.

(b) A motion for an examination under subdivision (a) shall specify the time, place, manner, conditions, scope, and nature of the examination, as well as the identity and the specialty, if any, of the person or persons who will perform the examination. The motion shall be accompanied by a meet and confer declaration under Section 2016.040.

(c) Notice of the motion shall be served on the person to be examined and on all parties who have appeared in the action.

Ca. Civ. Proc. Code § 2032.310

Added by Stats 2004 ch 182 (AB 3081),s 23, eff. 7/1/2005.

Section 2032.320 - Granting motion

(a) The court shall grant a motion for a physical or mental examination under Section 2032.310 only for good cause shown.

(b) If a party stipulates as provided in subdivision (c), the court shall not order a mental examination of a person for whose personal injuries a recovery is being sought except on a showing of exceptional circumstances.

(c) A stipulation by a party under this subdivision shall include both of the following:

(1) A stipulation that no claim is being made for mental and emotional distress over and above that usually associated with the physical injuries claimed.

(2) A stipulation that no expert testimony regarding this usual mental and emotional distress will be presented at trial in support of the claim for damages.

(d) An order granting a physical or mental examination shall specify the person or persons who may perform the examination, as well as the time, place, manner, diagnostic tests and procedures, conditions, scope, and nature of the examination.

(e) If the place of the examination is more than 75 miles from the residence of the person to be examined, an order to submit to it shall be entered only if both of the following conditions are satisfied:

(1) The court determines that there is good cause for the travel involved.

(2) The order is conditioned on the advancement by the moving party of the reasonable expenses and costs to the examinee for travel to the place of examination.
Ca. Civ. Proc. Code § 2032.320
Added by Stats 2004 ch 182 (AB 3081),s 23, eff. 7/1/2005.

Section 2032.340 - Mental examination of child less than 15 years of age; duration
(a) If any action involving allegations of sexual abuse of a minor, including any act listed in paragraphs (1) to (3), inclusive, of subdivision (a) of Section 1002, the mental examination of a child less than 15 years of age shall not exceed three hours, inclusive of breaks.
(b) Notwithstanding subdivision (a), the court may grant an extension of the three-hour limit for good cause.
Ca. Civ. Proc. Code § 2032.340
Added by Stats 2017 ch 133 (SB 755),s 2, eff. 1/1/2018.

Article 4 - FAILURE TO SUBMIT TO OR PRODUCE ANOTHER FOR PHYSICAL OR MENTAL EXAMINATION

Section 2032.410 - Party required to submit to examination
If a party is required to submit to a physical or mental examination under Articles 2 (commencing with Section 2032.210) or 3 (commencing with Section 2032.310), or under Section 2016.030, but fails to do so, the court, on motion of the party entitled to the examination, may make those orders that are just, including the imposition of an issue sanction, an evidence sanction, or a terminating sanction under Chapter 7 (commencing with Section 2023.010). In lieu of or in addition to that sanction, the court may, on motion of the party, impose a monetary sanction under Chapter 7 (commencing with Section 2023.010).

Ca. Civ. Proc. Code § 2032.410
Added by Stats 2004 ch 182 (AB 3081),s 23, eff. 7/1/2005.

Section 2032.420 - Party required to produce another for examination

If a party is required to produce another for a physical or mental examination under Articles 2 (commencing with Section 2032.210) or 3 (commencing with Section 2032.310), or under Section 2032.030, but fails to do so, the court, on motion of the party entitled to the examination, may make those orders that are just, including the imposition of an issue sanction, an evidence sanction, or a terminating sanction under Chapter 7 (commencing with Section 2023.010), unless the party failing to comply demonstrates an inability to produce that person for examination. In lieu of or in addition to that sanction, the court may impose a monetary sanction under Chapter 7 (commencing with Section 2023.010).

Ca. Civ. Proc. Code § 2032.420
Added by Stats 2004 ch 182 (AB 3081),s 23, eff. 7/1/2005.

Article 5 - CONDUCT OF EXAMINATION

Section 2032.510 - Attorney or party permitted to attend as observer

(a) The attorney for the examinee or for a party producing the examinee, or that attorney's representative, shall be permitted to attend and observe any physical examination conducted for discovery purposes, and to record stenographically or by audio technology any words spoken to or by the examinee during any phase of the examination.

(b) The observer under subdivision (a) may monitor the examination, but shall not participate in or disrupt it.

(c) If an attorney's representative is to serve as the observer, the representative shall be authorized to so act by a writing subscribed by the attorney which identifies the representative.

(d) If in the judgment of the observer the examiner becomes abusive to the examinee or undertakes to engage in unauthorized diagnostic tests and procedures, the observer may suspend it to enable the party being examined or producing the examinee to make a motion for a protective order.

(e) If the observer begins to participate in or disrupt the examination, the person conducting the physical examination may suspend the examination to enable the party at whose instance it is being conducted to move for a protective order.

(f) The court shall impose a monetary sanction under Chapter 7 (commencing with Section 2023.010) against any party, person, or attorney who unsuccessfully makes or opposes a motion for a protective order under this section, unless it finds that the one subject to the sanction acted with substantial justification or that other circumstances make the imposition of the sanction unjust.

Ca. Civ. Proc. Code § 2032.510

Amended by Stats 2005 ch 294 (AB 333),s 10, eff. 1/1/2006
Added by Stats 2004 ch 182 (AB 3081),s 23, eff. 7/1/2005.

Section 2032.520 - Additional X-rays of area taken

If an examinee submits or authorizes access to X-rays of any area of his or her body for inspection by the examining physician, no additional X-rays of that area may be taken by the examining physician except with consent of the examinee or on order of the court for good cause shown.

Ca. Civ. Proc. Code § 2032.520

Added by Stats 2004 ch 182 (AB 3081),s 23, eff. 7/1/2005.

Section 2032.530 - Right to record mental examination by audio technology

(a) The examiner and examinee shall have the right to record a mental examination by audio technology.

(b) Nothing in this title shall be construed to alter, amend, or affect existing case law with respect to the presence of the attorney for the examinee or other persons during the examination by agreement or court order.

Ca. Civ. Proc. Code § 2032.530

Amended by Stats 2005 ch 294 (AB 333),s 11, eff. 1/1/2006
Added by Stats 2004 ch 182 (AB 3081),s 23, eff. 7/1/2005.

Article 6 - REPORTS OF EXAMINATION

Section 2032.610 - Delivering of copies of reports required by demanding party

(a) If a party submits to, or produces another for, a physical or mental examination in compliance with a demand under Article 2 (commencing with Section 2032.210), an order of court under Article 3 (commencing with Section 2032.310), or an agreement under Section 2016.030, that party has the option of making a written demand that the party at whose instance the examination was made deliver both of the following to the demanding party:

  (1) A copy of a detailed written report setting out the history, examinations, findings, including the results of all tests made, diagnoses, prognoses, and conclusions of the examiner.

  (2) A copy of reports of all earlier examinations of the same condition of the examinee made by that or any other examiner.
(b) If the option under subdivision (a) is exercised, a copy of the requested reports shall be delivered within 30 days after service of the demand, or within 15 days of trial, whichever is earlier.
(c) In the circumstances described in subdivision (a), the protection for work product under Chapter 4 (commencing with Section 2018.010) is waived, both for the examiner's writings and reports and to the taking of the examiner's testimony.
  Ca. Civ. Proc. Code § 2032.610
Added by Stats 2004 ch 182 (AB 3081),s 23, eff. 7/1/2005.

Section 2032.620 - Motion for order compelling delivery of reports

(a) If the party at whose instance an examination was made fails to make a timely delivery of the reports demanded under Section 2032.610, the demanding party may move for an order compelling their delivery. This motion shall be accompanied by a meet and confer declaration under Section 2016.040.
(b) The court shall impose a monetary sanction under Chapter 7

(commencing with Section 2023.010) against any party, person, or attorney who unsuccessfully makes or opposes a motion to compel delivery of medical reports under this section, unless it finds that the one subject to the sanction acted with substantial justification or that other circumstances make the imposition of the sanction unjust.

(c) If a party then fails to obey an order compelling delivery of demanded medical reports, the court may make those orders that are just, including the imposition of an issue sanction, an evidence sanction, or a terminating sanction under Chapter 7 (commencing with Section 2023.010). In lieu of or in addition to those sanctions, the court may impose a monetary sanction under Chapter 7 (commencing with Section 2023.010). The court shall exclude at trial the testimony of any examiner whose report has not been provided by a party.

Ca. Civ. Proc. Code § 2032.620
Added by Stats 2004 ch 182 (AB 3081),s 23, eff. 7/1/2005.

Section 2032.630 - Waivers by demanding and obtaining report or taking deposition of examiner

By demanding and obtaining a report of a physical or mental examination under Section 2032.610 or 2032.620, or by taking the deposition of the examiner, other than under Article 3 (commencing with Section 2034.410) of Chapter 18, the party who submitted to, or produced another for, a physical or mental examination waives in the pending action, and in any other action involving the same controversy, any privilege, as well as any protection for work product under Chapter 4 (commencing with Section 2018.010), that the party or other examinee may have regarding reports and writings as well as the testimony of every other physician, psychologist, or licensed health care practitioner who has examined or may thereafter examine the party or other examinee in respect of the same physical or mental condition.

Ca. Civ. Proc. Code § 2032.630
Added by Stats 2004 ch 182 (AB 3081),s 23, eff. 7/1/2005.

Section 2032.640 - Receipt of existing report of any examination

A party receiving a demand for a report under Section 2032.610 is entitled at the time of compliance to receive in exchange a copy of any existing written report of any examination of the same condition by any other physician, psychologist, or licensed health care practitioner. In addition, that party is entitled to receive promptly any later report of any previous or subsequent examination of the same condition, by any physician, psychologist, or licensed health care practitioner.

Ca. Civ. Proc. Code § 2032.640

Added by Stats 2004 ch 182 (AB 3081),s 23, eff. 7/1/2005.

Section 2032.650 - Motion for order compelling delivery of medical reports

(a) If a party who has demanded and received delivery of medical reports under Section 2032.610 fails to deliver existing or later reports of previous or subsequent examinations under Section 2032.640, a party who has complied with Section 2032.610 may move for an order compelling delivery of medical reports. This motion shall be accompanied by a meet and confer declaration under Section 2016.040.

(b) The court shall impose a monetary sanction under Chapter 7 (commencing with Section 2023.010) against any party, person, or attorney who unsuccessfully makes or opposes a motion to compel delivery of medical reports under this section, unless it finds that the one subject to the sanction acted with substantial justification or that other circumstances make the imposition of the sanction unjust.

(c) If a party then fails to obey an order compelling delivery of medical reports, the court may make those orders that are just, including the imposition of an issue sanction, an evidence sanction, or a terminating sanction under Chapter 7 (commencing with Section 2023.010). In lieu of or in addition to the sanction, the court may impose a monetary sanction under Chapter 7 (commencing with Section 2023.010). The court shall exclude at trial the testimony of any health care practitioner whose report has not been provided by a party ordered to do so by the court.

Ca. Civ. Proc. Code § 2032.650

Added by Stats 2004 ch 182 (AB 3081),s 23, eff. 7/1/2005.

Chapter 16 - REQUESTS FOR ADMISSION

Article 1 - REQUESTS FOR ADMISSION

Section 2033.010 - Generally

Any party may obtain discovery within the scope delimited by Chapter 2 (commencing with Section 2017.010), and subject to the restrictions set forth in Chapter 5 (commencing with Section 2019.010), by a written request that any other party to the action admit the genuineness of specified documents, or the truth of specified matters of fact, opinion relating to fact, or application of law to fact. A request for admission may relate to a matter that is in controversy between the parties.

Ca. Civ. Proc. Code § 2033.010

Amended by Stats 2016 ch 86 (SB 1171),s 43, eff. 1/1/2017.

Added by Stats 2004 ch 182 (AB 3081),s 23, eff. 7/1/2005.

Section 2033.020 - Request for admission without leave of court

(a) A defendant may make requests for admission by a party without leave of court at any time.

(b) A plaintiff may make requests for admission by a party without leave of court at any time that is 10 days after the service of the summons on, or appearance by, that party, whichever occurs first.

(c) Notwithstanding subdivision (b), in an unlawful detainer action or other proceeding under Chapter 4 (commencing with Section 1159) of Title 3 of Part 3, a plaintiff may make requests for admission by a party without leave of court at any time that is five days after service of the summons on, or appearance by, that party, whichever occurs first.

(d) Notwithstanding subdivisions (b) and (c), on motion with or without notice, the court, for good cause shown, may grant leave to a plaintiff to make requests for admission at an earlier time.

Ca. Civ. Proc. Code § 2033.020
Amended by Stats 2007 ch 113 (AB 1126),s 12, eff. 1/1/2008.
Added by Stats 2004 ch 182 (AB 3081),s 23, eff. 7/1/2005.

Section 2033.030 - Number of admissions requested

(a) No party shall request, as a matter of right, that any other party admit more than 35 matters that do not relate to the genuineness of documents. If the initial set of admission requests does not exhaust this limit, the balance may be requested in subsequent sets.
(b) Unless a declaration as described in Section 2033.050 has been made, a party need only respond to the first 35 admission requests served that do not relate to the genuineness of documents, if that party states an objection to the balance under Section 2033.230 on the ground that the limit has been exceeded.
(c) The number of requests for admission of the genuineness of documents is not limited except as justice requires to protect the responding party from unwarranted annoyance, embarrassment, oppression, or undue burden and expense.

Ca. Civ. Proc. Code § 2033.030
Added by Stats 2004 ch 182 (AB 3081),s 23, eff. 7/1/2005.

Section 2033.040 - Requesting greater number of admissions

(a) Subject to the right of the responding party to seek a protective order under Section 2033.080, any party who attaches a supporting declaration as described in Section 2033.050 may request a greater number of admissions by another party if the greater number is warranted by the complexity or the quantity of the existing and potential issues in the particular case.
(b) If the responding party seeks a protective order on the ground that the number of requests for admission is unwarranted, the propounding party shall have the burden of justifying the number of requests for admission.

Ca. Civ. Proc. Code § 2033.040
Added by Stats 2004 ch 182 (AB 3081),s 23, eff. 7/1/2005.

Section 2033.050 - Declaration for additional discovery

Any party who is requesting or who has already requested more than 35 admissions not relating to the genuineness of documents by any other party shall attach to each set of requests for admissions a declaration containing substantially the following words:

DECLARATION FOR ADDITIONAL DISCOVERY

I, _____, declare:

1. I am (a party to this action or proceeding appearing in propria persona) (presently the attorney for _____, a party to this action or proceeding).

2. I am propounding to _____ the attached set of requests for admission.

3. This set of requests for admission will cause the total number of requests propounded to the party to whom they are directed to exceed the number of requests permitted by Section 2033.030 of the Code of Civil Procedure.

4. I have previously propounded a total of _____ requests for admission to this party.

5. This set of requests for admission contains a total of _____ requests.

6. I am familiar with the issues and the previous discovery conducted by all of the parties in this case.

7. I have personally examined each of the requests in this set of requests for admission.

8. This number of requests for admission is warranted under Section 2033.040 of the Code of Civil Procedure because _____. (Here state the reasons why the complexity or the quantity of issues in the instant lawsuit warrant this number of requests for admission.)

9. None of the requests in this set of requests is being propounded for any improper purpose, such as to harass the party, or the attorney for the party, to whom it is directed, or to cause unnecessary delay or needless increase in the cost of litigation. I declare under penalty of perjury under the laws of California that the foregoing is true and correct, and that this declaration was executed on _____.

_____ (Signature) _____

Attorney for

Ca. Civ. Proc. Code § 2033.050
Added by Stats 2004 ch 182 (AB 3081),s 23, eff. 7/1/2005.

Section 2033.060 - Request for admissions

(a) A party requesting admissions shall number each set of requests consecutively.

(b) In the first paragraph immediately below the title of the case, there shall appear the identity of the party requesting the admissions, the set number, and the identity of the responding party.

(c) Each request for admission in a set shall be separately set forth and identified by letter or number.

(d) Each request for admission shall be full and complete in and of itself. No preface or instruction shall be included with a set of admission requests unless it has been approved under Chapter 17 (commencing with Section 2033.710).

(e) Any term specially defined in a request for admission shall be typed with all letters capitalized whenever the term appears.

(f) No request for admission shall contain subparts, or a compound, conjunctive, or disjunctive request unless it has been approved under Chapter 17 (commencing with Section 2033.710).

(g) A party requesting an admission of the genuineness of any documents shall attach copies of those documents to the requests, and shall make the original of those documents available for inspection on demand by the party to whom the requests for admission are directed.

(h) No party shall combine in a single document requests for admission with any other method of discovery.

Ca. Civ. Proc. Code § 2033.060
Added by Stats 2004 ch 182 (AB 3081),s 23, eff. 7/1/2005.

Title 4 - CIVIL DISCOVERY ACT

Section 2033.070 - Service of copy of request

The party requesting admissions shall serve a copy of them on the party to whom they are directed and on all other parties who have appeared in the action.

Ca. Civ. Proc. Code § 2033.070
Added by Stats 2004 ch 182 (AB 3081),s 23, eff. 7/1/2005.

Section 2033.080 - Protective order

(a) When requests for admission have been made, the responding party may promptly move for a protective order. This motion shall be accompanied by a meet and confer declaration under Section 2016.040.

(b) The court, for good cause shown, may make any order that justice requires to protect any party from unwarranted annoyance, embarrassment, oppression, or undue burden and expense. This protective order may include, but is not limited to, one or more of the following directions:

(1) That the set of admission requests, or particular requests in the set, need not be answered at all.

(2) That, contrary to the representations made in a declaration submitted under Section 2033.050, the number of admission requests is unwarranted.

(3) That the time specified in Section 2033.250 to respond to the set of admission requests, or to particular requests in the set, be extended.

(4) That a trade secret or other confidential research, development, or commercial information not be admitted or be admitted only in a certain way.

(5) That some or all of the answers to requests for admission be sealed and thereafter opened only on order of the court.

(c) If the motion for a protective order is denied in whole or in part, the court may order that the responding party provide or permit the discovery against which protection was sought on terms and conditions that are just.

(d) The court shall impose a monetary sanction under Chapter 7 (commencing with Section 2023.010) against any party, person, or attorney who unsuccessfully makes or opposes a motion for a protective order under this section, unless it finds that the one subject to the sanction acted with substantial justification or that other circumstances make the imposition of the sanction unjust.

Ca. Civ. Proc. Code § 2033.080
Added by Stats 2004 ch 182 (AB 3081),s 23, eff. 7/1/2005.

Article 2 - RESPONSE TO REQUESTS FOR ADMISSION

Section 2033.210 - Requirements
(a) The party to whom requests for admission have been directed shall respond in writing under oath separately to each request.
(b) Each response shall answer the substance of the requested admission, or set forth an objection to the particular request.
(c) In the first paragraph of the response immediately below the title of the case, there shall appear the identity of the responding party, the set number, and the identity of the requesting party.
(d) Each answer or objection in the response shall bear the same identifying number or letter and be in the same sequence as the corresponding request. The text of that request need not be repeated, except as provided in paragraph (6) of subdivision (e).
(e) In order to facilitate the discovery process:

(1) Except as provided in paragraph (5), upon request by the responding party, the propounding party shall provide the requests for admission in an electronic format to the responding party within three court days of the request.

(2) Except as provided in paragraph (5), upon request by the propounding party after receipt of the responses to the requests for admission, the responding party shall provide the responses in an electronic format to the propounding party within three court days of the request.

(3) A party may provide the requests for admission or responses to the requests for admission requested pursuant to paragraphs (1) and (2) in any format agreed upon by the parties. If the parties are unable to agree on a format, the requests for admission or responses to the requests for admission shall be provided in plain text format.

(4) A party may transmit the requests for admission or responses to the requests for admission requested pursuant to paragraphs (1) and (2) by any method agreed upon by the parties. If the parties are unable to agree on a method of transmission, the requests for admission or responses to the requests for admission shall be transmitted by electronic mail to an email address provided by the requesting party.

(5) If the requests for admission or responses to the requests for admission were not created in an electronic format, a party is not required to create the requests for admission or responses in an electronic format for the purpose of transmission to the requesting party.

(6) A responding party who has requested and received requests for admission in an electronic format pursuant to paragraph (1) shall include the text of the request immediately preceding the response.

Ca. Civ. Proc. Code § 2033.210
Amended by Stats 2019 ch 190 (AB 1349),s 2, eff. 1/1/2020.
Added by Stats 2004 ch 182 (AB 3081),s 23, eff. 7/1/2005.

Section 2033.220 - Answers
(a) Each answer in a response to requests for admission shall be as complete and straightforward as the information reasonably available to the responding party permits.
(b) Each answer shall:

(1) Admit so much of the matter involved in the request as is true, either as expressed in the request itself or as reasonably and clearly qualified by the responding party.

(2) Deny so much of the matter involved in the request as is untrue.

(3) Specify so much of the matter involved in the request as to the truth of which the responding party lacks sufficient information or knowledge.

(c) If a responding party gives lack of information or knowledge as a reason for a failure to admit all or part of a request for admission, that party shall state in the answer that a reasonable inquiry concerning the matter in the particular request has been made, and that the information known or readily obtainable is insufficient to enable that party to admit the matter.

Ca. Civ. Proc. Code § 2033.220
Amended by Stats 2005 ch 22 (SB 1108),s 24, eff. 1/1/2006
Added by Stats 2004 ch 182 (AB 3081),s 23, eff. 7/1/2005.

Section 2033.230 - Objections
(a) If only a part of a request for admission is objectionable, the remainder of the request shall be answered.
(b) If an objection is made to a request or to a part of a request, the specific ground for the objection shall be set forth clearly in the response. If an objection is based on a claim of privilege, the particular privilege invoked shall be clearly stated. If an objection is based on a claim that the matter as to which an admission is requested is protected work product under Chapter 4 (commencing with Section 2018.010), that claim shall be expressly asserted.

Ca. Civ. Proc. Code § 2033.230
Added by Stats 2004 ch 182 (AB 3081),s 23, eff. 7/1/2005.

Section 2033.240 - Signing response under oath
(a) The party to whom the requests for admission are directed shall sign the response under oath, unless the response contains only

objections.

(b) If that party is a public or private corporation, or a partnership or association or governmental agency, one of its officers or agents shall sign the response under oath on behalf of that party. If the officer or agent signing the response on behalf of that party is an attorney acting in that capacity for the party, that party waives any lawyer-client privilege and any protection for work product under Chapter 4 (commencing with Section 2018.010) during any subsequent discovery from that attorney concerning the identity of the sources of the information contained in the response.

(c) The attorney for the responding party shall sign any response that contains an objection.

Ca. Civ. Proc. Code § 2033.240

Added by Stats 2004 ch 182 (AB 3081),s 23, eff. 7/1/2005.

Section 2033.250 - Time for service of response; time for response from date of service

(a) Within 30 days after service of requests for admission, the party to whom the requests are directed shall serve the original of the response to them on the requesting party, and a copy of the response on all other parties who have appeared, unless on motion of the requesting party the court has shortened the time for response, or unless on motion of the responding party the court has extended the time for response.

(b) Notwithstanding subdivision (a), in an unlawful detainer action or other proceeding under Chapter 4 (commencing with Section 1159) of Title 3 of Part 3, the party to whom the request is directed shall have at least five days from the date of service to respond, unless on motion of the requesting party the court has shortened the time for response, or unless on motion of the responding party the court has extended the time for response.

Ca. Civ. Proc. Code § 2033.250

Amended by Stats 2007 ch 113 (AB 1126),s 13, eff. 1/1/2008.

Added by Stats 2004 ch 182 (AB 3081),s 23, eff. 7/1/2005.

Section 2033.260 - Agreement to extension of time

(a) The party requesting admissions and the responding party may agree to extend the time for service of a response to a set of admission requests, or to particular requests in a set, to a date beyond that provided in Section 2033.250.

(b) This agreement may be informal, but it shall be confirmed in a writing that specifies the extended date for service of a response.

(c) Unless this agreement expressly states otherwise, it is effective to preserve to the responding party the right to respond to any request for admission to which the agreement applies in any manner specified in Sections 2033.210, 2033.220, and 2033.230.

(d) Notice of this agreement shall be given by the responding party to all other parties who were served with a copy of the request.

Ca. Civ. Proc. Code § 2033.260
Added by Stats 2004 ch 182 (AB 3081),s 23, eff. 7/1/2005.

Section 2033.270 - Request and response filed with court; retention of originals by requesting party

(a) The requests for admission and the response to them shall not be filed with the court.

(b) The party requesting admissions shall retain both the original of the requests for admission, with the original proof of service affixed to them, and the original of the sworn response until six months after final disposition of the action. At that time, both originals may be destroyed, unless the court, on motion of any party and for good cause shown, orders that the originals be preserved for a longer period.

Ca. Civ. Proc. Code § 2033.270
Added by Stats 2004 ch 182 (AB 3081),s 23, eff. 7/1/2005.

Section 2033.280 - Failure to timely serve response

If a party to whom requests for admission are directed fails to serve a timely response, the following rules apply:

(a) The party to whom the requests for admission are directed waives any objection to the requests, including one based on privilege or on the protection for work product under Chapter 4 (commencing with Section 2018.010). The court, on motion, may relieve that party from this waiver on its determination that both of the following conditions are satisfied:

(1) The party has subsequently served a response that is in substantial compliance with Sections 2033.210, 2033.220, and 2033.230.

(2) The party's failure to serve a timely response was the result of mistake, inadvertence, or excusable neglect.
(b) The requesting party may move for an order that the genuineness of any documents and the truth of any matters specified in the requests be deemed admitted, as well as for a monetary sanction under Chapter 7 (commencing with Section 2023.010).
(c) The court shall make this order, unless it finds that the party to whom the requests for admission have been directed has served, before the hearing on the motion, a proposed response to the requests for admission that is in substantial compliance with Section 2033.220. It is mandatory that the court impose a monetary sanction under Chapter 7 (commencing with Section 2023.010) on the party or attorney, or both, whose failure to serve a timely response to requests for admission necessitated this motion.

Ca. Civ. Proc. Code § 2033.280
Amended by Stats 2005 ch 294 (AB 333),s 12, eff. 1/1/2006
Added by Stats 2004 ch 182 (AB 3081),s 23, eff. 7/1/2005.

Section 2033.290 - Motion compelling further response
(a) On receipt of a response to requests for admissions, the party requesting admissions may move for an order compelling a further response if that party deems that either or both of the following apply:

(1) An answer to a particular request is evasive or incomplete.

(2) An objection to a particular request is without merit or too general.

(b)

(1) A motion under subdivision (a) shall be accompanied by a meet and confer declaration under Section 2016.040.

(2) In lieu of a separate statement required under the California Rules of Court, the court may allow the moving party to submit a concise outline of the discovery request and each response in dispute.

(c) Unless notice of this motion is given within 45 days of the service of the verified response, or any supplemental verified response, or any specific later date to which the requesting party and the responding party have agreed in writing, the requesting party waives any right to compel further response to the requests for admission.

(d) The court shall impose a monetary sanction under Chapter 7 (commencing with Section 2023.010) against any party, person, or attorney who unsuccessfully makes or opposes a motion to compel further response, unless it finds that the one subject to the sanction acted with substantial justification or that other circumstances make the imposition of the sanction unjust.

(e) If a party then fails to obey an order compelling further response to requests for admission, the court may order that the matters involved in the requests be deemed admitted. In lieu of, or in addition to, this order, the court may impose a monetary sanction under Chapter 7 (commencing with Section 2023.010).

Ca. Civ. Proc. Code § 2033.290

Amended by Stats 2018 ch 317 (AB 2230),s 5, eff. 1/1/2019, op. 1/1/2020.

Amended by Stats 2013 ch 18 (AB 1183),s 3, eff. 1/1/2014.

Added by Stats 2004 ch 182 (AB 3081),s 23, eff. 7/1/2005.

Section 2033.300 - Withdrawal or amendment of admission

(a) A party may withdraw or amend an admission made in response to a request for admission only on leave of court granted after notice to all parties.

(b) The court may permit withdrawal or amendment of an admission only if it determines that the admission was the result of mistake, inadvertence, or excusable neglect, and that the party who obtained the admission will not be substantially prejudiced in maintaining that party's action or defense on the merits.

(c) The court may impose conditions on the granting of the motion that are just, including, but not limited to, the following:

(1) An order that the party who obtained the admission be permitted to pursue additional discovery related to the matter involved in the withdrawn or amended admission.

(2) An order that the costs of any additional discovery be borne in whole or in part by the party withdrawing or amending the admission.

Ca. Civ. Proc. Code § 2033.300
Added by Stats 2004 ch 182 (AB 3081),s 23, eff. 7/1/2005.

Article 3 - EFFECT OF ADMISSION

Section 2033.410 - Matter conclusively established; binding only on party

(a) Any matter admitted in response to a request for admission is conclusively established against the party making the admission in the pending action, unless the court has permitted withdrawal or amendment of that admission under Section 2033.300.

(b) Notwithstanding subdivision (a), any admission made by a party under this section is binding only on that party and is made for the purpose of the pending action only. It is not an admission by that party for any other purpose, and it shall not be used in any manner against that party in any other proceeding.

Ca. Civ. Proc. Code § 2033.410
Added by Stats 2004 ch 182 (AB 3081),s 23, eff. 7/1/2005.

Section 2033.420 - Motion to pay reasonable expenses

(a) If a party fails to admit the genuineness of any document or the truth of any matter when requested to do so under this chapter, and if the party requesting that admission thereafter proves the genuineness of that document or the truth of that matter, the party requesting the admission may move the court for an order requiring the party to whom the request was directed to pay the reasonable expenses incurred in making that proof, including reasonable attorney's fees.

(b) The court shall make this order unless it finds any of the following:

(1) An objection to the request was sustained or a response to it was waived under Section 2033.290.

(2) The admission sought was of no substantial importance.

(3) The party failing to make the admission had reasonable ground to believe that that party would prevail on the matter.

(4) There was other good reason for the failure to admit.

Ca. Civ. Proc. Code § 2033.420

Added by Stats 2004 ch 182 (AB 3081),s 23, eff. 7/1/2005.

Chapter 17 - FORM INTERROGATORIES AND REQUESTS FOR ADMISSION

Section 2033.710 - Generally

The Judicial Council shall develop and approve official form interrogatories and requests for admission of the genuineness of any relevant documents or of the truth of any relevant matters of fact for use in any civil action in a state court based on personal injury, property damage, wrongful death, unlawful detainer, breach of contract, family law, or fraud and for any other civil actions the Judicial Council deems appropriate.

Ca. Civ. Proc. Code § 2033.710

Added by Stats 2004 ch 182 (AB 3081),s 23, eff. 7/1/2005.

Section 2033.720 - Official form interrogatories for victims receiving complete restitution payment

(a) The Judicial Council shall develop and approve official form interrogatories for use by a victim who has not received complete payment of a restitution order made pursuant to Section 1202.4 of the Penal Code.

(b) Notwithstanding whether a victim initiates or maintains an action to satisfy the unpaid restitution order, a victim may propound the form interrogatories approved pursuant to this section once each calendar year. The defendant subject to the restitution order shall, in responding to the interrogatories propounded, provide current information regarding the nature, extent, and location of any assets, income, and liabilities in which the defendant claims a present or future interest.

Ca. Civ. Proc. Code § 2033.720

Added by Stats 2004 ch 182 (AB 3081),s 23, eff. 7/1/2005.

Section 2033.730 - Advisory committee

(a) In developing the form interrogatories and requests for admission required by Sections 2033.710 and 2033.720, the Judicial Council shall consult with a representative advisory committee which shall include, but not be limited to, representatives of all of the following:

(1) The plaintiff's bar.

(2) The defense bar.

(3) The public interest bar.

(4) Court administrators.

(5) The public.

(b) The form interrogatories and requests for admission shall be drafted in nontechnical language.

Ca. Civ. Proc. Code § 2033.730

Added by Stats 2004 ch 182 (AB 3081),s 23, eff. 7/1/2005.

Section 2033.740 - Use optional; available through clerk of court; rules to govern use

(a) Use of the form interrogatories and requests for admission approved by the Judicial Council shall be optional.

(b) The form interrogatories and requests for admission shall be made available through the office of the clerk of the appropriate trial court.

(c) The Judicial Council shall promulgate any necessary rules to govern the use of the form interrogatories and requests for admission.

Ca. Civ. Proc. Code § 2033.740
Added by Stats 2004 ch 182 (AB 3081),s 23, eff. 7/1/2005.

Chapter 18 - SIMULTANEOUS EXCHANGE OF EXPERT WITNESS INFORMATION

Article 1 - GENERAL PROVISIONS

Section 2034.010 - Inapplicability to eminent domain proceedings

This chapter does not apply to exchanges of lists of experts and valuation data in eminent domain proceedings under Chapter 7 (commencing with Section 1258.010) of Title 7 of Part 3.

Ca. Civ. Proc. Code § 2034.010
Added by Stats 2004 ch 182 (AB 3081),s 23, eff. 7/1/2005.

Article 2 - DEMAND FOR EXCHANGE OF EXPERT WITNESS INFORMATION

Section 2034.210 - Generally

After the setting of the initial trial date for the action, any party may obtain discovery by demanding that all parties simultaneously exchange information concerning each other's expert trial witnesses to the following extent:

(a) Any party may demand a mutual and simultaneous exchange by all parties of a list containing the name and address of any natural person, including one who is a party, whose oral or deposition testimony in the form of an expert opinion any party expects to offer in evidence at the trial.

(b) If any expert designated by a party under subdivision (a) is a party or an employee of a party, or has been retained by a party for the purpose of forming and expressing an opinion in anticipation of the litigation or in preparation for the trial of the action, the designation of that witness shall include or be accompanied by an expert witness declaration under Section 2034.260.

(c) Any party may also include a demand for the mutual and simultaneous production for inspection and copying of all discoverable reports and writings, if any, made by any expert described in subdivision (b) in the course of preparing that expert's opinion.

Ca. Civ. Proc. Code § 2034.210
Added by Stats 2004 ch 182 (AB 3081),s 23, eff. 7/1/2005.

Section 2034.220 - Demand without leave of court

Any party may make a demand for an exchange of information concerning expert trial witnesses without leave of court. A party shall make this demand no later than the 10th day after the initial trial date has been set, or 70 days before that trial date, whichever is closer to the trial date.

Ca. Civ. Proc. Code § 2034.220
Added by Stats 2004 ch 182 (AB 3081),s 23, eff. 7/1/2005.

Section 2034.230 - Requirements of demand

(a) A demand for an exchange of information concerning expert trial witnesses shall be in writing and shall identify, below the title of the case, the party making the demand. The demand shall state that it is being made under this chapter.

(b) The demand shall specify the date for the exchange of lists of expert trial witnesses, expert witness declarations, and any demanded production of writings. The specified date of exchange shall be 50 days before the initial trial date, or 20 days after service of the demand, whichever is closer to the trial date, unless the court, on motion and a showing of good cause, orders an earlier or

later date of exchange.
Ca. Civ. Proc. Code § 2034.230
Added by Stats 2004 ch 182 (AB 3081),s 23, eff. 7/1/2005.

Section 2034.240 - Service of demand
The party demanding an exchange of information concerning
expert trial witnesses shall serve the demand on all parties who
have appeared in the action.
Ca. Civ. Proc. Code § 2034.240
Added by Stats 2004 ch 182 (AB 3081),s 23, eff. 7/1/2005.

Section 2034.250 - Motion for protective order
(a) A party who has been served with a demand to exchange
information concerning expert trial witnesses may promptly move
for a protective order. This motion shall be accompanied by a meet
and confer declaration under Section 2016.040.
(b) The court, for good cause shown, may make any order that
justice requires to protect any party from unwarranted annoyance,
embarrassment, oppression, or undue burden and expense. The
protective order may include, but is not limited to, one or more of
the following directions:

(1) That the demand be quashed because it was not timely
served.

(2) That the date of exchange be earlier or later than that
specified in the demand.

(3) That the exchange be made only on specified terms and
conditions.

(4) That the production and exchange of any reports and
writings of experts be made at a different place or at a different time
than specified in the demand.

(5) That some or all of the parties be divided into sides on the basis of their identity of interest in the issues in the action, and that the designation of any experts as described in subdivision (b) of Section 2034.210 be made by any side so created.

(6) That a party or a side reduce the list of employed or retained experts designated by that party or side under subdivision (b) of Section 2034.210.

(c) If the motion for a protective order is denied in whole or in part, the court may order that the parties against whom the motion is brought, provide or permit the discovery against which the protection was sought on those terms and conditions that are just.

(d) The court shall impose a monetary sanction under Chapter 7 (commencing with Section 2023.010) against any party, person, or attorney who unsuccessfully makes or opposes a motion for a protective order under this section, unless it finds that the one subject to the sanction acted with substantial justification or that other circumstances make the imposition of the sanction unjust.

Ca. Civ. Proc. Code § 2034.250
Added by Stats 2004 ch 182 (AB 3081),s 23, eff. 7/1/2005.

Section 2034.260 - Procedure and requirements of exchange

(a) All parties who have appeared in the action shall exchange information concerning expert witnesses in writing on or before the date of exchange specified in the demand. The exchange of information may occur at a meeting of the attorneys for the parties involved or by serving the information on the other party by any method specified in Section 1011 or 1013, on or before the date of exchange.

(b) The exchange of expert witness information shall include either of the following:

(1) A list setting forth the name and address of a person whose expert opinion that party expects to offer in evidence at the trial.

(2) A statement that the party does not presently intend to offer the testimony of an expert witness.

(c) If a witness on the list is an expert as described in subdivision (b) of Section 2034.210, the exchange shall also include or be accompanied by an expert witness declaration signed only by the attorney for the party designating the expert, or by that party if that party has no attorney. This declaration shall be under penalty of perjury and shall contain all of the following:

(1) A brief narrative statement of the qualifications of each expert.

(2) A brief narrative statement of the general substance of the testimony that the expert is expected to give.

(3) A representation that the expert has agreed to testify at the trial.

(4) A representation that the expert will be sufficiently familiar with the pending action to submit to a meaningful oral deposition concerning the specific testimony, including an opinion and its basis, that the expert is expected to give at trial.

(5) A statement of the expert's hourly and daily fee for providing deposition testimony and for consulting with the retaining attorney.
Ca. Civ. Proc. Code § 2034.260
Amended by Stats 2018 ch 92 (SB 1289),s 45, eff. 1/1/2019.
Amended by Stats 2017 ch 64 (SB 543),s 3, eff. 1/1/2018.
Added by Stats 2004 ch 182 (AB 3081),s 23, eff. 7/1/2005.

Section 2034.270 - Demand includes demand for production of reports and writings

If a demand for an exchange of information concerning expert trial witnesses includes a demand for production of reports and writings as described in subdivision (c) of Section 2034.210, all parties shall produce and exchange, at the place and on the date specified in the demand, all discoverable reports and writings, if any, made by any designated expert described in subdivision (b) of Section 2034.210.

Ca. Civ. Proc. Code § 2034.270
Added by Stats 2004 ch 182 (AB 3081),s 23, eff. 7/1/2005.

Section 2034.280 - Supplemental expert witness list

(a) Within 20 days after the exchange described in Section 2034.260, any party who engaged in the exchange may submit a supplemental expert witness list containing the name and address of any experts who will express an opinion on a subject to be covered by an expert designated by an adverse party to the exchange, if the party supplementing an expert witness list has not previously retained an expert to testify on that subject.
(b) This supplemental list shall be accompanied by an expert witness declaration under subdivision (c) of Section 2034.260 concerning those additional experts, and by all discoverable reports and writings, if any, made by those additional experts.
(c) The party shall also make those experts available immediately for a deposition under Article 3 (commencing with Section 2034.410), which deposition may be taken even though the time limit for discovery under Chapter 8 (commencing with Section 2024.010) has expired.

Ca. Civ. Proc. Code § 2034.280
Added by Stats 2004 ch 182 (AB 3081),s 23, eff. 7/1/2005.

Section 2034.290 - Demand and lists filed with court; retention of originals by demanding party

(a) A demand for an exchange of information concerning expert trial witnesses, and any expert witness lists and declarations exchanged shall not be filed with the court.
(b) The party demanding the exchange shall retain both the original of the demand, with the original proof of service affixed, and the original of all expert witness lists and declarations exchanged in response to the demand until six months after final disposition of the action. At that time, all originals may be destroyed unless the court, on motion of any party and for good cause shown, orders that the originals be preserved for a longer period.

(c) Notwithstanding subdivisions (a) and (b), a demand for exchange of information concerning expert trial witnesses, and all expert witness lists and declarations exchanged in response to it, shall be lodged with the court when their contents become relevant to an issue in any pending matter in the action.

Ca. Civ. Proc. Code § 2034.290
Added by Stats 2004 ch 182 (AB 3081),s 23, eff. 7/1/2005.

Section 2034.300 - Exclusion of evidence of expert opinion of party not in compliance

Except as provided in Section 2034.310 and in Articles 4 (commencing with Section 2034.610) and 5 (commencing with Section 2034.710), on objection of any party who has made a complete and timely compliance with Section 2034.260, the trial court shall exclude from evidence the expert opinion of any witness that is offered by any party who has unreasonably failed to do any of the following:

(a) List that witness as an expert under Section 2034.260.

(b) Submit an expert witness declaration.

(c) Produce reports and writings of expert witnesses under Section 2034.270.

(d) Make that expert available for a deposition under Article 3 (commencing with Section 2034.410).

Ca. Civ. Proc. Code § 2034.300
Added by Stats 2004 ch 182 (AB 3081),s 23, eff. 7/1/2005.

Section 2034.310 - Calling expert not previously designated as witness

A party may call as a witness at trial an expert not previously designated by that party if either of the following conditions is satisfied:

(a) That expert has been designated by another party and has thereafter been deposed under Article 3 (commencing with Section 2034.410).

(b) That expert is called as a witness to impeach the testimony of an expert witness offered by any other party at the trial. This impeachment may include testimony to the falsity or nonexistence of any fact used as the foundation for any opinion by any other party's expert witness, but may not include testimony that contradicts the opinion.

Ca. Civ. Proc. Code § 2034.310
Added by Stats 2004 ch 182 (AB 3081),s 23, eff. 7/1/2005.

Article 3 - DEPOSITION OF EXPERT WITNESS

Section 2034.410 - Generally

On receipt of an expert witness list from a party, any other party may take the deposition of any person on the list. The procedures for taking oral and written depositions set forth in Chapters 9 (commencing with Section 2025.010), 10 (commencing with Section 2026.010), and 11 (commencing with Section 2028.010) apply to a deposition of a listed trial expert witness except as provided in this article.

Ca. Civ. Proc. Code § 2034.410
Added by Stats 2004 ch 182 (AB 3081),s 23, eff. 7/1/2005.

Section 2034.415 - Production of materials

An expert described in subdivision (b) of Section 2034.210 whose deposition is noticed pursuant to Section 2025.220 shall, no later than three business days before his or her deposition, produce any materials or category of materials, including any electronically stored information, called for by the deposition notice.

Ca. Civ. Proc. Code § 2034.415
Added by Stats 2016 ch 467 (AB 2427),s 3, eff. 1/1/2017.

Section 2034.420 - Location of expert's deposition

The deposition of any expert described in subdivision (b) of Section 2034.210 shall be taken at a place that is within 75 miles of the courthouse where the action is pending. On motion for a protective order by the party designating an expert witness, and on a showing of exceptional hardship, the court may order that the deposition be taken at a more distant place from the courthouse.

Title 4 - CIVIL DISCOVERY ACT

Ca. Civ. Proc. Code § 2034.420
Amended by Stats 2008 ch 303 (AB 2619),s 1, eff. 1/1/2009.
Added by Stats 2004 ch 182 (AB 3081),s 23, eff. 7/1/2005.

Section 2034.430 - Payment of expert's hourly or daily fee

(a) Except as provided in subdivision (f), this section applies to an expert witness, other than a party or an employee of a party, who is any of the following:

(1) An expert described in subdivision (b) of Section 2034.210.

(2) A treating physician and surgeon or other treating health care practitioner who is to be asked during the deposition to express opinion testimony, including opinion or factual testimony regarding the past or present diagnosis or prognosis made by the practitioner or the reasons for a particular treatment decision made by the practitioner, but not including testimony requiring only the reading of words and symbols contained in the relevant medical record or, if those words and symbols are not legible to the deponent, the approximation by the deponent of what those words or symbols are.

(3) An architect, professional engineer, or licensed land surveyor who was involved with the original project design or survey for which that person is asked to express an opinion within the person's expertise and relevant to the action or proceeding.
(b) A party desiring to depose an expert witness described in subdivision (a) shall pay the expert's reasonable and customary hourly or daily fee for any time spent at the deposition from the time noticed in the deposition subpoena, or from the time of the arrival of the expert witness should that time be later than the time noticed in the deposition subpoena, until the time the expert witness is dismissed from the deposition, regardless of whether the expert is actually deposed by any party attending the deposition.
(c) If any counsel representing the expert or a nonnoticing party is late to the deposition, the expert's reasonable and customary hourly or daily fee for the time period determined from the time noticed in

the deposition subpoena until the counsel's late arrival, shall be paid by that tardy counsel.

(d) Notwithstanding subdivision (c), the hourly or daily fee charged to the tardy counsel shall not exceed the fee charged to the party who retained the expert, except where the expert donated services to a charitable or other nonprofit organization.

(e) A daily fee shall only be charged for a full day of attendance at a deposition or where the expert was required by the deposing party to be available for a full day and the expert necessarily had to forgo all business that the expert would otherwise have conducted that day but for the request that the expert be available all day for the scheduled deposition.

(f) In a worker's compensation case arising under Division 4 (commencing with Section 3201) or Division 4.5 (commencing with Section 6100) of the Labor Code, a party desiring to depose any expert on another party's expert witness list shall pay the fee under this section.

Ca. Civ. Proc. Code § 2034.430
Amended by Stats 2008 ch 303 (AB 2619),s 2, eff. 1/1/2009.
Added by Stats 2004 ch 182 (AB 3081),s 23, eff. 7/1/2005.

Section 2034.440 - Responsibility for fee charged by expert for preparing for deposition

The party designating an expert is responsible for any fee charged by the expert for preparing for a deposition and for traveling to the place of the deposition, as well as for any travel expenses of the expert.

Ca. Civ. Proc. Code § 2034.440
Added by Stats 2004 ch 182 (AB 3081),s 23, eff. 7/1/2005.

Section 2034.450 - Delivery of expert's fee

(a) The party taking the deposition of an expert witness shall either accompany the service of the deposition notice with a tender of the expert's fee based on the anticipated length of the deposition, or tender that fee at the commencement of the deposition.

(b) The expert's fee shall be delivered to the attorney for the party designating the expert.

(c) If the deposition of the expert takes longer than anticipated, the party giving notice of the deposition shall pay the balance of the expert's fee within five days of receipt of an itemized statement from the expert.

Ca. Civ. Proc. Code § 2034.450
Added by Stats 2004 ch 182 (AB 3081),s 23, eff. 7/1/2005.

Section 2034.460 - Service of notice accompanied by fee effective to require party to produce expert

(a) The service of a proper deposition notice accompanied by the tender of the expert witness fee described in Section 2034.430 is effective to require the party employing or retaining the expert to produce the expert for the deposition.

(b) If the party noticing the deposition fails to tender the expert's fee under Section 2034.430, the expert shall not be deposed at that time unless the parties stipulate otherwise.

Ca. Civ. Proc. Code § 2034.460
Added by Stats 2004 ch 182 (AB 3081),s 23, eff. 7/1/2005.

Section 2034.470 - Motion for order setting compensation of expert

(a) If a party desiring to take the deposition of an expert witness under this article deems that the hourly or daily fee of that expert for providing deposition testimony is unreasonable, that party may move for an order setting the compensation of that expert. Notice of this motion shall also be given to the expert.

(b) A motion under subdivision (a) shall be accompanied by a meet and confer declaration under Section 2016.040. In any attempt at an informal resolution under Section 2016.040, either the party or the expert shall provide the other with all of the following:

(1) Proof of the ordinary and customary fee actually charged and received by that expert for similar services provided outside the subject litigation.

(2) The total number of times the presently demanded fee has ever been charged and received by that expert.

(3) The frequency and regularity with which the presently demanded fee has been charged and received by that expert within the two-year period preceding the hearing on the motion.

(c) In addition to any other facts or evidence, the expert or the party designating the expert shall provide, and the court's determination as to the reasonableness of the fee shall be based on, proof of the ordinary and customary fee actually charged and received by that expert for similar services provided outside the subject litigation.

(d) In an action filed after January 1, 1994, the expert or the party designating the expert shall also provide, and the court's determination as to the reasonableness of the fee shall also be based on, both of the following:

(1) The total number of times the presently demanded fee has ever been charged and received by that expert.

(2) The frequency and regularity with which the presently demanded fee has been charged and received by that expert within the two-year period preceding the hearing on the motion.

(e) The court may also consider the ordinary and customary fees charged by similar experts for similar services within the relevant community and any other factors the court deems necessary or appropriate to make its determination.

(f) Upon a determination that the fee demanded by that expert is unreasonable, and based upon the evidence and factors considered, the court shall set the fee of the expert providing testimony.

(g) The court shall impose a monetary sanction under Chapter 7 (commencing with Section 2023.010) against any party, person, or attorney who unsuccessfully makes or opposes a motion to set the expert witness fee, unless it finds that the one subject to the sanction acted with substantial justification or that other circumstances make the imposition of the sanction unjust.

Ca. Civ. Proc. Code § 2034.470
Added by Stats 2004 ch 182 (AB 3081),s 23, eff. 7/1/2005.

Article 4 - MOTION TO AUGMENT OR AMEND EXPERT WITNESS LIST OR DECLARATION

Section 2034.610 - Generally

(a) On motion of any party who has engaged in a timely exchange of expert witness information, the court may grant leave to do either or both of the following:

    (1) Augment that party's expert witness list and declaration by adding the name and address of any expert witness whom that party has subsequently retained.

    (2) Amend that party's expert witness declaration with respect to the general substance of the testimony that an expert previously designated is expected to give.

(b) A motion under subdivision (a) shall be made at a sufficient time in advance of the time limit for the completion of discovery under Chapter 8 (commencing with Section 2024.010) to permit the deposition of any expert to whom the motion relates to be taken within that time limit. Under exceptional circumstances, the court may permit the motion to be made at a later time.

(c) The motion shall be accompanied by a meet and confer declaration under Section 2016.040.

    Ca. Civ. Proc. Code § 2034.610

Added by Stats 2004 ch 182 (AB 3081),s 23, eff. 7/1/2005.

Section 2034.620 - Conditions required to be satisfied to grant leave to amend or augment or amend

The court shall grant leave to augment or amend an expert witness list or declaration only if all of the following conditions are satisfied:

(a) The court has taken into account the extent to which the opposing party has relied on the list of expert witnesses.

(b) The court has determined that any party opposing the motion will not be prejudiced in maintaining that party's action or defense on the merits.

(c) The court has determined either of the following:

(1) The moving party would not in the exercise of reasonable diligence have determined to call that expert witness or have decided to offer the different or additional testimony of that expert witness.

(2) The moving party failed to determine to call that expert witness, or to offer the different or additional testimony of that expert witness as a result of mistake, inadvertence, surprise, or excusable neglect, and the moving party has done both of the following:

(A) Sought leave to augment or amend promptly after deciding to call the expert witness or to offer the different or additional testimony.

(B) Promptly thereafter served a copy of the proposed expert witness information concerning the expert or the testimony described in Section 2034.260 on all other parties who have appeared in the action.

(d) Leave to augment or amend is conditioned on the moving party making the expert available immediately for a deposition under Article 3 (commencing with Section 2034.410), and on any other terms as may be just, including, but not limited to, leave to any party opposing the motion to designate additional expert witnesses or to elicit additional opinions from those previously designated, a continuance of the trial for a reasonable period of time, and the awarding of costs and litigation expenses to any party opposing the motion.

Ca. Civ. Proc. Code § 2034.620
Added by Stats 2004 ch 182 (AB 3081),s 23, eff. 7/1/2005.

Section 2034.630 - Monetary sanction for unsuccessfully opposing motion

The court shall impose a monetary sanction under Chapter 7 (commencing with Section 2023.010) against any party, person, or attorney who unsuccessfully makes or opposes a motion to augment or amend expert witness information, unless it finds that the one subject to the sanction acted with substantial justification or that other circumstances make the imposition of the sanction unjust.

Ca. Civ. Proc. Code § 2034.630

Added by Stats 2004 ch 182 (AB 3081),s 23, eff. 7/1/2005.

Article 5 - MOTION TO SUBMIT TARDY EXPERT WITNESS INFORMATION

Section 2034.710 - Generally

(a) On motion of any party who has failed to submit expert witness information on the date specified in a demand for that exchange, the court may grant leave to submit that information on a later date.

(b) A motion under subdivision (a) shall be made a sufficient time in advance of the time limit for the completion of discovery under Chapter 8 (commencing with Section 2024.010) to permit the deposition of any expert to whom the motion relates to be taken within that time limit. Under exceptional circumstances, the court may permit the motion to be made at a later time.

(c) The motion shall be accompanied by a meet and confer declaration under Section 2016.040.

Ca. Civ. Proc. Code § 2034.710

Added by Stats 2004 ch 182 (AB 3081),s 23, eff. 7/1/2005.

Section 2034.720 - Conditions required to be satisfied to grant leave

The court shall grant leave to submit tardy expert witness information only if all of the following conditions are satisfied:

(a) The court has taken into account the extent to which the opposing party has relied on the absence of a list of expert witnesses.

(b) The court has determined that any party opposing the motion will not be prejudiced in maintaining that party's action or defense on the merits.

(c) The court has determined that the moving party did all of the following:

(1) Failed to submit the information as the result of mistake, inadvertence, surprise, or excusable neglect.

(2) Sought leave to submit the information promptly after learning of the mistake, inadvertence, surprise, or excusable neglect.

(3) Promptly thereafter served a copy of the proposed expert witness information described in Section 2034.260 on all other parties who have appeared in the action.

(d) The order is conditioned on the moving party making the expert available immediately for a deposition under Article 3 (commencing with Section 2034.410), and on any other terms as may be just, including, but not limited to, leave to any party opposing the motion to designate additional expert witnesses or to elicit additional opinions from those previously designated, a continuance of the trial for a reasonable period of time, and the awarding of costs and litigation expenses to any party opposing the motion.

Ca. Civ. Proc. Code § 2034.720
Added by Stats 2004 ch 182 (AB 3081),s 23, eff. 7/1/2005.

Section 2034.730 - Monetary sanction for unsuccessfully opposing motion

The court shall impose a monetary sanction under Chapter 7 (commencing with Section 2023.010) against any party, person, or attorney who unsuccessfully makes or opposes a motion to submit tardy expert witness information, unless it finds that the one subject to the sanction acted with substantial justification or that other circumstances make the imposition of the sanction unjust.

Ca. Civ. Proc. Code § 2034.730
Added by Stats 2004 ch 182 (AB 3081),s 23, eff. 7/1/2005.

Chapter 19 - PERPETUATION OF TESTIMONY OR PRESERVATION OF EVIDENCE BEFORE FILING ACTION

Section 2035.010 - Generally

(a) One who expects to be a party or expects a successor in interest to be a party to an action that may be cognizable in a court of the state, whether as a plaintiff, or as a defendant, or in any other capacity, may obtain discovery within the scope delimited by Chapter 2 (commencing with Section 2017.010), and subject to the restrictions set forth in Chapter 5 (commencing with Section 2019.010), for the purpose of perpetuating that person's own testimony or that of another natural person or organization, or of preserving evidence for use in the event an action is subsequently filed.

(b) One shall not employ the procedures of this chapter for purposes of either ascertaining the possible existence of a cause of action or a defense to it, or of identifying those who might be made parties to an action not yet filed.

Ca. Civ. Proc. Code § 2035.010

Amended by Stats 2016 ch 86 (SB 1171),s 44, eff. 1/1/2017.

Amended by Stats 2005 ch 294 (AB 333),s 13, eff. 1/1/2006

Added by Stats 2004 ch 182 (AB 3081),s 23, eff. 7/1/2005.

Section 2035.020 - Methods for discovery

The methods available for discovery conducted for the purposes set forth in Section 2035.010 are all of the following:

(a) Oral and written depositions.

(b) Inspections of documents, things, and places.

(c) Physical and mental examinations.

Ca. Civ. Proc. Code § 2035.020

Added by Stats 2004 ch 182 (AB 3081),s 23, eff. 7/1/2005.

Section 2035.030 - Petition

(a) One who desires to perpetuate testimony or preserve evidence for the purposes set forth in Section 2035.010 shall file a verified petition in the superior court of the county of the residence of at least one expected adverse party, or, if no expected adverse party is a resident of the State of California, in the superior court of a county where the action or proceeding may be filed.

(b) The petition shall be titled in the name of the one who desires the perpetuation of testimony or the preservation of evidence. The petition shall set forth all of the following:

(1) The expectation that the petitioner or the petitioner's successor in interest will be a party to an action cognizable in a court of the State of California.

(2) The present inability of the petitioner and, if applicable, the petitioner's successor in interest either to bring that action or to cause it to be brought.

(3) The subject matter of the expected action and the petitioner's involvement. A copy of any written instrument the validity or construction of which may be called into question, or which is connected with the subject matter of the proposed discovery, shall be attached to the petition.

(4) The particular discovery methods described in Section 2035.020 that the petitioner desires to employ.

(5) The facts that the petitioner desires to establish by the proposed discovery.

(6) The reasons for desiring to perpetuate or preserve these facts before an action has been filed.

(7) The name or a description of those whom the petitioner expects to be adverse parties so far as known.

(8) The name and address of those from whom the discovery is to be sought.

(9) The substance of the information expected to be elicited from each of those from whom discovery is being sought.

(c) The petition shall request the court to enter an order authorizing the petitioner to engage in discovery by the described methods for the purpose of perpetuating the described testimony or preserving the described evidence.

Ca. Civ. Proc. Code § 2035.030

Amended by Stats 2005 ch 294 (AB 333),s 14, eff. 1/1/2006

Added by Stats 2004 ch 182 (AB 3081),s 23, eff. 7/1/2005.

Section 2035.040 - Service of notice of petition

(a) The petitioner shall cause service of a notice of the petition under Section 2035.030 to be made on each natural person or organization named in the petition as an expected adverse party. This service shall be made in the same manner provided for the service of a summons.

(b) The service of the notice shall be accompanied by a copy of the petition. The notice shall state that the petitioner will apply to the court at a time and place specified in the notice for the order requested in the petition.

(c) This service shall be effected at least 20 days prior to the date specified in the notice for the hearing on the petition.

(d) If after the exercise of due diligence, the petitioner is unable to cause service to be made on any expected adverse party named in the petition, the court in which the petition is filed shall make an order for service by publication.

(e) If any expected adverse party served by publication does not appear at the hearing, the court shall appoint an attorney to represent that party for all purposes, including the cross-examination of any person whose testimony is taken by deposition. The court shall order that the petitioner pay the reasonable fees and expenses of any attorney so appointed.

Ca. Civ. Proc. Code § 2035.040

Added by Stats 2004 ch 182 (AB 3081),s 23, eff. 7/1/2005.

Section 2035.050 - Determining whether to make order

(a) If the court determines that all or part of the discovery requested under this chapter may prevent a failure or delay of justice, it shall make an order authorizing that discovery. In determining whether to authorize discovery by a petitioner who expects a successor in interest to be a party to an action, the court shall consider, in addition to other appropriate factors, whether the requested discovery could be conducted by the petitioner's successor in interest, instead of by the petitioner.

(b) The order shall identify any witness whose deposition may be taken, and any documents, things, or places that may be inspected, and any person whose physical or mental condition may be examined.

(c) Any authorized depositions, inspections, and physical or mental examinations shall then be conducted in accordance with the provisions of this title relating to those methods of discovery in actions that have been filed.

Ca. Civ. Proc. Code § 2035.050

Amended by Stats 2005 ch 294 (AB 333),s 15, eff. 1/1/2006
Added by Stats 2004 ch 182 (AB 3081),s 23, eff. 7/1/2005.

Section 2035.060 - Use of deposition

If a deposition to perpetuate testimony has been taken either under the provisions of this chapter, or under comparable provisions of the laws of the state in which it was taken, or the federal courts, or a foreign nation in which it was taken, that deposition may be used, in any action involving the same subject matter that is brought in a court of the State of California, in accordance with Section 2025.620 against any party, or the successor in interest of any party, named in the petition as an expected adverse party.

Ca. Civ. Proc. Code § 2035.060

Amended by Stats 2005 ch 294 (AB 333),s 16, eff. 1/1/2006
Added by Stats 2004 ch 182 (AB 3081),s 23, eff. 7/1/2005.

Chapter 20 - PERPETUATION OF TESTIMONY OR PRESERVATION OF INFORMATION PENDING APPEAL

Section 2036.010 - Generally

If an appeal has been taken from a judgment entered by a court of the state, or if the time for taking an appeal has not expired, a party may obtain discovery within the scope delimited by Chapter 2 (commencing with Section 2017.010), and subject to the restrictions set forth in Chapter 5 (commencing with Section 2019.010), for purposes of perpetuating testimony or preserving information for use in the event of further proceedings in that court.

Ca. Civ. Proc. Code § 2036.010
Amended by Stats 2016 ch 86 (SB 1171),s 45, eff. 1/1/2017.
Added by Stats 2004 ch 182 (AB 3081),s 23, eff. 7/1/2005.

Section 2036.020 - Methods of discovery

The methods available for discovery for the purpose set forth in Section 2036.010 are all of the following:
(a) Oral and written depositions.
(b) Inspections of documents, things, and places.
(c) Physical and mental examinations.

Ca. Civ. Proc. Code § 2036.020
Added by Stats 2004 ch 182 (AB 3081),s 23, eff. 7/1/2005.

Section 2036.030 - Requirements of motion

(a) A party who desires to obtain discovery pending appeal shall obtain leave of the court that entered the judgment. This motion shall be made on the same notice to and service of parties as is required for discovery sought in an action pending in that court.
(b) The motion for leave to conduct discovery pending appeal shall set forth all of the following:

(1) The names and addresses of the natural persons or organizations from whom the discovery is being sought.

(2) The particular discovery methods described in Section 2036.020 for which authorization is being sought.

(3) The reasons for perpetuating testimony or preserving evidence.
Ca. Civ. Proc. Code § 2036.030
Added by Stats 2004 ch 182 (AB 3081),s 23, eff. 7/1/2005.

Section 2036.040 - Order authorizing discovery
(a) If the court determines that all or part of the discovery requested under this chapter may prevent a failure or delay of justice in the event of further proceedings in the action in that court, it shall make an order authorizing that discovery.
(b) The order shall identify any witness whose deposition may be taken, and any documents, things, or places that may be inspected, and any person whose physical or mental condition may be examined.
(c) Any authorized depositions, inspections, and physical and mental examinations shall then be conducted in accordance with the provisions of this title relating to these methods of discovery in a pending action.
Ca. Civ. Proc. Code § 2036.040
Added by Stats 2004 ch 182 (AB 3081),s 23, eff. 7/1/2005.

Section 2036.050 - Use of deposition
If a deposition to perpetuate testimony has been taken under the provisions of this chapter, it may be used in any later proceeding in accordance with Section 2025.620.
Ca. Civ. Proc. Code § 2036.050
Added by Stats 2004 ch 182 (AB 3081),s 23, eff. 7/1/2005.

Title 5 - OF THE RIGHTS AND DUTIES OF WITNESSES

Section 2064 - Duty to attend and answer
A witness, served with a subpoena, must attend at the time

appointed, with any papers under his control lawfully required by
the subpoena, and answer all pertinent and legal questions; and,
unless sooner discharged, must remain until the testimony is
closed.

Ca. Civ. Proc. Code § 2064
Amended by Stats. 1907, Ch. 395.

Section 2065 - Notice that witness may be entitled to fees and mileage

Any witness who is subpoenaed in any civil or administrative action
or proceeding shall be given written notice on the subpoena that the
witness may be entitled to receive fees and mileage. Such notice
shall indicate generally the manner in which the request for fees
and mileage should be made.

Ca. Civ. Proc. Code § 2065
Added by Stats. 1979, Ch. 67.

Title 6 - OF EVIDENCE IN PARTICULAR CASES, AND MISCELLANEOUS AND GENERAL PROVISIONS

Chapter 1 - EVIDENCE IN PARTICULAR CASES

Section 2074 - Offer equivalent to actual production and tender

An offer in writing to pay a particular sum of money, or to deliver a
written instrument or specific personal property, is, if not accepted,
equivalent to the actual production and tender of the money,
instrument, or property.

Ca. Civ. Proc. Code § 2074
Enacted 1872.

Section 2075 - Receipt for payment of money or delivery of instrument or property

Whoever pays money, or delivers an instrument or property, is
entitled to a receipt therefor from the person to whom the payment

or delivery is made, and may demand a proper signature to such
receipt as a condition of the payment or delivery.

Ca. Civ. Proc. Code § 2075

Enacted 1872.

Section 2076 - Objection required

The person to whom a tender is made must, at the time, specify any
objection he may have to the money, instrument, or property, or he
must be deemed to have waived it; and if the objection be to the
amount of money, the terms of the instrument, or the amount or
kind of property, he must specify the amount, terms, or kind which
he requires, or be precluded from objecting afterwards.

Ca. Civ. Proc. Code § 2076

Enacted 1872.

Section 2077 - Rules for construing descriptive part of conveyance of real property

Section Two Thousand and Seventy-seven. The following are the
rules for construing the descriptive part of a conveyance of real
property, when the construction is doubtful and there are no other
sufficient circumstances to determine it:

One-Where there are certain definite and ascertained particulars in
the description, the addition of others which are indefinite,
unknown, or false, does not frustrate the conveyance, but it is to be
construed by the first mentioned particulars.

Two-When permanent and visible or ascertained boundaries or
monuments are inconsistent with the measurement, either of lines,
angles, or surfaces, the boundaries or monuments are paramount.

Three-Between different measurements which are inconsistent with
each other, that of angles is paramount to that of surfaces, and that
of lines paramount to both.

Four-When a road, or stream of water not navigable, is the
boundary, the rights of the grantor to the middle of the road or the
thread of the stream are included in the conveyance, except where
the road or thread of the stream is held under another title.

Five-When tide water is the boundary, the rights of the grantor to

ordinary high-water mark are included in the conveyance. When a
navigable lake, where there is no tide, is the boundary, the rights of
the grantor to low-water mark are included in the conveyance.
Six-When the description refers to a map, and that reference is
inconsistent with other particulars, it controls them if it appears
that the parties acted with reference to the map; otherwise the map
is subordinate to other definite and ascertained particulars.

Ca. Civ. Proc. Code § 2077
Amended by Code Amendments 1873-74, Ch. 383.

Chapter 3 - ADMINISTRATION OF OATHS AND AFFIRMATIONS

Section 2093 - Persons having power to administer oaths and affirmations

(a) A court, judge or clerk of a court, justice, notary public, and
officer or person authorized to take testimony in an action or
proceeding, or to decide upon evidence, has the power to
administer oaths and affirmations.

(b)

(1) A shorthand reporter certified pursuant to Article 3
(commencing with Section 8020) of Chapter 13 of Division 3 of the
Business and Professions Code has the power to administer oaths
and affirmations and may perform the duties of the deposition
officer pursuant to Chapter 9 (commencing with Section 2025.010)
of Title 4. The certified shorthand reporter is entitled to receive fees
for services rendered during a deposition, including fees for
deposition services, as specified in subdivision (c) of Section 8211 of
the Government Code.

(2) This subdivision also applies to depositions taken by
telephone or other remote electronic means as specified in Chapter
2 (commencing with Section 2017.010) and Chapter 9 (commencing
with Section 2025.010) of Title 4.

(c)

(1) A former judge or justice of a court of record in the state who retired or resigned from office may administer oaths and affirmations, if the former judge or justice requests and receives a certification from the Commission on Judicial Performance pursuant to paragraph (2).

(2) The Commission on Judicial Performance shall issue a certification enabling a former judge or justice to administer oaths and affirmations if the following conditions are satisfied:

(A) The former judge or justice was not removed from office; was not censured and barred from receiving an assignment, appointment, or reference of work from any California state court; did not retire or resign from office with an agreement with the commission that the former judge or justice would not receive an assignment, appointment or reference of work from any California state court; and, at the time of the former judge or justice's retirement, resignation, or request for certification, a formal disciplinary proceeding was not pending or was resolved on the merits in the judge or justice's favor after his or her retirement or resignation and before the request for certification.

(B) A medical certification provided to the commission by the former judge or justice pursuant to paragraph (3) establishes one of the following:

(i) The former judge or justice does not have a medical condition that would impair his or her ability to administer oaths or affirmations.

(ii) The former judge or justice has a medical condition that may impair his or her ability to administer oaths and affirmations, but the condition does not impair his or her ability at the present time.

(3) The Commission on Judicial Performance may require an

797

applicant to obtain a medical certification in order to receive or renew a certification to administer oaths and affirmations if, at the time of resignation or retirement, there is evidence in a disability application file or in a disciplinary investigation file of possible cognitive impairment affecting the judge or justice, or if the former judge or justice previously received a two-year certification to administer oaths and affirmations from the commission. The commission shall supply the required forms to an applicant upon request.

(4) If an applicant's medical certification indicates that the applicant has a medical condition that may impair his or her ability to administer oaths and affirmations, but the condition does not impair his or her ability at the time the medical certification is submitted with the application, the Commission on Judicial Performance shall issue a certification to administer oaths and affirmations pursuant to paragraph (2), but the certification is only valid for a period of two years from the date of issuance.

(5) Notwithstanding paragraph (1), a former judge or justice of a court of record who received a certification to administer oaths and affirmations from the Commission on Judicial Performance prior to January 1, 2018, may continue to administer oaths and affirmations until the expiration of the certification, at which time he or she may reapply for certification pursuant to paragraph (2).

(6) The Commission on Judicial Performance may charge a regulatory fee not to exceed fifteen dollars ($15) for each certification application submitted pursuant to this subdivision to cover its costs, including costs to review a medical certification.
(d) A rule or regulation regarding the confidentiality of proceedings of the Commission on Judicial Performance does not prohibit the commission from issuing a certificate as provided for in this section.
(e) The administration of an oath or affirmation pursuant to this section without pay does not violate Section 75060.6 of the Government Code.

Ca. Civ. Proc. Code § 2093

Amended by Stats 2018 ch 92 (SB 1289),s 46, eff. 1/1/2019.

Amended by Stats 2017 ch 82 (AB 740),s 1, eff. 1/1/2018.

Amended by Stats 2016 ch 86 (SB 1171),s 46, eff. 1/1/2017.

Amended by Stats 2015 ch 308 (AB 1028),s 1, eff. 1/1/2016.

Amended by Stats 2004 ch 182 (AB 3081),s 24, eff. 7/1/2005

Amended by Stats 2001 ch 812 (AB 223), s 12, eff. 1/1/2002.

Section 2094 - Administered by obtaining affirmative response to questions

(a) An oath, affirmation, or declaration in an action or a proceeding, may be administered by obtaining an affirmative response to one of the following questions:

(1) "Do you solemnly state that the evidence you shall give in this issue (or matter) shall be the truth, the whole truth, and nothing but the truth, so help you God?"

(2) "Do you solemnly state, under penalty of perjury, that the evidence that you shall give in this issue (or matter) shall be the truth, the whole truth, and nothing but the truth?"

(b) In the alternative to the forms prescribed in subdivision (a), the court may administer an oath, affirmation, or declaration in an action or a proceeding in a manner that is calculated to awaken the person's conscience and impress the person's mind with the duty to tell the truth. The court shall satisfy itself that the person testifying understands that his or her testimony is being given under penalty of perjury.

Ca. Civ. Proc. Code § 2094

Amended by Stats 2002 ch 806 (AB 3027),s 17, eff. 1/1/2003.

Amended by Stats 2000 ch 688 (AB 1669), s 13, eff. 1/1/2001.

Section 2095 through 2097 - [Repealed]

Ca. Civ. Proc. Code § 2095 through 2097

Repealed by Stats 2000 ch 688 (AB 1669), ss 14-16, eff. 1/1/2001.

Title 7 - UNIFORM FEDERAL LIEN REGISTRATION ACT

Section 2100 - Applicability of title

This title applies only to federal tax liens and to other federal liens notices of which under any Act of Congress or any regulation adopted pursuant thereto are required or permitted to be filed in the same manner as notices of federal tax liens.

Ca. Civ. Proc. Code § 2100

Added by Stats. 1979, Ch. 330.

Section 2101 - Filing notices

(a) Notices of liens, certificates, and other notices affecting federal tax liens or other federal liens must be filed in accordance with this title.

(b) Notices of liens upon real property for obligations payable to the United States and certificates and notices affecting the liens shall be filed for record in the office of the recorder of the county in which the real property subject to the liens is situated.

(c) Notices of federal liens upon personal property, whether tangible or intangible, for obligations payable to the United States and certificates and notices affecting the liens shall be filed as follows:

(1) If the person against whose interest the lien applies is a corporation, a limited liability company, or a partnership whose principal executive office is in this state, as these entities are defined in the internal revenue laws of the United States, in the office of the Secretary of State.

(2) If the person against whose interest the lien applies is a trust that is not covered by paragraph (1), in the office of the Secretary of State.

(3) If the person against whose interest the lien applies is the estate of a decedent, in the office of the Secretary of State.

(4) In all other cases, in the office of the recorder of the county where the person against whose interest the lien applies resides at the time of filing of the notice of lien.

Ca. Civ. Proc. Code § 2101

Amended by Stats. 1997, Ch. 892, Sec. 2. Effective January 1, 1998.

Section 2102 - Certification entitles notices to be filed

Certification of notices of liens, certificates, or other notices affecting federal liens by the Secretary of the Treasury of the United States or his or her delegate, or by any official or entity of the United States responsible for filing or certifying of notice of any other lien, entitles them to be filed and no other attestation, certification, or acknowledgment is necessary.

Ca. Civ. Proc. Code § 2102

Added by Stats. 1979, Ch. 330.

Section 2103 - Presentation of notices to filing officer

(a) If a notice of federal lien, a refiling of a notice of federal lien, or a notice of revocation of any certificate described in subdivision (b) is presented to a filing officer who is:

(1) The Secretary of State, he or she shall cause the notice to be filed, indexed, and marked in accordance with the provisions of Sections 9515, 9516, and 9522 of the Commercial Code as if the notice were a financing statement within the meaning of that code; or

(2) A county recorder, he or she shall accept for filing, file for record in the manner set forth in Section 27320 of the Government Code, and index the document by the name of the person against whose interest the lien applies in the general index.

(b) If a certificate of release, nonattachment, discharge, or subordination of any lien is presented to the Secretary of State for filing he or she shall:

(1) Cause a certificate of release or nonattachment to be filed, indexed, and marked as if the certificate were a termination statement within the meaning of the Commercial Code.

(2) Cause a certificate of discharge or subordination to be filed, indexed, and marked as if the certificate were a release of collateral within the meaning of the Commercial Code.

(c) If a refiled notice of federal lien referred to in subdivision (a) or any of the certificates or notices referred to in subdivision (b) is presented for filing to a county recorder, he or she shall accept for filing, file for record in the manner set forth in Section 27320 of the Government Code, and index the document by the name of the person against whose interest the lien applies in the general index.

(d) Upon request of any person, the filing officer shall issue his or her certificate showing whether there is on file, on the date and hour stated therein, any notice of lien or certificate or notice affecting any lien filed after January 1, 1968, under this title or former Chapter 14 (commencing with Section 7200) of Division 7 of Title 1 of the Government Code, naming a particular person, and if a notice or certificate is on file, giving the date and hour of filing of each notice or certificate. Upon request, the filing officer shall furnish a copy of any notice of federal lien, or notice or certificate affecting a federal lien. If the filing officer is a county recorder, the fee for a certificate for each name searched shall be set by the filing officer in an amount that covers actual costs, and the fee for copies shall be in accordance with Section 27366 of the Government Code. If the filing officer is the Secretary of State, the certificate shall be issued as part of a combined certificate pursuant to Section 9528 of the Commercial Code, and the fee for the certificate and copies shall be in accordance with that section.

Ca. Civ. Proc. Code § 2103

Amended by Stats 2012 ch 494 (SB 1532),s 2, eff. 1/1/2013.
Amended by Stats 2009 ch 606 (SB 676),s 1, eff. 1/1/2010.
EFFECTIVE 7/01/2001. Amended October 10, 1999 (Bill Number: SB 45) (Chapter 991).

Section 2104 - Fees

The fee charged for recording and indexing each notice of lien or certificate or notice affecting the lien filed with the county recorder shall be the same as those established by Article 5 (commencing with Section 27360) of Chapter 6 of Part 3 of Division 2 of Title 3 of the Government Code for the recording and indexing of documents. The fee for filing and indexing each notice of lien or certificate or notice affecting the lien with the office of the Secretary of State is set forth in subdivision (a) of Section 12194 of the Government Code.

The officer shall bill the district directors of internal revenue or other appropriate federal officials on a monthly basis for fees for documents recorded or filed by the county recorder or the Secretary of State.

Ca. Civ. Proc. Code § 2104

Amended by Stats. 1999, Ch. 1000, Sec. 13. Effective January 1, 2000.

Section 2105 - Federal tax lien notices filed prior to January 2, 1968

Filing officers with whom notices of federal tax liens, certificates and notices affecting such liens have been filed on or before January 1, 1968, shall, after that date, continue to maintain a file labeled "federal tax lien notices filed prior to January 2, 1968" containing notices and certificates filed in numerical order of receipt. If a notice of lien was filed on or before January 1, 1968, any certificate or notice affecting the lien shall be filed in the same office.

Ca. Civ. Proc. Code § 2105

Added by Stats. 1979, Ch. 330.

Section 2106 - Application and construction of title

This title shall be applied and construed to effectuate its general purpose to make uniform the law with respect to the subject of this title among states enacting it.

Ca. Civ. Proc. Code § 2106

Added by Stats. 1979, Ch. 330.

Section 2106.5 - Filing by electronic or magnetic means

This title shall be applied and construed to permit the transmission, filing, recording, and indexing of notices of federal tax liens and all certificates that relate to or affect those liens, including, but not limited to, certificates of release, discharge, subordination, and nonattachment, by electronic or magnetic means, using computerized data processing, telecommunications, and other similar information technologies available to the filing offices.

Ca. Civ. Proc. Code § 2106.5

Added by Stats. 1998, Ch. 463, Sec. 1. Effective January 1, 1999.

Section 2107 - Title of act

This title may be cited as the Uniform Federal Lien Registration Act.

Ca. Civ. Proc. Code § 2107

Added by Stats. 1979, Ch. 330.

Made in the USA
Las Vegas, NV
12 September 2024

95211092R00449